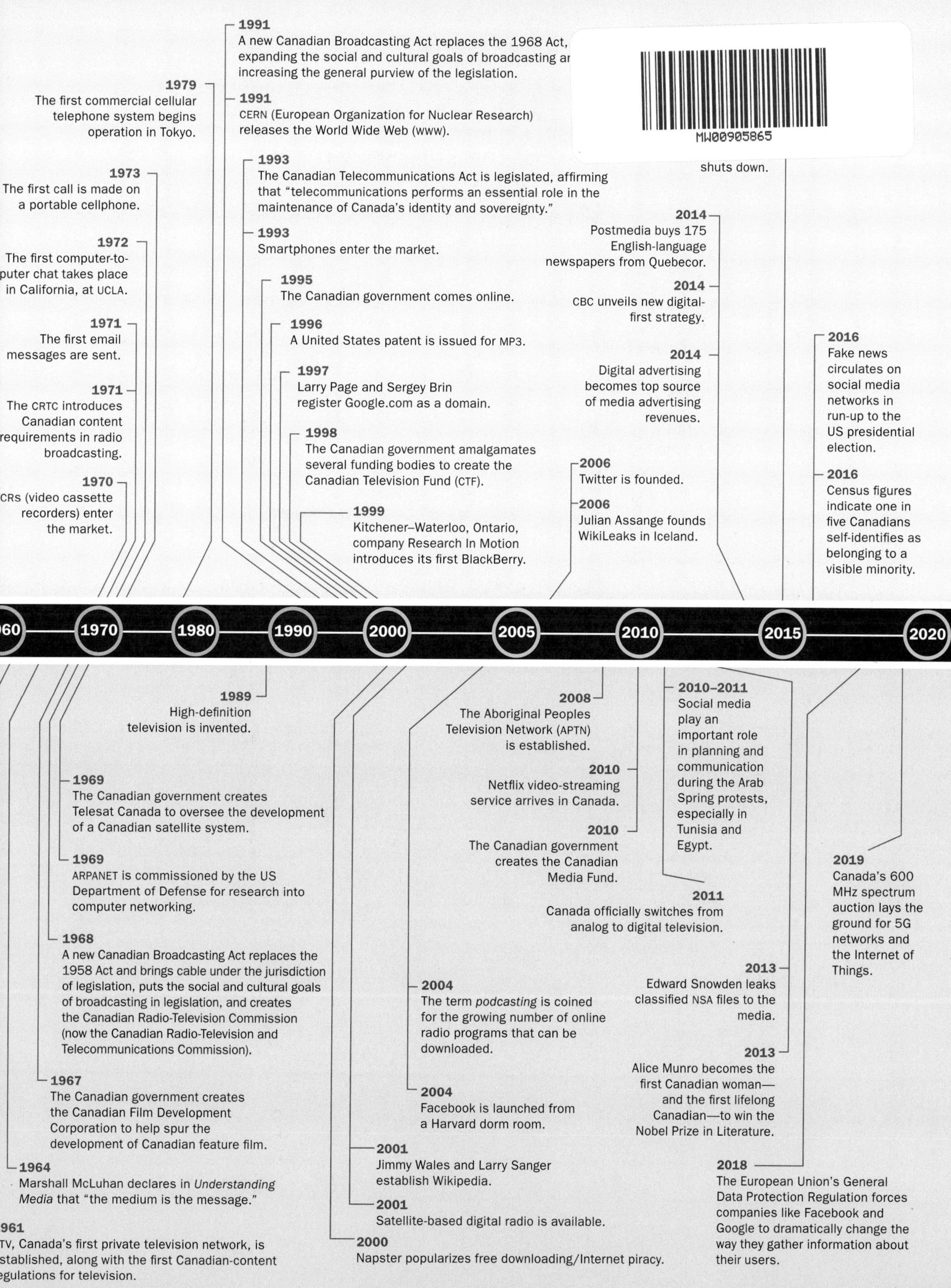

1991
A new Canadian Broadcasting Act replaces the 1968 Act, expanding the social and cultural goals of broadcasting ar increasing the general purview of the legislation.
1979
The first commercial cellular telephone system begins operation in Tokyo.
1991
CERN (European Organization for Nuclear Research) releases the World Wide Web (www).
MW00905865
shuts down.
1973
The first call is made on a portable cellphone.
1993
The Canadian Telecommunications Act is legislated, affirming that "telecommunications performs an essential role in the maintenance of Canada's identity and sovereignty."
1972
The first computer-to-puter chat takes place in California, at UCLA.
1993
Smartphones enter the market.
2014
Postmedia buys 175 English-language newspapers from Quebecor.
1995
The Canadian government comes online.
2014
CBC unveils new digital-first strategy.
1971
The first email messages are sent.
1996
A United States patent is issued for MP3.
2016
Fake news circulates on social media networks in run-up to the US presidential election.
2014
Digital advertising becomes top source of media advertising revenues.
1971
The CRTC introduces Canadian content requirements in radio broadcasting.
1997
Larry Page and Sergey Brin register Google.com as a domain.
1998
The Canadian government amalgamates several funding bodies to create the Canadian Television Fund (CTF).
2006
Twitter is founded.
1970
VCRs (video cassette recorders) enter the market.
2016
Census figures indicate one in five Canadians self-identifies as belonging to a visible minority.
1999
Kitchener–Waterloo, Ontario, company Research In Motion introduces its first BlackBerry.
2006
Julian Assange founds WikiLeaks in Iceland.
960
1970
1980
1990
2000
2005
2010
2015
2020
1989
High-definition television is invented.
2008
The Aboriginal Peoples Television Network (APTN) is established.
2010–2011
Social media play an important role in planning and communication during the Arab Spring protests, especially in Tunisia and Egypt.
1969
The Canadian government creates Telesat Canada to oversee the development of a Canadian satellite system.
2010
Netflix video-streaming service arrives in Canada.
2010
The Canadian government creates the Canadian Media Fund.
1969
ARPANET is commissioned by the US Department of Defense for research into computer networking.
2019
Canada's 600 MHz spectrum auction lays the ground for 5G networks and the Internet of Things.
2011
Canada officially switches from analog to digital television.
1968
A new Canadian Broadcasting Act replaces the 1958 Act and brings cable under the jurisdiction of legislation, puts the social and cultural goals of broadcasting in legislation, and creates the Canadian Radio-Television Commission (now the Canadian Radio-Television and Telecommunications Commission).
2013
Edward Snowden leaks classified NSA files to the media.
2004
The term *podcasting* is coined for the growing number of online radio programs that can be downloaded.
2013
Alice Munro becomes the first Canadian woman—and the first lifelong Canadian—to win the Nobel Prize in Literature.
1967
The Canadian government creates the Canadian Film Development Corporation to help spur the development of Canadian feature film.
2004
Facebook is launched from a Harvard dorm room.
2001
Jimmy Wales and Larry Sanger establish Wikipedia.
1964
Marshall McLuhan declares in *Understanding Media* that "the medium is the message."
2018
The European Union's General Data Protection Regulation forces companies like Facebook and Google to dramatically change the way they gather information about their users.
2001
Satellite-based digital radio is available.
1961
CTV, Canada's first private television network, is established, along with the first Canadian-content regulations for television.
2000
Napster popularizes free downloading/Internet piracy.

Media & Communication in Canada

Media & Communication in Canada

Networks, Culture, Technology, Audiences

Mike Gasher | David Skinner | Natalie Coulter

Ninth Edition

Oxford University Press is a department of the University of Oxford.
It furthers the University's objective of excellence in research, scholarship, and education by publishing worldwide. Oxford is a registered trade mark of Oxford University Press in the UK and in certain other countries.

Published in Canada by
Oxford University Press
8 Sampson Mews, Suite 204,
Don Mills, Ontario M3C 0H5 Canada

www.oupcanada.com

Third Edition published in 1996
Fourth Edition published in 2001
Fifth Edition published in 2004
Sixth Edition published in 2008
Seventh Edition published in 2004
Eighth Edition published in 2016
Second Edition published by McLelland & Stewart
@ 1991 Rowland Lorimer and Jean McNulty

Library and Archives Canada Cataloguing in Publication

Title: Media and communication in Canada : networks, culture, technology, audiences / Mike Gasher, David Skinner, Natalie Coulter.
Names: Gasher, Mike, 1954- author. | Skinner, David, 1956- author. | Coulter, Natalie, 1971- author. | Preceded by (work): Lorimer, Rowland, 1944- Mass communication in Canada.
Description: Ninth edition. | Preceded by Mass communication in Canada / Mike Gasher, David Skinner, and Rowland Lorimer. Eighth edition. 2016. | Includes bibliographical references and index.
Identifiers: Canadiana (print) 20190189746 | Canadiana (ebook) 20190189754 | ISBN 9780199033218 (softcover) | ISBN 9780199038688 (loose-leaf) | ISBN 9780199033256 (EPUB)
Subjects: LCSH: Mass media—Canada—Textbooks. | LCSH: Communication—Canada—Textbooks. | LCSH: Mass media—Textbooks. | LCSH: Communication—Textbooks. | LCGFT: Textbooks.
Classification: LCC P92.C3 L67 2020 | DDC 302.230971—dc23

Cover image: Adnan Salekin Saif/Getty Images
Cover design: Laurie McGregor
Interior design: Sherill Chapman

Oxford University Press is committed to our environment.
Wherever possible, our books are printed on paper which comes from responsible sources.

Printed and bound in the United States of America

1 2 3 4 — 23 22 21 20

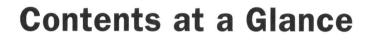

Contents at a Glance

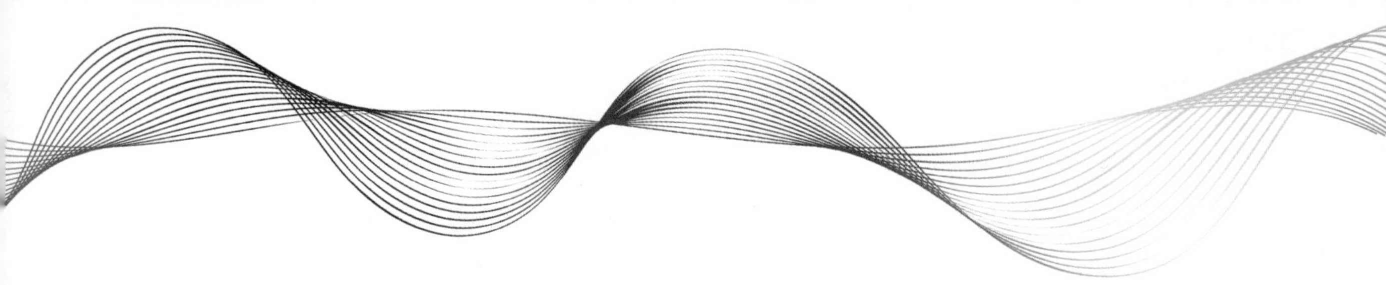

Contents

List of Boxes

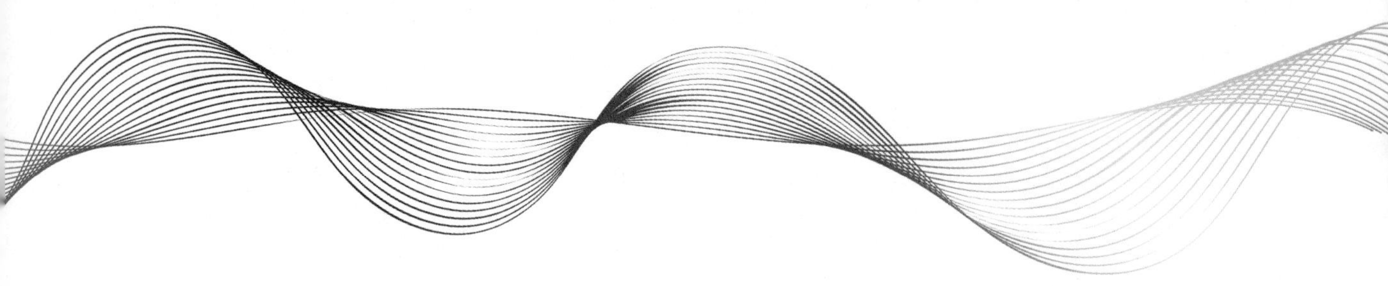

Preface

Given the rapidly changing mediascape, every revision of this textbook ends up as a significant overhaul. This time we have even changed the title. If, as outlined in Chapter 1, mass communication is still a key element of Canadian media digitization, the new media forms that have accompanied digitization have restructured the field to the extent that we thought that it was time to acknowledge the changes in the name of the book itself. So we have changed the title from *Mass Communication in Canada* to *Media and Communication in Canada*. If digitization has altered our communication habits, redrawn the map of our communications world, changed how we engage with media, and shaken to the core the communications industries themselves, digitization has also had an impact on every chapter in this book. Think, for example, of how anachronistic some of our terminology has become. Is it adequate any more to talk about media *consumers*, when many of us are also engaged in some form of media production, whether that entails posting and sharing content on social media sites, contributing reviews of movies and TV shows, submitting online comments about news stories, or developing our own podcasts and websites? When we talk about radio, television, film, books, magazines, or newspapers, do we mean the analog version, the online version, or the mobile version? What does watching TV or listening to music mean, when these activities can take place almost anywhere and anytime, using different devices? What, exactly, are we talking about? These questions preoccupied us at every stage of revising and updating this edition of the book.

This is not to suggest that in this time of transition everything is new. Certainly, one of the challenges in revising this textbook is separating what is fundamentally new and different from what only appears new. Yes, there are always new gadgets, new apps, or new services. But which of these truly alters how we communicate, and which is simply old wine in a new bottle?

The increase in our access to information is typically celebrated, but one of the things we believe to be fundamentally new is the extent to which we are under constant surveillance, as both government agencies and corporations exploit new media technologies to track, store, analyze, influence, and act upon our communications and our behaviours. One new development in this area is the extensive use of social media networks by foreign states, extremist groups, and their proxies to intervene in political debates and otherwise democratic elections.

Working conditions in the media industries have also changed fundamentally, in both the private and public sectors; secure and permanent positions are being replaced by precarious contract work, employers are demanding greater rights to sell and distribute that work across numerous platforms and through digital archiving, and workers are being asked to produce their work for multiple platforms while at the same time facing greater competition from the underpaid labour of freelancers and the free labour of interns and amateurs.

What is *not* new is the power that media corporations exert in an increasingly commercialized mediasphere. If there remains considerable talk about the democratization of communication thanks to the accessibility of digital media, corporations continue to consolidate their power by growing larger, by integrating their operations across the full range of analog and digital media, by using their human and capital resources to produce and distribute content with high production values, and by employing their promotional and marketing power to grab the attention of audiences and advertising markets. In other words, the tools available to citizens are also available to corporations, governments, and other organizations with the resources to fully exploit these tools.

Another thing that is not new is the way in which this book focuses on communication in Canada and adopts a critical perspective. With the Canadian population being relatively small and spread thinly across a vast geography bordering the United States, the media in this country are fundamental to understanding our friends, neighbours, and fellow citizens, as well as our place in the world. They are key to visualizing the unique circumstances that drive our problems, challenges, and ambitions. In other words, media sit at the heart of the forces that animate the Canadian polity. From this perspective, they are central to the democratic process, revealing and accommodating difference, and building common vision and goals. At the same time, Canadian governments at all levels draft laws, enforce regulations, fund institutions, and enact policies that shape our mediascape in fundamental ways. This can include prohibitions on things ranging from hate speech and online bullying to state and corporate surveillance, and it can include support instruments for particular media sectors and the production of certain kinds of content.

For all these reasons, having a Canadian focus, like the one we take in *Media and Communication in Canada*, Ninth Edition, is key to understanding the place and role of media in Canadian society.

Not only is this edition of *Media and Communication* fully updated with new examples, illustrations, and statistics, but it is also loaded with new content, reflecting both the shifting dimensions of the field of media and mass communication and the social and political implications of these shifts. Perhaps the biggest single challenge has been to document and analyze the growing influence that digitization and new media are having on our society; while we take digital media for granted today, they remain relatively new—for instance, the World Wide Web is only 30 years old—and they still coexist with analog versions. This is not to say that technology is the primary driver of social change, but media are certainly implicated in the shifting social, political, and economic dimensions of our society, and understanding their role in that regard is a key focus of this book.

A notable part of this edition's new content is a chapter devoted to advertising and promotional culture. Previous editions have discussed advertising and marketing, of course, but given the ubiquity of advertising and related forms of promotional messages carried by the media, we felt it deserved much more thorough treatment.

Part I, "The Sociocultural Context," situates media and mass communication within this larger context, and revisions in this section largely focus on how digitization and new media are implicated in the ways in which our daily lives and society are being restructured along social, political, economic, and geographic dimensions. We have also revised the theoretical elements of these chapters, more fully integrating them with the historical context of their development.

In Chapter 1, we provide a broad introduction to the themes and ideas presented in the book, defining terms such as *communication*, *mass communication*, and *convergence*. Here, we introduce key models for understanding the social dimensions of communication, and we consider the ways in which communication systems are central to orienting us within the world.

Chapter 2 takes a historical look at the relationships between communication, society, and culture. Terms such as *culture*, *society*, *capitalism*, and *information and communication technology* (ICT) are defined and discussed, and the roles of media and communication in the political and cultural dimensions of society are further elaborated. We examine different theories of the political role of media in this context, and we go on to consider the ways in which the distinctive elements of the social, political, and physical geographies of the Canadian state have nuanced the form and structure of the Canadian media.

Part II, "Theoretical Perspectives," surveys prominent theories pertaining to content, audiences, and media as vehicles for advertising and promotional culture, and technology.

In Chapter 3, we introduce terms that describe some basic characteristics of the process of communication and media content. Working with a model that describes communication as a process of encoding and decoding, we introduce a number of common theoretical and methodological perspectives used to study media content and illustrate how these theories relate to the production of meaning and the larger social practice of communication.

Chapter 4 addresses the dynamic interaction between media and audiences, such that audience members actively and selectively interpret media content based on frameworks of understanding they bring to that content. Such a perspective provides a means for explaining how media, audiences, and culture interact in a non-deterministic fashion and, particularly, how audiences engage with media.

Chapter 5 examines how advertising and promotional culture are deeply tied to the workings of both our economy and our culture, especially given their ubiquity and their symbiotic relationship with the media.

We have revised Chapter 6 to further emphasize the point that technology refers not merely to communications hardware and software, but as well to ways in which production practices are organized and, relatedly, to the point that all technologies are embedded within a social, cultural, political, and economic context.

Our discussion of technology serves as a nice bridge to Part III, "The Communication Environment," where we explore the structured context within which mass communication in Canada takes place today.

In Chapter 7, we review the history of cultural policy development in Canada. It has been updated to provide a better link between the approaches that characterized policy for most of the twentieth century and government responses to the circumstances facing the various communications sectors today. Chapter 8 surveys the challenges and policy responses across the various communication sectors. The ongoing convergence of Canada's cultural industries is central to this discussion, as are its impacts on what were once the separate media silos of telecommunications, broadcasting, music recording, film, new media, publishing, and the postal service.

Chapter 9 addresses media ownership and the economics of mass communication in a period when new business models are being explored, changing the game for media organizations, those who work for them, and audience members. In Chapter 10, we bring together a number of themes in the book by providing a concrete discussion of journalism as a particular, and significantly transformed, means of content production. We situate the practice of journalists in an evolving media environment that brings into play ideals, laws, settings, storytelling conventions, and economic imperatives.

Part IV, "An Evolving Communications World," is the last section of the book. It situates Canadians' communications within a global context. In Chapter 11, we define what globalization means and survey a number of theoretical currents while, at the same time, underscoring the point that the activities and institutions we have described throughout the book are not, and have never been, cut off from the rest of the world. Chapter 12 provides the conclusions and includes a concise summary of the ideas and perspectives covered in the book, while pointing the way to future study and directions of growth and development in the mass communication field.

While the renamed *Media and Communication in Canada* continues to evolve from the first edition published under the title *Mass Communication in Canada* in 1987, it also continues to bear the stamp of the vision and foresight of its original authors, Rowland "Rowly" Lorimer and Jean McNulty. Their goal of providing a rigorous, theoretically informed introduction to the field of communication studies from a Canadian perspective continues to be the guiding force behind this book. Canadians' experience of media is unique, and we believe it is critical that those studying the media in Canada understand and appreciate the particularities of the Canadian mediascape.

Those who have used this book in the past have no doubt noticed that Rowly's name has been replaced by a new author, Natalie Coulter. Rowly has retired from the School of Communication at Simon Fraser University and, after serving as the guiding force through the first eight editions of what came to be known as "the Lorimer book," has entrusted us with continuing, and building upon, its legacy. Aside from conceiving of the book's approach and its initial structure, Rowly was also a mentor to his co-authors. Mike Gasher had been an undergraduate student in the Canadian Studies program that Rowly directed, and Rowly later supervised Mike's MA thesis in Simon Fraser's communication program. When Mike completed his PhD in communication studies at Concordia University in 1999 and joined Concordia's journalism department as an assistant professor, Rowly invited him to co-author the fourth edition. David Skinner was an undergraduate student of Rowly's at Simon Fraser and had taught various versions of *Mass Communication in Canada* as a lecturer and later as a professor in the Department of Communication Studies at York University. David became a co-author as of the sixth edition, published in 2008. Mike and David have learned a great deal from Rowly Lorimer over the years: about all facets of the Canadian mediascape to be sure, but also how best to convey that information to students, both directly, as an instructor in the classroom, and through a textbook such as this.

With Rowly's retirement, Mike and David invited Natalie Coulter to join the team. Natalie, also a Simon Fraser alum, is an assistant professor in the Department of Communication Studies at York University. Her central research interests include girls' studies, critical advertising studies, and the media of children and young people. She is a founding member of the Association for Research on the Cultures of Young People, and is completing a SSHRC-funded research project entitled *The Embodied Tween: Living Girlhood in Global and Digital Spaces*. She is the author of *Tweening the Girl: The Crystallization of the Tween Market* (2014), co-editor of the special issue, "Locating Tween Girls," of the journal *Girlhood Studies* (2018), and co-editor of the collection *Youth Mediations and Affective Relations* (2018). Natalie has used earlier editions of *Mass Communication in Canada* as a textbook numerous times in courses she taught at both the college and university levels.

Acknowledgments

We—Mike, David, and Natalie—would like to thank our colleagues who provided the specialized box material included with the chapters, as well as our partners Dianne Arbuckle, Jennefer Laidley, and Troy Hammond for their constant support. We appreciate the helpful comments of both the named and anonymous reviewers of the text, including

Darren Blakeborough, University of the Fraser Valley
Andrea Braithwaite, University of Ontario Institute of Technology
Lisa Broda, University of Saskatchewan
Rita Isola, Capilano University
Sandra Jeppesen, Lakehead University
Ravindra N. Mohabeer, Vancouver Island University
Wade Nelson, University of Winnipeg
Kathryn Pallister, Red Deer College
Gregory Taylor, University of Calgary

We also thank the editorial, management, and sales teams at Oxford University Press Canada for their work and continued support of this book. We are particularly thankful to acquisitions editor Stephen Kotowych and the editor of the ninth edition, Lauren Wing, for their efforts in shepherding us through this revision.

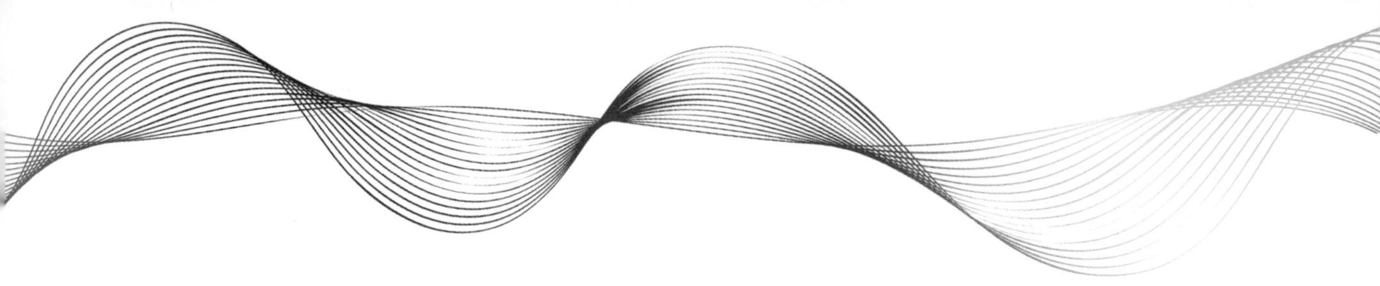

From the Publisher

The ninth edition of *Media and Communication in Canada* builds on the successful approach used in the previous editions that has served instructors and students well. It gives first-time students a comprehensive, engaging, and clear introduction to the study of media and communication, ensuring that they understand the subject matter in sociological, political, technological, and economic terms.

The coverage of the topics in the text retains the best features of the previous edition while adding new information on current trends and changes in media:

- New discussion of franchise formats in media (Chapter 3)
- New analysis of the changing nature of TV (Chapter 4)
- A brand new chapter on advertising and promotional media (Chapter 5)
- New discussion of the regulation of music streaming services (Chapter 8)
- Increased content on indigenous media and reconciliation (Chapters 8, 11)
- New discussion of fake news and the post-truth era (Chapter 10)
- Increased content on diversity, representation, and ethnocultural media (Chapter 10)

Thoroughly revised and updated, this authoritative guide explores the shifting nature of media and communication systems by examining traditional and new media, and a wealth of current media issues and trends. Highlighting historical and social contexts, theoretical perspectives, and cutting-edge research and debates, *Media and Communication in Canada* will help students think critically about the place and role of media and communication in their own lives and in Canadian society.

Contributed boxes from Canadian communication scholars give students an in-depth yet accessible look into the latest studies, media issues, and trends in the field:

Box 4.2	"Feminism and Media Studies" by Tamara Shepherd
Box 4.3	"Fan Studies" by Steve Bailey
Box 5.2	"Identity Politics" by Kisha McPherson
Box 6.4	"Platforms or Walled Gardens?" by Fenwick McKelvey
Box 8.4	"Copyright" by Sara Bannerman
Box 8.5	"The Video-Game Industry in Canada: A Snapshot" by Greig de Peuter and Chris J. Young
Box 9.5	"Precarious Labour" by Errol Salamon
Box 10.6	"Ethnocultural Media" by April Lindgren
Box 10.9	"Podcasting" by Andrea Hunter

5

Advertising and Promotional Culture

Advertising is capitalism's way of saying "I love you" to itself.
—*Michael Schudson*

Torontonian / Alamy Stock Photo

Opening Questions

- How are advertising and promotion a cultural force?
- What theoretical perspectives are used to study and understand the relationships between advertising and promotion and the media?
- How is advertising a form of ideology?
- How do advertising and promotion change in digital media?
- What are some of the ways that the media functions as a system to deliver audiences to advertisers?

A brand new chapter on advertising and promotional media examines the relationship between advertising and media.

136 | **Part II** Theoretical Perspectives

Fed Ex's holiday campaign #howtheholidaysarrive enlisted influencers like Julia Engel of the blog *Gal Meets Glam* to create content for the campaign.

Influencers engage in promotional culture by three means, according to Crystal Abidin's research on selfies and Instagrammers. First, they disseminate content by sharing, liking, retweeting, and pinning, depending on the social media platform. This requires no action from their followers but merely pushes out content. Second, they aggregate by inviting their followers to respond to a dedicated thread. This includes contests, surveys, or questionnaires, sometimes to win a prize. This amplifies the original content. And finally, they instigate by encouraging followers to generate or recreate content by uploading videos onto websites or feeds (2016). Abidin suggests that followers become "a network of advertorial capillaries by duplicating, amplifying, and multiplying" the influencer content to their own circle of friends (2016: 4). What this means is that it is not simply the influencers themselves but also their followers whose digital labour is exploited.

Promotion in digital capitalism relies on people to become creative labourers who do the work for little or no compensation. Instead, their creative work becomes part of the marketing and promotion of brands. For example, a growing form of advertising production is sourced from audience members as companies call on audiences to craft commercials themselves. Frito-Lay, for instance, has run consumer-produced ads, otherwise known as user-generated content, on the Super Bowl broadcast for several years, and companies such as Starbucks and General Motors have also capitalized on this trend of having consumers/fans produce digital content. If nothing else, the hype around such contests in itself generates an excitement for the brand and strengthens audience attention to those ads. In Canada, the brand Hotels.com famously had people create and upload videos of themselves as Captain Obvious, the brand spokesperson. The winning video was

A contemporary design reflects the digital, quickly changing world of communication in which we live.

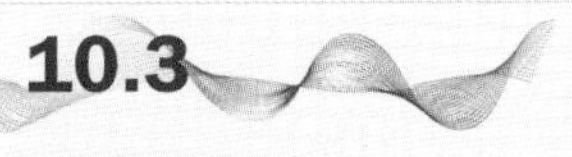

10.3 Fake News

The proper functioning of democratic society depends on a number of institutions providing its citizens with information that is factual, accurate, verifiable, trustworthy, and credible: government (through agencies such as Statistics Canada), the legal system (courts, police), the education system (through both research and teaching), the medical establishment (from doctors to researchers), and journalism. Factual information forms the basis of every kind of decision-making process.

If fake news has a long history—think of the trashy tabloid newspapers and celebrity magazines displayed at supermarket checkouts—it has become a much more serious problem given the ease with which social media networks can be deployed to fabricate or distort news reports and images.

The erosion of public trust is a serious threat, as media theorist Roger Silverstone argues: "For the media to be viable they have to be trusted by their addressees" (2007: 124). Once that trust is lost, Silverstone maintains, it is almost impossible to restore.

Bill Kovach and Tom Rosenstiel have described journalism as a "discipline of verification" as opposed to a "discipline of assertion." They write, "In the end, the discipline of verification is what separates journalism from entertainment, propaganda, fiction, or art" (2001: 71).

Methods of verification have taken on renewed importance given the increasingly open access to media networks, and social media in particular. The Knight Foundation (Hindman and Barash, 2018) conducted a study of "the fake news ecosystem" in the aftermath of the 2016 US presidential election, which was subjected to numerous and sophisticated disinformation campaigns. Analyzing 10 million tweets from 700,000 Twitter accounts linked to more than 600 "fake and conspiracy news outlets" in a 30-day period in spring 2017, the Knight Foundation concluded that "disinformation continues to be a substantial problem postelection." It tracked 4 million tweets linked to fake news and conspiracy producers, estimating that 70 per cent of the sites were automated (3–4).

The subsequent Donald Trump presidency in the United States has been noteworthy in prompting news organizations like the *Washington Post* (see Rizzo, 2018) and the *New York Times* (see Qiu, 2018) to publish regularly the results of fact-checking White House statements. And, of course, news consumers have greater capacity to do their own fact-checking (see Silverman, 2007).

New boxed content appears throughout to promote further learning.

Aids to Student Learning

Numerous features promoting student learning are incorporated throughout the book. They include the following:

Opening Questions help students focus their reading at the outset of each chapter by asking the questions that the chapter will explore and answer.

Summary sections review key concepts and objectives at the end of each chapter.

Lists of **Key Terms** highlight the important words in each chapter that students might want to explore further.

Related Websites and **Further Readings** offer more resources for students who seek to expand their knowledge of media and communication.

Study Questions at the end of each chapter are a great tool for study and review.

2

The History of Media

Social and Cultural Forms

The greatest power of the mass media is the power to ignore.
—*American essayist Sam Smith*

EQRoy/Shutterstock

Opening Questions

- What were the Renaissance and the Enlightenment? Why are they important to contemporary notions of citizenship and democracy?
- What were the roles and purposes of media as they developed in industrial society?
- How do libertarian theory, the social responsibility theory of the press, the mass society thesis, and critical political economy each conceive of the role(s) of the media in society?
- What are the distinctive characteristics of the Canadian state that have helped shape its communication systems?

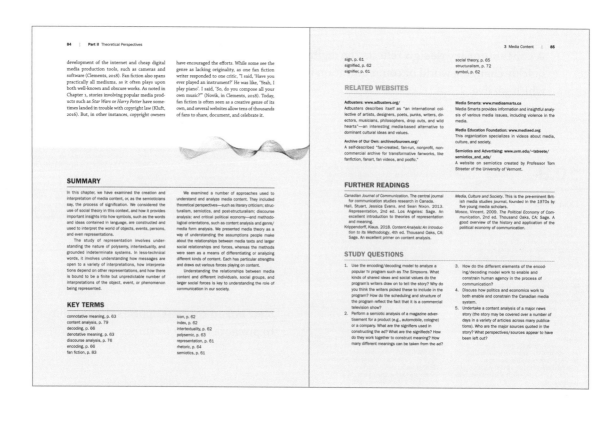

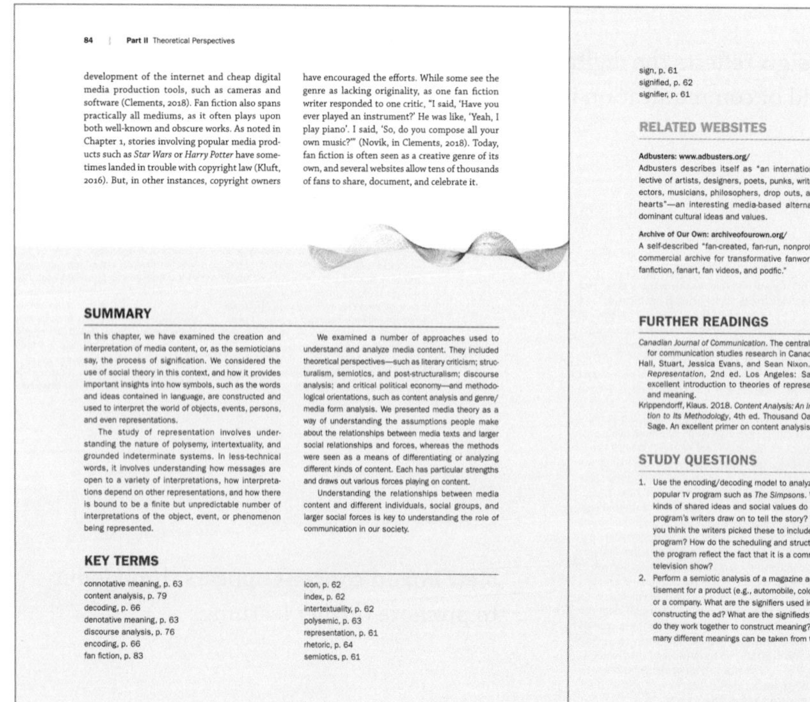

84 | **Part II** Theoretical Perspectives

development of the internet and cheap digital media production tools, such as cameras and software (Clements, 2018). Fan fiction also spans practically all mediums, as it often plays upon both well-known and obscure works. As noted in Chapter 1, stories involving popular media products such as *Star Wars* or *Harry Potter* have sometimes landed in trouble with copyright law (Kluft, 2016). But, in other instances, copyright owners have encouraged the efforts. While some see the genre as lacking originality, as one fan fiction writer responded to one critic, "I said, 'Have you ever played an instrument?' He was like, 'Yeah, I play piano'. I said, 'So, do you compose all your own music?'" (Novik, in Clements, 2018). Today, fan fiction is often seen as a creative genre of its own, and several websites allow tens of thousands of fans to share, document, and celebrate it.

SUMMARY

In this chapter, we have examined the creation and interpretation of media content, or, as the semioticians say, the process of signification. We considered the use of social theory in this context, and how it provides important insights into how symbols, such as the words and ideas contained in language, are constructed and used to interpret the world of objects, events, persons, and even representations.

The study of representation involves understanding the nature of polysemy, intertextuality, and grounded indeterminate systems. In less-technical words, it involves understanding how messages are open to a variety of interpretations, how interpretations depend on other representations, and how there is bound to be a finite but unpredictable number of interpretations of the object, event, or phenomenon being represented.

We examined a number of approaches used to understand and analyze media content. They included theoretical perspectives—such as literary criticism; structuralism, semiotics, and post-structuralism; discourse analysis; and critical political economy—and methodological orientations, such as content analysis and genre/media form analysis. We presented media theory as a way of understanding the assumptions people make about the relationships between media texts and larger social relationships and forces, whereas the methods were seen as a means of differentiating or analyzing different kinds of content. Each has particular strengths and draws out various forces playing on content.

Understanding the relationships between media content and different individuals, social groups, and larger social forces is key to understanding the role of communication in our society.

KEY TERMS

connotative meaning, p. 63
content analysis, p. 79
decoding, p. 66
denotative meaning, p. 63
discourse analysis, p. 76
encoding, p. 66
fan fiction, p. 83
icon, p. 62
index, p. 62
intertextuality, p. 62
polysemic, p. 63
representation, p. 61
rhetoric, p. 64
semiotics, p. 61
sign, p. 61
signified, p. 62
signifier, p. 61
social theory, p. 65
structuralism, p. 72
symbol, p. 62

3 Media Content | 85

RELATED WEBSITES

Adbusters: www.adbusters.org/
Adbusters describes itself as "an international collective of artists, designers, poets, punks, writers, directors, musicians, philosophers, drop outs, and wild hearts"—an interesting media-based alternative to dominant cultural ideas and values.

Archive of Our Own: archiveofourown.org/
A self-described "fan-created, fan-run, nonprofit, noncommercial archive for transformative fanworks, like fanfiction, fanart, fan videos, and podfic."

Media Smarts: www.mediasmarts.ca
Media Smarts provides information and insightful analysis of various media issues, including violence in the media.

Media Education Foundation: www.mediaed.org
This organization specializes in videos about media, culture, and society.

Semiotics and Advertising: www.uvm.edu/~tstreete/semiotics_and_ads/
A website on semiotics created by Professor Tom Streeter of the University of Vermont.

FURTHER READINGS

Canadian Journal of Communication. The central journal for communication studies research in Canada.

Hall, Stuart, Jessica Evans, and Sean Nixon. 2013. *Representation*, 2nd ed. Los Angeles: Sage. An excellent introduction to theories of representation and meaning.

Krippendorff, Klaus. 2018. *Content Analysis: An Introduction to Its Methodology*, 4th ed. Thousand Oaks, CA: Sage. An excellent primer on content analysis.

Media, Culture and Society. This is the pre-eminent British media studies journal, founded in the 1970s by five young media scholars.

Mosco, Vincent. 2009. *The Political Economy of Communication*, 2nd ed. Thousand Oaks, CA: Sage. A good overview of the history and application of the political economy of communication.

STUDY QUESTIONS

1. Use the encoding/decoding model to analyze a popular TV program such as *The Simpsons*. What kinds of shared ideas and social values do the program's writers draw on to tell the story? Why do you think the writers picked these to include in the program? How do the scheduling and structure of the program reflect the fact that it is a commercial television show?
2. Perform a semiotic analysis of a magazine advertisement for a product (e.g., automobile, cologne) or a company. What are the signifiers used in constructing the ad? What are the signifieds? How do they work together to construct meaning? How many different meanings can be taken from the ad?
3. How do the different elements of the encoding/decoding model work to enable and constrain human agency in the process of communication?
4. Discuss how politics and economics work to both enable and constrain the Canadian media system.
5. Undertake a content analysis of a major news story (the story may be covered over a number of days in a variety of articles across many publications). Who are the major sources quoted in the story? What perspectives/sources appear to have been left out?

Instructor and Student Supplements Accompanying the Text

Media and Communication in Canada is part of a comprehensive package of learning and teaching tools that includes resources for both students and instructors all available in the Ancillaries Resource Centre (ARC): www.oup.com/he/Gasher9e.

For the Instructor

An **instructor's manual** includes overviews of each chapter, learning objectives, sample lecture outlines, overviews of key concepts, lists of online resources, review questions, and suggestions for student assignments, activities, and debates.

A **test bank** offers a comprehensive set of multiple choice, true/false, short-answer, and discussion questions, with suggested answers, for every chapter.

PowerPoint slides summarizing key points from each chapter, and incorporating figures and tables from the textbook, are available to adopters of the text.

Instructors should contact their Oxford University Press sales representative for details on these supplements and for login and password information.

For the Student

A **Student Study Guide** offers chapter overviews, related websites, study questions, and self-grading quizzes.

To access these useful features, go to **www.oup.com/he/Gasher9e** and follow the links!

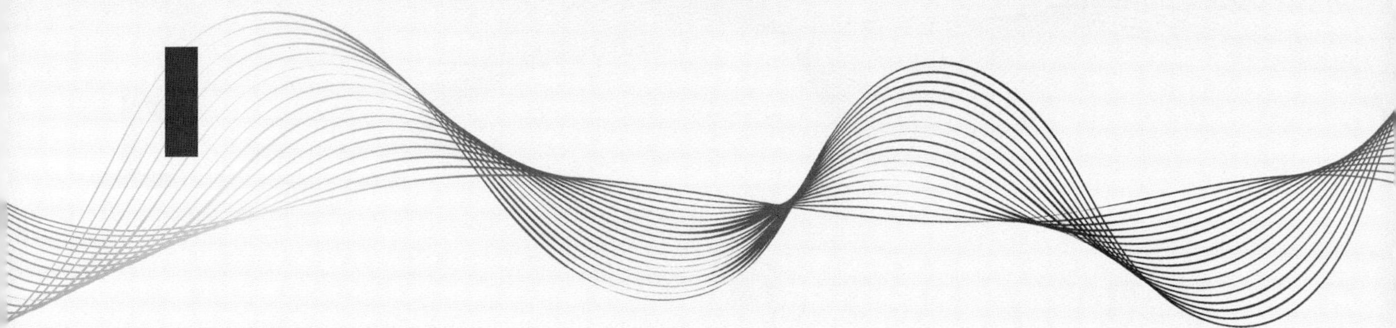

The Sociocultural Context

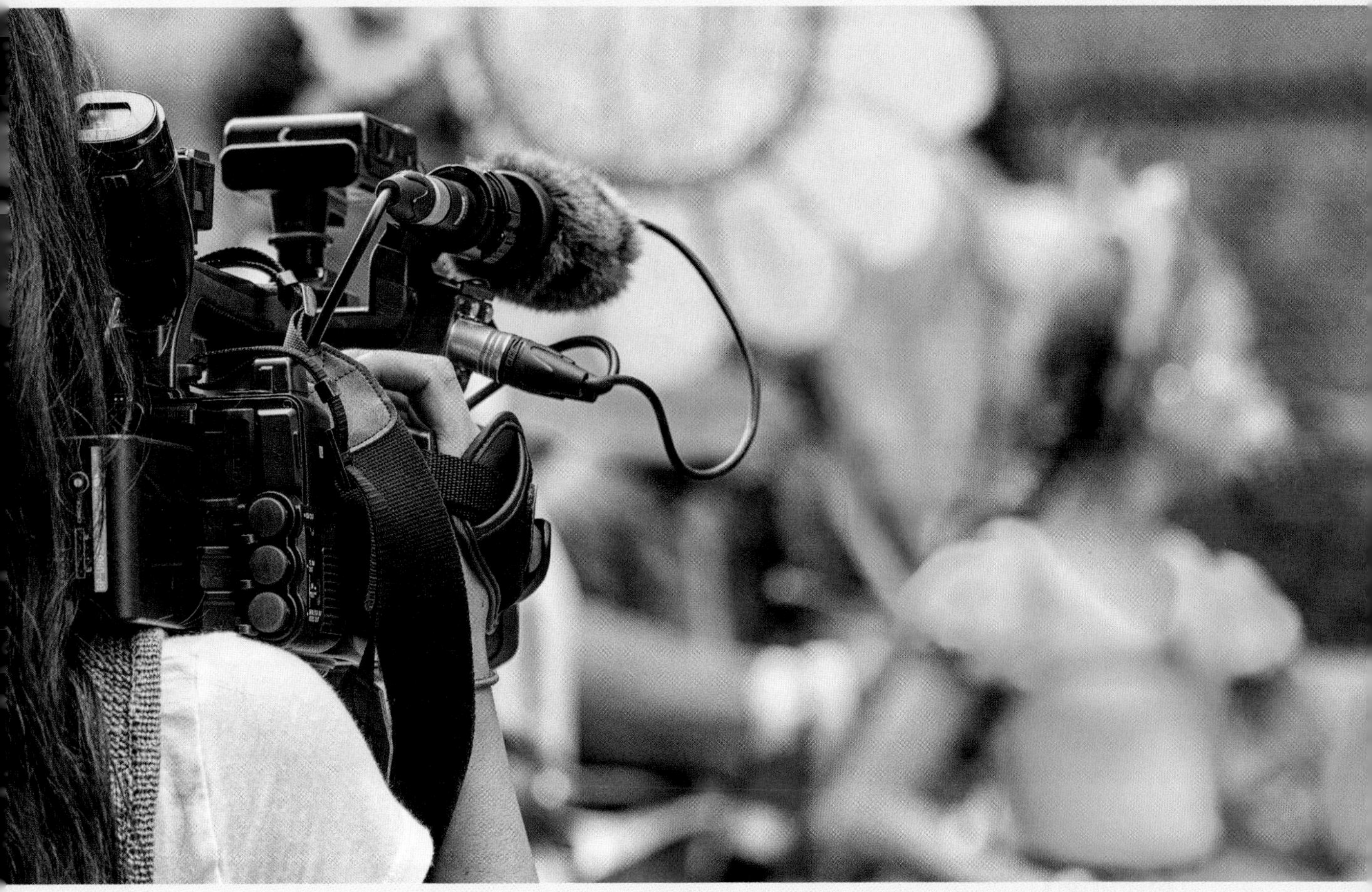

Rick Rudnicki/Alamy Stock Photo

1

Defining the Field

Without communication, what is there? —*Anonymous*

izusek/iStockphoto

Opening Questions

- What is communication?
- What are communication media?
- How important are media to our knowledge and understanding of the world?
- How have shifts in communication media contributed to changing our understanding of the world?
- What are some of the larger social roles of media?

Introduction

Media lie at the heart of our contemporary world. From cellphones to Facebook, television to blogs, newspapers to satellites, Twitter to Google, media and communication systems are central to our understanding of the world and how we coordinate our actions within it. In this textbook, we provide an introduction to the study of media and communication and their relationships to larger social institutions and processes. We examine their history, the ways in which they are woven into different elements and processes that form the dimensions of our lives, and various ways of interpreting how they shape and nuance our perspectives and experience of the world.

We introduce these themes and ideas in this chapter, illustrating the shifting nature of communication technology, considering how media and communication systems are central to the functioning and operation of our society, and examining the ways in which they orient us to the world. We examine traditional media, digital media, and social media, and we consider the ways they frame our perspectives. We provide definitions for terms such as *communication* and *convergence*, and we present two models of the process of communication. As you work through the text and our exploration of the field of communication, these definitions and models will provide the basis for building a common understanding of the subjects under study. Finally, in preparation for developing broader theoretical perspectives on media as social and cultural forms, this chapter goes on to outline and examine some of the social roles of media and communication.

Media in an Ever-changing Communications Universe

Media are central to the ways in which, as individuals, we come to know and understand the world. As Isaiah Berlin puts it, they are "part of the 'general texture of experience'" (Silverstone, 1999: 2). They are involved in almost all aspects of our lives—deciding on a career, getting an education, thinking about politics and government, finding the music we listen to, getting a job, purchasing clothes, planning a date, deciding what to eat and where to buy it, paying bills, and finding a place to live. Media help us decide what we need and want, why we care, and even who we are. They frame our focus on the world, draw us in, and entwine us in an artfully crafted patchwork of events and circumstances. From deep ocean trenches to inside volcanoes, and from local neighbourhoods to the surfaces of the moon and Mars, media carry us across space. They also play on how we experience time, providing windows on news and events unfolding currently in "real" time, as well as how we experience things that happened hours, days, or even years ago.

Statistics indicate how pervasive media are in people's lives. Canadians spend an average of 26.6 hours per week watching television and 16.6 hours per week listening to the radio

(CRTC, 2017); 90 per cent of Canadians use the internet, 74 per cent spend 3–4 hours a day online, and 42 per cent of households have five or more internet-connected devices (CIRA, 2018).

But not only are communication media key to our individual lives, they are also central to the larger organization and functioning of our society. Media help bind Canadians together with common ideas and understandings of our culture. From maple leaves to hockey to health care and beyond, they create what Benedict Anderson (1983) calls an "imagined community" and help construct and feed our conceptions about Canada and what it means to be Canadian. Media are the major means through which governments—federal, provincial, and municipal—communicate with residents and citizens. (It may surprise you to know that government is the largest single advertiser in this country!) They are the primary way that businesses develop and communicate with customers. Media are also key agents in globalization. They are the central vehicle for controlling the world economy and the movement of goods and services around the globe—for example, coordinating centres of production in China with markets in Canada. And media also introduce people to different cultures and keep immigrants in touch with the countries from which they moved. Media also work to generate a global cultural consciousness through blanket coverage of political and economic news from around the world, mass sports events such as the Olympics and soccer's World Cup, and global tragedies such as airline disasters, earthquakes, and hurricanes. They also help raise our consciousness about our roles in impending environmental disasters, like global warming. In this heavily mediated world, where the implications of one person's or country's actions can span the globe, "think globally, act locally" has become the new universal mantra, and media are the vehicles through which such actions are coordinated.

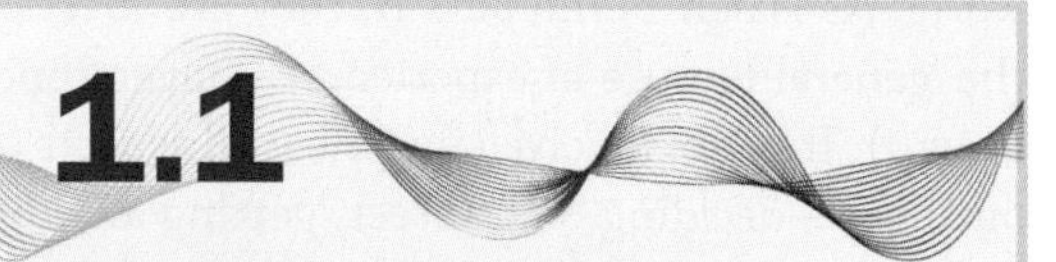

Canadians Are #1 in Internet Usage on the Planet According to the World Atlas

Canadians spend an average of 43.5 hours online per month, making us the top users of the internet globally. As we discuss in Chapter 11, however, what this average masks is how people living in urban centres, and those with higher incomes, have better access to the internet than those living in rural areas or those with lower incomes.

Average Hours Spent Online per Person per Month

Country	Hours
Canada	43.5
United States	35.3
United Kingdom	32.3
South Korea	27.7
France	26.6
Brazil	25.8
Germany	24.1
Russia	21.8
Japan	18.4
China	13.5
India	11.9

Source: World Atlas, 2017.

Twenty-five years ago, the internet was largely the purview of scientists and researchers. Today, along with the more traditional media—such as television broadcasting, film, newspaper and book publishing, and sound recording (music)—the internet is a key element of our lives. But while some writers argue that new internet-based media are making old media obsolete, the internet isn't so much replacing traditional media industries as it is incorporating them and serving as another vehicle for their distribution. Almost two decades ago, downloading music from sites such as Napster and Pirate Bay was thought to spell the death of the music industry; but that industry adapted, and the popularity and revenues of sites like iTunes indicate the industry is still very much alive. While blogging and citizen journalism were once seen as displacing newspapers and traditional news sources, today's bloggers and people writing about news on social media develop much of the material they publish and circulate from those traditional media. Similarly, as streaming services such as Netflix and Crave illustrate, television programs and networks, once seen as being displaced by internet programming, are finding a new means of distribution online.

The internet, however, does offer much more than traditional media. By joining computing power with transmission capacity, digital media platforms and companies such as Google, Twitter, Facebook, Instagram, YouTube, and Wikipedia have opened up new ways of seeing and understanding the world, extended personal relationships and social networks, and enabled once-passive consumers of media to become producers of content. Yochai Benkler (2006: 2) points out that this new information environment holds a number of promises "as a dimension of individual freedom; as a platform for better democratic participation; as a medium to foster a more critical and self-reflective culture; and, in an increasingly information-dependent global economy, as a mechanism to achieve improvements in human development everywhere." As we shall see, while such promises are a long way from being fulfilled, the struggle to reshape the institutions and organizations that provide form and focus to this information environment, and the media it supports, is ongoing.

fyv6561/Shutterstock

By June 2018, there were more than 2.23 billion monthly Facebook users and 328 million people active on Twitter monthly.

Back to the Future

It is easy for us to get caught up in the wave of digital media and its propensity for expanding the reach and speed of communication and to forget the internet is only one of many major electronic media innovations introduced in the last two centuries. As digital media ushered in various forms of social change and, in some instances, made older media obsolete, they, too, were seen as revolutionary and world-changing.

The telegraph, the world's first mode of electronic communication, was one of the most revolutionary of communication media. As James Carey (1989: 201) argues, "Perhaps the most important fact about the telegraph is [that it] permitted for the first time the effective separation of communication from transportation." No longer did letters and other forms of communication need to be transported physically by horse and rider, carrier pigeon, or ship. Instead, messages could be transported almost "at the speed of light" across vast distances. This innovation helped spur other changes, such as standard time zones and modern markets.

To be sure, the telegraph was a key technology in *shrinking space through time*—that is, reducing the time it took to accomplish particular tasks in space (see Figure 1.1). With the telegraph, transactions that might have previously taken weeks or even months to accomplish via mail could be completed in a few minutes. Rather than sending a written order by horseback, people could now transmit a short telegraphic message between Vancouver and Toronto and confirm the need for raw materials such as wood or iron ore to be shipped from the industrial periphery to factories in Canada's central core. Similarly, a telegram between Montreal and Halifax could initiate sending finished products such as stoves or furniture back out to the distant margins. Telegraph technology was also helpful in exerting political control over space. The news of uprisings and social discontent in distant colonies could be instantly communicated to central governments, and troops could be dispatched to quell such disturbances. Just as the internet and social networking sites today seem to shrink the distance between friends and colleagues, the telegraph shortened the time to accomplish or coordinate action at a distance, thus making the world seem smaller.

But the telegraph was not invented in a vacuum. From semaphore towers to smoke signals, it had many predecessors, although due to their vulnerability to bad weather and other natural hazards, none were as efficient (see page 7). But neither the invention of the telegraph nor its adoption as a major medium of communication happened overnight. Principles behind the technology were developed in the early eighteenth century, and proposals for telegraph systems were being written by around 1750. While a number of attempts to establish telegraph lines began in 1800, it wasn't until the 1830s that the first successful telegraphs were established, and they didn't become relatively common until the 1850s—a century after the technology was first conceived.

The development and adoption of the telephone and radio followed a similar track. The idea of the telephone, for instance, leaned heavily on earlier inventions, such as the speaking tube. And patents for a range of electronic means of transmitting voice messages by wire or over the air were filed years before the telephone and radio that we know today were actually developed for widespread commercial use.

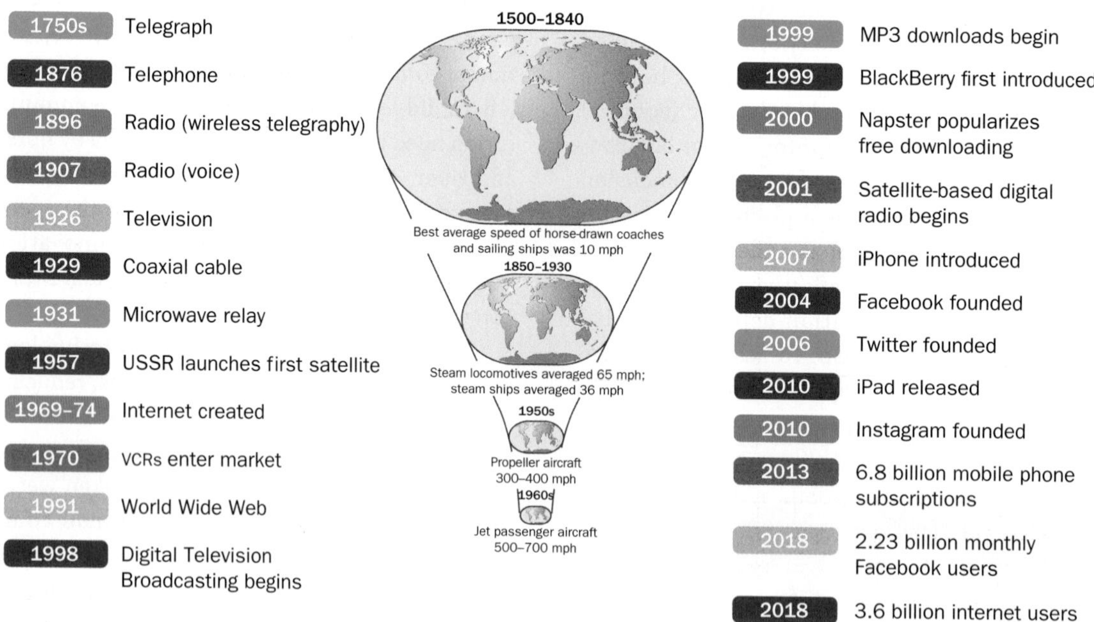

FIGURE 1.1 The Shrinking Globe

With the invention of each of these new media, the world seemingly gets smaller. Whether we are buying or selling goods and services, keeping in touch with friends and family, or relaxing with film, video, or music, digital media have increasingly helped make it easier to communicate with others and have thereby made the distances between people and places seem smaller. In other words, these technologies "shrink space" by reducing the time it takes to coordinate action across distance.

Source: Adapted from David Harvey, *The Condition of Postmodernity* (Oxford: Blackwell, 1989), 241, plate 3.1.

HIP/Art Resource, NY

Modern modes of communication build upon technologies of the past. The telegraph, for instance, was modelled on semaphore towers, like this one, which relied upon flags to communicate messages over distances. Invented in France in 1792, semaphore towers were a faster and cheaper form of communication than the mail. The arms on the top of the tower could be placed at various angles, creating shapes that were coded as letters or words.

As they began to be used widely, both the telephone and the radio were seen as inventions that shrank space. The telephone initially was marketed as a business tool and used to help coordinate the sale of goods and services. Like the telegraph, it was seen as a means of closing the distance between businesses and their customers, as salespeople used the phone to contact customers, and customers were able to call suppliers to order products. It is worth remembering that prior to the telephone, people living on the prairie in Saskatchewan would have to write letters to Eaton's department store in Toronto to order everything from clothes to pots and pans to houses and then wait weeks or even months for that order to be processed and delivered. With the widespread adoption of the telephone, much of that wait time was eliminated.

Radio, on the other hand—with its propensity for spreading ideas—was envisioned as creating common perspectives and understanding, or a common consciousness, between people. In a speech later that summer about the first Canadian national radio broadcast on 1 July 1927, Canada's sixtieth birthday, Prime Minister Mackenzie King talked about how the technology brought the people of Canada together through enabling them to hear speeches and other business of government in Ottawa. In doing so, he thought that people would become more interested and involved in the affairs of the country. As he said,

> On the morning, afternoon and evening of July 1, all Canada became, for the time being, a single assemblage, swayed by common emotion, within the sound of a single voice. . . . Hitherto to most Canadians, Ottawa seemed far off, a mere name to hundreds of thousands of our people, but henceforth all Canadians will stand within the sound of the carillon and within the speakers of Parliament Hill. May we not predict that as a result of this carrying of the living voice throughout the length and breadth of the Dominion, there will be aroused more general interest in public affairs, and an increased devotion of the individual citizen to the common weal. (Weir, 1965: 38)

From this point of view, we can see why Benedict Anderson (1983) considers communication technologies as central in helping create the "imagined community" of the nation-state.

Through the 1930s and '40s, radio became one of the major providers of news and entertainment. In living rooms across the country, families gathered around the radio after dinner to listen to radio plays, sporting events, and news. Whether broadcast from across town or across the country, radio brought people "closer" to distant events and circumstances while, at the same time, creating common points of reference for the population. Strangers meeting at school, work, on the bus, or at the coffee shop didn't seem so strange when it was discovered that they cheered on the same hockey team, laughed at the same jokes on the radio, and held similar concerns about the issues and events that gripped politics at city hall or Parliament in Ottawa.

Just like the telegraph and radio, television extended and deepened social ties, too. In 1969, TV showed images of humans' first footsteps on the moon, making history in connecting viewers to points beyond earth. But like all new communication technologies, there was some time between its invention and widespread adoption, and while television was first demonstrated in the mid-1920s, it wasn't until the 1950s that it began to elbow radio out of Canadian living rooms.

With the arrival of television, radio was seen by some as becoming obsolete and without any real future. With the development of new technology, however, radio receivers shrank from the size of large boxes to small packages that could be installed in the dashboards of cars or stuffed in jacket pockets. In this guise, radio took on a new life as one of the first mobile electronic media. In the process, radio largely moved from the foreground to the background, as people began listening to it while performing other activities like driving from one place to another, working on the job, or doing chores at home.

Cable television was first introduced in US cities in the late 1940s and early '50s. Coaxial cables carry much more information than regular copper wire, so they were used to bring multiple television channels to places where over-the-air television signals were blocked by buildings or natural barriers.

By the late 1960s, people began to see the cable's carriage capacity as the gateway to a wide range of new information services similar to those available over the internet today. These new visions of a heavily connected way of life were heralded as the *wired city*. As we discuss in later chapters, cable-based interactive television was at the heart of these plans, and through the 1970s, experiments in building communities where electronic communication was central to the fabric of everyday life took place in countries such as Canada, the United States, Japan, France, Germany, and Britain (refer also to the Telidon system on page 20). However, it wasn't until the 1990s and the widespread use of personal computers, digitized information, and the internet that the original vision of the wired city actually began to materialize.

From this brief history, we can see that media development and changes in communication are ongoing processes. Each advance in electronic communication technology was built upon previous technologies and, in many ways, continued to enhance the relationships established by the telegraph. Through helping extend people's reach and reducing the amount of time it takes to accomplish certain tasks and activities across space—such as ordering a book online rather than going to a bookstore, taking a course over the internet instead of commuting to a campus classroom, or skyping with friends and family in lieu of travelling distances to see them—media are said to shrink space through time. As media have changed, moreover, they have become increasingly pervasive in our lives, helping to shape how we see, understand, and act within the world. Whether the changes media have wrought in our lives are positive or negative is the subject of considerable debate.

Media and Technology: A Brave New World?

Promoters of digital media and communication technologies often present a particularly optimistic or *utopian* view of media development. They claim that communication technology increasingly delivers more choice in information and entertainment. From news to entertainment programs, whether via film, music, video games, or websites like Crave, Netflix, and iTunes, media offer more and more consumer choice and—as mobile technologies gain customers—services are increasingly available from any location. Digital communication systems also offer an increasingly available and convenient range of consumer products. From this perspective, access to education and government services is said to be better. And all of one's needs and desires can be met with a few clicks on a keyboard, as one can purchase food, clothes, shelter, pets, and sex online.

But wait, there's even more! Digital media are also often portrayed as ushering in truly participatory democracy on a global scale. With all the information available online, people are said to be able to inform themselves of the issues that affect their lives as never before. They can talk back to the institutions and people who hold power by telling governments and corporations what they think about issues and products. They can produce and circulate information that represents their point of view. The technology provides opportunities to vote on many issues. Supposedly, it offers true democracy where everybody knows and understands the issues that affect them, and has the ability to make their views known.

Others, however, are not so sanguine in their assessment of new media technology. They contend that communication systems designed on the basis of the profit motive or market principles primarily serve owners and investors, not citizens. For instance, because new (and old) commercial communication enterprises seek revenue from advertisers, they first serve the needs of those advertisers. Consequently only those media products that generate profits for advertisers are available. Owners of private media companies—radio or television stations, newspaper publishers, internet service providers, or social media platforms—are in business to make money for themselves and their shareholders, not to perform public service. All the better if they can perform some public service or provide some public good, but this is not their primary purpose.

As British media scholar and cultural critic Raymond Williams once noted, within such a media system people are free to say anything they want as long as they can say it profitably. Ideas and perspectives that fail to meet the logic of increasing profits—such as those calling attention to the drawbacks of consumer lifestyles or issues affecting the poor and cultural and ethnic minorities—are sidelined or left out altogether.

Media owners also want to attract the largest number of audience members or users for the least amount of money. In Canada, this has particular consequences. As you may have noticed, television broadcasters other than the CBC carry very little Canadian programming other than sports and news. Why is this? Is it because Canadians make bad television? If that were the case, why are so many American television programs filmed in Canada? No, as we shall see in later chapters, the problem isn't that Canadians make bad TV. (In fact, American media producers spend billions of dollars each year making film and television programs in Canada using Canadian workers.) Rather it is because, after recovering most of their costs in American markets, American programming is sold to Canadian broadcasters at a fraction of its cost of production, and a fraction of the cost of producing or purchasing Canadian programming. In other words, American shows dominate Canadian programming not because Canadians want or prefer such media fare, but because media companies make much more money carrying US programming than Canadian shows.

Privacy is another key issue (see Chapter 6). In such a heavily mediated world, people are constantly sharing information about themselves. Whether it's on social networking sites or blogs, where we share ideas, pictures, and experiences with our friends and colleagues, or on web surveys, sign-ups, and applications, companies and governments are recording or following our online activities. Our actions and preferences are constantly being monitored and often accessed by advertisers, parents, schools, insurance companies, government spy agencies, and police departments. As a result, some people are finding themselves inundated with commercial spam, kicked out of school, denied medical insurance, fired from a job, and even charged with crimes.

Access is yet another problem (see Chapters 6 and 8). There is little doubt that media are becoming the lifeblood of our society and that access to media is important not only for satisfying individual needs and desires, but also for educational purposes and to exercise one's rights as a citizen. But not everyone has access to media systems. In our cities, large numbers of families and individuals cannot afford to own the latest computers or to have internet service. In some small towns, places in Canada's North, and rural areas across the country, even dial-up internet service is not available, let alone the high-speed access that many of us take for granted. And in many developing countries around the world even phone service is a luxury that many cannot afford. This **digital divide** is one of the key issues facing media policy-makers today.

So, do media serve public purposes or are they mere profit centres for investors? Is technology going to help in creating a better, more equitable world, or is it going to widen the digital divide? In a larger sense, will the gap between rich and poor get worse? Ultimately, what are the implications of the ongoing monumental changes in communications? Are we collapsing into a totally commercialized society that cannot differentiate between the worthwhile and the trivial, or are we evolving into a more equitable, free, informed, and just world?

As we shall see, there are no easy answers to these and other similar questions.

Our Approach

In this book, we approach the study of media and communications from a *critical* perspective. Here, the term *critical* does not refer to the many complaints that can be levelled at the media for being too commercial or making too much violent material available on television or the internet. Rather, taking a *critical perspective* means that we look analytically at the ways media are implicated in our knowledge and understanding of the world.

Media Democracy Project

With the motto "Know the Media, Be the Media, Change the Media," Media Democracy Day strives to provide us with a critical perspective on media and the ways they shape and influence people's lives.

What role do media play in the construction of identity and the development of our tastes and desires? How do they inform our understanding of the places we live and work? What role do they have in political processes? Are television sitcoms, shows promoting celebrities, and other seemingly innocuous programs simply "entertainment" or do they have other influences or impacts on our lives? Does it matter who owns the media? How does advertising influence what we see in the media? What role do the media play in the economy? In globalization? In other words, whose or what interests do media serve and what role do they play in creating and maintaining social relationships, particularly relations of wealth and power? These are the kinds of questions we address in this book—our aim is to explore the centrality of media and communication both in society and in our lives.

But to understand the way media and communication systems are implicated in our lives, we must first understand what it is we are investigating.

What Is Communication? Some Definitions and Models

As we start to examine the field of communication we need to consider what exactly it is that we are studying. In this section, we define terms and provide some models for helping to understand the process of communication.

At a basic level, *communication* is the act of making something common between two or more people. It is something people actually do. It is a form of social action, in that it implies the involvement of two or more people in a process of creating or sending and receiving or interpreting a message or idea. This process has been conceived in several different ways.

The Shannon–Weaver Model of Communication

One of the first models for thinking about the process of communication was proposed in 1949 by Claude Shannon and Warren Weaver, communication engineers working for Bell Laboratories in the United States. Shannon and Weaver's so-called mathematical or transmission model of communication refers to the basic technical characteristics of the process of sending and receiving messages.

In the Shannon–Weaver model, seen in Figure 1.2, a person—the encoder or *source*—formulates a message by putting an idea into words (e.g., "What are you doing?"). The message is then sent through a particular channel or medium,

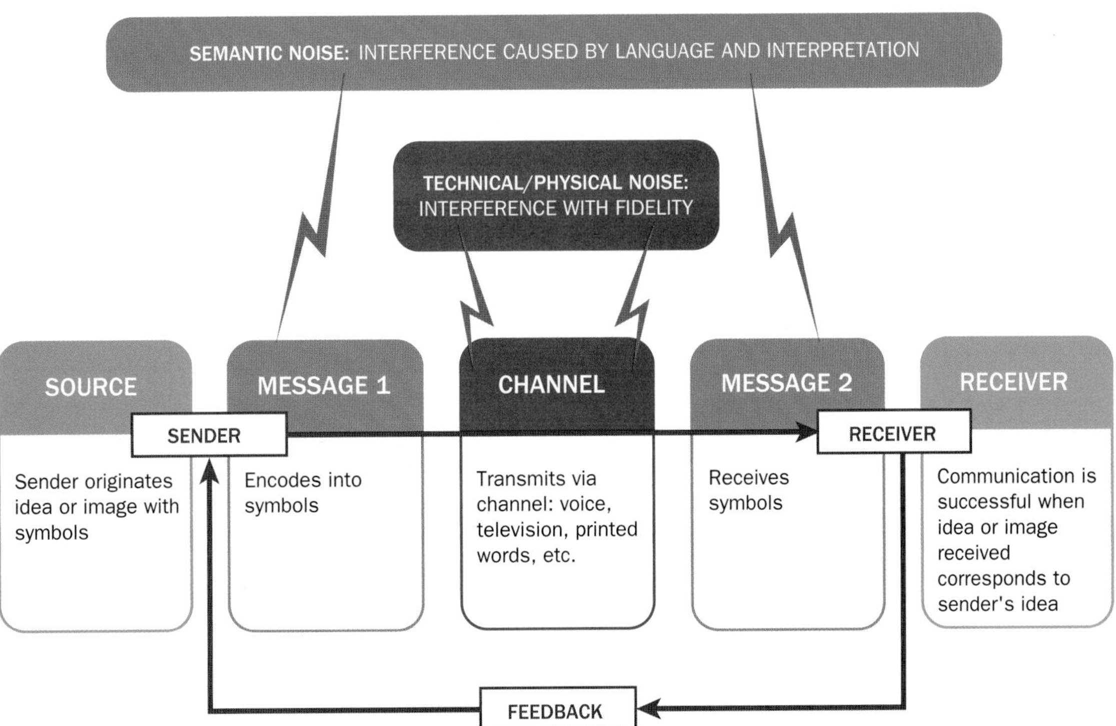

FIGURE 1.2 Shannon and Weaver's Mathematical Model of Communication (1949)

"The Communicative Process," adapted from Claude Shannon and Warren Weaver's *The Mathematical Theory of Communication*. A similar model based on verbal communication was proposed around the same time by Harold Lasswell: "Who says what to whom in what channel with what effect?"

Source: *The Mathematical Theory of Communication*. Copyright 1949/1998 by the Board of Trustees of the University of Illinois. Used with permission of the author and the University of Illinois Press.

such as email, voice mail, or text message. On the receiving end, the decoder receives and interprets the signals and, on the basis of the symbols sent, formulates meaningful content. The decoder may then give the encoder *feedback* by letting the encoder know that she or he has received the message. By sending a message back, the decoder becomes an encoder (e.g., replying, "Studying.").

Any interference in the transmission of the intended message (signified by the lightning bolts in the diagram) is referred to as *noise*. Noise may be loud background sounds that make it difficult for you to hear; a heavy, unfamiliar accent; static on the telephone line; or a typographical error in an email or text message.

This model's strength is its simplicity. It breaks the process of communication into a few very basic elements. It works well for engineers and technicians who speak in terms of the fidelity of messages and transmission technologies like cellphones and voice over internet protocol (VOIP). Because the model simplifies the process of communication so much, it works less well for researchers, social scientists, and others concerned with the social nature of communication, as we are here. In fact, except in terms of noise, it provides no consideration of the larger social context of communication.

Consequently, critics argue that while this model helps to identify basic elements of the complex process of communication, it is much too simplistic. Communication is a social process, and the ideas, symbols, and techniques that we draw on to construct messages are taken from our larger social experience. Language, culture, media forms—the elements that form the social context within which messages are constructed and interpreted—all work to frame and determine not only the meaning we make of them but also the kinds of messages that we create. For instance, no two languages approach the world the same way. Each language positions the speaker in sometimes subtly different ways of thinking about or being in the world. Similarly, there are differences in the way one's age, education, gender, race, or ethnicity nuance one's experience and understanding of the world. Not only can these kinds of social variables influence the way communication takes place, but they can also determine whether it takes place at all.

The Social Model of Communication

The social nature of communication can be seen in Figure 1.3. This model emphasizes social and media-related variables that inform the process of communication. The larger social environment

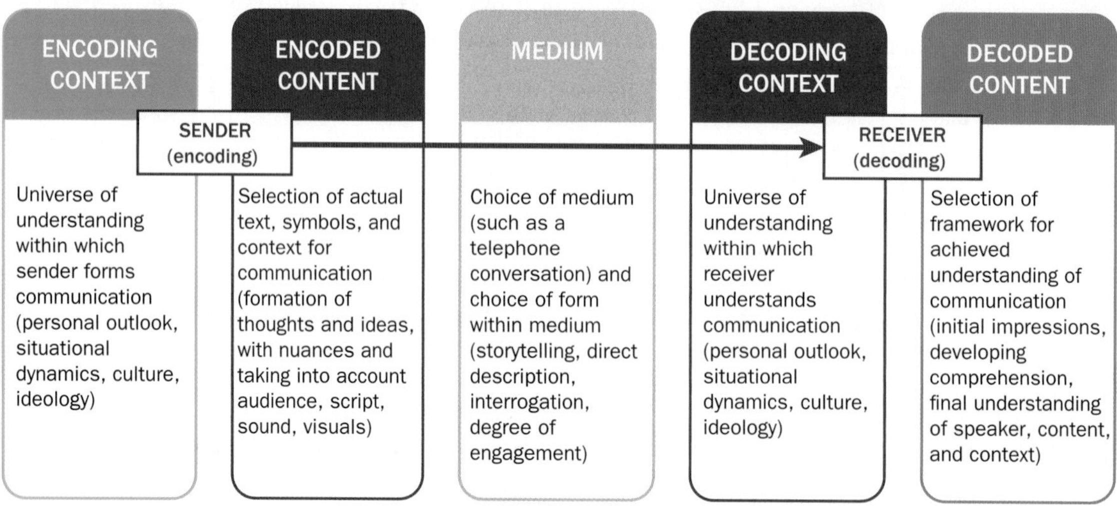

FIGURE 1.3 A Social Model of Communication

or milieu within which message formulation takes place is termed the *encoding context*. At the other end, the *decoding context* represents the ideas and understandings that the decoder brings to deciphering the encoded message. The nature of these larger frames of reference is the subject of theories of meaning generation and communicative interaction that we will explore in Chapters 4 and 5. From this perspective, successful communication is always contingent on the sender and receiver sharing some common idea or notion of the process or subject of communication, particularly in terms of language or experience.

As John Durham Peters (1999: 14) points out, "If meanings inhere not in words but in minds or references to objects, nothing can guarantee successful transit across the distance between two minds." For instance, if provided with the letters *a-p-p-l-e*, you would probably conjure the image of a juicy red (or green) fruit. However, the letters *p-o-m-a* would probably not have the same effect, unless you speak Catalan. So here we can see that sharing a common language is an important condition for effective communication. But even speaking the same language is no guarantee of common understanding. Words such as *love* and *happiness*, for example, can have very different meanings for different people.

However, from this perspective, not only is the process of communication structured by the social contexts of the sender and the receiver, it is nuanced by the medium of communication as well. Putting an idea into words, for instance, is not the same as painting a picture in an attempt to communicate the same idea. Nor is a television newscast item the same as a newspaper write-up of the same story. Each provides a different kind of information about the subject of the story. Similarly, a novel differs from its movie adaptation. The medium transforms the message by encouraging a certain structure in the encoding process, and further transforms it by making certain elements predominant for decoding. Television emphasizes the visual image. Writing emphasizes linearity and logic. Oral speech emphasizes social context, body language, and inflections of the voice.

The social model sees communication as both structured by and contingent on some shared social element or space. From this perspective, communication is a cultural form, a social practice intimately woven into a larger set of ideas, values, and understandings of the world. Exactly how dependent communication is on the larger social context within which it takes place is an issue we take up in every chapter.

Based upon these considerations, we will define **communication** as *the action of making a message or idea common to two or more people.*

Communication: Mass Audiences, and Mass Communication

Traditionally, forms of communication that address large audiences have been called "mass communication." Here the modifier *mass* tends to emphasize the meaning "large in scale," as in **mass audience**, mass action, or mass murder—so, **mass communication** means "communication on a large scale." Mass communication, however, can carry other meanings.

As we will see in Chapters 2 and 3, one common usage of the term *mass* sometimes is based on the perceived character of *audiences* for media as they emerged over time in the context of industrial society. As a consequence of industrialization in the eighteenth and nineteenth centuries, many people in Europe and, to some extent, in North America were uprooted from traditional, rural ways of life and moved to live in towns and cities where factories were located. This new way of life was fraught with problems. Removed from a traditional, essentially feudal and agricultural, way of life and the social values, customs, and bonds that gave that way of life form and function, people were viewed by some analysts in their new industrial context as a collection "of atomized, isolated individuals without traditional bonds of locality or kinship"

(O'Sullivan et al., 1983: 131). According to these early social theorists, within this mass society, the supposed lack of commonly held traditional social values left these individuals particularly vulnerable to "(i) totalitarian ideologies and propaganda; and (ii) influence by the mass media (largely comprising, in this period, newspapers and the emergent cinema and radio)" (131). Until the early twentieth century, this perspective had a strong impact on the development of communication theory, hence the term *mass communication* sometimes carries with it the idea that audiences for forms of large-scale communication are unsophisticated and vulnerable to manipulation. While, as O'Sullivan et al. go on to point out, "mass society theory has been refuted by historical evidence," this line of thinking still exists in many circles today.

John Thompson (1995: 24) points out that the notion of mass as large scale is problematic:

> It conjures up the image of a vast audience comprising many thousands, even millions of individuals. This may be an accurate image in the case of some media products, such as the most popular modern day newspapers, films, and television programs; but it is hardly an accurate representation of the circumstance of most media products, past or present. . . . The important point about mass communication is not that a given number of individuals (or a specific portion of the population) receives the products, but rather products are available in principle to a plurality of recipients.

With literally hundreds of television channels available to the average household, as well as the many other forms of information and entertainment available over the internet, mass audiences numbering in the tens of millions for any particular scheduled program are becoming rare. Despite the fact that there still are mass audiences for some media events and programs, such as the Olympics, soccer's World Cup, and the Academy Awards, today's media fare often targets much smaller audiences, such as programs on specialty channels devoted to sports, cooking, documentaries, or particular genre movies.

As discussed below, however, it is important to keep in mind that just because the audiences viewing some media products may be small does not mean those programs won't be seen by much larger aggregate mass audiences. People usually watch videos on YouTube, for instance, either by themselves or with one or two friends. Those single views, however, often add up to a mass audience of hundreds of thousands or even millions of people. Audiences for traditional media work the same way; for example, viewers might see a film in many different ways: at a theatre, on a streaming service, on a video-on-demand cable channel, downloaded from a website, on a smartphone or other mobile device, on a specialty channel, or on a regular television channel. Although each of these audiences may be relatively small, they often form a large, or mass, audience in the aggregate.

Mass Communication

In this context, the term *mass communication* has been used to describe the communication that happens by means of large traditional corporate media, such as mainstream movies, large daily newspapers, and broadcasting. O'Sullivan and his colleagues captured that meaning of mass communication:

> Mass communication is the practice and product of providing leisure entertainment and information to an unknown audience by means of corporately financed, industrially produced, state regulated, high-technology, privately consumed commodities in the modern print, screen, audio, and broadcast media. (O'Sullivan et al., 1983: 131)

This definition was written prior to the development of the internet, smartphones, Netflix, Google, Facebook, and blogs, but we, of course, know that times and technology have changed.

Beginning in the mid-1990s, when the internet began to be publicly embraced, the options for person-to-person communication on a mass scale expanded dramatically. Suddenly, it was possible to send an email to an address anywhere in the world that was connected with the internet. Transmission was instantaneous and generally free, obviating all the steps and costs in postal services, telegraph messages, and fax transmission. Gone were the constraints and pitfalls of sending traditional letters by post: there was no longer the need for writing paper; envelopes; postage stamps; mailboxes; mail pickup; sorting and handling by imperfect humans; travel by air, land, or sea; resorting; and delivery. Instead, dashing out a few lines on a keyboard and pressing "send" did the trick.

In quick succession, a number of technologies were added to early internet text-exchange protocols so that by the end of the 1990s, digital files of any type—text, sound, or image—could be exchanged between computers. By 2000, it had also become possible for any person, with a bit of effort and little more expense than a computer, some software, and internet access, to create a website that was accessible around the world. By 2005, blogs proliferated into the millions and wikis became common. By 2006, the term **Web 2.0** was being promoted to describe the invention of such interactive online applications. Today, online social media and networking services like Instagram, Twitter, Facebook, LinkedIn, and many others engulf us in a complex web of networked relationships.

While the internet started off as a means for person-to-person communication, the success of the World Wide Web and digital technology and their increasing use by the business community and other organizations, the web has become both a mass person-to-person communication system and a decentralized broadcast or distribution system. It has quickly evolved into a large-scale interactive communication system that allows people in Canada, or in many other countries, to create content for next to nothing and make it available to the world, now facilitated by ubiquitous search engines. These many and continuing developments have fundamentally changed the nature of mass communication.

Consequently, from our current perspective, the traditional definition of mass communication is incomplete. Today, *mass communication* is better understood simply as *the transmission and transformation of information on a large scale* no matter what specific media may be involved. Such a definition involves three aspects or forms of organization (Lorimer, 2002):

1. *Mass communication is the production and wide dissemination of information and entertainment*—the production of entertainment and information to large audiences by means of print, screen, audio, broadcast, audiovisual, and internet technologies or public performance for both private and public consumption. In certain instances (e.g., broadcasting and, less often, print) it is state regulated. Some examples are radio, television, newspapers, film, magazines, books, recorded and performed music, and advertising.
2. The second form allows for greater participation by many members of society as part of either their work or leisure. *Mass communication is the decentralized production and wide accessibility of information and entertainment.* Such communication is sometimes corporately financed, sometimes industrially produced, and sometimes, but not necessarily, intended for small or niche audiences. It may be undertaken by many individuals, organizations, and institutions and includes websites, podcasts, blogs, print, film, audio, broadcast, and public performances. YouTube stands as a case in point here. The site acts as a centralized platform where producers and consumers from around the globe meet to share information. The site gets 1 billon visits a month, and the most watched video—"Despacito" by Luis Fonsi—had over 5.5 billion views as of October 2018 (Statista). This is a "mass medium" with a "mass audience."

3. The third form of mass communication accents interactivity as its defining attribute. *Mass communication is the interactive exchange of information (or messages or intelligence) among a number of recipients.* This form of mass communication encompasses the increasing interactivity of interconnected, or *networked*, groups of people. Alvin Toffler (1980) introduced the term "prosumers" in the early 1980s, defining it as those people who both consume and produce a product. Interactive mass communication also emphasizes the rising role of the prosumer in the online world, where the line between producers and consumers is increasingly blurred (Toffler, 1980: 267, in Fuchs, 2012: 43). It includes applications such as Facebook, Instagram, and Twitter and encompasses a wide range of technologies, such as telephones, computers, tablets, and a range of mobile devices, as well as an expanding number of ways that the users of these media produce and contribute to the content that they carry—from Facebook, Twitter, and Instagram accounts, to uploading videos to YouTube, to playing massively multiplayer online role-playing games (MMORPG).

Such a three-part definition of mass communication—within the overall definition: the transmission and transformation of meaning on a large scale—positions traditional media as just one form of mass communication rather than as the central and dominant form. It recognizes the importance of interactivity and decentralization in today's media and illustrates what Chadwick (2013) refers to as the "hybridity" of media and media systems: the blended and shifting nature of media and media systems as older media technologies and practices merge with new ones.

Media, Mass Media, and New Media

A **medium** is *any vehicle that conveys information*. Language is a medium, for instance, as are pictures, photographs, and musical instruments. Any vehicle or object that imparts meaning or information can be considered a communication medium. **Media** is the plural of *medium*.

Mass media *are the vehicles through which mass communication takes place*. Historically, these have been understood as newspapers, magazines, cinema, television, radio, advertising, and sometimes book publishing (especially popular fiction) and music (the pop industry) (O'Sullivan et al, 1983: 130). The focus here was on the large institutions and organizations that make up traditional media. In the context of technological change and our three-part definition of mass communication, however, the different kinds of media involved in mass communication encompass much more than traditional television, radio, and film and now comprise services and products such as the internet, websites, and cellphones.

It is also important to note that mass communication can involve a number of different types of media at the same time. If we watch a YouTube video of someone singing a song, for instance, the media involved are the language in which the song is sung; the person's voice; the musical instruments, if used; the video itself; and the internet.

From this perspective, mass media can be seen as *any kind* of vehicle that conveys information on a large scale and so might include such things as buildings, statues, coins, banners, and stained-glass windows—any communication vehicle that comes in contact with a large number of people. These forms of mass media involve institutions communicating with many members of society. But while there are many such media of communication, we tend not to talk about them as media because their communicative role is secondary to housing people, commemorating history, serving as a medium of exchange, and so on (see Box 1.2).

The term *new media* (sometimes referred to as *digital media*) came into prominence in the mid-1990s with the advent of new digital forms of media. These media differ from the traditional mass media in that they do not focus on centralized institutional production and mass

1.2

The Various Ways We Communicate

Architecture, graffiti, memorial sculptures, public art, even clothing can be perceived as media of communication, even if their language isn't always accessible and their message isn't always clear. In some cases, these media evoke memories. The names of city streets—Papineau in Montreal, Granville in Vancouver, Yonge in Toronto—recall historical and political figures. Almost every town in Canada has some sort of war memorial serving as a symbol of personal remembrance and as a reminder to passersby of the sacrifice the town's citizens have made to Canada's past war efforts.

Building styles, too, can act as media or vehicles for communication of ideas and values. The number, size, and structural splendour of Montreal's churches, for instance, speak to the power and influence the Roman Catholic Church once wielded in Quebec. Christian churches are often built in the shape of the cross, and the stained-glass windows that adorn them usually relate stories from the Bible, both features acting as communication media.

In New York, the twin towers of the World Trade Center soared over surrounding buildings, providing a resounding symbol of America's power and primacy in the world economy, which is one of

© Monilu/istockphoto

the reasons why al Qaeda targeted them on 11 September 2001. The CN Tower, pictured below, is a clear reminder that Toronto is the country's communication centre because, apart from representing a major rail, air, and road transportation hub, it is a telecommunications tower serving 16 Canadian television and radio stations.

While these media draw much of their authority from being sanctioned and permanent community symbols, graffiti draws its communicative power from its ephemeral and rebellious qualities. Often dismissed simply as vandalism, graffiti nonetheless speaks to people. Sometimes, the message is a straightforward "I was here," as in the *tags*, or signatures, we see on city buildings, or in the names of people spray-painted on rock faces at various spots along Canadian highways. Other times, the message—often profane—may be one of protest or dissent. Whatever the case, graffiti serves very much as a "voice of the voiceless."

© Jruffa/Dreamstime.com

A church stained-glass window.

© Bcbounders/Dreamstime.com

Toronto's CN Tower.

dissemination. Instead, they decentralize opportunities to create and distribute media information. Any number of people, equipped with the right software applications, skills, and access to the internet, can produce new media content. But even though they are decentralized, these media still encourage wider participation and in some cases facilitate ongoing participation in the production and exchange of information. Digital new media created a "participatory culture" that is replacing more traditional "passive media spectatorship" (Jenkins, 2006: 3). In other words, digital **new media** are *technologies, practices, and institutions designed to facilitate broad participation—or interactivity—in information production and exchange (i.e., communication) on a mass scale*. Smartphone cameras, email, file sharing, text messaging, podcasts, blogs, wikis, websites, social media—all these and more make up digital new media.

But while digital media bring fresh capabilities to media production and exchange, they are also broadening the reach and capabilities of traditional mass media. For instance, websites and online delivery are important for newspapers. Books are now often sold and distributed in electronic form online, and these e-books are read on tablets, computers, and smartphones. Music is mostly marketed and distributed—or streamed—online, as opposed to by CD, tape, or vinyl record. And traditional media are using the technology to allow audience members to contribute news and other media content. This bringing together, or *convergence*, of media forms is a characteristic feature of today's media environment.

Convergence

Over the last several decades, the mediascape has been very rapidly transformed, a product of technological innovation, fundamental policy shifts, and massive corporate mergers. The term **convergence** was initially coined to describe the merging, or bringing together, of a wide range of previously separate and distinct communication technologies and media.

At a very basic level, this has entailed the merging of computer and transmission technologies—that is, technologies used to store, access, and transmit information—to create **information and communication technology (ICT)**. In the past, for instance, photographs were taken on film and circulated in hard copy. Video was recorded magnetically on tape. Music was distributed on tape or vinyl records. But in a few short decades, electronic **digital** technology has revolutionized all three of these things. What was recorded previously on distinct media forms now can be turned into the binary language of 1s and 0s and manipulated, transmitted, and read via the internet on computers. This *technological convergence* of voice, video, data, and other communication media is at the heart of new media and the changes that have gripped media industries over recent decades.

As we discuss in Parts III and IV of this book, changing media technology has been accompanied by changes in both government regulation and the structure of media industries, as companies that once operated in industries and fields held separate by technological and regulatory divides have restructured in an effort to gain competitive advantages in this shifting environment. In this context, *corporate convergence* has led to the growth of increasingly large media companies with investments in a range of different kinds of media. Whereas not so long ago, television, radio, cable systems, and newspapers were seen as quite different businesses, today's large companies, like Bell and Rogers, have interests in a range of media such as radio and television stations, magazines, cable systems, and telephone and broadband companies. Similarly, Quebecor owns newspapers, television stations, cable systems, magazines, cable and phone service, and music/video/book retail stores.

Convergence is also shifting the ways we understand and participate in media and media events. As the interactive features of digital media converge with traditional media, audiences can participate directly in the outcomes of programs such as *The Voice*, where they vote on which contestants get to continue on the show. On another front, program producers are also working to build audiences through *transmedia* storytelling techniques. Here, stories are both told and marketed across multiple platforms. *Star Wars* is one of the most successful examples of this type of technique (Guynes and Hassler-Forest, 2017). It is interesting to note that this form of storytelling is not new. The way in which stained-glass windows in churches echo Bible stories is an early example.

The convergence of new and traditional media also allows audience participation to extend directly into creating or remixing media products. In this regard, copyright critic Lawrence Lessig (2008: 29–33) argues that digital technologies have produced what he calls a more participatory read/write or "R/W culture." From this perspective, prior to interactive media, audiences necessarily had to assume a passive *read only* or RO relationship with media content. Now, equipped with new digital media tools, they are empowered to have a read-and-write, or RW, relationship with media and to remix or create their own

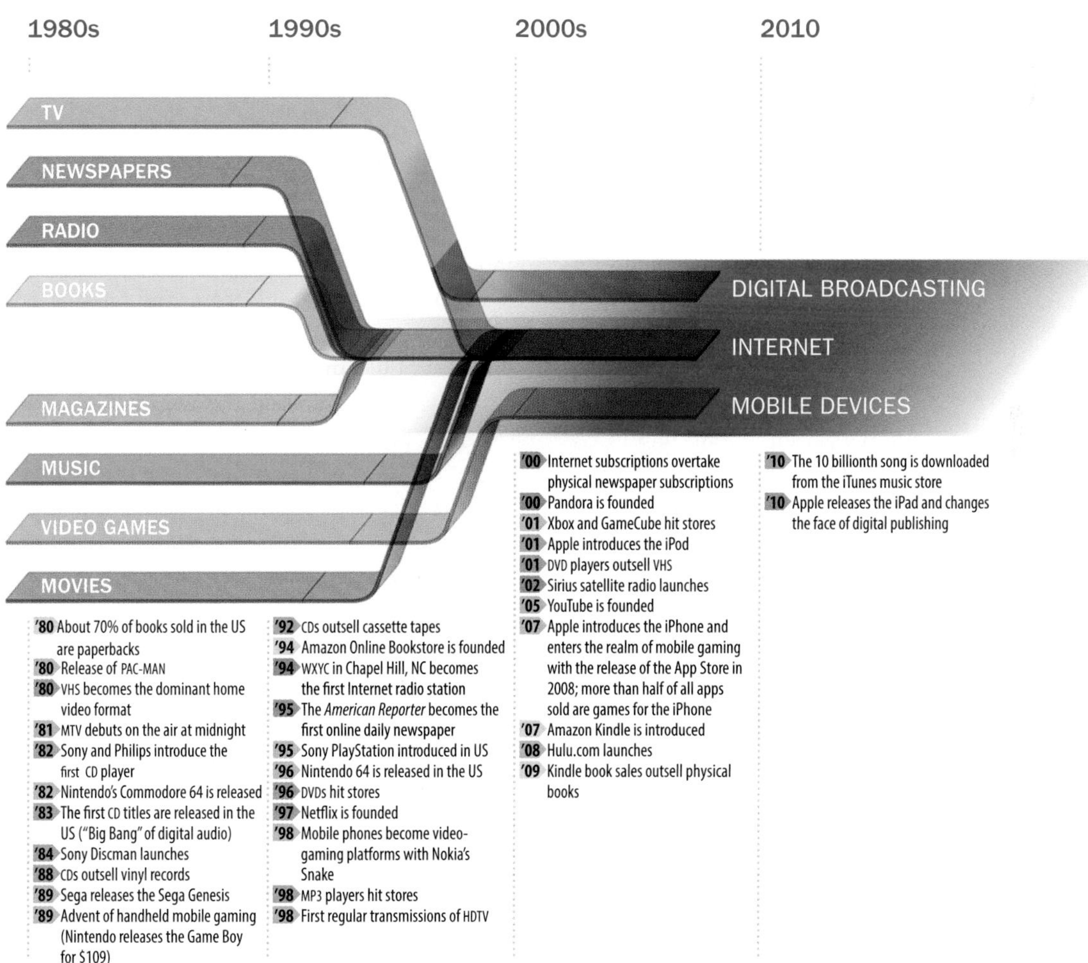

FIGURE 1.4 Convergence

Source: Rejan Dev and Oscar Villalon

media products, whether completely original or based on products of popular culture. Mash-ups, where artists splice together already published music and/or images to create a "new" song or video, are a popular but sometimes controversial element of this kind of work, as the copyright holders of the original work sometimes object to its being reworked in this manner (Murray, 2015). Similarly, in some cases, people producing fan fiction—where fans create stories using characters or settings from popular media products such as *Star Wars* or *Harry Potter*—have landed in trouble with copyright law (Kluft, 2016).

But fan-made media products that mimic the work of original content are not always frowned upon by the big media companies. As Joel Eastwood (2014) points out, "the recording industry is making more money from fan-made mash-ups, lip-syncs and tributes on YouTube than from official music videos. . . . Rather than order the video removed for copyright infringement, the record company can instead choose to run ads before and during the video, making money off the video's views." The money generated from these videos, however, goes to the companies holding the rights to the songs, not to the fans who made them.

The networked character of digital media is also helping develop a new political culture. As we discuss in Chapter 2, working with email and social media platforms such as Facebook and Twitter, activists in countries around the world have been able to bring pressure on governments to change unpopular laws or regulations, and in some cases even bring about changes in government (Lievrouw, 2011).

On a number of different fronts, then, convergence and the interactive media technologies that it has spawned are key features of today's media environment.

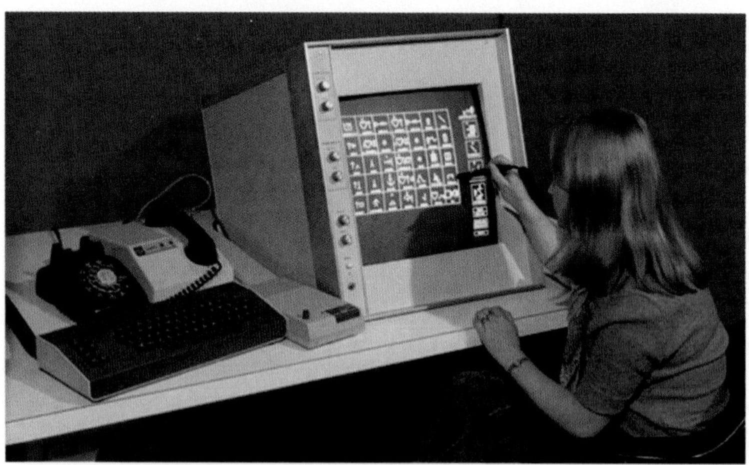

Telidon, from the Greek *tele* meaning "distant" and *idon* meaning "I see," was an early precursor to the personal computer, developed by the Canadian Communications Research Centre in the late 1970s. It was Canada's version of the home-based link to the cable-based "wired world." A number of countries, including Britain and France, developed similar teletext systems. Unlike today's personal computers, however, these systems had poor computing power and stored very little information, depending instead on external, usually distant, databases. Pictured here is a Telidon trial conducted in 1976. *(Communications Research Centre Canada, 1976.* Reproduced with the permission of the Minister of Public Works and Government Services Canada.)

Some Social Roles of Media

As we will explore in later chapters, mass media are an integral part of our **society** and **culture**—our ways of life—and images, ideas, and values gleaned from the media are deeply woven into the ways in which we understand and embrace the world. By way of introduction to these ideas, we will now focus on the ways in which media play an important social role across three dimensions of social life: politics, economics, and individual identity.

A Political Role

Most media theory sees the media as playing a central role in politics, and in later chapters we examine how media and journalism are vital to Canadian political life (see Chapters 7, 8, and 10). Here, we will consider some of the more general aspects of media and information in politics.

1.3

O Canada: Our Home and Naïve Land

Ipsos Reid/Dominion Institute History Quiz Reveals Canadians Know More about American History Than They Do about Canadian History

It appears that Canadians know more about the history and politics of their neighbours to the south than they do about their own country. According to a poll conducted in the format of a 20-question quiz by Ipsos Reid on behalf of the Dominion Institute, Canadians had a higher average percentage of correct scores on questions about the United States (47%) than they did on questions about Canada (42%).

The quiz featured 10 questions about each country, the topics ranging from the founding of each nation to the decade in which women's suffrage was granted.

Questions about Canada were paired with similar questions about US history, so that knowledge about the two countries could be compared. The largest discrepancy in knowledge had to do with heads of state. While 75 per cent of Canadians knew that George W. Bush, US president at the time, was the American head of state, only 21 per cent knew that the Canadian head of state was Queen Elizabeth II. On the other hand, Canadians were much more likely to know the first line of their own national anthem (53%) than the first line of the US anthem (25%). The best-answered Canadian questions dealt with John A. Macdonald being the first prime minister of Canada (61% answered correctly) and the year of Canadian Confederation being 1867 (61%). Canadians averaged 4.2 correct answers overall on the Canadian questions, and 4.7 correct answers overall on the US questions.

What might account for Canadians' poor knowledge about their own country? Could it result from the fact that much of the media content Canadians consume is made in the USA?

Source: Adapted from https://www.historicacanada.ca/sites/default/files/PDF/polls/canadaday.survey.dominioninstitute.1july08_en.pdf.

While politics is sometimes thought of as voting or specific debates over policy, a broader, more inclusive way of thinking about the term is as "the process through which people make collective decisions." This definition includes formal processes of government, but it also includes a much wider range of activities that frame and animate formal government policies and activities, as well as informal discussions of social norms and values. From this perspective, politics is a key element in many aspects of social life. Whenever we are discussing or otherwise engaged with issues of collective concern with other members of society, be it in a large or small group or simply with just one other person, we are engaging in politics.

Political activity takes place in the public sphere (Habermas, 1989), an abstract place where people are able to discuss and consider matters of common concern and interest. We say "abstract" because the public sphere is more of an idea than a specific place. In fact, any place where such discussion might take place can be considered part of the larger public sphere—whether that be media, coffee shops, auditoriums, public rallies and demonstrations, or parks.

Media are key elements of the public sphere because of the information they provide about public life (see Box 1.3). They are the central vehicle for the production and distribution of information about events taking place at different levels of government, and of information about other things such as wars, oil spills and other environmental disasters, natural disasters, visits of foreign dignitaries, and elections. Indeed, our knowledge of almost all events of public concern is, in some way or another, drawn from media sources—in fact, any decisions that we make regarding our larger collective interests are, to some degree, related to media.

While television, radio, newspapers, and websites offer news and information about political issues and events, some media provide more interactive venues to debate and discuss political ideas and concerns. At any given time, for example, a number of videos on YouTube provide different perspectives on public issues. These are greatly varied and might range from issues concerning the environment to gender issues, to media policy, and to social benefit regulations. Twitter and Facebook provide a similar, though more interactive, place for such discussions, and it is common practice for social activists and others to create Facebook pages addressing political issues. Although controlled by the editors and owners, the editorial pages of newspapers provide a more traditional forum for discussing ideas and concerns about political issues of the day.

In Canada, media owners have a long history of using their products to influence political discussion and action. An early English-Canadian example of communication famously used as a political instrument is William Lyon Mackenzie politicizing Upper Canadians through his newspaper, the *Colonial Advocate*, and eventually leading some of them into rebellion in 1837. Pierre Bédard similarly spread his political ideas in *Le Canadien*, the newspaper he helped to establish. As the leader of the Parti canadien (later the Parti Patriote), Bédard used *Le Canadien* as a nationalist party organ to oppose the Château Clique, the ruling elite group of Lower Canada. Even earlier, in 1778, through *La Gazette littéraire* (precursor to *La Gazette de Montréal* [1785]), Fleury Mesplet, a colleague of Benjamin Franklin, spread the ideals of the American Revolution in French Canada.

Many contemporary media owners have admitted to controlling the range of perspectives available in their newspapers and other publications. Moreover, at election time, *The Globe and Mail* generally supports the federal and provincial Conservative parties, while the *Toronto Star* supports the Liberals. In Quebec, *Le Devoir* is a staunch supporter of Quebec independence, whereas the Desmarais family's *La Presse* supports the federalist option and the federal Liberal party, in particular. When questioned about this, newspaper owners and management have defended their actions by arguing that control of editorial perspective is a privilege of ownership.

1.4

The Two-Step Flow of Communication

In a classic study in the 1950s, Elihu Katz and Paul Lazarsfeld argued that information from the mass media is transmitted or channelled to the larger population by "opinion leaders"—that is, people with better access to the media and greater understanding of the news and topics covered there than most people have. Such people may be family or community members, teachers, or religious leaders, and are then seen to be central in the larger diffusion or spread of ideas found in the media.

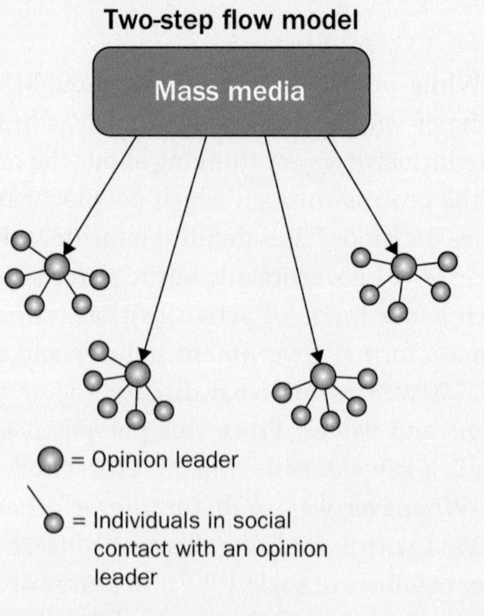

FIGURE 1.5 Katz and Lazarsfeld's Two-Step Flow Theory of Mass Communication

Source: Katz and Lazarsfeld, 1955.

Creative Touch Imaging Ltd./NurPhoto via Getty Images

On the campaign trail to his being elected Premier of Ontario in June of 2018, Doug Ford broke with tradition and declined to have a media bus accompany him. Instead, he hired his own "reporter" and posted campaign updates created by that person to his Facebook page.

Governments, too, strive to control media coverage and thereby public opinion. Elected officials commonly refuse to grant interviews and try to withhold information on controversial topics. Stephen Harper's federal Conservative government (2006–2015) was well known for trying to control public opinion in this manner, such as with its efforts to muzzle scientists employed by the federal government (Chung, 2013). More recently, Donald Trump—the president of the United States—has taken to branding news that puts him in an unflattering light as "fake news" (Nguyen, 2018). Similarly, when governments or politicians become dissatisfied with normal media coverage, they sometimes use social media or organize media channels to speak directly to the public (*Toronto Star*, 2018).

Government communication is generally constrained on one side by a concern with freedom of information, and on the other by people's right to privacy. Governments collect vast amounts of information through surveys, censuses, satellites, and mandatory reporting mechanisms, such as income-tax statements. Public access to some of that information, such as census data, which provides a comprehensive snapshot of the demographic characteristics of the population, is important because it is used by a great many organizations to plan and advocate for everything from social services to recreational programs to transit. Such information is the lifeblood of informed policy discussions, and without the proper census data it's almost impossible to make informed public-policy decisions. Similarly, access to government records and documents is important for journalists and others working to monitor the actions of government officials—these journalists need access to ensure that they can properly scrutinize the government and make sure those in public office are serving citizens' interests.

The US government in post-9/11 times, with little resistance from the country's freedom-loving citizens, put in place a series of measures, exemplified by the *Patriot Act*, for investigating the personal history of both Americans and those who have any dealings with the United States—ostensibly to help root out terrorists and related threats. Critics have warned that such a means of collecting information about the activities of citizens could lead to unwarranted charges of wrongdoing and the suspension of people's civil rights by the US government and its agencies. And in September 2017, Canada's privacy commissioner issued a warning that Canadians should be "very concerned" about having their cell phones and computers searched by border guards when crossing into the United States (CBC, 2017).

With the Conservatives' passage of Bill C-51 in June 2015, such concerns were echoed in Canada (Watters, 2015). This legislation increased the power of police and security agencies and has raised the possibility of greater surveillance and control of environmental groups and others opposed to government policy (McCarthy, 2015).

In this regard, websites like WikiLeaks provide a controversial vehicle for government or industry insiders to leak or release secret information to the press. Such information might expose government or industry wrongdoing, or it might reveal activities or information being kept secret for national security reasons. As the media coverage surrounding National Security Agency whistleblower Edward Snowden's release of thousands of classified documents illustrates,

AP Photo/Marco Garcia.

Edward Snowden worked for the US National Security Agency and leaked a series of documents that exposed massive spying by various governments, particularly his own, on the activities of their citizens.

the question of whether such information should be kept secret, particularly if it is information held by the government, is a source of intense controversy.

In short, media and the information they generate and distribute are central to the political landscape and vital to the public sphere.

An Economic Role

Media play an important economic role in our society and culture. Not only are they important industries in their own right, but they are also key elements of our consumer culture, a growing information economy, and, according to some, an information society.

Traditional media, such as radio and television stations, newspapers, and related telecommunications companies, are big business. In 2016, there were over 1,000 community newspapers and 84 daily newspapers with paid circulation in this country, and newspapers posted over $2 billion in advertising revenue in 2016. Canada has more than 1,100 radio and audio services, and Canadians have access to more than 600 Canadian and non-Canadian television services. The Canadian broadcasting industry alone brought in $17.8 billion in revenues in 2016, and the telecommunications and broadcasting industries reported a combined $65.8 billion in that year. If one adds digital media, such as computer, software, and video game companies, they and related organizations together employ hundreds of thousands of Canadians (Canada, 2017).

Media are also central to the larger economy in a number of ways. As the major purveyor of advertising, they are the primary way that people are acquainted and connected with the many products they purchase. In other words, they are the main vehicles through which our consumer lifestyle is symbolically negotiated. Media are also a central means for businesses to find employees and, through business radio and television programs, as well as business-related articles in web and hard-copy periodicals, they are one of the key vehicles through which people can better understand the economy and monitor the economic activities of both government and corporations. Corporations also conduct public-information and public-relations campaigns through media, raising their profile and attempting to promote positive public images.

Media generally also promote the larger interests of consumer culture. A good deal of the content is addressed directly to consumers, comparing or trumpeting the benefits of particular products. Similarly, much of the news is related to consumer issues, such as the price of gas and other commodities, or the effects of particular events on the economy. Other programs also valorize or aggrandize the benefits of consumer culture, illustrating the lavish lifestyles of the rich and famous and teasing the general public with luxuries to covet.

Perhaps most importantly, media and communication industries make up one of the fastest-growing sectors of the economy. For many, the recent rapid growth in information and communication technologies (ICTs) has signalled the rise of an **information society**, where the production, distribution, and consumption of information are the main drivers of the economy. As we discuss in later chapters, this development goes hand in hand with **globalization** and the deindustrialization of the traditional industrialized countries in the northern hemisphere, such as the United States, Canada, the United Kingdom, and the countries of Western Europe. From this perspective, media and information industries have not only been pivotal for facilitating the transfer of manufacturing industries to places such as China, India, and a number of other countries, but they are also essential to creating new economic activity in the old industrialized countries.

Over the last 20 years, numerous federal governments and their agencies have invested considerable time and resources in attempting to better understand the role of ICTs in the economy and to develop policies that ensure Canada doesn't get left behind or become disadvantaged in this shifting information environment. Recent efforts in this direction include strengthening copyright legislation, establishing a fund to promote the development of new media content, and developing a policy to promote the growth of digital and broadband communication applications, products, and infrastructure—in short, the basis of an expanded Canadian information economy (Canada, 2017).

For all these reasons, media and ICTs are sometimes referred to as the "shock troops" of global **capitalism** (see Box 1.5). Both directly and indirectly, they spread, advertise, and promote the benefits of capitalist society in newly industrializing countries in terms that seem to promise steady jobs and income, an endless supply and wide array of products, and the opportunity to live a rich and comfortable life.

An Individual Role: Media and Identity

Our understanding of our place in society—who we are, along with our likes, dislikes, desires, fears, and loyalties—can be thought of as aspects of identity. Identity may be innate and genetic, wrapped up in the physical features of our being; but in

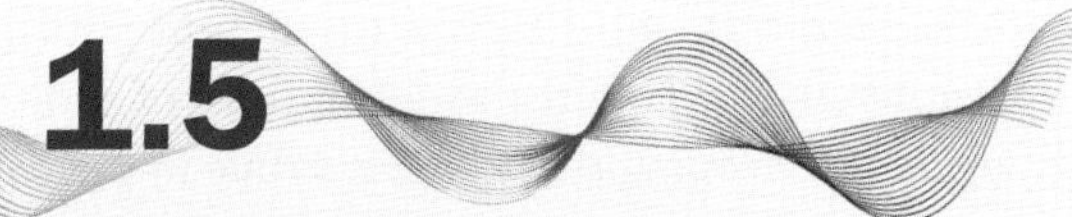

What Is Capitalism?

Capitalism is an economic system, or a system for the production, distribution, and consumption of goods and services. As Jim Stanford (2008: 34–5) points out in his book *Economics for Everyone*, "two key features . . . make an economy capitalist.

1. Most production of goods and services is undertaken by privately owned companies, which produce and sell their output in the hopes of making a profit. This is called PRODUCTION FOR PROFIT.
2. Most work in the economy is performed by people who do not own their company or their output, but are hired by someone else to work in return for a money wage or salary. This is called WAGE LABOUR.

. . .

Any economy driven by these two features—production for profit and wage labour—tends to replicate the following patterns, over and over again:

- Fierce *competition* between private companies over markets and profit.
- *Innovation*, as companies constantly experiment with new technologies, new products, and new forms of organization—in order to succeed in that competition.
- An inherent tendency to *growth*, resulting from the desire of each individual company to make more profit.
- Deep *inequality* between those who own successful companies, and the rest of society who do not own companies.
- A general *conflict* of interest between those who work for wages, and the employers who hire them.
- Economic *cycles* or "rollercoasters," with periods of strong growth followed by periods of stagnation or depression; sometimes these cycles even produce dramatic economic and social crises.

(continued)

Some of these patterns and outcomes are positive, and help to explain why capitalism has been so successful. But some of these patterns and outcomes are negative, and explain why capitalism tends to be economically (and sometimes politically) unstable.

In part, capitalism has its origins in the enclosure movement in rural England in the sixteenth century, when peasants lost their direct access to the land—the means of production—and instead had to exchange their labour for wages (Wood, 2002). Capitalism subsequently spread throughout Europe in the seventeenth and eighteenth centuries.

"In pre-capitalist societies, most people worked for themselves, one way or another. Where people worked for someone else, that relationship was based on something other than monetary payment (like a sense of obligation, or the power of brute force). And most production occurred to meet some direct need or desire (for an individual, a community, or a government), not to generate a money profit" (Stanford, 2008: 35).

One of the key effects of private ownership of media is that profit is the primary goal of such organizations. Without a profit, the company will go out of business. Hence, much of the organization and its products are oriented toward this goal. As we shall see, this has powerful effects on the range and kinds of information found in the media, as well as how that information is presented.

other ways, it is a learned process, the product of our personal history, experience, and interactions with other people and institutions in the world. One might say that most of our identities are constructed through these social interactions, as we learn about the world and work to fit ourselves into it. In other words, much of our identity is socially constructed; we negotiate and interact with social and cultural processes and institutions. Elements in this process include family, work, social class, education, gender, race, ethnicity, and religion.

People have particular social roles—as adults, children, fathers, mothers, and so on. Culturally, we see ourselves as having unique traits in terms of race, ethnicity, habits, and customs. Politically, we are citizens and members of society. Economically, we are workers and consumers. As one of the principal vehicles through which we come to know and understand the world, media—particularly mass media—play a large role in helping develop these identities. As audience members, we are exposed to ideas, perspectives, and ways of thinking about and understanding the world. Via news, films, music, cartoons, nature programs, and so on, media provide an environment in which to explore the world and how we connect with it. Through media, we enlarge our understanding of our place in the world. We can take political positions; develop a sense of national pride and patriotism; explore gender issues; develop ideas and interests around sexuality; and take a position on the environment. Any number of our understandings of the world and our place(s) within it may be negotiated and/or enhanced through the media.

Consumer culture underwent a dramatic expansion through the twentieth century (see Chapter 2). Media were in the forefront of spreading and developing that culture. While in the past people were necessarily more self-sufficient and dependent on family and neighbours to provide life's necessities, today it feels natural for people to satisfy their needs, wants, and desires through the

Justin Kase zsixz/Alamy Stock Photo.

Advertising strives to link specific products to how we feed, clothe, entertain ourselves, and make ourselves sexually and socially attractive. It encourages us to literally purchase who we are, or who we want to be.

marketplace. As Leiss and colleagues (2005: 4–5) argue, "Material objects produced for consumption in the marketplace not only satisfy needs, but also serve as markers and communicators for interpersonal distinctions and self-expression." Media generally encourage that view of the world, reflecting consumer culture back to us in many ways. Advertising in particular strives to link specific products to how we feed, clothe, and entertain ourselves and make ourselves sexually and socially attractive. It encourages us to literally purchase who we are, or who we want to be. As some writers argue, not only is this a growing trend but it is also leading to deepening psychological crises and increasing social inequality, and is accelerating the destruction of the planet (Coulter, 2014; Jhally, 1997). Consequently, understanding the ways in which media encourage us to understand ourselves is an important element in the study of mass media and mass communication.

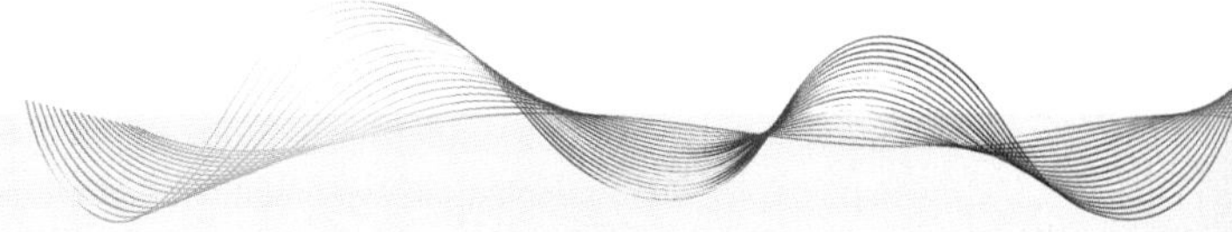

SUMMARY

Media and communication have central importance in our society and culture and continue to evolve. In this chapter, we have offered two different models of communication as a means of building a common understanding of the subjects under study, as well as a number of definitions of communication media and processes. We also have provided here an updated definition of the term *mass communication* as *"the transmission and transformation of information on a large scale"* and described three different forms of mass communication in this context. With the aim of providing an overview of the larger field of communication explored in this book, we also described some of the different roles media play in the context of our society.

KEY TERMS

capitalism, p. 25
communication, p. 13
convergence, p. 18
culture, p. 20
digital, p. 18
digital divide, p. 10
globalization, p. 25
information and communication technology (ICT), p. 18
information society, p. 24
mass audience, p. 13
mass communication, p. 13
mass media, p. 16
media, p. 16
medium, p. 16
new media, p. 18
society, p. 20
Web 2.0, p. 15

RELATED WEBSITES

Alliance of Canadian Cinema, Television and Radio Artists (ACTRA): www.actra.ca
An association of more than 21,000 professionals working in Canadian media, its website offers insights into the issues facing these Canadian industries.

Berne Convention (copyright): www.law.cornell.edu/treaties/berne/overview.html
This site includes the pre-eminent world statute on copyright, including all its various clauses and levels.

The 1991 Broadcasting Act: http://laws-lois.justice.gc.ca/eng/acts/b-9.01
This is the legislation that governs broadcasting in Canada. Part II is particularly important, as it lays out the general purposes and goals of the system as well as the responsibilities of the different institutions and organizations within it.

Canadian Media Guild: www.cmg.ca
This is the site of the union that represents workers at the CBC as well as various other media companies across the country. It has a number of interesting features and provides insight into the kinds of issues facing media workers today.

Canadian Association of Journalists: www.caj.ca
This site provides journalists with professional information and, from time to time, it takes up issues of interest to all Canadian journalists.

Canadian Broadcast Standards Council (CBSC): www.cbsc.ca
The CBSC sets broadcasting standards, such as how much advertising broadcasters can put in a program.

Canadian Radio-television and Telecommunications Commission (CRTC): www.crtc.gc.ca
The CRTC provides everything you might want to know about its activities regulating Canada's media.

CBC: Who We Are, What We Do: cbc.radio-canada.ca/en/vision/mandate
This site highlights the mandate of the Canadian Broadcasting Corporation.

Canadian Centre for Policy Alternatives: www.policyalternatives.ca
A progressive think tank that works on issues of social and economic justice.

Public Library of Science (PLOS): www.plos.org
PLOS is a non-profit organization that is making the world's medical and scientific literature freely available to everyone via its website.

Society of Composers, Authors, and Music Publishers of Canada (SOCAN): www.socan.com
The SOCAN site presents information for musicians, users of music, and the general public.

FURTHER READINGS

Hamilton, Sheryl N. 2014. "Considering critical communication studies in Canada." In *Mediascapes: New Patterns in Canadian Communication*, 4th ed., edited by Leslie Regan Shade. Don Mills, ON: Nelson, 4–24.

Lipton, Mark. 2014. "Doing media studies." In *Mediascapes: New Patterns in Canadian Communication*, 4th ed., edited by Leslie Regan Shade. Don Mills, ON: Nelson, 25–42.

Martin, Michel. 2004. "Communication and social forms: The development of the telephone, 1876–1920." In *Communication History in Canada,* edited by Daniel J. Robinson. Don Mills, ON: Oxford UP, 66–76.

Pattinson, John Richard. 2018. "Popular Music and Canadian National Identity." *Canadian Journal of Communication,* vol. 43, no. 2, pp 221–44. doi: 10.22230/cjc.2018v43n2a3110

Winseck, Dwayne. 2004. "Back to the future: Telecommunications, online information services, and convergence from 1840–1910." In *Communication History in Canada*, edited by Daniel J. Robinson. Don Mills, ON: Oxford UP, 53–65.

STUDY QUESTIONS

1. How does communication technology "shrink space through time"?
2. What were some of the predecessors to the internet? What characteristics made them predecessors?
3. Define communication and mass, as used in this chapter.
4. Explain mass communication and its three parts.
5. What is the fundamental difference between the transportation and social models of communication?
6. How do not-for-profit broadcast institutions differ in their basic purpose and mission from profit-driven institutions?
7. What is convergence? What are some of its different forms?

2

The History of Media
Social and Cultural Forms

The greatest power of the mass media is the power to ignore.
—American essayist Sam Smith

EQRoy/Shutterstock

Opening Questions

- What were the Renaissance and the Enlightenment? Why are they important to contemporary notions of citizenship and democracy?
- What were the roles and purposes of media as they developed in industrial society?
- How do libertarian theory, the social responsibility theory of the press, the mass society thesis, and critical political economy each conceive of the role(s) of the media in society?
- What are the distinctive characteristics of the Canadian state that have helped shape its communication systems?

Introduction

In this chapter, we consider the nature of the relationships between communication, society, and culture. After defining key terms, we trace the historical roots of media development and illustrate that today's media are the product of dramatic shifts in the ways in which people understood the world and their relationships to it. This change in worldview—and the institutions of science, industry, and government that it gave rise to—is the fertile ground within which the media developed. We examine different theories of the political role of media in this context, and we go on to consider the ways in which the distinctive elements of the social, political, and physical geographies of the Canadian state have nuanced the form and structure of the Canadian media. In this way, we illustrate that today's media are deeply intertwined with larger social and cultural forms.

Society, Culture, and Media

Set at the intersection between people and different social groups, organizations, and institutions, the media are vital elements of both society and culture. But while these terms are often used in the context of media and communication studies, what exactly do they mean? And what is their relationship to media and communication? Spending a little time thinking about this now will ease discussion later in the book.

Society is used in two main senses: (1) as a "general term for the body of institutions and relationships within which a relatively large group of people live" and (2) as an "abstract term for the conditions in which such relationships are formed" (Williams, 1976: 291). From this perspective, Canadian society is the product of a complex weave of institutions and relationships:

- particular cities and neighbourhoods
- municipal, provincial, and federal levels of government
- the legal system
- educational institutions
- transportation systems
- the health-care system
- businesses and corporations
- sports teams
- not-for-profit and voluntary organizations
- religious organizations
- and (of course) media

In other words, we share institutions and organizations—they connect and bind us together. Within the larger geographic dimensions of the country—and beyond—this complex weave of relationships and dependencies provides the common bonds that are the foundations of Canadian society.

Culture, on the other hand, "is one of the two or three most complicated words in the English language" (Williams, 1976: 87). One study found over 160 definitions circulating in the academic literature. We will do our best to sidestep this quagmire, limiting ourselves to three somewhat overlapping senses of the term.

An early English variant of the term *culture* was drawn from an agricultural usage, where it meant "the tending of something, basically crops or animals" (87). This notion of tending, growing, or developing was transferred to people so that culture became thought of as developing one's mind; in particular, "a general process of intellectual, spiritual, and aesthetic development" (90). That's the first sense.

The second sense centres on the works and practices that are the focus of this process of development: intellectual and artistic works, such as music, painting, sculpture, and dramatic arts. Traditionally, however, this definition has been limited to classical or fine art forms, such as symphonies, ballet, classic literature, and Shakespeare's plays. These *high* cultural forms are sometimes contrasted with more everyday, and generally popular, forms of music, painting, writing, television programs, and so on, which are termed *popular culture* (see Chapter 7). *Folk culture* represents yet another kind or dimension of culture and generally refers to traditional or ethnic practices and arts, such as storytelling, singing, carving, weaving, dance, and traditional costumes. One of the problems with this classification is that it sometimes carries elitist connotations whereby high culture is seen as superior, more intellectual, and more "refined" than popular or folk culture.

The third definition has its roots in anthropology and is generally used to indicate a "particular way of life, whether of a people, a period, a group, or humanity in general" (Williams, 1976: 90). From this perspective, culture includes "knowledge, belief, art, morals, law, custom, and any other capabilities and habits acquired by man as a member of society" (E.B. Tylor, in Thompson, 1990: 128). Canadian culture is multi-layered. At one level, we have a broad set of shared ideas and values regarding what it means to be Canadian, such as shared official languages, symbols (e.g., the Canadian flag), laws, games, customs, institutions, songs, and holidays. At another level, we have regional differences in culture and perspective: British Columbia, the Prairies, and Ontario all have distinctive ways of life. Quebec, with its French language and histories, is particularly distinctive. Further, we have elements of indigenous cultures deeply woven into many common ideas and concepts, as well as contributions that various immigrant groups have made to Canadian ways of life. This third definition—"culture as a way or ways of life"—is the one we use in this book.

Media are a vital link in how we both see and understand our relationships with our society and culture. Canada is the second-largest country in the world. Bounded by water on three sides, it is more than 9,000 kilometres wide and has a total area of 9.9 million square kilometres. Given the vast scale of the country, many of our ideas and understandings of what makes up both our society and culture are created or reinforced through our interaction with media, and media content is woven both into and from the complex social and cultural fabric that blankets this geography.

© Baytchev/Dreamstime.com.

Often, when we talk about "cultured" people, we mean those who know a lot about forms of high culture such as fine art, ballet, opera, or classical music. But we're all "cultured" people, sharing a way of life with others around us.

By permission of Rogers Media.

Hockey Night in Canada, Punjabi edition, illustrates the multi-layered character of Canadian culture.

For instance, our understanding of the international, national, regional, and local events and circumstances that shape our lives are drawn from the screens of smartphones, televisions, computers, and tablets, as well as from the pages of newspapers and magazines. Both news and entertainment exploit stereotypical Canadian images and ideas—like the prairies, the Rocky Mountains, the Parliament buildings, moose, beavers, long winters, and universal health care—to draw us into the narratives they create. Advertising often strives to link products like beer and coffee with Canadian symbols and icons—such as maple leaves and hockey—to illustrate that they are key elements of our culture. And, at a more general level, film and television content employs a range of cultural figures and stereotypes we immediately recognize—such as the nuclear family, mischievous kids with a dislike for school, greedy and cold-hearted bosses—to construct stories and humour.

In other words, media are a key vehicle through which we see, share, understand, and enjoy our relationships with our society and culture.

Because it is largely through media that we come to know our society and culture, there are many types of government policies and support programs to help ensure that media are Canadian-owned and that they reflect Canadian ideas and perspectives. Concerns in this regard are twofold. First is the threat that foreign media will simply eclipse or overrun local or national media. Such is the case with Canadian film and television products. Less than 5 per cent of the films screened in Canadian theatres are Canadian, while a large majority of the television programs Canadians watch—particularly drama—are produced elsewhere, mainly in the United States. As we will see, the reasons for this state of affairs have very little to do with consumer choice; instead, because there is generally more money to be made from screening US films in Canadian theatres, Canadian films have very little access to theatres—especially outside Quebec. Similarly, because US sitcoms, reality TV, and one-hour dramas can be purchased from the United States for a fraction of their production cost, most of this kind of programming on Canadian television—particularly on the private networks—is American, not Canadian. If Canadians want to see their society and culture reflected in their media, government regulation is necessary.

A second, related concern is that by consuming foreign media products, Canadians come to know more about foreign societies and cultures than their own. Polls often find, for instance, that

Keith Homan/Shutterstock.

By permission of Hockey Canada

Companies like Molson and Tim Hortons associate their products with Canadian symbols to demonstrate their connection to Canadian culture.

despite the fact most people in Canada are proud to be Canadian and think of themselves as quite distinct from Americans, Canadians often know more about US history than about Canadian history, and they know more about how the US government and law enforcement work than about their own (see Box 1.3). While it is difficult to link this phenomenon entirely to media consumption, it does raise questions about the effects of having Canadian media so heavily dominated by US content. But before we consider the peculiarities of the Canadian media system, we need to better understand the social and cultural dimensions of media development in general, and for insight into this we turn to the history of media in Western society.

The European Roots of Media and Western Society

While papermaking and movable type were first developed in Asia, it might be said that modern mass media began to emerge in mid-fifteenth-century Europe with Johannes Gutenberg's development of the printing press in Mainz, Germany, in 1454. This advance in technology is often used to designate the end of the Middle Ages and the beginning of the **Renaissance**—a transition from a social order where people were subservient to a powerful Church and monarch to one that was more sympathetic to the freedom of individuals and ideas. The Renaissance and the movements and conceptual developments that followed it—humanism, the Reformation, the Counter-Reformation, the **Enlightenment**, and the **Industrial Revolution**—paved the way for liberal-democratic industrial societies and modern forms of media.

A major aspect of the Renaissance was the rediscovery and revival of learning and literature from antiquity, especially the Greek and Roman empires, which had been lost and suppressed during the Middle Ages. This recovered knowledge helped to reorient social perspectives concerning the place of humankind and nature in the cosmic order. Led by Italian thinkers and artists, the Renaissance was the beginning of a reassertion of reason and the senses that had characterized classical Greece. Emerging from the Renaissance was *humanism*, a broad philosophy that celebrated human achievement and capacity. Although often couched in religious contexts, humanism—through art, sculpture, and architecture—celebrated the human form and encouraged an empirical understanding of the world—*empirical* in that this perspective allowed that people might come to understand the world through individual observation and experience rather than through religious texts and emissaries of the Church. The great works of art and architecture that characterize the period were grounded in these ideas, and they led to Western culture's knowledge of such things as mathematics, mechanics, and geometry, an awareness of perspective, and a theory of light and colour. In the practice of this empirical knowledge, humanism emphasized people's abilities to know and understand the world beyond what had been the teachings of the Church.

At this point in European history, the dominant **ideology** (see Chapter 4) held that the world was ordered by a divine hand and that

Much of Renaissance (*re-naissance*, meaning "born again") architecture and design was taken from Greek and Roman designs. In what other ways have the Greeks and Romans influenced our culture?

true knowledge of the world came from God or through his emissaries on earth: the Pope and the priests of the Church. In the feudal system of production that dominated the period, social position and responsibilities were inherited by birth—royalty and aristocrats held their stations and governed according to a doctrine of divine right (see Figure 2.1). By demonstrating the abilities of individuals to understand and shape the world, humanism sowed the seeds of a secularized society within this traditional order.

The dissemination of humanist ideas was facilitated by the technologies of writing and printing, which allowed individuals to develop and record their ideas and communicate them in a manner understandable by many. Printing presses were established throughout Europe over the next centuries and encouraged the spread of literacy. As literacy spread, so, too, did the thirst for ideas. With printing, ideas rejected by the ruling elite in one regime could be exported into others, leading to destabilization. As American historian Robert Darnton (1982) has demonstrated, a regular business of printing books in Switzerland and smuggling them into France was an important precursor to the French Revolution.

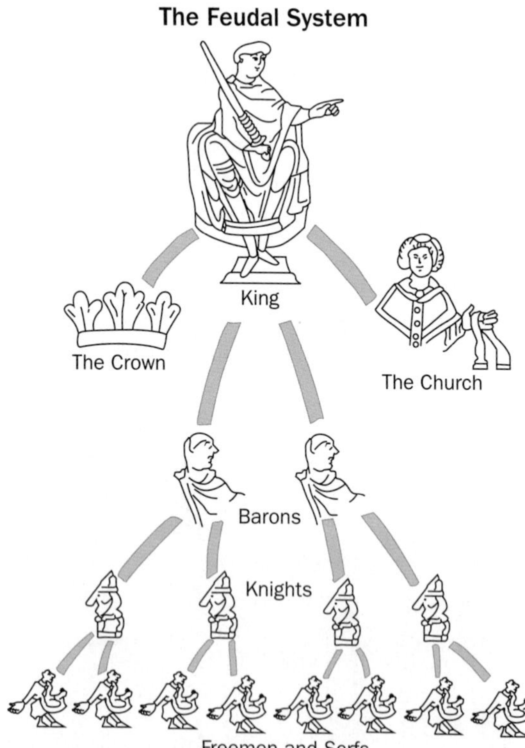

FIGURE 2.1 Feudal system

Feudal society had a well-defined class structure and social positions, and responsibilities were inherited by birth. In what ways do you think this differs from the way our society is structured today? In what ways do you think it's similar?

Source: © Reading Museum (Reading Borough Council). All rights reserved.

In the early eighteenth century, humanism combined with logic and empiricism to introduce the Enlightenment, sometimes otherwise known as the Age of Reason. The Enlightenment was distinguished by an intellectual approach based on a scientific and rational perspective on the world. It heralded a fundamental shift in worldview that championed science over religion and justice over the abuse of power, and a social contract that specified individual rights and freedoms over the absolutist rule of monarchs and popes.

In this regard, the writings of Enlightenment philosophers, such as John Locke (1632–1704), Voltaire (1694–1778), Jean-Jacques Rousseau (1712–1788), and Adam Smith (1723–1790), worked to undermine the inherited right of monarchs and the Church to control government. They argued that people possessed natural, inalienable social rights, and they upheld the market over feudal forms of production and exchange.

These shifts in social ideas that characterized the Enlightenment were fuelled by an emerging elite competing with the aristocracy for power. This prosperous and educated **bourgeoisie**—or new land-owning class—had been working to build a market economy and colonial trade from about the sixteenth century onwards. Through the eighteenth and early nineteenth centuries, the Enlightenment's legacy of scientific reason combined with the growing wealth of the bourgeoisie to fuel change in social and political structure. First with the American War of Independence (1775–1783), and later with the French Revolution (1789–1799), Europe and

North America were gripped in conflict as a new social order took shape. The result was a massive upheaval in European society that laid the groundwork for yet another change in social structure, the shift from an agrarian to an industrial society—a transformation that, again, was fertilized by communication.

Beginning with the invention of the printing press and onward, the spread of knowledge based on a humanist understanding of the world prepared Western society for profound political and social change, from feudalism to capitalism, from farming to industry, from medieval to Renaissance and then to an Enlightenment worldview. In the realm of politics, the acquisition of such knowledge allowed a new class of citizens to emerge and gain enough education to compete with the aristocracy for the right to govern. Similarly, in culture, talented and knowledgeable creative artists brought forward secular literary, musical, and artistic works that were appreciated by the viewer for their visions and understandings of the world rather than their religious significance.

A nineteenth century drawing of Johannes Gutenberg (1398–1468), the inventor of the European movable-type printing press, inspecting a page produced by his printing press. Why is the printing press so important in Western history? What kinds of changes did the invention of the printing press bring about?

It was in this context that what Jürgen Habermas called the *public sphere* took form (refer to Chapters 1 and 10). And, because they inform the public about the important issues of the day, it was under these circumstances that knowledge- and information-based institutions—or, in other words, the media—became, and have remained, essential to the larger process of government.

The Industrial Revolution, Communication, and Social Form

Paralleling the Enlightenment's giving rise to new ways of thinking about people's relations to each other and to the world, the Industrial Revolution introduced a major change in social organization. With the application of growing scientific knowledge to production, industry began to dominate in the late eighteenth century in Western Europe.

As landlords moved to turn their lands to commercial agriculture, serfs, tenant farmers, and others dependent on those lands for their livelihoods were forced to migrate, either into

During the Industrial Revolution, young men started leaving the farms of their families to work in urban factories or on infrastructure like the Firth of Forth Road Bridge near Edinburgh. Life changed dramatically during this time, and people looked to different forms of media to close the geographical and social distances created by these new workspaces and serve new social interests and needs. In what ways are media responding to social change today?

the swelling cities and towns where the new "manufactories" were being built or across the oceans to developing colonies, which increasingly served as sources for raw materials in industrial production. New forms of transportation, such as railways and steamships, provided means for moving people, raw materials, and finished goods, while new forms of communication, such as the telegraph and newspapers, provided vehicles for coordinating buyers and sellers, workers and employers, and governments and citizens.

The growth of industry complicated social relationships as urbanization and migration stamped the landscape with the spatial and temporal edifices and rhythms of industrial production. This production demanded the coordination of social action across increasing physical distances, as both raw materials for factory processes and foodstuffs for rising populations converged on burgeoning urban centres.

Industrial life also redrew the dimensions of family life. The traditional extended family, wherein mother and father, children, grandparents, and aunts and uncles might live in close proximity—even in the same home—gave way to the more streamlined family unit we know today (sometimes called the *nuclear family*), a more flexible form of social organization that was more easily moved from place to place in pursuit of work opportunities.

Industrial production also shifted the temporal dimensions of social life. Work in a rural, agricultural setting is ongoing, requiring a paced way of life in which the work and daily living must adjust to daily and seasonal cycles, structured by the necessary tasks of caring for livestock, raising crops, and sustaining and maintaining the family and the household. Industrial production demanded a different temporal division of the day so that a new distinction arose between work and leisure time.

It was in this context that modern communication media took form. In the face of the changes wrought by the new industrial way of life, the media developed what Raymond Williams has called "specialized means" to close the geographical and social distances created by industrial production and to serve new social interests and needs. As Williams (1974: 22–3) illustrates, "the press [developed] for political and economic information; the photograph for community, family and personal life; the motion picture for curiosity and entertainment; [and] telegraphy and telephony for business information and some important personal messages." Let's consider the forces behind the development of each of these media.

As we discussed in Chapter 1, in the context of developing industrial society, the telegraph greatly enhanced the coordination of people and goods across vast distances. It was a key advance in what Karl Marx described as people's abilities to "shrink space through time." It forestalled the necessity of physically sending messages from one place to another and enabled communication virtually at the speed of light. Both government and industry could respond much more quickly to developing events, accomplishing so much more in shorter periods of time that it seemed as though space—or the distances between places and things—had actually shrunk. Governments more quickly learned of revolts in far-flung parts of their territories and responded with troops, thereby securing more readily the supply of resources and markets. Manufacturers could order raw materials from suppliers a continent away, while orders for goods could be taken from cities and towns scattered across the country. The telephone built upon and enhanced the economic relations created by the telegraph, and although today we think of the telephone as primarily for personal communication, it was first and foremost, and generally remains, a business tool.

On the face of it, the photograph was a simple technique for capturing images on light-sensitive glass or paper. But as the new emerging economic system tore traditional kin and friendship ties apart, it became a way of constructing and remembering family and community. As Susan Sontag (1999: 177) points out,

> Photography becomes a rite of family life just when, in the industrializing countries of Europe and America, the very institution of the family starts undergoing radical change. . . . Those ghostly traces, photographs, supply the token presence of dispersed relatives. A family's photograph album is generally about the extended family—and often it is all that remains of it.
>
> With the rise of large commercial newspapers in the late nineteenth century, the photograph also becomes a way of familiarizing readers with political and business leaders—of "putting a face to the name"—as well as, through images, linking them with far-off events. In these ways photography helped sew the seams of the emerging industrial-based social fabric.

Motion pictures—an extension of the photographic image—were given cultural freedom to grow by the new rhythm of the industrial day that divided time between work and leisure. As people moved into cities and towns and took up industrial ways of life, an increasing number of urban dwellers had free time and disposable income. Entrepreneurs worked to find ways to capitalize on these circumstances, and new products or **commodities** (see Box 2.1) were created to sell to this growing body of consumers. Through the early twentieth century, among these new commodities was the motion picture. The motion picture was also the product of the economies of scale engendered through industrial production (see Box 2.3). Many copies or prints of the same film could be shown simultaneously in widely scattered cities and towns, thereby spreading the cost of production among many audience members.

Of all the modern media given both form and function by the development of industrial society, however, the newspaper or "the press"—named after the printing press—was the earliest to develop, and it was the most pervasive.

Two young sisters pose in an early photograph most likely taken by a studio camera. Large plates coated with light-sensitive chemicals were replaced at the back of the camera for each succeeding photograph. Most photographers developed their own plates and images until George Eastman in 1888 developed the Kodak camera with celluloid film that could be returned to the manufacturer for developing. This, in turn, led to cameras being bought and used by an increasing number of individuals.

The Beginnings of the Modern Media: The Newspaper, or "Press"

In the eighteenth and early nineteenth centuries, some degree of organization was brought to the cacophony of publishing voices created by the printing press, as newspapers began to align with (and sometimes even be owned by) political parties, labour unions, and religious groups. This pattern—the emergence of many newspapers, then their reduction to a few, often politically aligned, publications—has been repeated in

2.1

The Commodity and Communication

One of the most dynamic features of capitalism as an economic system is the way it works to convert things for which we find need and uses in our lives into products for which we must pay market prices. Critical commentators call this *the commodification of everyday life*—that is, what Karl Marx highlighted as the process of turning "use value" into "exchange value" (see Mosco, 2009). Others celebrate this process as the entrepreneurial spirit of capitalism.

Think of all the different elements of the process of communication that have been commodified over the last few years. Television and radio used to arrive free over the air. Now the monthly cable or satellite bill can eat up a day's pay. Time spent in movie theatres—particularly the interval between people taking their seats and the feature film starting—has been commodified, as the theatre owners have used advertising to turn that time into a product they can sell to advertisers. Internet access is purchased by the month or by the byte. Telephone service has evolved into an ever-increasing array of products, such as voice mail, text messaging, and various web-based telecom services. Even the ring tones for cellphones have become products for sale. And, increasingly, information itself—such as news, government reports and statistics, and course readings—is becoming a product for sale.

As we shall see in the following chapters, this ongoing commodification of communication products and processes lies at the heart of what people call the *information economy* or the *communication revolution* and is seen as a key factor in economic growth. However, it creates a growing divide between the communication haves and have-nots, between the information-rich and the information-poor. And, given that communication products and processes play key roles in our knowledge and understanding of the world, the commodification of communication and information—or turning both information and access to it into products we have to pay for—can't help but undermine people's abilities to exercise their full rights and responsibilities as citizens.

many Western countries at various points in their histories. And just as this pattern has repeated itself, so has the subsequent transition of control of newspapers to business interests.

In Canada, newspapers in the early and mid-nineteenth century were generally under the control of partisan political interests. As Robert Hackett and Yuezhi Zhao (1998: 20) observe in *Sustaining Democracy? Journalism and the Politics of Objectivity*,

> Often owned by a group of wealthy partisans . . . papers had the explicit purpose of representing a political party. Overall, they tended to serve the ruling political and business elites. . . . Newspapers often counted on financial support from government patronage or direct party subsidies. Shaped by party affiliations, the journalism of the time was replete not only with special pleading for the politicians who financially supported each paper, but also with vicious personal attacks on political foes.

By the early twentieth century, however, the cost of producing newspapers drove them into the control of business. Perhaps the largest influence on this shift in ownership was the development of industrial society. Around the end of the nineteenth century, the growth in industry and urban populations led to developments in both mass production and mass marketing.

The modern newspaper in Canada is rooted in the period from 1890 to 1920, when among other things, a rapidly expanding urban population, increased literacy, the economic boom of the Laurier era, and a growing national market for consumer goods contributed to the profitability of new newspaper ventures" (Sotiron 1997: 4). Newspaper publishers found that providing marketers with a vehicle to reach the increasing numbers of consumers was more profitable than direct alliances with political parties, and advertising soon became their major source of revenue. As modern newspapers evolved within industrial society, they crossed the boundary between the public life of work and community and the private home. In this configuration, papers began to serve multiple roles.

Not only were they the source of political and community news but they also provided a wide range of other information important to people confronted with an increasingly complex society. Want ads linked job seekers and employers, merchandise and service ads linked the swelling ranks of workers with a growing number of products, and personal ads helped people locate partners and friends in the increasingly impersonal urban environment.

New technologies animated these changes. Cheap newsprint and faster printing presses lowered the cost of producing newspapers, while the telegraph and later the telephone were conduits for the information needed to fill pages and attract readers. Thus, just as the photograph, the motion picture, the telegraph, and the telephone took form and function in the emerging structure of industrial society, so, too, did newspapers (Schudson, 1978).

Journalism also changed to meet the new industrial regime. In news, *objectivity* replaced partisan reporting as papers sought to reach a wider readership and increase circulation and profits (see Hackett and Zhao, 1998; Schudson, 1978). The use of headlines and photographs to capture the attention of potential readers became popular, as did partitioning newspapers into different sections and offering a range of different features—such as serialized novels—to attract a diverse readership.

As the press became more a business than a service, publishers also promoted their own interests, emphasizing the freedom to pursue profitability in the marketplace unencumbered by state restrictions (see Chapter 8). Journalists developed a complementary ethic by stressing their need for independence from the state for reportage and analysis. This dual business and journalistic thrust has allowed the press to establish some distance from the politicians of the day. This is not to say that in claiming their independence, newspapers, and the media as a whole, represent the interests of all citizens. On the contrary, as we will see in the following chapters, the media generally represent the interests of the power elites in society—mostly business types, but also the agendas of the political and intellectual elites.

While newspaper readership has declined in recent years, the electronic media that dominate our lives today are very much a product of this history. Controlled by corporate interests, the profit motive plays a strong role in shaping media form and content. Still, however, just as they have since the early days of industrial society, media continue to provide a key link between people, governments, and the larger society within which they live.

Perspectives on the Media

From the beginning, the media have played a key role in the shifting relations of social power. During the Renaissance, the printing press was used to undermine the traditional power of the Catholic Church. As newspapers developed through the seventeenth and eighteenth centuries, governments in Britain and Europe used a range of measures to censor and control the circulation of news in order to maintain social and political control. Through the late eighteenth and early nineteenth centuries, liberal writers such as John Milton, Jeremy Bentham, James Mill, and John Stuart Mill advocated that a press independent from government regulation (a "free press") was central to good government and democracy.

It was in this context that in a speech to the British House of Commons, Edmund Burke referred to the press as "**the fourth estate**," meaning that alongside the other "estates," or institutions of social governance—the clergy, the nobility, and the commons—the press played an important role as a kind of political watchdog, guarding the rights of citizens through publicly reporting on affairs of state. Over the last few centuries, consequently, freedom of the press from government interference became an important political ideal, and it is reflected in the *Canadian Charter of Rights and Freedoms,* the Constitution of the United States, and the United Nations' Universal Declaration of Human Rights. Although newspaper readership has declined in recent years, newspaper and television news organizations remain the largest producers of news and public affairs content, and the bulk of the news available on the internet originates from these sources. In this context, the term *press* is taken to represent the news media as a whole. And while the term may conjure up old-fashioned images of huge metal presses hammering out reams of ink-stained paper, it is important to remember that the press still plays important social and political roles in society.

But while newspapers have historically contributed to political freedoms, they have over time come to be operated as commercial enterprises, and there has been a growing concern that corporate interests—namely, the pursuit of private profit—have dominated over the public interest in their operation. Press barons of the late nineteenth century were known to sensationalize news, and sometimes even to make it up, in their efforts to attract readers. And today there are many examples of how news production and, sometimes, perspectives in news media are tilted toward the interests of the shareholders of media companies rather than to the general public.

More recently, another issue undermining the legitimacy of the press, particularly in the United States, is that of **fake news**. As we discuss in later chapters, the term is used in two senses: (1) to describe particular news items that are totally fabricated, usually to undermine a political foe or de-legitimate an idea; or (2) to describe particular news outlets that a politician or political party sees as generally undermining the general image or message they would like to portray to the public.

Despite these problems, the press is still central to social and political life. However, defining the exact social role of the press, and subsequently that of the media, is a matter of some debate and depends largely on one's theoretical perspective, and different theories of society take different approaches to understanding the role of the media in that context. In this section, we consider four perspectives on media and society.

The first two—the libertarian theory of the press and social responsibility theory—focus primarily on the news media and draw on liberal theories of society to consider what they believe to be the ideal role these media should play in social and political life, as well the social conditions necessary to realize that role. Drawing from early Enlightenment philosophers, these two theories emphasize the freedom of the individual and the idea that the media, too, should enjoy relative freedom from both government and commercial interests so that it might

While newspaper readership has been declining in recent years, newspaper and television news organizations remain the largest producers of news and public affairs content, and the bulk of the news available on the internet originates from these sources.

provide unbiased perspectives on events and circumstances. Focusing on the media in general, the second two perspectives—the mass society thesis and political economic theory—downplay the importance of the individual and instead focus on the ways in which larger social forces impact both the way in which people understand society and how the media represent it.

Although quite different in character, these theories or perspectives underpin the ways in which many people think of the social and political roles of the media today. As you may recognize, liberal theory, and particularly the social responsibility theory of the press, is the dominant way of thinking about the media and its role in society. The point to consider here, however, is not which of these theories is the correct or "true" perspective on the media and society but rather the insight that each brings to the analysis.

Libertarian Theory

Such philosophers as John Locke (1632–1704), David Hume (1711–1776), and John Stuart Mill (1806–1873) nourished the liberal concepts of agency and the free will of individuals. Modern libertarians took those concepts a step further and foregrounded the idea that individual freedom is the first and foremost social goal to be sought. Libertarians are highly suspicious of the state and of government regulation; they maintain that limiting the powers of the government and other impediments to individual action will create the most advantageous situation for all.

Libertarian theorists tend to see media as an extension of the individual's right to freedom of expression and, hence, as independent voices that help to make government responsible to the people. The media do so by supplying information to people such that they might judge government's performance and, come election time, vote accordingly. Apart from this watchdog role, libertarians also see the media as assiduous pursuers of free speech. From this perspective, freedom of speech is considered one of the most important of all freedoms; and while it may result in problems and difficulties in the short term, as in the case of pornography and hate speech, libertarians maintain it is the best way to preserve freedom and the rights of all citizens. In striving to ensure distance between the government and the media, libertarians place media in the hands of private citizens. The rights to publish and to free expression are fundamental rights of citizenship and must not be tampered with, particularly by government.

One of the main problems with this perspective, however, is that in the face of the overarching importance placed on freedom of speech or expression, there is little concern for the fact that in the course of media production and operation, the corporate sector promotes its own interests—those of developing markets and of accruing profits—which are placed above the interests of the people, society, and the government of the day. Consequently, rather than allowing journalists to dedicate themselves to "serving the people," privately controlled media tend to maximize their own interests as private, profit-oriented corporations, thereby undermining the libertarian ideal they often claim to uphold.

Social Responsibility Theory

The social responsibility theory of the press was originally put forward in the United States in 1947 by the Commission on Freedom of the Press (or Hutchins Commission)—a non-governmental inquiry into the state of the US media. The study was motivated by a concern that left to their own devices, the media companies were not upholding the broad public principles that libertarian theory claimed they would and that a new vision or understanding of the role of the media in society had to be formulated. While also drawing on liberal theories of society and the libertarian theory of the press, the study concluded that the libertarian arrangement often fails to produce media that are generally of benefit to society. The commission thus put together a broad set of civic-minded principles to guide newspaper operations. It stopped short, however, of recommending government enforcement of those principles, instead allowing that media should be self-regulating.

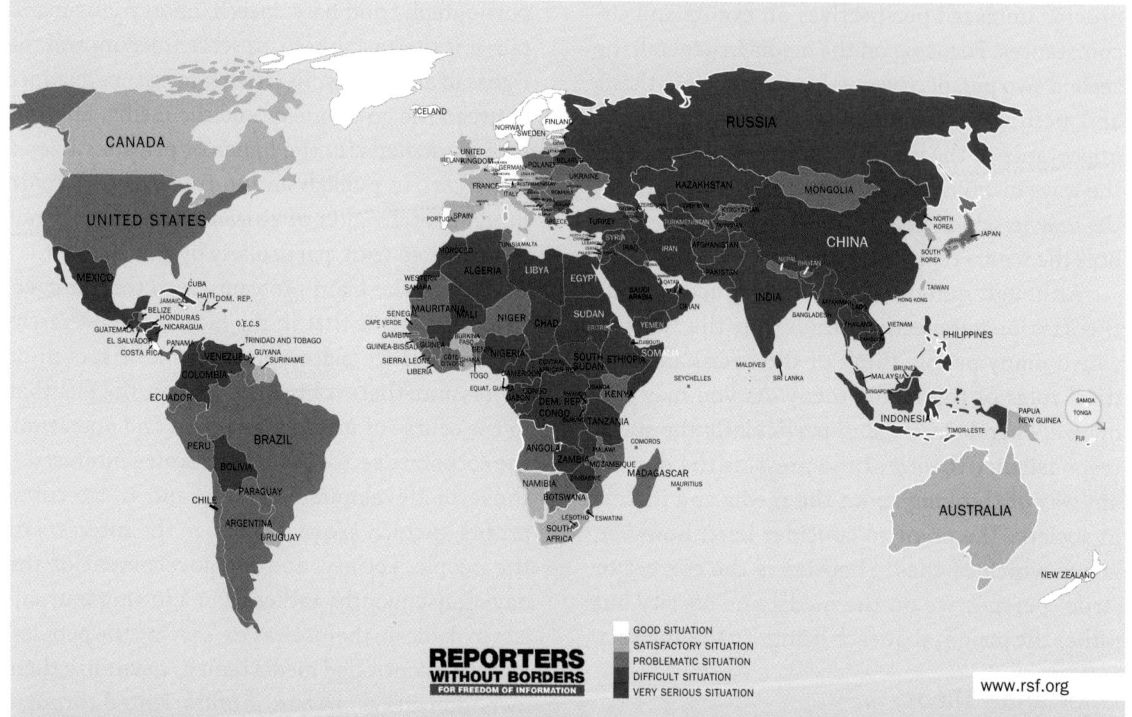

FIGURE 2.2 Reporters Without Borders: Press Freedom Index

Reporters Without Borders is a non-profit organization based in France that monitors attacks on the media and freedom of information. Every year, it produces a "Press Freedom Index" that strives to track the freedom of information in countries around the world. As Christophe Deloire, the organization's secretary general, points out, the index "is a reference tool that is based on seven criteria: the level of abuses, the extent of pluralism, media independence, the environment and self-censorship, the legislative framework, transparency and infrastructure."

Source: Reporters Without Borders World Press Freedom Index 2018.

In Canada, there has been a long-standing concern that corporate interests might be superseding the public interest in the press and, as we discuss in Chapter 7, there have been a number of government-sponsored inquiries in this regard. In taking up this concern, the 1981 Kent Royal Commission on Newspapers (Canada, 1981: 235) explained the social responsibility theory well, pointing out that as newspaper publishing began to be taken over by big business, the notion of social responsibility was born of a need to fight against the potential for big business to impose its perspectives on news reporting and maintaining press independence.

While, as we will see, there are no formal laws laying out the exact role of the media in Canadian society, social responsibility theory is perhaps the most common way of thinking about it (see Chapter 8). However, exactly what the dimensions of media responsibility are in this country and how they might be either taken up by or imposed on the private corporations that own a large part of Canada's media remain the subject of public debate.

The Mass Society Thesis

For many writers during the Industrial Revolution, the new way of life was without cultural foundation. As they saw it, cut free from a traditional feudal agricultural way of life and the social values, customs, and bonds that gave that life form and function, people in the new industrial context became a collection of isolated individuals—an undifferentiated "mass" society within which no assumptions about social order and people's place and function in it were held in common.

In this state of social atomization and potential moral disorder, the newfound social and political powers of the masses were regarded by the social elite of the day as somewhat threatening to the existing cultural order. The nature of the perceived threat to the establishment varied from writer to writer. For some, it was viewed as a potential state of anarchy, a breakdown of social order. Others expressed concern that these people were commonly subject to manipulation and easy targets for totalitarian social and political movements. In this way, media are seen as a unifying force in society, a means of conjoining minds in common cause and action, although not necessarily toward positive ends.

Through the early twentieth century, this perspective wound its way into a range of academic disciplines and had a strong impact on early communication theory. To a large extent, it framed new media of the day, such as radio and film, as part of a new "commercial" or **mass culture** where media content is simply an unsophisticated commercial product designed to placate the masses with cheap entertainment and, through advertising, incorporate them into a more consumer-oriented way of life.

The major problem with this perspective is that it is elitist—privileging the idea that the high cultural values held by the more educated and affluent members of society are superior to those of poorer and less educated citizens. At the same time, it also assumes that the more affluent are better able to see through and resist the slick sales pitches of advertisers and the propaganda of authoritarian governments. As we shall see in Chapter 4, underlying these conceptions of the purpose of mass media was an unsophisticated vision of the relationship between media and audiences—one that assumes the media have a direct effect on people's behaviour—and a perspective that has been firmly proven to be untrue.

Political Economy and Marx

In the early to mid-nineteenth century, as capitalist industry was introducing massive social change in Europe, Karl Marx argued that the capitalist system was built on a set of social relations in which politics and economics were inextricably linked. Modern Western societies, Marx argued, were characterized by a new and revolutionary mode of production—industrial capitalism—in which scientific techniques, applied to the mass production of an ever-increasing range of goods (or *commodities*, in Marx's terms), created wealth for the owners of capital (see Box 2.1). In Marx's analysis, industrial society is organized around the reproduction of capital—that is, the creation of surplus or profits from productive activities. This tends to create two main classes: capitalists, the owners of the means of production (factories, commercial property, and so on), and workers, who, because they don't own productive property, must sell their labour power to capitalists. Marx argued that this system of production generally serves the interests of the capitalists (a tiny fraction of the population), while workers (the vast majority of people) are exploited by the capitalists. They can be fired at any time and for whatever reason, and they have to fight to squeeze a living wage out of industrialists.

As Marx saw it, modern capitalism transformed all aspects of life, particularly at the political level, as government and the structure of the state increasingly came to represent the interests of capital. New laws were enacted to protect private property, particularly the productive property of capitalists. Labour legislation laid the legal framework for relations between capital and labour. Taxation raised funds for creating infrastructure—roads, railways, canals, harbours, and communication systems—that kept the wheels of commerce moving. Schooling was redefined along industrial models in order to teach people the skills necessary to become productive workers. And when workers rebelled through strikes or some other form of civil disobedience, the police force could be called upon to restore order.

At the heart of a Marxist analysis of modern society is a belief in the possibility of a better life that could be shared by all—a life that is blocked by the private appropriation of wealth. Material abundance could be available to all if the techniques of modern manufacturing were somehow regulated with everyone's interests in mind.

Marx's ideas shaped the political life of the twentieth century throughout the world. In most European democracies, political parties tended to develop in one of two directions: those that represent the interests of the owners of productive property and those that represent the interests of workers. Although the Russian system of authoritarian state socialism clearly failed, communist and socialist parties still command strong showings in elections in European countries and elsewhere in the world. Marx's emphasis on the fundamental importance of economic life on the structure and other elements of social life remains a substantial and important contribution to social theory.

Writers working from Marx's analytic legacy are critical of the ways in which the structure of society affords benefits—wealth and power—to some groups of people over others; hence the term *critical political economy*. In particular, critical political economy focuses on the ways in which the allocation, production, distribution, and consumption of social resources enable and constrain social action. That is, it is concerned with the way the ownership and control of society's resources—especially political and economic resources—give owners a larger say in the form and direction society takes than to those lacking control over such controls.

Critical political economy is concerned with the ways in which the media support dominant interests in society, helping them maintain power and control (see Chapter 4). In contrast to the libertarian and social responsibility theories of the press, which argue that the media can and should have a relatively independent place in the political and economic processes that govern society, critical political economy argues that in capitalist societies, the media are a key institution in

David Hume Kennerly/Getty Images Reportage.

Lars Niki/Getty Images for United States Olympic Committee.

In the US, the **conservative** industrial billionaire Koch brothers are part of a network of rich corporate donors who planned to spend $400 million on influencing the American mid-term elections in 2018.

Drawing from the work of Karl Marx (pictured here on an East German stamp), critical political economy argues that in capitalist societies, the media are a key institution in promoting capitalism and in helping maintain social inequality. How do you see this at work in the media today? In what ways do the media challenge social inequality?

promoting capitalism and in helping maintain social inequality (Mosco, 2009).

From this perspective, media support the capitalist system and the inequalities it perpetuates in a number of ways—first, and perhaps most obviously, by promoting the sale of commodities (see Box 2.1). Advertising is pervasive in the media and provides a constant barrage of messages that encourage people to purchase goods/services and to support the capitalist system. Second, more generally, the media promote a consumer lifestyle. Woven throughout media content, be it news, entertainment, or advertising, is a constant refrain that the consumer lifestyle—that is, satisfying one's wants, needs, and desires through the market—is the best and perhaps only way to be happy. And third, news, information, and entertainment programming generally assume that the existing economic system and the institutions and social relations it entails are the best and most legitimate way of doing things. Social problems, such as unemployment, poverty, and corruption, are seen as the fault of particular events or individuals—not the system itself. Consequently, in all these ways, the media and media content are seen as one of the main vehicles in helping to legitimate and support our political and economic systems.

Which of these perspectives is the true or correct one? The short answer is that there is no single true perspective. As we have seen, the social roles and structure of the media are complex. To some extent, social responsibility theory—with its belief that the media play an important role in democratic societies in terms of informing the public—is the dominant way of thinking about the media and its role in society in Canada. But all four perspectives continue to influence the ways in which people think about the media today. To understand what role media play in any particular instance, we need to examine the specific relations of power in which they are implicated.

Media and Canadian Realities: History and Structure

Just as larger social, political, and economic events, such as the Enlightenment and the Industrial Revolution, have shaped communication media in general, so, too, have the development and structure of the Canadian state, as well as a distinctive Canadian culture, nuanced the structure and operation of media in Canada.

In the early nineteenth century, European settlement of the geography that is now Canada took the form of a collection of colonies scattered across the vast northern half of North America. Industry at that point was largely devoted to the export of staples or raw materials for manufacturing in Britain and the United States. In this context, the lines of communication followed the lines of commerce and ran either overseas to Britain or north–south into the United States. But by the mid-nineteenth century, both Britain and the United States had enacted trade restrictions on the colonies, forcing them to look to themselves for development. In the face of these pressures, Canadian Confederation in 1867 was the first step to building an economic unit out of these colonies.

In 1879, Prime Minister John A. Macdonald introduced Canada's National Policy, a set of initiatives designed to turn the idea of an east–west economy into a reality. The National Policy had three particularly important components:

1. the building of a transcontinental railway;
2. a tariff designed to limit the entry of manufactured goods from the United States and Britain; and
3. efforts to entice immigrants to settle the prairies.

The railway was to provide a reliable line of transportation for people and goods across the country, and particularly to move raw materials from the margins of the country to the industrial heartland in Central Canada where they would be manufactured into goods and shipped back out to market. In other words, the railway was to bind the country into a cohesive political economic unit with a "ribbon of steel." The tariff was used to tax materials and manufactured goods entering the country. Its purpose was to protect Canadian industries in their infancy by keeping cheap competitive goods outside the country. At the same time, it encouraged foreign investment, as non-Canadian companies wishing to tap into the expanding Canadian market were encouraged to build factories and produce goods here in order to avoid the tariff. The tariff was necessary because Canada had a much smaller population than either Britain or the United States and did not have the **economies of scale** (see Box 2.3) necessary to produce goods at a price that could compete with similar goods produced in those countries. Finally, immigration policy actively sought settlers from Central and Eastern Europe to populate the Prairie provinces, both to develop the land and raise grain for the central Canadian market and to serve as a market for the manufactured goods of Ontario and Quebec (See Box 2.2: "A Dark Side of Canadian History").

Despite these measures, because of the large size of the country and the small population, it was often difficult to wring profits from business in Canada, so the government often had to step in to encourage private investment. For instance, the Canadian Pacific Railway (CPR) was issued a wide range of government payments and subsidies to encourage the building of the transcontinental railway. Similarly, because of the large investment necessary, Bell Telephone was given a monopoly on long-distance telephone service in Central Canada so that it might exploit economies of scale when building that system.

Still, it was all but impossible for the government to attract private investment in some areas. When private investment could not be found, both the federal and provincial governments frequently undertook some businesses themselves, often in the form of Crown—or government-owned—corporations. Canada's second national railroad, for example, the Canadian National Railway (CNR), bolstered service to some areas and brought a railway option to others not served by the Canadian Pacific Railway (CPR). Canada's first transcontinental airline, now Air Canada, was a Crown corporation, as was the first national broadcaster, the Canadian Radio Broadcasting Commission. Later, the country's first satellite company, Telesat Canada, was also a government initiative. In short, historically, because of the unique features of the Canadian state, the government has often taken a strong hand in shaping the economy. At the federal level, these efforts have been motivated by a strong nationalist sentiment.

This tradition of nation building is reflected in the structure of Canada's media industries. In the same way that the railway was seen as binding Canada physically, broadcasting in the 1930s was envisioned as bringing the country together through a common Canadian consciousness or perspective on the world (see Box 2.4). Consequently, the government set up the Canadian Radio Broadcasting Commission, which later

2.2 A Dark Side of Canadian History

As James Daschuk illustrates in his book *Clearing the Plains: Disease, Politics of Starvation and the Loss of Aboriginal Life*, John A. Macdonald's efforts to drive the railway across the country and encourage European settlement of the prairies came at great cost to the indigenous peoples who lived there. As he points out,

> A key aspect of preparing the land was the subjugation and forced removal of indigenous communities from their traditional territories, essentially clearing the plains of aboriginal people to make way for railway construction and settlement. Despite guarantees of food aid in times of famine in Treaty No. 6, Canadian officials used food, or rather denied food, as a means to ethnically cleanse a vast region from Regina to the Alberta border as the Canadian Pacific Railway took shape. (Daschuk [quoted in *The Globe and Mail*], 2013)

University of Toronto/Thomas Fisher Rare Book Library.

became the Canadian Broadcasting Corporation (CBC), to create a national broadcasting network and Canadian programming—two activities the private sector was unable to undertake profitably at the time.

Later, various policy measures in the magazine, newspaper, publishing, music, film, and telecommunications industries—including online media—were undertaken with similar objectives in mind: to help build and strengthen a common Canadian culture. In other words, they were enacted with nationalist purposes in mind. As we shall see, however, the government record in building and strengthening Canadian culture is spotty at best, and while government policy has often been framed by strong language that claims concern for Canadian culture, it has not always been backed with strong action.

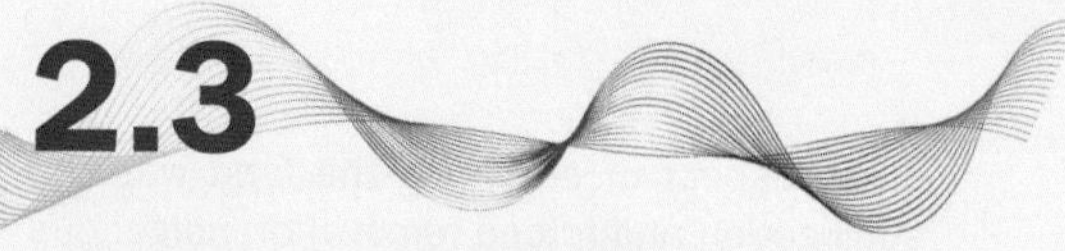

Economies of Scale

Economies of scale reflect the fact that the greater the quantity of a particular product is made, the less each one costs to produce. Much of the cost of an industrial product is in setting up the factory that will produce it. Whether one is producing cars, stoves, or matches, buying the real estate on which the factory is located, building the building in which it will be housed, and then designing and creating the machinery that will make the product represent a much greater investment than the raw materials that go into the product. For instance, if, when putting together a factory for making stoves, it costs $1 million and the labour and raw materials that go into each stove cost $100, the cost of manufacturing one stove will be $1,000,100. If 10,000 stoves are produced, the cost of each stove would be $200 ($1,000,000 divided by 10,000 equals $100 + $100 in raw materials). If 1,000,000 stoves are produced, however, the cost falls to $101 each ($1,000,000 divided by 1,000,000 equals $1 + $100 in raw materials). Consequently, because the United States over the years has had a population roughly 10 times the size of Canada's, manufactured goods coming out of the United States have been cheaper than those made in Canada. As we will see, these economics also apply to media products.

Distinctive Characteristics of the Canadian State

Before considering some of the larger political principles and cultural concerns that underpin the Canadian media, we need to understand the distinctive characteristics of the Canadian state that have shaped the development of its communication systems. We have already looked at two of these characteristics: the *vastness of the country* and the *small size of Canada's population*. These geographic and demographic facts have pressed governments to invest in expensive national transmission systems so that Canadians can stay in touch with each other.

A third significant characteristic, derived in part from the size of the country, is Canada's *regionalism*. Canada is not just a country of physical geographic variety; it is a vast country of regional cultures. From the disparate French and British colonies scattered throughout what is now Canada grew a "confederation." This nation required means of internal communication, but not those in which messages would be generated only from a central point and fed to outlying regions. Each region needed to generate its own information such that the region's particularities might be reflected to the whole. This would help bring the country together—or such has been the ideal.

Canada is also a nation of *two official languages* (English and French), which is now enshrined in the country's *Constitution Act, 1982*. But Canadians have committed themselves to more than a freedom of language choice for individuals. They have committed themselves to providing federal government services, including broadcasting, in both official languages. Bilingual government services and bilingual broadcasting channels (not just programs) are a testament to the right of any Canadian to live and work wherever she or he may wish. They are also a continual reminder to all that we are officially a bilingual country.

In 1971, during Pierre Trudeau's first term as prime minister, Canada also officially became a *multicultural country* and, although it was long in coming, an increasing number of media programming services have been tailored to various ethnic communities.

A final, important characteristic of Canada's communication environment is its proximity to the United States. Economies of scale in media production (see Box 2.5), coupled with shared language in Anglophone Canada and some similar basic political and economic philosophies,

2.4 Broadcasting and Nation-Building

In the face of an overwhelming spillover of US programming into Canada, the federal government set up the Canadian Radio Broadcasting Commission (CRBC), and later the Canadian Broadcasting Corporation (CBC), to build a national broadcasting network and create Canadian programming. In introducing the 1932 *Broadcasting Act* to the House of Commons—the legislation that created the CRBC—Prime Minister R.B. Bennett (1932: 112) outlined what the government saw as the purposes of that legislation:

> This country must be assured of complete Canadian control of broadcasting from Canadian sources, free from foreign interference or influence. Without such control radio broadcasting can never become a great agency for communication of matters of national concern and for the diffusion of national thought and ideals, and without such control it can never be the agency by which consciousness may be fostered and sustained and national unity still further strengthened. . . . No other scheme than that of public ownership can ensure to the people of this country, without regard to class or place, equal enjoyment of the benefits and pleasures of radio broadcasting.

Early on, Canadian legislators recognized radio's ability to operate on the principle of free speech and its potential to create a national community.

have combined with this proximity to yield a large influx of US media products into Canada. More US television programming is available to the majority of Canadians than is Canadian programming. On most Canadian commercial radio stations, more US than Canadian music is available to listeners. On virtually all magazine racks in Canada, more US magazines are available to the reader than Canadian magazines, this despite the fact that more than 2,000 magazines are published in Canada. Over 95 per cent of the films screened in Canadian theatres are foreign productions, mainly American ones.

Our proximity to the United States and the resultant spillover of US cultural products are a major factor to be considered when assessing Canada's communication environment. Unlike many Canadian media outfits, US media companies favour, for economic reasons, distributing homemade products over imports. Consequently, the United States has less tolerance for products that are not recognizably American, and so the counter-flow—Canadian ideas/products moving stateside—has been very limited.

In the face of the challenges posed by these characteristics of Canadian media markets, Canada has a fairly strong record of achievement in forging a national communication system. Table 2.1 provides a chronology of dates of important communication achievements, including many Canadian firsts.

2.5 The Economics of Media Representation

As in other industries, economies of scale underlie media production. Much of the cost of producing a magazine or book, for instance, is in paying the writers, editors, photographers, and typesetters to create the "first copy." After that, these initial expenses are spread across the number of copies produced. So, if the cost of gathering and putting together all of the material that goes into a particular magazine is $50,000 and 50,000 copies of that magazine are printed, the editorial cost of each magazine is $1.00. But if 500,000 magazines are printed, the cost falls to only 10 cents per copy. Similar economics apply to film and television, where the "cost per viewer" is spread over the number of audience members.

Because the market for media products in the United States is roughly 10 times the size of the market in Canada, the cost per reader or audience member for those products is often significantly less in the United States than it is for Canadian production aimed primarily at a Canadian audience. It is therefore often much more profitable for Canadian distributors of media products to sell US books, magazines, TV shows, and films than those made specifically for the Canadian market. As a result, US media products are often more commonly available in Canada than homegrown versions. It is not because Americans make better media products than Canadians that our markets are overrun with US fare; it's simply because more money can be made from selling them in Canada than from producing our own.

Each of these developments strengthened links between Canadians and was a factor in nation building and cohesion. But just as important as the technological achievements in building the system are the legislative achievements behind that technological expansion, the 1932 *Broadcasting Act* and the 1993 *Telecommunications Act*. These statutes gave voice to the public interest in the development of these communication systems and set in law the public goals and ambitions that underlie them. Still, addressing the needs of all the different regions and peoples of the country has been difficult, particularly in the North, where, as Lorna Roth (2005: 221) notes, "When first introduced in the 1960s and '70s, television temporarily stalled indigenous self-development by introducing yet another Southern medium devoid of First People's images, voices, and cultural activities."

But while privately owned media organizations have generally welcomed government support through various forms of regulation, they have not always been enthusiastic about assuming particular responsibilities in return for that support. In the broadcasting field, for instance, support for private broadcasters and Canadian ownership of broadcast outlets has been a constant theme of successive Broadcasting Acts and media regulation. But with the exception of CBC, broadcasters and the large media corporations of which many are now a part have been more interested in importing and distributing US programs than in producing Canadian content because that is where the profits lie. Similarly, while the government has played a strong role in helping build the telecommunications system that supports the internet, the private companies that own much of that infrastructure have not always been cooperative in terms of working to balance the public interest against their own private interest (see, for example: Klass et al, 2016; Moll and Shade, 2008, 2011; Vipond, 2011; Raboy, 1990; Weir, 1965; Babe, 1990; Rutherford, 1990; Peers, 1969, 1979).

These realities continue to present challenges to government, business, and other social groups in creating communication systems that serve all Canadians in a fair, equitable, and comprehensive manner.

TABLE 2.1
Some Important Achievements in Canadian Communication History

Year	Achievement
1885	A transcontinental railway
1901	A transatlantic radio link
1927	A trans-Canada radio network
1932	A trans-Canada telephone network First Broadcasting Act is passed
1948	World's first commercial microwave link
1956	World's first tropospheric scatter transmission system
1958	A transcontinental television service A transcontinental microwave network
1959	First Canadian communications satellite experiment, including use of the moon as reflector
1968	Founding of the Canadian Film Development Corporation
1970	Beginning of fibre optic research
1972	A domestic geostationary communications satellite
1973	First nationwide digital data system World's first digital transmission network (Dataroute)
1976	Bill C-58: legislation to help Canadian magazine industry
1990	Completion of a 7,000-kilometre coast-to-coast fibre optic network, the longest terrestrial fibre network in the world
1991	Canadian Broadcasting Act passed
1993	Canadian Telecommunications Act passed
1996	Launch of the first North American commercial digital radio service
1999	Aboriginal Peoples Television Network launched
2005	Canadian Television Fund founded
2010	Canadian Media Fund set up
2018	86% of Canadians have a broadband connection in their home

Media and Canadian Culture

We can now turn to examining the relationship between Canadian culture and Canada's media—including the government's administration and regulation of them. This relationship is interesting and complex.

As we have seen, the media are set at the intersection between people and the different social groups, organizations, and institutions that make up our society. Media are thus primary vehicles in communicating the depth and breadth of the ways of life—or culture—of Canadians. The federal government notes that culture "includes the knowledge, beliefs, art, morals, customs and all other capabilities acquired by a particular society" (from a report on Canada's cultural industries titled *Vital Links* [Canada, 1987: 11]). To this schema we might add the laws, institutions, and organizations that give society form, making culture a way, or ways, of life. In Canada, we have a distinctive set of institutions—such as governments, schools, universities, media, the health-care system—that give Canadian culture form, as well as the distinctive ideas, values, and beliefs that exist within that larger framework of social institutions.

Media are central to how we come to understand and share culture, and, in a large industrial nation such as Canada, the media are intricately woven into the social fabric. They are the means through which the exchange of ideas, experience, images, and interpretations and perspectives on the world takes place. Indeed, it is generally through the media that we come to know our society, its institutions and organizations, and the other people with whom we share our national culture. For this reason, the media industries—such as those involved in radio and television broadcasting, digital media, film, music, newspapers, magazine and book publishing—are often called *cultural industries*. As we discuss in Chapter 8, Canada's cultural industries provide an information base around which various communities and other social groups that make up our society can coalesce and interact, at the best of times contributing to social cohesion and a sense of belonging on the part of all members of society.

Canada's modern communication system is historically rooted in transportation. While John A. Macdonald and his government had the CPR built primarily to ensure the flow of goods and immigrants, with the influx of both came the flow of information—through the mail and the telegraph. The post office instituted inexpensive second-class mail rates to encourage the circulation of newspapers and magazines, which helped

vm/iStockphoto.

The media are central to how we come to understand and share culture. For this reason, media industries, such as television broadcasting, are often called *cultural industries*.

knit the country together. These, and other commercial communications—like the Eaton's department store catalogue—gave Canadians a sense of connection with their compatriots elsewhere in the country. For instance, people on the Prairies or the West Coast ordering a pump organ from Clinton, Ontario, or a wood stove from Sackville, New Brunswick, gave Western Canada an economic link and a social connection to Eastern Canada.

From these humble beginnings, successive federal governments have over the years implemented a range of policies to encourage the development of Canadian media and a media system operating on an east–west axis. Today, many of the laws and regulations that address the cultural industries are administered by Heritage Canada (see Figure 2.3), the federal government department responsible for this field of legislation.

While Canadian governments have nodded to the importance of media and cultural products in the life of the nation, they have not been consistent protectors and supporters of Canada's cultural industries. One of the main points of concern has been competition from US media products (Armstrong, 2016; Grant and Wood, 2004). Foreign content has always been an important part of the flow of information within the Canadian nation, but it has also been the subject of controversy. Tables 2.2 and 2.3 list the top programs in the English and French television markets for the period 9–15 April 2018. The figures provide a sense of the size of the audiences for each program. In Quebec, Canadian programming dominates, with 26 of 30 programs being made in Canada. Of the remaining four, two are from France and two are from the US, and none of the Canadian programs are news or sports. In the rest of Canada, US shows dominate overwhelmingly, with only 11 programs of 30 being Canadian made. Of the 11 Canadian programs, however, 3 are sports and 3 are news, meaning that only 5 out of 24 programs other than news and sports are Canadian.

Culturally, such foreign media products have worked to make Canadians and their public institutions strangers in their own land as consumption of American news, film, and television products have made American laws, politicians, and political and legal organizations often more familiar than our own.

Canadian government investment in communication has traditionally stressed telecommunications transmission and technology. In the 1990s, amid budget cuts to public broadcasting, the federal government spent millions upgrading transmission networks. More recently, the federal government's focus has been on developing a policy for promoting Canadian creative industries, which are taken to include books, music, magazines, film, television, performing and visual arts, video games, and virtual reality and augmented reality industries (Canada, 2017). We will consider this policy—the *Creative Canada Policy Framework*—more closely in Chapter 7. Meanwhile, as that document states, it is worth noting that the cultural sector provides 630,000 jobs for Canadians and contributes $54.6 billion per year in economic activity to the economy.

Historically, from a cultural perspective, the federal government's commitment to the development of communication technology has been a mixed blessing (Charland, 1986). Within

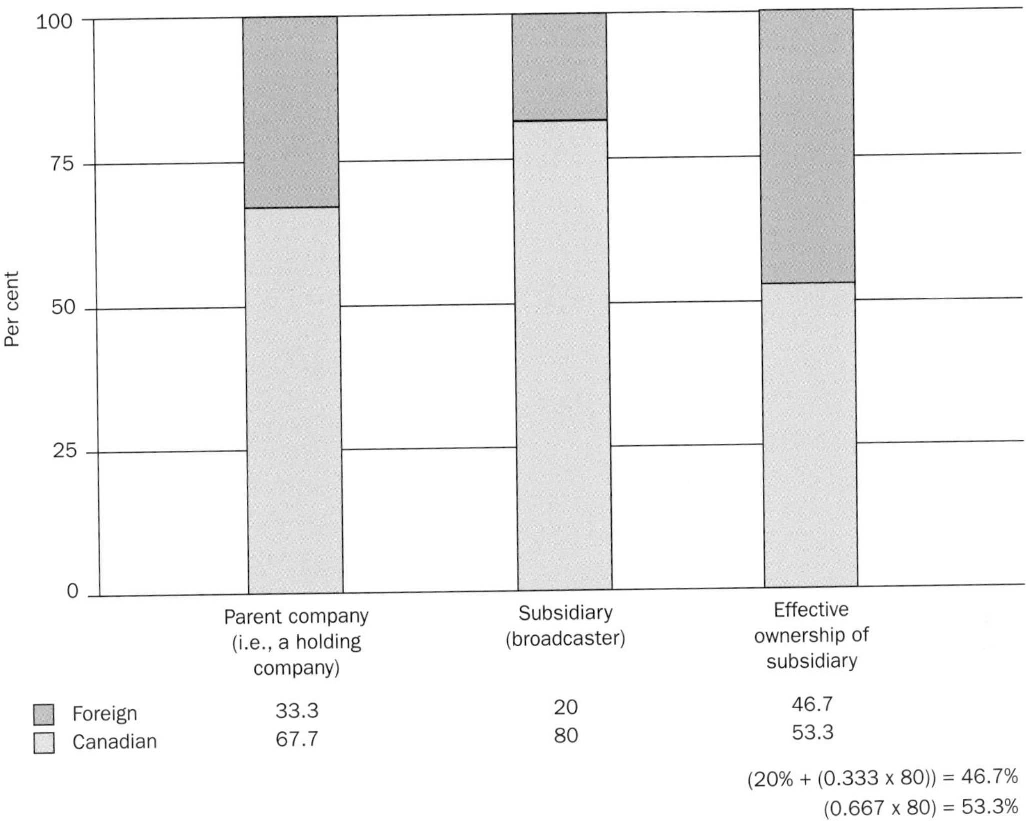

FIGURE 2.3 Maximum allowable foreign ownership of a Canadian broadcaster

As free trade between nations continues to increase, so does foreign ownership. This figure illustrates how Canadian law allows effective ownership of a broadcaster up to as much as 46.7 per cent through indirect ownership (of a holding company) and direct ownership of a broadcaster that is a subsidiary of the holding company. An uptick in the allowable percentage of foreign ownership would potentially give majority control to a foreign interest. Because it is more difficult to hold companies that are headquartered outside the country accountable to domestic laws and regulations, rules requiring that Canadian media companies have majority Canadian ownership have been common in Canadian media regulation. Foreign ownership is often seen as a key problem in maintaining cultural sovereignty, and many other countries, including the United States, have similar regulations.

Canada, the telecommunications infrastructure has served private-sector growth. Through the insistence of the CRTC, some cultural benefits have emerged from that growth, but by and large, privately owned electronic media have been reluctant contributors to national cultural goals. Canadians have never been in a position, however, to produce enough programs and other content to fill the transmission capacity that has been developed in electronic media. Even if Canadian producers could somehow produce the programs, there would not be enough money in the pockets of advertisers, the public, and governments to pay for the range of choice available in the infrastructure. In Anglophone Canada, American media products slip seamlessly into that vacuum. For as little as one-tenth the cost of producing a season of half-hour television dramas in Canada, US producers can provide a high-quality program with high ratings and ever-so-attractive stars, complete with on- and off-line advertising that spills over the border in US media products. It is a self-promoting cultural machine that often

TABLE 2.2
Top English-Language Programs, Canada, 9–15 April 2018

Rank	Program	Broadcast Outlet	Day	Total (thousands of viewers)
1	*The Big Bang Theory*	CTV	Th	3,215
2	*Young Sheldon*	CTV	Th	2,624
3	*Roseanne*	CTV	Tu	2,278
4	*Survivor*	Global	W	2,019
5	*Rick Mercer Report*	CBC	Tu	1,595
6	*Grey's Anatomy*	CTV	Th	1,444
7	*CTV Evening News*	CTV	MTWTF	1,428
8	*Station 19*	CTV	Th	1,393
9	*CTV Evening News: Weekend*	CTV	SS	1,372
10	*Designated Survivor*	CTV	W	1,357
11	*SWAT*	Global	Th	1,332
12	*Criminal Minds*	CTV	W	1,266
13	*Seal Team*	Global	W	1,264
14	*Law & Order: SVU*	CTV	W	1,242
15	*The Crossing*	CTV	M	1,216
16	*Hawaii Five-O*	Global	F	1,214
17	*MacGyver*	Global	F	1,212
18	*Chicago Med*	Global	Tu	1,209
19	*NHL Playoffs, Round 1*	CBC	WTFSS	1,209
20	*Blue Bloods*	CTV	F	1,206
21	*Big Brother Canada*	Global	M	1182
22	*Master Chef Canada*	CTV	Tu	1,166
23	*Big Brother Canada*	Global	Th	1,139
24	*Lucifer*	CTV	Su	1,099
25	*Big Brother Canada*	Global	W	1,097
26	*The Voice*	CTV	M	1,096
27	*CTV National News*	CTV	MTWTFSS	1,090
28	*Chicago PD*	Global	W	1,067
29	*Baseball Blue Jays*	Sportsnet	MTu	995
30	*Hockey Central Saturday*	CBC	Sa	932

*Based on confirmed program schedules and preliminary audience data. Demographic: All persons 2+.

Source: © 2018 Numeris.

makes it difficult to "discover" Canadian-made products in the media mix available to Canadians (Canada, 2017).

While Canadian governments provide subsidies and have enacted legislation to protect Canadian media products and support producers, they have been reluctant to impose heavy restrictions on private enterprise or to restrict the ability of foreigners to do business in Canada. Consequently, as we have seen, only in Quebec is the regional culture thoroughly reflected in the media (see Table 2.3).

TABLE 2.3
Top French-Language Programs, Quebec, 9–15 April 2018

Rank	Program	Broadcast Outlet	Day	Total (thousands of viewers)
1	*La Voix*	TVA	Su	2,017
2	*Unité 9*	SRC	T	1,663
3	*District 31*	SRC	MTWT	1,496
4	*1res fois*	SRC	Th	1,177
5	*Hubert & Fanny*	SRC	Tu	1,173
6	*Tout le monde en parle*	SRC	Su	1,148
6	*VLOG*	TVA	Su	1,048
8	*Ruptures*	SRC	M	1,047
9	*Les Morissette - Captation du spectacle*	SRC	M	1,004
10	*Enfants de télé-Best*	SRC	W	922
11	*Lâcher prise*	SRC	M	901
12	*En direct de l'univers*	SRC	Sa	887
13	*La Poule aux Oeufs d'or*	TVA	W	866
14	*Facture, La*	SRC	Tu	864
15	*Les Petits Doués*	TVA	Th	804
16	*Deuxième chance*	SRC	Sa	785
17	*Le Tricheur*	TVA	MTWTF	763
18	*Infoman*	SRC	Th	728
19	*TVA Nouvelles (18h –LV)*	TVA	MTWTF	720
20	*La petite vie*	SRC	Sa	673
21	*Film de Gars*	TVA	F	658
22	*TVA Nouvelles (18h –SD)*	TVA	SS	633
23	*Arrive en Campagne*	TVA	W	632
24	*Épicerie*	SRC	W	606
25	*Maxim Martin Enfin*	TVA	Su	605
26	*Ici Laflaque*	SRC	Su	599
27	*Du Talent à Revendre*	TVA	F	589
28	*Ma Maison Bien-Aimée*	TVA	M	573
29	*Ninja Warrior Le Parcours Ultime*	TVA	Tu	555
30	*TVA Nouvelles (17h)*	TVA	MTWTF	527

Source: © 2015 Numeris.

As the internet continues to provide an expanding choice of largely foreign news and entertainment products, such as CNN and MSNBC, Netflix, and Amazon Prime, the proportion of Canadian alternatives continues to shrink. Exactly what impact this situation might have on the ways in which we see and understand our country and its place in the world is yet to be determined.

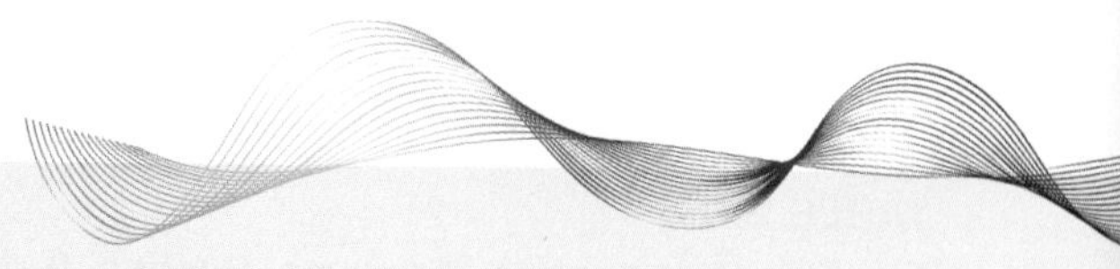

SUMMARY

The evolution of the modern media began in the mid-fifteenth century with Gutenberg's development of printing by means of movable type. Printing with movable type was an important element of a social shift that saw the eclipse of feudalism and the dawning of the Renaissance, followed by the Enlightenment, and the Industrial Revolution. Government by divine right of monarchs was replaced with the notion of the *consent of the governed*. From the fifteenth century onward, the printing press and other media have served an important social role in gathering information and informing citizens. As we have seen, however, different theories of society have envisioned this communication role and function in different ways.

In the course of their development, the press and, subsequently, other communication media have been given form and function by a larger set of social circumstances and events. The rise of industrial society, along with urbanization, increased literacy, and the eight-hour workday, provided the context within which contemporary media took form. In Canada, the development of modern media was further shaped by basic geographical and social realities, such as our vast, sparsely populated, bilingual, multicultural, and regional country, situated next to the United States—the world's largest economy and most aggressive exporter of entertainment and information products.

After years of subsidies and support, as we will see in Chapter 8, magazine and book publishers, filmmakers, and sound-recording artists are, to a degree, increasing their domestic market share and making a mark on the world stage. These successes are fragile, however, and require the ongoing support of governments. Canadians must remind themselves that they are not alone in taking action to regulate the mass media and to stimulate cultural industries. While efforts to define and protect cultural industries have weakened in the face of growing transnational business and trade agreements, the struggle still continues for many countries to maintain control over their own cultural development.

KEY TERMS

bourgeoisie, p. 34
commodities, p. 37
conservative, p. 44
economies of scale, p. 46
Enlightenment, p. 33
fake news, p. 40
ideology, p. 33
Industrial Revolution, p. 33
mass culture, p. 43
Renaissance, p. 33
the fourth estate, p. 39

RELATED WEBSITES

CIRA: *Canada's Internet Factbook*: cira.ca/factbook/
A compendium of facts and figures on the internet in Canada put together by the Canadian Internet Registration Authority (CIRA), a not-for-profit organization that manages the .ca internet domain on behalf of all Canadians.

***The Canadian Encyclopedia*: www.thecanadianencyclopedia.ca/en**
An encyclopedia focused specifically on the history and peoples of Canada. Something quite unique, particularly in a country that is awash in foreign media products.

Canadian Heritage: www.canada.ca/en/canadian-heritage.html
Every Canadian student concerned with culture, the media, and heritage should visit the federal government's Canadian Heritage website.

J-Source, The Canadian Journalism Project: j-source.ca
A website devoted to Canadian journalism and journalism issues.

Demonstrating the Gutenberg Printing Press: www.youtube.com/watch?v=7XLWIeZgU3s
A video demonstrating the use of a Gutenberg press.

Milton's *Areopagitica*: http://www.gutenberg.org/ebooks/608
An important work on censorship by the English poet John Milton.

Rabble.ca
A vibrant Canadian site of alternative news and views.

FURTHER READINGS

Armstrong, Robert. 2016. *Broadcasting Policy in Canada*, 2nd ed. Toronto: University of Toronto Press. A comprehensive account of the history and dimensions of broadcasting policy in Canada.

Canada. 1981. *Report of the Royal Commission on Newspapers* (Kent Commission). Ottawa: Minister of Supply and Services. This dated but most recent royal commission on the press brings forward many issues that are still important today. Its background papers are also very informative.

———. 2003. *Our Cultural Sovereignty: The Second Century of Canadian Broadcasting*. Report of the Standing Committee on Canadian Heritage. Ottawa: Communication Canada Publishing. This report provides good background on the history, structure, and problems facing Canadian broadcasting.

———. 2017. *Creative Canada: A Vision for Canada's Creative Industries*. Ottawa: Department of Canadian Heritage. Available at: https://www.canada.ca/en/canadian-heritage/campaigns/creative-canada.html. An important policy document that strives to chart the future for Canada's cultural (and creative) industries.

Starr, Paul. 2004. *The Creation of the Media: Political Origins of Modern Communications*. New York: Basic Books. This Pulitzer Prize–winning book explores the weave of politics, economics, and technology in the making of the US media.

Wagman, Ira, and Peter Urquhart. 2012. *Cultural Industries.ca: Making Sense of Canadian Media in the Digital Age*. Toronto: James Lorimer. A good overview of Canada's cultural industries.

Weir, Ernest Austin. 1965. *The Struggle for National Broadcasting in Canada*. Toronto: McClelland & Stewart. As the title suggests, the author presents an account of the development of public broadcasting in Canada and of the political and cultural milieu out of which this regime was established.

Williams, Raymond. 1974. *Television, Technology and Cultural Form*. Glasgow: Fontana Collins. Focusing on the development of television, Williams illustrates how technological development is the product of a broad set of social forces.

STUDY QUESTIONS

1. Define the terms *society* and *culture*.
2. Describe how modern media took form during the development of industrial society.
3. Describe some of the ways in which the federal government has played a central role in developing both the economy and the media in Canada.
4. Provide some examples of economies of scale in media organizations.
5. Describe four perspectives on the role of the media in society and their connections to larger theories of society.
6. Describe the distinctive characteristics of the Canadian state and the impacts they have had on the development of domestic media.

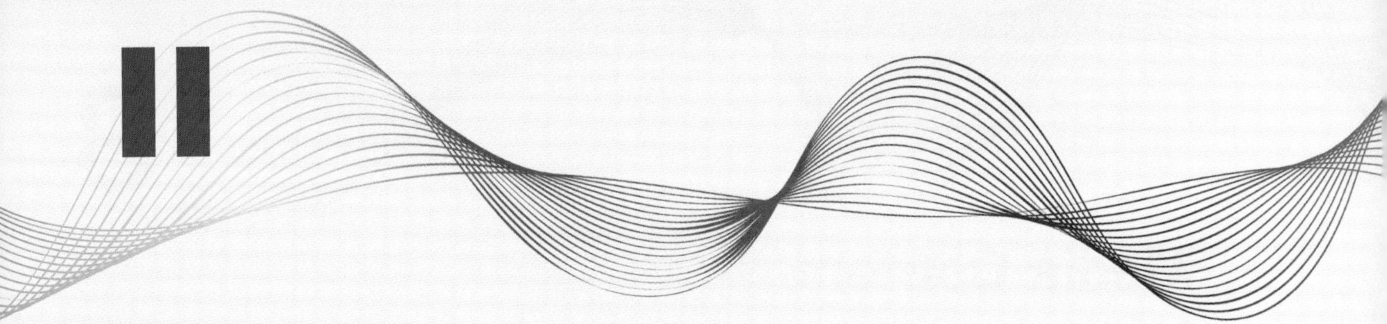

II

Theoretical Perspectives

TommL/iStockphoto

3

Media Content

Studying the Making of Meaning

The philosophers have only interpreted the world, in various ways; the point is to change it. —*Karl Marx*

TommL/iStockphoto

Opening Questions

- Do the media provide a full, unbiased perspective on the world?
- What do we mean when we say that media *represent* the world?
- What is *social theory* and what is its purpose?
- What is an *encoding/decoding* model?
- What is human agency, and what does it mean to say that social structures and process can be both "enabling" and "constraining"?
- What are some of the main theoretical perspectives on media content?

Introduction

In Chapters 3 and 4, we build on earlier discussions of communication theory to offer rigorous definitions of terms such as *social theory* and illustrate some of the main approaches to the study of media content and audiences. In this chapter, we begin by introducing terms that describe some basic characteristics of the process of communication and media content. Working with a model that describes communication as a process of encoding and decoding, we introduce a number of common theoretical and methodological perspectives used to study media content, and we illustrate how these theories relate to the larger social practice of communication. We also examine several key content genres, such as news, soap operas, reality TV, and fan fiction.

A geographic map is *representation,* or "re-presentation," of a place that it seeks to describe. In other words, it is a particular kind of portrayal or "presentation" of a place.

Representation and Signification

When we study communication, and particularly communication content, we are generally studying practices or processes of **representation**. What is representation? It's the act of putting or *encoding* ideas into words, paintings, sculpture, film, plays, television programs, or any other medium of communication. A picture of a plane crash is not the crash itself, obviously, but a *representation* of that crash. A map is not an actual place but a drawing or a picture that *represents* that place. An advertisement for an SUV (sport utility vehicle) is not the vehicle but a representation of a way of looking at or thinking about such a vehicle. Even a live telecast of a hockey game or some other sporting event is not the game itself but a series of carefully chosen and constructed images, camera angles, and commentary that represent the event in an audiovisual package.

Using any medium of communication, a person selects certain elements of reality to describe the object, event, person, or situation he or she wishes to represent. Representations are, to a large extent, simplifications and interpretations of the objects and events they describe. (The accompanying map, for instance, doesn't describe every rock, valley, and tree in the actual landscape it represents. Rather, it illustrates broad features and landmarks and distances between them.)

The person receiving or *decoding* that communication then uses what he or she knows of what is described and what that person knows of the system of representation—most often, language—to come to an understanding of what was encoded by the sender.

A more rigorous or detailed way of thinking about representation is as a process of signification. Signification is using signs to make meaning. What's a **sign**? Anything with meaning: a word, an image, a sound, a painting, even things themselves, like dark clouds on the horizon. The Swiss linguist Ferdinand de Saussure—sometimes considered the founder of **semiotics** or the science of signs—posited that signs are composed of two elements: the signifier and the signified. The **signifier** is the thing that we see, hear, or feel:

TABLE 3.1
Semiotics: Signifier, Signified, and Sign

Signifier	Signified
· Thing that we see hear, or feel · sound · image on screen · bumps on paper	· The mental concept we draw from the signifier · music · blog · Braille

Sign
Combination of signifier and signified created through the process of signification · sound = music · image on screen = blog · bumps on paper = Braille

the image on a screen, sounds, or small bumps on paper. The **signified** is the idea or mental concept we draw from those signifiers: the ideas in a blog, in music, or in Braille words. Together, the signifier and signified make up the sign,

The process of signification is the process of making meaning. Indeed, from this perspective, the whole of our experience of the world is a process of signification as we translate situations and things we encounter into meaning: dark clouds mean rain, a short chapter means less homework, an angry parent means trouble.

C.S. Peirce categorized signs into three different types: icon, index, and symbol. An **icon** looks like the object it describes. For instance, both maps and photographs are icons. An **index** is related to the object it represents. Smoke is an index of fire and a sneeze is an index of a cold, allergy, or irritant. A **symbol** is a sign that bears no direct resemblance to what it signifies. Words are symbols, as is the image of an apple when it is used to represent something other than fruit, such as knowledge or a particular brand of electronic products.

Intertextuality, Polysemy, and the Indeterminacy of Representation

The idea that a sign can represent or signify more than one thing raises the indeterminacy of representation (defined more fully below). For instance, to some people the image of a sporty SUV might signify or represent luxury, adventure, or sex appeal; to others, environmental disaster. The sound of falling rain might signify or represent either a soothing summer's evening or an impending flood. The meaning of any particular sign is not guaranteed but is dependent on the context of its use and interpretation.

In other words, signs do not exist in isolation—they are either explicitly or implicitly part of larger "texts" or sets of signs and symbols. Images of SUVs are often found in advertisements that portray them as part of mountain adventures or happy family outings. The melodic splash of rain is often used to establish a mood in music, film, or television programs. In other words, the meaning of these signs is itself given form by its relation to other signs in the context of a larger symbolic system. If we are confronted by images and sounds without this kind of grounding, to make meaning out of them we often supply our own context, drawn from memory and imagination.

The idea that meaning is made in the context of larger symbolic systems draws our attention to two other important elements of the process of signification. The first is the **intertextuality** of the process of making meaning. Intertextuality refers to the meaning we make of one text depending on the meanings we have drawn from other sets of signs we have encountered (Kristeva, 1969; Barthes, 1968). That is, meaning is grounded in the relationships we find between different texts. Our understanding of the picture of the SUV as a family vehicle is dependent on our combining knowledge of the SUV as a mode of transportation and the representation of the people in the image as a family. Folding the two signifiers together—SUV and happy family—creates the signified "family vehicle." Similarly, our understanding of the ways automobile exhaust emissions are related to global warming might also lead us to interpret the SUV as an instrument of environmental degradation. Thus, our past experience—our individual histories—provides the backdrop for interpreting the signs and symbols we encounter in everyday life.

oksana.perkins/Shutterstock.

What does the image in this ad signify to you? What do you think it was intended to signify to audiences?

The second important point to note here is that making meaning is an active process. Making the connection between signifier and signified, joining past and present experience, requires active participation. When the meaning of things appears obvious, even natural, it still requires active work. We make or create meaning. Even when it seems the meaning of a television program, social media post, or film scene is obvious and that everyone should "get it," making meaning from that representation requires effort or work on the part of the person viewing it.

Because signs can be open to a variety of interpretations, they are said to be **polysemic**—that is, having "many meanings" (Jensen, 1990). As noted, depending on the context, an image of an apple might be interpreted as knowledge, as a computer company, or simply as fruit. The different types or levels of meaning drawn from such an image may be denotative and connotative, where **denotative meaning** refers to the literal or most obvious interpretation of the sign and **connotative meaning** refers to the range of other less obvious or more subjective meanings that may be drawn.

Advertisements exemplify the purposive use of signs to create different levels of meaning. For instance, by using seemingly ordinary women in its ads instead of the professional models who generally represent the standards of beauty in soap and cosmetic advertising, Dove's Real Beauty Campaign, launched in 2004, attempted to change the usual advertising meaning of beauty. While drawing some controversy because of other products the Dove brand's owner—Unilever—also marketed, for over a decade the Real Beauty Campaign was often credited with helping "re-signify" the concept of beauty in advertising (Bahadur, 2017).

However, in the fall of 2017, Dove released a Facebook ad for a body wash that showed a black woman peeling off her shirt to reveal a white woman underneath. Recalling skin whitening creams and other race-based products, the ad was quickly branded as racist by many, forcing Dove to retract it and issue an apology (Bach, 2017).

Here then is a good example of the polysemic nature of signs and the ways in which their larger social context provides a framework for their interpretation. While for years Dove's ads successfully played upon larger social conventions of beauty to promote their products, the 2017 body wash ad had the effect of signifying the brand as racist—throwing the sincerity of the larger campaign and the brand itself into question. The fact that signs are polysemic highlights the importance of context for the creation and interpretation of meaning. The social and cultural conditions surrounding the production of media texts, as well as those involved in their consumption, play into the meaning generated from them.

Similarly, the fact that any given sign can have many meanings illustrates the *indeterminacy of representation* (see Figure 3.1). On the one hand, the meaning of signs and the messages of which they are a part is indeterminate because there is a multiplicity of ways of representing an object, action, or event—another representation can always be made. On the other hand, they are indeterminate because there is no *necessary* correspondence between the meaning encoded in a particular message by the sender and that decoded by the receiver.

By permission of Edelman.

This image has been commonly associated with Dove's Real Beauty Campaign. In what ways do these women differ from conventional models? What does this presentation mean to you? Were you aware of the controversy surrounding this ad as discussed in this chapter? If so, did that change your perception of the campaign?

In other words, because decoding messages requires active participation on the part of the person or people receiving the message, there is no guarantee that the receiver will actually get or understand the intended meaning. Nevertheless, each representation is grounded in a specific context as the person or medium doing the representing works to guide the audience or receiver of the message toward a specific or preferred meaning.

There are many factors determining polysemy, or the indeterminacy of representation. Different media provide different systems for making meaning, and one system of representation cannot encompass the full spectrum of the meaning of another. For instance, a painting cannot be fully translated into a prose essay, or even poetry. Nor can a sculpture be completely transformed into a photograph or a hologram. Inevitably, something is lost.

Polysemy and the indeterminacy of representation tend to lead the study of communication away from the foundations of science and social science toward the foundations of interpretation we find in the humanities. It is concerned more with **rhetoric** (how things are said) and hermeneutics (how things are interpreted) than with "truth" (see Box 3.1, "Media/Culture Binding").

In the study of communication, the importance of a statement is not limited to whether it predicts events, can be refuted by others, or generates interesting hypotheses—all standards used in science. What is important also entails how an act of communication selects and *represents* or *reconstructs* something, and what gives a particular representation its force, its ability to persuade, or its attractiveness. Whatever makes a particular novel, painting, or film more popular or revered than another, or even a novel more "powerful" than a film, cannot be satisfactorily discussed by reference to the relative "truth" of

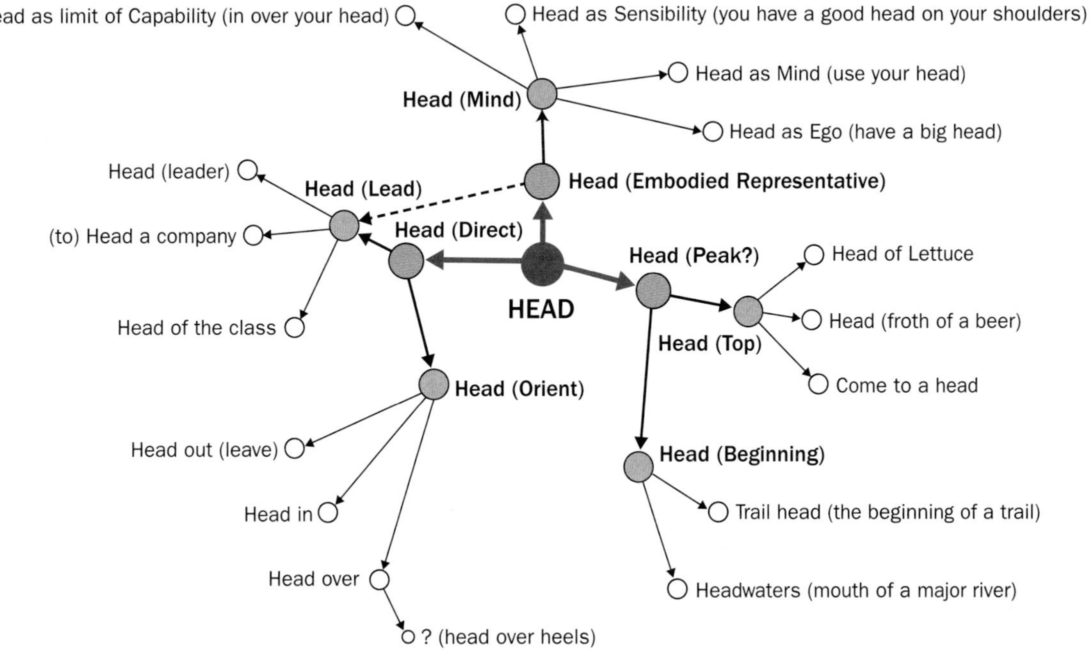

FIGURE 3.1 Polysemy and the indeterminacy of representation

This diagram illustrates some of the many meanings of the word *head*. When you see the word, how do you decide which meaning is being used?

Source: Ryan Dewey. HEAD: Polysemous Network for an Open Class Lexical Item. 2010. Used by permission. RyanDewey.org.

each communication. Such media and individual works are discussed by communication scholars in terms of their rhetorical force or the nature or style of their representation.

If we compare media in this way, the visual dimension of film and television quite consistently adds a specific sense of reality that another medium, such as print, cannot provide. What film and television gain in that dimension, however, they often lose in subtlety, character development, and room for imaginative play when compared to print. Similarly, the discussion of abstract ideas changes when one moves from books to the popular press or to television. Television invites a pluralism of sight, sound, and personage that is partially present in radio and absent in print—more than a few minutes of the same person talking on television, no matter what the visuals, tends to undermine the speaker's credibility or, at least, the viewers' interest. Just the opposite seems to hold for print—a single authorial voice will more readily elicit a reader's attention and understanding. The characteristics of different media tend to nuance the crafting of content in particular ways.

Communication Theory as Social Theory

In studying the process of communication, we often draw on social theory, and particularly communication theory, for helping us to understand how processes of communication are nuanced and operate.

What is **social theory**? Generally, it is a representation of the social world; a set of ideas about how the world is organized and functions. We all have ideas about how the world works, but our assumptions are often fragmentary and contradictory. Take, for instance, common-sense proverbs such as "many hands make light work" and "too many cooks spoil the broth." While they both purport to provide a way of understanding and approaching work, they offer contradictory perspectives on how to do so. In contrast, social theory strives to offer rigorous, logical explanations of elements of the social world. It is a representation of the world that attempts to provide a systematic and comprehensive explanation of the relationships between individuals, social groups, and the world around them.

What is the purpose of social theory? At one level, it provides explanations of how things work and why things are the way they are. At another level, such explanations guide action: to alleviate social problems and improve the quality of life or to construct social policy. To paraphrase Karl Marx, "The purpose of social theory is not simply to understand the world but to change it," and change it in a progressive manner that makes things more egalitarian and provides more equal access to the fruits of our society for all citizens.

As a kind of social theory, communication theory is a way of representing the complex process of communication. It is a way of trying to understand the different forces that contextualize and give form to human communication.

There is, however, a wide variety of communication theories. Some are elements of larger theories of society, such as the libertarian, social responsibility, mass society, and Marxist political economy we examined in the previous chapter. Others offer only partial explanations of the process of communication, such as the semiotic explanation of the process of signification discussed above. Some provide simple, highly abstract perspectives, such as Shannon and Weaver's model of communication that we outlined in Chapter 1 (see Figure 1.2), which asserts that communication both begins and ends with individuals. Others, such as the social model of communication (see Figure 1.3), illustrate the process of communication as given form by a great many factors and variables.

To provide a better understanding of the variety of ways different theories approach and envision the process of communication, we will now turn our attention to another model of communication.

The Encoding/Decoding Model

As we have seen, mass communication is a process that involves both **encoding**, or creating media messages, and **decoding**, or interpreting

mindscanner/Shutterstock.

them. While these are active processes, in each of these moments a range of social institutions and forces serves to frame or contextualize the ways in which messages are constituted and the ways in which people make meaning from them.

Drawing from Stuart Hall's (1993) discussion of this process, Figure 3.2 illustrates some of the key elements involved in it. Please note, however, that although the diagram displays these pieces of the process as individual parts, all of these parts are interrelated in reality. As we saw in Chapter 2, communication media are integral to the societies of which they are a part, not separate or distinct technical systems. Similarly, the professional values of media workers are woven between organizational and technical imperatives, not ideas separated or distinct from social context. For purposes of illustration, however, we have abstracted the process of communication from this larger social context and exploded its pieces to highlight the different roles that each plays. Each of these pieces is described below.

First is the shared field of social institutions and knowledge, or culture, within which the media system operates—the general social milieu in which we live. It comprises language and social customs: ideas we hold about gender, family, and work as well as the laws, regulations, and other social processes and structures that frame and animate society and the ways we think and act in the world. To a large part, these are the elements of what we referred to as industrial society in Chapter 2. Or these things might be thought of as culture, or the ways of life that make up our society.

Certainly, the ways in which each media producer and consumer experiences and draws on this larger social milieu are not the same; they

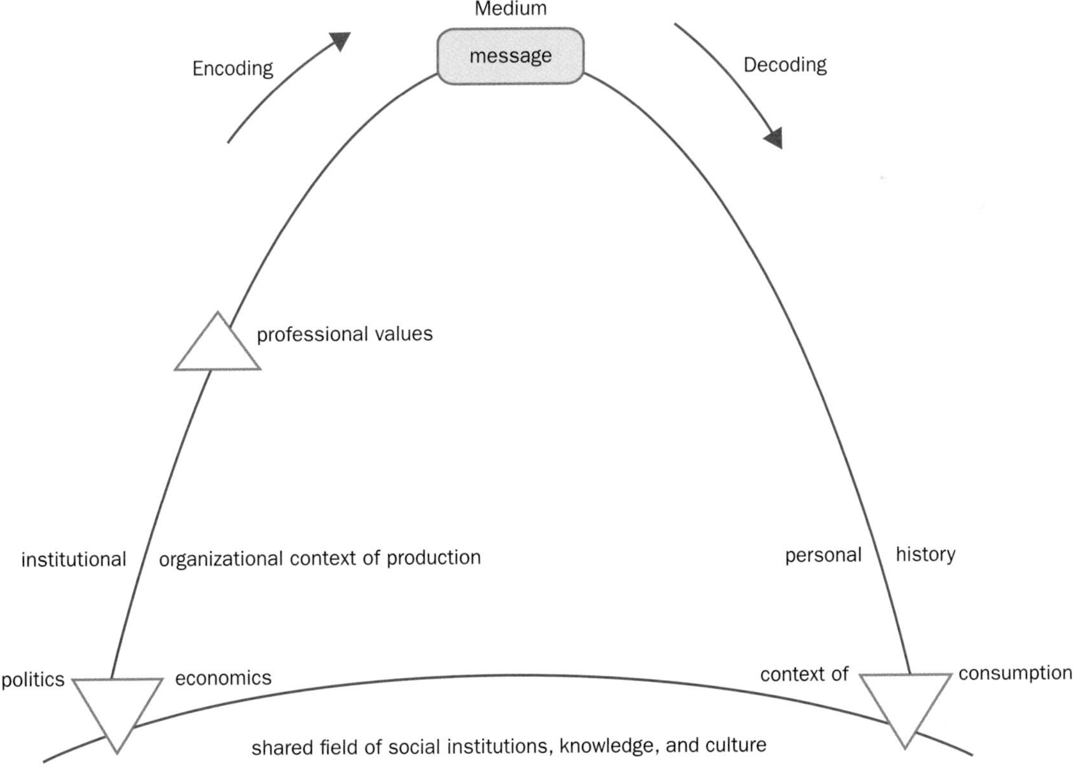

FIGURE 3.2 **Encoding and decoding**

Source: Adapted from Hall, 1993.

are often quite different. For instance, a fashion magazine draws upon a very different set of ideas and circumstances to create its product than the producers of a television program like *The Simpsons*. This larger social milieu, however, does provide a common field of referents for people to draw on and to make meaning from.

Second, broad political and economic processes contextualize how the process of media production is undertaken. On the political side, we would include specific laws and regulations that frame the way media organizations operate and what media professionals do: libel laws, copyright, and media ownership regulations. In the case of broadcasting, we would include the *Broadcasting Act* and the regulations promulgated by the CRTC; for film, distribution regulations; and for newspapers, ownership regulations. As we saw in Chapter 2, each medium operates in a specific legal and regulatory context that informs the way its products are created.

On the economic side, we are concerned with the ways in which the drive for profits, or commercial forces, can impinge on production. As we have seen, the economies of scale enjoyed by US producers help flood Canadian markets with their media products. All of these political and economic circumstances influence media content or, in other words, the ways in which media products represent the world.

Third is the institutional or organizational context within which media messages are created. Here, we might consider the ways in which organizational mandates or imperatives frame what media organizations do and the products they create. The National Film Board (NFB), for example, is guided by its mandate "to produce and distribute and to promote the production and distribution of films designed to interpret Canada to Canadians and to other nations." This purpose underlies all of the work the NFB produces. Similarly, as laid out in the *Broadcasting Act*, CBC's mandate guides the public broadcaster's actions. Private broadcasters and other media have profits as their motive. Hence, both the ways their resources are

National Film Board of Canada.

The NFB's mandate, "to produce and distribute and to promote the production and distribution of films designed to interpret Canada to Canadians and to other nations," guides the ways in which the organization's products are "encoded."

organized and the media products they produce reflect that imperative.

A fourth dimension of influence on the way media represent the world comprises the professional values that guide media producers. Media professionals are guided in their practices by specific ideas about the characteristics of the products they create. Journalists go to journalism school to learn how to identify newsworthy events and produce news reports. Similarly, television writers working on situation comedies, soap operas, and other program genres are governed by assumptions and guidelines as to how those programs are structured.

Fifth, as we have discussed, the medium through which representations are communicated can have great influence on the form and structure of ideas and information. Telling a story in a novel is quite different from telling it in a film. Radio addresses audiences quite differently than television or newspapers. News is often presented online in a different way than in traditional media.

Finally, at the level of decoding, the context of consumption, where and by whom media products are consumed, influences the meaning that is made from them. Age, education, family background, religion, gender, race, and ethnicity are all elements of one's background or "history" that can play on how media messages are decoded. Moreover, much of this personal history is social experience—that is, experience drawn from the larger field of social institutions, knowledge, and culture. For Stuart Hall, these factors could result in interpretations or "readings" of messages that range from "dominant," such as those that are in complete agreement with the ideas/perspectives contained in the message, to "oppositional," such as those that are in total disagreement with those ideas.

Again, while the encoder's and decoder's experiences of this field may be vastly different, it does provide a common set of *referents*—ideas, situations, and circumstances that can be referred to or represented in media products. Consider again *The Simpsons*, which is broadcast in many countries and a number of different languages around the world. The culture and institutions found in these countries are often quite different, yet people in these different places are able to decode the meaning from this program and share in its humour. How so? To a large extent, this is because the show's writers draw on a set of characters and circumstances familiar to all those people. The program focuses on a typical nuclear family—father, mother, and three children—who live in a typical American town and lead a typical life that includes homemaking, working, going to school, spending time with friends, and getting into trouble. In other words, both the characters and the situations they encounter are stereotypes of lives in an industrial society that many recognize and to a degree understand, even though they may not live like that or approve of the stereotyping. In creating the program, *Simpsons* writers draw on ideas familiar to a very diverse group of people. And, in large part, the wide appeal of that program depends on their ability to find common points of knowledge and understanding in the midst of that diversity.

As a social model of communication, the encoding/decoding model draws our attention to the fact that the process of communication is given form by social factors. Individuals who work in a particular institutional and organizational context employ professional values to construct media messages that draw on social knowledge supposedly shared by their intended audience; then, the messages are delivered through particular technical systems to audience members with particular social backgrounds. In turn, these individuals draw upon social knowledge accrued through their

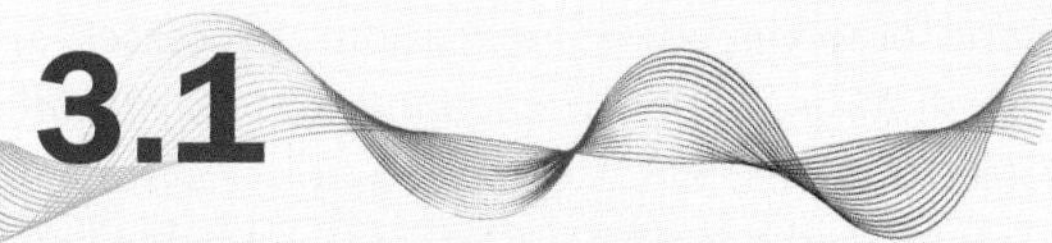

Media/Culture Binding

The media interact with everyday life in various ways. They inform us about politics, life in other cultures and places, how people kiss, how people smoke, how people rob banks, how children and others play with toys, how people dance. The list of human behaviours modelled in media is endless. But the interaction is not a one-way process. The media draw their content from the real lives of particular individuals and groups. In an example that captures this relation well, renowned writer and semiologist Umberto Eco looked at it this way:

1. A firm produces polo shirts with an alligator on them and it advertises them.
2. A generation begins to wear polo shirts.
3. Each consumer of the polo shirt advertises, via the alligator on his or her chest, this brand of polo shirt.
4. A TV broadcast (program), to be faithful to reality, shows some young people wearing the alligator polo shirt.
5. The young (and the old) see the TV broadcast and buy more alligator polo shirts because they have "the young look."

Which is the mass medium? The ad? The broadcast? The shirt? *Who is sending the message?* The manufacturer? The wearer? The TV director? The analyst of this phenomenon? *Who is the marketer?* This is not to imply that there is no marketing plan, but rather that it does not emanate from one central source.

Source: Eco, 1986, 148–50. (Some paraphrased from the original)

Courtesy of adbusters.org.

Adbusters often employs semiotics to create subvertisements: ads slightly changed, or subverted, to expose the negative effects of the products they promote. Here, the signifier—the vodka bottle—has been modified to shift its signified from the usual party atmosphere depicted in liquor ads to something less alluring.

personal histories to decode the messages and deploy that information in their lives.

This model is useful for understanding how certain theories envision the process of communication. Few theories claim to explain the influence of all of these different dimensions on that process. Rather, they focus on how a number of those elements work to determine how the media operate and the influence they have.

Agency and Structure: A Key Concern in the Study of Communication

A central consideration of social theory in general, and media and communication theory in particular, is the relationship between *agency* and *structure*. To put this another way, can people generally undertake whatever actions they choose? That is, do they have unlimited agency? Or do the structures and processes in which people live and work determine the range and character of the actions they can undertake? This is a pivotal question for trying to explain how society operates.

Take the economic system, for example. The economy enables people to earn money, which, in turn, can help increase the number of things they can do. Go to university, take a trip, buy a house—money can increase the range of action one might undertake or, in other words, it can increase a person's *agency*. The education system can act in a similar way: with a good education, people can better understand how the world works and improve their position within it. Well-educated people can understand how the political system works and who or what interests benefit from its current structure; they can understand how the media system works and who or what interests it supports; they can understand how the economic system works, and they can use all that knowledge to help better their position in society.

As a number of researchers have pointed out, however, social institutions, processes, and structures are both *enabling* and *constraining* (see Giddens, 1984). In our economic system, for example, those with money are enabled to access a wide range of goods and services. Those without money are not as capable. So, our economic system constrains those who are, for one reason or another, unable to access money. The education system functions in much the same way. Those who have access to education generally have better access to wealth and power in our society than those who don't.

The issue of agency/structure is also a key question for trying to understand and explain how media systems operate. In terms of media and communication, it might be summarized like this: can people generally encode whatever ideas and meanings they want into media messages and programs? Or do the structures and processes in which people live and work determine the range and character of the messages and ideas they can produce?

Language itself provides a structure for communication, a set of words and rules for communicating. While that structure is enabling because it allows the communication of a vast range of ideas, it is also constraining in that we can communicate in that language only if we correctly enact its vocabulary. If you have ever struggled to express to yourself in a language you barely understand—to order a meal, secure a hotel room, or change money—you know how constraining not being fluent in a language can be.

Work environments can carry similar consequences. While the job of being a reporter at a large news organization can be constraining in that one has to adhere to editorial policies and professional values regarding what kinds of events constitute news, how to write a news story, and organizational rules and deadlines, it also is enabling because it allows one to write about changing events and circumstances on a daily basis from a range of perspectives, and because the material one writes will be read regularly by thousands of people.

Understanding the relationship between agency and structure, the ways in which communication processes and institutions work—to enable and constrain the ways in which communication takes place and the ideas that can be communicated—is one of the central concerns of communication theory.

Perspectives on the Study of Content

Over the years, a number of perspectives have been developed and used to study media content. A few of the more historically important perspectives are discussed in this section: literary criticism, structuralism, semiotics, and post-structuralism; discourse analysis; critical political economy; content analysis; and media form or genre analysis. Some of these perspectives are drawn from larger theories of society and communication. Others are better understood as methods or approaches for examining media content and might be used in concert with larger theories. Here, our purpose is to simply introduce these ideas and provide some understanding of the history of their development. In particular, we consider how they address the encoding of media messages and the larger set of social and linguistic forces coming to bear on the production process.

Rather than provide a comprehensive review of the different theories of content at play in the field of communication studies, this section is meant to help introduce the range of perspectives brought to bear on that study. Should analysis focus on the author/writer? On the text/content itself? Or on the larger set of social circumstances that influence the author/writer? There is no easy answer to these questions and the multiplicity of perspectives underscores the importance of the notion that it is not which one of them is the correct perspective, but rather what useful insight each brings to the analysis of media content.

Literary Criticism

Literary criticism is the study and interpretation of texts. It explores the different ways texts can be analyzed and understood. Its roots reach back to when written records first emerged. As soon as something is recorded, it becomes open to interpretation and discussion. Major movements and changes in world history have focused on examinations and re-examinations of particular texts. Martin Luther, for example, challenged the interpretation of the Bible by the Roman Catholic Church and the right of the Catholic Church to control access to and to be the sole interpreter of the scriptures. Similarly, from the Sung dynasty (900 BCE) and thereafter in China, official interpretations of classic Confucian texts were promoted, and unofficial versions were banned.

Debates in literary criticism have been particularly important for communication studies and for the study of content because they draw our attention to the various ways meaning might be drawn from texts. Should texts be read simply in terms of the intentions of the author? Or might meanings decoded by readers other than what the author intended be considered legitimate "meanings" of the text? Might texts be viewed as the product of forces that impinge on the author, like language and culture?

One of the traditional modes of criticism is to view texts in terms of the presumed intention of the author. From this perspective, interpretation tries to uncover what the author consciously had in mind, as expressed in the text. Taking this one step further, Freudian analysis of the text purports to explain what the author had subconsciously in mind. Here, the text is treated only as the specific product or vehicle of an individual author/creator whose works have particular characteristics and might be cross-compared with the work of other writers (e.g., the novels of Jane Austen, the plays of Shakespeare).

Doumic Studio.

Auteur theory views the structure and content of a film as the specific vision of the director.

This approach spread to film studies, with the director carrying the authorship mantle. For instance, from this perspective one might analyze the films of Alfred Hitchcock, the Coen brothers, or Quentin Tarantino to uncover and compare the peculiarities of each director's style or practice. Such an approach in film analysis became known as *auteur theory*, which focuses on the personal vision of the director and treats that person as the creative originator of the film.

In the early twentieth century, a variant of literary criticism, New Criticism, gained prominence. From this perspective, analysis is confined to the texts per se, and both authorial intention and reader response are disregarded in favour of a close reading aimed at revealing ambiguities and multiplicities of meanings within the work itself. More recently, emerging schools of literary criticism have incorporated concepts from linguistics, sociology, and anthropology to extend debates into a wide range of factors (including language and culture) that can be drawn into the interpretation of content. However, while this perspective acknowledges the indeterminacy of representation and the polysemic nature of signs and texts, analysis is generally confined to the text itself and does not consider relationships between the text and external factors like the personal history of the author or larger social or cultural factors that may have influenced its production.

Structuralism, Semiotics, and Post-structuralism

In the 1950s and '60s, a perspective known as *structuralism* became dominant in the social sciences and humanities, especially in the fields of linguistics, anthropology, sociology, psychology, and literature. In the analysis of media content, the aim of **structuralism** is to discover underlying patterns or structures that shape both texts and genres; to try to uncover common linguistic or thematic patterns that give them form—a quite different perspective from the one about New Criticism described above. Here, the author is viewed primarily as a vehicle that enacts the extant rules of language and culture in the creation of her/his work (or life). To put it another way, from a structuralist perspective, to a large extent we do not speak language so much as *language speaks us*. In other words, the agency of the author, reader, or audience member is not seen by structuralists as a key factor in how meaning is created.

An early and seminal work exemplifying structuralist principles was that of the Russian folklorist Vladimir Propp. In the 1920s, Propp collected over 400 traditional tales from different parts of Europe and showed how they all had a similar narrative structure. First, he identified a set of basic (lexical) elements (all stories have certain similar items): a hero or heroine, a villain, a helper. Second, he described the motifs that propel the narrative from beginning to end. Thus, something must happen to set the hero (usually male) in motion: at some point, the villain will disrupt the hero's plans, and at another juncture, the hero will receive aid from a helper (who may or may not be female) to overcome the obstacles in his way. Propp was able to reduce the apparent complexity of a great number of different stories to a simple set of underlying narrative elements that could be combined in a strictly limited number of ways (see Propp, 1970). The structural analysis of narrative has subsequently been applied to all manner of stories, including James Bond novels and films (Eco, 1982; Bennett and Woollacott, 1987), romantic novels (Radway, 1984), and soap operas (Geraghty, 1991). Figure 3.3 illustrates structuralism at work in the romance genre.

Once narrative structures and surface elements were identified, Propp and other structuralists were able to identify common themes that recurred in stories from all over the world. The magical union of strength and beauty, power in two forms, is a good example of a myth to be found in virtually all cultures. In this instance, the male embodiment of spiritual and bodily strength (usually a prince) grows up in his kingdom. The female embodiment of beauty and perceptiveness (a princess) grows up in her kingdom. One or both may be disguised in a certain way (a frog prince, a pig princess) or confined (Sleeping Beauty, Cinderella), sometimes as a result of immature vulnerability (plotting by unworthy usurpers, innocence). An event, story, or intervention of some sort induces one (usually the male in a patriarchal society or the female in a matriarchal society) to set out on a quest, sometimes purposeful, sometimes not. The seeker finds the sought (the object of his or her dreams, again evidence of divine blessing) and recognizes her/him by virtue of her/his or both of their inner senses, inherent kindness, or nobility. This something not only confirms the union, but it also confirms the special qualities of both seeker and sought, which befits them to rule others (divine right of kings). The children of the union are, of course, very special, since they inherit the qualities of both.

Such myths live on. Perhaps the most recent incarnation of the myth of the prince/princess ascending the throne would be the courtship and marriage of British Prince William and Kate Middleton, a commoner.

So powerful are such myths that US film stars have handlers who build up their mythological identity (or public persona) by counselling them to accept only certain roles. Some pursue a particular type of character (e.g., Michael Cera, Melissa McCarthy), while others pursue versatility (e.g., Meryl Streep, Christian Bale).

Another influential scholar in the field of structuralism was the Swiss linguist Ferdinand de Saussure, mentioned earlier. Saussure developed what was later seen as the structural analysis of language (1974). Saussure proposed that language could be scientifically studied in the abstract as an underlying set of linguistic structures (*langue*, in his terms) and combined together by any native speaker to produce an utterance (*parole*). As he argued, "Language is a system of signs that express ideas, and is therefore comparable to a system of writing, the alphabet of deaf-mutes, symbolic rites, polite formulas, military signals, etc.

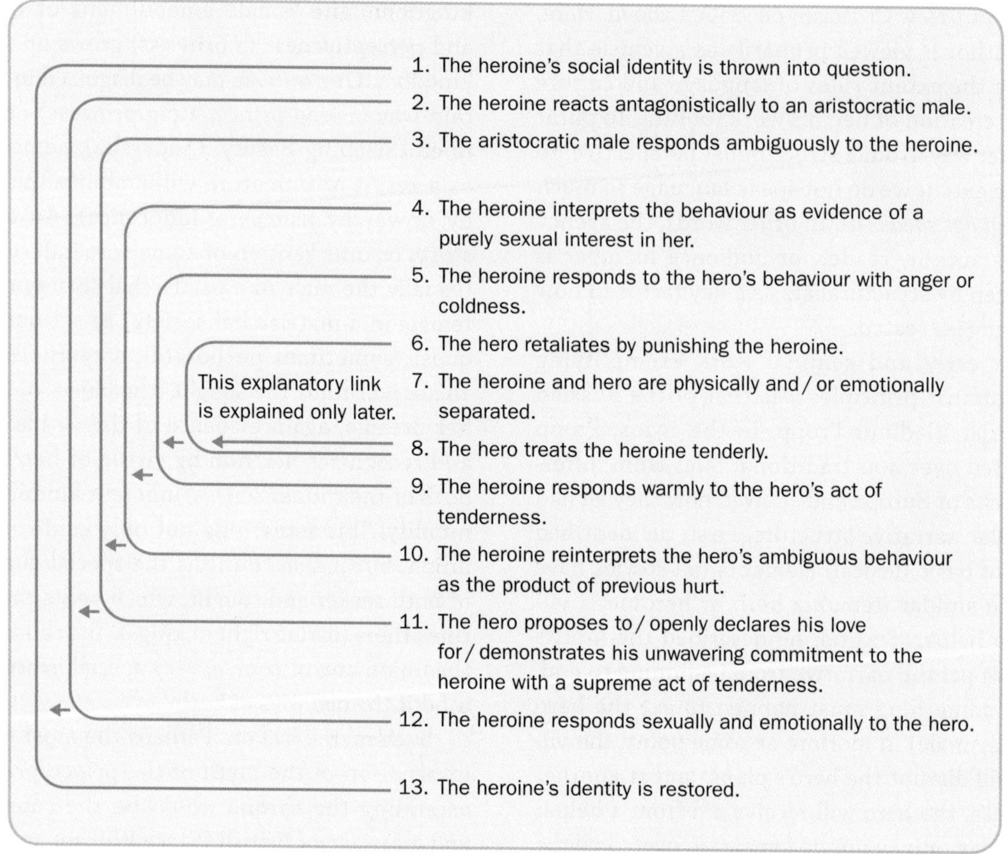

1. The heroine's social identity is thrown into question.
2. The heroine reacts antagonistically to an aristocratic male.
3. The aristocratic male responds ambiguously to the heroine.
4. The heroine interprets the behaviour as evidence of a purely sexual interest in her.
5. The heroine responds to the hero's behaviour with anger or coldness.
6. The hero retaliates by punishing the heroine.
This explanatory link is explained only later.
7. The heroine and hero are physically and / or emotionally separated.
8. The hero treats the heroine tenderly.
9. The heroine responds warmly to the hero's act of tenderness.
10. The heroine reinterprets the hero's ambiguous behaviour as the product of previous hurt.
11. The hero proposes to / openly declares his love for / demonstrates his unwavering commitment to the heroine with a supreme act of tenderness.
12. The heroine responds sexually and emotionally to the hero.
13. The heroine's identity is restored.

FIGURE 3.3 The narrative logic of the romance

Structuralist analysis was able to identify common themes that reoccurred in stories around the world, casting doubt on the idea that such stories are simply the product of individual imagination.

Source: From Janice A. Radway, *Reading the Romance: Women, Patriarchy, and Popular Literature.* Copyright © 1984, new introduction © 1991 by the University of North Carolina Press. Used by permission of the publisher, www.uncpress.unc.edu.

But it is the most important of all these systems" (Saussure, in Silverman, 1983: 4–5). To better understand this system, he proposed a science of signs—*semiotics.*

For Saussure, meaning is made in the difference between signs. Given that symbols bear no necessary relation to what they represent, the only way to identify the symbol is by knowing what it is not. A red light at a traffic intersection, for example, is not a green light (see Silverman, 1983).

Anthropologist Claude Lévi-Strauss extended the structuralist formula into social interaction and claimed to show in his work "not how men think in myths, but how myths operate in men's minds without their being aware of the fact" (Lévi-Strauss, 1969: 12). The point is that words carry preconceived ideas, or *signifieds,* about things and thereby provide a frame or screen for interpreting the world. From this perspective, one can begin to see why structuralism sometimes claims that people are "spoken" by the language they use rather than the other way around.

As we have seen, based on the sign (signifier/signified), a semiotic analysis distinguishes between two levels of meaning: the denotative and the connotative. Using this schema, Roland Barthes (1972) famously decoded ideological meanings in everything from wrestling and striptease to the paintings in the Louvre, television shows, popular novels, and advertisements.

MAYBAYBUTTER/iStockphoto.

According to Saussure's idea of semiotics, the only way to identify a red traffic light is by knowing what it is not—in this case, a green light.

By making connections between the images found in everyday media and the ideologies of bourgeois capitalist society, Barthes strove to uncover the ways that popular culture promotes dominant ideas and values.

Consider a picture or ad portraying an SUV as a family vehicle that can be used for city transportation and country adventure. From Barthes's perspective, the ad not only represents the SUV as a part of family life, but also draws on a deeper, more subtle set of assumptions and values—another order of connotations. Based on the notion that the meaning of the ad is found in the differences between the images that it contains and possible alternatives, underlying the ad are ideas such as the following: the nuclear family is the natural and dominant social unit; private vehicles are a preferred mode of transportation; and people's domination of nature is both a legitimate and pleasurable leisure activity. Social issues—such as what constitutes a family in this day and age and the forms of environmental damage caused by the use of gas-powered vehicles—are ignored, buried under these more dominant contemporary social myths. In other words, the text positions the reader in reference to the objects in the ad in particular ways and encourages a very specific reading, or understanding, of those objects. From this perspective, by accepting the idea that the SUV is the perfect family vehicle, not only are you accepting the obvious premise of the ad, but you are absorbing the baggage of these underlying ideas as well. Through the 1970s and '80s, Barthes-style semiotic analysis became the preferred way of reading cultural texts (e.g., see Williamson, 1978, for an analysis of advertisements).

While both structuralism and semiotics provide useful insights into the ways in which language structures the form and content of communication, perhaps their biggest shortcoming as modes of analysis is how they underplay the importance of the particular in favour of the general—of langue in contrast to parole. Hence, the way in which they underplay human agency and the roles of the individual speaker and listener (or producer and consumer) in creating and interpreting messages became a key source of criticism.

Beginning in the 1960s, post-structuralism emerged as a critique of the idea that a consistent structure to texts exists and that the process of encoding somehow fixes or solidifies meaning for the decoder. A number of the main proponents of post-structuralism had been structuralists earlier, among them Roland Barthes.

For post-structuralists, "meaning" is made in the act of decoding and thereby is the purview of the reader or audience member. Whatever sense is to be made of any particular word, image, or sound is the product of the people interpreting those signs and depends on the perspective(s) they bring to the task. Women may interpret content differently from men, homosexuals differently from heterosexuals, children differently from adults, and so on. Understanding texts involves *deconstructing* them to uncover the possible play on differences they contain. Meaning is never fixed in content. It remains as fluid as the next reader makes it. In semiotic terms, post-structuralism argues that signs have come undone and that signifiers can no longer be said to have specific signifieds. Take again the SUV ad. Who cares about the happy-heterosexual-family symbolism seemingly bestowed on the vehicle by the advertising company? With one look at the ad's description of its spacious interior and stylish appointments, perhaps an LGBTQ environmentalist group will decide that this is the perfect mode of transportation for getting its members to their latest waterfowl habitat recuperation project in the mountains.

This is the point made by Barthes in his famous essay "The Death of the Author" (1977b). Since the text becomes meaningful only in the act of being read and understood, the source of meaning, Barthes argued, is the reader—not the author, as auteur theory would propose. One effect of this startling reversal in approach was the empowerment of the reader or audience. No longer chained to the dull task of trying to find out what Shakespeare "had in mind" when he wrote *Hamlet* (an impossible task anyway, argued Barthes), the reader or audience member was now drawing from her/his own experience, free to create his/her own meanings and open up rather than close down the meaning of a text. Gone was any notion of a "true" or "authentic" meaning of the text, or that meaning was somehow locked into the text itself. Set against the multiplicity of possible interpretations by readers or audience members, texts were polysemic and had any number of different possible meanings. The conception of reading also changed from the passive absorption of the text's imposed meaning to an active exploration of its possibilities.

As we illustrate in Chapter 4, this shift in interpretation parallels a shift in the ways audiences are viewed in terms of their relation to media content.

Discourse Analysis

Discourse analysis is another perspective with a long history, dating back more than two millenniums to the discipline of *rhetorica*, or rhetoric. The study of rhetoric was focused on making speeches more effective and generally addressed the planning, organization, specific operations, and performance of speech in political and legal settings (van Dijk, 1985, vol. 1: 1; see Murray, 2012). From this perspective, it sought to understand how language engaged audiences.

Combining elements of rhetorical theory and structuralism, discourse analysis focuses on how language, as a system of representation, provides us with a particular perspective or "position" in the social world. It posits that language is a kind of structure and that, by being inside that structure, language gives us a particular view of the world. Today, there are many strands of discourse analysis at play in communication studies (see van Dijk, 2014; Fairclough, 2010; van Dijk, 1997). A major stream focuses on specific instances of language use and their relationship to social power. Another, following the work of Michel Foucault, considers how specific modes of language use bind our ways of thinking and become "sedimented" into specific institutions and relations of social power.

The first of these modes of analysis points to how particular patterns and conventions of language usage become taken for granted and considers how these patterns serve as larger frames of reference to shape our experience and understanding of the world. Discourse analysis has, for example, been used to illustrate the gendered character of language—the long-standing prevalence of words like chair*man*, fire*man*, fisher*man*, and so on—and to demonstrate through historical referents how this kind of language has supported patriarchal forms of domination in society. Hence, today, to promote more egalitarian relationships, we use gender-neutral language: *chair*, *chairperson*, *firefighter*, *fisher*.

This type of analysis also provides a way of understanding how particular elements of media content work together to create a larger perspective on, or way of seeing, social events and circumstances. A discourse analysis of federal election coverage, for example, might look at all of the different kinds of media content focusing on the election—coverage of debates, polls, editorials, news stories—and analyze the ways in which different leaders and parties are treated in that coverage. Were they given equal time/space? Were the views of one party or leader given more favourable or sympathetic treatment than others?

Similarly, discourse analysis might explore the ways in which texts position different discourses and the power relations inherent in that positioning. In their article, "'It's Not Easy Being Green': The Greenwashing of Environmental Discourses in

Advertising," Jennifer Budinsky and Susan Bryant illustrate how some companies borrow from the language of environmentalism to frame their still environmentally destructive products as "friendly" to the environment (Budinsky and Bryant, 2013). For instance, Clorox, a company heavily involved in the sale of environmentally damaging chemicals, promotes a "green" line of such products. And despite the fact that automobiles remain one of the main contributors to global warming, carmakers such as Ford and Toyota promote seemingly environmentally friendly cars. As the authors point out, the language of environmentalism is often used in advertising to hide or smooth over the connection between consumers' continued purchase of damaging products and the ongoing deterioration of the environment.

The second type of discourse analysis has a more structuralist character and argues that, in the form of ideas or sets of ideas, discourse (language) becomes a way of knowing the world and, in turn, a way of controlling it. In a series of studies that includes histories of madness, prisons, and sexuality, Michel Foucault (1980, 1988, 1995) illustrates how, through making crime, madness, and sex into objects of scientific inquiry and discipline, the "knowledge" or ideas generated from these inquiries become a vehicle to control action and behaviour.

As ways of thinking and being in the world, discourses become "sedimented," or structured, into institutions and organizations. They become rules and regulations that govern our lives and our ways of thinking, seeing, and being in the world. In this way, words move from being simply ideas to becoming disciplining social practices. Consider how the idea of education, for instance, has become sedimented or structured into particular practices, objects, and institutions, such as classes, textbooks, and schools or universities. In other words, the idea of education has taken form in very specific physical spaces (classrooms), activities (attending lectures), and practices (writing exams and essays).

By this account, we live immersed in discourse, like fish in water, with its invisible currents shaping and determining much if not all of our lives, as language—in the form of ideas—takes on a life of its own. At the personal level, larger social discourses frame our ideas, hopes, and desires. Our identities are given form by the discourses of which we are a part: what it means to be male, female, Canadian, and so on. From this perspective, media content can be seen as part of these larger discursive formations, part of the social mechanism through which norms, values, and other ideas about how the world "is" and "should be" are circulated and reproduced.

Critical Political Economy

Working from the Marxist perspective that the media generally support private capital and the dominant interests in society (see Chapter 2), writers in the field of critical political economy have approached the media from a number of directions (see Mosco, 2009). In the 1970s, for instance, Dallas Smythe noted that in contrast to the seeming fact that the purpose of the media is to serve the interests and tastes of audiences—that is, to inform and entertain people—the product from which private broadcasters and newspapers draw the balance of their income is audiences, from which Smythe concluded that the real business of commercial media companies is selling audiences to advertisers. From this perspective, media serve the interests of owners, not the public at large. As he argues,

> The capitalist system cultivates the illusion that the three streams of information and things are independent: the advertising merely "supports"' or "makes possible" the news, information, and entertainment, which in turn are *separate* from the consumer goods and services we buy. This is untrue. The commercial mass media *are* advertising in their entirety . . . both advertising and the "program material" reflect, mystify, and are essential to the sale of goods and services. The program material is produced and distributed in order to attract and hold the attention of the audience so that its members may be counted (by audience survey organizations which then certify the size and character of the audience produced) and sold to the advertiser. (Smythe, 1994: 9)

A similar argument can be made about social media. Take Google, for example. As Fuchs (2012) points out, while Google's search engine appears to provide a public service, the company's real business is using the information users enter into the search engine to develop profiles of things they seemingly want or desire, and then selling advertisers access to those users based upon those wants or desires. Hence, if you search about guitars, you get ads for guitars accompanying YouTube channels you watch and other material you may download from the internet. If you search about a particular place or city, you get ads from travel companies trying to sell you a trip to that location accompanying your online fare. In other words, the system is purposefully constructed to turn your curiosity and interests into sales opportunities.

The point here is that the capitalist system's drive for profits structures or limits the kinds and forms of media available to us. If the service offered by the company or organization cannot turn a profit—either through advertising, subscription fees, or some other form—it will fade and disappear from the public realm. MySpace, Friendster, and Eons offer examples in this regard.

Focusing specifically on news media, in their book *Manufacturing Consent: The Political Economy of the Mass Media,* Edward Herman and Noam Chomsky (2002: 2) argue that there are five political, economic, and organizational "filters" that come to bear on US news media to ensure that the content they produce works in favour of political and economic elites:

1. the concentration of ownership of the media in the hands of a few large private corporations
2. the media's dependence on advertising as their principal source of revenue
3. the media's reliance on government and business elites as sources of news and opinion
4. "flak," or negative feedback, from powerful established interests when the news plays against their interests
5. strong belief in the "miracle of the market" as a means to satisfy social needs and desires. As they state, the model "traces the routes by which money and power are able to filter out the news fit to print, marginalize dissent, and allow the government and dominant private interests to get their messages across to the public."

As Herman and Chomsky point out, taken together these factors work to ensure that news content generally supports the social status quo and helps maintain the legitimacy of both our form of government and economy.

The political economy of communication has also been employed to illustrate how global entertainment media undermine local cultures (Mirrlees, 2013); how patterns of media ownership limit the range and character of media available in society (Winseck, 2017); how new media technologies are being used to reshape global media industries (Winseck and Jin, 2012); how corporate interest generally overrides the public interest in Canadian telecommunication policy (Moll and Shade, 2011, 2008; Winseck, 1998; Babe, 1990); why the Canadian media are generally dominated by US products (Pendakur, 1990; Smythe 1981); how corporate media generally represent a narrow range of perspectives and opinions (Hackett and Gruneau, 2000); and how political economic factors shape Canadian television production (Quayle, 2015; Bredin, 2013; Druick and Kostopoulos, 2008).

In sum, the main point made by critical political economy is that the larger political and economic relationships that govern society reach down to structure not only the ways in which the media operate but also how they represent the world to us. With a little practice, it is relatively easy to see the "truth" of this perspective. If a privately owned media outlet fails to make a profit, for example, eventually it will likely go out of business, taking whatever ideas or perspectives it circulates with it. Hence, only those television programs that are profitable, or most profitable, get shown. Similarly, as we have discussed, because there is much more money to be made from running US television and film products than from screening similar Canadian fare, both small and large screens in Canada are overrun with Hollywood content. In the face of these factors, governments have taken a number of steps to help ensure that a wide range of ideas and perspectives find voice in this country, including the creation of our publicly funded broadcaster: the CBC/Radio Canada.

The Cultural Critique

One of the key strengths of both structuralism and political economy is the way they provide a means of understanding how media content is the product of a larger set of material social circumstances. Indeed, as the encoding/decoding model illustrates, media producers can't just create whatever content they want. The agency of media producers in the production process is guided by a whole set of factors, such as the available budget, professional values or norms, and a host of other social and cultural factors. But while political economy points to economics as the key or overriding determinant in production and the way content is created, other perspectives, such as cultural studies, take a broader perspective (see Chapter 4).

Why, for example, are there more male media executives than female ones? And as we discuss below, why are minorities consistently under-represented or misrepresented in television advertising? How is it that racial stereotypes—often negative (Hirji, 2014)—can be found in news coverage? These are not questions that a political economic analysis can easily answer. Instead, we need to look to perspectives that foreground the way other social factors or determinants, such as gender, ethnicity, and race, influence the ways in which the media and media content represent the world to us. Understanding the ways in which these issues play out in the production of media content and the larger impact that this misrepresentation may have on people's lives is an important element of communication research.

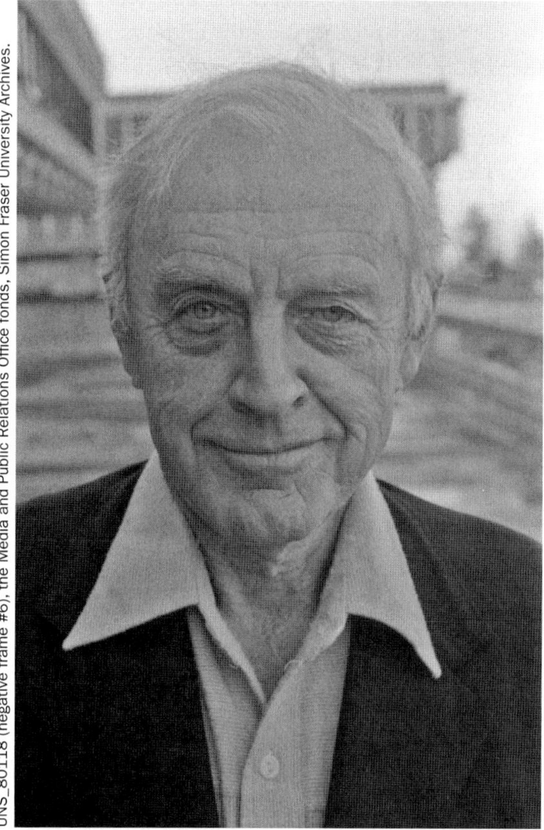

UNS_80118 (negative frame #6), the Media and Public Relations Office fonds, Simon Fraser University Archives.

Dallas Walker Smythe (1907–1992) was a groundbreaking Canadian political activist and researcher; his field was the political economy of communication.

Content Analysis

While it merits our attention here because it is often employed as a method for analyzing media content, *content analysis* is not a theory. Rather, it is used in conjunction with such approaches as discourse analysis or critical political economy to identify the specific characteristics of media content, such as how particular people, social groups, or places are framed or treated in news stories and what is either included or left out of particular stories or television programs (Richter et al., 2011; Krippendorf, 2004).

Content analysis emphasizes the quantitative aspects of media content, specifically the number of occurrences of a particular category of phenomenon. For instance, what places (cities, provinces, or countries) are covered in news stories? What kinds of subjects are covered? What sources do reporters quote or draw on in writing a story? Are some politicians quoted more than others? Are some think tanks called on more than others? How often are minorities covered in news stories? How are they covered?

The system of analysis works this way. First, the analyst determines the variables to be measured. Variables may include things like the general subject or theme of a story; the particular people, places, or events represented; whether these things are framed or treated in a positive or negative light; and the sources or experts quoted. The researcher then sets up units of analysis—phrases, sentences, paragraphs, column inches, and so on—and counts these variables and perhaps their relation to other aspects of content, such as pictures or long pieces with prominent placement. On the basis of frequency of occurrence in one or more media products (e.g., newspapers, TV news programs), the analyst can provide a reading of the media treatment of an issue over time. For instance, a study published in 2018 based on a content analysis of 80 ads produced by Canada's oil sands industry found that the advertising campaigns shifted over time from "linking industry's interest in oil with a visual commitment to preserving, reclaiming, and restoring the natural environment" to "undertak[ing] a multidimensional campaigning strategy, the most prominent of which is lifestyle messaging that celebrates oil's ubiquity in consumer culture" (McCurdy, 2018). Similarly, employing discourse analysis, Felt (2017) analyzed the content of news reports to consider how they helped construe cyberbullying as a Canadian social problem.

Content analysis can also help illustrate what has been left out of media coverage. For instance, in a study done in 2000, NewsWatchCanada found that over a six-month period on CBC and CTV television newscasts, "right-wing think tanks received 68 per cent of all references while left-wing think tanks received 19.5 per cent" (Hackett and Gruneau, 2000: 204). While these statistics don't tell us what the news stories were about, they illustrate that during the specified period, right-wing sources were consulted or referred to more than three times to one. Similarly, a content analysis of the online editions of Canada's self-described national newspapers—*The Globe and Mail*, the *National Post*, and *Le Devoir*—showed that their coverage was not national at all, but largely confined to the cities and provinces in which they were based and the activities of federal government institutions (Gasher, 2007).

And, in a comparison of their coverage of climate change, Gunster (2011) found that mainstream and independent or alternative media in British Columbia took quite different perspectives.

Other studies illustrate both a general lack of representation of people of colour in mainstream Canadian media, and that when they are represented, it is often in the form of stereotypes (Hirji, 2014; Jiwani, 2010). Similarly, a recent study of Canadian television found that while the portrayal of diversity had improved in recent years, there was still a lack of representation of people with disabilities and indigenous peoples (See Pedwell, 2017).

In another instance, a content analysis focusing on the coverage of Latin America in the US press over time revealed that the dominant definition of news—what was most often reported about Latin America—was natural disasters, such as earthquakes and volcanoes. During the 1970s, there was a gradual shift toward a focus on dictators and banana republics. Such analyses are revealing not only in terms of the trivialization of the definition of *news* for an entire region of the world but also in terms of the significant absences—the failure to offer any serious account of the economic, political, or social developments of that region.

As can be seen from these examples, content analysis can be a valuable tool for helping to uncover systematic biases or problems in the ways in which the media represent particular perspectives or social groups.

Genre, or Media Form

Another type of analysis that can be used as a complement to any of the above frameworks is derived from Marshall McLuhan's notion that "the medium is the message." The presentation of meaning is constrained by both how the medium itself structures and carries content and the genre or content type, of which any particular piece of content is a part.

In terms of the medium, Heyer (2003) illustrates that analysis focuses "on a consideration of the properties embodied in the carriers of that content and the influence those properties have on production, transmission, and reception." Genre analysis looks to the way artistic or professional conventions structure or dictate the production and consumption of content. But when examining particular types of content, there is not always agreement on how to distinguish conventions from the influence of the medium (see Meyrowitz, 1994).

Take, for instance, the differences between the presentation of news on television and in the newspaper. Although they belong to the same broad content genre—news—the way in which television and newspapers present their content is quite different. On television, the news team focuses on creating compelling visuals and a story that can be told quickly and simply. A newspaper story, on the other hand, depends for its strength on elements such as a logical presentation of the facts and thorough analysis. Is this difference a product of the medium (television versus newspaper) or convention (the way in which the journalists choose to present the story)?

A television anchor could present the written text of a newspaper story on television, although the full reading may seem time-consuming and boring for the viewer, compared to the fast-paced visuals of a regular TV news clip. Indeed, online media do often present news in textual form on screen. On the other hand, there are obviously considerable differences between paper and an electronic screen, and these differences can have important influences on how information is presented (see Heyer, 2003; see also Box 1.2).

In any event, apart from the influence that the medium may have on content, understanding the larger cultural and economic histories of media genres and forms provides important insights on both the character of their content and their larger cultural significance.

Advertising

Perhaps the most dominant and pervasive media genre is advertising. It has profound significance in our market-based, consumer society and animates much of the economy, linking producers and consumers by creating awareness and demand for products and services. Advertising lies at the very foundation of the commercial media, financing the production and distribution of most information and entertainment. For a surcharge paid on consumer products (the cost of ads is built into the cost of products), advertising has become the central means for financing the media. With media like newspapers, television, radio, and websites, as well as cable, satellite, and mobile delivery systems, consumers pay only a small portion, if any, of the cost of content. Rather, the bulk is paid by advertisers, who hope that audiences pay attention to the content they sponsor and, more particularly, to the advertising messages that content includes. Similarly, in their quest

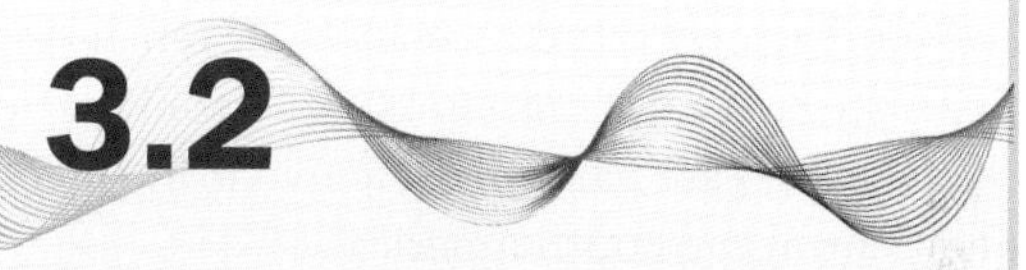

On Orson Welles's *War of the Worlds*

Paul Heyer has created an interesting text/audio analysis of Orson Welles's *War of the Worlds* controversy. In October 1938, Welles broadcast a radio program that was seemingly a live report of a Martian invasion of earth. Thousands of people mistook the report as real, and a degree of public panic ensued. Heyer's work is a media form analysis that discusses the intuitive understanding Welles had of radio as a medium. Heyer's 2003 article, "America under attack 1: *The War of the Worlds*, Orson Welles, and 'media sense'," is in *Canadian Journal of Communication*, vol. 28, no. 2, pp. 149–65. It is accessible online at www.cjc-online.ca/index.php/journal/article/view/1356/1421.

to monetize, or make money from, their services, new media companies like Facebook, YouTube, Google, and Twitter have been feverishly working to find ways to generate advertising revenue from their services. In fact, as we will see in later chapters, the sometimes surreptitious means through which new media organizations are collecting and selling information about users has given new life to the old adage, "If you are not paying for the product (or service), the product is you."

In any event, because advertising is such a pervasive form of media content, we devote an entire chapter (Chapter 5) to discussing it. Meanwhile, let's consider the characteristics of several other common media genres.

Soap Operas

Developed at the beginning of the 1930s in the early days of commercial radio, soap operas were a popular cultural form designed to socialize a home-confined female audience with disposable income into the art of consuming, especially household cleaning products (Williams, 1992; LaGuardia, 1977). Today, televised French- and Spanish-language versions—téléromans or telenovelas—are particularly popular in Quebec and Central and South America.

Soaps are one of the most analyzed of all the narrative genres on television. They have been of particular interest to feminist scholars because they are a preferred form of entertainment for female viewers in many countries. Analysis has concentrated on the form and content of soaps and on the pleasures they offer viewers.

Over time, academic perceptions of soaps have changed. At first, they were considered the epitome of that commonly criticized aspect of television that echoes the mass society thesis: trivial, mindless entertainment. Gradually, however, just as the pleasures offered by other forms of popular culture, such as films, magazines, sports, and other television fare were legitimized as valid pastimes, so, too, were soaps viewed in a more positive light (Geraghty, 1991; Radway, 1984).

Music Videos

In a fashion similar to the soaps, music videos emerged because producers wanted to socialize an audience into purchasing their product. The difference between the soaps and music videos is that, with videos, the product to be purchased is part of the promotional vehicle used to bring it to the attention of the audience. Music videos are visually enhanced versions of the recorded music that audiences are intended to purchase. They provide a visual track to the sound recording and sometimes, as in the case of Michael Jackson's groundbreaking song "Thriller," or, more contemporarily, some rap and hip-hop videos, they are highly crafted works of art in their own right.

As media content, music videos give viewers an entry point to popular culture. They provide examples of current clothing and accessories, how to behave, what expressions to use, and are also sometimes used as a form of social critique (Doherty, 2018). In highlighting material for imaginative creation, music videos complement fashion photographs and magazines. Viewers make individual interpretations and inject a dynamism built on popular music, enhancing the frozen-in-time quality of fashion photographs (see Goffman, 1959; Fornas et al., 1988). As James Curran (1990: 154) has remarked, "[popular] music is viewed as a laboratory for the intensive production of identity by adolescents seeking to define an independent self." In this vein, researchers often examine these videos to see what subcultural trends they appear to be following or animating, and to assess their role in shaping individual and cultural values (see Jhally, 1997).

Reality TV

A genre that has enjoyed increasing popularity over the last 20 years is reality-based television. As a category of content, reality TV encompasses a range of different types of programming, including game shows, talent searches, cooking and food programs, sports, lives of celebrities, talk shows, hidden cameras, hoaxes, and a "day or week in the life" of prominent personalities.

BIG BROTHER CANADA

Insight Productions Ltd.

Format reality TV shows like *Big Brother Canada* are standardized programs created to be licensed internationally (see Quail, 2015). They provide relatively inexpensive content for the increasing number of television stations and networks that characterize today's media universe.

Reality TV sometimes has the patina of a documentary style and focuses on "real-life," unscripted situations. At other times, plot and narrative structure are achieved through editing or having subjects participate in contrived scenarios. Other traditional narrative techniques, such as characterization, are achieved through focusing on people with outlandish personalities and jobs or by careful screening and casting of participants.

For producers and television networks, a prime attraction of reality TV is its low cost. With neither expensive actors to pay nor high-priced sets and special effects to create, reality-based television is one antidote to the difficulties presented by today's fragmenting television market, where the increasing sea of program choice means shrinking audiences and ad dollars for many individual stations and networks. Most of the cast members of these programs work for nothing, and the sets or locations require little preparation. A key component of this genre is franchise formats. As Quail (2015:186) points out, "Formats—program concepts, created by a production team for the purpose of licensing internationally to national production firms—are standardized television shows with multiple international iterations . . . (and) in one year, a format can be adapted in numerous markets; for example, The Weakest Link has 60 simultaneous versions." As she goes on to illustrate, in Canada this type of program includes "Toronto-based Insight Productions . . . Big Brother Canada, Amazing Race Canada, Canadian Idol, Project Runway Canada, Canada's Got Talent, Intervention Canada, and Top Chef Canada" (190).

Meanwhile, on the decoding side of the equation, reality TV shrinks the distance between program and audience as ordinary people become television stars, and videos and other material created by non-professionals are used in television programs. The emergence of this television genre sparked a range of research into its political economic origins and cultural significance (Quail, 2015; Baltruschat, 2009; Murray and Oulette, 2004).

Fan Fiction

Fan fiction comprises works that use characters or settings from films, books, television shows, comics, or other media products that were originally the products of other creators. While works of this type can be traced back hundreds of years, they have become particularly popular with the

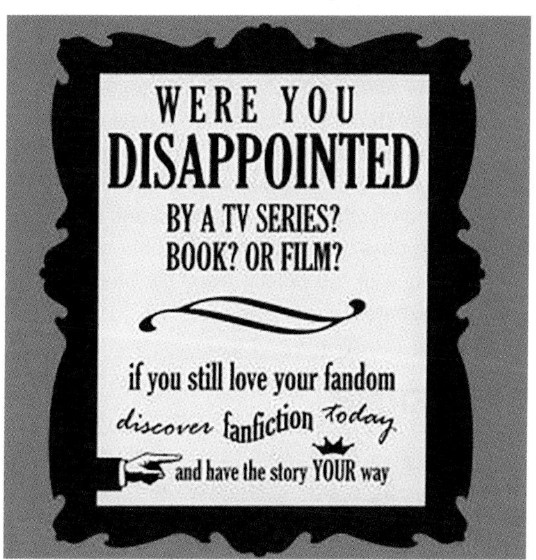

Fan fiction is an increasingly popular media genre where creators employ characters or settings originally developed by other people.

development of the internet and cheap digital media production tools, such as cameras and software (Clements, 2018). Fan fiction also spans practically all mediums, as it often plays upon both well-known and obscure works. As noted in Chapter 1, stories involving popular media products such as *Star Wars* or *Harry Potter* have sometimes landed in trouble with copyright law (Kluft, 2016). But, in other instances, copyright owners have encouraged the efforts. While some see the genre as lacking originality, as one fan fiction writer responded to one critic, "I said, 'Have you ever played an instrument?' He was like, 'Yeah, I play piano'. I said, 'So, do you compose all your own music?'" (Novik, in Clements, 2018). Today, fan fiction is often seen as a creative genre of its own, and several websites allow tens of thousands of fans to share, document, and celebrate it.

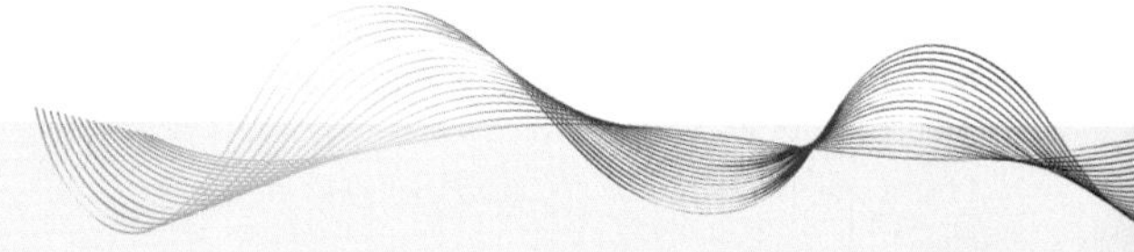

SUMMARY

In this chapter, we have examined the creation and interpretation of media content, or, as the semioticians say, the process of signification. We considered the use of social theory in this context, and how it provides important insights into how symbols, such as the words and ideas contained in language, are constructed and used to interpret the world of objects, events, persons, and even representations.

The study of representation involves understanding the nature of polysemy, intertextuality, and grounded indeterminate systems. In less-technical words, it involves understanding how messages are open to a variety of interpretations, how interpretations depend on other representations, and how there is bound to be a finite but unpredictable number of interpretations of the object, event, or phenomenon being represented.

We examined a number of approaches used to understand and analyze media content. They included theoretical perspectives—such as literary criticism; structuralism, semiotics, and post-structuralism; discourse analysis; and critical political economy—and methodological orientations, such as content analysis and genre/media form analysis. We presented media theory as a way of understanding the assumptions people make about the relationships between media texts and larger social relationships and forces, whereas the methods were seen as a means of differentiating or analyzing different kinds of content. Each has particular strengths and draws out various forces playing on content.

Understanding the relationships between media content and different individuals, social groups, and larger social forces is key to understanding the role of communication in our society.

KEY TERMS

connotative meaning, p. 63
content analysis, p. 79
decoding, p. 66
denotative meaning, p. 63
discourse analysis, p. 76
encoding, p. 66
fan fiction, p. 83
icon, p. 62
index, p. 62
intertextuality, p. 62
polysemic, p. 63
representation, p. 61
rhetoric, p. 64
semiotics, p. 61

sign, p. 61
signified, p. 62
signifier, p. 61
social theory, p. 65
structuralism, p. 72
symbol, p. 62

RELATED WEBSITES

Adbusters: www.adbusters.org/
Adbusters describes itself as "an international collective of artists, designers, poets, punks, writers, directors, musicians, philosophers, drop outs, and wild hearts"—an interesting media-based alternative to dominant cultural ideas and values.

Archive of Our Own: archiveofourown.org/
A self-described "fan-created, fan-run, nonprofit, noncommercial archive for transformative fanworks, like fanfiction, fanart, fan videos, and podfic."

Media Smarts: www.mediasmarts.ca
Media Smarts provides information and insightful analysis of various media issues, including violence in the media.

Media Education Foundation: www.mediaed.org
This organization specializes in videos about media, culture, and society.

Semiotics and Advertising: www.uvm.edu/~tstreete/semiotics_and_ads/
A website on semiotics created by Professor Tom Streeter of the University of Vermont.

FURTHER READINGS

Canadian Journal of Communication. The central journal for communication studies research in Canada.

Hall, Stuart, Jessica Evans, and Sean Nixon. 2013. *Representation*, 2nd ed. Los Angeles: Sage. An excellent introduction to theories of representation and meaning.

Krippendorff, Klaus. 2018. *Content Analysis: An Introduction to Its Methodology*, 4th ed. Thousand Oaks, CA: Sage. An excellent primer on content analysis.

Media, Culture and Society. This is the pre-eminent British media studies journal, founded in the 1970s by five young media scholars.

Mosco, Vincent. 2009. *The Political Economy of Communication*, 2nd ed. Thousand Oaks, CA: Sage. A good overview of the history and application of the political economy of communication.

STUDY QUESTIONS

1. Use the encoding/decoding model to analyze a popular TV program such as *The Simpsons*. What kinds of shared ideas and social values do the program's writers draw on to tell the story? Why do you think the writers picked these to include in the program? How do the scheduling and structure of the program reflect the fact that it is a commercial television show?
2. Perform a semiotic analysis of a magazine advertisement for a product (e.g., automobile, cologne) or a company. What are the signifiers used in constructing the ad? What are the signifieds? How do they work together to construct meaning? How many different meanings can be taken from the ad?
3. How do the different elements of the encoding/decoding model work to enable and constrain human agency in the process of communication?
4. Discuss how politics and economics work to both enable and constrain the Canadian media system.
5. Undertake a content analysis of a major news story (the story may be covered over a number of days in a variety of articles across many publications). Who are the major sources quoted in the story? What perspectives/sources appear to have been left out?

4

Perspectives on Media and Audiences

What the media are selling, in a capitalist society, is an audience.
—1970 Special Senate of Canada Committee on the Mass Media

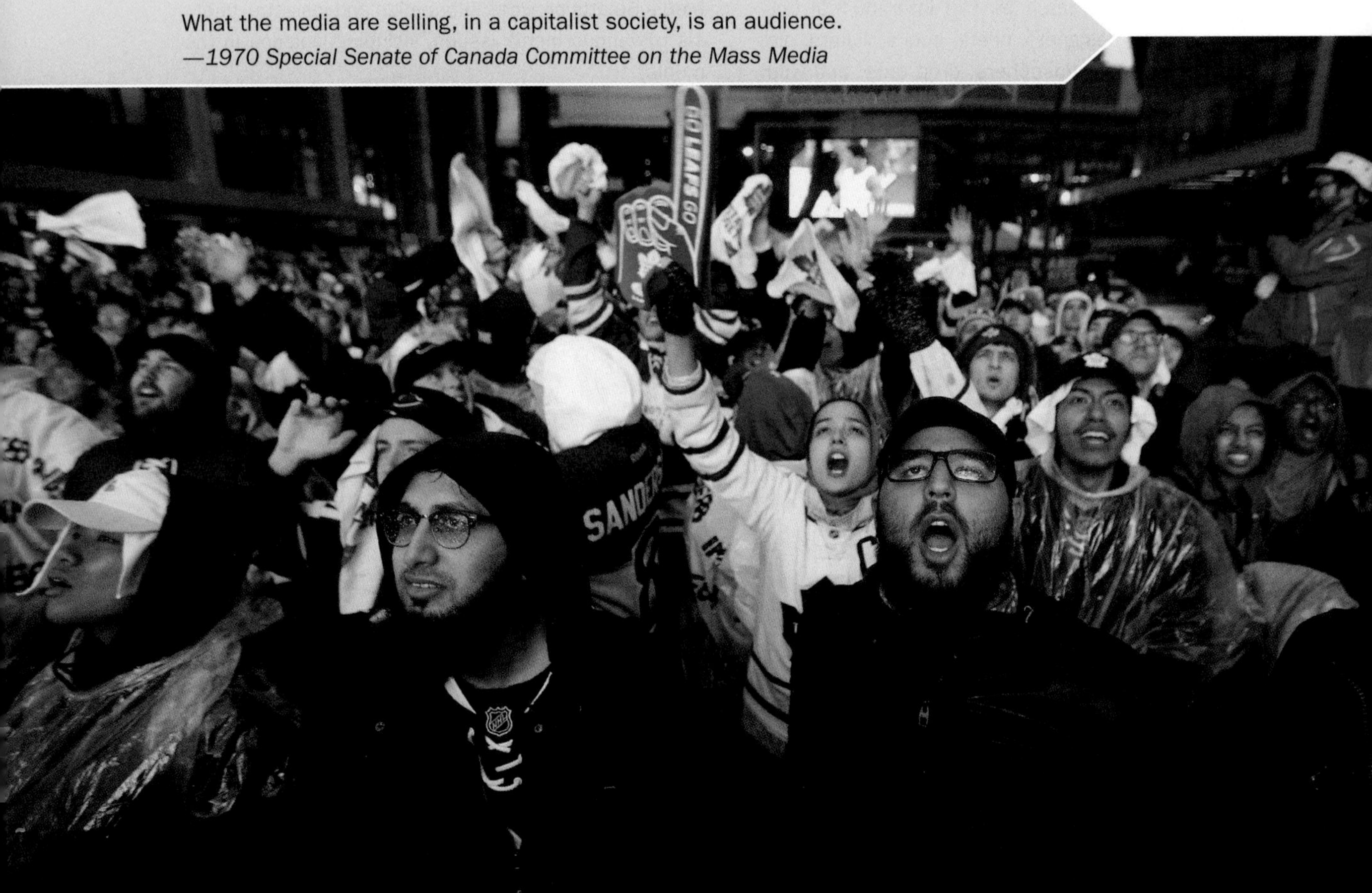

Steve Russell/Toronto Star via Getty Images

Opening Questions

- What are the relationships between media and audiences?
- How are audiences researched?
- What theoretical perspectives are used to study and understand the relationships between media and audiences?
- Can social media users be thought of as audiences?
- What are some of the issues associated with social media tracking their users?
- What are some of the shortcomings of the media industry's audience research?

Introduction

As we have seen, media weave through our lives at many levels. At the political level, they help frame and animate our understanding of the events and circumstances that define citizenship, how society is organized politically, and our role and purpose in that organization. At the level of culture, media play on our knowledge of particular ways of life, social groups, gender, and racial and ethnic distinctions. They also collude in our understanding of social roles (e.g., mother, father, child, teacher), organizations, and institutions. They address us as fans and devotees of particular media personalities and types of programs. And economically, they position us as consumers. In all these ways, media frame and animate our sense of identity and provide an understanding of ourselves in relation to others and the world. By and large, however, the media address us as audiences—that is, as sets or groups of individuals for whom their content is designed. Media seek audiences: sometimes to inform, other times to enlighten, still other times to entertain, and usually as targets to sell to advertisers, or as customers who will pay a fee for the receipt of content.

With the explosion of often interactive digital media choices, people are gaining more control over the terms of their participation as audience members and able to contribute to media production. In both traditional and social media, user-generated content is providing an expanding part of our media choice. Still, even in some instances with social media, the overarching relation is one where content is designed for consumption by specific groups or types of individuals, generally with a profit motive in mind.

Media audiences are of particular interest to academic and industry researchers. Scholars and social scientists seek to understand the nature of the interaction between the media and their audiences; what audiences do with media content; how they engage with television, social media, books, magazines, and music; how media influence perceptions and understandings of the world; and how they guide or influence social action.

Glasshouse Images / Alamy Stock Photo.

Ever since the radio became a common household item, researchers have been interested in studying how audiences interact with media.

Members of the industry have a different agenda. They want to know the size and the **demographic** characteristics (e.g., age, gender, ethnicity) as well as other attributes of particular audiences, such as education, income level, and purchasing patterns, so they can pinpoint the characteristics of the audience or "product" they are selling to advertisers and marketers. Industry members also want to know how audiences respond to audience-building techniques so they can understand how to attract larger audiences or audiences with specific characteristics.

Similarly, social media companies such as Facebook and Google want to develop profiles of their users so they can better target advertising to those persons' interests, needs, and desires. Given the vast range of information that social media companies are able to gather about their users from their posts and searches, advertising sales by social media have rapidly outpaced those of traditional media such as newspapers and television.

Meanwhile, audience members themselves have their own agendas, often dividing their attention between screens as they watch television, chat with friends on Facebook, and check out the latest Instagram posts, all at the same time.

In this chapter, we explore approaches to media audiences. It begins with a brief overview of the different ways that audiences have been understood through history, and goes on to consider some of the complexities of the relationships between audiences, media, and culture. We then examine several different academic perspectives on the audience, as well as contemporary industry and corporate perspectives. We close the chapter with a critical discussion of some of the shortcomings of industry conceptions of audiences and a consideration of the shifting nature of media/audience relationships.

Shifting Perspectives on Audience

Notions of what an audience comprises, and the relationships between audiences and different kinds of performances, spectacles, media, and media content, have shifted radically over time and can vary dramatically between cultures. Theatre in early Greece, for instance, was both political and intellectual in content, and "'the public was an active partner, free to comment, to be commented upon, to assist, or to intervene' with the on-stage production" (Sullivan, 2013: 11). At the same time, these audiences were also sometimes "talkative and unruly . . . [sometimes] disrupting performances by shouting, jeering, throwing fruit, and worse" (Arnott, 1989: 6). By comparison, "Roman theater was designed for nonpolitical spectatorship" (Sullivan, 2013: 10). And in the declining years of the Roman empire, "Instead of encouraging citizen participation, the goal was to stave off popular rebellion by refocusing the attention of the masses on ritualized violence and entertainment" (11). In Shakespeare's sixteenth-century England, theatre audiences were also noisy and unruly as well as divided by class, with the wealthier patrons seated well above the poorer folks who stood on the ground in front of the stage. On another front, traditional theatre performances in Japan and China might last for hours or even days.

By vastly increasing the number of books in circulation, Gutenberg's printing press helped create a new kind of audience (Sullivan, 2013: 9). With printing, the act of communication between the originator of a message and its recipient(s) became increasingly *mediated*. In other words, it was unhinged or disconnected from specific time and place such that "the writer addressed him- or herself to an invisible collectivity of readers who may exist in different locales, historical time periods, and cultural contexts" (12).

As we have seen, with the development of industrial society and mass media, such as newspapers, radio, and television, an increasing number of these new kinds of audiences took form. Within the context of the mass society thesis that we discussed in Chapter 2, these audiences were envisioned as large, anonymous, and generally undifferentiated groups or masses (*mass audiences*). They were generally much larger than public gatherings for performances or political events had been previously and, as McQuail (2010: 58) points out, they were seen as having some particular characteristics:

> (The mass audience) was very widely dispersed, and its members were usually unknown to each other or to whoever brought the audience into existence. It lacked self-awareness or self-identity and was incapable of acting together in an organized way to secure objectives. . . . It did not act for itself but was, rather, "acted upon" (and thus an object of manipulation). It was heterogeneous in consisting of large numbers from all social strata and demographic groups, but also homogenous in its choice of some particular object of interest and according to the perception of those that would like to manipulate it.

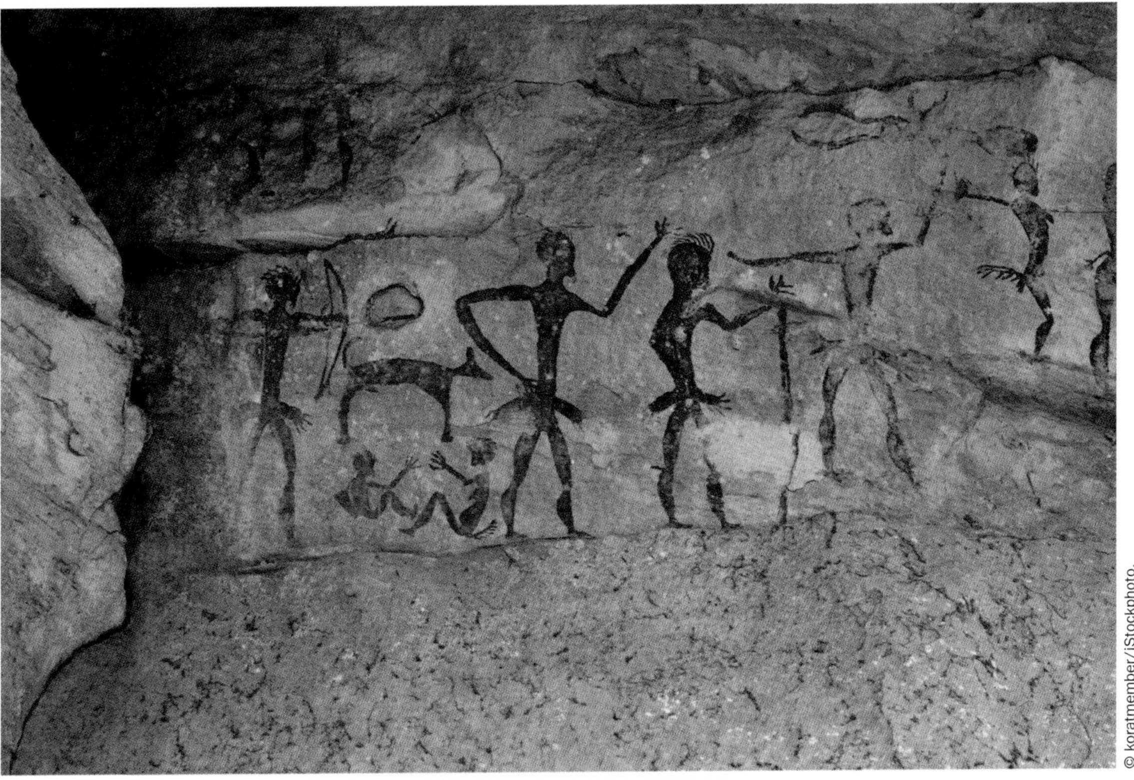

© koratmember/iStockphoto.

Are cave paintings like this one in Isan, Thailand, a form of mediated communication meant for a specific audience?

As advertisers and marketers struggled to better target customers for their products through the mid-twentieth century, however, a more nuanced vision of audiences took shape and they were segmented into particular demographics: groups of a particular age, sex, education, or income level. Industry research focused on finding ways to appeal to these market niches. And, in an attempt to capitalize on the information gathered from this research, through the 1980s and early '90s, marketing combined with technological innovation to create an increasing number of media outlets—from magazines, to newspapers, to cable and satellite channels—devoted to appealing to particular demographics.

At the same time, as illustrated in our discussion later in this chapter of the different academic perspectives on audiences, communication researchers began to take a closer look at the ways in which audiences interacted with media products. In the process, they discovered that media consumption was much more nuanced than had been previously thought. As we illustrated in Chapter 3, advertisers moved to incorporate these findings into their appeals to consumers.

Over the last 20 years, digitization and media convergence have been used to increasingly break down the distance between media production and consumption. On television, game shows, such as CBC's *Canada's Smartest Person Junior*, invite audience members to test their skill at challenges confronted by contestants. Talent competitions like *The Voice* employ audience members to pick winners. Television dramas have enrolled audiences to help pick endings and plot lines. And, of course, internet sites like YouTube allow all members of what was once thought of as the "passive" audience to become media producers themselves.

As Napoli (2011: 12) points out, what is particularly interesting about this shift in audience relations is that

> it represents in some ways a return to a conceptualization of the audience that was predominant in the pre-mass media era . . . [when] early manifestations of the audience were very much participatory and interactive. . . . Theatre audiences, for example, once engaged in a wide variety of activities, ranging from singing songs to yelling instructions and insults at performers to yelling at (and fighting with) each other. . . . It was only with the development of electronic mass media . . . that the dynamic between content provider and audience became increasingly unidirectional.

Photo by Nikki Ormerod.

Lilly Singh—aka Superwoman—is a Canadian YouTube star with over 14 million subscribers.

But while new technology has offered audiences increasing choice and participation, as we have discussed in previous chapters, it has also served to fragment audiences. People now watch programs on an increasing range of screens—from laptops to tablets to phones—and, when watching TV, they are often multi-tasking, using their laptops or other devices at the same time. One US study found that 77 per cent of people watching TV were also using their computers (Reuters, 2013).

Audience fragmentation presents a serious challenge to broadcasters, as fragmentation leads to a lowering of the advertising rates they can charge for any one program. To combat this issue, they are working to *re-aggregate* audiences across different platforms. For instance, after paying $5.2 billion in 2013 for the broadcast rights to *Hockey Night in Canada*, Rogers now broadcasts the program on City and CBC, and streams it on Sportsnet NOW. As a result, fans can catch a game in myriad ways, including on any device that can access the internet. Similarly, to help keep audience attention riveted to particular television programs, producers are increasingly offering online components to their broadcast programs, such as backstories for lead characters, series-themed games, and videos on the making of the program.

But just as interactive media technologies have given audience members more control over the range and character of their media consumption, so, too, have those technologies allowed companies and governments to track the movements and interests of media consumers. As we discuss in Chapter 6, privacy experts warn that this information can make us vulnerable in a number of ways. For example, present and future employers might search out information on our media preferences and online activities to help judge our suitability for particular jobs. Insurance companies might look for clues as to the potential risk we might pose in terms of health care and life insurance. And police forces and governments might examine our purchases and activities to consider the potential threats we might pose to what they define as the public good.

The character of audiences will continue to shift as media technologies alter the relationships between the production and consumption of media products. But as we discuss in the next section, how audiences interpret media is not simply a matter of technology.

Making Meaning in Context: Culture, Media, Audience

As they *decode* media content, audience members do not accept all of what they see or hear—regardless of whether that content is the facts of a news story or the general portrayal of society and its values in a film, television show, or novel. Watching television, reading books or magazines, listening to music, and so on are largely casual or leisure activities, and no research has ever shown that the media have the power to induce audience members to act against or outside their will.

Media–audience interaction is probably best thought of as a sometimes energetic, sometimes passive engagement between audience members and the media. Insofar as decoding media content requires audiences to have some understanding of a larger set of social values and institutions, this interaction also takes place at a social or cultural level. From this perspective, audience members, the media, and cultures can be conceived of as a closely woven meaning-generating system.

Let us consider the example of a young woman, home early from classes, who tunes into WWE on TV to find Undertaker and Brock Lesnar throwing each other around the wrestling ring. No one is home, least of all her brother, who left the television on this channel the day before. Though normally not a fan of wrestling, she is captivated by the spectacle for several minutes. But she quickly finds that the bout is nothing special. "Boring," she thinks, and reaches for the remote.

This example illustrates many of the elements of meaning generation. As our protagonist is confronted with this wrestling program, she immediately recognizes the scene and the characters and can sense if anything appeals to her in this action soap opera directed at young men. She analyzes the material on the screen by interpreting the events in her terms and then reacts accordingly.

Is this interaction complex and multidimensional? Yes. After some consideration, our viewer finds little in the scene that appeals to her. The fact that none of the advertising accompanying the program is relevant to her illustrates that advertisers don't expect it to be relevant to her. The interaction is also mediated by the context, and by the choices found in the moment. Were she at a friend's house and the friend wanted to watch, she might stay with the program a while longer. But here at home by herself, she wonders what the other channels have to offer. At the same time, she might be wondering, What's happening on Facebook? Twitter? What is in the fridge? When is her next assignment due? In assessing whether to watch, her perspective is framed by her understanding of the other activities available to her at the time, her knowledge of wrestling, and her interest in the spectacle. The young woman considering her other options, her sighs of boredom, her flopping down on the couch in the first place all are part of the meaning she is making of the situation she is in.

Given these media–audience dynamics, where does culture as an active, meaning-generating system figure in this scenario? Cultural dynamics play themselves out in the young person's vision of herself and the relevance of the program to her. Also, the fact that the program is aired and commands vast audiences is part of a cultural dynamic. Finally, the very scene of these modern gymnasts/gladiators, dressed as stereotypical heroes and villains, heaving each other around in a sensational action theatre, draws on a wide range of cultural ideas and values.

Building on our discussion of the encoding/decoding model in the previous chapter, we can see from this example that audience interpretations of media content derive from at least the following factors: (a) the social background or history of the audience member; (b) her/his current state of mind; (c) the social situation, or context, within which the media consumption is taking place; and (d) the text or content, including the range and character of media options available. Given these criteria, we are able to understand the possible roots of our viewer's behaviour. Nevertheless, a particular part of her individual personality or attitude in that moment might have caused her to behave differently. We cannot know exactly how she will react. (In fact, a Google search will quickly illustrate that, although they make up a minority of the fan base, there are many female wrestling fans.) The point of analyzing media–audience relations, however, is not to predict audience behaviour but rather to understand it.

Culture is a key element in this meaning-generating system. The individual's cultural milieu works to help create identity through acting as the reference point to a host of factors. As we have discussed, culture is a set of ideas and values, or way of life, through which people understand and relate to the larger set of organizations, institutions, and relationships among which they live. It is a dynamic derived from the wealth, history, and present-day attitudes and actions of groups and individuals in their respective social milieux. By conducting daily interactions in their social milieu, people generate meaning through a constant process of selection, re-stylization (or appropriation), and transformation.

Within this context, the study of audiences can be approached in many different ways. We will examine six academic approaches to the audience: (1) effects research; (2) uses and gratification research (U&G); (3) Marxist analysis and the Frankfurt School; (4) British cultural studies; (5) feminist research; and (6) reception analysis. As with the perspectives on content we examined in the last chapter, the point here is to provide an overview of some of the main ways audiences have been approached by researchers, as well as to illustrate some of the key issues audience research has raised—not to present a comprehensive review of these perspectives.

Effects, Agenda Setting, and Cultivation Analysis

Early studies of the media following World War I (1914–1918) presupposed media to have direct **effects** on human behaviour and attitudes. Fuelled by the success of propaganda campaigns during the war, which seemed to indicate that the masses would believe almost anything they were told, researchers posited the "magic bullet," "hypodermic needle," or "inoculation" theory of communication, built on the idea that media could inject ideas into people's heads.

This perspective was supported by the social science of the day, which, on the one hand, subscribed to the mass society thesis—which, as we have seen, characterized people, particularly the lower classes, as easily manipulated—and, on the other hand, embraced early behaviourist conceptions of psychology that saw human behaviour as a simple response to external stimuli. The early success of newspaper and radio advertising, which stimulated demand for the growing range of products generated by industry during the interwar period, added credence to this idea.

But while the success of war propagandists and early advertisers seemed to demonstrate that people were easily swayed by media suggestion, studies conducted after World War II (1939–1945) found that the impact of media messages on individuals was weak and, if anything, acted to reinforce existing ideas and beliefs rather than to alter opinions. In a review of effects research published in 1960, Joseph Klapper, a respected media researcher of the day, concluded that "mass communication does not ordinarily serve as a necessary or sufficient cause of audience effects, but rather functions through a nexus of mediating factors" (cited in McQuail, 2010: 457).

Having found weaker effects than anticipated, researchers undertook the task of reanalyzing the relations between media and audiences and began to look for more diffuse, indirect effects. Working in this vein in the early 1960s, Bernard Cohen argued that news "may not be successful in telling people what to think, but it is stunningly successful in telling its readers what to think about" (cited in Croteau and Hoynes, 2003: 242). For example, the front-page headlines of *The Globe and Mail* (and presumably, to some extent, the *National Post* and the *Ottawa Citizen* as well) play a significant role in what questions are asked the next day in the House of Commons, as do the lead stories on the national television news networks. This idea that the media serve an **agenda-setting function**, that they work, selectively, to draw the public's attention to particular events and circumstances, has gained a measure of credibility among media researchers.

Beginning with George Gerbner in the late 1960s and '70s (1969, 1977), researchers have also examined the effects of viewing behaviour on people's conception of social reality—a perspective that has evolved into what is called **cultivation analysis**, wherein content is studied for its ability to encourage or cultivate particular attitudes in viewers toward particular people or perspectives (see Potter, 2014; Signorielli and Morgan, 1990). For instance, Gerbner's work illustrated that people who watch a great deal of television overestimate the amount of violence in society and tend to have a "bunker mentality" to protect themselves from what they perceive to be a violent world. In spite of the broad acceptance of Gerbner's work, however, certain British studies (e.g., Wober and Gunter, 1986) have not been able to replicate his findings.

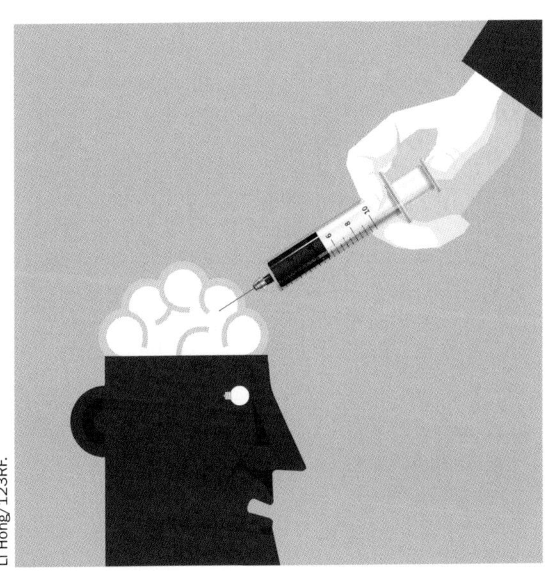
Li Hong/123RF.

Early media effects research was based on the now discredited premise that the media could inject ideas into peoples' heads.

Effects analysis, which abstracts the process of communication from its social context and tries to draw a straight line between sender and receiver, has been greatly criticized, essentially because researchers have not been able to identify clear, strong effects from media exposure. Just as the Shannon and Weaver model of communication discussed in Chapter 1 was shown to be too simplistic to account for the many influences on the ways media messages are constructed, so, too, is the effects model not able to illustrate the many influences on decoding. From this perspective, human agency is reduced to a simple reaction to content without consideration of how a larger set of social characteristics and forces (e.g., age, gender, education, mental condition) bears on media reception.

Research on agenda setting suffers from similar defects. It offers no explanation for how or why the media select what they will cover or what forces might be at play to help sensitize audience receptivity to messages. For instance, as the encoding/decoding model outlined in Chapter 3 illustrates, the media draw their material from a larger set of social circumstances; that is, from the larger cultural context within which they reside. Perhaps the news agenda is set in this context by local, national, and world events. On the other hand, perhaps the agenda is set by public or audience demand, or possibly it is an interaction of media institutions, audiences, and this larger set of social circumstances. In short, the effects tradition of media research raises more questions than it answers. Little attention is paid to the social circumstances—such as poverty, inequality, racial discrimination, alcoholism, child and sexual abuse, or extreme misogyny—that animate real-life violence.

Uses and Gratification Research

Uses and gratification research (U&G) began both as a response to findings of limited effects and as a reaction to the growing concern, rooted in the mass society debates, that popular culture—the wide variety of new television, radio, and musical content that started to gain popularity in the 1950s—was undermining or debasing audience tastes (Sullivan, 2013; Blumler and Katz, 1974). Based in social psychology, instead of focusing on the question *What do media do to audiences?* the central question of the U&G approach is *What do audiences do with the media?* The underlying premise was to focus on the agency of audience members and explore their motivations in the active selection of media content. Take, for example, two university students who decide to see an action movie after their last exam of the semester. They are not yet at the theatre to see the film, but a U&G approach already sees the students' activities as relevant. Going to a movie provides a good chance to relax, get together with friends, enjoy whatever is of interest in the movie, and go out for a coffee afterwards to socialize. Movies give people a chance to talk about other, related interests.

But while U&G theory puts more emphasis on agency than does effects theory, it still focuses on abstracting media consumption from the larger social context. Media consumption is reduced to an individual desire, process, or relationship. The influences of larger social, cultural, or ideological factors are not fully explored. Moreover, U&G theory is **functionalist**: that is, it is based on the assumption that media function to serve some kind of audience need, and then researchers set out to discover what that need is. No account is taken of the larger social origins of this supposed need or of how the process of media consumption plays into a larger set of social forces and institutions. For instance, certain facts—that the leisure time within which media are consumed is a product of industrial

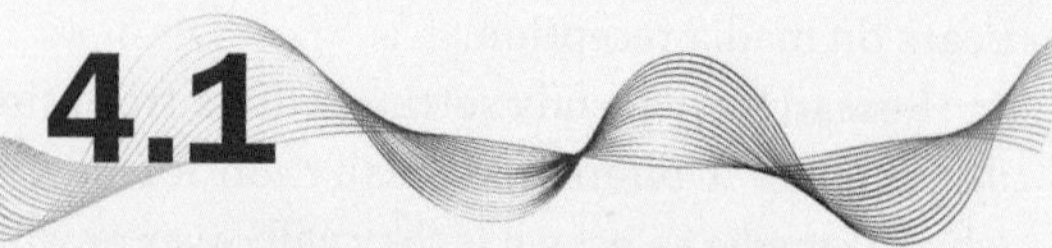

4.1 The Language of Movies and Television

Part of the structuring process of each media form is that it develops conventions or a "language" the audience comes to understand. Sometimes film scripts themselves make fun of these conventions, as in the *Deadpool* movie series. The following are examples of conventions that North American audiences have come to learn from watching many hours of film and television content.

- All police investigations require at least one visit to a strip club.
- All beds have L-shaped sheets to allow the man to bare his chest and the woman to hide hers.
- Ventilation systems are perfect hiding places. They reach every part of a building, are noiseless to enter and easy to move along both horizontally and vertically, and no one thinks to look there.
- When alone, foreigners speak English to one another.
- All women staying in haunted houses are compelled to investigate strange noises in their most revealing underwear.
- Cars that crash almost always burst into flames.
- Any person waking from a nightmare sits bolt upright.
- All bombs are fitted with large time displays that indicate exactly when they are to go off.
- You can always find a chainsaw if you need one.
- Having a job of any kind ensures that a father will forget his son's eighth birthday.
- Any lock can be picked easily unless it is on a door to a burning building in which a child is imprisoned.
- The more a man and woman hate each other initially the greater the chance they will fall in love in the end.

Source: Adaptation of "A sampler of one-liners and true facts," by Gary Borders, *The Daily Sentinel* (Nacogdoches, TX). Reprinted by permission of the author.

society and its division between work and leisure, or that much media content is focused on working to sell products to consumers—are not considered. To put it another way, the larger social purposes of media and how audience uses and understandings of media are shaped by other social conditions are outside the frame of these types of analysis.

Marxist Analysis and the Frankfurt School

As we have seen, Marxism envisions society as animated by a set of social forces based on capitalist forms of production (see Chapter 3). Working from this larger frame, Marxist perspectives generally focus on how the media support dominant interests in society, helping them maintain power and control over time. Consequently, Marxist perspectives don't focus on media–audience relations per se or on the ways media interact with, or impinge on, the agency of individual audience members. Instead, Marxist critics consider the ways in which media integrate audiences into the larger capitalist system.

One of the most far-reaching and influential Marxist critiques of twentieth-century media and culture comes from a group known as the **Frankfurt School**. The leading members of this group of intellectuals were Max Horkheimer, Theodor Adorno, and Herbert Marcuse; their ideas were formed in the 1920–1940 interwar period (Jay, 1974). At first, they worked at the Institute for Social Research attached to the University of Frankfurt, but when Hitler came to power, because they were Jews and their ideas were fundamentally out of step with fascism, they had to leave Germany, eventually settling in the United States for the duration of the war.

These theorists argued that capitalist methods of mass production had profound impacts on cultural life. Capitalist methods had been applied, in the nineteenth century, to the manufacture of the necessities of life; that is, to material goods like machinery and clothing. As we have seen, beginning in the 1920s—although interrupted by the Great Depression and World War II—capitalist forms of mass production yielded an increasing range of cheap commodities, coupled with reasonably well-paid factory jobs that enabled people to purchase these goods. With the help of advertising, families were persuaded that the acquisition of cars, household appliances, and fashionable clothing and accessories was essential to modern life. New forms of mass communication such as cinema, radio, and photography (in newspapers and magazines), complete with formulaic and commercial content, became woven into this way of life, celebrating and helping integrate people into it. At the same time, these new mass-produced cultural products displaced older, high-cultural forms of leisure and entertainment, such as symphonies, ballet, theatre, poetry, and great literature. Adorno and Horkheimer pooled these developments of this new industrial culture together under an umbrella term: "the culture industry" (Adorno and Horkheimer, 1977 [1947]).

The Frankfurt School argued that, through such developments, industrial capitalism penetrated deeper into cultural life and began creating a ready-made way of life. Thus, people's wants and desires were both created and satisfied through the marketplace. Building on the concerns of the mass society theorists that industrial society heralded a loss of social and cultural values, Adorno and Horkheimer saw marketers rushing to fill this void with an endless parade of commodities.

But for these theorists, this new way of life was devoid of any deeper meaning or understanding of the world. The pleasures derived from consumption of these commodities lasted only as long as it took for them to come to market. They argued that the distinctions between different makes, models, and brands of everything from cars to toasters are largely illusory and based on quickly shifting styles rather than on substantive differences in their qualities or characteristics. Popular films and music were seen to be simple and formulaic, their plots and rhythms easily recognized and understood. And in the ongoing churn of the market, no lasting relationships or deeper understandings of the world might be made.

From this perspective, culture and the media serve only one master: capital. All culture becomes a product of industrial capitalism and the guiding logic is one of corporate profit. Audiences are fed meanings by advertisers and manufacturers, and the possibility of the media acting as a venue for democratic discussion of issues of public concern disappears. Audience members are seen as little more than cultural dupes, or as Smythe (1994: 9) puts it, unpaid "workers" for the capitalist "consciousness industry" who are inexorably drawn, via the media, into a prepackaged world where choice is simply an illusion that supports this domination. (For a critique of this reading of Adorno and Horkheimer, see Gunster, 2004.)

The Frankfurt School members have been accused of cultural elitism and of pessimism. Perhaps most importantly, because they see people as easily manipulated by media, their perspective provides little room for human agency. The audience is simply a tool of the capitalist economy. Today, very few people would suggest that the *culture industry* (a useful term) has the entirely negative effects that the Frankfurt School claimed it did. Nevertheless, the members of the Frankfurt School rightly pointed out the importance of analyzing culture as integral to capitalism and critically questioned its impact and effect on contemporary cultural life.

The issues they addressed have continuing relevance. Since they first developed their analysis, the expansion of elements of the cultural industry has spread the influence of consumer culture throughout the world; from blue jeans to films to Disney-style theme parks, particular cultural icons and narrow cultural expressions are the currency of global culture. People around the world watch the same movies, wear the same clothing brands, and eat the same fast foods. Consequently, despite the seeming "choice" we have as consumers, as long as one has the money to participate, commercial culture is eerily the same in many places around the world. Here then, the trends the Frankfurt School identified years ago conjoin us in one grand commercial culture.

At the same time, contemporary Marxist-inspired research also explores how digital media such as Facebook and Google have worked to incorporate those platforms into this larger commercial culture and turn the thoughts and desires of their users into commodities that can be sold to advertisers (Fuchs, 2013; Cote and Pybus, 2011).

British Cultural Studies

British cultural studies began as a reaction to Marxist and other media theories that downplayed the role of human agency and discounted the apparent pleasures of popular culture. The impact of the growing mass culture in postwar Britain, particularly on the working class, was of interest to a number of intellectuals in the 1950s, including Richard Hoggart (1992 [1957]) and Raymond Williams (1958). To advance his concerns, Hoggart established the small post-graduate Centre for Contemporary Cultural Studies at the University of Birmingham, which his colleague Stuart Hall took over in the late 1960s. Hall's work in the 1970s with graduate students in what came to be called the **Birmingham School** of cultural studies was increasingly influential and largely defines what is today known as cultural studies.

Two main lines of development can be identified in the short history of British cultural studies from the 1950s to the present: the analysis of working-class culture, particularly the culture of young working-class males, and then, in response to feminist critiques at the centre, the analysis of young working-class females (Women's Studies Group, 1978; see also Turner, 1990; McGuigan, 1992; Storey, 1993; Schulman, 1993). A central concern was the use of mass culture, by both sexes, to create and define gendered identities. What clothing you chose to wear, the kind of music you listened to, whether you had a motorcycle or a scooter—these things helped create your image and define your personality. This emphasis on individual agency, and the relations of social power that enable and constrain that agency, also helped give rise to the study and concern for gender and identity politics (Waylen et al., 2016).

Instead of individuals being manipulated by the products of mass culture—as the Frankfurt School had argued—cultural studies turned the relationship around. Individuals could take these products and manipulate them, subvert them, to create new self-definitions. The classic study of this process is Dick Hebdige's *Subculture: The Meaning of Style* (1979), which looked at how young, white working-class males created identities for themselves through music: from mods and rockers in the 1950s and '60s through to punk and beyond in the 1970s.

Cultural studies paid particular attention to the ambiguous relationship between musical styles and social identities and to the embrace of black music and the culture of young, black males by young, white working-class males—much like the hip-hop culture of recent years. While cultural studies illustrated that the appropriation of meaning was much more complex than previously thought, it also demonstrated that social forces and institutions worked in complex ways to help reproduce the dominant order. For instance, in his classic study of an English high school, Paul Willis (1977) shows how rebellion against established authority leads working-class youth to working-class jobs.

An important strand in the study of contemporary culture has been analysis of film and television. In the 1970s, the British Film Institute's journal *Screen* put forward a structuralist-inspired analysis of film, arguing that how a story is told (through techniques of editing, visual images, and so forth) controls and defines how it might be viewed. In other words, they argued that the narrative techniques of cinema—often called *film language*—subtly but powerfully imposed their meanings on the viewer, who cannot avoid being "positioned" to see the film in a particular way. The notion of **position** refers particularly to the point of view constructed for the viewer through filmic techniques—that is, how the viewer is "put in the picture." In a classic analysis of Hollywood movies, Laura Mulvey (1975) argued that the pleasures of this kind of cinema were organized for a male viewer and that women (both in the storyline and as objects to be looked at) were merely instruments of male pleasure—objects of a male gaze.

Stuart Hall and his students, undertaking an analysis of how television and other media work, developed a more open kind of analysis. They argued that media content is structured to relay particular meanings—preferred readings—to audiences, but that it is quite possible for audiences to refuse that meaning and develop their own interpretation of what they hear and see (Glasgow Media Group, 1976).

Ideology, Primary Definers, and Negotiated Meanings

The key concept in such analyses is **ideology**. Ideology is one of those words that has had a number of definitions over the years (see Eagleton, 2007; Larrain, 1979, 1983; Thompson, 1980 [1963]). The term is generally taken to mean "a coherent set of social values, beliefs, and meanings that people use to decode the world—for example, neo-liberalism or socialism." There are number of variations on this definition, however, each with its own nuances.

A Marxist interpretation of the term *ideology* focuses on how a particular set of ideas, values, and beliefs support the dominant or ruling class. From the Marxist viewpoint, capitalism promulgates such ideas as "the poor are lazy," "unions and strikes are bad for society," and "capitalism is the only viable economic system." In reality, these ideas can be proven to be not true. Many people who work very hard for minimum wage are, by definition, still poor. The eight-hour workday and forty-hour work week were hard-won concessions from industry, largely as a result of union activity. And, there are indeed many ways to organize an economy other than around capitalist relations of production. Still, ideas like this persist and manage to augment the inequality problem in our society. For instance, why is there a growing gap between lower- and higher-income people in our society today? Why have people allowed the average income to stagnate for the last 20 years while high-income earners continue to make more? Why don't the poorer people stand up for themselves and demand better wages, a fairer tax system, and vote for politicians who will deliver these things? The answer, in a Marxist analysis, is ideology—that despite growing inequality, people, particularly those who are poorer, believe that society is fair and/or there is nothing to be done about this state of affairs.

Chris So/*Toronto Star* via Getty Images.

Can talent and other reality-TV competition shows like *Dragons' Den* challenge the status quo? In what ways do they uphold the dominant ideology?

Through accepting these kinds of ideological misrepresentations of social reality, Marxists argue that members of the working class are prevented from understanding how they are exploited or oppressed and come to accept the values of the ruling class. In other words, through accepting the above assertions as true, people have been lured into a *false consciousness* regarding how capitalist society works. From this point of view, ideology is a way of representing the world to oneself, a set of ideas that one uses to impose order on society and to decide what place different people and groups should occupy in the social order. By presenting versions of social reality that represent the existing order as natural, obvious, right, and just—in short, as the way things are and ought to be—the effect of ideology is to maintain the status quo, or to accept the domination of the powerful over the powerless. Just as accepting the idea that "the poor are lazy" serves to make it appear that people who are poor are deservedly so.

In the face of the social unrest of the 1960s and '70s—the civil rights movement in the United States, the rise of feminism throughout the Western world, and the student movement in North America and several European countries—some social scientists began to argue that there was more than one form of ideological oppression at play. Not only did ideology keep the workers in a subordinate position but, given these protests, it had also been doing the same for women, people of colour, and other social groups. Through their acts of protest, these groups illustrated that they had started to see through the ideology that had kept them in subordinate social positions and now had their own ideas about how the social world should be structured, and what their positions in that world should be. In other words, they had their own ideologies.

While these protests did have some positive impact on changing the unfair structure of society, to a large part the existing order, or status quo, has been maintained. Hence, with an eye on this struggle for social power, the question for researchers became *Amid all of these possible competing ideologies, why is it that the one that generally helps keep wealthy white males in positions of power seems to prevail?*

Exploring this question in the British context, cultural-studies researchers argued that British television was a key vehicle in helping reproduce the dominant ideological or value system—loosely understood as a paternalistic, class-based consensus that believed in the monarchy, the Anglican Church, Parliament, and the rule of law, among other things (Hall, 1980; Hall et al., 1978). For these researchers, television news and current-affairs programs are major vehicles for reproducing dominant values: powerful **primary definers** (interviewed politicians, experts, military figures) are routinely allowed to frame the issues, express their opinions, and offer interpretations of events and circumstances (Hall et al., 1978). Alternative or oppositional interpretations of events are seldom, if ever, allowed expression. An extreme example of this in Britain was the banning of members of Sinn Fein (the political wing of the Irish Republican Army [IRA]) from British television (see Curtis, 1984; Schlesinger, 1983).

Working from this idea, we can see that news isn't the only culprit here. Television dramas, films, song lyrics, popular novels, and so on can be seen as a set of morality tales from which we are to take lessons in what constitutes desirable and undesirable behaviour. Think about police shows and dramas that underscore that certain kinds of behaviours are bad or immoral. Talent and other reality-TV shows tend to perpetuate the idea that hard work and dedication to training or selling a start-up business idea will pay off in stardom or big contracts—even though the fact that the number of star-quality or business-wizard contestants those programs recruit demonstrates that hard work and talent don't guarantee success.

Moreover, when viewed from the perspective of the dominant ideology, media products and ideas that fail to conform to the values inherent in that set of ideas are often seen to be dangerous and cause negative effects. Consider, for instance, the range of things that Walmart has reportedly banned from its shelves, including albums by Kanye West, Sheryl Crow, and Marilyn Manson (Kleinman, 2012). It would appear that the work of these musicians doesn't meet with what Walmart executives consider should be the dominant set of social values, or what they see as the dominant ideology.

Despite the fact that media products may reflect the dominant ideology, Stuart Hall et al. (1978) and the cultural studies perspective argue that different people may decode them in very different ways. Indeed, as protesters from the 1960s to today demonstrate, not all people decode either the media or social life in the same way. Depending on their social background (e.g., gender, class, race, ethnicity, culture), they often hold different or competing ideas about how the world should be ordered and their place within it. In other words, they articulate meaning differently. Consequently, although the dominant ideology may be reflected in media products, it doesn't mean that people receiving and interpreting those products must accept that perspective as their own way of looking at the world. (Indeed, just because Walmart executives see some popular musicians as subversive doesn't mean other people are reading them that way.)

A study by David Morley (1980)—a graduate of the school—was an important step in establishing the Birmingham School perspective. Morley looked at how viewers of a BBC news and current-affairs program called *Nationwide* interpreted or decoded the program. He found, as Hall had suggested, three different responses: *dominant*, *negotiated*, and *oppositional*. Some viewers accepted what was presented in the program at face value, which accented national unity, strong family values, and suggested that Britain was essentially a nation of white, middle-class families living in suburbia. In other words, they accepted the program's preferred meaning. Other viewers, however, took a more critical or negotiated view of the program and did not see it as wholly representing British society; a few groups of viewers (notably young blacks) rejected the *Nationwide* premise altogether.

Spurred by the work of the Birmingham School, from the 1980s to the present day the cultural-studies approach to media analysis has helped foreground research on how audiences make sense of media products (Barker, 2012; Lee, 2003). Embracing a broad definition of ideology, the approach rejects the strongly deterministic view of the Frankfurt School and the journal *Screen*, instead stressing that media consumption is an active process and that different people interpret media differently. Hence, to understand how people interpret media, one must talk to people themselves and uncover the broad social and cultural conditions that frame the way they make meaning in the world. It also illustrates how culture is more than simply a range of prepackaged ideas and experiences spoon-fed to us by industry and advertisers—it is actually a rich and dynamic field, filled with a complex range of social meanings.

4.2

Feminism and Media Studies

By Tamara Shepherd

Broadly speaking, feminism describes a range of theories and modes of advocacy that share a concern with the equal rights and treatment of women. Historically, feminism tends to be seen as a series of movements or waves, which describe critical moments of ideological and political struggle. Within these waves, diverse forms of media have played a central role both as tools for furthering feminist advocacy and as battlegrounds for conflicts over gendered representation.

The first wave describes a period around the late nineteenth and early twentieth centuries, when women famously fought for and eventually won the right to vote. Women's suffrage, which can be traced to earlier proto-feminist texts in literature and philosophy, was the issue that served to crystallize concerns about women's status in education, property ownership, and marriage. Correspondingly, it was print media that played a key role in translating feminist ideas into protest activities, with feminist periodicals and pamphlets serving to articulate the political agenda of suffragettes in a largely male public sphere. A women's production culture comprised print, along with some early silent films, contributing to the media framing of feminism as a collective identity, thereby facilitating collective action.

Philip Scalia / Alamy Stock Photo.

For media studies, feminism's second wave becomes even more salient, as it coincides with other political struggles around representation and rights between the 1960s and mid-1970s. Ideologically, second-wave feminist thought drew from contemporary philosophical currents in psychoanalysis and Marxism to critique the imaginary "ideal woman." This ideal woman was represented widely across popular media forms, especially in advertising, magazines, cinema, and television. Critiques of such representations helped form the basis for activism, where feminist protest took shape around issues such as pay discrimination and reproductive rights.

Starting around the 1980s, the more radical strains of the second wave helped plant the

Feminist Media Research

Like Marxism, feminism is deeply critical of the character of modern societies, which, it argues, are based on fundamental inequalities (Beauvoir, 1957 [1949]; Friedan, 1963). But where Marxism locates the root of inequality in capital ownership and class division, feminism points to the male domination of society (patriarchy) as the root of profound inequalities and injustices in the world. And, in fact, such inequalities are pervasive aspects of modern life. For instance, on average, women make about 87 cents for every dollar men make (Israel, 2017).). In a recent survey of the 100 most influential companies on the Toronto Stock Exchange, BNN Bloomberg found that only one of those companies had a female CEO (Erlichman, 2018). In the 2015 federal election, only 88 of 338 people elected to Canada's federal Parliament were women. And men committing violence against women is much more prevalent than the reverse scenario.

Despite the fact that such inequalities have been known and documented for many decades, how is it that patriarchal values continue to hold sway? Communication researchers have studied how media and cultural products can contribute to normalizing the oppression of women and perpetuating these differences. As Kimmel and Holler (2011: 241) point out in their book *The Gendered Society*, the "media are part seeds for the third wave. Here, feminists worked to extend the critique of patriarchy to consider how it oppressed other social groups based on intersections of race, ethnicity, ability, and sexual orientation. Taking cues from postmodern and post-structural theory, the third wave sees identity as a more multiple and fluid concept, meaning that stereotypical media representations of race and gender needed also to be critiqued in terms of how they help perpetuate forms of discrimination under white capitalist patriarchy.

Yet at the same time that the third wave expanded considerations of gendered discrimination, popular news media mounted a conservative backlash against the radicalism of the second wave. Sensational depictions of second-wave feminists as "bra burners" and "man haters" were common as conservatives attempted to reverse women's flight away from the home and into the workforce. Simultaneously, some strains of media studies shifted their focus toward lowbrow culture and domestic audiences, offering feminist analyses of previously vilified cultural forms, such as television talk shows and romance novels. Rather than critiquing the producers of stereotypical media texts, feminist studies of popular audiences identified moments of pleasure, community formation, and identity construction within women's domestic consumption of popular media, arguing that these everyday experiences were politically empowering. This latter strand of third-wave feminism is still dominant today.

From this vantage point, the more recent post-feminist movement is seen as incorporating feminism into dominant power structures of patriarchal capitalism. Coinciding with a neo-liberal focus on the individual (rather than the collective) as the primary unit of political agency, post-feminism champions a woman's individual choice as ultimate empowerment. Consolidated in popular music through acts like the Spice Girls and television programs like *Sex and the City*, the late-1990s post-feminist boom saw feminism as a taken-for-granted position that no longer needed to be fought over since women were now fully "equal," at least in Western society.

Yet women and other marginalized groups are, of course, *not* treated equally. Patriarchy still dominates most places in the world, and so the message of earlier waves of feminism continues to be crucial for creating new representations and new forms of political action. In media studies, a key strand of recent research has considered how these representations are conditioned by gendered labour in media industries, inviting an alliance between feminist and labour movements in their resistance of capitalist patriarchy. At the same time, related theoretical perspectives such as queer, disability, and post-colonial studies point toward the ways in which feminist media studies have helped sustain the critique of structures of domination in both the production and consumption of print and electronic media, moving images, and new media technologies.

Tamara Shepherd is an Assistant Professor in the Department of Communication, Media and Film at the University of Calgary.

of a gigantic cultural apparatus that reproduces gender inequality by making it appear that such inequality is the natural result of existing gender differences. First the media create the differences; then the media tell us that the inequality is the natural result of those differences."

As Tamara Shepherd details in Box 4.2, feminism is often seen as a series of waves or movements, each with its own relationship to media and media studies. This section provides a very short review of some of this work as it relates to the second and third waves. For instance, as part of what Shepherd describes as the second wave of feminism, Judith Williamson's groundbreaking work (1978), *Decoding Advertisements: Ideology and Meaning in Advertising*, examines how advertising plays a central role in promoting ideological perspectives that perpetuate gender stereotypes. And, following in this vein, Jean Kilbourne's *Killing Us Softly* video series documents how television and print advertising provides distorted perspectives on femininity (Jhally, 2010).

In later work, feminist researchers developed the idea of gendered narratives, exploring how some types of stories (narrative genres) appeal or speak to male readers or viewers while other types appeal to female readers and viewers (Radway, 1984, is the key text). David Morley (1986) studied TV viewers in family settings and discovered a consistent profile of male and female preferences. One principal program category was television soap operas, with their largely female viewing audiences, and many studies have since examined what women enjoy in such programs (Seiter et al., 1989). As Kimmel and Holler (2011: 241) illustrate, today's media markets reflect these differences: "there are women's and men's magazines, chick flicks and action movies, chick lit and lad lit, pornography and romance novels, soap operas and crime procedurals, guy video games and girl video games, blogs and 'zines—and, of course, advertising that is intricately connected to each of these formats."

As Andrea Press (2000: 28–9) observes, **feminist research** approaches the media from at least three, sometimes overlapping, dimensions. The first looks at "feminism, difference and identity" and "highlights the experiences of those who have remained unheard and gives voice to that which has remained unspoken." Here, analysis focuses on how media representation and social discourse override or frame out particular perspectives and voices. A second strand of research, "feminism and the public sphere," emphasizes the "role of the media in facilitating—or hindering—public debate," particularly in terms of "giving voice to those previously unheard, such as women, under-represented groups, and others whose ideas have not previously entered public debate." For instance, in the new media field, Shade (in Grossberg et al., 2006: 291) points out, "There are tensions in gender differences, whereby women are using the Internet to reinforce their private lives and men are using the Internet for engaging in the public sphere." The third dimension, "new technologies and the body," considers "broader questions about media, technology, and the relationship of both to the body" (Press, 2000: 29). Recent research has also focused on *cyberfeminism*, which, as Gajjala and Oh (2012: 1) point out, covers "how power plays not only in different locations online but also in institutions that shape the layout and experience of cyberspace."

At a more general level, contemporary feminist media scholarship examines how media consumption is woven into the fabric of everyday life, how media products and institutions are both shaped by and give form to particular perspectives and ideas on gender and sexuality, and how women and other social groups deploy media, along with other facets of their experience, to make meaning of their lives (see Gajjala and Oh, 2012; Sarikakis and Shade, 2008; Hermes, 2006). As Sawchuk (2014: 73) illustrates, feminism has proven itself over the years to be "not simply an extraneous add-on to the media agenda, but intrinsic to the study of communication." Moreover, as Shepherd points out, with its attention to the ways in which social relations spin unequal relations of power, feminism has also been key in helping develop other important critical perspectives on communication such as queer, disability, and post-colonial studies (see Cavalcante et al., 2017).

Bbernard/Shutterstock.

Reception analysis looks at the social setting in which audiences respond to the products of contemporary popular culture. The dynamics of power relations between males and females, parents and children, and older and younger siblings have been studied in relation to, for example, who has access to the remote control.

Reception Analysis

In the 1980s, cultural and feminist studies of the mass media increasingly looked at how audiences made sense of cultural products, how they interpreted what they read, saw, and heard. But it became apparent that to do this it was necessary to attend not simply to the product itself (the novel, the film, the TV drama) but also, more generally, to the context in which the consumption of the cultural product took place. **Reception analysis** thus takes into account the social setting in which audiences respond to the products of contemporary popular culture. In this way, it is somewhat similar to uses and gratification theory. However, rather than emphasizing what use or gratification an audience member gains from media exposure, reception analysis focuses on how he or she actively interprets what the media text has to offer and how media consumption is reintegrated into the personal dimensions of her or his life. As Gray (1999: 31) puts it, this work "place[s] media readings and use within complex webs of determinations, not only of the texts, but also those deeper structural determinants, such as class, gender, and . . . race and ethnicity. These studies have also shed light on the ways in which public and private discourses intersect and are lived out within the intimate and routine practices of everyday life."

Reception analysis has been of particular interest to feminist scholars in a number of ways. For instance, when US researcher Janice Radway studied American women readers of romantic fiction, she found that they emphasized how the activity of reading became a special, personal time when they left behind domestic chores and responsibilities to husbands and children, and created a time and space for themselves and their own pleasure. They saw it as a moment of self-affirmation (Radway, 1984). This discovery points to the importance of attending to what lies outside the cultural products themselves. The meaning of romance fiction for Radway's readers was something more than the form and content of the stories themselves. Instead, meaning was found in the ways that the act of reading resonated with other important elements of their lives.

In the same way that Radway examined romance reading, work was undertaken on how family members use radio, TV, newspapers, magazines, video players, and satellite dishes. It showed that these media can be used for a range of purposes that have little to do with their content (see Cavalcante et al, 2017). Here, the attention is directed toward what the audience brings to a viewing or decoding, the social context, and the act of viewing. Parents may watch a TV program with a child to nourish their relationship rather than to learn what the program is about. The dynamics of power relations between males and females, parents and children, and older and younger siblings have been studied in relation to, for instance, who has access to the remote control for the TV or who can record programs (Morley, 1986). In some families, and at some times, a switched-on television functions as a conversation stopper or mediator, rather than as a source of watched programming (see Bryce, 1987; Modleski, 1984)

Other researchers, such as Roger Silverstone (1981) and John Hartley (1987), have discussed how television provides the basis for symbolic participation in a national community or sometimes, as in the cases of Belgium, Switzerland, and Canada, an international linguistic community. Along similar lines, more recently, Garnage (2018) examines how soap operas have become a "shared cultural resource" in the lives of Sri Lankan women, while Al-Mahadin (2017) examines "the role sonic environments play in mediating constructs as diverse as national identity, class, religion, and ethnicity." Researchers are also exploring how social media are changing people's perception of themselves: on one hand, offering new avenues for identity formation; on the other, having the "potential to distort an individual's sense of self and sense of other people" (Thomas, 2016; see also Mathieu, 2015; Sullivan, 2013: 182).

Thus, from the perspective of reception analysis, an "audience" is not so much an identifiable

4.3

Fan Studies

By Steve Bailey

One important recent development in the study of media audiences has been the development of the distinct field of "fan studies" that emerged in the 1980s and '90s. Fan studies has roots in a number of earlier scholarly perspectives in the study of communication and culture, most notably work in the British cultural studies tradition. Scholars such as Paul Willis and Dick Hebdige became interested in the role that passionate attachments to forms of media culture played in the composition of a social identity and in the behaviour of individuals with such deep interests in particular performers, programs, and other cultural objects. Hebdige, for example, looked at the ways that subcultures formed around appreciation for certain styles of clothing or genres of music. Another important influence was the work of literary scholar Janice Radway, author of *Reading the Romance*, who studied avid female readers of romance novels, a genre considered to be of low quality and little interest by mainstream work in literary studies. The recognition that this mode of consuming mediated messages, required specific forms of research, and had distinct characteristics was then extended into a recognized field of fan studies. Part of this effort was designed to move the study of fandom away from one that views fans as pathological or stereotypically obsessive in their interests and studies them as manifestations of one segment of a larger audience community.

Tara Walton/Toronto Star via Getty Images.

Dressed as Stormtroopers from the *Star Wars* movies, a man and his son attend Fan Expo, a three-day conference for sci-fi, anime, and horror show lovers held in Toronto.

Scholars of media fandom, or "fanthropologists," as they are sometimes jokingly called, tend to rely on research methods associated with anthropology and qualitative sociological approaches, especially ethnography. They often study fans in natural social situations, such as concerts, fan conventions, or other social gatherings, and they tend to favour methods such as interviews and detailed questionnaires to gather data on fan behaviour. Increasingly, scholars of fandom have examined a range of "secondary texts" produced by fans, such as fan fiction, artwork inspired by a particular cultural object or performer, and other forms of cultural production. The crucial work in the development of fan studies was Henry Jenkins's 1992 book *Textual Poachers*, which explored these types of activities in considerable detail. The creative work of fans is analyzed to help understand how they relate to the objects of their interest and passion and to make better sense of the importance of fandom in the development of worldviews, forms of identity, and social behaviour. This area of fan research has become increasingly intertwined with scholarship examining "participatory culture," which involves the examination of a variety of forms of cultural consumption that involve productive activities on the part of consumers, such as recording comical "filk" songs that parody mainstream culture, or performing unauthorized modifications of commercial video games.

Most recently, scholars of media fan cultures have focused a great deal of attention on the impact of the internet on fan communities. The rise of virtual culture has allowed for the formation of large international fan communities connected through websites, email lists, and other forms of new media communication. This technological shift has greatly expanded the number of individuals who participate in some form of fan culture and has also allowed for the development of a wide range of cultural practices, such as the making and distribution of video and audio mash-ups of popular culture, works by fans.

Steve Bailey is author of *Media Audiences and Identity: Self-Construction in the Fan Experience*. New York: Palgrave Macmillan, 2005. Reproduced with permission of Palgrave Macmillan.

group transfixed on a particular text or program as it is a variable set of individuals, whose lives (and conceptions of the meaning of media consumption) are structured between media texts and the shifting dimensions and determinants of their own lives. In other words, from this perspective media are seen as one element in a larger set of institutions, technologies, and discourses that provide the means through which people live their lives.

As media become increasingly mobile, and both places and forms of reception increasingly diverse, it will be interesting to see how these shifting contexts of reception influence how we understand both media and our relationship to it.

Industry Audience Research

While academics have had their own reasons for studying mass media audiences, media institutions themselves have long been keenly interested in finding out what people read, listen to, and watch. This information has obvious economic value: the more precise the information they have about their audiences, the greater the possibilities to sell these audiences to advertisers. As the CRTC notes, it also uses such data to "assess the effectiveness of its policies by understanding the reach of programming across the country and across various demographics" (CRTC 2017). At the same time, as we shall see, using the information that users put into their platforms, digital media such as Facebook and Google have been able to develop user profiles that can seemingly be used to target advertising messages more efficiently than employing traditional audience research techniques. They are thus able to use that information to heavily undermine the income of broadcast media.

Traditionally, audience research concentrated on audience size: the bigger the audience for a television program, the more attractive it would be to advertisers. But since the 1970s, industry researchers have tried to provide more accurate information about what kinds of viewers are attracted to which programs. Such information can be particularly valuable. For instance, a program may not reach a mass prime-time audience, yet it may have a strong viewership among young, affluent professionals. That program may then command premium prices on advertisements—more than the ads on the program with the larger audience.

Audience attributes other than simple purchasing power can also be attractive to advertisers. For instance, for the makers of Barbie, an audience of prepubescent girls and their mothers is of great value. As Sullivan (2013: 98) notes, increasing pressure to target specific people has led to even more refined techniques for segmenting audiences, such as *psychographics* and *lifestyle measurements*. *Psychographics* "refers to the general association of personality or psychological traits with groups of consumers" (98). *Lifestyle measurements* "define a group of individuals according to their product and media consumption habits. . . . Individuals might be classified as 'frequent travelers,' [for example,] if they make more than four airline trips per year" (98).

Such segmentation has been given impetus by the explosion of new broadcast channels. (Targeting broadcast audiences with very specific demographics is called **narrowcasting**.) Over the last 30 years, the number of television channels available to Canadian audiences has mushroomed from less than 20 to hundreds. This has led to severe audience fragmentation as viewers have been scattered across this expanding television landscape; the increasing draw of the internet has also further fragmented the audience. In 1969, 35 per cent of the English-speaking television audience watched CBC, while 25 per cent watched CTV. By 2015–2016, the CBC share had fallen to 5.1 per cent, and CTV, Global, and other non-specialty channels garnered about 25 per cent of the viewing audience (CRTC, 2017). This increasingly fragmented audience has given rise to more innovative techniques for tracking and targeting potential customers.

As we discussed at the beginning of this chapter, the reality of fragmented audiences has put pressure on broadcast companies to find innovative ways to reach large numbers of people. This has led to concentration of media ownership as companies work to reach or re-aggregate audiences by owning a number of different television channels or media outlets. We will examine this phenomenon more closely in Chapter 9. But for now you should note that in Canada, audience fragmentation has also led to vertical integration among media corporations, as cable and satellite distributors have been purchasing television networks and specialty channels in an attempt to help distribute the cost of programming across different broadcast outlets. Similarly, the proliferation of mobile media has also motivated telecommunications companies to acquire broadcast properties, as they move to obtain content for the new mobile services they are offering.

Three concepts or measures are commonly used to gather data on how many people are watching or listening to particular programs:

1. **reach**: the number of audience members available during a particular program period;
2. **share**: the percentage of the audience *reach* who are watching a particular program during a specific time period; and
3. **viewing time**: the number of hours spent viewing during a day, week, or longer period of time.

Share is generally the most important statistic, as it describes what percentage of the available audience is tuned in to a particular program.

But while such ratings measure the number of people watching or listening, they don't provide information as to why people tune in to particular programs. As Savage (2014: 137) illustrates, this information is usually gathered through three methods: *surveys*, *focus groups*, and *program tests*. All three methods can be used either before or after programs have been broadcast.

Traditionally, media consumption was measured by means of diaries kept by audience members, in which people made notes about the TV or radio programs they followed. In 1993, BBM Canada (formerly the Bureau of Broadcast Measurement) introduced the people meter, an electronic device that sat on top of televisions and measured audience viewing habits. The meters showed that audience members were spending less time with media than they reported in the diaries. Because of this, ad rates had to be readjusted. In 2009, BBM introduced portable people meters that track audience members by recording inaudible codes embedded in broadcast programming.

While audience research measurement techniques for broadcast programming are growing more sophisticated, it is also becoming increasingly difficult to track people as they move between different media, particularly to online program distributors such as Netflix, YouTube, and Apple TV. Without such information, neither industry nor government agencies like the CRTC can rigorously measure or understand the impact these services are having on Canada's mediascape.

Some Limits of Industry Audience Research

Conducting traditional audience research that focuses on measuring the size and demographic character of viewer groups has its limitations, particularly when it comes to understanding the needs and desires of target viewerships. While it tells producers how successful they have been in reaching particular types of people, it offers little understanding of the ways media engage audiences with their social and political environments. True, their demographic characteristics may be known and their degree of attentiveness estimated, but because audience members are not conceived as citizens who might benefit from, or even require, certain information to help them make informed social and political decisions, the range of media content offered is limited. For instance, questions that industry audience research does not address in this regard include the following: *Do the media in general impart values that reflect the ideals of society and contribute to its improvement and survival? Do they adequately inform citizens about domestic and international affairs? Do they allow us to see our own achievements or to know about ourselves so that we understand how we can make a contribution to society?*

Such questions are important because the greater use that society and individuals make of the media, the greater are the media's responsibilities in informing people of the larger political, economic, social, and environmental forces that contextualize their lives. If audiences are seen only within limited frameworks (e.g., to be entertained but not enlightened), then the media's contribution to society is limited. Moreover, access to the media—particularly television—is increasingly costly, leaving many people with reduced access, particularly in terms of Canadian programming. As we illustrate in Chapter 8 with our discussion of the cultural industries, such questions are particularly relevant in Canada, where media have been traditionally viewed as performing important public functions. Reducing media to a simple calculus of the marketplace serves to undermine our knowledge and understanding of the many dimensions of public life, as well as our abilities to participate in it.

At the same time, as noted above, traditional forms of audience research that work to develop demographic profiles of audience members appear to be, at least in some cases, more expensive and less effective at targeting consumers than the information gathered by digital media such as Facebook and Google. Consequently, there is an ongoing shift of advertising revenue from traditional forms of media such as newspapers and television to digital media such as Facebook and Google (see Winseck, 2018).

The Shifting and Vanishing Audience: Opportunities and Risks

Because people today have more and more choice between different types of media and also find growing degrees of interactivity in these media, conceptions are changing of both media and audiences. As we have seen, television is becoming interactive, as game shows allow audiences to play along with on-stage contestants, and dramas provide apps that extend and develop characters and storylines. Audiences increasingly access sports programs from a range of devices. In some cases, they can even choose the camera angles they watch games from. And adding yet another dimension to the experience, social media sites like Facebook and Twitter provide venues for kibbitzing about particular plays, players, and statistics.

On the web, the distinction between producer and audience is particularly blurry now that it's commonplace for people to upload video and create blogs, podcasts, games, webcam sites, and other material for public consumption. With these interactive forms of media, the audience "vanishes," drawn up into the content itself. This is, of course, particularly true on social media such as Facebook, Instagram, and Twitter, where—except for the advertisements—the content is generally created by users. (While still a popular place to upload video, YouTube is looking increasingly like traditional television, as both individuals and large corporations stock the site with their own *channels*, complete with commercials and audience research that draws upon traditional forms of measuring broadcast audiences. See Box 4.5, "Monetizing the Web: Turning the Audience into Media Professionals.") This shift in the relationship between media producer and media audience member has caused some researchers to call non-professionals who create content for various media **prosumers**—meaning people who are both media producers and media consumers at the same time. As García-Galera and Valdivia (2014) illustrate, the opportunities to create and distribute media content afforded by contemporary digital media are much greater than those experienced by any previous generation.

At the same time, as noted in Chapter 1, the networked character of social media adds a whole new dimension to traditional conceptions of audience. Whereas, as McQuail (2010) noted earlier

4.4 The Audience Commodity

When Dallas Smythe wrote about the "**audience commodity**" in 1977, he was referring to the way audiences were packaged for sale to advertisers. His contention was that the time audiences spent watching television, reading newspapers, and consuming other media was, in reality, unpaid labour time and that it was this unpaid labour that media companies exploited when they sold audiences to advertisers.

Whether or not watching television, listening to the radio, or reading a newspaper could be counted as unpaid labour quickly became a hot topic of debate in critical media studies circles and continues to be a contentious issue today. With the rise of the internet and social media, however, Smythe's ideas have taken on new significance. On sites like Facebook, Twitter, Instagram, and Google, it is precisely the unpaid labour of people posting and searching for material that yields the information these companies sell to advertisers and other interested parties. Computer programs pore over these entries, looking for information on users' interests, hopes, and desires, which, in turn, is sold to advertisers, marketers, and almost anyone else who will pay for it. As a number of researchers have pointed out, users are performing unpaid labour in this way—labour that is directly translated into an information commodity that is sold to these companies' customers (see McGuigan and Manzerolle, 2014). And, as the Canadian Media Concentration Research Project (CMCRP) illustrates, Google and Facebook are increasingly successful in expediting this process of commodification, having captured nearly three-quarters of the $6.2 billion Canadian internet advertising market in 2017—up from two-thirds in 2016 (CMCRP, 2019).

iStockphoto/Petar Chernaev.

Because the posts you make on sites like Facebook and Twitter form the basis of information products they sell to advertisers and others, that activity can be seen as performing unpaid labour for those corporations.

in this chapter, historically the "mass audience" "lacked self-awareness or self-identity and was incapable of acting together in an organized way to secure objectives." Networked through social media, audience members can now communicate with each other. While the impacts of this shifting relationship are still being worked out, one of the most striking features of the transformation of the audience from a passive content receiver to an active content creator is how the business models of many of these media companies depend on the material that audiences create. As Cohen (2008: 8) puts it, "the business models of Web 2.0 ventures depend on the performance of free labour; without it there would be no content and therefore no profit." Indeed, much of the information or content that one puts into the web—whether a Facebook post, a Google search, or pictures of one's favourite things—is what drives these businesses. Computer programs pore over these entries, developing profiles of peoples' interests, hopes, and desires, which, in turn, are sold to advertisers, marketers, and almost anyone else who will pay for such information.

For instance, based upon users' posts on Facebook, the organization sells a service called "lookalike audiences," which allows companies or other organizations to locate people who have similar characteristics to their existing customers, audiences, or other groups of people they want to reach or know about. As Facebook notes, "A Lookalike Audience is a way to reach new people who are likely to be interested in your business because they're similar to your best existing customers" (Facebook, 2018).

Users, however, have little or no control over how the information they post to the internet is used, as one woman found out when she became

4.5

Monetizing the Web: Turning the Audience into Media Professionals

People spend over a billion hours each day watching YouTube videos. At the same time, 500 hours of video are uploaded each minute for a total of 82.2 years of video uploaded a day (Hale, 2019)

But while YouTube is still a favourite place for people to upload videos they have made of their pets or antics with their friends and family, it is also becoming increasingly commercialized. Following the opening of a series of new studios for creators in places like Los Angeles, London, Tokyo, and Toronto in recent years, one estimate is that the platform paid out $5 billion in advertising to creator/contributors in 2015 (Ingham, 2016). And now the company appears to be moving to focus attention on its more popular creators.

In an effort to try to rein in extremist and offensive content, the company is raising the bar on which creators will qualify for advertising sales. In the process, critics argue, the platform may lose many of its contributors. As noted in *Wired*, the new policy

> discourages everyone else from building a channel from the ground up, subscriber by subscriber, week by week, the way so many original YouTubers did," says Matt Wallace, a writer and YouTuber with a modest audience. . . . If YouTube loses its small, upcoming creators, the site's community will inherently change. It will likely become more commercialized; filled with popular creators diligently adhering to advertiser guidelines, brands, and media companies. "To me," says Wallace, "that all signals an end to the artistic, cultural, and sociopolitical merit YouTubers worked so hard to establish, back when the popular perception of YouTube was that it was a website filled with cat memes."
>
> (Matsakis, 2018)

pregnant and began searching for information on babies. She soon found herself confronted by pop-up ads on her computer from companies that wanted to sell her baby clothes, toys, and other things related to child-rearing. But when she suffered a miscarriage and lost the baby, the ads didn't stop and became a cruel reminder of what had happened to her (Anderssen, 2014). As we discuss in Chapter 6, information given up on the internet can also be used for more nefarious purposes, as insurance companies, employers, and law-enforcement agencies scour information scraped from the internet for clues that individuals may pose threats to profitability or public safety. Years ago, being an anonymous member of the mass audience may have seemed boring because nobody was paying any attention to you, but drawing attention as an active audience member on the internet today comes with risks.

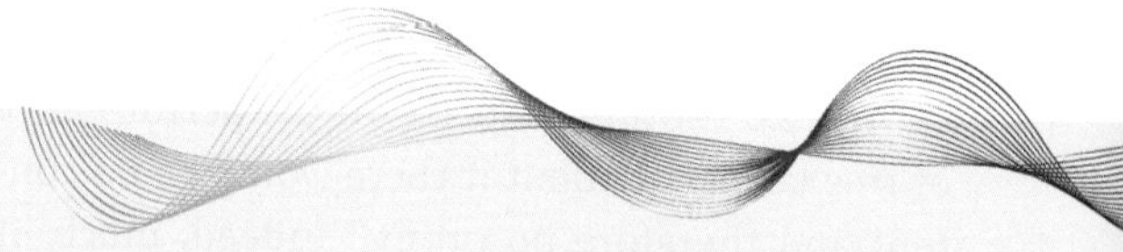

SUMMARY

The interaction between media and audiences is a dynamic interaction in which audience members actively and selectively interpret media content based on frameworks of understanding they bring to that content. Such a perspective provides a means for explaining how media, audiences, and culture interact in a non-deterministic fashion and, particularly, how audiences engage with media.

Generally, academic research on audiences is framed by precepts and ideas drawn from larger social theories. The theoretical approaches reviewed in this chapter reflect this orientation. Set in the context of theories of mass society, effects research highlights the direct impact of the media on the behaviour of audience members. Uses and gratification research focuses on what audience members tend to do with media content. Marxist research and the Frankfurt School draw attention to how the production of media and cultural products influences the ways in which they represent the world and the relations of power they help engender. Cultural studies accents the agency of individuals and the multiplicity of social factors that come to bear on how audiences interpret media and incorporate them into their lives. Feminist research brings forward the gendered nature of narratives and, like cultural studies, explores how the audience member is positioned by the narrative. And against the backdrop of contemporary social theories that accent human agency, reception analysis tends to consider the many ways media and media content are woven into the lives of audience members. Industry research largely generates quantitative measures on the nature of audiences, their size, age, location, education, family income, use of certain products, use of leisure time, and so on.

All these approaches to the audience offer information and insight for explaining and understanding, but not predicting, the relationships between media and audiences, which depend not only on what audience members bring to the text, but also on the culturally specific character of that material.

Understanding internet users and usage is a growing area of inquiry. It is clear that digital communication technologies and the growing convergence between broadcasting and the web are having dramatic impacts on how audiences are constructed, as well as on the role of media in forms of communication and citizenship. In this context, the role and purposes of digital media are ongoing sites of struggle among industry, audiences, public-interest groups, and policy-makers How this struggle will play out remains to be seen.

KEY TERMS

agenda-setting function, p. 93
audience commodity, p. 108
audience fragmentation, p. 90
Birmingham School, p. 96
British cultural studies, p. 96
cultivation analysis, p. 93
demographic, p. 87
effects, p. 92
feminist research, p. 102
Frankfurt School, p. 95
functionalist, p. 94
ideology, p. 97
narrowcasting, p. 105
position, p. 97
primary definers, p. 98
prosumers, p. 107
reach, p. 106
reception analysis, p. 103
share, p. 106
uses and gratification research (U&G), p. 94
viewing time, p. 106

RELATED WEBSITES

Numeris: en.numeris.ca
Formerly BBM, this is the website for the largest broadcast audience research company in Canada.

Cultural Theory: British Cultural Studies: www.youtube.com/watch?v=zyUYG1J3tKI
This short lecture by Professor Ron Strickland of Illinois State University provides a good introduction to British cultural studies.

The Frankfurt School: www.marxists.org/subject/frankfurt-school/index.htm
This website provides a history of the Frankfurt School and discusses some contemporary theorists carrying on the school's legacy. See particularly the entries for Theodor Adorno and Max Horkheimer.

Vividata: www.vividata.ca
A not-for-profit organization representing the interests of Canadian publishers, advertising agencies, and advertisers, this company helps facilitate advertising sales for magazines and newspapers through surveying audiences for these media across the country. As their website states, "Vividata surveys over 40,000 Canadians, aged 14+, annually to capture their news and magazine readership." Visit their website to get a better understanding of how they accomplish this task.

FURTHER READINGS

Barker, Chris, and Emma A. Jane. 2016. *Cultural Studies: Theory and Practice.* 5th ed. Thousand Oaks, CA: Sage.

Cavalcante, Andre, Andrea Press, and Katherine Sender. 2017. "Feminist reception studies in a post-audience age: returning to audiences and everyday life." In *Feminist Media Studies,* vol. 17, issue 1, pp. 1–13. The lead essay in a special edition of the journal that examines contemporary feminist audience studies.

Napoli, Philip. 2011. *Audience Evolution*. New York: Columbia University Press. A detailed analysis of the shifting nature of audiences.

Radway, Janice. 1984. *Reading the Romance*. Chapel Hill, NC: University of North Carolina Press. Radway's book is a classic analysis of how women readers use romantic fiction, and demonstrates the contribution scholars can make to understanding the interaction between the media and people's lives.

Savage, Philip. 2014. "Audiences are key." In *Mediascapes: New Patterns in Canadian Communication*, 4th ed. Edited by Leslie Regan Shade. Don Mills, ON: Nelson, 127–49.

Sullivan, John L. 2013. *Media Audiences: Effects, Users, Institutions, and Power*. Thousand Oaks, CA: Sage. A good introduction to the study of audiences.

STUDY QUESTIONS

1. Describe how each of these perspectives approaches the audience, in fewer than 50 words:
   - effects research
   - Frankfurt School
   - cultural studies
   - feminist studies
2. "Some reception studies (e.g., Radway, 1984) appear to describe the interaction between audiences and content as secondary to the tangential actions surrounding the interpretation of content. The act of reading counts more than what the person derives from the content itself." Comment on this observation in relation to other methods of analysis.
3. Which of the perspectives on audiences would you use for writing an essay about the role of television in family life? Why?
4. Which of the perspectives on audiences corresponds most closely to your own views, and why?
5. Are you concerned about social media companies monitoring your activities on their sites? Why or why not? Discuss.

5

Advertising and Promotional Culture

Advertising is capitalism's way of saying "I love you" to itself.
—*Michael Schudson*

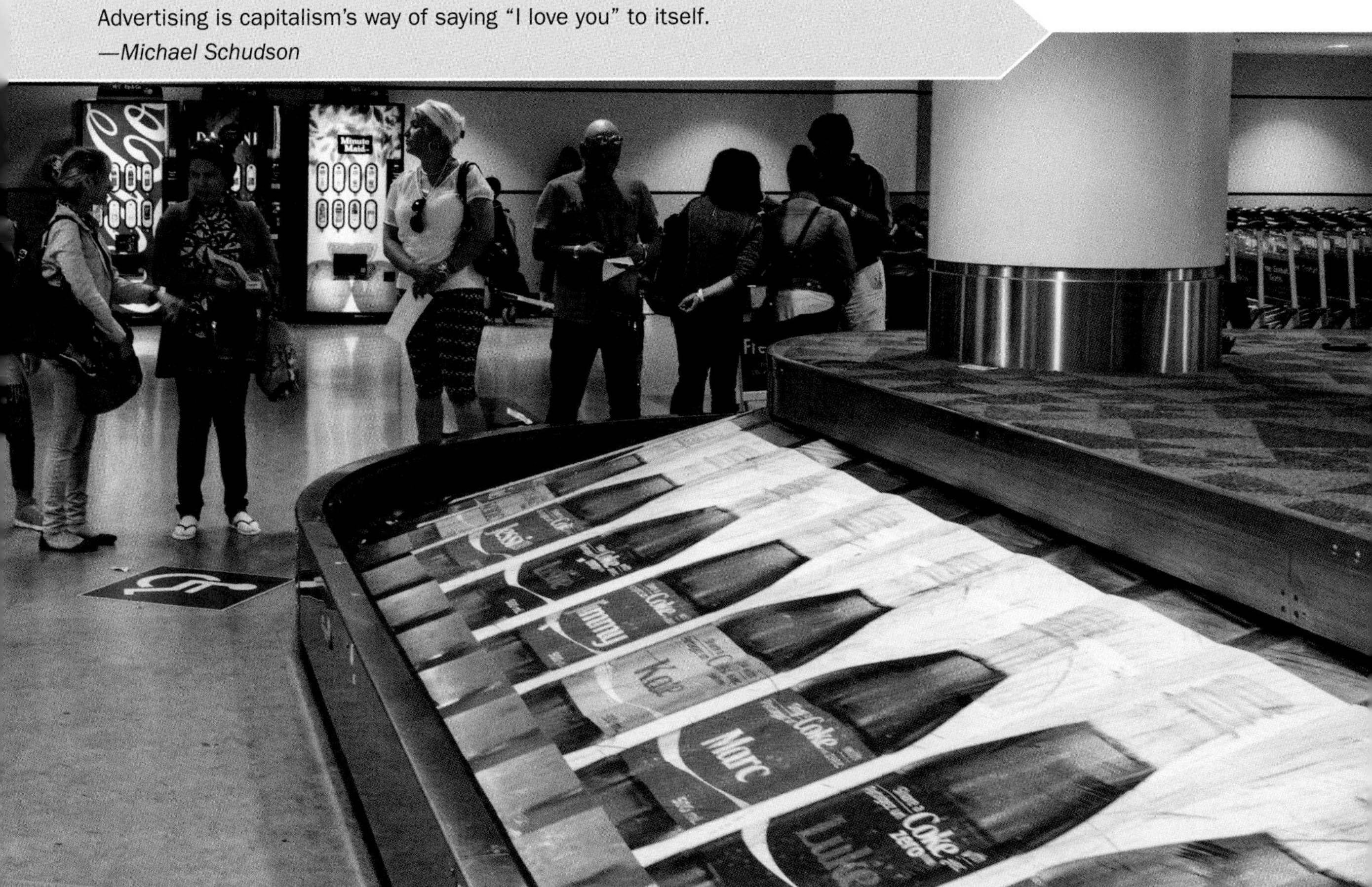

Torontonian / Alamy Stock Photo

Opening Questions

- How are advertising and promotion a cultural force?
- What theoretical perspectives are used to study and understand the relationships between advertising and promotion and the media?
- How is advertising a form of ideology?
- How do advertising and promotion change in digital media?
- What are some of the ways that the media functions as a system to deliver audiences to advertisers?

Introduction

In this chapter we examine how advertising and promotional culture are deeply tied to the workings of both our economy and our culture. In today's global marketplace, with many transnational corporations such as Nike, Disney, and McDonald's, advertising is central to how capitalism functions—not just as an economic system, but as a cultural force that persuades us to participate in the cycles of consumption. The inner workings of advertising and promotion are constantly shifting and changing as capitalism takes on new forms, as new technologies are developed, and as corporations take up new strategies of engagement. Advertising and promotion are not static entities, but are in constant flux. What was true at the time of writing this chapter may have changed by the time you read it. The chapter concludes with questions on the ecological impacts of advertising and promotional culture.

What is Advertising and Promotional Culture?

It is hard to picture our world without thinking about all of the spaces and places in which we encounter advertising. Ads are on the sides of buses that pass us on the streets; they are on billboards that loom over us on the highways; they take up the first 10 minutes of every movie we see in theatres; they pop up in our social media feeds; we see them on the backs of the doors when we sit in public bathroom stalls; and sometimes athletes even temporarily tattoo their bodies with ads that will reach audiences while they are under the camera's gaze. From the massive advertisements that wrap entire streetcars to the small ads that appear on stickers on bananas, advertisements surround us.

Advertisements are ubiquitous in our society and dominate a huge amount of public space. Advertising has crept into spaces well beyond the traditional forms of media. For example, public buildings are named after corporate brands. Think of Rogers Place in Edmonton and the Bell MTS Place in Winnipeg. Festivals like the TD Toronto Jazz Festival are essentially **branded** events, and street corners have become places of "branded experiences," where brand ambassadors dole out free samples of new products. Advertising has colonized much of our public space. It takes over places such as subway stations or skylines and fills them with corporate messages. Over the past century, advertising has become a powerful cultural force.

Advertising is commonly understood to mean advertisements. The term **advertising** refers to a type of message or speech with the underlying goal of promoting a specific product. It is a system of promotional messaging designed for and brought to the attention of the people that advertisers want to reach, with the goal of increasing sales. To gain this attention, companies pay to place the advertisements in some sort of media, such as a television program, a page in a newspaper, the pre-roll of an online video, or a sponsored search result.

Torontonian/Alamy Stock Photo.

Advertising takes over many public spaces and places, like this advertising wrap of a streetcar in Toronto.

Advertising as a System of Industries

But there is more to advertising than just advertisements. Advertising consists of a whole system of industries that work with one another. First and foremost, there are the brands and companies that want to promote their products: these are the advertisers. But there are many more industries that participate in the promotion of products. Think about all of the cultural workers involved in selling a simple bottle of Coca-Cola. There are the packaging designers who design the bottle, the client brand teams who define the product and guide the brand, the agencies who develop the communications and brand identity, the merchandisers who place it in the stores, social media managers who are the voice of the brand online, market researchers who study Coca-Cola's current and future consumers, and media companies who deliver an audience to watch the company's ads.

It is also easy to think of products and brands—the Tim Hortons, Coca-Colas, and McDonald's of the world—as the only advertisers. But there are other entities that are also advertisers. Governments advertise a range of items, from policy changes to public service announcements (PSAs). Public interest groups, such as the World Wildlife Fund (WWF) or Mothers Against Drunk Driving (MADD), also advertise their social messages. Political parties advertise their political ideas and seek your vote. And third-party advertisers, like the Canadian Association of Petroleum Producers (CAPP), advocate for support on particular issues, such as expanding the fossil fuels industry.

Advertising is not a monolithic institution. Instead, it is a complex system of businesses, institutional structures, and agencies that work toward a common goal of the promotion of specific goods or services. Because of this complexity, the advertising industry is bigger than simply the creation and placement of ads. The logic and rhetoric of advertising have crept into many other areas of society and culture. Branding, for instance, has moved beyond the confines of simply advertisers communicating a company identity and has extended to other areas of life—universities, countries, or even our own selfhoods can all have branded identities. The boundaries between media content and advertising have in many ways collapsed. It is no longer clear—with product placement, advertorials, native advertising, and social media—where the media content stops and advertising starts. Furthermore, **public relations** now extend into virtually every corporate, public, private, or governmental enterprise. It no longer works to call all of these activities *advertising*; instead, we add the term **promotional culture** as way of articulating how the boundaries between advertising, marketing, promotion, the media, and public relations are blurring and destabilizing.

Advertising as a Form of Discourse

Advertising is a form of **discourse** (see Chapter 3 for more on discourse). It is a means of messaging with the goal of promotion. When something like advertising is called *discourse*, it refers to a system of messaging that articulates thoughts, ideas, beliefs, and practices that shape the way we as society come to understand our world. It is a system of messaging that advocates for the consumption of goods and services. A century ago, in North America and Western Europe, religious discourse touched the lives of most citizens through church sermons, political oratories, the forms of scholarship promoted in schools, the types of stories told, and the advice and logics of family elders. Religious rhetoric was ubiquitous and held moral authority. But today it is promotional discourse that holds this power. Over the course of the last century, advertising has become the dominant and most privileged form of discourse. For example, advertising is central to how our media systems (including social media) function. Most media depend on advertising revenue, so promotional messages are often woven into the content of the media. Furthermore, promotional culture is ubiquitous in our daily landscape (we even wear clothing covered in logos), and as a society we have come to expect and even enjoy advertising messages in our everyday lives.

5.1 Word of Mouth Marketing

Advertisers are always looking for new ways to promote their brands or products for the cheapest cost. "Word of mouth" advertising, the idea that customers tell their friends and colleagues about a product, has a long history. In the early twentieth century, advertisements tried to encourage testimonials and endorsements. Packard Motors (an auto manufacturer in the 1930s) used the slogan "Ask the man who owns one."

Things escalated in the 1970s when a psychologist named George Silverman noticed that in focus groups with physicians for new pharmaceutical products, skeptical doctors would change their minds if encouraged by a colleague who has had a good experience with a drug. Silverman pioneered Word of Mouth Marketing (WOMM) by developing advertising campaigns that encouraged peer networking as part of the promotion. Part of the reason that advertisers like word of mouth is that it is cheap, it costs little to have others tout the values of a product, but it also is considered more reliable. People trust recommendations more when they are given by someone in their personal network then by an advertising campaign or a celebrity. There is even a Word of Mouth Marketing Association (WOMMA), started in 2004.

With the advent of social media, word of mouth marketing has exploded as a marketing strategy and it forms a key component of many advertising campaigns. Hype, buzz, and viral are really terms that refer to word of mouth marketing, implying that people are talking about, sharing, liking, and promoting something.

Many of us make decisions based on the recommendation of our online networks (I just went to a restaurant because my friend posted it on Twitter). With social media it is much easier for businesses to encourage people to promote their products through WOMM. Pinterest, for example, went from 3,000 followers in 2010 to over 200 million in 2018. One of the strategies the company used was the "Pin It Forward" campaign, which encouraged users to invite their friends to the site.

Of course, as companies note, it is also easy to share negative campaigns. The example of musician Dave Carroll, whose guitar was broken by United Airlines, is a good one here. After not receiving compensation for the broken guitar, Carroll created a music video for YouTube called "United Breaks Guitars." It received over 17 million views, went viral, and caused United Airline stock to fall dramatically.

Companies encourage and try to stimulate people to talk about their products or brands positively. Perhaps one of the most successful media and entertainment brands (intellectual properties, or IPS) to do this is the *Harry Potter* (HP) franchise. Its massive success (estimated to be worth $25 billion) has largely been due to its fans promoting the franchise. There was very little formal advertising, given the size of the franchise's worth. There are so many aspects to HP word of mouth; many of them seem to be organic and not a direct campaign. For example, think of a young girl holding a Harry Potter–themed birthday party. By the time she blows out the candles on her "Sorting Hat" cake, she has educated her friends on the Harry Potter brand. Before the party, a few of her friends might have seen a movie, or maybe even read a book, but by the end of the party they have all made wands, identified their house, and know their patronus. They are now all educated in the HP franchise.

The themed birthday party is worth more to IPS than simply the merchandise of the party; it becomes a moment of brand awareness. Children's media and entertainment companies know this. In 2017, a market research company for the industry declared to an audience of close to 400 industry members, "Get your superfans to evangelize your IP, they do the work for free," and gave the example of the birthday party.

And it is not just children. Brands such as Nike and Red Bull actively recruit student brand ambassadors to subtly promote products. Who knows? Maybe the person sitting next to you right now, who is telling you how great their new shoes are, is really a brand ambassador paid to seed word of mouth marketing campaigns.

Advertising and promotion have also infiltrated many non-market spaces. One only has to think of the creep of corporations sponsoring or subsidizing elementary school activities and events to appreciate how commercial messaging has penetrated supposedly non-commercial spaces.

As a privileged form of discourse, advertising is subject to a series of laws, codes, and agencies that protect companies' rights to advertise, such as components of the Canadian *Broadcasting Act*, the Canadian Code of Advertising Standards, and the industry lobby group **Advertising Standards Canada**. Throughout this chapter, this idea of advertising as a privileged form of discourse will be explored in much more depth.

Advertising in Modern Culture

Advertising is an integral component of modern culture. It creates a vast system of symbols and ideas that reflect and shape our cultural values and understandings. Its unsurpassed communicative powers circulate and recirculate cultural meanings, symbols, and references. What this means is that advertising takes meaning from culture, reinscribes it with new meanings, and circulates it back through culture.

Take, for example, an advertising icon like the Marlboro Man, who has been at the centre of the Marlboro advertising campaign since 1955. He is an archetypal figure, drawn from American history. The images of the Marlboro Man enjoying a well-earned cigarette after a day's hard work of riding horses and conquering the American prairie has shaped how we understand such notions as masculinity, what constitutes work, our relationship to nature, and, of course, the erasure of indigenous peoples from the American prairie. Such ideas are circulated, in part, by the Marlboro Man and are rearticulated in popular culture. Tim Hortons provides another example of circulated meanings. The company's advertisements have long articulated a nostalgic view of Canada tied to ice, winter, and rural community. Even though these images are exclusionary—as only certain types of people fit into them—they have still contributed to how we think about Canada.

Economic and Cultural Impacts

The impact of advertising in our contemporary culture is broad and wide reaching. To start, we can think about two specific impacts of advertising: economic and cultural. The complexity of these two impacts was perhaps best summed up by American sociologist Philip Slater (1970: 165) in the 1970s:

> Our economy is based on spending billions to persuade people that happiness is buying things and then insisting that the only way to have a viable economy is to make things for people to buy so they'll have jobs and get enough money to buy things.

Slater's quote reveals the influence of advertising on both the economy (viable economy, creating jobs) and culture (happiness can be found in buying things). Of course, the integration of economics and culture is much more complex than Slater's quote suggests. Throughout this chapter we will further explore this economic and cultural entanglement in advertising.

Advertising and the Economy

Advertising is a fundamental component of our economic systems and structures. It is at the core of contemporary capitalism and has profound significance in our market-based consumer economy. It animates much of the economy by creating consumer awareness and demand for products and services. Advertising lies at the very foundation of the commercial mass media, financing the production and distribution of most information and entertainment.

Advertising is a large component of the global economy. It has been estimated that global advertising spending in 2018 was US$534.8 billion. North America is the largest regional market, followed by Asia Pacific and Western Europe. Some of the largest advertising companies in the world have thousands of employees worldwide. London-based WPP Group owns some of the largest marketing companies in the world, including Ogilvy &

Mather and J. Walter Thompson (now Wunderman Thompson), with over 205,000 employees in 2016, while Omnicom Group (BBDO Worldwide, DDB Worldwide, and TBWA) has over 75,000 employees (worldatlas.com). Most of Canada's biggest advertising agencies, such as Leo Burnett, BBDO, and Publicis, are owned by international conglomerates. And these are just the advertising agencies. This does not include all of the other companies and industries that are a part of the wider industries of promotional culture, such as the in-house marketing teams of brands, public relations companies, and market research companies.

Statistics like these illustrate how big a global industry advertising is, and how central it is to the economy. Nor do these statistics include those companies that work in the media, which is an essential component of the advertising industry. It is easy to overlook how advertising works as part of the media system. There are many ways to finance a media enterprise such as a magazine, a radio station, a television station, or a YouTube channel. They include being funded by government/taxpayers (e.g., CBC Radio), being paid for solely through subscriptions, tickets, or purchases (e.g., books, video games, or concerts), and a system where the bulk is paid by advertisers who direct the audience's attention to sponsored content and, more particularly, to the advertising messages that content includes.

While this may seem simple on the surface, let's pull apart what is really happening here. Simply put, media companies produce content that audience members watch, listen to, read, or click on. The advertiser pays for a small slice of this attention with a surcharge paid on consumer products (the cost of ads is built into the cost of products). In this system, advertising has become the central means for financing much of the media. Since it is the advertisers that, in effect, "write the cheques" for the media, the media create content that attracts audiences and also appeals to advertisers. Advertisers like it when the audience is in a "buying mood" at the moment when the show (story or column) flips to the advertisement.

It is important not to confuse advertising spots with free speech. Media companies control the messages in the advertising spots. Even if one has the money to buy the advertising spot, media companies will not sell it if the advertisement is deemed to be antithetical to the media company's business model of creating a nice, safe, pleasing space for advertisers to place their messages. Canadian media activist group **Adbusters** experienced this in the early 2000s when it tried to buy advertising space for political purposes, such as environmental advertising campaigns with messages telling consumers not to buy cars because of their high ecological footprints. Media companies such as CTV, Global, ABC, MTV, and Fox refused to sell them space, citing concerns that the ads didn't fit their business models. One company even stated, "Your spots are counterproductive to what we do. We sell advertising." This prompted Adbusters co-founder Kalle Lasn to state, "In a totalitarian system, you aren't allowed to talk back to the government; in the capitalist system, you can't talk back to the sponsor." The ideological power of promotional culture is evident here. One can question how much things have changed in the digital mediascape. Are there possibilities to talk back to corporations?

At the core of its business model, the media's main role is not to create or disseminate content but to deliver audiences to advertisers. The product of the media industry is the audience. In effect, selling an audience is the core of the media's business model. When Canadian economist Dallas Smythe wrote about the "audience commodity" in 1977, he was referring to the way that audiences were packaged for sale to advertisers (see Chapter 3 for more on Smythe's work). His contention was that the time audiences spent watching television, reading newspapers, and consuming other media was, in reality, time that was sold. When a person's time is sold, we call that *work* or *labour*. What Smythe was arguing was that audiences perform unpaid labour time that media companies exploit when they sell audiences to advertisers. Smythe's work was instrumental in understanding how media industries are productive for capitalism and bound up in the processes of commodification.

Sut Jhally (1987) built upon Smythe's work and suggested that the living room was a factory, arguing that the labour of the audience sitting in their living rooms watching television is sold. Each viewer sells 8 minutes of every 30 minutes of their time to advertisers (following standard advertising spots on TV), assuming of course that viewers do not change the channel during a commercial break. Jhally argues that instead of thinking about what television and other media forms deliver to the home, we must think about what they extract from the home. They extract profits made from audience members' time, particularly those audience members who have the means and desires to buy particular products.

With the rise of the internet and social media, however, Smythe and Jhally's ideas have taken on new significance. On sites like Facebook, Twitter, Pinterest, and Google, it is precisely the unpaid labour of people posting and searching for material that yields the information these companies sell to advertisers and other interested parties. Digital platforms pore over these entries, looking for information on these users' interests, hopes, and desires, which in turn is sold to advertisers, marketers, and almost anyone else who will pay for it. As a number of researchers have pointed out, users are performing unpaid labour in this way—labour that is directly translated into an information commodity that is sold to these companies' customers (see McGuigan and Manzerolle, 2014).

One of these researchers is Italian theorist Tiziana Terranova, who has suggested that in the digital economy online users (no longer called an audience) perform the creative labour that becomes the content of the internet. This is not employed labour, but work freely given to companies. In the digital economy "knowledge is inherently collective," Terranova argues, but "selectively compensated" (2012: 41). Most of us who create content online fail to get financially compensated for that time even though companies are making profits from our creation of content. Take Facebook, for example, which makes money from selling our personal data to advertisers, who can precisely target us with their advertising campaigns. Lee McGuigan (2019) notes how today there are many scholars in Canada whose work is heavily influenced by Smythe's theory on the commodification of media. These scholars are concerned with issues such as data mining, how the work of digital journalists is shifting away from traditional forms of employment, and how data controls market process. Work by people such as Elmer (2003), Cohen (2008), and Zwick and Knott (2009) reveals the complex circuitries of advertising in the media marketplace.

Advertising and Culture

Advertising is deeply tied to our culture. It is an ideological system of meaning-making that, as a cultural power, often shapes, informs, reflects, and moulds our views on social issues. Advertising is deeply woven into contemporary culture. The Marlboro Man, discussed in the previous section, is a good example of this. Not only is he an icon used to sell cigarettes, but the image of a lone cowboy has also become part of our cultural imagination. Raymond Williams has argued that advertising is the official art of modern capitalist society. Advertising and promotional culture takes up most of our cultural landscape. It is what we see in the streets, it shapes what creative content we consume in our free time, it is at the core of the stories we tell about ourselves, and it commands the services of a large body of creative workers (writers, designers, artists, filmmakers, etc.). In the same way that the Renaissance was defined and shaped by great artists like Leonardo da Vinci or Michelangelo, the creative outputs of advertising reflect and define this contemporary moment.

In an essay entitled "Advertising: The Magic System," Williams (1980) argues that advertising is a system of magic. He calls it a "system of magical inducements and satisfaction, functionally very similar to magical systems in simpler societies, but rather strangely coexistent with a highly developed scientific technology" (175). The magic of advertising is that it promises to meet non-material needs like fun, love, happiness, and health. The story told in an advertisement for tires, for example, is not that tires are wheels that go on a car, but instead that the right tires ensure the protection of one's family from tragedy. The advertisement is selling a story of family and love, of safety and security, and assuming that the targeted reader is male, a story of fatherly obligations and masculinity.

Advertising tells stories and in doing so responds to and shapes the way we see things. The strategic work of advertising is based on constant surveillance of our changing culture. Trends, fashion, cultural values, social attitudes, and individual behaviours are all monitored and scrutinized by market intelligence and fed back to the industry in the form of market data. This data is used by the industry to shape promotional messaging and new advertising campaigns. This system keeps the industry flexible and dynamic, as it is able to quickly respond to societal shifts and changes. Advertising is a constitutive part of the social change and cultural transformations that have occurred in the past century.

A good example of advertising's role in cultural transformations is the 2018 Nike campaign featuring Colin Kaepernick, the famed former NFL quarterback who protested the treatment of Black Americans and police brutality by taking a knee during the NFL national anthems, sparking controversy nationwide. The campaign was a reincarnation of Nike's classic "Just Do It" campaign with the tagline, "Believe in something. Even if it means sacrificing everything." Nike's decision to use Kaepernick as its spokesperson would not have been made lightly. The company would have consulted reams of data and conducted focus groups before making such a choice. Nike's Kaepernick campaign has been praised by some for taking on the issue of racial relations and for legitimizing protest against racialized police brutality, but others have criticized the campaign, suggesting that the ad's vague reference to "believe in something" dilutes Kaepernick's revolutionary messaging of anti-Black racism, as "something" could easily be anything. The "something," it is argued, could be applied to racist beliefs, as well. While the actual impact of the campaign is debated by scholars, it has contributed to how we understand Kaepernick, his protest, social conversations on race, and potential ways to address systemic anti-Black racism. The campaign could either be a part of erasing the revolutionary potential of Kaepernick's protest and Black Lives Matter or it will strengthen these debates and bring more awareness and understanding to racism and police brutality. Either way, the Kaepernick campaign is not separate from, or simply a response to, cultural change, but rather plays a constitutive role in social transformation.

Nike's decision to use Kaepernick was not simply an altruistic agenda of wanting to be part of social change.

Richard Levine / Alamy Stock Photo.

Nike's advertisement featuring Colin Kaepernick is displayed in New York City, with its tagline "Believe in something, even if it means sacrificing everything."

The company's goal is to ultimately move more Nike product, both in the United States and globally, where Kaepernick is recognized as a hero. Nike sales increased an estimated 31 per cent after the campaign was first revealed (Gleeson, 2018). The controversial campaign yielded a huge surge of Nike followers on Instagram and likes on its Facebook and Twitter pages—an estimated US$43 million in media exposure in the first 24 hours (Novy-Williams, 2018). While the campaign strengthens Nike's brand as a company at the forefront of cultural revolution, cultural critics like Naomi Klein have been skeptical of the long history of Nike in "aggressively mining" young Black men as a source of borrowed meaning and identity (2000: 73).

The cultural impacts of advertising and promotional culture can be profound. Messages such as those in the Kaepernick "Just Do It" campaign are not haphazard but highly controlled. While the numbers are not available publicly, Nike clearly spent millions of dollars on the campaign.

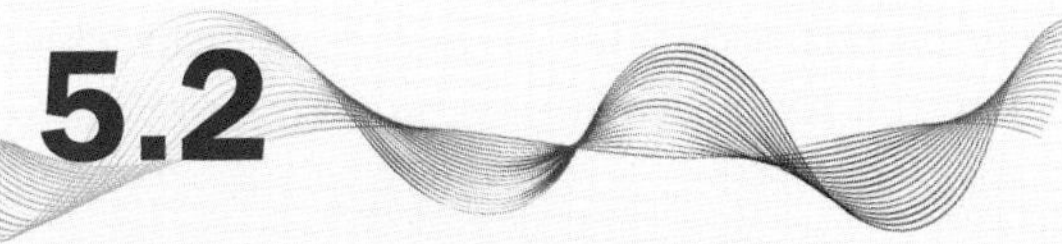

Identity Politics

By Kisha McPherson

Identity politics is a hot-button topic in media and popular culture. It is not surprising that much of the discourse on identity politics has been generated within contemporary media, as identity and its relationship to power within any society is often constructed through and within media forums.

In broad terms, identity politics refers to the process and positions that people assume based on their race, sexuality, ethnicity, religion, etc., rather than on issues based on broader, non-specific policies. Many academic fields such as women's studies, disability studies, and race and ethnic studies emerged out of identity politics. Identity politics illuminates the need for separate and distinct scholarship focused on aspects of identity that broader academic fields fail to address.

Many of the concerns surrounding identity are based on whether or not claims made by specific groups about their experiences are valid, and, if they are, who has the right to speak on or make claims about specific identities. We are regularly confronted with issues related to race, gender, sexuality, and ability, among other identity classifications. Identity politics presents us with complicated questions: Who has the right to speak on or make claims about specific identities? Do you have to identify as Black to speak on or about a Black person's lived experience? Must a person be female to make arguments for or against abortion, and what is acceptable for the female body? All of our identities have direct relationships with power within our society, and power is the foundation of politics and identity.

My research explores the voices and concerns of Black girls in Canada. Identity politics, as it is described here, is a consistent theme in the narratives and accounts that relate to the Black youth experience in the Greater Toronto Area (GTA). Thinking more about aspects of identity that often construct the experience of being Black, for example, there are debates on who has the right to participate in conversations about race and engage in Black cultural expression.

A "durag" is a hair maintenance product that was invented to help create waves in Black hair and keep it neat. Black cultural production is extremely popular in urban spaces like the GTA, and this often blurs the lines between what has a specific purpose for Black people, and what is just fashionable and cool. This also creates a tension that is related to identity politics because Black people lack the level of power that their cultural production creates within the urban spaces and broader society. Today, durags are commonly worn by Black people. However, Black people who wear durags are often stereotyped as "thugs" or "ghetto," racialized labels that do not have the same political consequences on the lives of non-Black people wearing durags.

This is the story of identity politics. As many argue for an inclusive, equitable society in which identity politics is not necessary, the example of the durags, who can and should wear them, also provides us with an example of how the politics of identity affects the lived experiences of people.

There would have been a vast contingent of creative labourers designing the images and honing the messages in order to convey the ad's exact meaning, and there would have been extensive market research into how the campaign is read by audiences.

This is not to suggest something so simplistic as advertising manipulates or has direct effects on consumers (see Chapter 4 for more on the effects of the media). Despite the company's best efforts, Nike cannot control the way people respond to the campaign, or the way the campaign is understood by the public. Assuming that advertising has such manipulative power fails to address the complicated ways in which we make meaning. Instead, advertising should be understood as part of the complex circuitry of cultural meaning-making. As part of this circuitry, advertising influences, shapes, reflects on, and responds to the ways in which we understand aspects of identity, such as gender, race, ethnicity, sexuality, and age. It also shapes how we make meaning of multiple aspects of our world, such as nature, science, family, the body, countries and nations, cities, and so many more things.

In other words, advertising is a form of ideology (see Chapter 4 for more on ideology). It is a way of shaping our relationship to material things—to "our stuff." When we call something an ideology, we are really stating that it is a system of beliefs and values that shape the way an individual or group understands the world around them. An ideology is a way in which people orient themselves to the world. Many scholars argue that advertising is a form of ideology that orients people to the idea that material items can bring happiness, success, pleasure, and love.

As a privileged form of discourse, advertising also sells the message that the purchasing of goods is a way of life. Dallas Smythe suggested that the "basic myth of our culture is that consumption is the goal of life." The Frankfurt School (see Chapter 4), a group of academics critical of the workings of capitalism, stated that the triumph of advertising "is that consumers feel compelled to buy and use its products even though they see through them" (Horkheimer and Adorno, 1946). Other theorists contend that advertising is ideological, as it places the audience in the role of the buyer and socializes them to identify as consumers.

Many of these scholars who reflect upon advertising as ideological push these ideas further to think about how this ideology is integral to the workings of contemporary capitalism. As a form of promotional discourse, the logics of consumer culture are so omnipresent in our culture that consumption seems to be natural to it. It is normalized as part of our culture, and we do not even think of it as ideology or a belief system. Instead, advertising seems to be a natural way of life.

A Brief History of Advertising

Today, we live in a consumer society. This means that the institution and structures of contemporary culture are organized around the activities of consumption. While the actual origins of modern consumer culture have been hotly debated, it was in the late nineteenth and early twentieth centuries that consumption became solidified as the main organizing principle of culture and society. Prior to this, during the Industrial Revolution (eighteenth and nineteenth centuries), the focus was on increasing production through the development of factories and a labour force of factory workers.

During the turn of the twentieth century, the Industrial Revolution began to wane and was replaced by a consumer society. Industry leaders and government agencies began to believe that encouraging the population to consume was the avenue for economic expansion. By the 1880s, workers' wages had increased and there was a rise in literacy rates, which opened up opportunities to position workers as potential consumers. During this time, advertising agencies were founded and began to supply industry with creative services and market research. Together these services helped propel the industry to new heights.

Advertising in Canada has a long history. Early newspapers contained advertisements, but advertising was not their main source of income. The *Halifax Gazette,* the first newspaper published in Canada, in 1752, contained ads for a grocer, a job printer, and a tutor. But these early advertisements were not much more than descriptions of goods and services; they looked very similar to the classified advertisements that appear in the backs of newspapers today.

At first, advertising in Canada had an image problem. It was not well respected as a profession. It was seen as being unscientific, manipulative, and untrustworthy. To counter this, a group of ad workers formed an organization in 1911 called the Toronto Ad Club. The club united male advertising workers (female workers were not invited) to help the industry improve its image. Essentially, the club's goal was to advertise advertising. The Toronto Ad Club campaigns successfully professionalized the industry. Canadian newspapers and publishers began to realize that their main market was not readers looking for information, but rather advertisers looking for media that sympathized with their corporate goals (Johnson, 2018: 24). Advertising historian Russell Johnston traces the rich history of the advertising industry in Canada and suggests that Canadian advertising "came of age between 1900 and 1918." It was also at this time that Canadian department stores— most notably Eaton's, Simpson's and the Hudson's Bay Company (HBC)—became some of Canada's largest advertisers. These stores helped revolutionize the ways Canadians thought about and experienced advertising, shopping, consumer culture, and modernity (Belisle, 2011).

An early Hudson's Bay Company flyer.

After the First World War, advertising began to shift its approach. Instead of providing information on products, advertising messages began to persuade consumers that they had desires and needs. Advertising worked to encourage people to alter their daily patterns of life to include consumption of products and services. Advertising created messages to introduce unknown products into the daily patterns of everyday life, to create reasons for use, to tell people how and why to use them. According to cultural historian Stuart Ewen (1976), advertising's task was to *create* demand in consumers, as opposed to simply reflecting their innate desires. Ewen uses a quote from the 1930s advertising trade journal *Printer's Ink* to illustrate this point: "Advertising helps to keep the masses dissatisfied with their mode of life, discontented with the ugly things around them. Satisfied customers are not as profitable as discontented ones" (39). The implications of advertisers thinking that the role of advertising is to "keep the masses dissatisfied" is profound.

Of course, the types of goods that advertising told consumers they needed were not goods developed in the best interests of consumers, or of society for that matter, but a response to the requirements of the "capitalist productive machinery" (36). So, the solution to dissatisfaction, consumers were told, was mass-produced products that were cheap to produce and to transport. The messages in these ads also reassured and accommodated people to the twentieth-century way of life. Roland Marchand (1985) called advertising in the early twentieth century "the apostle of modernity." The ads told people not what the product could do, but of a way of life made possible. Advertising was a story of lifestyle—not product—information, a lifestyle that fit with the capitalist demands of a market-placed economy.

In the early decades of the twentieth century, advertising became a social force that was not only supported by consumerism but also created consumerism. By the end of 1945, advertising was embedded as an important business practice, and all brands had marketing strategies. The second half of the century saw the rapid expansion of the advertising industry, fuelled by the development of new technologies (such as television, satellite TV, and the internet), the formation of governmental policies that protected commercial speech (such as the deregulation of the media in the 1980s), the expansion of public relations as a corporate strategy, and the intensification of branding over production by contracting out production.

This section by no means covers the extensive history of advertising in Canada; it offers only a few key highlights. But what is revealed here is that advertising—and by extension consumer culture—was not a predetermined historical trajectory but a carefully executed political act. Political decisions, institutional structures, and economic systems were all put in place to support, protect, and legitimate advertising and promotional culture, and to develop a consumer society.

Commodities, Brands, and Markets

When we think critically about advertising and its role within our culture and economy, it is essential to pull back and think about how the broader structures of capitalism work, since advertising is central to today's capitalist system. Karl Marx's 1867 work, *Das Kapital*, provides a helpful starting point in unpacking the intricate workings of capitalism. While it may seem illogical to use a text that was written well before the twentieth-century institutionalization of advertising, Marx provides such a deep exploration of the inner workings and logics of capitalism that scholars often return to his work to unpack the complexities of today's capitalist systems.

Goods as Commodities

One of the key concepts of Marx's work that helps to explain how advertising fits in with the workings of capitalism is the notion of **commodity fetishism**. Marx argues that a main feature of capitalism is that production is separated from consumption as an inevitable outcome of mass production. Prior to capitalism, when people consumed commodities they usually knew where and how the good was produced and who produced it. In capitalism, the human labour of commodities is a series of fragmented tasks: workers produce raw materials, transport the raw materials, transform the materials into products in factories, and then ship and distribute the products to retailers. The labour and conditions of production are masked or hidden to the consumer and are not part of the meaning of the product. Instead, the product, or commodity, becomes enchanted with new meanings that appear to be inherent in the commodity itself. Meanings such as fashion, strength, athleticism, wealth, and love—all human qualities—are attached to the commodity. It is advertising's role to help empty the commodity of its story of production and replace it with carefully chosen cultural meanings. As Jhally so eloquently interprets Marx, the fetishism of commodities is a "disguise whereby the appearance of things in the marketplace masks the story of who fashioned them and under what conditions" (Jhally,1987: 50). The commodity is "a unity of what is revealed and what is concealed in the processes of production and consumption" (Leiss et al, 1990: 257).

Take, for example, a Tim Hortons cup of coffee. The simple cup of coffee has a much deeper meaning than being a cup of water that comes from filtered coffee beans. Hidden in the cup is the labour of the coffee farmers and the political conditions that allow for land to be used to produce coffee. Also hidden is the labour that picks, processes, and packages the beans, as well as the conditions of this labour (where the workers live, how many hours they work, and the health and safety conditions of the work). There are the workers who deliver the coffee to Tim Hortons stores, those who create the cups, and those who produce the raw materials used to create the cups and lids.

When we drink a Tim Hortons coffee, we see very little of its production. Instead, we see its symbolic meanings: Canadian nationalism and patriotism that is committed to local communities, loyalty to family, and a sense of economic worth. Tim Hortons coffee carries such iconographic weight that politicians are invariably seen drinking out of Tim Hortons cups as a means to articulate that they are in touch with "ordinary citizens" (Comrack and Cosgrave, 2018: 101). It has taken decades of iconic advertising campaigns to solidify the meanings of a Tim Hortons cup of coffee so deeply in our collective psyche. Of course, it should be noted that this labour of the company's marketing strategies, the market research, product development, and all other creative labour is also hidden in the commodity.

The conditions of production hidden in commodities have many real-life consequences. Consider the hidden labour in the shiny screens of the latest iPhones. Jack Linchuan Qiu's recent book entitled *Goodbye iSlave: A Manifesto for Digital Abolition* (2016) details the exploitative labour practices for the millions of workers who produce these technologies. Qiu argues that these practices are new forms of slavery in which workers are forced to work (and live) in factories, where they experience wage theft, abusive management, squalid living conditions, and are often child labourers. These factories, like eighteenth-century slave ships, have nets to stop workers from jumping to their deaths. For Qiu, slavery is not a metaphor: the iSlave is the victim of a new form of slavery adapted to today's global capitalist system. Its functions are embedded in governmental policy, the workings of state institutions such as schools and the police, and in the practices of transnational corporations such as Apple, Nintendo, and Intel.

Products as Brands

At the heart of promotional culture and commodity fetishism in the twentieth century is the brand. More than simply goods, commodities are now brands. At a basic level, a brand is a promise, a set of values and expectations attached to a name/logo. Branding is about giving products and companies human characteristics, a frame that echoes the notion of commodity fetishism. **Branding**, as Naomi Klein points out in *No Logo* (2000), is the "core meaning of the modern corporation." It is a form of promotional culture that goes beyond advertising to include sponsorships and logo licensing (5).

Originally, branding emanated from the concept of branding cattle to distinguish one person's cattle from another. It became a way for mass-produced products to be differentiated from one another. In the 1800s, as goods such as soap, or wax, began to be packaged, shipped, and sold in far-off stores, manufacturers created names and logos for consumers to identify their products. The roots of branding are located in these early days of mass markets, when the railroad could ship goods well beyond these sites of production. Brand labels allowed customers to familiarize themselves with the producer through the brand name, as opposed to having a local connection. Today, branding has taken on new forms to include trademarks, licensing, and brand loyalties. The modern brand is a complex entity at the heart of promotional culture. As Asquith and Hearn (2012: 246) illustrate,

> The term "brand" is most commonly understood to stand for a distinct form of marketing practice, intended to link products

> and services to resonant cultural meanings through the use of narratives and images. In recent years, the practices of branding have moved from attempting to directly discipline consumer taste to working more indirectly by constructing a particular ambience for consumption, comprised of sensibilities and values, which may then condition consumer behaviour. A brand no longer refers to a simple commodity but to an entire "virtual context" for consumption. . . . While the object of the logo or trademark was initially to guarantee quality, it has now become the sign of a definite type of social identity, which summons consumers into relationship with it.

Iconic Canadian brands include Hudson's Bay Company, Tim Hortons, Molson Canadian, lululemon, Roots, Canada Dry, Bombardier, Mountain Equipment Co-op, and Canada Goose. Each of these brands has a complex set of signifiers and meanings that have been heavily invested in by corporations. These brands are worth a great deal more than what they tangibly own (real estate, production facilities, materials, etc.). A brand's value is based in the intangible: its image and meaning, its consumers' recognition of and loyalty to the brand, and the promise of the brand. This is often called **brand equity**. In the corporate world, there are multiple ways that companies might determine a brand's equity based on a variety of metrics. But really, when one thinks about it, brand equity is simply the workings of commodity fetishism. The brand's value is not a reflection of its production but instead of its enchanted meanings, which can be transferred to other products.

A case in point here is brand licensing, the practice in which a brand rents out the use of its name or logo for manufacturers to use on new products. For example, the iconic Canadian clothing company Roots has licensed its brand to select manufacturing partners that produce items such as watches, home furnishings, and perfume. Roots does not actually make the products; it simply allows its name to appear on the products. Licensing is such big business that the Licensing Industry Merchandisers' Association (LIMA) estimates that annual revenue generated globally for licensing in 2017 was US$271.6 billion.

A famed illustration of brand equity occurred in 1988 when the Philip Morris Company (Marlboro, Maxwell House, Miller beer) bought Kraft (Sealtest ice cream, Velveeta cheese, Miracle Whip) for $12.6 billion, six times what the company was worth on paper. The value in Kraft was not in the physical assets of the company, but in the value of the brand (brand equity). Consumers, according to this logic, buy brands, not products. The acquisition of Kraft typified the dramatic shift in business culture in the 1980s when companies' business models changed from producing products with branding as an add-on to being solely brands by outsourcing production.

Nike was a leader in this shift. Instead of owning the factories that produced Nike athletic wear, Nike contracted out production to factories. These factories were often located in countries with weak labour laws, cheap taxes, and poor regulations on pollution, where goods could be made as cheaply as possible. Since Nike had not invested in factories or its workforce, it could easily shift labour contracts from one factory to another. This made Nike extremely flexible, and factories began to undercut one another in order to win the lucrative Nike contracts. This business practice has had serious consequences on the livelihoods of millions of people globally and has dramatically shaped the workings of global capitalism.

Freed from the pressures of maintaining a factory workforce and production facilities, Nike invested in its brand. It hired superstar athletes like Michael Jordan to endorse its products, created iconic campaigns such as "Just Do It," expanded into virtually every sport, and opened exclusive retail outlets called NikeTown. The brand is so prolific, and so emblematic of the era of branding, that Klein called Nike a "superbrand."

Branding extends beyond products and companies: churches, universities, countries, political parties, and even people have brands. Parks

Canada, an agency of the Government of Canada that oversees the protection and presentation of the country's cultural and natural heritage, has an iconic beaver logo. The first version of the logo, designed in the 1970s and retired from corporate use in 2000 following a redesign exercise, carried such resonance that in 2012 the agency licensed the use of the retired logo to produce a line of clothing that was sold by the Hudson's Bay Company. Parks Canada received 8 per cent of the wholesale price of each item.

Parks Canada is only one of thousands of examples of public institutions that have been caught up in promotional culture. Andrew Wernick's (1991) critical text *Promotional Culture* demonstrates how the logics of the advertising and promotion industry have infiltrated every facet of social life, including those spaces that are supposedly outside the market. The university is a good example. Wernick outlines that in the 1980s the university underwent a general organizational shift, so that it was "imaged and packaged just like any other marketed product" (156). Ideally, the university is a public institution that functions for the common good of society through the exploration of new ideas and education of the population. But it has become implicated in the logics of promotion and brand culture. Today, universities invest in expensive brand campaigns as they compete for students and donors. They design new buildings, student spaces, and even programs and degrees to appeal to students instead of focusing on social goals.

Parks Canada

Parks Canada's logo reflects the brand's Canadian identity of authenticity, ruggedness, wilderness, and simplicity.

Intellectual thought is rerouted through the promotional vortex of social media, where scholars post ideas and thoughts, circumventing the peer review process, and professors are often evaluated on various citation metrics, not the social value of their scholarship. The "promotionalized university," Wernick points out,

> is a site which brings together the market for commodities in the ordinary sense with other forms of competition (for status, for example) of a more purely symbolic kind. For that reason, too, the forms of promotion and exchange which have come to characterize the institution are not just pervasive, but multiple and condensed: as complex in their articulation as they are profound in their organizational and subjective effects (Wernick, 1991:158).

Arguably, it is not just universities but all aspects of social life that have become "promotionalized," to use Wernick's term. Take for example the Canadian Museum of Civilization in Gatineau. In 2012, the Canadian government under Conservative Prime Minster Stephen Harper renamed it the Canadian Museum of History. This was part of a wider move of the Harper government to brand Canadian identity and history in the image of the Conservative party. As part of the change, the museum shifted its narrative away from one that gave space to multiple civilizations, including indigenous peoples of Turtle Island, to a focus on a colonial version of Canadian history as a narrative of national progress (Brady & Aronczyk, 2015). This example reveals the ideological nature of branding. It is not just about promoting the museum as a means to increase visitors. Instead, branding is implicated in pushing a narrative of the nation that was tied to the Harper government's political agenda.

Subverting Brands

While the brand is at the epicentre of global capitalism, it is also its "Achilles heel," as Naomi Klein's work *No Logo* so eloquently states. Since the brand is really an imaginary meaning, it can be usurped for new meanings beyond the powers of the corporations that own the brand. Often these new meanings are political and challenge the hegemonic power of the corporations. This is called **subvertising**, a political act of culture jamming, in which logos, slogans, or images are reworked to subvert—or jam—corporate messaging. Sometime this may take the form of graffiti, where a billboard for McDonald's with the slogan "I'm loving it" is changed to "I'm gaining it," or an iPhone ad is manipulated to become iAddict. Sometimes cultural jamming campaigns are more sophisticated, such as when ads for Nike shoes are edited to replace sports imagery with images of abhorrent working conditions and child labour. These subversive campaigns can be very powerful acts of resistance, as they can attach new meanings to brands.

Many commentators question the impact of counterculture activities like culture jamming, arguing that it fails to make any substantial economic or political change. They observe that rebellious messages of culture jamming are easily usurped and taken up by the corporations that use the messaging to articulate a rebelliousness and authenticity. A perfect example is how graffiti artists (the ultimate cultural critics) loan their visions to advertising campaigns, or how corporations take the language of critique on Twitter and use it to write tweets that support their own companies. Marx once wisely observed that capitalism thrives because, to further its own means, it always solves the problems it creates.

Thousands of wildlife birds from different origins were weighed down with oil giving them deadly hypothermia since oil destroys the insulating quality of their feathers...
How many species will die for Shell?

An example of a subvertisement that presents Shell's brand image as one that causes environmental damage.

Consumers as Markets

Mass Audiences

Prior to the 1980s, much of the mainstream media was geared toward gathering mass audiences. The larger the audience, the more expensive the time or space the media could sell to advertisers. The more attention that could be sold, the more lucrative the advertising spot. This fits with Smythe's concept of the audience as a commodity, discussed earlier. Bigger audiences meant bigger profits. For Canadian network stations like CTV or CBC, it was worth it to spend money to gather mass audiences. Market researchers and media companies spent vast amounts of time and resources trying to find these mass audiences and to understand their motivations.

In this system, ratings become critical. Ratings are a tool to estimate the size and demographic of an audience. In Canada, the main audience measurement organization for television is Numeris (previously known as the Bureau of Broadcast Measurement, BBM Canada). Founded in 1944 by the Canadian Association of Broadcasters, Numeris has faced stiff competition from its American competitor, Nielsen, with which it joined briefly in the 1990s.

From the 1980s through the turn of the century, rating companies like Numeris and Nielsen were the lifeblood of the mass media and were central to creating revenue; the higher the ratings, the more revenue the media received. The ratings of a publication or television show justified the sale of advertising space. But the gathering of ratings is not without bias. Smythe's

David Cooper/Toronto Star via Getty Images.

Hockey Night in Canada (HNIC) has had some of the highest ratings in Canada since it began broadcasting in 1952. In 2013, Rogers Media bought the rights to HNIC for 12 years for $5.2 billion.

version of the audience as a commodity assumes that the science behind gathering these ratings is an unbiased scientific representation of an audience whose members are all considered equally. Scholars such as Eileen Meehan have argued that there is actually tremendous bias in these rating systems, and audience members are not considered equally. Meehan used feminist perspective to demonstrate that audience data was highly gendered and racist. While the female commodity audience was valued during the daytime, resulting in the media gearing programming to women performing housework at home (think of soap operas and talk shows), it was the prime-time audience that was highly prized. It was assumed that white males aged 18–34 made the most important spending decisions, so advertisers coveted this consumer demographic and the media developed content that catered to it. Even though the goal of the media was to get large ratings, it was essential to a television show's success that the audience included a large number of this coveted demographic. As Meehan states: "Television was largely in the business of men – counting them, characterizing them, selling to them, and programming for them. As long as 'society' defined men as the proverbial breadwinners, that social reality governed the decisions of advertisers, networks and the ratings monopolist" (Meehan, 2005: 318). This is an important consideration in the field of communication and media studies as it reveals how the pursuit of this demographic shaped the decisions made in the type of content produced, who was getting hired, and what kinds of stories got told.

Niche Audiences

While there is a long history of the pursuit of the mass audience, it is slowly disappearing. Over the course of the twentieth century and into the twenty-first, the mass audience has fractured into smaller and tighter market niches as a result of media fragmentation and advancements in market research. There are a few key moments in this shift. In the 1950s, the radio industry lost its big national advertisers to television. To compete with television's massive audiences, radio stations began to appeal to narrow sets of demographics, often based on their music preferences. In the 1960s, mass-consumer magazines began to struggle. Instead, special-interest lifestyle magazines with smaller audiences flourished and were filled with advertisements for highly selective ranges of products that fit the readers' lifestyles. *Playboy* and *Seventeen* magazines are perhaps most iconic examples of this shift.

In the 1970s, advances in sociology and psychology contributed to new ways of understanding consumer behaviour. Developments in computer technologies also allowed for new methods of surveying consumers' values, lifestyle choices, patterns, and habits. In the 1980s, the expansion of cable and satellite television meant that audiences had more major networks to choose from (e.g., Global, CTV, CBC), along with a wide array of niche channels, such as MuchMusic (launched in 1984), TSN (1984), YTV (1988), and the History Channel (1995). This fragmentation and

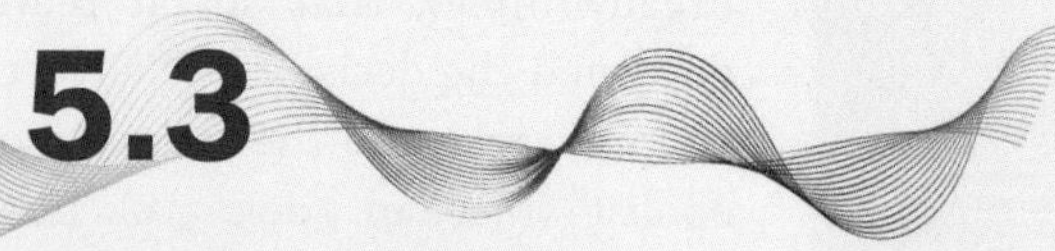

5.3 Ratings, Analytics, and Click Farms

Quantitative data on ratings, clicks, shares, and likes are critical to digital media companies too. Many digital media companies generate their own numbers. For example, on YouTube you can see how many views, likes, and shares a video has received, or how many subscribers a YouTube channel has. Many websites generate their own analytics. But when it comes to using these numbers to decide on the cost of buying and placing advertising, companies do not trust other companies to provide "in-house" analytics on the number of unique browsers who visit a site.

Instead, many companies purchase the services of an external company like Comscore. Comscore claims that it is a reliable third-party source for providing audience measurement of digital media. As digital audiences move across platforms, it has become increasingly difficult to measure them.

But online data cannot really be trusted. In recent years it has come to light that there are various ways digital media publishers, or social media influencers for example, can artificially boost their numbers. Click farms have cropped up; for a price, one can purchase clicks on specific sites. At these click farms either workers or bots will click on a specific site to generate profitable analytics or create an impression of popularity that might actually induce something to go viral. Click farms will also provide an array of bogus followers to increase the relevancy of an influencer. There is also the suggestion that click farms may be hired by a company's competition to deplete its advertising budget. Since sometimes companies only pay digital publishers when an ad is clicked on (pay-per-click), an artificially high number of clicks will cost a larger amount of money.

Various politicians, brands, and celebrities have been outed for inflating their numbers of followers by using these services. Scholars have also recently documented politicians who create fake grassroots activity online, as part of a strategy to create the impression of local, grassroots support for a particular cause.

In response to these fraudulent activities, a number of social media companies such as Facebook, Instagram, and YouTube have tried at various points to scrub fake accounts off their platforms. But it seems that despite dramatic purges, these companies are not very successful in eradicating this fraud in the long term.

A click farm.

splintering dramatically intensified the development of digital media, a topic we will explore in the next section.

Despite this trend of fracturing audiences into smaller segments, there are still events that gather mass audiences. The largest Canadian audience to date occurred on February 28, 2010, during the Winter Olympics gold medal men's hockey game. The game averaged 16.6 million Canadians who watched Canada defeat the US 3–2 in overtime. In total, close to 26.5 million Canadians tuned in at some point during the game—nearly two-thirds of the Canadian population. With such large numbers, the game was hailed as "ratings gold" for CTV by the press the following day.

Market Segmentation

In understanding market segmentation, it is critical to think through what is actually meant by a market segment. **Market segmentation** is the organization of consumers into smaller, tighter groups based on their demographic characteristics, lifestyles, and social values. Business executive turned author Michael J. Croft simply defines market segmentation as "the process of identifying different groups of users within a market who could possibly be targeted with separate products or marketing programs" (1994:1). The value in segmenting consumers into narrow audiences means that the media can deliver a tight and precise audience to an advertiser. Media companies try to appeal to advertisers by claiming that they can deliver a desirable group of consumers, one so narrow, precise, and in the right frame of mind, that the advertiser will not waste money paying to reach audience members who are not interested in the product. Media firms sell their audiences to advertisers by claiming that virtually every audience member is a potential customer for the advertiser. Think of the Golf Channel, which not only delivers a very narrow demographic of consumer (male, wealthy, white) but also a consumer thinking about golf at that exact moment. So, advertisements for golf equipment, tourist sites related to golf, and even cars that fit golf clubs would appeal to the Golf Channel audience.

On the surface, the above definition of market segmentation appears to be a rational and straightforward summary, but this "process of identifying" is complex and deeply ideological. First, it is ideological to define people as a market, or consumers with purchasing power, rather than as citizens possessing a set of rights. Second, market segments are not actual living people but rather artificial groupings of imagined people, organized and defined according to the logics and needs of the marketplace. Essentially, market segments are socially constructed categories of meaning. They are a way of making sense of a population for the purposes of selling products and maximizing profits. Market segmentation is a means of apprehending human activity and a form of social organization in which the consumer becomes the object of the "market research gaze" (Cook, 2004:19), where the object (in this case, the consumer) is seen through the eyes of the gazer (in this case, the advertiser).

The types of quantitative and qualitative information gathered and collated on groups of people are based on their position as consumers. Each bundle of information is considered pertinent or viable by market researchers only if it is ultimately relevant to their purchasing practices. Market segmentation is a means of analyzing group characteristics and translating these characteristics into valuable information to be exploited for the benefit of those companies trying to sell to them. Daniel Cook calls this a "commercial epistemology." An **epistemology** is a theory of knowledge—of what gets defined as knowledge and the sources and structures of that knowledge (2009).

A *commercial epistemology* means that the industries of the marketplace—such as marketers, advertisers, market researchers, the media, and retailers—define, demonstrate, and articulate what information counts and what is not valuable as knowledge. It is these industries that identify and articulate a market segment as a process of "knowing" (Cook, 2011). This knowing is deeply ideological, as it both describes and constructs the market segment according to the needs and logics of the marketplace and does not consider social aspects that are not relevant to the marketplace. These industries spend huge amounts of time on market research; they collect data on consumers' views, preferences, and consumption habits in order to be able to categorize consumers into separate markets. There are multiple ways in which market researchers conduct research: they gather data from online sources and social media feeds, conduct focus groups and surveys, and even observe people in their own homes. This data provides the basis for the imagined consumers that make up a market segment. In Canada, there are many market research companies, such as the Quebec firm Léger or the Toronto-based Environics and Numeris.

Market Segmentation of Children

The focus of Cook's work on market segments and commercial epistemologies is the children's market. Children, it can be argued, have been at the epicentre of the expansion of market segmentation. For starters, childhood has been segmented into smaller and tighter marketing niches based on age and gender. Marketers, for example, reference the baby market, the toddler market, the preschool market, the pre-tween market, the tween market, and the teen market. Each of these markets is further subdivided based on gender. For example, there are strict distinctions between the boy tween and the girl tween markets. Marketers make sense of and give meaning to psychosocial and biological developments of young people and define them in terms of markets. The tween market did not exist prior to the 1980s, nor did the teen market prior to the 1950s, or—as Cook (2004) argues—the toddler market prior to the 1930s. It was the industries of advertising and promotional culture that first defined and articulated these stages of childhood, which eventually have been taken up as authentic categories of life history. Today, toddlers, tweens, and teens are all bona fide stages of youth, but they were first defined and articulated as markets before they were legitimated as specific stages of childhood. Of course, it is important to remember that these conceptions of markets are rarely intersectional (to include race, class, sexuality, and so forth). Most of the construction of the children's market has assumed that the child consumer is white, middle class, able-bodied, and heterosexual.

Commercial epistemologies are not simply about defining the children's market according to the industry's needs. There is also a moral objective in the process. Naming children as markets, learning about their preferences and desires, and then creating products that cater to these desires provides a means for the advertising industry to legitimate its presence in children's lives and legitimate the child as a consumer subject. The moral implication made by advertising is that the market is only providing what children naturally want, a perspective that makes it more palatable to treat children as consumers. Defining the child as a market naturalizes consumption and frames the subjectivity of being a consumer as a natural state of humanity. If the child is defined as a consumer, consumption can be assumed to be a natural component of human development. Here one can see how advertising performs an ideological service that not only defines people as consumers but also naturalizes the act of consumption as central to humanity. An alternative would be to think of the subject position of being a consumer as an artificially constructed subjectivity imposed by the hegemonic structures of consumer capitalism.

Market Segmentation in the Age of Big Data

The complexity of market segmentation has intensified with the expansion of the digital into our everyday lives. The amount of data on individual consumers that can be harnessed instantaneously has exploded. The processes of market segmentation, and even how we think of markets, have shifted dramatically. Online advertising has become increasingly personalized, targeted, and interactive. Websites, social media feeds, and marketers are able to direct specific advertisements to specific people. In traditional media, advertising is expensive, and the audience is not guaranteed. In digital media, advertising is much cheaper, companies can track audiences with precise accuracy, and they can directly target consumers with precision. With digital, companies can build relationships with loyal groups of followers or consumers by communicating with them directly.

Social networking sites (SNS) are an important part of the matrix of digital advertising. SNS derive profit out of their knowledge about users and their social contexts. The *social context* is both the demographic profile of the user and anyone they "friend"—their social relations (friends, family, professional acquaintances, etc.) (Langlois, 2014). Instead of selling a commodity or entertainment, social networking sites financialize the self. What a social media site like Facebook is actually selling is the self. Facebook is really an advertising platform that allows companies to micro-target consumers. Every post, like, online quiz, game, or social connection becomes a data point that can be aggregated to deliver narrow and specific advertising opportunities for companies.

Social media has the possibility to micro-target to such intensity with such focus that Cambridge Analytica, for example, stated in 2016 that it had over 5,000 personalized data points that it could deliver to hyper-targeted advertising campaigns on social media sites (Lapowski, 2017). Facebook has come under fire many times recently for harvesting personal data on its platform that is then used by other companies for more nefarious practices. The most infamous example may be when Cambridge Analytica, encouraged by Donald Trump's electoral campaign team, manipulated Facebook advertising content for various voter segments, directly targeting voters in swing states, which in effect shaped the way they voted and likely the outcome of the 2016 election in the United States.

Online advertising is dominated by Facebook and Google. Both platforms have multiple points to connect with consumers. At the time of writing this chapter, Facebook owns WhatsApp and Instagram, and Google owns YouTube, but also has Gmail, its search engine, platforms for mapping, and document storage/editing. In recent years, Amazon has become one of the largest companies in online advertising. It is third in the digital ad market behind Alphabet Inc. (Google) and Facebook Inc. Amazon's ad revenue was estimated to be US$5.83 billion in 2018.

The conflation of advertising with knowledge of consumers and retail is worrisome. Nearly half of all online sales in the US are on Amazon, generating a wealth of consumer data. A big chunk of Amazon's ad business comes from its retail site, where companies pay to be listed high up in the search results. Add to this the fact that Amazon has a number of in-house products that get

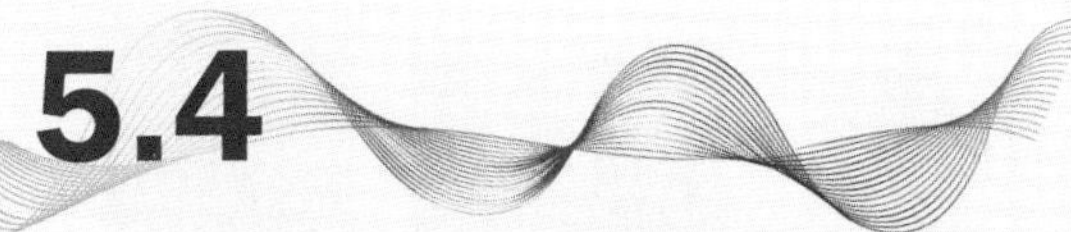

The Internet of Things

As the digital, internet connected world moves beyond just our computers to everyday objects such as fridges, lights, thermostats, cars, speaker systems, toasters, and even children's toys being digitally connected, there are new opportunities for advertisers to gather data on people. This extension of the internet to other objects is often referred to as the Internet of Things (IoT). IoT devices that seem benign in effect become forms of data gathering and surveillance for companies to track our patterns and behaviours. For example, think about what the GPS connectivity of a car offers to a car company that can log where the car has been, how far and fast it has gone, how often, where it stops for gas, etc. These companies can sell this information to third parties, and we as consumers are not aware that our data has been commodified, packaged, and sold. Furthermore, it is not clear who has access to this data or how it is being used. Or if this information is hacked, who can access it? Going well beyond the issues of simply turning our everyday lives into market research opportunities, the IoT raises huge concerns about surveillance and control, and who is watching us. A well-known example of this is the Google Home or Amazon Alexa smart speaker, which is always on, always "listening," and always gathering information on what is happening in the home and feeding this information back to the company that uses it for target advertising.

These smart devices can track conversations that occur around the device, both when activated, but also when background chatter seems to be enough to activate the system. In 2018, police in the US investigating a murder actually subpoenaed the recordings made by a device. Hackers and identity thieves have also been able access these recordings.

a special space on the search results page (and probably also benefit from data on the purchasing patterns for their competitor's products). Furthermore, Amazon's virtual assistant, Alexa, has tremendous potential as a marketing platform and data harvester. These examples all highlight how in today's age of rapid change in corporate strategies and quick technological advancement, the marketization of our media practices moves swiftly, often without the public's knowledge of such shifts.

The business of advertising has shifted from being about how to make creative ads to breaking through the clutter and captivating audiences, to figuring out how to collect information about consumer behaviour and how to monetize this behaviour. Advertising agencies rely on programmatic advertising, which is, in a sense, automated real-time auctions for online advertising space, data analytics (the collection, storage, and analysis of consumer behaviour), and the development of algorithmic formulas that learn how to target consumers based on their profiles and habits (Aronczyk, 2018).

The reliance on all of this harvested data and artificial intelligence is worrying to those who think about racism and sexism. Safiya Umoja Noble has documented how data discrimination is a real social problem. In her 2018 work *Algorithms of Oppression*, Noble traces how search engines "reinforce oppressive social relationships and enact new modes of racial profiling" (1). Often we think of search engines and data as neutral, but as Noble points out, these systems are actually deeply embedded with racist and sexist processes. Noble's works are full of examples of systemic

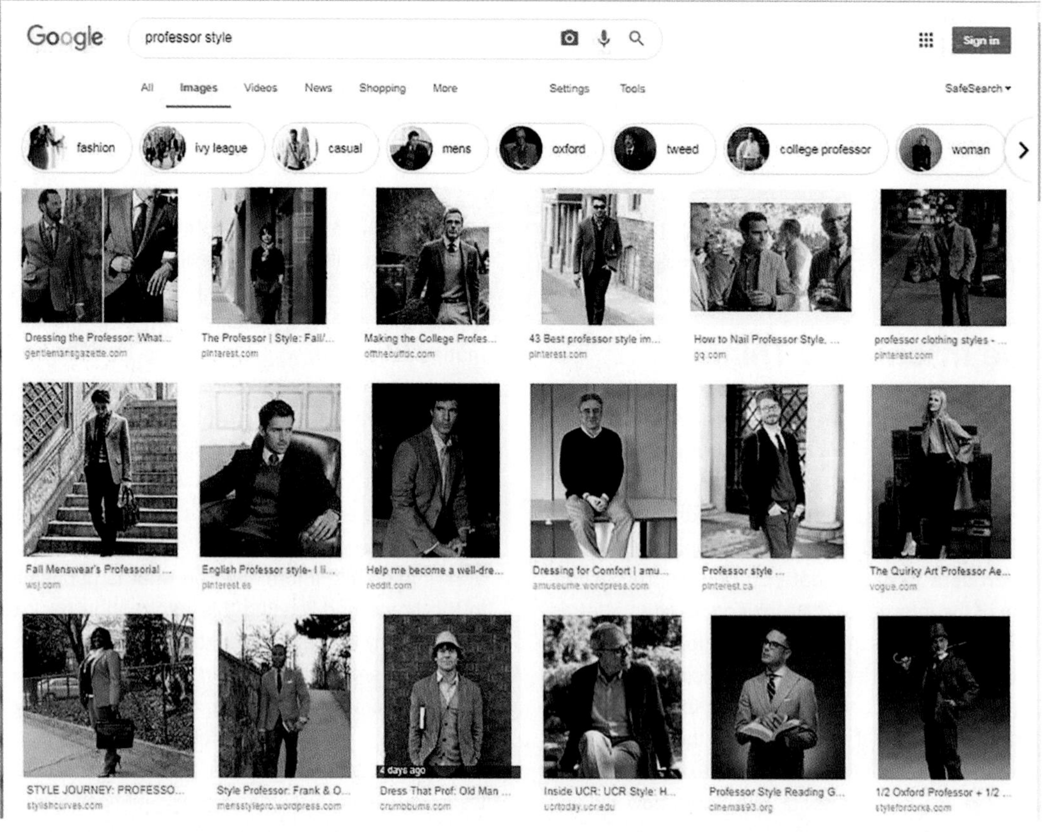

A May 2019 screenshot of the Google search "professor style," pictured here, still shows the dominant image of a white male, echoing Noble's original study.

racism and sexism of **algorithms**. Particularly poignant are the examples for Google's autosuggest search results (done in 2013) that complete phrases when googling such phrases as "why are Black women so . . ." in comparison to "why are white women so . . . ." The autosuggestions that completed these terms were radically different. Black women, Google suggested, were angry, loud, mean, lazy, annoying, and bitter. White women were pretty, beautiful, mean, skinny, fake, and nude. Another example Nobel cites is that when googling images using the keywords *professor style*, the search results reveal images of people who are almost exclusively white.

Advertising is undergoing dramatic changes as companies are in data-driven relationships with consumers. While it might seem benign that our digital data is used to sell us more goods, it is not. There are deep social and political implications to this. Perhaps the most problematic is how there is increasing perception that the personal data collected by private media companies constitutes the "sum of who we are as public people" and that this data should be used to shape public policy. For example, organizations like the United Nations are asking private companies to "donate" their consumer data for the "public good" to be used to make decisions about how to shape various policies on climate change and the environment (Aronczyk, 2018). Aronczyk and Noble's work reminds us that Google, Facebook, YouTube, and most other digital platforms are also advertising platforms geared solely to engage with people as consumers, not as fully formed citizens with rights that extend beyond the marketplace.

Celebrities and Influencers

The shape of promotional culture is changing drastically in the digital environment. While many of the basic premises of promotional culture have stayed the same, it has taken on new forms and intensities in recent years. Think about what is means for a person to have the power to influence people's consumer habits. There is a long history of celebrities endorsing and promoting products. Famous examples include Ronald Reagan shilling for Chesterfield Cigarettes in the 1940s, Bob Hope pitching for American Express in the 1950s, and Brooke Shields selling Calvin Kleins in the 1980s when she coyly stated, "Nothing comes between me and my Calvins." But these types of endorsements take much different forms as they circulate in digital spaces. There are still traditional celebrities who endorse products and have tremendous influence in the marketplace: LeBron James or Taylor Swift come to mind, as they have massive sway in the marketplace and large commercial deals with various companies. But with digital media, the ability of individuals to persuade people to buy things has expanded to include individuals who gather large followings on social media. Instead of being celebrities who have gained fame offline and bring it to the digital space, influencers build their fame and their followers *in* the digital space.

A social media **influencer** is defined as a person who generates a form of celebrity capital by "cultivating as much attention as possible and crafting an authentic personal brand via social networks, which can subsequently be used by companies and advertisers for consumer outreach" (Hearn and Schoenhoff, 2016: 194). Influencers maintain a relationship with their audience that is more intimate, and seemingly more "real" and authentic, than that of celebrities. The distinction between celebrity and influencer is not clear-cut; the borders between the two are fuzzy, but influencers provide companies with a veneer of authenticity that celebrities often do not. Celebrities can become influencers and influencers can become celebrities, like the famous Canadian YouTuber Superwoman (aka Lilly Singh), who started posting videos on YouTube in 2010 after graduating from York University. Now with an estimated 2.8 billion views, she is also an author, has acted on television shows and films, is a brand ambassador for Pantene, and at the time of writing this, was announced to host a late-night show on American network television. Singh is the quintessential influencer-turned-celebrity. Only a few influencers reach the heights that Singh has and are able to transcend the boundary to become celebrities.

https://www.instagram.com/p/-m1gpYPssb/.

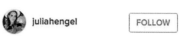

Fed Ex's holiday campaign #howtheholidaysarrive enlisted influencers like Julia Engel of the blog *Gal Meets Glam* to create content for the campaign.

Influencers engage in promotional culture by three means, according to Crystal Abidin's research on selfies and Instagrammers. First, they disseminate content by sharing, liking, retweeting, and pinning, depending on the social media platform. This requires no action from their followers but merely pushes out content. Second, they aggregate by inviting their followers to respond to a dedicated thread. This includes contests, surveys, or questionnaires, sometimes to win a prize. This amplifies the original content. And finally, they instigate by encouraging followers to generate or recreate content by uploading videos onto websites or feeds (2016). Abidin suggests that followers become "a network of advertorial capillaries by duplicating, amplifying, and multiplying" the influencer content to their own circle of friends (2016: 4). What this means is that it is not simply the influencers themselves but also their followers whose digital labour is exploited.

Promotion in digital capitalism relies on people to become creative labourers who do the work for little or no compensation. Instead, their creative work becomes part of the marketing and promotion of brands. For example, a growing form of advertising production is sourced from audience members as companies call on audiences to craft commercials themselves. Frito-Lay, for instance, has run consumer-produced ads, otherwise known as user-generated content, on the Super Bowl broadcast for several years, and companies such as Starbucks and General Motors have also capitalized on this trend of having consumers/fans produce digital content. If nothing else, the hype around such contests in itself generates an excitement for the brand and strengthens audience attention to those ads. In Canada, the brand Hotels.com famously had people create and upload videos of themselves as Captain Obvious, the brand spokesperson. The winning video was viewed over 25,000 times. The winner received a $1,000 gift card and an all-expense-paid trip to Toronto, which is really a pretty cheap means of producing content.

Digital advertising changes the ways that we may think about Smythe's theory of audience as a commodity. In digital, the audience's labour goes beyond simply attention. Now the audience is a user, and as a user its digital activity—whether as influencers or producers of content, or simply producing data points in social media spaces—is monetized. It is no longer the living room that is the factory, but our smartphones and laptops.

Product Placement, Branded Content, and Native Advertising

Advertising used to be seen as distinct from other forms of content, but as creeping commercialism has become more and more a part of our culture, and competition between media outlets has become fiercer, the line between advertising and other forms of content has become fuzzy. The distinction between these two has become so blurred that it can be very difficult to distinguish between the two. There are various forms of this.

One form, called **product placement**, occurs when a company negotiates placing its product or brand into fictional or non-fictional content. Hollywood films have a long history of getting paid to place products into the content of the film. Some of the most successful have been Tom Cruise's Ray-Ban sunglasses in the 1983 movie *Risky Business*, BMW in the James Bond series, and Domino's Pizza in *Teenage Mutant Ninja Turtles*. Product placement also occurs outside films: the judges on *American Idol* always drink Coke, musicians such as Lorde incorporate alcohol brands like Grey Goose into their lyrics, and video games are often full of product placements, such as the Mercedes-Benz car options in *Mario Kart 8*. The amount of money these companies have paid for product placement is not known to the public, and often these contracts are secret deals.

Product placement has intensified to *product integration*, where a brand or product is integrated right into the heart of the media content instead of being simply a prop. Here the brand is woven into the story or plotline. For example, *Cast Away,* perhaps one of the most notorious examples of product placement, is basically a film about FedEx and a brand of volleyballs. Or, in a 2015 episode of *Modern Family* called "Connection Lost," the entire storyline of the episode was told though the interface of a lead character's MacBook Pro as she connected with the show's other characters on their Apple products, which not only showcased Apple products but also educated the consumer on the ways to use Apple products.

Another way that the lines between advertising and content blur is with **native advertising**, the practice of creating advertisements that look and feel like actual content. Native advertising may take the form of **advertorials**—advertisements that look like editorial content—search engine ads that pose as search results, or ads that imitate content in our social media feeds. It is often difficult to tell online when content is native advertising. Sometimes small notes at the top of the piece state that the content is "sponsored," but often it is really challenging to tell the difference.

There is also *branded* or *sponsored content*, a form of advertising in which creative content is designed to build awareness for a specific brand. In the earlier days of 1920s broadcasting, advertisers fully sponsored shows such as the Colgate Comedy Hour or the plethora of radio shows created and developed by Canadian National Railways. Much of this ended with the advent of public radio in 1934. In the past few decades, there has been a resurgence of sponsored content. As a recent example, *The Lego Movie* is an entire film that stars the Lego brand. As another example, in 2014, the *New York Times* ran what appeared to be a long-read article written by Melanie Deziel, an editor for the *Times'* "brand studio." The article seemingly focused on women's prisons and was entitled "Women Inmates: Why the Male Model Doesn't Work," but it turned out that the article was commissioned to promote Netflix's upcoming season of *Orange is the New Black*. The same year, the alternative rock band OK Go produced an innovative video for their song "I Won't Let You Down," which featured Honda's self-balancing unicycles. The video has over 38 million views and includes footage with Honda executives. There are also the Red Bull extreme sports events, such as Red Bull Crashed Ice and the Red Bull Global Rallycross Championship. In all of these examples, the brand is woven right into the content and appears to be part of the story.

Sponsored content can also take many creative forms, particularly in the digital space. The Kardashians come to mind, as so many of the family's posts feature brands. Or take the power couple Priyanka Chopra and Nick Jonas. The couple has many private endorsement deals, so it is not clear what is sponsored, but their engagement and wedding highlighted many brands, from the Tiffany wedding ring and bridal shower at Tiffany's Blue Box Café in New York, to Nick's bachelor party with a carefully staged photo of him posing with a vodka brand, to the couple's reference that they first bonded over their love of Ralph Lauren.

These examples show how the blurring between commerce and creative content has intensified in the digital space. This blurring creates many new opportunities for corporations that have been slowly turning away from traditional advertising to digital marketing. According to the Canadian Marketing Association's (CMA) 2017 report on digital marketing, there are 14 components of digital marketing. This includes search engine optimization as a way to improve the ranking on a website search engine listing, mobile marketing, social network marketing, pay-per-click sponsored advertisements, branded content / native advertising online, and customer-facing websites. One of the concerns here is how much power these companies have in determining the content of our media. This is not only concerning from the standpoint of colonizing creativity, but also in terms of driving the types of stories or issues that resonate in popular culture and shape our larger culture. The expansion of advertorials, infomercials, product placement, and other forms of promotional content illustrates how the relationship between content and advertising has intensified over the years. Clear distinctions between culture and commercialism cease to exist, and it is becoming increasingly difficult to determine the difference between public and commercial space.

https://www.instagram.com/p/Bjjq1b8gfuF/.

An Instagram post by Priyanka Chopra Jonas with incredible reach (over 1 million likes alone) promotes both In-N-Out burgers and Chanel.

The Power of Advertising

From the early days of the late nineteenth century, when advertisements were small boxes of type lauding the value of a product, to today, where celebrities are brand ambassadors who subtly (or not so subtly) feature brands in their social media posts, advertising has extended its reach into every nook and cranny of culture so that it is now

5.5

Smart Cities and Surveillance Capitalism

In 2017, Sidewalk Labs, a company owned by Alphabet (Google), announced that it was selected by Waterfront Toronto to develop Toronto's valuable eastern waterfront. Sidewalk Labs claims that it will develop a smart city, combining urban design with digital technology to address the challenges that face cities. Sidewalk Labs also claims that it has undertaken an extensive public consultation process that informs its plan. While this may all seem wonderful, the idea of a smart city run by Google has raised many critical questions about the role of technology companies in public spaces.

A smart city is a city that is constantly gathering data on its citizens. For example, Sidewalk Labs uses a what it calls a "next-generation urban planning tool" called Replica, which maps out individuals' travel patterns based on "de-identified location data." It can track, according to Replica's website, the total number of people on a road or street, how they are travelling, and the locations they travel to and from. At the time of writing this, Sidewalk Labs was negotiating with the state of Illinois to sell it this tool, and has offered to bring it to Toronto for free. This of course raises questions about the value of this data to Alphabet (which owns Google Maps, Chrome, Android OS, and YouTube). While data from Replica is to be provided to city planners, Sidewalk Labs promises that this data will be disconnected from personal identifying data, but it is not clear how true this is. Nor is it clear how the data will be used, or who it will be sold to. Despite this promise, Toronto city counsellor Joe Cressy states that it shouldn't be up to private companies to direct rules on how data is collected in the private and public realm.

To entice citizens to support its proposal, the company has promised Toronto many lucrative things, such as moving its Canadian headquarters to Toronto. At the same time the company has been negotiating around changing the size of the project and access to tax revenues and development fees that would otherwise go into public funds.

As companies like Google begin to take over our public services, they are able to hold the public hostage in order to get what they want. And as cities around the world, not just Toronto, are collecting more and more data on their citizens through private companies (the privately developed Presto transit cards are another example), we have to question how this data is being used to drive specific consumer habits. Alphabet is essentially a media company that, at the end of the day, sells advertising. How does this data fit into this overall objective? The gathering, commodifying, selling, and owning of data, often collected under the guise of making experiences better for the consumer (in what is sometimes called surveillance capitalism), will be an important civic issue in the decades to come. At the time of writing this chapter, an airport in China has put in place a facial recognition kiosk, which you can stand in front of, and have it identify you and give you information on your upcoming flight. And McDonald's just revealed that it is buying technology from a company named Dynamic Yield that will read licence plates to "optimize menu displays" at the drive-thru windows. Many smartphones have fingerprint scanners to make accessing our phones and tablets easier, while Pokémon GO herded players to specific sites of restaurants or stores, some of which paid to have players directed there.

difficult to determine where its reach ends. The goal of this system is ultimately to activate our individual buying impulses so advertisers can sell us more products, more efficiently than before.

Advertising has more profound impacts than simply telling us product information and communicating the utilitarian features of goods. It is an entire cultural system, a social discourse whose unifying theme is the meaning of consumption. The implications of the power of advertising and its hegemonic ideology of consumption is extensive, as it reaches to all aspects of our society, culture, politics, and economy.

The power of advertising is much greater than simply being a persuasive encouragement for consumers to choose between brands—Pepsi or Coke, Tim Hortons or Starbucks. Instead, it is a much larger ideological system with tremendous power, protected by political structures and funded by powerful economic engines.

Jhally has argued that "20th century advertising is the most powerful and sustained system of propaganda in human history and its cumulative cultural effects, unless quickly checked, will be responsible for destroying the world as we know it" (2006, 101). Jhally's words are prophetic and ring true. Our voracious appetites for consumer goods have had a huge impact on the environment. At the time of writing this chapter, the United Nations released a report stating that to avoid absolute catastrophe the world must make dramatic changes in how we consume, by 2030. Advertising and promotional culture must play new roles in how we think about consumption and our subjectivity as consumers.

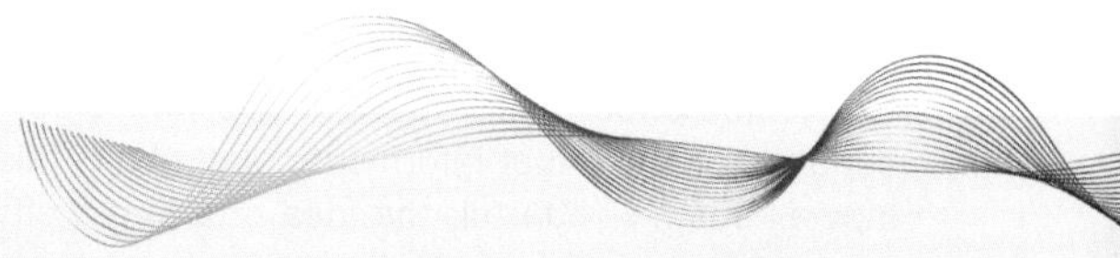

SUMMARY

In this chapter we have tried to show how advertising and promotion is a much stronger cultural force than simply selling people more products. It is a privileged form of discourse that is allocated special rights and access to people. It has organized and defined categories of people through the vehicle of market segmentation. It has shaped the types of content produced by the media and the way the media are organized. It has impacted the way digital media and social media sites function. It articulates and circulates symbols, meanings, and stories that help mould our social ideas and values. And it functions as an ideological force that legitimizes and maintains mass consumption as a key activity of modern life.

KEY TERMS

Adbusters, p. 118
advertising, p. 114
Advertising Standards Canada, p. 117
advertorials, p. 137
algorithms, p. 135
branded, p. 114
brand equity, p. 126
branding, p. 125
commodity fetishism, p. 124
discourse, p. 115
epistemology, p. 131
influencer, p. 135
market segmentation, p. 131
native advertising, p. 137
product placement, p. 137
promotional culture, p. 115
public relations, p. 115
subvertising, p. 128

RELATED WEBSITES

Ad Standards Canada: adstandards.ca

Ad Standards Canada is a not-for-profit, self-regulatory body of the advertising industry in Canada. This website features the Canadian Code of Advertising Standards, a code that industry members agree to adhere to. The website also highlights background information on the codes and the councils that devise them, and features official complaints made by the public against advertisements that may have failed to adhere to the codes. It is an important resource for anyone working in the advertising industry in Canada.

***Strategy*: strategyonline.ca**

Strategy is a magazine about advertising in Canada. *Strategy's* website hosts the digital version of the magazine and reports on new and innovative advertising campaigns. It contains articles on social and technological issues that face the industry, and it provides background on different advertising agencies and marketing companies.

Cannes Lions: www.canneslions.com

Every June in Cannes, the Cannes Lions International Festival of Creativity celebrates the "creative communications industry." Its annual Cannes Lion awards are given to the top advertisements and campaigns in the world, which can be viewed on this website. You can also view festival exhibits, and watch talks and panels that often feature top industry executives and influencers who provide insight into the direction of advertising worldwide.

FURTHER READINGS

Asquith, Kyle, editor. 2019. *Advertising, Consumer Culture, and Canadian Society: A Reader*. Don Mills, ON: Oxford UP.

Klein, Naomi. 2000. *No Logo: Taking Aim at the Brand Bullies*. Toronto: Knopf Canada.

McAllister, Matthew P., and Emily West, editors. 2013. *The Routledge Companion to Advertising and Promotional Culture*. New York and London: Routledge.

Schor, Juliet B., and Douglas B. Holt, editors. 2000. *The Consumer Society Reader*. New York: New Press.

Sivulka, Juliann. 2012. *Soap, Sex, and Cigarettes: A Cultural History of American Advertising*. Boston: Wadsworth Cengage Learning.

STUDY QUESTIONS

1. In what ways is the media basically a tool to deliver audiences to advertisers?
2. How is advertising and promotion an ideology?
3. Find an example of a product and describe it using the concept of commodity fetishism. What is hidden in the commodity? What cultural meanings are attached to the commodity? Look at the advertisements for the commodity and explain how the ads create meanings that are attached to the brand.
4. What are some current examples of advertising campaigns that are influencing or shaping our cultural ideas and values?
5. Does the audience perform labour in digital media? How should the ways in which we think about audience shift when thinking about the digital? Are digital users still an audience? Why or why not?
6. How do you think advertising and promotion should change to address the current climate change crisis?

6

Communication Technology and Society

Theory and Practice

I used to write, I used to write letters, I used to sign my name
—*Arcade Fire*

Rawpixel.com/Shutterstock

Opening Questions

- How do we define *technology*?
- What does it mean to say technology is socially embedded?
- What is technological determinism?
- What is a constructivist approach and why does it prevail today in studies of technology?
- What does *media convergence* mean?
- In what significant ways do digital media differ from analog media?
- What do the surveillance capacities of new media technologies mean for Canadian society?

Introduction

What we typically refer to by the generic term *the media* are technologies: devices connected to social, political, and economic structures, enabling communication across time, across space, and with an unlimited number of interlocutors. When we think about communication technology, the tendency is to conjure exciting new gadgets and cool software applications, even revolutionary change. It is an exciting time for students of communication, who can monitor the transitions underway in how we communicate, reflect on the challenges all cultural industries face in the shift from fixed and wired analog systems to mobile and wireless digital forms, and participate first-hand in the existential experiments media organizations are undertaking to find new ways to conduct their affairs.

In this chapter, we seek to address the question "What's going on?" But in doing so, we want to provide much-needed perspective on the subject of communication technology, by broadening the view of what we mean by "technology" and by situating technological change within a context informed not simply by science and engineering but also by politics, economics, culture, and history. As compelling as the digital age may be, it is not the first time that seismic shifts have occurred in the communication field, nor is it necessarily the most consequential period—the jury is still deliberating on that, given the need to think about how the changes we are witnessing today compare to the invention of the printing press in the middle of the fifteenth century and its subsequent role in the Enlightenment, or the developments in rapid succession of photography, telegraphy, telephony, cinema, and radio in the nineteenth century, which altered profoundly and permanently our senses of time and space. What we need to resist is the idea of the "technological sublime," what Jennifer Daryl Slack and J. Macgregor Wise define as "the almost religious-like reverence paid to machines" (2007: 17).

Perspectives on Technology

The word *technology* is from the Greek *techne*, meaning "art, craft, or skill." This etymology reminds us that technology refers to much more than tools or devices. Rather, the term encompasses the devices *as well as* a knowledge or understanding of their use or operation, an understanding of how they fit into a larger set of social circumstances or way of life. Technology, then, should be seen as woven into the circumstances and rhythms of social life.

Slack and Wise (2007: 72) remind us that technologies are inherently social and cultural—it is people who create, use, and program technologies, in activities that always reflect values and choices. The original creators of technologies may be scientists, engineers, or backyard inventors, but the context in which their creation occurs will inform what they are trying to create and the purposes they envision their technology serving.

Creation requires time, skills, money, and often infrastructural support, investments that demand some kind of compensation. Clearly, the research and development that corporations fund is aimed at either saving money through resulting efficiencies or generating revenues by bringing new products or services to market. But even the research of public-sector scientists is aimed at serving institutional demands, typically those of funding agencies that have identified particular needs and encourage investigation in specific directions (e.g., finding a cure for cancer, understanding the social impact of screen violence). Users, too, whether individuals or organizations, shape technological development, both through the demands or needs they express and, ultimately, how they adapt the technology to their daily lives. Communication technologies, for example, are often envisioned and promoted as serving idealistic purposes like public education or democracy, but wind up being employed just as frequently for entertainment, amusement, or commerce. As the Canadian physicist Ursula M. Franklin puts it:

The authors wish to thank John Maxwell for his work on previous iterations of this chapter. John is an associate professor and director of the Master of Publishing Program at Simon Fraser University.

Aleutie/iStockphoto.

Do you agree with Slack and Wise that our society has an "almost religious-like reverence" for machines?

> What needs to be emphasized is that technologies are developed and used within a particular social, economic, and political context. They arise out of a social structure, they are grafted on to it, and they may reinforce it or destroy it, often in ways that are neither foreseen nor foreseeable. (1996: 57)

Here, technology belongs to a larger social system, and our predominant means of communication can tell us a lot about our culture. Two Canadian scholars, Harold Innis and Marshall McLuhan, were the first communication theorists to bring serious attention to the idea that the ways in which people communicate might actually shape a society and its culture, focusing on the form of communication rather than on its contents.

Innis (1950), a political economist, argued that each medium has a particular bias and thereby sets the basic parameters for the functioning of any society. In this regard, he claims that oral communication and early hieroglyphic writing on clay tended to maintain cultural practices through time and emphasize a close-knit society that preserved outlooks, values, and understandings over long periods. In his words, Innis saw these media as having a time bias; their use necessitated direct and close contact, privileging the temporal endurance, as opposed to the spatial extension, of social relations. For instance, the ways in which oral societies preserve knowledge and cultural integrity are fundamentally different from those of literate society. But the capacity of oral societies to preserve the past, to transform that past as necessary, and to base law in custom illustrates their stability and their tendency to preserve, extend, and adapt culture.

6.1

Time Bias

Societies have both history and geography—or, as Harold Innis would say, societies occupy both time and space. One way societies occupy time and space is through their communication media, which, Innis argued, have characteristic biases that make some more conducive to carrying messages through time (e.g., heavy, durable materials like clay or the brick walls of buildings) and others more conducive to carrying messages through space (e.g., light, easily transportable materials like parchment or paper). Time-biased media are time-binding media in that they connect us to the past through their enduring images and messages. Think of the stained-glass windows in churches that relate biblical tales, war memorials that ask us to remember fallen ancestors, or buildings that carry the names of their founders etched in stone or concrete. Similarly, historical murals, such as those in Chemainus, British Columbia, or Vankleek Hill, Ontario (see the accompanying photo), offer residents and visitors a sense of the town's past.

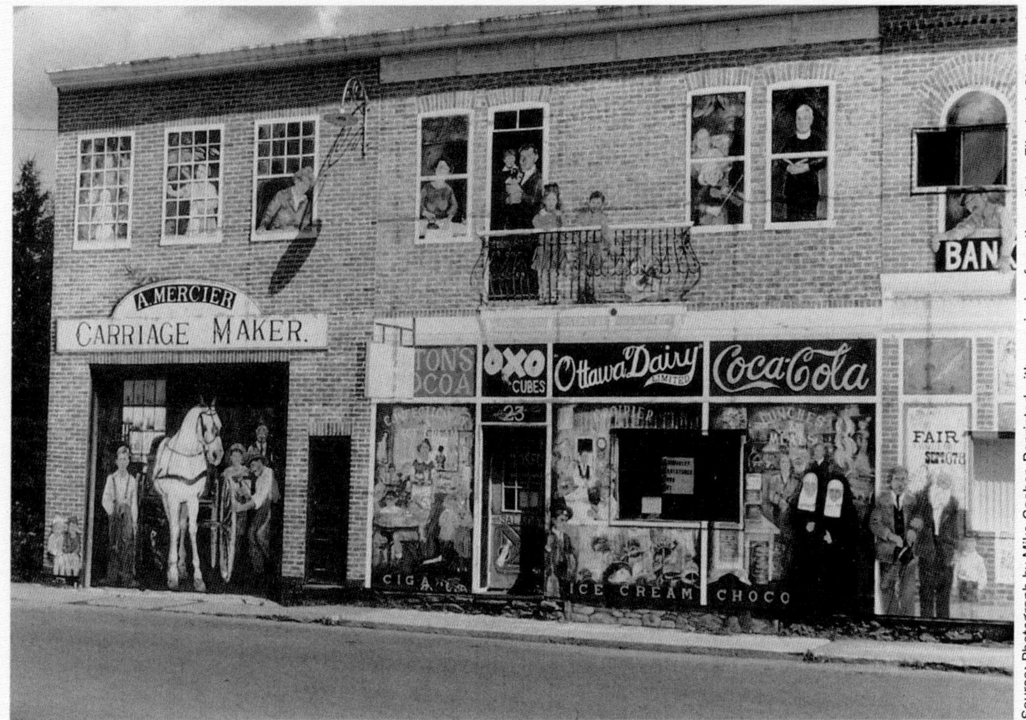

Source: Photograph by Mike Gasher. Reprinted with permission from the artists: Elisabeth Skelly and Odile Têtu.

Historical murals, such as this one in Vankleek Hill, Ontario, offer residents and visitors a sense of the town's past.

Written communication, on the other hand, favours the establishment and maintenance of social relations through space, such as empires and power blocs spread over large geographic areas and across different cultures. Innis used the Roman Empire as his example. To conquer and then coordinate and administer such a vast empire required a written system for recording and communicating messages on a portable medium that could be transported across vast distances. Laws were created, written down accurately, and then transported to the far reaches of the empire. In this way, Roman society spread "through space," what Innis called a space bias. As he states:

> A medium of communication has an important influence on the dissemination of knowledge over space and over time and it becomes necessary to study its characteristics in order to appraise its influence in its cultural setting. According to its characteristics it may be better suited to the dissemination of knowledge over time than over space, particularly if the medium is heavy and durable and not suited to transportation, or to the dissemination of knowledge over space than over time, particularly if the medium is light and easily transported. The relative emphasis on time or space will imply a bias of significance to the culture in which it is imbedded. (Innis, 1951: 33)

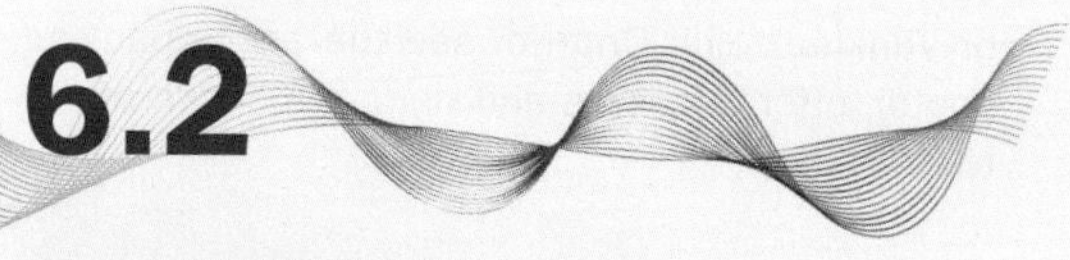

Space Bias

The notion of space bias does not come easily to some, perhaps because the word *bias* most commonly has negative connotations. Innis used the word to mean "tendency" or "emphasis." The following footprint diagram in Figure 6.1 illustrates the space bias of satellite technology. By beaming down a signal to a particular area of the earth's surface, a satellite creates, at least to some degree, a community—of all those people receiving the same signal. People choose whether to watch and which channel to watch, of course, and different satellite footprints (the terrestrial areas covered by specific satellite signals) can carry the same content. The broadcast of a news program from a particular city to widespread geographic areas, however, creates an artificial spatial extension of that city. In some ways, CNN and BBC are extensions of Atlanta and London, respectively, just as in the print medium *The Globe and Mail* is, to a degree, an extension of Central Canada. These are all instances of space bias.

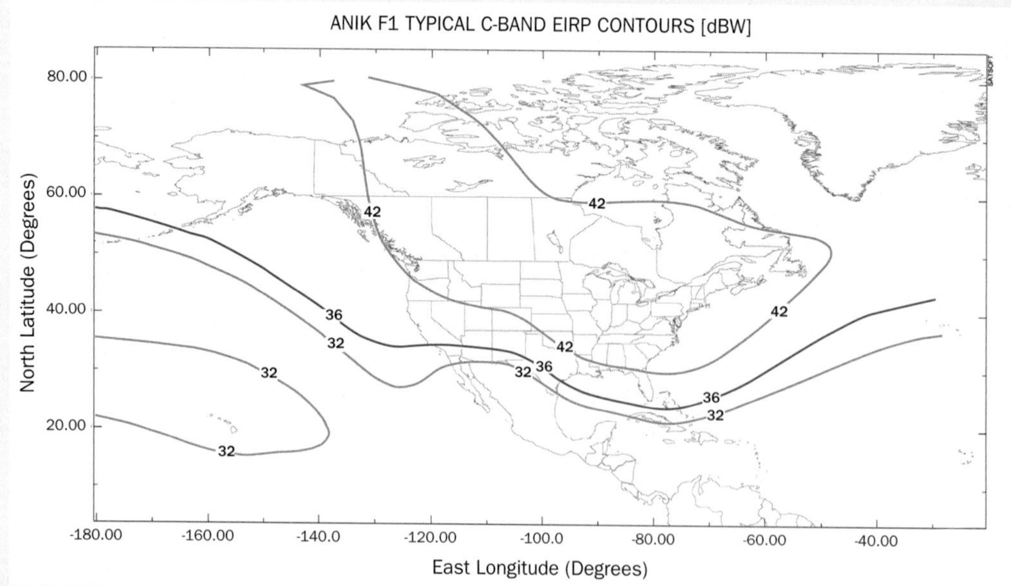

FIGURE 6.1 The Anik F1 satellite

Telesat Canada's Anik F1 satellite creates a primary spatial community encompassing virtually all of Canada and much of the United States. As the map shows, weather signals extend that community to the rest of North America.

Source: Footprint courtesy of Telesat Canada.

McLuhan, a scholar of English literature, took up Innis's core ideas and adapted them to the modern period. McLuhan first studied the impact of printing, capturing its influence on society by coining the term *typographical man*, which referred to Western culture after the invention of printing with movable type (in Europe) by Johannes Gutenberg in the fifteenth century. The printed book was a tremendously powerful means of communicating knowledge; McLuhan and others have argued that the printed book transformed Western societies so that working with this medium encouraged particular ways of thinking—namely, logical, linear thought, as well as individualism, conceptuality, science, and monotheism (McLuhan, 1962).

Next, McLuhan turned to an analysis of electronic society. He studied the impact of radio, television, photography, and cinema on what we think of as modern societies. McLuhan argued that electronic media created, for the first time in history, the possibility of instant communication between any two points on the globe: he referred to this reality as the *global village*. In using the term, he meant that electronic society has vast information-gathering and transmission capacities sufficient to make us intimately aware of the activities of people around the world. McLuhan referred to electronic communication as an "outered nervous system," and saw such media as extending our senses of sight, touch, vision, and hearing. McLuhan expressed his ideas in a distinctive, aphoristic, and provocative way; his books were read widely outside the academy, and he had a great impact on 1960s politics, advertising, and media in North America and Europe.

Both Innis (1950) and McLuhan (1962), as well as academics in the Toronto School (of communication theory) who followed in their wake (e.g., Goody, 1977; de Kerckhove, 1995), placed their emphasis on the ways in which particular forms of media influenced the structure and development of societies. They drew attention to media form—their material properties—rather than content.

Slack and Wise (2007: 127–29) encourage us to think about technology in terms of "articulation," getting past the idea of technologies as mere things. Technologies instead are products *and* practices that assume their specific form thanks to their particular connections, their place in a network of related activities. They are, in other words, embedded—socially, culturally, politically, and economically. The **cyborg** metaphor, for example, emphasizes how humans and human activity articulate with technologies (see Box. 6.3).

In his classic work *Television: Technology and Cultural Form* (1974), Raymond Williams makes a similar point, arguing that technology reflects the overall organization of society. Television, for instance, offers programs to fill our leisure time and advertising to fuel the consumption of a vast range of goods and services, thereby driving and maintaining the mass society that industrialization created.

This also means that specific devices change their purpose and function, depending on the context in which they are embedded. A laptop computer, for example, may be perceived and used as a word processor and research tool in the workplace, and a games console and video platform at home. On a larger scale, the same medium can assume a very different form and purpose, depending on the country or political system in which it operates. If television, for example, is a medium of general information and entertainment in Western democracies like Canada, it is strictly a medium of propaganda in totalitarian regimes like North Korea. It is the same device, but situated in a different context and resulting a different outcome.

These perspectives on technology draw attention to the complex network of ideas and practices of which technologies are a part.

Thinking about Technology

In *Questioning Technology* (1999), philosopher Andrew Feenberg provides an account of the major conceptual frameworks social scientists and philosophers have used to think about technology. His analysis provides four main ways to understand technology: instrumentalism, determinism, substantivism, and critical theory. A fifth perspective, constructivism, is closely related to critical theory.

Instrumentalism is a relatively naive position, which views technology as a value-neutral tool that can shorten the path to natural ends or social goals; technology here is simply a means to an end, a simple tool for our use.

Technological determinism holds that technology operates according to an inexorable logic inherent in the technology itself, "an autonomous functional logic that can be explained without reference to society" (Feenberg, 1999: 77; see also Croteau and Hoynes, 2014: 299–300). Technology here is associated with notions of progress, perceived as a straightforward track toward improvement, and the effects of technology are attributed by determinists to the technology itself, rather than to human decisions about how it is developed and employed. It is a determinist view, for example, that the internet enhances individual freedom and democracy, ignoring the same technology's potential for disseminating propaganda, the power of governments and corporations to control its use, and the fact that not all citizens have the same access to networked computers or comparable skill in using them (see Hindman, 2018). From the determinist perspective, human control over the exact direction of technological development is minimal—the technology has a life of its own.

In a stance related to technological determinism, **substantivism** claims that technology operates according to its own inherent logic, but this logic does not necessarily represent

TABLE 6.1
Views on Technology at a Glance

Instrumentalism	Determinism
· perceives technology as value-neutral · sees technology as a simple means to an end · emphasizes technology's efficiency as a tool for our use	· sees technology operating according to a logic inherent to the technology itself · sees technology as having a life of its own; it is what it is · sees its use and adoption largely divorced from societal forces · is associated with notions of progress
EXAMPLE: A cup is simply a vessel to contain water, coffee, or tea.	**EXAMPLE:** The internet fosters individual freedoms and democracy.

Substantivism
· is similar to determinism in that technology is the driving force behind its use and implementation · contends that technology has its own inherent logic, largely divorced from societal forces · maintains that effects of technology can be positive or negative
EXAMPLE: Widespread use of the automobile leads to car culture (urban sprawl, congestion, air pollution, dependence on fossil fuels).
Critical Theory
· emphasizes societal choice over all aspects of technology (its development, use, incorporation within societal structures) · avers that technology does not have a life of its own or an inherent logic, but is shaped by societal forces, including economics, politics, culture
EXAMPLE: Radio developed as a medium of broadcasting as opposed to point-to-point communications.
Constructivism
· is related to critical theory · sees that technology is socially constructed, shaped by societal forces in any given society and historical period · contends that any technology has both a technical and a social logic · maintains that technology is embedded within particular societies
EXAMPLE: Green technologies were developed in societies concerned with climate change.

Cyborgs

We typically associate cyborgs—or cybernetic organisms—with science-fiction characters in movies or video games: Alex Murphy (*RoboCop*); Max Da Costa (*Elysium*); Ava (*The Machine*); Jax, Kano, and Sub-Zero (*Mortal Kombat*); Master Chief (*Halo*); Matthew Kane (*Quake IV*).

One of the reasons these characters resonate so powerfully is that it is not much of a stretch to see ourselves as part human, part machine, particularly in a technologically advanced and affluent society such as Canada. In a well-known essay, Donna Haraway (1991) insists that we *are* cyborgs. The cyborg is "a creature of social reality as well as a creature of fiction," she writes, arguing that "we are all chimeras, theorized and fabricated hybrids of machine and organism; in short, we are cyborgs" (149–50). Haraway celebrates the cyborg as a model for challenging standard divisions of identity:

> Late-twentieth-century machines have made thoroughly ambiguous the difference between natural and artificial, mind and body, self-developing and externally designed, and many other distinctions that used to apply to organisms and machines. (152)

The cyborg metaphor is a clear manifestation of the idea that technology comprises much more than machinery, but it is tied as well into techniques or ways of performing tasks and reflects the larger sociocultural environment in which machines and ways of doing things are embedded.

To take a simple but far-reaching example, the priority society places on health care and lifespan longevity can be seen in the efforts expended on developing technologies to improve life (e.g., eyeglasses, hearing aids, prosthetics), extend life (e.g., pacemakers, immunization, antibiotics, organ transplants), and even create life (e.g., fertility treatments, cloning).

If technological systems can enhance personal comfort and make it easier to communicate and to travel, there is a flip side. In the workplace we can very much feel like the proverbial cogs in the machine, especially if our job is one in a series of repetitive, mechanical steps and does not require thinking, judgment, or creativity—or, if our jobs are made redundant by technology, as happened in the newspaper industry when computerization displaced many printers' jobs (see McKercher, 2002).

This is what Harry Braverman (1974) famously described as **deskilling**, the process by which previously skilled jobs are broken into a series of much simpler and discrete tasks that can be performed by semi-skilled or unskilled workers.

Braverman attributed this process largely to the **scientific management** movement in the late nineteenth century, which he defined as "a science of the management of others' work under capitalist conditions" (90). Scientific management is sometimes called *Taylorism*, after Frederick Winslow Taylor, who sought to improve economic efficiency through increases in labour productivity. In the early twentieth century, Taylor conducted a series of time and motion studies to break down work-related tasks into their component parts and determine the most efficient means of organizing such tasks (see Taylor, 1997 [1911]). Taylorism was ideally suited to industrialized, mass-production processes that combined workers and machinery in various forms of assembly line.

progress or improvement. Take the automobile, for example; the availability of mass-produced cars in the early twentieth century led to the development of large-scale infrastructure (roads, highways, suburbs, shopping malls) designed with cars and car travel in mind. We now live in a car culture, where urban sprawl, air pollution, and dependency on fossil fuels have become significant problems with no easy solution. The structure prompted by the technology's adoption becomes self-reinforcing: the easiest way to live in what has become a car culture is to drive a car. We become, in a sense, slaves to the machine.

None of instrumentalism, determinism, or substantivism is adequate to fully explain technology. Proponents of **critical theory** insist we have choices about how we develop technology, shape its development, use it, incorporate

elenabs/iStockphoto.

How might we think about smartphones using the five perspectives on technology explained here?

it within larger systems, and engage with it to a greater or lesser extent. The theorists Herbert Marcuse and Michel Foucault opened up the opportunity to think about technology and technological development as something other than an external force, making it possible to conceive of technology as existing within society, as integral to society in the same way as religion, education, culture, economics, and political systems. Technology is thus subject to the same kinds of criticism and reform.

This twofold notion—that technology exists within society and that social forces and political decision-making can control both the nature of the machines that emerge and their usage—means that technology develops in a **socially contingent** manner. In other words, technology arises and takes a particular form depending on the dynamics of the society in which it emerges—which may include rejection. Critical theory sees technology as offering possibilities from which society chooses a course of action, raising issues of power, control, and freedom that society must address. As we discuss in Chapter 7, Canada was compelled to make choices about how to perceive and organize the new technology of radio in the 1920s—whether it would function as a medium of local or national broadcasting, as an industry or as a public service. We as a society continue to make such choices.

Today, **constructivism** largely prevails in studies of technology. Constructivists argue that technology is socially constructed and shaped by social forces. There are always viable alternatives to our research and development priorities, the form technology will take, and the uses to which it will be put. Constructivists argue that to succeed, any given technology must have a technical *and* a social logic. We can see this today in the example of technologies employing alternative energy sources, such as hybrid and electric cars, intended to respond to environmental concerns. Governments can encourage conservation measures and green energy projects, and automotive manufacturers can produce vehicles powered by alternative fuels, but it is society at large that will determine their viability and their precise uses.

The constructivist perspective seeks to recover a sense of history when regarding any technology. The telephone, for example, was once conceived as a broadcast receiver, and after a long history as a point-to-point oral communication device, in its current smartphone iteration it serves as a point-to-point written communication device, camera, sound recorder, video screen, music player, notepad, agenda, GPS, and computer tablet. Given this history, David Croteau and William Hoynes argue that "the development and application of new media technologies is neither fixed nor fully predictable." While a new medium's inherent technical capacities provide constraints and parameters, these technologies

© stephenmeese/iStockphoto.

Green energy technologies like wind turbines and solar panels are a response to concerns about the world's dependency on fossil fuels. How do technologies like this relate to social forces?

are ultimately defined by social forces, including legislation, policy, social norms, market pressures, and how they come to be used by people (2014: 300; see also Flew and Smith, 2014; Goggin, 2011). For these reasons, Wiebe Bijker claims that what we call a machine or a technology is better understood as a **socio-technical ensemble** (Bijker, 1993: 125).

Technology and Western Society

All cultures and societies can be seen as being based on tightly integrated technologies. Sociologist of science Bruno Latour suggests that what distinguishes modern society from so-called traditional societies may be the size and scope of our socio-technical ensembles, rather than any qualitative difference in the way people think or how cultures act (see Blok and Jensen, 2011).

So enthusiastic is the acceptance of technology by Western, especially North American, society that some would argue the world is increasingly in the clutches of the technological imperative—that is, we have convinced ourselves that we should continuously develop new technologies and apply them broadly for a better life. Rather than change our ways, we tend to assume that technological solutions will be found for problems like climate change or the degradation of the oceans. Furthermore, development of technology in Western society is usually a deliberate attempt to create material objects, interventions, or systems that allow the developer to reap financial reward; the economies of Western nations are wrapped up intimately with the innovation, development, and promotion of new technologies. One result is that the technological distance between countries of the Global North and Global South in communication has been increasing. This gap is part of what we call the **digital divide,** a term referring to the disparities between technological *haves* and *have-nots*, and which we discuss at greater length in Chapter 11. These gaps between haves and have-nots can be measured between countries, but also within domestic populations (see van Dijk, 2012).

The enthusiastic acceptance of technology by technologically oriented societies is sometimes so complete that both analysts and the general public accept the projections about the future of society based on technological capacity. This is a straightforward example of technological determinism. Technological determinists, for instance, have argued that the internet leads to greater democratization (e.g., Shirky, 2008, 2010; Bruns, 2008); in fact, this assertion is hotly disputed (Hindman, 2018; Grofman *et al.*, 2014; McChesney, 2013; Dahlberg and Siapera, 2007). Greater amounts of information do not equate automatically with a better-informed citizenry or a healthier democracy, as we have seen recently in the manipulations of social media to influence election results, disseminate falsehoods, and create moral panics (discussed in greater detail in Chapter 10). We can identify in a general sense what new technologies enable—for example, the internet enables the collection and rapid

Rawpixel/iStockphoto.

Media are socio-technical ensembles in the sense that they are embedded, and largely defined by, how they are used in any given society.

dissemination of information—but precisely how those enabling capacities will be employed or how far they extend is unpredictable. We need to ask, *What kind of information will be collected and disseminated, and who will undertake these tasks, and with what intent?*

Determinism fails to consider that technology does not drop out of the clear blue sky or from the head of some genius. Rather, it is derived from specific and typically collective efforts to solve problems or find opportunities. Technological determinism also ignores the role of state and institutional control over the industrialized application of technology. As is apparent, the internet can as easily be used for dictatorship or terrorism as for democracy; it can further bigotry as easily as it can enable enlightened debate. If governments wish, they can enact policy so that a certain technology (e.g., the internet) can be used only in certain ways (e.g., for legal forms of communication), and hence, with certain consequences (e.g., clamping down on child pornography or organized crime). Such control is not just in the hands of governments—often, corporate interests exercise their power to shape technological systems in order to preserve market influence (see Box 6.4). But users, too, play a role.

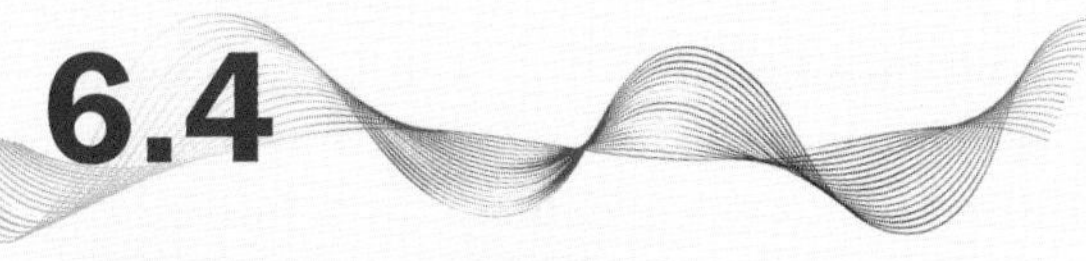

6.4 Platforms or Walled Gardens?

By Fenwick McKelvey

Apple Inc. is best known as a computer company, but today what the company really sells is access to its own private ecosystem. Your Macbook or iPhone work best together, as part of the rest of its integrated line-up of computer products and services (e.g., iTunes, iWatch, iPad, iCloud, as well as physical and online stores). It is a business model often called a "platform" because Apple charges to access its ecosystem, and each of its products directs revenue to its other services. Critics call it a "walled garden." As *Newsweek* explained it, "Instead of making a one-time sale, each iPad sold becomes a recurring revenue stream for Apple" (Lyons, 2010, p. 49). The iPad encourages users to buy their videos from iTunes, and those videos will run only on Apple devices. On an iPhone, users can only buy apps sold through its official store, of which Apple earns a commission on every purchase. Apple's control over its walled garden extends to developers too, who rely on Apple to access customers (Nieborg and Helmond, forthcoming). Critics of the walled garden question who it keeps out as much as who it lets in. In 2011, Apple rejected the game *Phone Story*, a humorous but critical look at the process of manufacturing an iPhone. The game's stages included mining conflict minerals to working in China in a Foxconn factory to make the phone. Apple banned the game allegedly for "excessively objectionable or crude content," among other things (Dredge, 2011). The power and profitability of Apple's walled gardens has inspired many other technology firms, with Facebook, Google, Amazon, and Snap all experimenting with devices and services to create their own private ecosystems that now not only sell you access but also mine your data and sell advertising. This is the new normal in what's called the "platform economy" (Srnicek, 2017).

Fenwick McKelvey is an associate professor in the Department of Communication Studies at Concordia University in Montreal.

The Dangers of Technology and Technological Hubris

Implicit in our everyday perspective on technology is the notion that technology can transform society for the good—that it inherently contributes to progress. But as Jacques Ellul (1964) points out, the consequences of the transformative dynamic of a given technology can be hard to discern in its initial application. Antibiotics serve as a good example. While antibiotics have been a godsend to public health, we now understand that strains of antibiotic-resistant bacteria have emerged precisely because of our overuse of these drugs.

The 1912 sinking of the *Titanic* is perhaps the most famous symbol of **technological hubris**—the massive ship was viewed by many so-called experts as unsinkable because it was the latest and greatest product of human ingenuity. This example of hubris cost more than 1,500 lives.

In communication, similar issues surround the limitations of technology; as Ellul warns, the positive and negative effects of technology are inseparable. While more people are able to access vast amounts of information, economies of scale come to influence what information is available; thus, information attracting only a limited audience tends to disappear or, more likely, is not gathered and stored in the first place. Community newspapers across Canada are disappearing for precisely this reason; their operations are often too small for those owners who seek greater returns on their investment, with the result that many communities have lost reliable sources of information about local current affairs. The control systems of the large producers tell them that they can make more money elsewhere, especially as more and more segments of society are subjected to a commercial logic (see Chapter 9). In a similar vein, elements as mundane as the number of hours one might spend sitting in front of a computer or TV screen, or the lack of socialization involved in working from home, may have considerable unanticipated health consequences when multiplied throughout society.

Media Convergence

For much of their history, media technologies operated in distinct fields, organized as discrete industries, owned and controlled by industry-specific organizations, and governed by particular sets of laws and policies (see Chapters 7 and 8). This history gives the impression that these **media silos** were products of the technologies themselves, that the technical specifications of analog media determined their application and their organization. But if their technical composition was not irrelevant, it was not determining. Technology did not prevent newspaper publishers from using their printing presses to publish magazines or books, or from moving into other media spheres. In fact, newspaper publishers were among the first to get into the radio broadcasting business in the 1920s and '30s. Similarly, there were two visions for radio in its earliest years: point-to-point communications and broadcasting. If broadcasting became the predominant industry form, point-to-point was used for things like marine communications as well as police, fire, and ambulance services. Even the internet was first devised as a system for military communications. The history of convergence demonstrates that these **silos** were social constructs.

The word *convergence* means coming together, such as two rivers converging to form one larger river. **Media convergence** refers to either the merging of previously distinct media technologies through digitization and computer networking, or a business strategy by which the media properties of a communication conglomerate work together (see Gasher, 2013). Media convergence has a longer history than is generally acknowledged. Some newspaper publishers did engage in other kinds of printing and, as mentioned above, newspaper companies were among the first organizations to invest in radio stations. Radio broadcasters later entered the television business (e.g., CBC/Radio-Canada). Hand in hand with these developments, we have seen a long-term trend toward corporate convergence.

© Manakin/iStockphoto.

The *Titanic*, which sank after hitting an iceberg in the North Atlantic in 1912, remains a potent symbol of technological hubris. The arrogant belief that it was unsinkable resulted in the loss of more than 1,500 lives. Do arrogant beliefs about technology still exist? What kinds of "unsinkable" technologies still exist in our world?

If, early in the twentieth century, independent newspapers became part of chains and independent radio stations became part of networks, it became common in the latter part of the century for companies like Quebecor and Bell—originally the Bell Telephone Company of Canada, now Bell Canada Enterprises (BCE)—to expand into other communication industries and even into unrelated fields. Quebecor, for example, began as the publisher of a single community newspaper in Montreal in 1950, and subsequently evolved into a communication conglomerate with subsidiaries in newspaper, magazine, and book publishing; television broadcasting; cable television distribution; and music retailing (see Chapter 9).

Digitization and computer networking facilitated this transition. Digitization is the process by which all forms of information—textual, visual, aural—are translated into a common language of 0s and 1s, so that content produced originally for one digital platform can be used on all other platforms. Computer networking ties all of these digital platforms together on our various devices. The result is what we are witnessing today: the breaking down of meaningful distinctions between media forms. We listen to music on our smartphones, we watch television on our laptops, and we read books on our e-readers.

As we detail in Chapters 7 and 8, governments are significant players in the convergence game. Historically, public policy—laws, regulations, conventions—has supported media silos between, for example, broadcasting and telecommunications, between publishing and broadcasting; government agencies continue to patrol these boundaries where cross-media ownership and corporate concentration are concerned.

Policy decisions in the communication sphere are guided by three central issues: (1) ensuring that the needs of the public and of cultural and national groups are met, (2) ensuring that Canada has viable cultural industries, and at the same time (3) ensuring that certain businesses do not become too powerful and thwart the participation of others and prevent further social and technological development. These are precisely the concerns prompted by the market power of Apple, Google, Microsoft, Amazon, and Facebook, media companies operating internationally and which in 2016 became the world's five most valuable corporations (Mosco, 2017: 10-11; see also Mosco, 2014; Taras, 2015; Hindman, 2018).

While convergence has obvious implications for media economics, policy formation, and the specific cultural industries, Henry Jenkins (2006) perceives a cultural transformation as well. What he terms "convergence culture" entails "a shift in the way we think about our relations to media" and "may have implications for how we learn, work, participate in the political process, and connect with other people around the world" (22–3).

The Internet and Digitization

While we take the internet and digitization for granted today, it is important to remember that these technological shifts are still relatively new—we celebrated the thirtieth anniversary of the World Wide Web in 2019—and that we as a society continue to adapt to these evolving forms of communication. The internet presents challenges for traditional conceptions of communication technology and industries: in its starting assumptions, its structure, and the ways in which people are using it. The sheer size of the internet today means that how it differs from older communication models represents a major shift in the way we must think about communication media. For instance, according to International Telecommunication Union statistics for 2017, 48 per cent of the world's population now uses the internet (ITU, 2017), and it is structured as an international, rather than national, communication system (see Figure 6.2).

The foundations of the internet were laid in the United States in the 1960s, when large amounts of Cold War–era government funding were poured into the new computer-science departments at universities. Researchers at the time were interested in developing an interactive

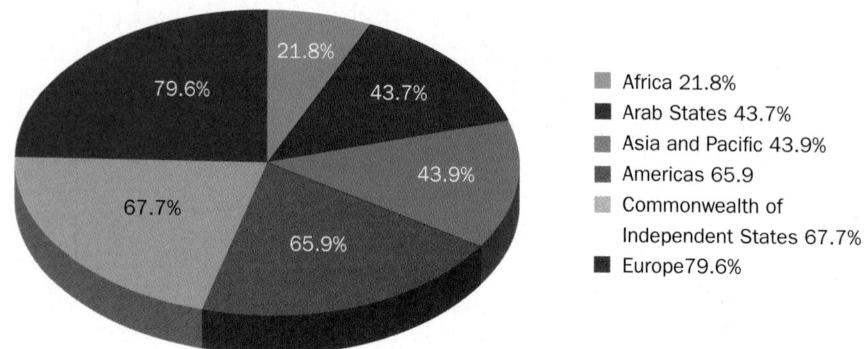

FIGURE 6.2 Internet users in the world, distribution by world regions, 2017

Internet World Stats (www.internetworldstats.com/stats.htm)

computer network. The original **ARPANET** project (circa 1969) connected computer systems at five US universities, enabling information and message exchange between them (see Figure 6.3). One of the key ideas behind the network was that if, in the event of a nuclear attack, one or more of its nodes were destroyed, the network could still function. ARPANET grew into what we now know as the internet—the international network of computer networks—through the 1970s and early '80s, by which time most of the underlying technological infrastructure in use today had been worked out.

Demonstrating a particular socio-technical ensemble, a number of interesting features of the early internet shaped how it works today. First, the internet was developed as a **peer-to-peer system**; there is no central control point in the network. The internet is arranged like a web, in which points on the network are redundantly interconnected; the route by which any particular piece of information travels is guided by software rather than by the physical connections, and all points on the internet are equals or peers. The internet trades information units called *packets*, which are something like envelopes with "To:" and "From:" labels on them. Network software reads these address labels and makes decisions about how to transfer packets along the web. Furthermore, these packets are like sealed envelopes; the contents are important only to the computer systems at either end of a transmission. The internet is thus described as an end-to-end architecture, with the network itself remaining neutral about what is being transferred. This feature is called *network neutrality* and ensures that all data being transferred receives equal treatment by the network. The concept of net neutrality is at the heart of how the internet is to be defined, whether as a public good supporting democracy or as a commodity belonging to the market economy (Schulte, 2011: 48).

An interesting feature of the internet is that it has existed for much of its life as a publicly funded system, first in the United States, and today in most other countries as well. Since the mid-1990s, however, more and more of the internet is made up of corporate, for-profit components, while substantial chunks worldwide still are run by governments or academic institutions. This has given the internet a different character from large-scale corporate media, and effective corporate control of the internet remains limited.

A second significant feature of the internet is that its underlying technologies have for the most part been developed and released non-commercially as open systems and as **open-source software**. This means that the software, standards, and protocols making the internet run are not owned or controlled by any one party but, rather, are publicly available.

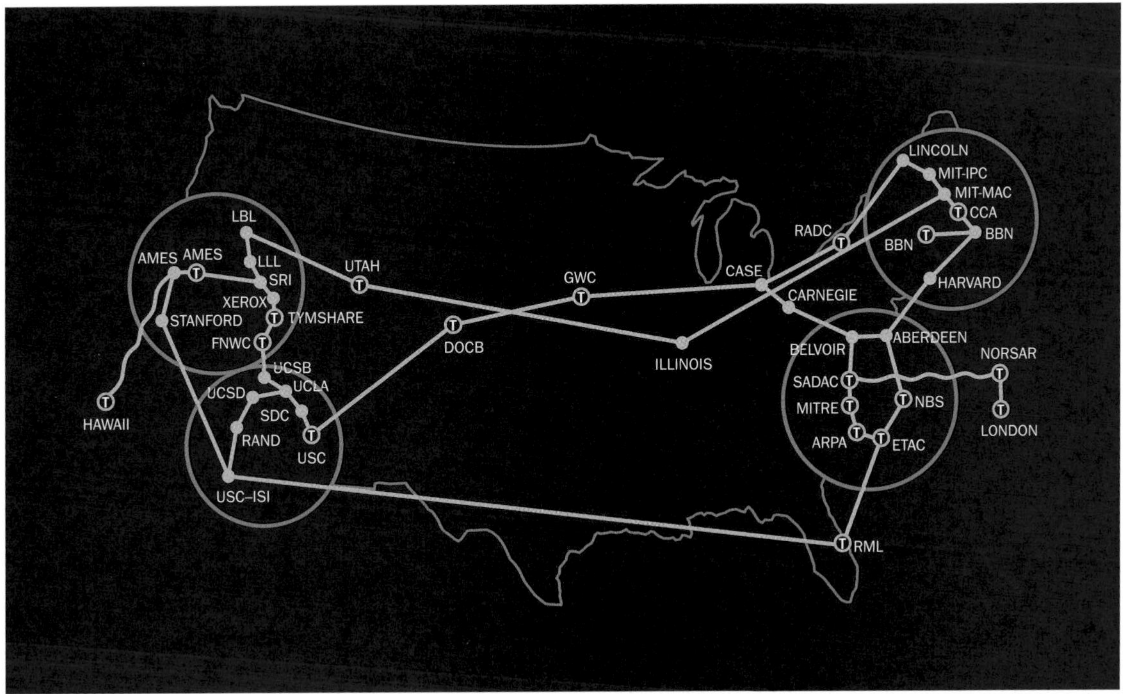

FIGURE 6.3 ARPA geographic map, September 1973

The original ARPANET project connected computer systems at five US universities, enabling information and message exchange between them. One of the key ideas behind the network was that if, in the event of a nuclear attack, one or more of its nodes were destroyed, the network could still function.

Source: Courtesy of the Computer History Museum.

This model of systems development has proved enormously successful for the internet itself, but it also has cultural implications. In a world in which works—text, music, video, and so on—are stored and transferred digitally and can be copied and distributed globally in an instant for almost no cost, traditional conceptions of copyright and intellectual property have become increasingly problematic, especially for century-old industries that have grown up around a more traditional copyright landscape, treating content as a form of private property. Into the legal battles that result from technological change comes the **open-source** movement, bringing with it a completely different sensibility about how and by what terms works should be circulated and exchanged. We discuss copyright in greater detail in Chapter 8.

With regard to internet usage by the general public, the World Wide Web emerged as an internet application in the early 1990s and quickly grew to be the largest user of internet bandwidth. The web, which provides a friendly interface to the internet, grew in its first decade to the point where it allowed for an almost infinite number of niche audiences to access content of interest to them. For much of the web's first decade, its basic model was a simple page-delivery system. However, its increasingly interactive capability has transformed users into veritable webmasters.

The web's status as a new, interactive mass medium—Web 2.0—comes to the fore when we consider the extent to which it enables consumers of media content to become producers as well. Some have termed this trend "prosumption" or "produsage" and celebrate it as an important step toward the democratization of communication and the erosion of corporate media power (see Lessig, 2008; Bruns, 2008; Jenkins, 2006). Examples of sites and applications that enable individuals to produce their own content abound: Wikipedia, YouTube, Facebook, Twitter, Instagram, Spotify, Strava, as well as countless websites, blogs, and citizen journalism sites. Axel Bruns's four key principles of produsage are (1) inclusive rather than exclusive production; (2) a "heterarchical" network structure rather than a hierarchical, top-down structure; (3) always unfinished and continuing production; and (4) freely available, community-held content in an information commons (Bruns, 2008).

While there is no doubt we enjoy increased capacity to participate in the production, distribution, and sharing of media content, the extent to which this represents democratization, threatens corporate power, or provides us with an information commons—a space open to all—is highly debatable. David Croteau and William Hoynes (2014) note, first of all, that the extent of content production by users is vastly overstated. They remind us of the 1 per cent rule, which claims that "for every person who creates content, there are 99 who do not" (307). For his part, Christian Fuchs (2009) maintains that user interactivity actually *extends* corporate power in what he calls "the Internet gift economy." Fuchs explains that in exchange for free access to these commercially owned sites and web applications, users contribute free content, which enhances the sites' commercial value. Fuchs writes, "The more users make of advertisement-based free online platforms and the more time they spend online producing, consuming, and exchanging content, communicating with others, the higher the value of the prosumer commodity they produce will become, the higher the advertisement prices will rise, and the higher the profits of the specific Internet corporations will be" (2009: 82; see also Elmer, 2004; Hindman, 2018; Powers and Jablonski, 2015). Fernando Bermejo (2011) sees in this a "double articulation" of audience labour, in that "users are producers of content that attracts other users while, at the same time, generating data about themselves that is used to turn them into consumers" (273–4).

That said, interactivity is a defining feature of digital media, and it is clear that some industries (e.g., publishing, sound recording) have been shaken to the core by our new-found capacity to bypass traditional production and distribution channels. Interactivity serves for the moment as an example of the unforeseen consequences of technological development in the media sphere and how specific devices and applications are socially embedded, tied into larger cultural, political, and economic matrices.

Another defining feature of digital media is mobility. The ongoing transition from wired to wireless has implications for the form and content of media, and how we engage with them. As a highly connected society, we are still coming to terms with what it means to be able to carry our devices wherever we go and access wireless networks in an increasing number of places. For one thing, mobility alters fundamentally the spatial and temporal bounds of our communications (see Crow et al., 2010: 10). We can work at home and play while at work, and we are confined less and less to the schedules set by others, whether that means watching our favourite TV series when we want—through time-shifting or binge viewing—or responding to texts or email messages either as they arrive or during a set time in the day. The flip side, of course, is that we are increasingly contactable, whether by employers on our time off or by telemarketers. Mobility also encourages further technological convergence. Rather than our needing separate devices for specific purposes, each of our mobile devices offers multiple functions. As we noted earlier, the hand-held smartphone allows us to read an e-book, watch television, make a short video, surf the web, play games, or, yes, talk to someone.

A third defining characteristic of digital media is individualization. If the legacy media—especially cinema, radio, television—were typically experienced collectively, digital media are much more personal. This trend began in the 1980s with the personal computer, but it gradually included cellphones (phone numbers belong to individuals rather than households), MP3 players (with their personalized playlists), and the screens—either cellphone or computer—on which TV shows, sports events, and movies are increasingly viewed, and on which games are played. A significant part of the attraction of these devices is precisely their personalization; we can adapt them to our own particular needs and use them as we see fit (see Goggin, 2011; Crow et al., 2010).

Technological Change: A Cost–Benefit Analysis

If there has been a note of caution in our discussion of technology so far, it is for good reason. As much as we marvel at the scope and pace of technological change in the media sphere—none of the authors would wish to return to the days when a textbook such as this would be researched within the physical confines of libraries and written on a typewriter—history teaches us that benefits always come with costs or trade-offs.

Increased Communication Capacity, Speed, and Flexibility

For many of us, it is easier to communicate and to find information than ever before. We now speak in terms of bandwidth and nanoseconds, how quickly and globally we can communicate.

Canada is and always has been at the forefront of communication technology, beginning with the first phone call made in the world by Alexander Graham Bell from Brantford, Ontario, to Paris, Ontario, in 1876; the first transatlantic telegraph message from Poldhu, England, to Signal Hill in St. John's, Newfoundland, in 1901; and the first radio broadcast, by Canadian Reginald Fessenden, on Christmas Eve in 1906. Canada was the first nation to launch a domestic communication satellite, and the federal government has maintained a commitment to both speed and capacity in the country's communications.

At the same time, we need to recognize that the digital divide that van Dijk (2012) analyzes pertains not only to the different nations of the world, but also between populations—even within countries like Canada that boast advanced communication infrastructure. We discuss the digital divide further in Chapter 11, but it is worth noting here that when it comes to internet access and usage, which many of us take for granted, there remain discrepancies among Canadians depending on income and educational levels, age, and community size. If Statistics Canada determined that 83 per cent of Canadian households had internet access in 2012 (the most recent statistics available), only 58 per cent of households with incomes of $30,000 or less enjoyed access. Similarly, only 28 per cent of Canadians 65 and over in the lowest income quartile used the internet, compared to 95 per cent aged 16 to 24 in the same income category (Statistics Canada, 2013). If the precise figures have no doubt changed since 2012, the trends they highlight remain pertinent. These distinctions become especially meaningful as government service outlets, schools, banks, insurance companies, and retailers presume access and disadvantage those without it. Some shops, for instance, now refuse cash, excluding those without a credit card or debit card.

Increased Flexibility in Production and Distribution

Over the last three decades, the traditional, centralized, capital-intensive model of media has been eroded by digital media. In the late 1980s, desktop publishing brought layout and the design of books and magazines to anyone with a computer, a laser printer, and some basic skills. In the mid-1990s, the web brought a new form of global distribution online at minimal cost. In the late 1990s and early 2000s, inexpensive digital tools transformed music and video production, and independent producers were increasingly able to reach audiences directly via social networking sites such as MySpace and Facebook. YouTube, Twitter, Instagram, and numerous others have furthered this trend, complemented by the proliferation of hand-held mobile devices.

But the emergence and growth of these corporate aggregators has resulted in the reintroduction of intermediaries, countering the initial trend. Some call it **re-intermediation**, prompted by the filtering capacities of these services. A good example is Spotify, which presents a new mechanism for filtering, sorting, and—more importantly—promoting music available online. YouTube provides another example, whereby hundreds of millions of video clips are available for free. These re-intermediators have established their own brand identity and presence. With the burgeoning of content, the traditional challenges of producing, manufacturing, and distributing product are being replaced by the provision of a wide range of content filtered, organized, and capable of being sampled and remixed in new ways. What makes this possible is not just a wealth of content but an enormous increase in the amount of readily available information about the content, through blogs, reviews, tags, comments, and cataloguing data (see Anderson, 2006).

But if these services make available vast quantities of both professional and user-generated content, those who own and manage them nonetheless reassert their power to determine the terms for access to their services. This includes whether we can download content and at what price, whether and how much they will compensate content producers, and, ultimately, whether they will prohibit certain materials on, for example, moral or political grounds.

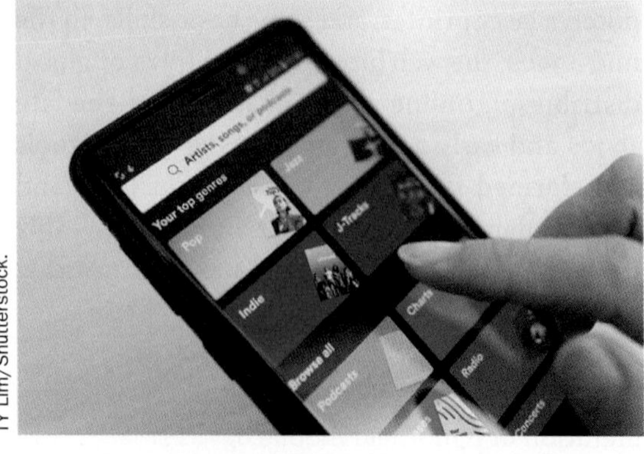

TY Lim/Shutterstock.

YouTube and Spotify are good examples of re-intermediation: the reintroduction of online intermediaries who specialize in aggregating or packaging content.

(See Box 6.4) They have reasserted themselves as gatekeepers, even if that role has been modified. Martin Hirst, John Harrison, and Patricia Mazepa (2014) argue that these practices result in the organization of information according to economic priorities, place information under private control and/or management, and assume for their own commercial purposes the role of public information repositories—a role traditionally held by true public institutions such as libraries and archives—by providing "free" content.

Models and Databases: Controlling Things and Processes

Computers are and always have been about models; the earliest computers were used to construct a model to allow projections of reality. Today, the mother of all information technologies is the database—most commonly, the relational database that structures information as collections of rows and columns and the web of interrelations between them. By collecting a large amount of real-world data as it is produced, and placing this material in a database, one can develop a sophisticated model with an immense amount of power to analyze what has gone before, understand what is happening currently, and predict what will happen next. Google's statistically improbable phrases (SIPs) allow discourse communities to be identified and publications of interest to be brought to the attention of consumers. Law-enforcement agencies use the same techniques to try to identify criminal activity. Each time an individual goes on a deadly rampage—for example, the April 2018 van attack on Yonge Street and the August 2018 Danforth Avenue shootings in Toronto—some wonder whether analysis of websites might allow prior identification of potential murderers.

Developing and analyzing databases of information in an effort to create new systems and processes of control is a growing field of study. Manufacturing relies on computer modelling and feedback. The emerging field of bioinformatics merges computer science with genetics, as researchers populate vast databases with genetic information, seeking to understand genetics through constructing computer-based models of the human genome. The combination of anthropological techniques (ethnography) with biological data into ethnobiology is allowing two different realms of information to be merged.

Such activities are sometimes referred to as **topsight**, and the pursuit of topsight is one of the major thrusts of high technology today. Every electronic transaction is recorded, and the sum total of transactions creates a body of data, which in turn can be mined for valuable information. This information can then be used by the person who collects it, or it can be sold to another party. Yet, effectively, such activities represent a scaling up of such processes and the consequent loss of interpersonal relationships, whether with small businesses or government agencies. What is advantageous for the organization—directing phone calls automatically, having ATMs do the work of bank tellers—may prove alienating or intimidating to individuals.

System Vulnerability

The storage capacity of today's computers, whether we are talking about the hard drive on our laptops or remote, cloud-based servers, can make life easier in many ways, as can such services as online shopping and electronic banking. But our move to a digital world introduces certain vulnerabilities. There is considerable concern today about the theft of data and the spread of malicious software, commonly known as malware, which can contaminate computer systems. Systems exist to protect sensitive data like credit card numbers and passwords. Usually, such data are encrypted before being transmitted over the network. But whatever can be encrypted can also be cracked, given enough effort. Practical, real-world data security is concerned with making things secure enough to make it not worth an attacker's while. Nothing is ever 100 per cent secure, however. The Canada Revenue Agency, which houses the personal data of millions of Canadians, was the victim of the so-called Heartbleed security bug in 2014, resulting in the theft of 900 social insurance numbers from its servers (Leblanc and Ha, 2014), and the CRA shut down its online tax services for two days in 2017 over fears of a software security risk (Harris, 2017).

As if attempts to disrupt normal internet activity by technically defeating a system via spam, viruses, and encryption cracking were not enough, we must also consider the role of human beings in the techno-social internet ensemble and examine the vulnerabilities of millions of online users. One of the most common examples of online fraud is **phishing**. You receive an email message seemingly from your bank or preferred email service in which you are asked to update information or renew your account. All you need to do, the message tells you, is click on the provided link and log in with your username and password. The problem is that the site you are asked to connect to is not the bank or your email service, and so when you type in your username and password, you are unwittingly providing this information to the people behind the scam. For very *little* investment, even a small percentage of people who respond by following the link and logging in can pay off for these crooks.

Extreme fraud involves stealing the identity of another. Identity theft entails collecting enough information on someone so that the fraud artist can begin to assume that person's identity. The relative instability of identity and authentication schemes on the internet leads to opportunities for fraud on both small and large scales.

Surveillance versus Privacy

Digital technologies permit sophisticated and pervasive monitoring of both public and private spaces, as well as the tracking of individuals' behaviour. Minna Tarkka (2011) describes "a totalizing grid and mesh of surveillance" comprising geographic information systems, Global Positioning Systems (GPS), radio frequency identification, and closed-circuit television systems (131). This surveillance grid has some obvious social benefits when it comes to things like personal, home, and national security, or crime prevention and law enforcement.

Surveillance tools and practices also benefit governments, which rely on statistical data for policy formation, and government agencies interested in tracking long-term social, economic, health, or environmental trends. They also help meteorologists warn of threatening weather systems and assist air-traffic controllers in doing their jobs. One of the reasons the disappearance of Malaysia Airlines flight MH370 has been such a compelling news story since 2014 is the fact that it continues to defy all of these surveillance systems.

There is a fine line, however, between these benefits and more invasive strategies that compromise our right to privacy. We are learning more and more about the extent to which government agencies and corporations are encroaching on this right, legally and illegally. Privacy is interpreted in the most general terms as the right to be left alone and is considered a basic human right, included in Section 8 of Canada's *Charter of Rights and Freedoms* as well as Article 12 of the Universal Declaration of Human Rights.

Canadians' privacy is governed by two specific pieces of legislation: the 1983 *Privacy Act*, which permits individuals access to personal information held about them by the federal government and imposes fair information obligations on the government in terms of how it collects, maintains, uses, and discloses personal information under its control; and the 2001 *Personal Information Protection and Electronic Documents Act*, which seeks to balance the privacy rights of individuals with the needs of organizations to collect and use information for economic purposes (Holmes, 2008: 4–5).

In a study of Canada's privacy laws, Nancy Holmes writes, "To experts in this area, privacy is equated with the right to enjoy private space, to conduct private communications, to be free from surveillance and to have the sanctity of one's body respected. To most people, it is about control—what is known about them and by whom" (1).

All laws and policy documents are subject to interpretation, of course, and Canadians share with citizens around the world an increasing concern about the protection of their privacy. The Communications Security Establishment Canada (CSEC) was little known to most Canadians until it made the news in 2013 when the extent of its electronic spying activities was revealed. CSEC is a security and intelligence agency mandated by the *National Defence Act* to

> acquire and use information from the global information infrastructure for the purpose of providing foreign intelligence, in accordance with Government of Canada intelligence priorities; to provide advice, guidance and services to help ensure the protection of electronic information and of information infrastructures of importance to the Government of Canada; to provide technical and operational assistance to federal law enforcement and security agencies in the performance of their lawful duties. (CSEC, 2014)

Even though CSEC is prohibited by law from spying on Canadians, documents leaked by former US National Security Agency (NSA) contractor Edward Snowden revealed that CSEC had used the free Wi-Fi system at an unidentified Canadian airport to track the metadata of randomly selected Canadians as a way of identifying foreign security threats, something to which CSEC later admitted. Metadata is the electronic equivalent of the "To" and "From" addresses on a letter envelope. The Snowden documents alleged further that Stephen Harper's government allowed the NSA, in coordination with CSEC, to spy on delegates to the 2010 G8 and G20 summits in Toronto, and that CSEC conducted industrial espionage against the Brazilian ministry of mines and energy (Fekete, 2013; McDiarmid, 2013; Greenwald, 2014).

Context here is important. Canadian governments have a long history of opening mail, eavesdropping on telegraph and telephone conversations, monitoring programs and personnel at Crown corporations like the CBC and NFB, reading and collecting publications, and sending covert representatives to political, labour, and cultural meetings, public demonstrations, and protests (Hirst et al., 2014: 275). And in the aftermath of the 9/11 attacks on New York City and Washington, such surveillance has been intensified in the so-called War on Terrorism. For example, Canada passed its *Anti-Terrorism Act* in December 2011, enlarging and extending the surveillance powers of the Canadian Security Intelligence Service (CSIS) (Hirst et al., 2014: 278–9).

6.5

Edward Snowden: Hero or Traitor?

In November 2013, a *Globe and Mail* editorial asked whether Edward Snowden should be considered a hero. Snowden is the former US National Security Agency subcontractor who leaked top-secret information about the NSA's domestic surveillance activities to *The Guardian* and *The Washington Post* in 2013. Snowden was charged by the US government under the *Espionage Act*, but he has been living in Russia seeking to avoid extradition (see Greenwald, 2014).

People like Snowden, journalist Glenn Greenwald, and WikiLeaks founder Julian Assange have turned the tables on these powerful and secretive state agencies by exposing details about their activities and sharing publicly some of the data they would prefer to keep secret. They defend their actions in the name of democracy and citizens' right to privacy. The states and the state agencies they are surveilling, however, accuse them of traitorous behaviour, undermining their efforts to maintain national security. Do you think Edward Snowden is a hero or a traitor?

Sarah Lynn Mayhew, SLM Art.

By blowing the whistle on surveillance activities by the NSA and CSEC, Edward Snowden became both a hero and a controversial figure around the globe.

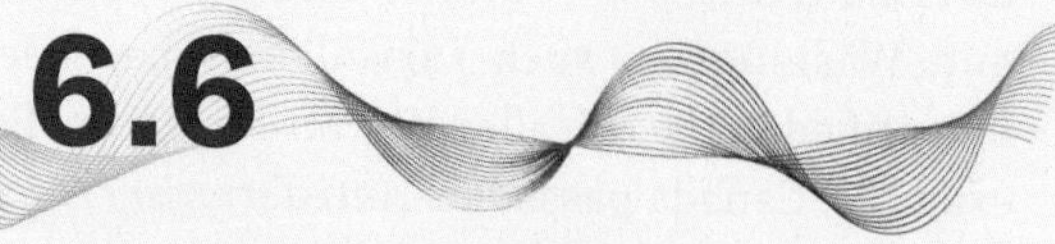

A Panoptic Society?

It is worth asking whether the surveillance technologies available to governments, border-control agents, military and police forces, and private corporations, constitute a form of panopticism.

The English philosopher of utilitarianism Jeremy Bentham developed the Panopticon in the late eighteenth century as a model form of prison. The prison would feature a central guard tower surrounded by an annular building of prisoners' cells. The cells would have windows front and back, allowing light to shine through. The idea was that the prisoners would be visible at all times to the guards, but the guards could not be seen by the prisoners. Because the prisoners would not know when they were being observed, they had to assume they were being watched constantly, and thus would discipline themselves.

In his classic work, *Discipline and Punish*, Michael Foucault (1995 [1979]) posits Bentham's Panopticon as "the diagram of a mechanism of power reduced to its ideal form" (205). The major effect of the Panopticon, Foucault writes, is "to induce in the inmate a state of conscious and permanent visibility that assumes the automatic functioning of power" (201). The Panopticon, though, was more than a prison; it was also a laboratory that "could be used as a machine to carry out experiments, to alter behaviour, to train or correct individuals" (203).

Applied to the surveillance techniques of society at large, panopticism implies that citizens will assume they are constantly being watched and will therefore behave accordingly, internalizing the state's regulatory power. We have to ask whether we want this, especially in a democratic society, because it could impede citizens' sense of freedom, inhibit their lawful right to express criticism and dissent, and their right to peaceful protest, and provide law-enforcement agencies grounds to infringe upon these freedoms.

We can see elements of panopticism in our own participation in social media, in what is called peer-to-peer or interpersonal surveillance. By voluntarily posting personal information to social media sites, and through the content we post or share, we render ourselves visible, not only to our social media "friends," but as well to marketers, corporations, and governments, agencies capable of using such data for profiling. In a study based on interviews with Facebook users, researcher Daniel Trottier (2012) compared this visibility to a form of surveillance. "As law enforcement branches, marketers, employers, and governments take a continued interest in sites like Facebook, the visibility produced by interpersonal social media surveillance will undoubtedly augment the scope and capacity of other kinds of social media surveillance" (331).

China is in the process of formalizing such surveillance into a "social credit" system, whereby citizens' personal data will be used to establish a

Innocent Canadians can pay the price when they get caught up in this web. Canadian Liberal senator David Smith was flagged as a "potential terrorist" on a no-fly list in 2012 when, ironically, he attempted to board a flight from Toronto to Ottawa to attend a meeting of the Special Anti-Terrorism Committee, of which he is the former chair (Hirst et al., 2014: 287). The most notorious case, however, is that of Maher Arar, a Canadian software engineer who was taken into custody by US authorities as he passed through a New York airport on a flight to Montreal following a 2002 vacation in Tunisia. Accused of having links to terrorism, he was held incommunicado in the United States for 12 days before being shipped off to Syria where he was tortured over a period of 10 months. A subsequent commission of inquiry exonerated Arar, but it was unable to verify reports that the RCMP and unidentified Canadian officials were implicated in his rendition by passing information about Arar to US authorities and, subsequently, damaging his reputation by leaking information to Canadian journalists. Nevertheless, both the RCMP and the Canadian government issued public apologies to Arar, and the Canadian government awarded him more than $10 million in compensation for his ordeal.

Canadian government departments and police forces remain active in monitoring Canadians' activities in cyberspace. Canada's rating of their trustworthiness, with points earned for good behaviour—e.g., paying taxes, proper parenting, donating to charity—and points deducted for bad behaviour—e.g., not paying taxes or fines, committing traffic offences or more serious crimes (Kobie, 2019; McDonald, 2019). First established in 2014, China's social credit plan is currently a series of data collection systems run by local governments and private businesses. These systems require users to opt in, but a comprehensive, and mandatory, government-run plan is envisioned as early as 2020 (Kobie, 2019). A report by Associated Press claimed that 17.5 million travellers were barred from buying airline tickets and another 5.5 million were barred from purchasing train tickets in 2018 for "social credit offences" (McDonald, 2019).

Courtesy the artist and David Zwirner, New York.

Canadian artist Stan Douglas's *Panopticon, Isla de Pinos* shows Presidio Modelo, a now-abandoned Cuban prison modelled on Bentham's Panopticon. How is Bentham's Panopticon like the surveillance state? What are the advantages and disadvantages of surveillance for society?

Supreme Court ruled unanimously in June 2014 that internet users have a reasonable expectation of privacy and that government and police officials were violating Canadians' constitutional privacy rights by obtaining information about the identities of telecom subscribers without a warrant (MacCharles, 2014). The ruling followed a report by Rogers Communications that it had received 175,000 requests for subscriber information in 2013, a figure that represented 1.75 per cent of its 10 million subscribers (Greenwood, 2014).

As we discussed earlier in this chapter, corporations are also collecting information on users of digital networks, primarily for marketing

iStockphoto/Alija.

In recent years, there has been an increasing presence of a wide-ranging security apparatus: security guards, security checkpoints, security cameras, and radar cameras at roadway intersections. Does the increase of security make you feel more or less safe?

purposes, turning users into commodities. What we typically think of as digital services provided to us for free (e.g., search engines, social media, Wi-Fi access in cafés and airports) actually come at a cost; we divulge personal information in exchange for access in what Greg Elmer (2004) terms "a digitized and networked information economy" (4–5).

Social networking sites like Facebook, LinkedIn, Twitter, Instagram, and Pinterest are among the most popular digital media applications, and texting has replaced telephone calls and emails for many kinds of interpersonal communication. If these sites and applications have become indispensable tools for keeping abreast of what's happening in all aspects of daily life, from our circles of family and friends to the worlds of news, sports, entertainment, and celebrity gossip, they leave us vulnerable to people who are not our friends.

Recent and highly publicized cases of cyberbullying have led to a public outcry and proposed legislation by the federal government. Rehtaeh Parsons of Dartmouth, Nova Scotia, hanged herself and died in hospital in 2013 after photos of her alleged gang rape at age 15 were distributed online. In 2012, Amanda Todd of Port Coquitlam, British Columbia, killed herself at age 15 after repeated instances of cyberbullying, including being blackmailed into exposing her breasts during a video chat session with a stranger, photos of which were posted to Facebook. If these are particularly extreme cases of online harassment, they demonstrate the extent to which digital interactivity can be used for ill as well as for good.

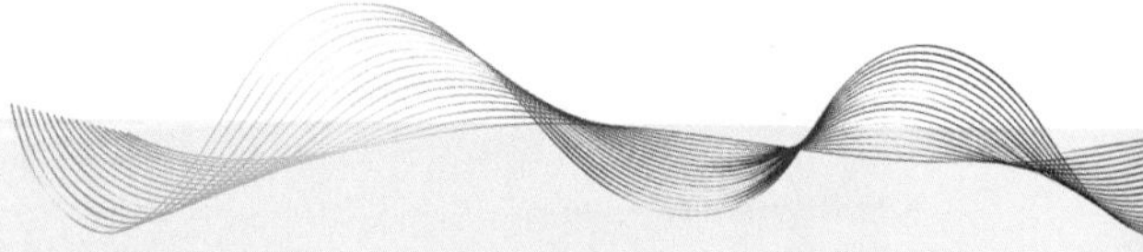

SUMMARY

We live in an age when technology—and communication technology especially—occupies a very central place in our lives, and it is important to understand what we mean by technology and the relationship between technology and human activity.

We began this chapter with some theoretical perspectives that emphasize the practical, social, situated nature of technology. We reviewed several theoretical perspectives on technology, including instrumentalism, determinism, substantivism, critical theory, and constructivism. We discussed the limitations of the first three in particular, and how theorists increasingly see technology as a phenomenon that, like other areas of social practice, is best understood as socially constructed. We noted how technologies can be seen as socio-technical ensembles, as phenomena that have technical elements but are social in their application or manifestation. We emphasized how technology changes things rather than simply solves problems; positive and negative consequences of technology are always intertwined and, to some extent, unpredictable.

Communication technology is closely linked to control, and public policy in the past century has had a major impact on the particular socio-technical ensembles and the resulting industries with which we now live. Media convergence is breaking down media silos and generating new policy challenges that require twenty-first-century approaches.

The social rationales most often used in favour of technological development highlight democracy and education. But the realities of technological communication systems, once they are introduced, involve various forms of commercial exploitation. History is repeating itself in this regard; in spite of the democratic potential of new media forms, corporations—some new, some old—remain key players in shaping cyberspace.

This is not to suggest that the game is over, or that opportunities for exploiting digital technologies for more progressive goals have been foreclosed, but it is a reminder to think about what is "new" about new media. We concluded the chapter by demonstrating that new media forms entail both new possibilities and new problems. There has been very little consideration of the macro implications of the development of the information sector. This lack of prior consideration is part of the technological imperative, which assumes that any unforeseen problems can be solved in time by still newer technological solutions. Today, for example, we hear such arguments in regard to climate change and environmental degradation. The blithe acceptance by society of technology because it means economic gain, at least for some, blinds us to considering the desirability of technological developments for society as a whole, whether those developments involve health, entertainment, war, fashion, or life itself.

KEY TERMS

ARPANET, p. 156
constructivism, p. 150
critical theory, p. 149
cyborg, p. 147
deskilling, p. 149
digital divide, p. 151
digitization, p. 155
instrumentalism, p. 148
media silos, p. 154
media convergence, p. 154
open-source software, p. 156
peer-to-peer system, p.156
phishing, p. 161
re-intermediation, p. 160
scientific management, p. 149
silos, p. 154
socially contingent, p. 150
socio-technical ensemble, p. 151
substantivism, p. 148
technological determinism, p. 148
technological hubris, p. 153
topsight, p. 161

RELATED WEBSITES

Canarie: www.canarie.ca
The Canarie website carries a wealth of information on Canada's data network.

International Telecommunication Union (ITU): www.itu.int/en/ITU-D/Statistics/Pages/facts/default.aspx
A useful source of current data on internet usage worldwide.

Office of the Privacy Commissioner of Canada: https://www.priv.gc.ca/en/
An information-rich site pertaining to privacy issues and initiatives affecting Canadians, including tips on protecting your privacy.

Wikileaks: wikileaks.org
A non-profit organization that provides an online platform for the publication of leaked documents and other original source material, accompanied by news stories providing the data with context.

***Wired* magazine: www.wired.com**
Wired is an influential source of news and commentary on new media. The magazine's masthead touts Marshall McLuhan as its patron saint.

FURTHER READINGS

Crow, Barbara, Michael Longford, and Kim Sawchuk, editors. 2010. *The Wireless Spectrum: The Politics, Practices and Poetics of Mobile Media*. Toronto: University of Toronto Press. A collection of essays examining what wireless, mobile technologies mean for the day-to-day lives of individuals and the public at large.

Feenberg, Andrew. 1999. *Questioning Technology*. New York: Routledge. An analysis of the nature of technology, including a review of various theories that attempt to explain technology.

Flew, Terry, and Richard Smith. 2018. *New Media: An Introduction*, 3rd Canadian ed. Don Mills, ON: Oxford UP. An introduction to the social, political, and economic impacts of new media through the years.

Hirst, Martin, John Harrison, and Patricia Mazepa. 2014. *Communication and New Media: From Broadcast to Narrowcast*. Canadian ed. Don Mills, ON: Oxford UP. An assessment of the implications of media convergence through the lens of political economy.

Jenkins, Henry. 2006. *Convergence Culture: Where Old and New Media Collide*. New York and London: New York UP. An analysis of contemporary sociocultural transformations resulting from media convergence.

McChesney, Robert W. 2013. *Digital Disconnect: How Capitalism Is Turning the Internet Against Democracy*. New York: The New Press. A critical view of what the internet's commercialization means to its democratic potential.

Powers, Shawn M., and Michael Jablonski. 2015. *The Real Cyber War: The Political Economy of Internet Freedom*. Urbana, IL: University of Illinois Press. A critical analysis of the battle by states for control of information resources.

Slack, Jennifer Daryl, and J. Macgregor Wise. 2007. *Culture and Technology: A Primer*. New York: Peter Lang. An accessible discussion of current debates that demonstrate the interplay between technology and culture.

STUDY QUESTIONS

1. What is determinism and why is it inadequate to our theoretical understanding of technology's place in society?
2. How do we define technology, and what does it mean to say technology is socially, cultural, politically, and economically embedded?
3. We cited the sinking of the *Titanic* in 1912 as an example of technological hubris. What is technological hubris? Cite a more contemporary example.
4. What are the trade-offs we make when we access free websites and other digital applications?
5. What is constructivism, and why is it the prevailing theory of technology today?
6. What are the pros and cons of society's increased surveillance capacities?

III

The Communication Environment

wellphoto/iStockphoto

7

The Formation of Public Policy

The cornerstone of Canada's approach . . . is the premise that culture is a way of life and an essential element of a community's survival. —*Sarah Armstrong*

WesRaymondPhotography/iStockphoto

Opening Questions

- What does it mean to say that mediated communication is a highly structured activity?
- What is communication policy?
- How is communication policy developed?
- What role does the public play in policy development?
- What ideas guided communication policy development in Canada for most of the twentieth century?
- What has changed in terms of the way the Canadian government develops communication policy?
- Why is policy now developed in a global context?

Introduction

Media communications take place in a constructed environment, informed by communication technologies, but also by laws, policies, conventions, economic imperatives, guiding ideals, and public pressures. Communication policy is established by international regulatory bodies and national and regional governments to ensure that media serve not only their owners and content creators but individual citizens and society as a whole. These policies establish rights and responsibilities individually and collectively. If media workers have the right to freedom of expression, they also have a responsibility to respect individuals' privacy and laws pertaining to libel, copyright, hate speech, and so on. If media owners have the right to a reasonable return on their investment, laws and policies compel owners to exert responsibly their market power and to respect the larger social and cultural goals of their community.

Policy development in any one jurisdiction is always part of a larger, international policy context because mediated communication takes place across borders— increasingly so today. **Copyright** laws are believed to have been introduced in the late fifteenth century, and international telephony has been regulated since the early twentieth century. Policy is particularly germane today when digital technologies enable media content to penetrate every region of the globe in an instant.

The policy discourse in Canada, articulated through a series of royal commissions, task forces, public hearings, and committee reports, serves as the country's collective response to the question, *What is communication for?* The answers to this question help us understand the logic behind policy decisions, laws, and regulations.

In Canada, communication policies can be developed by governments in committee, subject to usual parliamentary procedures, or by public agencies like the CRTC. More significant policy initiatives, the emergence of new problems in the communication field, or the advent of new media technologies typically prompt federal and provincial governments to call for public hearings. This allows governments to collect information, to gauge opinion—from the public, the business community, the research community, and people directly involved—and to receive specific recommendations.

These consultative exercises inform, but do not determine, communication policy. Typically, the resulting reports contain background information, valuable data, arguments from various perspectives, and pertinent recommendations

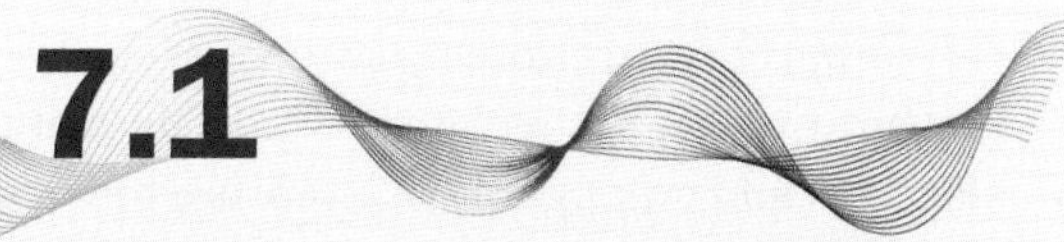

Defining Terms: Legislation, Regulation, Policy

The term **legislation** refers to acts, statutes, or laws that have been passed by Parliament or a provincial legislature. The *Broadcasting Act* and *Telecommunications Act* are examples of legislation.

Regulations are "the rules that address the details and practical applications of the law. The authority to make regulations related to an Act is assigned within that Act. Just like statutes, regulations have the full force of law" (Law Central Alberta). For instance, the structure of the CRTC and its powers to make regulation are described within the *Broadcasting Act*, and it uses those powers to make regulations derived from terms and ideas laid out in that legislation.

Policy is a blanket term referring to the set of rules, laws, and practices that govern a particular activity. For instance, the rules, laws, and practices governing broadcasting are called broadcasting policy.

An *order-in-council* is an order typically formulated by the federal cabinet and authorized by the Governor General. Orders-in-council are commonly used to make appointments, such as appointments to a royal commission (Forsey, 2006).

to governments that emerge from months—often years—of study. The recommendations range from the pragmatic to the idealistic, from those that represent mere tinkering with the status quo to much more radical propositions. The government of the day weighs the political, economic, legal, and sociocultural implications of these recommendations and decides if and how to act. Many of our most prominent cultural institutions—the NFB, the Canada Council, Telefilm Canada, the CRTC, the CBC—emerged from such recommendations.

Canadian government interventions in the communication field have been guided for most of the past century by a logic that frames the media, culture, and society in terms of the nation-state. While this framing has never gone unchallenged, it has faced particularly strong opposition in recent years on three fronts: the fiscal, the technological, and the philosophical. First, can Canada afford to promote and protect indigenous cultural activity? In an era of deficit reduction at all levels of government, the cultural sector has not been spared budget cuts. Increasingly, too, governments are looking to the private sector to fulfill Canadians' communication needs. The flip side of this question is, of course, can Canadian governments afford *not* to intervene? Second, with the rise of powerful, pervasive, and global communication networks, is it technologically feasible, even possible, for governments to intervene in communicative activities that stretch beyond their borders? For the time being at least, Ottawa has answered affirmatively, but the question remains pertinent. Finally, should Canadian governments be involved in cultural production in the first place, given the costs, the private-sector alternatives, the global climate of liberalized trade, and concerns about what state intervention might mean for the independence of cultural producers?

In order to address these questions, we need to understand how and why Canada's communication policy structure emerged. In this chapter, we situate the Canadian policy discussion within a global context. Next, we trace the historical trajectory of communication policy in Canada through four defining twentieth-century policy documents. This section reveals the bases on which communication policy was forged until the 1980s: the project of building a nation and a national culture, and the concern that a strict market approach to communications would lead to further dominance of the Canadian mediascape by the United States. We conclude the chapter with a discussion of how those themes, while they remain pertinent, no longer resonate as they once did with the public, cultural producers, or governments. If they're still part of the discussion, new policy challenges, such as **globalization**, and Canada's increasingly diverse population, have arisen. In Chapter 8, we will look at the policy picture from the perspective of each of the communication sectors in turn, particularly as digitization and the emergence of the internet are breaking down the clear distinctions between sectors.

Back to the Future

The instantaneous global communication enabled today by ubiquitous digital technologies resurrects communication policy themes that have been played out for more than 500 years, since the invention of the printing press in the mid-fifteenth century. It is important to understand that all countries patrol their communication borders: to protect national security, to prevent the illegal circulation of certain materials (e.g., child pornography), to ensure the integrity of financial data, to protect national cultural industries, and so on.

International communication scholar Cees Hamelink describes communication policy as a by-product of global contact between peoples, companies, and governments. Most of this contact prior to 1800 came about through meetings of individual traders, merchants, and diplomats. But following the significant expansion of trade markets in the eighteenth century, greater need arose for multilateral state governance (Hamelink, 1994: 5–6).

Each of the communication sectors required its own form of international governance. As early as the sixteenth century, the postal system in Europe was regulated by bilateral agreements to facilitate and standardize the circulation of letters across borders. Expanding shipping and railway networks necessitated a more formal, multilateral agreement. A first meeting in Paris in 1863 and a subsequent meeting in Berne, Switzerland, led to the **Berne Convention** and the founding of the General Postal Union in 1874 (renamed the Universal Postal Union in 1878) and "introduced basic norms and rules that still hold today" (7).

Similarly, the development of telegraphy in the early nineteenth century required standardization and cooperation across borders. Again, this began with bilateral agreements, and the agreements between European countries in the 1850s provided the template for the 1865 International Telegraph Convention. Telephony was incorporated into the agreement in 1903, and in 1932 the International Telegraph Union and the International Radio-Telegraph Union merged to become what we know today as the **International Telecommunication Union** (8–9).

The first international conference to discuss radio communication ("wireless radio-telegraphy"), held in Berlin in 1903, led to the 1906 Berlin Radio Convention, adopted by 27 countries. The convention allocated frequency bands within the earth's electromagnetic spectrum for use by specific services (e.g., marine communication, emergency communication) at a time when radio was used for two-way, point-to-point communication rather than the broadcasting we are familiar with today. A subsequent radio conference in Washington in 1927 drafted a new Radio Convention and Radio Regulations to address a range of issues raised by radio broadcasting, from **frequency allocation** to station ownership and state control (9–10).

The printing press prompted the notion of **intellectual property**, and it is believed that the first copyright laws emerged in Vienna in the late fifteenth century. Most of the earliest copyright laws protected only national citizens' works. The US *Copyright Act* of 1790, for example, did not protect foreign authors' works, which led to the rampant pirating of books by best-selling English authors, most famously Charles Dickens, as Box 7.2 explains (Hamelink, 1994: 11). A series of bilateral agreements on intellectual property rights were signed between 1840 and 1866, when the First International Convention on Copyright in Berne—the Berne Convention—granted protection to foreign-published works. Further discussions produced the Berne Treaty on copyright in 1886 (13).

The founding of these international governing institutions was fraught with struggles over questions of political and economic sovereignty, and over questions of communicative power, as they continue to be today. As cultural production became large-scale cultural industry in the twentieth century, there were both cultural and economic concerns about media imperialism; already by the last half of the nineteenth century, for example, three news agencies dominated the production and circulation of international news, dividing global territories among themselves and thus monopolizing the framing and definition of current events. By 1914, the major Hollywood film companies had captured 85 per cent of the world film audience (McChesney, 1997: 12–14). The United Nations Educational, Scientific and Cultural Organization (UNESCO) became the principal forum for discussion about how to resolve political tensions produced by the expansion of the world communication system, particularly between east and west during the Cold War and between the Global North and Global South that persist today. The World Trade Organization has become the venue for discussions of the economic implications of communicative exchange.

It should be noted that subnational governments also develop policy particular to their needs, Quebec being the most obvious Canadian example. If governments privilege the collective concerns of their jurisdictions—sovereignty,

7.2 Charles Dickens

Mass pirating of English-language books by foreign, especially English, authors persisted throughout the nineteenth century, despite the urgings of British (and some American) authors and politicians for the US Congress to recognize international copyright. Charles Dickens's *A Christmas Carol*, for example, sold for $2.50 in England and for six cents in the United States (Vaidhyanathan, 2001: 50). In January 1837, 55 British writers petitioned US Congress, but a proposed bill to protect their intellectual property on US soil was opposed by publishing houses in the States and went nowhere (51).

In 1842, Dickens himself toured the United States. "At many stops, Dickens pleaded for international copyright. Yet his audiences were filled with fans who had happily paid very low prices for American-printed, leather-bound copies of his work, from which Dickens earned nothing. Dickens was asking his readers to pay more money for his product, and they were in no mood to do so" (51). Dickens's account of his US tour, *American Notes* (1842), sold 50,000 pirated copies in the United States in three days.

The historical American recalcitrance with respect to international copyright seems ironic today when the United States, one of the world's largest producers of cultural materials, chastises and pursues legal remedies against countries like China that flout intellectual property agreements.

Pirated movies are sold around the world for a fraction of their retail price, none of the profits going to the people who produced them.

identity, the economy—**non-governmental organizations** like Amnesty International and Reporters Without Borders foreground basic individual human rights, including the **right to communicate**, privileging the universal application of such rights according to such conventions as the **Universal Declaration of Human Rights** (see Box 7.3).

The Canadian Public in Public Policy Formation

The formation of communication policy necessitates a tricky balancing act between individual and collective needs, and between universal principles and national and regional exigencies. Increasingly, too, policy formation is governed by

7.3 Universal Declaration of Human Rights

The Universal Declaration of Human Rights was the first global statement outlining the basic elements of non-negotiable human rights and the foundation for international human rights law. Its first draft was written by a Canadian, John Peters Humphrey, a legal scholar who served as the director of the Human Rights Division of the United Nations Secretariat. The 30-article document was adopted by the United Nations General Assembly on 10 December 1948. Canada was one of 48 countries voting in favour of the declaration.

Article 19 of the declaration speaks most directly to communication: "Everyone has the right to freedom of opinion and expression; this right includes freedom to hold opinions without interference and to seek, receive, and impart information and ideas through any media and regardless of frontiers." The full document can be found at www.un.org/en/universal-declaration-human-rights/.

It is useful to remember, though, that in spite of its title, the declaration's various articles are far from universally accepted. United Nations membership in 1948 was one-quarter of what it is today, as most of the Global South was unrepresented, and only four African countries were members (Fowler, 2014).

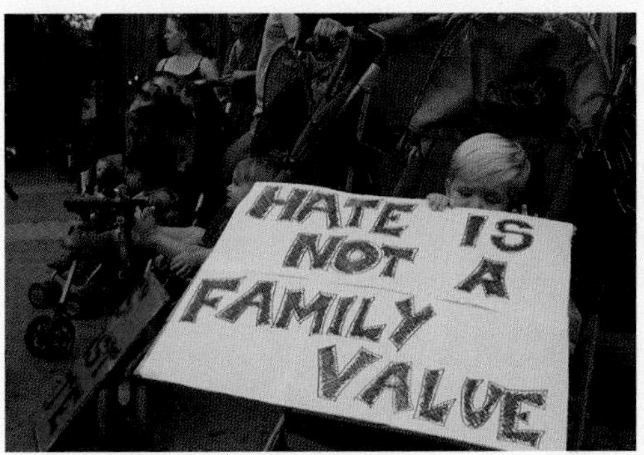

Richard Levine/Alamy Stock Photo.

While Canada supports universal free speech, this does not include speech that promotes violence or hatred toward identifiable groups.

international trade agreements. For a country as diverse as Canada, it is especially perilous. How do you accommodate the individual and collective communication needs of a relatively small yet extremely diverse population occupying the world's second-largest country, most of whom live close to the border with the United States, the world's richest and most powerful media empire? How do you ensure Canadian voices are heard without foreclosing Canadians' access to the international mediascape? And how do you ensure Canadians' voices are heard on all of these questions in the policy development process?

The issue of whether public opinion matters to policy formation is an important one in a country that has gone to considerable effort and expense establishing **task forces** and **royal commissions** to study issues ranging from foreign investment to national cultural development. The CRTC, for example, is legally required to conduct public consultations (Raboy and Shtern, 2010: 88). While most analysts would agree that public opinion is important, how it matters is not clear. Is public consultation merely a public relations exercise, or does it play a part in policy decisions?

A consideration of who constitutes "the public" participating in such inquiries must be central to any discussion of this policy institution. While hearings are open to anyone wishing to participate, they most often attract interested parties—industry stakeholders, labour leaders, researchers, organized pressure groups—rather than the general public.

As we will see in the reading of four key twentieth-century policy documents that follows, answers to the question *What is communication for?* are both important and subject to change. These documents, and the hearings that produced them, give us a sense of the particular social, political, and economic contexts in which policy debates took place, as well as a taste of the policy discourse and how it evolves over time.

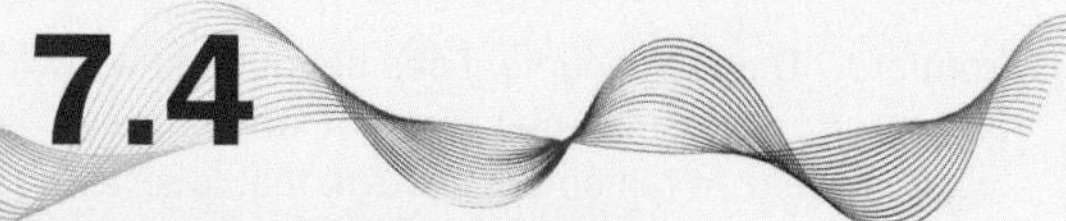

7.4

Major Communication Policy Documents

The following are key communication policy documents that have informed governments for the past 80-plus years. The reports, available through most public and university libraries, are written in a clear and accessible style and are valuable to researchers for the data and analysis they contain, but also for the language they use to talk about the respective roles of the public and private sectors in producing and delivering communication services to Canadians.

1929 Report of the Royal Commission on Radio Broadcasting
1951 Report of the Royal Commission on National Development in the Arts, Letters and Sciences
1957 Report of the Royal Commission on Broadcasting
1961 Report of the Royal Commission on Publications
1968 Report on Book Publishing
1969 Report of the Task Force on Government Information
1971 The Uncertain Mirror: Report of the Special Senate Committee on Mass Media
1971 Instant World: A Report on Telecommunications in Canada
1977 The Publishing Industry in Canada
1977 The Film Industry in Canada
1977 Disney Report on Federal Tax Issues of Concern to the Arts Community in Canada
1978 English Educational Publishing in Canada
1978 French Educational Publishing in Canada
1981 Report of the Royal Commission on Newspapers
1982 Report of the Federal Cultural Policy Review Committee
1983 Towards a New Broadcasting Policy
1984 The National Film and Video Policy
1984 Report on the Taxation of Visual and Performing Artists and Writers
1985 Report of the Film Industry Task Force
1986 Report of the Task Force on Broadcasting Policy
1986 Report of the Task Force on the Status of the Artist
1986 Report on Funding the Arts in Canada to the Year 2000
1986 Report of the Task Force on the Non-theatrical Film Industry
1986 Sex-Role Stereotyping in the Broadcast Media: A Report on Industry Self-Regulation
1987 Vital Links: Canadian Cultural Industries

The Aird Commission, 1929

The Aird Commission—officially, the Royal Commission on Radio Broadcasting—represents a watershed moment in communication policy history because it was the first public consultation of its kind, and it resulted in the recommendation that a national and publicly owned broadcasting network be introduced into a field that up until then was dominated by local and privately owned radio stations (Vipond, 1992). As Marc Raboy (1990) has noted, after the Aird Commission, broadcasting policy in Canada became national policy. But the Aird Commission has significance beyond broadcasting. Besides proposing the initial blueprint for a Canadian radio network, Aird recommended, and helped to initiate, a particular pattern of cultural governance. Historian Mary Vipond (1992: 219) comments, "A new view of the role of the government vis-à-vis culture and the media was thereby implied. Never before had the state been assigned such control over a cultural field."

Through the 1920s, when radio broadcasting was still in its infancy, the airwaves became increasingly crowded as signals from much more powerful US radio stations interfered with those of their weaker Canadian counterparts. At the same time, the content of some religious broadcasts became a growing political concern. As a result of these issues, the Canadian government recognized the need for a more comprehensive approach to broadcast policy. The minister of marine and fisheries, P.J. Arthur Cardin, asked ministry officials

1987 Communications for the Twenty-First Century: Media and Messages in the Information Age
1988 Canadian Voices, Canadian Choices: A New Broadcasting Policy for Canada
1991 Report of the Task Force on Professional Training for the Cultural Sector in Canada
1992 Report of the Standing Committee on Communications and Culture: The Ties that Bind
1992 Report of the Advisory Committee to the Canada Council for Racial Equality in the Arts
1992 Report of the Department of Communications: New Media, New Choices
1992 Report of the Task Force on Museums and First Peoples: Turning the Page
1994 Report of the Task Force on the Canadian Magazine Industry: A Question of Balance
1995 Competition and Culture on Canada's Information Highway: Managing the Realities of Transition
1996 Report of the Information Highway Advisory Council
1996 Making Our Voices Heard: Mandate Review Committee (CBC, NFB, Telefilm)
1996 Building the Information Society: Moving Canada into the 21st Century
1996 Report of the Task Force on the Future of the Canadian Music Industry
1997 Preparing Canada for a Digital World: Information Highway Advisory Council
1999 Report of the Feature Film Advisory Committee
1999 Report of the Cultural Industries Sectoral Advisory Group on International Trade: New Strategies for Culture and Trade
1999 Report of the Standing Committee on Canadian Heritage: A Sense of Place, A Sense of Being
1999 Report of the CRTC: Building on Success: A Policy Framework for Canadian Television
2000 From Script to Screen
2001 Report of the National Broadband Task Force: The New National Dream
2002 Canadian Content in the 21st Century: A Discussion Paper about Canadian Content in Film and Television Productions
2003 Our Cultural Sovereignty: The Second Century of Canadian Broadcasting. Report of the Standing Committee on Canadian Heritage
2006 Final Report on the Canadian News Media: Report of the Standing Committee on Transport and Communications
2006 Final Report of the Telecommunications Policy Review Panel
2014 Digital Canada 150

to prepare a report with recommendations for federal broadcasting policy. That departmental report, submitted 15 November 1928, recommended the establishment of a royal commission (Bird, 1988: 37). Less than a month later, Sir John Aird, president of the Canadian Bank of Commerce, was appointed chair, and was joined by two other commissioners: Charles A. Bowman, editor of the *Ottawa Citizen*; and Augustin Frigon, an electrical engineer who was director of Montreal's École Polytechnique and director-general of technical education for the province of Quebec (Canada, 1929a: 2). The royal commission held public sessions in 25 Canadian cities between April and July 1929 (Canada, 1929b: 5–6, 18–21).

The Aird Commission remained faithful to the agenda that had been established in its mandate. Most significantly, the commission rendered radio a government institution. Citing public support for placing broadcasting "on a basis of public service," the commissioners argued that only some form of public ownership could satisfy "both the interests of the listening public and of the nation" (Canada, 1929b: 5–6). Not only would radio broadcasting in Canada be a public service national in scope, Aird proposed that it be federally owned and operated with "provincial authorities" exercising full control over programming (6–7).

A national company would own and operate all stations in Canada, and each province would have a provincial radio broadcasting director as well as a provincial advisory council. The national company—the Canadian Radio Broadcasting Commission—would have a 12-member board of directors, three directors representing the Dominion and one from each province (7). The proposed CRBC would also have the capacity for chain broadcasting to permit national broadcasts (8). In addition to the existing licence fees on radio receivers—a user-pay system—the CRBC would be financed by a federal subsidy, a proposed $1 million for five years (10).

Marc Raboy (1990: 7) has argued that the significance of the Aird Commission is that it "infused broadcasting with a national purpose." The Aird commissioners described the purpose of their inquiry as "to determine how radio broadcasting in Canada could be most effectively carried on in the interests of Canadian listeners and in the national interests of Canada" (Canada, 1929b: 5), thereby invoking the order-in-council that established their mandate. The Aird report, in other words, was not the Canadian government's first word on radio broadcasting; nor were the commissioners starting with an entirely blank slate in their attempts to develop Canada's first comprehensive broadcasting policy.

Alexandra Studio/Library and Archives Canada/PA-122227.

Members of the Aird Commission, from left to right: Charles Bowman, Sir John Aird, Donald Manson (commission secretary), Dr. Augustin Frigon.

The medium of radio was also perceived as an instrument of national purpose. "In a country of the vast geographical dimensions of Canada, broadcasting will undoubtedly become a great force in fostering a national spirit and interpreting national citizenship" (Canada, 1929b: 6). Radio's potential to promote national unity was cited as one of the reasons radio should be subsidized by Ottawa (10).

Programming, too, was categorized in the terms of the nation-state. It would be predominantly Canadian and would have a considerable educational component, unlike the local and regional programming that had characterized private radio in Canada up to that point. Aird determined that the primary purpose of the CRBC "would be to give Canadian programs through Canadian stations" (10). Closely tied to the issue of Canadian programming was Aird's call for an emphasis on educational programming, meaning "education in the broad sense, not only as it is conducted in the schools and colleges, but in providing entertainment and of informing the public on questions of national interest" (6–11).

The Aird report attributed its findings to "the people" and thus asserted that the report spoke for the people of Canada, even though the consultation process was limited in scope and attracted primarily interest groups (e.g., radio station owners and managers, broadcasting equipment manufacturers, radio club spokespeople). The report is full of attributions to public opinion.

Besides its recommendation to nationalize radio, the Aird Commission raised two themes that would surface in subsequent reports and that inform Canadian communication policy to the present day: the relationship between communication media and commerce; and the cultural threat represented by close proximity to the United States.

Aird detected two problems with the structure of radio as a local, private enterprise. First, the private stations suffered from a lack of revenue, which "tended more and more to force too

7.5

Canadian Radio League

The release of the Aird report in October 1929 coincided with the beginning of the Great Depression, which delayed serious consideration of its recommendations. The **Canadian Radio League**, founded in 1930 by Graham Spry and Alan Plaunt, led a campaign to support the Aird Commission's central recommendation of a national public radio system under Spry's famous slogan, "The State or the United States." Spry (1931) illustrated the nationalist purpose he foresaw for the technology of broadcasting:

> Here is an agency which may be the final means of giving Canada a national public opinion, of providing a basis for public thought on a national basis. . . . There is no agency of human communication which could so effectively unite Canadian to Canadian and realize the aspiration of Confederation as radio broadcasting. It is the greatest Canadianizing instrument in our hands and its cultural influence . . . is equally important.

The Canadian Radio League lobbied politicians and government officials and mustered support for public broadcasting in the face of counter-arguments by the private broadcasting industry. R.B. Bennett's Conservative government passed the *Canadian Radio Broadcasting Act* in 1932, establishing the Canadian Radio Broadcasting Commission, which took over the radio facilities of the Canadian National Railway and established a rudimentary network of private and public stations broadcasting in French and English. The CRBC, however, struggled from a lack of funding, a weak mandate, and administrative problems. A new *Canadian Broadcasting Act* was passed in 1936, establishing a restructured Canadian Broadcasting Corporation as a Crown corporation and ensuring its financial stability through a $2.50 radio licence fee.

much advertising upon the listener." Second, stations were crowded into urban areas, where the revenue potential was greatest, resulting in the duplication of service in some areas and other, less populous areas being "ineffectively served" (6). Aird was especially critical of the commercialization of the radio airwaves through advertising, and the report recommended the elimination of "direct advertising," though it was more tolerant of indirect advertising, or sponsored programs. But, the "ideal program should have advertising, both direct and indirect, entirely eliminated" (10).

The distaste of the Aird Commission for advertising was matched by its displeasure that the majority of programs heard by Canadians originated in the United States. "It has been emphasized to us that the continued reception of these has a tendency to mould the minds of young people in the home to ideals and opinions that are not Canadian" (Canada, 1929b: 6). By international agreement, Canada had in 1929 only six exclusive and 11 shared broadcast wavelengths, and Aird recommended a more equitable division of the broadcast spectrum with the United States (11).

In sum, Aird took a huge step in advocating state intervention in the cultural sphere. By endorsing the idea that radio broadcasting should be established on the basis of a national public service and governed by a national institution, the Aird report proposed a framework patterned after that of the nation-state itself and dramatically extended the state's power into cultural affairs. Aird also introduced into the policy discourse two recurrent topics: commercialization and Americanization. These themes would form the central tenets of communication policy formation in Canada up to the present day.

The Massey–Lévesque Commission, 1949–1951

In the wake of World War II, Louis St Laurent's federal government commissioned in 1949 the most sweeping study of the cultural field in Canadian history, a study that was to include within its scope museums, libraries, archives, historical sites, monuments, scholarship, voluntary societies, crafts guilds, and the mass media. The study was struck at a time when, after the devastation and expense incurred by the war, both government and industry were reorganizing, and the foundations of what would become today's consumer and popular culture were being formed. The co-chairs of what was officially named the Royal Commission on National Development in the Arts, Letters and Sciences, 1949–1951, were Vincent Massey, chancellor of the University of Toronto, and Georges-Henri Lévesque, dean of the Faculty of Social Science at Laval University in Quebec City. The Massey–Lévesque Commission held 224 meetings, 114 of them public; received 462 briefs; and heard 1,200 speakers. The briefs included submissions from 13 federal government institutions, seven provincial governments, 87 national organizations, 262 local bodies, and 35 private commercial radio stations, and it drew on a series of background research studies (Canada, 1951: 8).

The order-in-council establishing the Massey–Lévesque Commission, like the Aird Commission two decades earlier, gave it an agenda that situated the broad spectrum of cultural activity within the national interest. The commissioners were asked to examine and make recommendations upon six areas: the operation and future development of such federal agencies as the National Film Board, the National Gallery, the National Museum, the Public Archives, and Library of Parliament; Canada's relations with UNESCO and other international bodies; relations between the government and national voluntary associations; methods to make people in foreign countries more aware of Canada; measures to preserve historical monuments; and "the principles upon which the policy of Canada should be based, in the fields of radio and television broadcasting" (Canada, 1951:, p. xxi; see also Shea, 1952: 10–11).

The Massey–Lévesque Commission took for granted the state's governance of the cultural sphere in the national interest. At one point, in fact, the report questioned whether culture and citizenship could even be distinguished as separate realms (Canada, 1951: 31).

Massey–Lévesque restated the principles on which national public radio had been established; it even recommended that the new broadcast medium, television, follow radio's model (301–2). The commission not only reinforced the cultural policies that had turned radio and, subsequently, cinema (the National Film Board was established in 1939) into governmental realms of activity, but greatly broadened state jurisdiction in the cultural sphere. One recommendation, for example, was the establishment of a new federal institution, the Canada Council for the Arts, to lend funding support to the arts, humanities, and social sciences (377–8). As the Canada Council's proposed mandate suggested, Massey–Lévesque brought a number of activities within the purview of the national interest. Universities, for example, were assigned "special responsibility for certain national problems" and were seen as "recruiting grounds for the national services." Massey–Lévesque further recommended the establishment of a national botanical garden, a national zoological garden, and a national aquarium (326).

Culture, the report emphasized, is also part of what it means to be a self-respecting nation-state. Cultural activities, the report stated, "lie at the roots of our life as a nation," and they are "the foundations of national unity" (284). For the Massey–Lévesque Commission, however, the idea of culture was somewhat different from the one that we have been using in much of this book. Rather than seeing culture as a general "way or ways of life," the commissioners saw activities like classical music, painting, sculpture, and dramatic arts as the epitome of cultural achievement. Cast from an elitist cultural perspective, cultural expression in the Massey–Lévesque report (271) is the search for essence, the search for a "Canadian spirit," a bond that defines as Canadian in their soul the constituents of the nation-state, no matter what their language, ethnicity, race, and so on.

Used with permission of Paul Robles/Art Bank.

The Canada Council for the Arts, one of the recommendations of the Massey–Lévesque Commission, continues to promote arts in Canada. In addition to other activities, the council shows off new and old works of art in its Art Bank.

Cultural phenomena and institutions that were not under state control, and particularly emerging popular cultural forms, were portrayed by Massey–Lévesque as potentially harmful influences. Here, most of the commission's angst was reserved for feature films, which it described as "not only the most potent but also the most alien of the influences shaping our Canadian life" (Canada, 1951: 50). What is not explained in the report is why it recommended no action in the feature-film sector, given the Canadian industry's domination by Hollywood.

The commission acknowledged differences within Canada, but it was divided as to their significance. Canada's demographic and geographical diversity inspired creativity; but difference was perceived as a potential threat to national unity. Regional difference should contribute to national unity rather than "sectionalism":

> Canadian sectionalism is not yet a thing of the past, but it is certain that the energetic efforts of the Canadian Broadcasting Corporation in providing special regional programmes and informative talks, and in introducing a great variety of Canadians to their fellow citizens, have done much to bring us nearer together. From Vancouver Island to Newfoundland and from the Mackenzie River to the border, Canadians have been given a new consciousness of their unity and their diversity. (Canada, 1951: 280)

Massey–Lévesque confessed an interest in First Nations arts and crafts "for its own sake and because it affects the well-being of an important group of people" (239), but endorsed the suggestion that "the Indian can best be integrated into Canadian life if his [sic] fellow Canadians learn to know and understand him through his creative work" (243).

As Aird had done, Massey–Lévesque placed the educational dimension in the foreground of cultural activity, and assumed responsibility for it. The commission's explicit intention was that Ottawa support and promote cultural work of "merit." For example, the report discussed film "chiefly as a means of furthering national unity and popular education" (50), which may partly explain its neglect of the feature-film sector. The commission expected a higher standard of programming from public radio than from private radio (286). One of the dangers the commission perceived in private commercial broadcasting was that such a system may produce "many programs which are trivial and commonplace and which debase public taste" (280–1).

Also like Aird, Massey–Lévesque purported to speak for the people; many of its comments were attributed to the oral and written submissions it received. "We believe we have heard the voice of Canada." Despite this enthusiasm, the report notes, on the same page, that most of the evidence came from organized groups (Canada, 1951: 268).

Massey–Lévesque also spoke to the issues of commercialization and Americanization. Faced with complaints from the private sector about government monopolizing film production and radio and television broadcasting, the report responded that the NFB and the CBC were protecting the nation "from excessive might divert listeners to US stations (290–1). These comments were echoed with regard to television.

Massey–Lévesque expressed apprehension about the US cultural presence in Canada. The report argued that Canada is culturally dependent in its "uncritical use of American educational philosophy" (16–17), in reading more foreign than domestic periodicals (17–18), and in the reliance of Canadian newspapers on foreign, principally American, news services for their international news coverage (62–3).

Massey–Lévesque introduced financing to the cultural debate, a topic that has become central to policy discussions in our time. Unlike today, however, the financial bind was confined to the cultural institutions themselves and wasn't a reflection of the government's overall fiscal health. The commission recommended stable, long-term state funding to address CBC's problem and to maintain its independence from government (293–4). Similarly, the commission recommended that Ottawa assist the universities through annual contributions based on provincial population figures (355).

In sum, Massey–Lévesque endorsed the federal government's initial cultural interventions and recommended that Ottawa expand its responsibility in this field, framing the arts, letters, and sciences in terms of Canada's national interest. Not only specific media like radio, television, and documentary film were deemed part of the state's cultural dominion, but cultural activity in general was also appropriated within the federal government purview. The commission defined cultural production as a requisite element of nationhood, and thus perceived the cultural sphere as state jurisdiction.

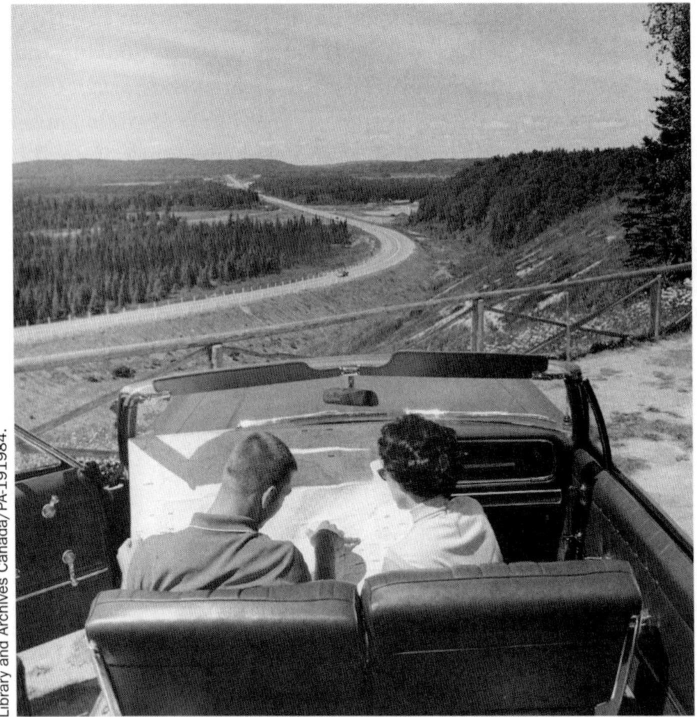

Library and Archives Canada/PA-191984.

The Massey–Lévesque Commission desired to help Canadians create a national identity through cultural institutions for the arts and sciences, much as the Trans-Canada Highway made transportation and travel easier across the country. In what ways have national cultural institutions helped form a Canadian identity?

commercialization and Americanization" (58). "Broadcasting in Canada, in our view, is a public service directed and controlled in the public interest by a body responsible to Parliament" (282–3).

The commission shared Aird's distaste for broadcast advertising, while acknowledging its importance as a source of revenue, particularly with the recommended introduction of the more costly medium of television to CBC'S portfolio. Massey–Lévesque, for instance, recognized that complete elimination of advertising from the national radio network was "impracticable," depriving Canadian companies of a national audience for their advertisements and the CBC of more than $2 million in advertising revenue. To ban commercial advertising from the national radio network, the commissioners argued, risked lowering the standard of programming and

Cast from a culturally elitist perspective, Massey–Lévesque posited private enterprise as antagonistic to the nation-building project in Canada and counterproductive to its framing of culture as national culture. More importantly for the commission, the commercialization of culture would mean its Americanization, casting the very project of nationhood itself in peril.

The Fowler Commission, 1956–1957

The Fowler Commission—officially, the 1957 Royal Commission on Broadcasting—resulted from a Massey–Lévesque recommendation that the subject of television broadcasting be reconsidered by an independent investigating body within three years of the beginnings of television broadcasting in Canada. Again, the commission's agenda was largely set; the December 1955 order-in-council establishing the Fowler Commission insisted that "the broadcasting and distribution of Canadian programmes by a public agency shall continue to be the central feature of Canadian broadcasting policy" (Canada, 1957: 293).

Chaired by Robert Fowler, the commission held 47 days of hearings in 1956 in 9 of the 10 provinces (bad weather cancelled the hearings in Newfoundland). Fowler was asked to make recommendations on seven points, including CBC television policy, the provision of adequate programming for both public and private television, financing (how much and from what sources), and the licensing and control of private television and radio "in the public interest" (293–4).

Fowler's initial question was *Is there a need for the state regulation of broadcasting in Canada?* The commission responded in the affirmative and cited public support for this conclusion. "We are satisfied that for Canada this is a legitimate and proper function of the state, and under our constitution it is a function of Parliament" (81).

Fowler explained its conclusion in four ways. The first was technological imperative. Rejecting the "freedom of the press" analogy, which the Canadian Association of Radio and Television Broadcasters (CARTB) had used to push for a devolution of state control of broadcasting, Fowler noted that the limited number of available radio and television frequencies necessitated allocation and a state licensing system (100–2).

Second, Fowler portrayed broadcasting as too powerful a medium to permit a laissez-faire approach. "Broadcasting is too important and its influence too great, to have the basic decisions as to those persons who shall be in charge of broadcasting removed from the control of those who are directly responsible to the Canadian people" (100–2).

A third justification for state regulation was "to restrain commercial forces from the excesses to which they may go" (84–5). This meant prohibiting too much advertising and encouraging a stronger commitment on the part of private broadcasters to "the public interest"—encouraging them to produce Canadian programming rather than just import cheaper US fare (86).

Finally, Fowler argued that state-regulated broadcasting was the only way to ensure Canadian broadcasting:

> If we want to have radio and television contribute to a Canadian consciousness and sense of identity, if we wish to make some part of the trade in ideas and culture move east and west across the country, if we seek to avoid engulfment by American cultural forces, we must regulate such matters as importation of programmes, advertising content and Canadian production of programmes. (Canada, 1957: 110)

While defending the national public service structure of broadcasting, the Fowler Commission nevertheless revealed some cracks in its foundation: the growing hostility of private broadcasters; complaints about CBC's centralization in Montreal and Toronto; and the subsumption of difference—regional, French–English, ethnic—within the national whole. Fowler gave little weight to criticisms of CBC's concentration in Central Canada, describing Montreal and Toronto as "necessarily" being "the two principal programme production centres in Canada" (Canada, 1957: 71). Conceding that ideas programs could more easily be decentralized, Fowler maintained that arts programs benefited from Central Canadian concentration.

The Fowler report acknowledged that Canadian broadcasting had to be representative. Regional needs had to be met and the commission emphasized the need for programming "as diversified and designed to satisfy as many different tastes (minority as well as majority) as economics and practicability may allow" (75). Consistent with this, Fowler proposed a board of broadcast governors with at least one of the 15 members from each of Canada's five regions: the Maritimes, Quebec, Ontario, the Prairies, and British Columbia (94).

The broadcasting system Fowler envisaged was not without cost, particularly as television service meant substantially higher expenses. The commission portrayed national public broadcasting as a necessity for Canada, and similarly deemed the broadcasting system it favoured as worth the expense, especially in the context of a prosperous economy (9). Fowler's major recommendation was increased and stable multi-year financing, based on 10-year forecasts of cost estimates (265–6).

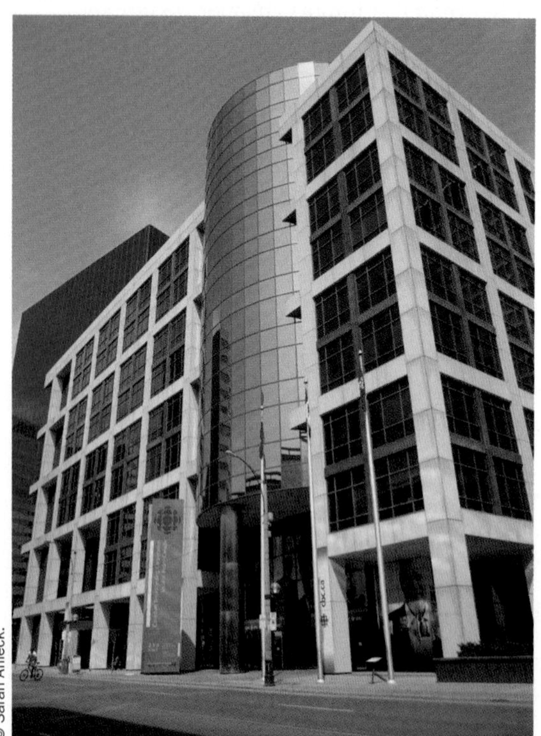

© Sarah Affleck.

The Fowler Commission gave little weight to criticisms of CBC's concentration in Montreal and Toronto, saying that decentralization would result in lower quality. In what ways does the internet change this conversation?

The Fowler Commission adopted a pragmatic, yet condescending, view of the commercialization of Canadian broadcasting. By the mid-1950s, selling goods had become one of the "four principal functions" of the broadcasting system (Canada, 1957: 44), yet the alliance of these four functions clearly was uneasy. Fowler described as "a conflict of interest and motives" the private broadcaster's "uncomfortable conflict between his desire to render a public service and his sound business instincts" (85).

Fowler maintained the rhetoric of Aird and Massey–Lévesque in portraying the United States as a threat to Canadian culture: "No other country is similarly helped and embarrassed by the close proximity of the United States" (7–8). Like Aird and Massey–Lévesque, Fowler posited the privatization of broadcasting as the Americanization of Canadian radio and television (230–3).

In sum, the Fowler Commission further reinforced the three themes that had legitimized state intervention in the cultural sphere in Aird and Massey–Lévesque. Fowler insisted that broadcasting remain a national service governed by the state, and rejected the private-enterprise alternative by casting the full-scale commercialization of Canadian broadcasting as its Americanization. Fowler also hinted at a new force in the communication policy debate: economics.

The Applebaum–Hébert Committee, 1981–1982

The Federal Cultural Policy Review Committee was established in August 1980 by Minister of Communications and Secretary of State Francis

Fox, led by composer Louis Applebaum and author-publisher Jacques Hébert. He insisted that the scope of Applebaum–Hébert be "broad and include all the main programmes of the Federal Government" (Canada, 1982: 369). Its mandate was to pick up where Massey–Lévesque had left off three decades earlier (3–5).

Like the commissions discussed above, however, Applebaum–Hébert was not without an agenda. Rising out of the recession of the late 1970s, the committee was a product of the end of the post–World War II economic boom; underneath it rested a concern for finding ways to reduce the cost of cultural support. At the same time, the interests in maintaining the elite cultural activities championed by Massey–Lévesque had been dulled by the rise of a new popular culture that championed and celebrated commercial cultural forms. In the face of the movement of industry from Canada, the United States, and Europe to places with lower labour costs and fewer environmental regulations, culture and information industries held the promise of helping rebuild the economy (see Chapter 11).

The committee published and distributed 50,000 copies of a discussion guide in December 1980 in order to stimulate public participation in its hearings. The guide "defined the field of inquiry," provided a historical overview of federal cultural policy, "outlined challenges and options facing Canadian cultural policy in the years ahead," and invited submissions (Canada, 1982: 370). Applebaum–Hébert held public hearings in 18 cities in every province and territory in 1981 (370).

The Applebaum–Hébert report represents a significant shift in thinking about the state's cultural role in general, and in attitudes toward the specific guiding principles by which state intervention had to this point been motivated and justified. While Applebaum–Hébert endorsed a role for the state, it redirected it. Conspicuously absent from the report was the anti-commercial and anti-American rhetoric characteristic of the Aird, Massey–Lévesque, and Fowler reports.

The Applebaum–Hébert report sought to balance what it perceived as a continuing need for an active state role in the cultural sphere with a concern for cultural producers' independence from state influence and control. The committee insisted that federal agencies such as the Canada Council for the Arts, CBC, the National Arts Centre, the NFB, and the Canadian Film Development Corporation should be exempt "from political direction in the form of ministerial directives of either a general or a specific nature" (Canada, 1982: 35–8). The committee also insisted on the independence of cultural producers related to funding. "If cultural life is to be autonomous and self-directed, it is important that it not become excessively dependent on one source of support—and especially on one government source" (57). In the performing arts, for example, Applebaum–Hébert envisaged the following income sources: "box office receipts, governments at all levels, and private donations from individuals, corporations and foundations" (174).

Yet, the committee was not completely consistent on the autonomy question. Applebaum–Hébert endorsed collaboration between cultural affairs and international trade promotion, and between travelling performing artists and Canadian business interests abroad. The committee proposed a Canadian International Cultural Relations Agency to administer international cultural relations under the secretary of state for external affairs (334–7).

Looking at Applebaum–Hébert now, it is striking for the absence of a national identity or a national unity discourse, though the report did tie the preservation of heritage properties to Canadians' "sense of place and continuity with their past" (110), and the committee regretted the absence of Canadian materials in the country's cultural institutions.

Nevertheless, Applebaum–Hébert maintained state governance as a central tenet. The committee was not deterred by the current economic recession that created pressure on governments to curtail spending. Reflecting its support of a cultural role for the state, it recommended the creation of a federal ministry of culture (46–7), the establishment of a contemporary arts centre (148), the introduction of a depreciation allowance and purchasing incentives to stimulate private demand for contemporary visual art (151), and greater support for Canadian magazines (225–6).

With regard to two central cultural institutions, however, the Applebaum–Hébert report advocated a retreat by the state. The committee recommended that the NFB be transformed into a research and training centre, delegating the bulk of its production activities to independent producers (256–5), and it recommended that the CBC relinquish all of its television production activities, with the exception of its news programs, in favour of acquiring shows from independent producers (292–4). While these recommendations were not adopted, they exemplified the commission's embrace of the commercialization of culture.

The Applebaum–Hébert report is particularly noteworthy for the break it made with the neat equation between the state's interests and those of the Canadian public in the cultural domain. Besides divorcing cultural producers from the nation-building project, Applebaum–Hébert acknowledged, and portrayed positively, **regionalism** and multi-ethnicity, referring in its opening chapter to "the different cultural traditions that Canadians so cherish" (Canada, 1982: 8).

Applebaum–Hébert also signalled an important shift in attitudes concerning the private sector's place in cultural production. Laying the ground for the commercialization of culture, the report placed new emphasis on building audiences and markets for Canadian cultural products. Applebaum–Hébert was less interested in resisting commercialism's encroachment than in devising means by which to create space for Canadian voices. Building audiences was proposed as a strategy to increase public support for both culture and federal cultural policy.

Finally, Applebaum–Hébert demonstrated none of the anti-American sentiment of previous commissions. The report lamented the dominance of US cultural products in the Canadian marketplace, not because of any pernicious American influence, but because Canadian cultural works were correspondingly under-represented—in publishing (Canada, 1982: 224), in sound recording (240), in television broadcasting (249–50), and in cinema (252–8). In spite of this, Applebaum–Hébert refused a protectionist stance, preferring to recommend proactive strategies by which Canadian cultural products could capitalize on the US-dominated industrial infrastructure, which the committee accepted as part of the cultural landscape.

Applebaum–Hébert maintained to a considerable extent the logic of state governance of the cultural sphere, but it did not do so unquestioningly. It shifted the state's role away from that of proprietor and regulator of culture toward the more comfortable roles of custodian, patron, and, especially, catalyst. Applebaum–Hébert is also remarkable for the extent to which it

www.thelightcone.com.

The Applebaum–Hébert Committee emphasized that in order for cultural life to be autonomous, it needs funding from places other than the government, like box office receipts or investments from private donors. How does changing where funding comes from change the arts and what it communicates?

abandoned the three motivating themes that had been the basis of Canadian cultural policy for the preceding half-century. The committee discarded the schema that equated state governance of culture with its Canadianization, and the market governance of culture with its Americanization. In its place it set the stage for culture as industry and the growing commercialization of culture in general. Following this trend, in 1987 the federal government published a report, *Vital Links: Canadian Cultural Industries*. Here Canadian film, book publishing, periodical publishing, sound recording, and broadcasting were clearly framed as commercial enterprises (Canada, 1987).

Re-evaluating State Involvement in the Cultural Sphere

There has been a shift in social values, a shift that applies specifically to three of the ideological pillars on which Canada's cultural policies have been based. The first of these pillars equated the interests of the state with the interests of the Canadian public. The second rejected the wholesale commercialization of cultural production in Canada. The third conceived of the United States as a force of cultural imperialism to be resisted.

The first signs of a change could be detected in the Fowler Commission's report, which noted the rise of private-sector opposition to state intervention, concerns about the centralization of Canada's principal cultural institutions, and the problem of satisfying regional and minority cultures within a larger national communication policy apparatus. The Applebaum–Hébert report may have best encapsulated the policy shift in its credo that "the essential task of government in cultural matters is to remove obstacles and enlarge opportunities" (Canada, 1982: 75). This has become the prevailing theme of approaches to policy development since the 1980s.

In part, this change in outlook is the product of the commercialization of culture in the post–World War II era, but additionally, Canadian nationalism has undergone change during this time. The immediate postwar period and the years leading up to centennial celebrations in 1967 could be described as a period of strong Canadian nationalism, but that sentiment was rivalled in the 1960s and '70s by a growing regionalism. The 1960s saw the emergence of a strong Quebec nationalist movement that had both militant and progressive elements. The sense of Quebec's distinctiveness grew through the 1980 referendum on sovereignty, the repatriation of the Canadian constitution in 1982, and the Meech Lake (1987) and Charlottetown (1992) constitutional accords. Quebecers' sense of themselves as a distinct people was fuelled, too, by early successes at finding a French-speaking voice in popular music (Robert Charlebois, Beau Dommage, Offenbach), film (Claude Jutra, Pierre Perrault, Gilles Carle), literature (Hubert Aquin, Anne Hébert, Réjean Ducharme, Marie-Claire Blais), theatre (Michel Tremblay, Robert Lepage), and television (*La Famille Plouffe*). Protected by language and promoted by a star system that English Canada has never been able to emulate, Quebec's communication sector is another mark of the province's distinct status.

This period, too, marked the rise of Western regionalism, particularly in Alberta. The Pierre Trudeau government's National Energy Program of 1980—a unilateral attempt by Ottawa to assert federal control over an industry under provincial jurisdiction—confirmed for many the view that the resource-based industries of the Western and Atlantic provinces were economically subservient to Central Canada's manufacturing sector, producing intense resentment especially in Alberta and British Columbia, which were seeking to assert their growing economic and political power.

As so many of Canadians' communication needs became served by commercial media through the 1970s and '80s, the argument that commercialization threatened Canadian culture became harder and harder to sustain. Even Canada's public television broadcaster, the CBC, has come to resemble a commercial service, with its menu of professional sports, Hollywood movies and game shows, and derivative reality-TV programs. Recessions in the late 1970s and early 1980s compelled governments to rethink their spending on cultural programs and organizations. As both the Fowler and Applebaum–Hébert reports signalled, economics had become a significant factor in policy discussions, and fiscal restraint has been a predominant theme of governments since the 1980s.

In this context, political ideologies have become much more fiscally conservative. After years of state intervention under Pierre Trudeau's Liberals, Brian Mulroney's Progressive Conservatives in the 1980s declared Canada open for business, embracing free trade with the United States and less state intervention—what is misleadingly termed **deregulation** (see Box 7.6)—in all sectors of the economy. International agreements liberalizing trade have had significant implications for government communication policy, because national policies have become subject to scrutiny by international trade bodies such as the **World Trade Organization**.

By permission of the Avanti Group.

The popular Radio-Canada talk show *Tout le monde en parle*, with hosts Guy A. Lepage (left) and Dany Turcotte, provides a weekly glimpse into Quebec's political and cultural life. It is part of a star system that the media in English Canada have never been able to rival.

Communication policy can now be seen as being formulated in a global context.

While, as we will see in Chapter 8, concern over the influence of US giants on the Canadian mediascape remains, "communication policy in Canada has always been heavily influenced by proximity to the United States, now that proximity has become global" (Abramson and Raboy, 1999: 776). The 1995 G7 meeting in Brussels was "a point where the governance of markets and [communication] technologies intersected" (781). This "post-Brussels shift" is significant because Canadian communication policy is "increasingly formulated in multilateral international fora," which results in "the globalization of Canadian communication policy."

Related to this is the dispersal of policy-making among different ministries within the Canadian government (787). The federal government's digital media policy, Digital Canada 150 (Canada, 2014e), for example, was developed by Industry Canada. The policy primarily addresses access and economic opportunity concerns. Its five priorities are connecting 98 per cent of Canadians with high-speed (i.e., 5 Mbps) internet access; providing protection against cyberbullying and malware; creating economic opportunity for Canadian businesses; providing greater access to government materials and data online; and giving Canadians greater online access to Canadian cultural materials (Canada 2014a–d).

The other dimension to globalization, of course, is the global circulation of digitized communications, which will be a central theme in our discussion of the cultural industries in Chapter 8. For example, there is pressure on the Canadian government to impose the same taxation and financing rules on foreign online media companies operating in Canada that apply to domestic film and television companies. In a particularly contentious case in 2018, the Department of Canadian Heritage refused to impose a sales tax on the popular streaming service Netflix, instead agreeing to Netflix spending $500 million over five years on Canadian productions, an amount the company was believed to be already spending (Kelly, 2018).

7.6

Deregulation or Reregulation?

The term used most commonly to describe governments' retreat from intervening in the marketplace—whether in communications, health care, education, or anywhere else—is *deregulation*. The term implies that these sectors of the economy are gradually being freed from regulation because governments are withdrawing their powers of surveillance and control to allow market forces to hold sway.

But market forces are also a form of regulation, producing simply an alternative form of governance. Some commentators prefer to use the term *reregulation*, because it more accurately and precisely captures the process that is taking place. Reregulation suggests that these sectors continue to be regulated, but market regulation is being substituted for state regulation.

A further challenge to Canadian policy-makers is addressing the increasing diversity of the country's population, if the communication media are to serve as a vehicle for social cohesion. As we discuss further in Chapter 11, Canada is a country of immigrants in which one-fifth of the population self-identifies as visible minority, and where there are great distinctions between urban and rural populations. In the 1950s, 95 per cent of immigrants came from Europe and the United States; since the 1990s, 60 per cent have come from Asia. More than half of Canada's youngest people (under age 20) have ethnic origins other than British, French, Canadian, or Aboriginal (Statistics Canada, 2016; see also Baeker, 2002: 181). As policy researcher Greg Baeker notes, "For ethno-racial and visible minorities with diasporic links to other nations, the privileging of the historical (time) and territorial (space) claims of Aboriginal and English- and French-speaking Canadians fails to reflect the reality of Canada today" (183).

In the face of this shifting context and the increasing importance of the cultural sector to the economy, the federal government announced the development of a new cultural policy framework—Creative Canada—in 2017. The framework is the first step in an ambitious project to restructure cultural policy for the digital age. Here the government expands the scope of cultural industries policy beyond "books, magazines, newspapers, audiovisual (film and television), [and] music" to include "a wider range of industries that contribute to the creative sector: design, fashion, architecture, video games, digital media and multiplatform storytelling – transmedia" (Canada, 2017). As the document states, "[t]he intent is to recognize their role as employers and producers in the creative economy." Consequently, the policy field is now said to encompass the "creative industries," rather than just the "culture industries." We will have a closer look at this change in Chapter 8.

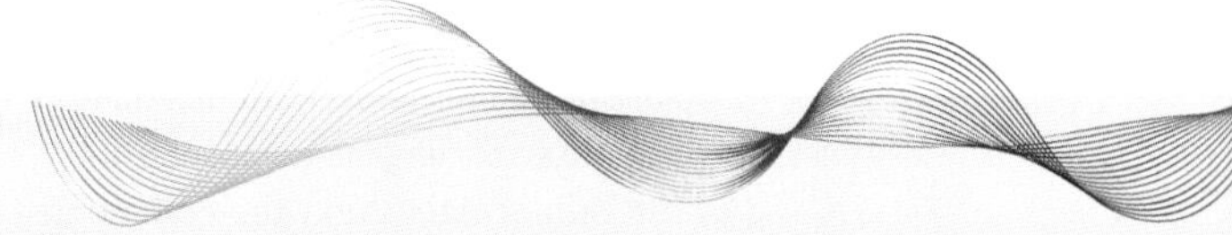

SUMMARY

We may wonder why communication policies, regulations, and laws are necessary. We have provided in this chapter a historical explanation, tracing the origins of, and rationale behind, state involvement in the communication sphere.

Communication takes place within an environment constructed by laws, policies, conventions, economic imperatives, guiding ideals, and public pressures. Communication policy establishes the rules by which mediated communication occurs, and dates back to the first days of the printing press in the fifteenth century, when books began to be produced on a large scale and were traded across borders. Policy is developed at both the local and global levels, as governments need to respect international covenants dealing with the circulation of cultural products while addressing their own particular exigencies.

Communication policy in Canada has historically framed the media, culture, and society in terms of the nation-state, so that communication policy is always also *national* policy, serving the promotion of a national culture. Priorities, though, can shift through time, and we have in this chapter traced policy development through four pivotal moments of the twentieth century. If policy was driven initially by the need to develop within Canadians a strong sense of nation and national culture, which treated commercialization and Americanization as threats to those aims, the thematic rationale began to shift in the 1970s and '80s. The financial burdens of state intervention became much more of an issue, regionalism became a rival sentiment to nationalism, and Canadians became accustomed to the commercialization and the Americanization of media. By the 1970s, most US commercial popular culture was less foreign to Canadians than the products of their own culture in many areas.

While US domination of the Canadian communication marketplace continues to be defined as a problem by policy analysts, it no longer resonates the same way with Canadian governments or with the Canadian people. The context of policy formation has shifted significantly since the 1980s. The greater integration of world markets has resulted in an increasing tendency to perceive and regulate communication products and services as commodities like any other good or service, undermining preferred treatment of domestic industries. Canadian governments have been advocates of liberalized trade and have spread the responsibility for policy development to ministries, such as Innovation, Science and Economic Development Canada, ministries that are primarily concerned with international trade and economic development. Digitization, too, has drawn all communication activity into a global sphere. A further shift has occurred in how we regard Canada's population; our increased diversity and the need for reconciliation with Canada's Indigenous peoples require much more flexible and inclusive policies to serve all Canadians' communication and cultural needs.

KEY TERMS

Berne Convention, p. 173
Canadian Radio League, p. 179
copyright, p. 171
deregulation, p. 188
frequency allocation, p. 173
globalization, p.172
intellectual property, p. 173
International Telecommunication Union, p. 173
legislation, p. 171
non-governmental organizations, p. 174
policy, p. 171
regionalism, p. 186
regulations, p. 171
right to communicate, p. 174
royal commission, p. 175
task force, p. 175
Universal Declaration of Human Rights, p. 174
World Trade Organization, p. 188

RELATED WEBSITES

Canadian Radio-television and Telecommunications Commission: www.crtc.gc.ca/eng/home-accueil.htm
The CRTC governs broadcasting and telecommunications in Canada; its website is an excellent source of information about recent decisions and upcoming hearings.

Department of Canadian Heritage: www.canada.ca/en/canadian-heritage.html
Heritage is the government ministry responsible for communications and culture. Its website contains information on all of the cultural industry sectors as well as information on the ministry's funding programs.

Innovation, Science and Economic Development Canada: www.ic.gc.ca/eic/site/icgc.nsf/eng/home
This is the government ministry responsible for economic activity in Canada, a portfolio that includes economic aspects of culture and communication, such as intellectual property and the internet. Its website is a good source of information about the ministry's programs and policies.

Friends of Canadian Broadcasting: www.friends.ca
Friends is a lobby group dedicated to the preservation and promotion of Canadian identity and culture on radio and television. Its website is a good guide to current broadcast policy changes and the issues raised by those changes.

Canadian Centre for Policy Alternatives: www.policyalternatives.ca
This is an independent research centre advocating policies for social and economic justice. Its series of policy papers includes studies touching on communication and culture.

FURTHER READINGS

Abramson, Bram Dov, and Marc Raboy. 1999. "Policy globalization and the 'information society': A view from Canada." *Telecommunication Policy*, 23. This article situates Canadian communication policy formation within a new global context.

Canada, Department of Canadian Heritage, 2017. *Creative Canada Policy Framework.* Available at: https://www.canada.ca/en/canadian-heritage/campaigns/creative-canada/framework.html.

Hamelink, Cees J. 1994. *The Politics of World Communication*. London: Sage. This book provides a comprehensive summary of global communication policy development from its earliest manifestations to the late twentieth century.

Raboy, Marc. 1992. *Missed Opportunities: The Story of Canada's Broadcasting Policy*. Montreal and Kingston: McGill-Queen's UP. Here is a history of broadcast policy development in Canada and a critique of its framing as national policy.

———, and Jeremy Shtern, editors. 2010. *Media Divides: Communication Rights and the Right to Communicate in Canada*. Vancouver: UBC Press. This book situates Canadian communication policy within the larger movement dedicated to the democratization of communication and establishing the concept of communication rights.

Vipond, Mary. 1992 *Listening In: The First Decade of Canadian Broadcasting, 1922–1932*. Montreal and Kingston: McGill-Queen's UP. The brief but fascinating history of Canadian radio prior to the establishment of a national broadcaster is detailed in this work. This document outlines the federal government's vision for developing a "creative industries" policy.

STUDY QUESTIONS

1. What purpose(s) does communication policy serve?
2. Why is governance of mediated communication not simply left to market forces?
3. What were the predominant themes motivating communication policy development through the first half of the twentieth century? Why were these themes predominant?
4. To what extent do these themes remain pertinent today?
5. How has the policy development context changed since the 1990s?
6. What has led to the increasing commodification of cultural products and communication services?
7. In what ways does the pervasiveness of the internet alter policy considerations in Canada?

8

Communication Policy

Sector by Sector

The central objective, then as now, centres on how to reconcile economic and socio-cultural objectives in view of technological innovations. —*Daniel J. Paré*

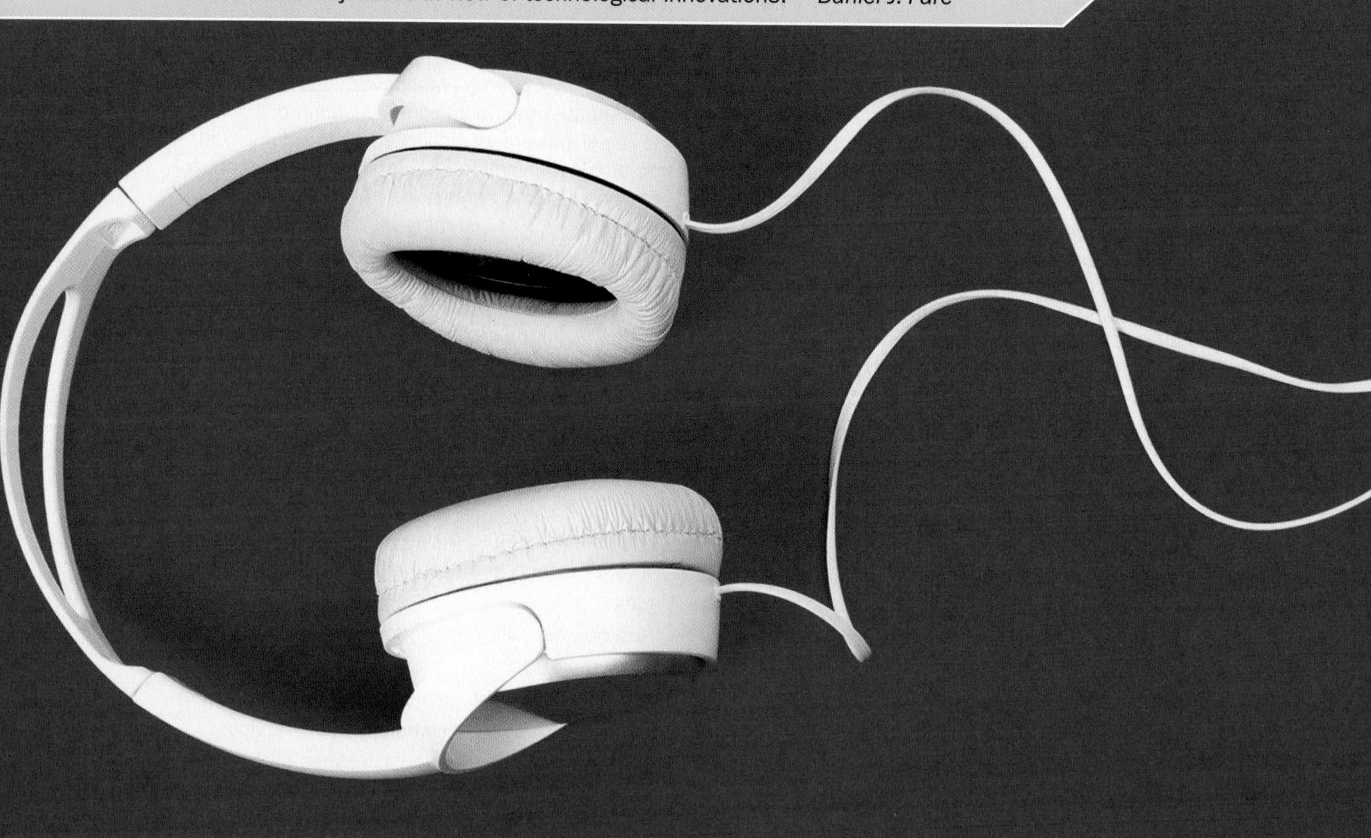

FabrikaCr/iStockphoto

Opening Questions

- What new challenges confront Canada's policy makers?
- What does it mean to say that media technologies, media forms, and media industries have converged?
- How do international trade agreements affect communication policy formation?
- How does the increasing diversity of Canada's population inform communication policy?

Introduction

If, as we discussed in Chapter 7, the development of media and communication policy must always take into account the environment within which communication takes place—technologies, laws, existing policies, conventions, economic imperatives, guiding ideals, public pressures—policy formulation must also adapt to change. One of the most significant changes of the past two decades has been **convergence**, which in the context of communication means the digital merging of previously distinct analog technologies, media forms, and media industries (see Chapter 6). A second dramatic change has been pressure for countries like Canada to revise and formulate communication policy in conformity with new international trade covenants. Finally, reconciliation with indigenous peoples, coupled with new global migration patterns, calls for further diversifying Canadian communication networks and policies. What has not changed, though, is a central policy aim: ensuring that Canadians have the full citizenship, cultural, and economic opportunities that a national media and communication system might afford.

As we have discussed in earlier chapters, digitization is the translation of information from various analog formats into patterns of 1s and 0s that can be transmitted along cables, fibre optic networks, telephone lines, and over the air, then reconstructed by various kinds of electronic receivers, such as computers, cell phones, tablets, and so on. In the past, it made sense to talk about distinct media forms—magazines, radio, television, cinema—as completely separate industries. But these media silos are breaking down rapidly. Almost all media content today is produced digitally, with the result that it can be distributed both in its conventional form (e.g., hard-copy magazines, over-the-air radio and television, celluloid film) and digitally, typically via the internet. The internet, though, is not simply an alternative delivery mechanism; it has become our central medium, transforming and bundling media content of every type and from every source, serving as the feeder system to all our digital devices. It is common now to hear people say they no longer read newspapers or watch television; they *do*, in fact, but the newspaper articles they read are retrieved through social media sites and read on their laptops or tablets or phones, just as the television shows they watch might be streamed through Netflix or YouTube.

As shown on p. 194, this technical convergence of media forms has been aided and abetted by the corporate convergence of media companies, which are no longer in the newspaper or television business exclusively but are producing content for audiences on a variety of media platforms. CBC, for example, which for 70 years was a broadcasting company, transformed itself into a multimedia company in 2009, with the greater integration of its radio, television, and online operations, and in 2014 announced its intention to prioritize its digital platforms. The Montreal media company Quebecor, which began as a newspaper publisher, owns magazines, newspapers, a book publisher, a web portal, a cable distributor, and a television network (among other media properties); it uses its portal—www.canoe.ca—to showcase content from a range of its media holdings.

One of the most attractive features of digital technology is its capacity for **interactivity**. As users of these communication services, we are quickly adapting to a mediascape in which we have increasing choice about how—and when and where—we listen to music or watch television or read a book. There has always been a participatory element to audiences' consumption of media products, but digital technology allows more and more people to become producers, whether in creating their own videos, music compilations, websites, or blogs, or in simply manipulating the output of media professionals (e.g., creating mash-ups, using recorded music as a soundtrack for a home video). In a similar vein, it has lowered the barriers to entry for more sustained communication projects like citizen journalism and other alternative media formulations (see Lessig, 2008). If communication

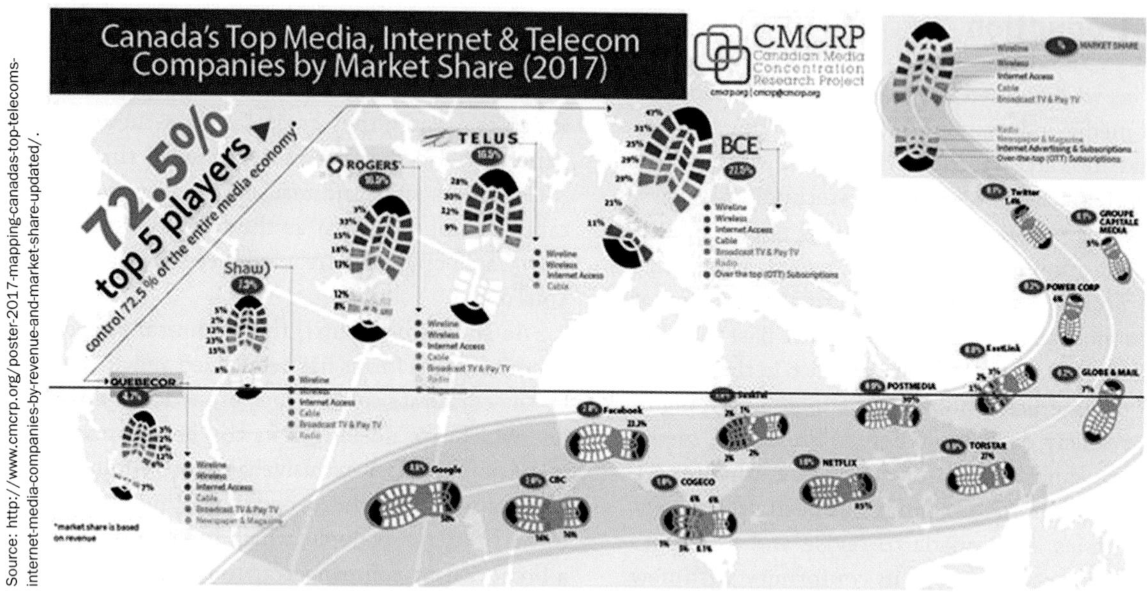

Source: http://www.cmcrp.org/poster-2017-mapping-canadas-top-telecoms-internet-media-companies-by-revenue-and-market-share-updated/.

As illustrated in this chart published by the Canadian Media Concentration Research Project, 72.5 per cent of Canada's media economy is controlled by five companies.

policy is to be relevant and effective, it must take these changes to what is called the media ecology into account.

A second significant change to the policy environment since the 1980s has been pressure to liberalize international trade and to eliminate protectionist legislation, including rules and regulations pertaining to the fields of communication and culture. Canada signed a free-trade agreement with the United States in 1987, and then endorsed the North American Free Trade Agreement (NAFTA) with the States and Mexico in 1994. NAFTA was replaced by the Canada–United States–Mexico Agreement (CUSMA) in 2018, although at the time of writing it still required ratification by the national governments before becoming law.

Other trade agreements that have bearing on Canada's media and communication industries include the Comprehensive and Progressive Agreement for Trans-Pacific Partnership (CPTPP) and the Canada-European Union Trade Agreement (CETA). Canada is also a member of the World Trade Organization (WTO), which has its own international framework for multilateral trade dating from 2007. These agreements seek to encourage international trade in goods and services across all sectors, and in so doing, create an open market by abolishing national policies perceived as discriminatory. However, one of the most contentious areas in these trade deliberations is cultural policy, which is designed precisely to discriminate on the basis of nationality in order to protect and promote indigenous cultural and creative industries, which, as we have seen, include film, television, radio, publishing, magazines, newspapers, and music.

The United States is not only Canada's largest trade partner and closest neighbour, but it is also the world's foremost advocate for breaking down trade barriers, particularly in industries like television, film, music, and publishing, where it has dramatic economies-of-scale advantages, and is a net exporter. (The United States is less enthusiastic about free trade in areas in which it is a net importer, such as softwood lumber.) The enormous quantity of cultural materials US companies produce and their ability to recover their costs of production in their own domestic market—the world's richest—provide US **cultural industries** with tremendous advantages in the global marketplace. For example, for Canadian television networks, buying and broadcasting US programs is generally one-tenth the cost of producing their own; the star power and promotional heft behind those American productions compounds this structural advantage. If there were no measures to promote the production and distribution of Canadian cultural products, there would be little room for Canadian creators in their own mediascape, as was the case in the early to mid-twentieth century.

For this reason, Canadian negotiators insisted on a cultural exemption in the original 1987 free-trade agreement with the United States, and in NAFTA and the more recent CUSMA. This exemption, however, is highly qualified and not really an exemption at all, as it comes with a key proviso that allows for one of the signatories to take a form of retaliation "of equivalent commercial effect" in response to protectionist measures. In other words, the United States could argue that a Canadian policy measure causes a US cultural industry financial damage, and seek redress from the Canadian government. Moreover, CUSMA extends free-trade provisions to "digital trade," which includes products such as "a computer program, text, video, image, sound recording, or other product that is digitally encoded" (Chapter 19). How this might affect Canadian cultural industries and markets remains to be seen.

While there is no general exemption for cultural industries under the WTO, both the CPTPP and CETA have some provisions in this regard. On another front, the United Nations Educational, Scientific and Cultural Organization (UNESCO) has adopted a Convention on the Protection and Promotion of the Diversity of Cultural Expressions, and Canada was the first country to ratify it in 2005. But this convention has not been signed by the United States, and to date has no bearing on international trade law.

Serving the communicative needs of Canadians is also challenging, both for media producers and governments. There are great differences among Canadian communities: between rural, suburban, and urban communities; between our major cities; and between our provinces and regions. Forging a media system that, in the words of Dwayne Winseck, maintains spaces for "civil discourse and the mutual understanding that democracies depend on to survive" (Winseck, 2010: 377) is further complicated by our increasingly ready access to international communication goods and services.

With the growing economic importance of media and communication products and services, there will continue to be pressure on countries like Canada to conform to strict market regulation of the cultural industries, rather than adhering to a regulatory regime that sees in these industries both economic and cultural dimensions. To some extent, this is reflected in the Department of Canadian Heritage's 2017 *Creative Canada Policy Framework* (discussed in Chapter 7), where a series of proposed policy measures to bolster Canada's creative or cultural industries—ranging from new tax credits and production funds to copyright reform, to strengthening public broadcasting—are laid out.

In this chapter, we provide brief profiles of the major communication sectors and examine sector-specific policy challenges in full recognition of the convergence of media forms and media industries well underway. But we also pick up where Chapter 7 left off, recognizing, too, that policy priorities are not only shaped by technological and industrial exigencies but are ultimately driven by our collective response generated by one persistent question: *What is communication for?* As we have seen, the answer to this question is rooted in the history and geography of the Canadian state, as Canadian creators and policy-makers have worked to develop a media system that allows Canadians to see and understand both themselves and the world beyond.

Telecommunications, Broadcasting, and the Internet

Telecommunications is governed in Canada by the 1993 *Telecommunications Act*. Under the terms of the Act, telecommunications is defined as "the emission, transmission or reception of intelligence by any wire, cable, radio, optical or other electromagnetic system, or by any similar technical system." Consequently, in formal terms, both the internet and broadcasting can be seen as kinds of telecommunication. However, as we shall see, neither the relations between these different fields of communication, nor how they should be treated in terms of law and regulation, is entirely clear.

Until 1996 telecommunications and broadcasting were treated as separate industries: telecommunications devoted solely to the transmission of information, and broadcasting to the production and distribution of media content. Under the law at the time, telecommunications companies were not allowed to create media content. The primary reason for this was to avoid any possible conflicts between content and carriage; that is, to ensure that telecommunications companies or "carriers" did not favour their own content (media products) over their rivals', and that all media or message producers had fair and equal access to electronic distribution networks. At the time, this rule was particularly important because many telecommunications companies enjoyed monopolies in the geographic areas where they operated. Hence, if they refused to carry or transmit television, radio, or newspaper companies' products, it might severely restrict the ability of those companies to operate outside any particular town or city. In other words, there might not be any television or radio networks, newspaper chains, or news wire services other than those owned by the monopoly telecommunications companies.

To further ensure that all parties had reasonable access to telecommunications services, companies offering these services to the public were designated "common carriers" and obliged by law to carry any message (content) that a company or individual wished to send, at an equitable cost. (As we will see, however, the internet is not subject to **common-carriage** rules.)

In the 1990s, however, these rules began to change. First, the government began to allow competition in telecommunications markets. Under the old regime, private telephone companies were granted monopoly status in designated Canadian territories, with the understanding that they would provide equitable telephone service at reasonable rates to both urban and rural markets, subsidizing toll-free local calling with the long-distance rates they charged. That system was gradually transformed, however, and in September 1994 the CRTC ruled that competition must be the basis for the provision of all telecommunication services, including local telephone service (Telecom Decision 94-19). This decision required companies to separate the costs of providing any single service (e.g., local phone service) from those for any other service (e.g., long-distance phone service), meaning that companies would no longer be allowed to cross-subsidize services. The idea behind this decision was that competition would help bring the cost of telephone service—particularly long-distance service—down.

Second, in 1996 the federal government issued a Convergence Policy Statement (Canada, 1996). This announcement stated the government's intention to break down the barriers between telecommunications, broadcasting, and cable markets. Not only did this allow telephone companies to offer cable television services, and cable television companies to offer telephone service, but it also led to telephone and cable companies buying television, radio, and newspaper companies as they worked to develop new economies of scale and scope.

Coupled with the technological convergence of media industries facilitated by digitization, the corporate manoeuvring that resulted from these policy changes is well illustrated on p. 194, where we can see that the five largest media companies in Canada have a wide range of media holdings, including wireline and wireless telephone services, cable and satellite television delivery, television, radio, publishing, and internet service provision. It's interesting that, while as illustrated they have quite diverse holdings today, in the 1980s Quebecor was primarily a publishing (newspaper) company, Shaw was a cable-TV company, Rogers was a cable-TV company, Telus was a telephone company, and Bell was a telephone company.

A third important development took place in May 1999 when the CRTC issued its new media exemption order, which basically exempted internet-based content from regulation (CRTC, 1999). At the time, the commission noted that internet-based content had "not had any detrimental impact on conventional radio and television audiences . . . [and that] the effect of new media on television audience size will be limited at least until such time as high-quality video programming can be distributed on the Internet." Today, of course, "high-quality video programming" is readily available on the internet, and how to deal with this impact is one of the major issues facing media regulation today.

Given the shifting character of both the technological and corporate media environments, the federal government struck a panel to review the Broadcasting and Telecommunications Acts in June 2018 (Canada, 2018c). As noted in the terms of reference, the review will consider how to "best support the creation, production and distribution of Canadian content in both French and English—and focus on updating and modernizing the broadcasting system by exploring how all players are reflected within it and can contribute to it." The panel is scheduled to report its findings in January 2020. From there, it will probably be at least another year or two before any legislative changes might be made. In the interim, telecommunications and broadcasting will remain legislatively separate, but converging on both the technological and corporate fronts.

Telecommunications

The historical core of the telecommunications sector is the telephone industry, but the telecommunications sector has become the veritable backbone of a growing range of applications, from conventional and wireless telephony to the provision of internet services. There is no better illustration of media convergence, and how telecommunications has evolved, than the new generations of smartphones, which act as telephones, cameras, video and audio players, and personal computers all in one small, hand-held device, linked into networks owned and controlled by communication conglomerates.

Telecommunications is a $50 billion industry with six subsectors: local wireline telephone service, long-distance wireline telephone service, internet services, data transmission, private line, and wireless services (CRTC, 2018). The five largest companies—Bell, Quebecor, Rogers, Shaw, and Telus—generate 72.5 per cent of telecommunications revenues. Wireless services form the largest and fastest-growing sector, accounting for about half of Canadians' spending on telecommunications. In 2017, household spending on communication averaged $222.83 per month. Approximately 99 per cent of Canadians have access to wireless networks, which cover about 20 per cent of Canada's land mass (CRTC, 2018); 87 per cent of Canadian households have internet service, and 88 per cent have mobile telephones. However, if mobile access to the internet is an important resource in our increasingly digital society, then lower-income households are at a disadvantage. As noted by the Canadian Media Concentration Research Project, "nearly one-in-three households in the lowest income quintile do not subscribe to a mobile wireless service, while only one-in-seven of those on the next rung up stand in the same position. By contrast, mobile wireless service is nearly universal for the most well-off in society" (CMCRP, 2018).

As with broadcasting, the **Canadian Radio-television and Telecommunications Commission (CRTC)** is charged with enforcing the rules laid out in the *Telecommunications Act*. However, there are specified limits on the CRTC's powers. For instance, the *Telecommunications Act* requires the CRTC to rely on market forces "to the maximum extent feasible" and to regulate "where there is a need to do so, in a manner that interferes with market forces to the minimum extent necessary" (CRTC, 2010: 5). At the same time, the Act also allows that the federal government retains the right to vary, rescind, or refer back for reconsideration all CRTC decisions.

Some of the key policy issues in telecommunications today are convergence, affordability and access, and foreign investment.

Regarding convergence, as noted, communication policy historically segregated carriage services (telecommunications, governed by the *Telecommunications Act*) from content services (broadcasting, governed by the *Broadcasting Act*). However, the 1996 Convergence Policy led to the

The telecommunications sector began as the telephone industry. What other applications does it have now?

8.1

Telecommunications Act, Section 7*

The foundation for Canadian telecommunications policy is contained in Section 7 of the 1993 *Telecommunications Act*. Notice how the Act specifies how the system should serve both social and economic purposes. As it states:

7. It is hereby affirmed that telecommunications performs an essential role in the maintenance of Canada's identity and sovereignty and that the Canadian telecommunications policy has as its objectives

    (a) to facilitate the orderly development throughout Canada of a telecommunications system that serves to safeguard, enrich and strengthen the social and economic fabric of Canada and its regions;

    (b) to render reliable and affordable telecommunications services of high quality accessible to Canadians in both urban and rural areas in all regions of Canada;

    (c) to enhance the efficiency and competitiveness, at the national and international levels, of Canadian telecommunications;

    (d) to promote the ownership and control of Canadian carriers by Canadians;

    (e) to promote the use of Canadian transmission facilities for telecommunications within Canada and between Canada and points outside Canada;

    (f) to foster increased reliance on market forces for the provision of telecommunications services and to ensure regulation, where required, is efficient and effective;

    (g) to stimulate research and development in Canada in the field of telecommunications and to encourage innovation in the provision of telecommunications services;

    (h) to respond to the economic and social requirements of users of telecommunications services; and

    (i) to contribute to the protection of the privacy of persons.

* Notes omitted.

Source: Government of Canada *Telecommunications Act*, Section 7; lois.justice.gc.ca/PDF/T-3.4.pdf. 2010. Reproduced with the permission of the Minister of Public Works and Government Services Canada, 2011.

corporate convergence of the country's largest telecommunication and broadcasting companies, and today these companies are in direct competition with one another in the creation, purchasing, and delivery of content to media platforms. This vertical integration between content and carriage raises an important set of issues, including the ability of independently owned TV networks and stations to access distribution networks. These issues are discussed in Chapter 9, where we consider the implications that different forms of ownership pose for media form and content.

In the face of rising complaints over how corporations were treating their mobile phone customers, the CRTC introduced a Wireless Code governing consumer rights in 2013 (CRTC, n.d.). The purpose of the code is to make the rules and regulations governing mobile services more easily understandable for customers and to promote better customer relations within the industry. But while these rules have helped smooth customer relations, they have done little to address concerns about affordability and access. It is a common complaint that "Canadians pay some of the highest prices in the industrialized world for cellphone plans" and other mobile services (Harris, 2018). Given the wide range of plans available on the market, industry representatives sometimes dispute the truth of this claim. At the same time, however, industry representatives also argue that because of the vast size of the country and our relatively small population, it is more costly to deliver service in Canada than it is in more densely populated markets such as Europe, where they can take advantage of much larger economies of scale. Still, at the time of writing, the CRTC is working with the industry to try to find ways to bring prices down (Paddon, 2018).

Increasing competition in mobile communication markets is often touted as one way to bring prices down. However, because of the high cost of building new telecommunication networks, finding companies willing to make such investments has proven difficult. Moreover, while competition might bring prices down in heavily populated areas of the country, it would do little or nothing for people living outside those centres, where the high cost of building networks has led to hundreds of thousands of Canadians not having access to basic digital communication services. Finding ways to address this digital divide is an important policy priority (CBC, 2018; Harris, 2018).

The *Telecommunications Act* stipulates that telecom companies must be Canadian-owned and controlled. In part, this is a recognition of the increasing importance of telecommunications services, and of the sensitive data these services carry as Canadian citizens, governments, and businesses conduct more and more of their affairs online. The CRTC has argued that Canadians consider communication services "essential," and that it is difficult to separate concerns about telecommunications network infrastructure from concerns about the content that infrastructure carries (CRTC, 2010: 214–5). At the same time, however, increasing foreign ownership of Canadian telecommunications companies is also sometimes touted as a way to lower costs and increase access. But despite the fact that, as outlined above, increased competition does not necessarily guarantee benefits in this regard, foreign ownership holds other pitfalls for the Canadian system. Perhaps the most important of these is the difficulty regulators might encounter when making foreign companies comply with Canadian regulations. The internet provides a case in point. To ensure that the media serve the broad public interest, regulation attempts to strike a balance of rights and responsibilities whereby in exchange for the licence to carry on business, companies agree to meet with regulations that promote Canadian interests and perspectives within Canada's media systems, such as adhering to content regulations or contributing to production funds. As has been clearly illustrated with web-based companies like Netflix, getting foreign media companies to respect national regulatory regimes can be very difficult (CBC, 2014). Indeed, it was problems like these that gave rise to ownership regulations in the first place (Bernard, 1982).

Broadcasting

Broadcasting in Canada is a $17.9 billion industry that includes radio and television as well as the distribution services of cable and satellite (CRTC, 2017). Distribution is the largest sector of the industry, accounting for 49 per cent of revenues, followed by television (41%) and radio (10%). The five largest ownership groups dominate the industry—BCE, Shaw (including Corus), Rogers, CBC, and Quebecor—with 81 per cent of the revenue.

In terms of distribution, 76 per cent of Canadian households subscribed to a cable, internet protocol television (IPTV), or satellite service provider in 2016 (CRTC, 2017). And while the numbers of cable and satellite subscribers declined 3.8 per cent and 7.1 per cent, respectively, from 2015 to 2016, IPTV subscribers increased by 13.8 per cent. Also, while traditional television viewing has decreased by approximately 1 hour per week over the last 5 years, weekly internet television viewing has increased by approximately 2.5 hours over the same period (CRTC, 2017).

Radio is the smallest broadcasting subsector in terms of revenues. It is also popular and profitable. There are more than 1,100 audio services in Canada, and Canadians listened to radio an average of 16.6 hours per week in 2016 (CRTC, 2017). There are many different types of radio operators in Canada: private commercial, national and local public, community, campus, indigenous, and religious broadcasters. Private commercial radio accounts for 75 per cent of the audience in an average week, with the public broadcaster, CBC/Radio-Canada, accounting for 16.1 per cent (CRTC, 2017). The average profit margin for private radio companies in 2016 was 18.6 per cent (5.3% for AM stations, 21.9% for FM stations).

Canadian television offers more than 600 domestic and international services across conventional, pay, pay-per-view, video-on-demand, and specialty TV options. The average viewer watched 26.6 hours of television per week in 2016, with specialty services accounting for the largest audience share in English Canada (CRTC, 2017).

Every country in the world regulates broadcasting, in part because the over-the-air broadcast spectrum is finite and requires management of assigned airwaves, not only for standard radio and television services but also for emergency services used by such agencies as police, fire, ambulance, and the military. As we discussed in Chapter 7, however, the Canadian government, like many others around the world, regulates broadcasting as well because it serves national, cultural, and political goals. Section 3 of the 1991 *Broadcasting Act* lays out those goals—it is reprinted in Box 8.2.

Access to content produced by Canadians is "the underlying principle of the broadcasting objectives." The CRTC states, "Canadian content must not only exist, it should also be available to all Canadians both as participants in the industry and as members of the audience" (CRTC, 2013). The commission ensures that Canadian content is both produced and distributed within the system through a number of policies, including Canadian-content regulations (See Table 8.1) for radio and television broadcasters, the carriage of Canadian services by cable and satellite providers, and minimum Canadian ownership of broadcast networks. In 2016, broadcasters spent $1.7 billion on Canadian productions, and distributors contributed $428 million to production (CRTC 2017).

The CRTC's regulatory duties derive from Section 5(2) of the *Broadcasting Act*, requiring the commission "to regulate and supervise the broadcasting system in a flexible manner that, among other things, takes into account regional concerns, is adaptable to technological developments, and facilitates the provisioning of broadcasting programs to Canadians" (CRTC, 2010: 5). These duties include

- defining categories of broadcasting licences
- issuing and renewing licences, up to a maximum of seven years
- modifying existing licence conditions

- suspending or revoking licences (the CBC licence excepted)
- licensing cable distributors and satellite delivery systems
- hearing complaints about the broadcasting system
- reviewing mergers of media companies

Much of the CRTC's work focuses on turning the broad policy ideas laid out in the *Broadcasting Act* into specific rules and regulations (see Armstrong, 2016: 75–88). In this regard, the CRTC is not simply a rubber-stamp agency, and has on occasion punished licensees who have been found violating their terms of licence with shortened terms of licence and, on rare occasion, revoking a licence (88–92).

As we saw in Chapter 7, ensuring Canadians' access to Canadian content in the broadcast realm has been a key function of regulation since its inception. Today, Canadian-content regulations stem from the CRTC's obligation under the *Broadcasting Act* to ensure that each licence-holder makes "maximum use . . . of Canadian creative and other resources in the creation and presentation of programming." The CBC's programming, according to the Act, should also be "predominantly and distinctively Canadian."

TABLE 8.1
Canadian Content

The commonly used phrase **Canadian content** is an unfortunate misnomer because, for regulatory purposes, it refers not to the content of a song or film or television program, but to the people who produce it. In other words, the content itself can touch on any subject, and does not have to concern Canada at all. For music or audiovisual programming to qualify as Canadian content, it must be produced by Canadian citizens according to specific requirements by the Canadian Audio-Visual Certification Office (CAVCO), for film and television content, and the CRTC's MAPL criteria for musical content.

For instance, as outlined below, under CAVCO regulations, for a creative series to be recognized as a Canadian production, a total of at least six points must be allotted according to the following scale. Points are awarded for each Canadian who rendered the services.

Non-animated Productions (Live Action)	Points Awarded
Director	2
Screenwriter	2
Lead performer for whose services the highest remuneration was payable	1
Lead performer for whose services the second highest remuneration was payable	1
Director of photography	1
Art director	1
Music composer	1
Picture editor	1
Animated Productions	
Director	1
Design supervisor (art director)	1
Lead voice for which the highest or second highest remuneration was payable	1
Camera operator where the camera operation is done in Canada	1
Music composer	1
Picture editor	1
Layout and background where the work is performed in Canada	1
Key animation where the work is performed in Canada	1
Assistant animation and in-betweening where work is performed in Canada	1

Source: *Report of the Auditor General of Canada*, November 2005, Office of the Auditor General of Canada. Reproduced with the permission of the Minister of Public Works and Government Services, 2015. www.nfb.ca.

8.2

Broadcasting Act, Section 3: "Broadcasting Policy for Canada"

3.(1) It is hereby declared as the broadcasting policy for Canada that

(a) the Canadian broadcasting system shall be effectively owned and controlled by Canadians;

(b) the Canadian broadcasting system, operating primarily in the English and French languages and comprising public, private and community elements, makes use of radio frequencies that are public property and provides, through its programming, a public service essential to the maintenance and enhancement of national identity and **cultural sovereignty**;

(c) English and French language broadcasting, while sharing common aspects, operate under different conditions and may have different requirements;

(d) the Canadian broadcasting system should

(i) serve to safeguard, enrich and strengthen the cultural, political, social and economic fabric of Canada,

(ii) encourage the development of Canadian expression by providing a wide range of programming that reflects Canadian attitudes, opinions, ideas, values and artistic creativity, by displaying Canadian talent in entertainment programming and by offering information and analysis concerning Canada and other countries from a Canadian point of view,

(iii) through its programming and the employment opportunities arising out of its operations, serve the needs and interests, and reflect the circumstances and aspirations, of Canadian men, women and children, including equal rights, the linguistic duality and multicultural and multiracial nature of Canadian society and the special place of aboriginal peoples within that society, and

(iv) be readily adaptable to scientific and technological change;

(e) each element of the Canadian broadcasting system shall contribute in an appropriate manner to the creation and presentation of Canadian programming;

(f) each broadcasting undertaking shall make maximum use, and in no case less than predominant use, of Canadian creative and other resources in the creation and presentation of programming, unless the nature of the service provided by the undertaking, such as specialized content or format or the use of languages other than French and English, renders that use impracticable, in which case the undertaking shall make the greatest practicable use of those resources;

(g) the programming originated by broadcasting undertakings should be of high standard;

(h) all persons who are licensed to carry on broadcasting undertakings have a responsibility for the programs they broadcast;

(i) the programming provided by the Canadian broadcasting system should

(i) be varied and comprehensive, providing a balance of information, enlightenment and entertainment for men, women and children of all ages, interests and tastes,

(ii) be drawn from local, regional, national and international sources,

(iii) include educational and community programs,

(iv) provide a reasonable opportunity for the public to be exposed to the expression of differing views on matters of public concern, and

(v) include a significant contribution from the Canadian independent production sector;

(j) educational programming, particularly where provided through the facilities of an independent educational authority, is an integral part of the Canadian broadcasting system;

(k) a range of broadcasting services in English and in French shall be extended to all Canadians as resources become available;

(l) the Canadian Broadcasting Corporation, as the national public broadcaster, should provide radio and television services incorporating a wide range of programming that informs, enlightens and entertains;

(m) the programming provided by the Corporation should

(i) be predominantly and distinctively Canadian,

(ii) reflect Canada and its regions to national and regional audiences, while serving the special needs of those regions,
(iii) actively contribute to the flow and exchange of cultural expression,
(iv) be in English and in French, reflecting the different needs and circumstances of each official language community, including the particular needs and circumstances of English and French linguistic minorities,
(v) strive to be of equivalent quality in English and in French,
(vi) contribute to shared national consciousness and identity,
(vii) be made available throughout Canada by the most appropriate and efficient means and as resources become available for the purpose, and
(viii) reflect the multicultural and multiracial nature of Canada;

(n) where any conflict arises between the objectives of the Corporation set out in paragraphs (l) and (m) and the interests of any other broadcasting undertaking of the Canadian broadcasting system, it shall be resolved in the public interest, and where the public interest would be equally served by resolving the conflict in favour of either, it shall be resolved in favour of the objectives set out in paragraphs (l) and (m);

(o) programming that reflects the aboriginal cultures of Canada should be provided within the Canadian broadcasting system as resources become available for the purpose;

(p) programming accessible by disabled persons should be provided within the Canadian broadcasting system as resources become available for the purpose;

(q) without limiting any obligation of a broadcasting undertaking to provide the programming contemplated by paragraph (i), alternative television programming services in English and in French should be provided where necessary to ensure that the full range of programming contemplated by that paragraph is made available through the Canadian broadcasting system;

(r) the programming provided by alternative television programming services should
(i) be innovative and be complementary to the programming provided for mass audiences,
(ii) cater to tastes and interests not adequately provided for by the programming provided for mass audiences, and include programming devoted to culture and the arts,
(iii) reflect Canada's regions and multicultural nature,
(iv) as far as possible, be acquired rather than produced by those services, and
(v) be made available throughout Canada by the most cost-efficient means;

(s) private networks and programming undertakings should, to an extent consistent with the financial and other resources available to them,
(i) contribute significantly to the creation and presentation of Canadian programming, and
(ii) be responsive to the evolving demands of the public; and

(t) distribution undertakings
(i) should give priority to the carriage of Canadian programming services and, in particular, to the carriage of local Canadian stations,
(ii) should provide efficient delivery of programming at affordable rates, using the most effective technologies available at reasonable cost,
(iii) should, where programming services are supplied to them by broadcasting undertakings pursuant to contractual arrangements, provide reasonable terms for the carriage, packaging and retailing of those programming services, and
(iv) may, where the Commission considers it appropriate, originate programming, including local programming, on such terms as are conducive to the achievement of the objectives of the broadcasting policy set out in this subsection, and in particular provide access for underserved linguistic and cultural minority communities.

(2) It is further declared that the Canadian broadcasting system constitutes a single system and that the objectives of the broadcasting policy set out in subsection (1) can best be achieved by providing for the regulation and supervision of the Canadian broadcasting system by a single independent public authority.

Source: Government of Canada *Broadcasting Act*, Section 3, http://laws.justice.gc.ca/PDF/B-9.01.pdf. 2010. Reproduced with the permission of the Minister of Public Works and Government Services Canada, 2011.

The Canadian-content quota has never been well received by the private broadcasters, who have protested each requirement vigorously and sought to minimize their carriage of Canadian-produced materials (see Babe, 1979). In March 2015, the CRTC removed content regulations on daytime television for conventional stations and relaxed them for some specialty services in the hope that requiring fewer hours of Canadian programming would spur broadcasters to spend more money on "big-budget" productions that might be sold internationally (CRTC, 2015). Conventional television licensees are still required to air at least 50 per cent Canadian programming in the evening hours. Specialty- and pay-TV channels will typically require 35 per cent.

The principal battleground for disputes over Canadian-content quotas has been English-language television, where Hollywood productions are readily available, cheap to buy, and popular with audiences and advertisers. Over the years, the federal government has engineered a number of programs to help boost production of Canadian content (see Armstrong, 2016: 94-117). The most recent iteration of these efforts is the Canada Media Fund (CMF), which had a funding budget of approximately $342 million in 2017–2018. These funds are derived from contributions from both cable and satellite broadcasters—which must contribute 5 per cent of their revenues to the fund—and the federal government. The CMF has two funding streams: the Convergent Stream, which supports the creation of convergent television and digital media content for consumption by Canadians anytime, anywhere; and the Experimental Stream, which "encourages the creation of leading-edge, interactive, digital media content and software applications." (CMF, n/d).

Inclusion was one of the central themes informing discussions leading up to the adoption of a revised *Broadcasting Act* in 1991, as evidenced in Section 3 (1) (d) (iii) (see Raboy, 1995). The Canadian broadcasting system should

> through its programming and the employment opportunities arising out of its operations, serve the needs and interests, and reflect the circumstances and aspirations, of Canadian men, women and children, including equal rights, the linguistic duality and multicultural and multiracial nature of Canadian society and the special place of aboriginal peoples within that society. (Canada, 1991)

A signal achievement in the diversification of Canadian broadcasting was the establishment of the Aboriginal Peoples Television Network (APTN), which was licensed as a national network in 1999, a world first. APTN provides a range of news, variety, and dramatic programming, and broadcasts in English, French, and a variety of indigenous languages. More than 85 per cent of its programming originates from Canadian producers (APTN, 2018; see also, Roth, 2005).

pixinoo/Shutterstock.

Over-the-top services like Netflix and Amazon Prime are creating new challenges for broadcast regulations in Canada.

The CRTC is not broadcasting's only regulator. The Canadian Broadcast Standards Council (CBSC) and Advertising Standards Canada (ASC) are industry associations providing a measure of self-regulation. The CBSC, for example, has policies on equitable portrayal, violence, ethics, and journalistic independence, although it investigates only when complaints are made (CBSC, 2018). The ASC administers the Canadian Code of Advertising Standards, which includes the Broadcast Code for Advertising to Children. This children's code contains guidelines pertaining to the factual presentation of products and services, product prohibition, sales pressure, comparison claims, and limits on the amount of advertising per program (Advertising Standards Canada, 2015). In Quebec, television advertising on children's programming is prohibited under the Quebec *Consumer Protection Act* (Armstrong, 2016: 164–165).

Internet

As we have seen, the internet is clearly an element of the Canadian telecommunications system. Telecommunications companies not only sell access to the internet, but many of them also own the wires, cables, and exchanges that make up its physical components. Of course, the internet is much more than the physical resources of any one of these companies, and comprises a vast network of both private and public servers and networks as well as an increasingly vast range of content and applications.

According to the Canadian Internet Registration Authority (CIRA), 86 per cent of Canadians have broadband connection at home, and 52 per cent have five or more internet-connected devices in their home; 74 per cent of Canadians spend 3–4 hours per day online, and 53 per cent subscribe to Netflix, 16 per cent to Spotify, 12 per cent to Apple Music, and 10 per cent to Amazon Prime video. Many people also access both newspapers and magazines online (CIRA 2018). Almost 24 million Canadians report using Facebook at least monthly, and 21.2 million regularly use YouTube (CRTC, 2017).

We have already considered some of the issues presented by internet platforms, in Chapter 6, such as privacy, surveillance, and online bullying. But perhaps one of the most discussed issues in recent years is net neutrality. **Net neutrality** refers to internet service providers (ISPs) treating all content and applications equally, without degrading or prioritizing service based on their source, ownership, or destination. Concern over a non-neutral network rises from fears that internet service providers have a financial interest in discriminating against corporate competitors or different classes of users. Indeed, this is what early telecommunications policy surrounding common carriage sought to prevent: imbalanced power relations stemming from control over communication resting with those who own the networks of communication.

Problems in this area can take several forms. Throttling, or traffic shaping, is one such problem. While some management of internet traffic may be desirable to alleviate congestion, there is a concern that ISPs might unfairly slow traffic from some sources or to some users in order to discourage their use. This can happen when an ISP thinks that a customer is using too much

Route66/Dreamstime.com.

In what ways has satellite technology played an important role in closing the gaps between Canada's regions?

data or a company is offering a service that competes with one owned by the ISP. Another issue is "zero rating." As the CRTC (2017b) points out, this is "where data from a certain source (e.g., a particular website or application) is discounted or not counted at all against a customer's monthly data cap, while all other data is counted against the cap." Similar to traffic shaping, this can be a particular problem where an ISP owns a video-streaming service and doesn't levy data charges on material streamed from that service but does so from others, thereby encouraging customers to subscribe to that service over their competitors. The CRTC has introduced a number of regulations to combat these problems (see CRTC, 2017b; CRTC, 2009).

The internet presents some serious challenges to Canada's media industries as well. Perhaps the biggest concerns in this regard are over-the-top, or OTT, services. OTT refers to media content that is delivered outside of or "over-the-top" of traditional distribution networks, such as cable and satellite. Such services include Netflix, Spotify, and Amazon Prime. As noted above, because these services are delivered through the internet, they are covered by the CRTC's 1999 New Media Exemption Order, which means they are not subject to regulation. Consequently, these companies are not obligated to meet with Canadian-content regulations or contribute to Canadian production funds. Nor do they pay Canadian taxes, such as GST. They also fragment Canadian audiences and undermine monies that flow into the media system, such as subscription and advertising revenues. One of the historical hallmarks of broadcast regulation has been the ability of regulators to ensure that corporations riding the development of new technologies such as television, cable, and satellite have been responsible to the overall goals of the system, as laid out in broadcast regulation. But this has not been the case with the internet.

This problem was compounded by a 2012 Supreme Court decision that ISPs—such as Bell, Rogers, and Telus—were not broadcasters, thereby exempting them from broadcast regulation. The hope of producers had been that because ISPs distribute film and video products on their networks—much the same way cable and satellite distributors do—they would be subject to the same regulations and therefore have to contribute to production funds, etc. In other words, the hope was that ISPs might be taxed and the proceeds of that tax put toward the production of Canadian film and video products.

The implications of having internet-based film and video companies like Netflix and Amazon Prime exempt from taxes are profound because, as we have seen in the face of cheap American media content, Canadian media producers are dependent on a complex series of taxes and subsidies, and without these regulations there are serious concerns about the viability of much of Canada's media production industry.

It would appear, however, that this battle is not over, as Canadian media producers continue to push for some sort of "Netflix tax" that would help make these **streaming** companies responsible to the objectives of the *Broadcasting Act* (Jackson, 2017). How this will play out in the face of the new CUSMA trade provisions related to "digital trade" and the ongoing review of the Telecommunications and Broadcasting Acts remains to be seen.

Recorded Music

A great proportion of radio broadcasting is, of course, recorded music. There has been a significant symbiosis between radio broadcast policy and policies designed to encourage the production and dissemination of Canadian music. Historically, the most important policy development for Canadian recorded music was the CRTC's establishment in 1971 of Canadian-content quotas for radio, recognizing the link between radio airplay and record sales. The quotas were a response to the under-representation of Canadian recording artists on Canadian radio stations at the time. In 1968, for example, Canadian music accounted for between 4 and 7 per cent of all music played on Canadian radio, in a period when the popular music scene was exploding and Canadian musicians like Gordon Lightfoot, Leonard Cohen, Neil Young, Joni Mitchell, and The Guess Who were part of the explosion (Filion, 1996: 132). A points system known as MAPL was devised to determine whether or not recordings qualify as Canadian, based not on their actual content, but on who produces them (see Box 8.3).

Radio's primacy as a promotional vehicle has been waning since the 1980s as, initially, music video stations (MuchMusic and MusiquePlus in Canada) became popular television hubs for music fans; more recently, a combination of MP3 players, social media sites, online radio, and streaming audio services have gained prominence. Websites permitting bands to upload and promote their music provide a much more diverse spectrum than conventional radio can muster, with its limited, mainstream genres. The CBC Radio 3 playlist (www.cbc.ca/listen/cbc-music-playlists/56-cbc-radio-3), for example, streams music from independent Canadian musicians, many of whom receive little or no mainstream radio airplay. And both download sites like Apple's iTunes and streaming sites like Spotify and YouTube make available a tremendous array of music that no bricks-and-mortar record shop can match.

With digitization allowing the easy distribution of music over the internet, illegal copying and downloading of music took a serious toll on industry revenues and artists' incomes. Revenues from the sales of recorded music and live performance fell from $736 million in 2003 to just $437 million in 2013 (Music Canada, 2013).

Paul Patterson.

The Broadcast Code for Advertising to Children contains guidelines pertaining to the factual presentation of products and services, product prohibition, sales pressure, comparison claims, and limits on the amount of advertising per program. Do you think books like these should be classified as advertising?

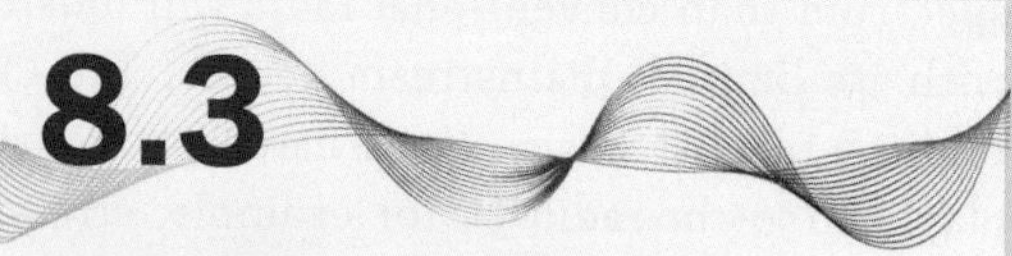

The MAPL System—Defining a Canadian Song

Canadian-content regulations focus on the factors of production and work to ensure that Canadians have the opportunity to participate in media production.

The CRTC defines a Canadian musical selection in its radio regulations. Within these regulations, four elements are used to qualify songs as being Canadian: *music*, *artist*, *performance*, and *lyrics* (MAPL).

To qualify as Canadian content, a musical selection must generally fulfill at least two of the following conditions:

- M (music): the music is composed entirely by a Canadian
- A (artist): the music is performed, or the lyrics are sung, principally by a Canadian
- P (performance): the musical selection consists of a live performance that is recorded wholly in Canada, or performed wholly in Canada and broadcast live in Canada
- L (lyrics): the lyrics are written entirely by a Canadian

There are several other special considerations whereby a piece of music may qualify as being Canadian, including an instrumental composition written by a Canadian, or a performance of an instrumental composition written by a Canadian.

Source: Adapted from www.CRTC.gc.ca/eng/info_sht/r1.htm.

There has been some recovery recently, however, with $569.5 in revenue in 2017. Digital music, and streaming in particular, has led this recovery. In 2007, digital sales accounted for just 10 per cent of the Canadian industry's revenues, but by 2017 they represented almost 65 per cent of industry revenues, with streaming comprising most of that and almost half of overall revenue (Music Canada, 2012, 2017).

A 2017 report by Music Canada, titled *The Value Gap*, illustrates that that there is a series of problems with the structure of regulation at both the national and international levels that are currently affecting the incomes of artists. One of the main issues lies with the way free music-streaming services, such as YouTube, are exempted from paying revenues to rights holders. As a result of this regulatory discrepancy, in 2015 YouTube returned only an estimated US$1 per consumer to music rights holders, while Spotify returned an estimated US$20 per consumer (Music Canada, 2017: 24).

Besides Canadian-content regulations, a second significant policy measure was the establishment in 1982 of the Foundation Assisting Canadian Talent on Recordings, which became known as FACTOR/Musicaction when a French-language component was added (www.factor.ca, musicaction.ca). Among other things, these organizations manage the Canada Music Fund, which is dedicated to helping

- build community support and skills development of creators
- support the production and distribution of "specialized music recordings reflective of the diversity of Canadian voices"
- provide project-based support to new emerging artists
- develop the business skills of Canadian music entrepreneurs
- ensure the preservation of Canadian musical works
- support recording-industry associations, conferences, and awards programs
- monitor industry performance

Cinema

The film industry has enjoyed the same kind of symbiotic relationship with television as the music industry has had with radio. Given the long-standing difficulty Canadian-made feature films have had in penetrating Canadian

Copyright

By Sara Bannerman

Intellectual property grants rights in creations of the human mind. Copyright is one type of intellectual property, granting rights to the creators of literary, artistic, and scientific works such as music, films, computer programs, and books like *Harry Potter*. Neighbouring rights are granted to broadcasters, makers of sound recordings, and performers like Rihanna. Patent law grants rights to inventors like Steve Jobs in their inventions, whereas trademark law grants rights in words or symbols associated with the sale of goods or services, like the Nike swoosh.

Copyright's purpose is to encourage the creation and dissemination of creative works. It grants creators the right to authorize, and thus benefit financially, from the reproduction, public performance, publication, or production of their works. It grants the moral right to be associated with the work as its creator. Copyright owners can sue those who infringe on their rights.

Digital technology facilitates the copying and distribution of digital content, challenging copyright enforcement. At the same time, online service providers play a growing role in enforcement, notifying users of alleged infringement and, in some cases, preventing the upload of copyright content or, when court-authorized, revealing identities of infringers to copyright owners.

Copyright law, to some extent, balances the rights of creators with the rights of the public. After all, new ideas emanate from the social whole and build on previous creative works. The term of copyright is therefore limited, ensuring that copyright works eventually enter the public domain. Copyright applies to the expression of ideas, not ideas themselves, so that ideas remain free for all to use. Copyright law establishes user rights, including *fair dealing*, which permits copyrighted materials be fairly used without permission for the purposes of research, education, private study, criticism or review, news reporting, parody, or satire. User rights permit time shifting (recording television programming for later viewing), format shifting (converting works to other formats), and the use of copyright works in the creation of non-commercial, user-generated content such as mashup videos or home movies as long as there is no adverse effect on the original work.

Sara Bannerman is Canada Research Chair in Communication Policy and Governance in the Department of Communication Studies and Multimedia at McMaster University.

movie theatres, television has been their most reliable means of distribution. And yet, like music, digital platforms are becoming more and more significant outlets for all forms of audiovisual production. To what extent Canadian films will succeed in reaching audiences this way, and whether their creators and producers will be adequately compensated, remain open questions.

The Canadian theatrical film industry is relatively small, generating just $318 million in spending during the 2016–2017 fiscal year, and producing 92 feature films (60 in English, 32 in French), the lowest number in a decade. The average budget for English-language features was $3.2 million, and $3.5 million for French-language features (CMPA, 2017: 58–60).

Governments' principal policy contributions have come in the production sector of the film industry, rather than in the distribution or exhibition ends. More than half (60%) of the financing of Canadian feature films comes from government-funding programs: Telefilm Canada (22%), provincial tax credits (20%), the federal tax credit (7%), and other public-funding sources (11%). Telefilm Canada provided $101 million for the development, production, distribution, marketing, and promotion of 88 Canadian features, $68 million of which was concentrated on production (CMPA, 2017: 64–66).

Federal and provincial governments in Canada have been sponsoring motion-picture production since the earliest years of the twentieth century, and Ottawa has operated a national film-production organization continuously since 1918. Canada, however, has been much more successful in the spheres of industrial and documentary film production—for example, films produced by the NFB, founded in 1939, have won 12 Academy Awards (see Table 8.2)—than in the higher-profile domain of dramatic, feature-length film production: the kinds of movies we see in our theatres. In this latter area, Hollywood is the dominant player in the Canadian market, accounting for 87.7 per cent of box-office receipts in 2016–2017, compared to Canadian films' 1.8 per cent share, a 10-year low (CMPA, 2017: 104). Even though directors like Deepa Mehta, Bruce McDonald, Léa Pool, Atom Egoyan, François Girard, Denis Villeneuve, Sarah Polley, Mina Shum, Denys Arcand, Jean-Marc Vallée, and Xavier Dolan have given renewed vigour to Canadian feature filmmaking since the early 1980s, domestic films have averaged only between 2 per cent and 6 per cent of box-office revenues, and less than 5 per cent of screen time in Canadian cinemas. Canadian films' share of viewing time on television is better, but also meagre: 9.5 per cent on pay television, 6.9 per cent on conventional television, and 2.7 per cent on specialty channels (CMPA, 2017: 104).

TABLE 8.2
The National Film Board's Academy Awards

National Film Board filmmakers have won 12 Academy Awards (and 1 honorary Oscar) to date, in addition to 73 nominations. You can watch many of the following films on the NFB website (www.nfb.ca):

FILMS

Year	Title (Director)
1941	Churchill's Island (Stuart Legg) Best Documentary Short Subject
1952	Neighbours (Norman McLaren) Best Documentary Short Subject
1977	The Sand Castle (Co Hoedeman) Best Animated Short Film
1977	I'll Find a Way (Beverly Shaffer) Best Live Action Short Film
1978	Special Delivery (John Weldon, Eunice Macaulay) Best Animated Short Film
1979	Every Child / Chaque enfant (Eugene Fedorenko) Best Animated Short Film
1982	If You Love This Planet (Terre Nash) Best Documentary Short Subject
1993	Flamenco at 5:15 (Cynthia Scott) Best Documentary Short Subject
1993	Bob's Birthday (Alison Snowden, David Fine) Best Animated Short Film
2004	Ryan (Chris Landreth) Best Animated Short Film
2006	The Danish Poet (Torill Kove) Best Animated Short Film

OTHER CATEGORIES

Year	Award
1989	Honorary Oscar in recognition of NFB's fiftieth anniversary
1999	Technical achievement to NFB scientists Ed H. Zwaneveld and Frederick Gasoi and two industry colleagues for the design and development of the DigiSync Film Keykode Reader

Source: www.nfb.ca.

In a sense, our own domestic cinema is foreign to Canadian audiences. For most of its history, the Canadian film market has been treated as an extension of the US market. The industry has been characterized by vertical integration, in which the same Hollywood studios that produce feature films also own film-distribution companies and movie theatres. Vertical integration ensures the distribution and exhibition of Hollywood studio films, making it very difficult for independent film producers to compete. Until 2004–2005, the same companies that owned major Hollywood studios also owned Canada's principal theatre chains—Famous Players and Cineplex Odeon—and the distribution companies that supplied those theatre chains with films.

Today, Cineplex Entertainment is Canada's only significant chain, with 164 theatres and 1,676 screens across the country. The company purchased the 24 theatres belonging to Canada's second-largest chain, Empire Theatres, in 2013. Landmark Cinemas has 45 theatres with 317 screens, while Cinémas Guzzo operates 10 theatres with 141 screens. The way Canadians watch movies is clearly changing, and theatre attendance is declining; box-office revenues were $993 million in 2016, but the exhibition industry's total revenues were $1.76 billion as theatres diversified to include live-event screenings, arcade games, indoor driving ranges, and expanded food concessions (CMPA, 2017: 104).

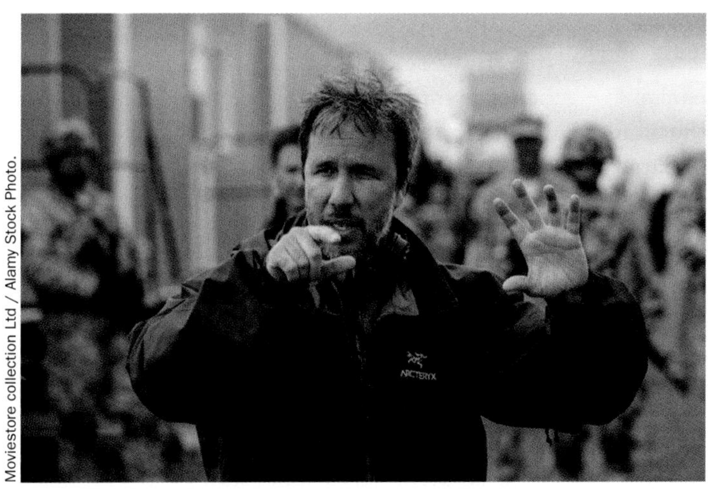

Moviestore collection Ltd / Alamy Stock Photo.

Canadian Denis Villeneuve has directed major Hollywood films such as *Arrival* and *Blade Runner 2049*, along with Canadian features *Incendies, Polytechnique*, and *Maelström*.

After decades of Hollywood dominance on our theatre screens, Canadians have come to associate cinema with Hollywood cinema, rendering "foreign" all those films made by other countries, including Canadian-made films. In 2016–2017, the most recent year for which figures are available, Canadian films accounted for a paltry 1.8 per cent of the box office: 0.8 per cent in the English-language market, where competition with Hollywood films is heaviest, and 8.7 per cent in the French-language market (CMPA, 2017: 104–12). No English-language Canadian film penetrated the top 10 in box-office receipts in 2016, but the Canadian film *Les 3 p'tits cochons 2* earned $2.87 million at the box office to place eighth among French-language screenings (114).

Although the primary federal policy concern in the postwar period has been increasing the production and distribution of Canadian feature films for theatrical, home video, and television release, provincial governments—most notably in Quebec, Ontario, and British Columbia—have instituted programs to encourage Hollywood producers to locate their film and television productions in such cities as Montreal, Toronto, and Vancouver (see Gasher, 2002; Elmer and Gasher, 2005). Every province now participates in what has become the largest segment of Canada's $8.38-billion film, television, and digital production industry. These foreign location service productions accounted for $3.76 billion in spending in 2016–2017, the highest level yet, producing 183 feature films, 149 television series, and 86 television movies and mini-series (CMPA, 2017: 5). British Columbia surpassed Ontario to become Canada's largest centre for film and television production (17).

History

In the early years of the last century, Ottawa perceived cinema as a medium of nation-building. The first state-sponsored films in Canada were tools to promote immigration from Britain to settle the Prairies; motion pictures are believed to have played a key role in Canada, attracting three million immigrants between 1900 and 1914. Early films were also used to lure industry and investment capital (Morris, 1978: 133–5). The use of film as a medium of propaganda during World War I led governments to play an increasing role in film production, and Canada became the first country in the world with government film-production units, although Ottawa consistently rejected calls to curtail US monopolization of the commercial film sector. The establishment of the National Film Board of Canada, under the direction of John Grierson in 1939, entrenched the state as a producer of films for nation-building purposes.

Increasingly since the end of World War II, the federal government has been called upon to address the commercial film sector. The first serious attempt by the Canadian government to stimulate indigenous feature-film production was the establishment of the Canadian Film Development Corporation (CFDC, now Telefilm Canada) in 1967. The CFDC was mandated to invest in Canadian feature-film projects; loan money to producers; present awards for outstanding production; support the development of film craft through grants to filmmakers and technicians;

and "advise and assist" producers in distributing their films (Magder, 1985: 148).

Canadian governments have been reluctant to impose protectionist measures on the film industry, even though Ottawa heard repeated calls for screen quotas in Canadian movie theatres throughout the twentieth century. Part of the problem, certainly, is that the operation of movie theatres falls under provincial jurisdiction. But there really is no public appetite for reducing in any way Hollywood's stranglehold on the Canadian market. Most Canadians—including francophones in Quebec—believe that attending the movies means going to Hollywood films. And this has been exacerbated by the reality that until at least the late 1980s, there was probably not a large enough stock of quality Canadian features to warrant a quota.

Television has been a friendlier platform for Canadian movies, thanks to Canadian ownership and Canadian-content regulations, CBC's inherent interest in Canadian content, and the licensing in the 1980s of pay-TV and specialty channels devoted to broadcasting feature-length films. In recognition of the promise television held, the federal government in 1983 altered the mandate of the Canadian Film Development Corporation. The federal Department of Communications introduced the $35-million Canadian Broadcast Development Fund, to be administered by the CFDC, which later that year changed its name to Telefilm Canada to reflect its new emphasis on television. While the sum of money in the broadcast fund may not appear significant, it increased considerably the ability of production companies to access other sources of investment, and it encouraged Canadian film producers to look more and more to television production.

Since the early 1980s, Ottawa has been gradually ceding its leadership role in the film policy field to the private sector and the provinces. Even though Telefilm remains the single most important source of film funding, no film can be made with Telefilm money alone. Filmmakers find themselves tapping half a dozen sources of funding to get their films made. Canada's major broadcasters have become important sources of financing for both project development and film and television production. These funding sources include the Harold Greenberg Fund, the Quebecor Fund, the Bell Fund, the Telus Fund, and the Rogers Group of Funds (see cmpa.ca/funding-opportunities/).

Canada's provincial governments have adopted a two-track film strategy. Every province in the country has a film office to promote it as a location for film and television production, primarily to Hollywood producers. In addition, the provinces provide development, production, and post-production support to Canadian producers through such funding vehicles as grants, loans, direct investment, and tax credits on labour costs.

Reminiscent of the late 1940s and early 1950s when television arrived, movie theatres today compete with increasingly sophisticated high-definition and wide-screen home theatres, as well as a growing number of online movie services, such as Netflix. As they did at

© Hxdbzxy / Dreamstime.com.

In what ways are filmmakers attempting to make the cinema experience *different* from home viewing? In your opinion, do these methods work?

8.5

The Video-Game Industry in Canada: A Snapshot

By Greig de Peuter and Chris J. Young

From Pokémon GO on the smartphone to Fortnite on consoles, video games and gaming platforms are not only increasingly pervasive, but also seriously lucrative. Globally, annual game-industry revenue is predicted to surpass $180 billion in 2022 (Wijman, 2018). Games can be hugely expensive to make, and game development is a notoriously risky business. Profits, however, are potentially massive. Take, for example, *Grand Theft Auto V*. Released in 2013, *GTA V* cost an astounding $266 million to produce, but it raked in $800 million in sales during its first *day* on the market: "That was the biggest launch day ever for any piece of entertainment—any movie, any record, anything at all," reported *Fast Company* (Kamenetz, 2013). So whereas "crisis" is a common theme in coverage of the movie and music industries, the video-game sector appears to be thriving. As game-based movies and music-based games demonstrate, however, video games mix and merge with other media in an ever-more-convergent entertainment complex.

The big money-maker is the mobile side of the business, which captured 55 per cent ($59.2 billion) of the industry's $108.4 billion in 2017 (SuperData, 2018). Apple's App Store, Google's Play Store, and Tencent's MyApp dominate the market on iOS and Android smartphones. The meteoric rise of the mobile sector coincides with the emergence of the Asian gaming market. Chinese behemoths Tencent and NetEase, relatively unknown a decade ago, dominate the charts with titles that rake in billions of dollars. The dominance of the free-to-play model with in-game purchases is largely responsible for these enormous profits. This has led to free-to-play PC games like *League of Legends*, establishing Tencent alongside traditional publishers Activision-Blizzard and Valve. The emergence of live-streaming and Esports has also contributed to growth in the PC sector, with titles like PlayerUnknown's *Battleground* gathering over 100 million unique viewers monthly on Twitch, YouTube, and other streaming services (SuperData, 2018). Live-streaming and Esports competitions increasingly build popularity around a select few franchises, which shape how games are consumed and monetized for non-player audiences.

Once the dominant sector of the industry, the console side of the business continues to amass substantial profits, an oligopoly currently dominated by Microsoft (xbox One), Nintendo (SWITCH), and Sony (PS4). Console makers have tended to price their hardware below cost in an effort to build market share and in turn generate profit from game software licensed to play on their proprietary systems. The creative fuel of the business is game development, an industrial subset that includes the console makers' in-house game studios, a multitude of third-party studios that produce games under contract to publishers, and a mushrooming population of indie developers that distribute games online through console marketplaces (e.g., PlayStation Store).

There is a long-standing power imbalance between most developers and publishers, since the latter finance game production (and thus influence the games that get made) and market games (which can affect a developer's commercial fate). Game development also displays a high level of ownership concentration, with large developer–publisher conglomerates frequently dominating the bestsellers list. Game development tends to favour companies with deep pockets; budgets for developing a console title average $12.5 million (Nordicity, 2017: 21), and a rule of thumb is that 10 per cent of the games earn 90 per cent of the money.

Canada is a significant node in the globalizing game industry, particularly in game development. According to a Nordicity (2017: 2) report funded by the Entertainment Software Association of Canada, the games industry contributed $3.2 billion to the Canadian economy in 2017. Nordicity reports that there are 596 game companies in Canada (2). However, 38 per cent are micro-enterprises with no more than four staff, 40 per cent are small operations with between 5 and 25 employees, 11 per cent are medium-sized firms with between 26 and 59 staff, 7 per cent are large firms with between 60 and 99 staff, and the remaining 4 per cent are vast entities (6), most of which are satellites of developer–publisher behemoths, such as Ubisoft, which employs approximately 4,000 people in Canada (Yerema and Leung, 2018). The game business may be booming in Canada, but in key aspects the seat of economic power is elsewhere. Although more than three-quarters of game businesses in the country are Canadian-owned

(continued)

(Nordicity, 2017: 13), the biggest ones tend to be foreign-owned. Electronic Arts (US), Disney (US), Nexon (South Korea), and many additional mega-publishers have extended their presence in Canada by buying up smaller homegrown studios. This is part and parcel of ownership concentration, a process that has been especially pronounced in the console-game-development sector. Although the technology industry has a pull-yourself-up-by-your-bootstraps reputation, the multinational firms that dominate game development in Canada are supported by significant state subsidies. In the late 1990s, Quebec's promise of tax breaks enticed the France-based Ubisoft to set up in Montreal what has grown into one of the largest studios in the world. And in 2010, Ubisoft opened a studio in Toronto after the province of Ontario offered the company incentives valued at $263 million, on the condition that Ubisoft create 800 jobs by 2020. Government assistance, said one Ubisoft executive, is simply "part of the equation" when deciding where to expand (cited in Ebner, 2009).

Canada's digital play business directly employed 21,700 people in 2017 (Nordicity, 2017: 2). Nordicity's profile suggests that the nation's game workforce is decently paid (average salary: $77,300), relatively young (average age: early thirties), and has high levels of formal education (2017: 4). By all accounts, working in game development is challenging and rewarding. Still, the industry doesn't entirely live up to its work-as-play image; one Canadian studio owner acknowledges that game companies have a "reputation for treating people badly" (cited in Gooderham, 2009). Especially controversial is overwork, a problem publicized a decade ago by an infamous blog post by the anonymous "EA Spouse" (later revealed as game designer Erin Hoffman) that detailed endemic excessive hours at game-industry giant Electronic Arts (EA). The game workforce is also profoundly gendered: merely 16 per cent of the games workforce in Canada is female, and women hold a narrow 5 per cent of technical roles (Nordicity, 2015: 40). Redressing this imbalance in game production is essential to respond to sexism in game culture, an enduring problem most recently exposed in the so-called Gamergate controversy in 2014, in which a number of women in the industry were subjected to misogynist attacks (see Wingfield, 2014).

A burgeoning game market does not guarantee employment security. A game that flops in the market can result in huge job losses. Studio closures and job cuts at major market–listed developers have been familiar industry news stories since the economic crisis of 2008. The game-development workforce is also stratified: at one end of the hierarchy are celebrity designers; at the other are those who play-test games for bugs—the workers most likely to earn the lowest company wage, to be hired on a temporary basis, and to be excluded from benefits programs. Lower production costs for mobile games hold promise for a renaissance in independent games, but indie game development remains a "precarious business" (Gouglas et al., 2010: 17). Risk is acute for rookie studios whose fate hangs on a single project. While game-production activity dots the country, nearly 80 per cent of game companies in Canada are in British Columbia, Quebec, and Ontario (Nordicity, 2017: 10). Within these provinces, the sector is primarily clustered in three cities: Vancouver, Montreal, and Toronto. In British Columbia, there are some 5,900 game workers at 152 studios (Nordicity, 2017: 10, 7). The more than 10,800-strong game-labour force in Quebec, the country's largest, is concentrated in Montreal—and its nucleus is Ubisoft. Ontario hosts a large number of studios (171), but the employment base (3,800) is significantly smaller compared to BC and Quebec (Nordicity, 2017: 7, 10). Lacking access to a major employer like EA in the Vancouver area, developers in Toronto struck out on their own in droves, launching studios specializing in lower-cost platforms such as mobiles.

Ultimately, however, the geography of video-game production is international; a new game concept might be conceived of in Canada, based on intellectual property owned by an entertainment company headquartered elsewhere, funded from another country, developed with inputs from multiple far-flung locales, and marketed to a global audience. Virtual games, in turn, depend on actual hardware, most of which is manufactured in lower-wage regions—and, when discarded, game-machine components eventually snake their way to e-waste villages in the Global South. So although it has a strong Canadian presence, the video-game industry spreads around the planet—and its pleasures and its pains are very unevenly distributed.

Greig de Peuter is an assistant professor in the Department of Communication Studies at Wilfrid Laurier University.

Chris J. Young is the Digital Scholarship Librarian at the University of Toronto Mississauga.

the dawn of television, filmmakers and theatre operators are seeking ways to make the cinema experience distinct from rival viewing platforms (e.g., by experimenting with 3-D, huge screens, digital sound). The future of movie theatres is focused on this competition.

Publishing

The book, magazine, and newspaper publishing industries face numerous challenges, especially in the ongoing transition from analog to digital production and distribution. For more than 500 years, publishing has meant the printing, transportation, and storage of bulky, physical reading materials, and a substantial portion of the costs associated with publishing are contained in the production and distribution of these materials: printing presses, paper, ink, transport, and the skilled tradespeople who carry out these processes. These costs are compounded in a country like Canada, with a huge land mass and a relatively small and widely dispersed population. As more and more people access reading materials electronically—e.g., via tablets, smartphones, and e-readers—there is great potential for publishers to reduce production costs and, at the same time, expand their audiences. In this transitional period, however, most publishers produce both hard-copy and digital editions with no assurance that the burgeoning market for digital publications will generate the revenues that hard-copy publishing has provided, at least any time soon. The newspaper industry is discussed in the next two chapters, so our focus here is on book and magazine publishing.

Book Publishing

Canada's publishing market is the 12th-largest in the world. Book publishing is a $2.1-billion industry in Canada, with 1,200 publishers selling over 51 million books annually (Nawotka, 2018; BookNet Canada, 2018; IBISWorld, 2018). Foreign-owned publishers accounted for almost 54 per cent of revenues in 2016, with Canadian-owned publishers responsible for 46 per cent. It is important to note that 80 per cent of Canadian-authored titles are published by the Canadian-owned publishing sector (Association of Canadian Publishers, n.d.). The industry is heavily concentrated in Toronto and Montreal; publishers in Ontario accounted for two-thirds of industry revenues in 2016 (the most recent data available) (Statistics Canada, 2018; Nordicity, 2018).

Digitization is a promising development in many respects: whether through online book sales, digital publishing, on-demand publishing, self-publishing, direct orders, or supply-chain management programs, digitization holds out the promise to reduce printing, storage, and transportation costs; facilitate book promotion; increase author–reader interaction; and make more books available to more Canadians (Lorimer, 2012: 260–86). Nevertheless, printed titles captured 75 per cent of books sales in 2016, with e-books accounting for just 13.7 per cent (Statistics Canada, 2018).

By permission of Café Books.

Canada's independent booksellers depend on customer service to compete with the convenience of online services like Amazon.

Digitization also entails significant challenges for bricks-and-mortar booksellers, and it affects the author–publisher relationship. Online retailers like Amazon are convenient for buyers, but they reduce customer traffic to local bookstores, which specialize in customer service—and online retailers can demand from publishers greater discounts than are typically available to smaller sellers (Lorimer, 2012: 226). The Amazon website also hosts "third-party sellers," whose sales of new and used books can cost authors royalties and publishers revenues (see Patch, 2018). Smaller independent bookstores in Canada are already competing with a national monopoly bookseller in Chapters/Indigo, as well as the big-box retailers Walmart and Costco. While online retailers can attract increased attention paid to authors and facilitate the sale of their books, they can also reduce royalty rates through direct negotiation with authors and increase the availability of second-hand books, for which authors receive no royalties (see Boggs, 2012: 98–9). On the book-production side, researcher Jeff Boggs argues that the emergence of online-only publishers can have a detrimental impact on the Canadian industry because they operate beyond Canadian copyright law, which governs the physical importation and distribution of books in the Canadian market. "Digital books can be bought from websites in other jurisdictions, reducing demand for titles in Canada's copyright space" (Boggs, 2012: 98).

The most vulnerable sector of the business pertains to the publishing of original Canadian titles, and this is the principal role of Canadian-owned publishers. Industry scholar Rowland Lorimer insists that a number of market distortions hamper the viability of a domestic industry for Canadian works, necessitating government programs offering both industrial and cultural support. The first market distortion is the importation of run-on copies of foreign-published book titles; because these books are priced based on their large sales volumes, they create downward pressure on the price of Canadian books destined for a much smaller domestic market. The second market distortion is the frequent inclusion of the Canadian market when US companies purchase the North American publishing rights to popular international book titles; this represents a lost opportunity for Canadian publishers in their own market. Third, Canada has only one national bookstore chain, and the business model of Chapters/Indigo privileges high-volume sales, leaving little shelf space for the non-mainstream and mid-list titles in which Canadian publishers tend to specialize (Lorimer, 2012: 48–9). Lorimer describes the organization of Canadian book production as "essentially feudal": "With or without publishers' approval, authors toil away without a wage to complete books for a small share of the return—often, for unestablished authors, as little as 5 per cent of retail price" (316). A survey by the Writers' Union of Canada found that the average Canadian writer in 2018 earned $9,380 annually from their writing, 27 per cent less than in 2015, meaning that even prize-winning writers need second jobs. The survey blamed the rise of free photocopying by educational institutions and contraction in the publishing industry (Sumanac-Johnson, 2018; see also McSween, 2017).

French-language publishers have been far more successful in getting their books to readers. This advantage is due in part to the fact that they do not face the same head-to-head competition from the United States as English-language publishers do. But there are two other factors. One is Quebec's Bill 51, passed in 1981, to protect Canadian-owned booksellers. Bill 51 establishes an accreditation system whereby public institutions like schools and libraries are required to order their books from accredited local retailers (rather than directly from publishers or through wholesalers). Accredited publishers, distributors, and retailers are also eligible for Quebec government assistance programs (Québec, 2018). The French-language publishing industry also uses an efficient book-ordering system, called the système d'offre. Based on agreements between distributors and retailers, newly published books are automatically shipped to bookstores in predetermined numbers. The distributors assume the shipping costs and the retailers assume the costs of returning unsold books. This system ensures the timely and consistent diffusion of new French-language books by Canadian authors.

The federal government supports book publishing through both legislation and funding programs. Lorimer describes the *Copyright Act* as "the main structural support for the industry" (2012: 166). Revised in 2012, the Act grants "sole supplier status" to Canadian importers and distributors, giving them exclusive rights to provide books to wholesalers and retailers. The government's principal funding program is the Canada Book Fund, which distributes $39.5 million in annual funding. The Canada Book Fund has two components: Support for Publishers, which aids the production and promotion of Canadian-authored books through financial assistance to Canadian-owned and controlled publishers; and Support for Organizations, which assists in the promotion of Canadian-authored books by industry organizations and associations through programs for marketing, professional development, strategic planning, internships, and technology projects (Canada, 2018a; Dewar, 2017). The Canada Council for the Arts, a Crown corporation founded in 1957, provides grants each year to Canadian writers in a variety of genres. The National Translation Program for Book Publishing is a fund to support the translation of Canadian-authored works: between English and French in Canada, and from English and French to other languages in international markets (Canada Council, 2018). The Public Lending Right provides annual payments to Canadian authors based on the presence of their books in libraries.

The federal government also protects the Canadian book industry through ownership restrictions, with policy dating from 1974. The current investment policy restricts foreign investment in new businesses to Canadian-controlled joint ventures, prohibits the direct acquisition of a Canadian-controlled business by a non-Canadian, reviews indirect acquisitions based on the net benefit to Canada, and requires non-Canadians wishing to sell an existing book-industry venture to ensure that Canadian investors have full and fair opportunity to bid. The *Investment Canada Act* "requires that foreign investments in the book publishing and distribution sector be compatible with national cultural policies and be of net benefit to Canada and to the Canadian-controlled sector" (Canada, 2017).

As in other communication spheres, each of the provinces and territories has its own support system for writing and publishing. Ontario, for example, has the Ontario Arts Council, which offers grants to writers, publishers, and literary organizations; the Ontario Book Publishing Tax Credit; the Trillium Book Award to reward excellence among Ontario writers; and the Ontario Media Development Corporation's various funds to support book sales and industry development (see Ontario Arts Council, 2018; Ontario Media Development Corporation, 2018).

Revenu Québec offers a tax credit for book publishers and does not impose provincial income tax on writers' royalty payments. Quebec's Société de développement des entreprises culturelles (SODEC) has a number of funding programs, including those for book publishing, book exports, and book fairs (SODEC, 2018).

Magazines

Magazine publishing in Canada is a $2-billion industry, producing more than 1,500 titles and employing 8,200 workers (IBISWorld, 2017). Magazine readership is declining—Canada had 15.9 million magazine readers in 2016 compared to 17.2 million in 2014, with only 44 per cent of those aged 21–34 reading magazines, compared to 67 per cent in the 50–69 age group (Statista, 2018).

Faced with significant competition and high distribution costs, the magazine industry is one of Canada's most volatile and diverse media sectors. Some magazines are published by large media corporations like Transcontinental, Quebecor, and Rogers, while others are produced by foundations, associations, and artists' collectives.

New magazine titles appear each year, but many don't last long. Canadian magazines earn about 75 per cent of their revenue from advertising and roughly 25 per cent from circulation, although this varies greatly from magazine to magazine.

The precariousness of the Canadian magazine industry is reflected in its labour practices. Magazines tend to have much smaller editorial staffs than newspapers, and so depend for a considerable amount of their content on freelance writers, photographers, and illustrators. Freelancers are typically contracted article by article, meaning they are constantly pitching story ideas in the quest for the next assignment. And the rates they are paid—from 30 cents per word at smaller magazines, to $1 or $2 per word at larger-circulation publications—have remained roughly the same since the 1980s (Coxon, 2018; Cohen, 2012). In April 2014, the Ontario Ministry of Labour served notice that unpaid magazine internships were in contravention of the *Employment Standards Act*, prompting the cancellation of gratis internships at a number of magazines, including *Toronto Life*, *The Walrus*, and *Canadian Geographic* (*Masthead*, 2014). Unpaid internships are common at Canadian magazines; on the one hand, they provide students and other aspiring journalists and writers an opportunity to gain experience and contacts that might not otherwise be available to them, but on the other hand, they can be exploitative, using interns' free labour instead of paying them, or others, for the same work.

Magazine policy is driven by the same logic as policy in book publishing: first, the need to create space in a relatively small and dispersed market for Canadian voices on a range of topics, from current affairs to popular culture, from the arts to sports and leisure activities; and second, the desire to support a domestic industry. The most important policy instrument for magazine publishers is Section 19 of the *Income Tax Act*.

The key source of government funding comes from the Department of Canadian Heritage's Canada Periodical Fund, which replaced both the Canadian Magazine Fund and the Publications Assistance Program in 2010. The fund contains three elements: Aid to Publishers, which supports content creation, production, distribution, online activities, and business development for Canadian magazines (print and online) and non-daily newspapers; Business Innovation, which provides monies for small and mid-sized magazines (print and online); and Collective Initiatives, which funds organizations' efforts to increase the overall sustainability of the Canadian magazine and non-daily newspaper industries (Canada, 2018b).

Federal assistance for periodical publishing has dropped dramatically. In an analysis of Canada's periodical funding programs, Patricia Elliott notes that there has been a 97 per cent reduction in project grants since 2001, and a 90 per cent decrease in the number of magazines receiving distribution support since 1990 (Elliott, 2017). Elliott cites two interrelated causes: pressure from the United States to reduce Canadian cultural subsidies—seen as unfair barriers to competition in a context of free trade between the two countries—and an internalization by governments of neoliberal economic doctrine, characterized by free trade, deregulation, marketplace logic, and the withdrawal of the state from economic activity (808). One of the biggest blows to the magazine industry was the cancellation in 2009 of Canada Post's $15-million subsidy to the Publications Assistance Program, which provided discounted postal rates to eligible publications, a significant aid given the industry's reliance on subscriptions (811–14). Distribution has become the fastest-rising cost for magazine publishers.

Postal Service

The postal system typically is overlooked by communication scholars, even though it is our oldest mass medium and a key way of developing and maintaining social, political, and economic networks and relations across space. The post office continues to move more than 8 billion pieces of correspondence—letters, notices, invoices, parcels—each year to more than 16 million residential and business addresses (Canada Post, 2018: 22, 281). Its history remains closely bound to the history of transportation in Canada (see Gendreau, 2000). The post office was one of the first federal government departments established after Confederation in 1867, but both the French and British colonial regimes had postal service in the earliest days of the colony. The French relied on ships to transport mail across the Atlantic Ocean from France and along the St Lawrence River valley in the seventeenth and eighteenth centuries. Mail was carried overland by travellers and fur traders forming a "human network of communication" (Willis, 2000: 36–7). The British established a formal postal system along the St Lawrence River valley in 1763 under the governance of a deputy postmaster general. Service was introduced to Nova Scotia in 1785 (Willis, 2000: 39–40). Canada Post was created as a Crown corporation in 1981 after having been run directly as a department of the federal government since 1868. Governed today by the *Canada Post Corporation Act* (1985), it has the exclusive right to collect and deliver letters up to 500 grams in Canada (Canada Post, 2014: 18). Canada Post, however, competes with other private direct-marketing and courier companies in these growing industry sectors (see McKenna, 2014).

Solidago/iStockphoto.

Rather than door-to-door service, Canada Post is increasingly using community mailboxes like the one pictured here as a cost-saving measure. What are the advantages and disadvantages of the new system?

Not surprisingly, the physical delivery of such items as letters, documents, greeting cards, invoices, and bank statements has been in decline since 2006, largely replaced by electronic mail, including Canada Post's own epost service, and Canada Post suffers for it (Canada Post, 2014). The Crown corporation reported a loss of $269 million for 2013. However, it made a profit of $199 million before taxes in 2017, its fourth consecutive year of profitability, although its volume of deliveries dropped for a fifth straight year. Not surprisingly, the delivery of letters continues to decline—3 billion pieces in 2017 compared to 5 billion in 2006—but driven by the need to deliver online purchases, parcel delivery increased by 24.5 per cent by volume in 2017, and the delivery of direct-marketing materials grew by 4 per cent over 2016. The growth areas for the company are its parcel service—with deliveries up 6.9 per cent in 2013, thanks to the increasing popularity of online shopping—and its digital services: epost, as well as Canadapost.ca and its mobile app (Canada Post, 2018: 281–4).

Canada Post is part of a global network of national postal services operating on the basis of equitable, universal service to citizens. An international agreement established the General Post Union in 1874 (later renamed the Universal Postal Union), ensuring the free transportation of mail within member countries and the standardization of charges collected by each country for mail service between members (Hamelink, 1994: 7). As a Crown corporation providing what is considered to be a key communication service, Canada Post is required by the federal government to undertake special obligations. These include the provision of free mail service between Canadian citizens and designated members of government; reduced postal rates for the shipping of books between libraries; the transportation of nutritious, perishable foods and other essential items to isolated northern communities; and the free mailing of materials for the blind (Canada Post, 2018: 251). Given the fiscal challenges Canada Post faces—decreasing amounts of mail, an increasing number of Canadian addresses, regular annual deficits, free electronic mail alternatives, increasing competition from private courier services—it will be interesting to monitor in coming years the extent to which the federal government continues to support the policy principle of equitable and universal service in a communication network that ties together every Canadian community.

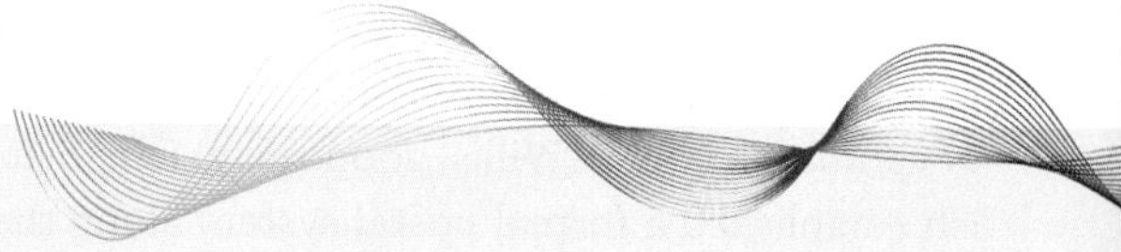

SUMMARY

Through this examination of specific policy sectors, we can see that the task of providing Canadians with a range of opportunities to produce and receive communications, while ensuring the viability of Canadian cultural industries, presents governments with constant challenges.

We began the chapter by outlining three significant changes affecting the media landscape in recent years, changes that have far-reaching implications for Canadian communication policy: the convergence or merging of previously distinct technologies, media forms, and media industries; **trade liberalization**, which puts pressure on Canada to make its policies, laws, and regulations conform to international trade agreements; and diversifying Canada's media systems to meet the needs of the country's peoples. What has not changed is Canada's central policy priority of ensuring that Canadians benefit from the opportunities that mass communication affords.

We have provided here a profile of each of the major communication sectors—telecommunications, broadcasting, the internet, recorded music, cinema, publishing, and postal service—and have outlined their respective policy challenges, providing current information about these industries and policy responses by governments. Each of the sectors had things in common (e.g., new services, digitization) as well as distinctions particular to their field.

It is clear that each of these sectors is still caught in the throes of shifting technological circumstances. These changes are impacting almost every facet of their operations, including their revenue streams, the kinds of work they entail, and the policy environments necessary to help them thrive.

KEY TERMS

Canadian content, p, 201
Canadian Radio-television and Telecommunications Commission (CRTC), p. 197
common carriage, p. 196
convergence, p. 193
cultural industries, p. 195
cultural sovereignty, p. 202
interactivity, p. 193
net neutrality, p. 205
streaming, p. 206
trade liberalization, p. 220

RELATED WEBSITES

Canadian Radio-television and Telecommunications Commission: www.crtc.gc.ca/eng/home-accueil.htm
The CRTC website contains a wealth of information about the broadcasting and telecommunications industries, as well as industry studies, press releases, and current decisions rendered.

Department of Canadian Heritage: www.canada.ca/en/canadian-heritage.html
This site is that of the government ministry responsible for the arts and cultural industries. It contains information on a number of cultural industry sectors as well as news releases and speeches pertaining to the ministry.

Innovation, Science and Economic Development Canada: www.ic.gc.ca/eic/site/icgc.nsf/eng/home
This site belongs to the federal ministry responsible for industry, which includes some of the cultural industries such as telecommunications and new media. The site contains industry profiles as well as research reports and statistical data.

Music Canada: www.musiccanada.com
This site belongs to a non-profit trade organization serving the music industry and musicians in Canada. Music Canada contains news and research material pertaining to all aspects of the sound recording industry in Canada.

Association of Canadian Publishers: https://publishers.ca/
This site belonging to the Association of Canadian Publishers is a good source of publishing industry news and policy information.

FURTHER READINGS

Armstrong, Robert. 2016. *Broadcasting Policy in Canada*, 2nd ed. Toronto: University of Toronto Press. This is an accessible, comprehensive, and current portrait of the policy picture for broadcasting in Canada. It covers every aspect of broadcast regulation in detail, and situates Canadian policies with respect to international trade and cultural agreements.

Canada, Department of Canadian Heritage. 2017. *Creative Canada Policy Framework*. Available at: https://www.canada.ca/en/canadian-heritage/campaigns/creative-canada/framework.html. This is the federal government's latest policy plan for Canada's creative/cultural industries.

Canadian Journal of Communication. Canada's premier source for current research on communication issues in all areas. Current and back issues can be accessed online at www.cjc-online.ca/index.php/journal.

Lorimer, Rowland. 2012. *Ultra Libris: Policy, Technology, and the Creative Economy of Book Publishing in Canada*. Toronto: ECW Press. This is a comprehensive study of book publishing in Canada, with an emphasis on policy instruments that have been developed to support the Canadian publishing industry.

Music Canada. 2017. *The Value Gap: Its Origins, Impacts and a Made-in-Canada Approach*. This report outlines the problems facing the Canadian music industry and provides a comprehensive plan for putting more money in the hands of creators.

Wagman, Ira, and Peter Urquhart, editors. 2012. *Cultural Industries.ca: Making Sense of Canadian Media in the Digital Age*. Toronto: James Lorimer. This book consists of chapters on each of the cultural industries in their transition to digital, as well as a section pertaining to questions of media research.

STUDY QUESTIONS

1. Is the development of digital platforms helping or hindering Canada's media companies?
2. What is net neutrality, and why, has it become an important issue?
3. While online services have increased choices for media consumers, they are hurting some producers of music, television programming, and published materials. Why is this the case?
4. The CRTC has decided not to regulate the internet. Does this mean that the internet is not subject to any form of regulation?
5. How have your media usage habits changed in recent years?
6. What are the most important communication concerns facing Canadians? What can be done about those concerns?

9

Ownership and the Economics of Media

You can say that at times freedom in our kind of society amounts to the freedom to say anything you wish, provided you can say it profitably. — *Raymond Williams*

Islemount Images / Alamy Stock Photo

Opening Questions

- How has the context of media economics changed in recent years?
- How do media organizations participate in the economy?
- What resources do media organizations require?
- What roles do advertising and subscription fees play for the mass media?
- What fundamental distinctions are there between publicly owned and privately owned media?
- What do we mean by *precarious labour*?
- What do we mean by the democratization of media?

Introduction

The economics behind the production, distribution, and consumption of media content is one of the central preoccupations of our time. The basic principles haven't changed; media economics is about ensuring that the communication needs and desires of society are met through a system that remains accessible and affordable to citizens while at the same time ensuring that producers and distributors at all levels are adequately compensated.

But the context of media economics has changed dramatically in recent times, owing to a number of interrelated factors. Mainstream media companies are increasingly part of concentrated conglomerates, placing renewed emphasis on revenue generation. The provision of access to media platforms—internet service, wireless networks, cable and satellite connections—occupies the largest part of the media economy. Declines in advertising support threaten the survival of analog media, and subscriptions are becoming more significant to companies' revenue streams. Media content producers face vastly increased competition because our access to content is almost unlimited. At the same time, budget-conscious governments are withdrawing subsidies and other supports, increasingly allowing **market** regulation of the communication sector to prevail. Media workers face a more competitive and precarious **labour** market as media companies rely increasingly on flexible contract work, and the demand for skilled labour is influenced by so-called *prosumers*: consumers of media content who have become producers as well, supplying content for free. And consumers insist on increased choice of what content is available to them, as well as how, when, and where. The ground is shifting dramatically, as we signalled in the preceding chapters, and the search for new and sustainable economic models is on.

All forms of mediated communication require resources: time, capital, labour, technology, and materials. What economists seek to understand is how these resources interact to meet society's communicative needs and desires.

The media economist Robert G. Picard identifies four groups served by the media: owners, audiences, advertisers, and workers (1989: 8–9)—to which we would add a fifth: governments. Each of these groups is multi-layered. The category of media owners, for instance, can range from the complex management groups of large, converged, and publicly traded corporations—such as Quebecor or Rogers—to community groups or individuals with their own websites. Some of these groups are motivated primarily by profit, others by some kind of public service or social purpose. Media owners include governments (e.g., CBC/Radio-Canada, the NFB), political groups (e.g., the Doug Ford government's social media service Ontario News Now), non-profit foundations (e.g., *The Walrus*, published by The Walrus Foundation), non-governmental organizations (*Greenpeace Magazine*), cooperatives (e.g., the Atlantic Filmmakers Cooperative), and individual business people (e.g., Brunswick News). One of Canada's largest French-language newspapers, *La Presse*, was converted from a commercial venture to a non-profit in 2018 (Nelson and Van Praet, 2018). Regardless of who they are or what their motivation is, media owners participate in some way in the economy.

We used to think of audiences as passive consumers of media products and services. But research has demonstrated that audiences are much more active in the ways they choose, receive, draw meaning from, and make use of media than was previously understood. Audiences have become even more active in the era of digital media, which allow media consumers to also become media producers, whether by engaging in online discussion groups, putting together music compilations, sharing commercial TV or film on YouTube, alerting followers to breaking news via Twitter, or going much further in producing mash-ups or blogs, sampling music, or documenting their own daily lives on social media. Regardless of the nature of their media use, members of the audience are crucial to the economic vitality of the media.

Advertisers use media not only to promote the goods and services they want to sell, but as well to project a certain kind of brand identification. Think of the number of companies using advertising to foster a "green" image. From an economic standpoint, advertisers generate revenue for media organizations in their quest to speak to audiences about the products and services they want to sell; what they are buying when they advertise is access to media audiences.

Media workers are a heterogeneous group, ranging from the star directors and actors of a Hollywood blockbuster to those who make their living in the film industry as carpenters, electricians, drivers, and hairdressers. Some media workers, in other words, have a central and direct role to play in the creation of the content we see on our screens, while many others play indispensable roles in media support networks—running printing presses, entering data, selling advertising, applying makeup, maintaining servers. Some of these workers are paid royalties or have an ownership stake and, therefore, have a clear and direct financial interest in the welfare of the enterprise. Others are paid an hourly wage for a contract of limited duration. So workers can have very different stakes in the operation, the mission, and the overall welfare of the media organization.

dmitro2009/Shutterstock.

The role of media workers varies widely. What kinds of work are required to produce a feature film?

Through their cultural-policy apparatus, governments adopt guidelines and laws that compel media organizations to serve the needs and wants of national or regional constituencies, as we saw in Chapters 7 and 8. This has meant ensuring that Canadians have access to the cultural and economic opportunities that participation in the media affords. And Canadian governments recognized early the media's role in fostering a sense of national identity; Benedict Anderson (1983) has highlighted the role of media in creating "imagined communities," and this continues to be a central driver in cultural policy today.

Particularities of Media Economics

Resources are the ingredients media producers require in order to generate and disseminate communicative content; media economics studies how these resources are acquired, allocated, and paid for. Typically, these resources fall into five categories: *time*, *labour*, *technology*, *capital*, and *materials*. Some media forms are more resource-intensive than others and therefore demand greater investment. Motion-picture production, for example, typically requires large crews encompassing a diverse collection of highly skilled workers, elaborate costumes and sets, considerable amounts of advanced technology, and significant levels of **capital** investment. Other media forms have much lower barriers to entry; a novel can be produced by a lone individual, and a simple website can be produced single-handedly with a personal computer; the key resources here are time and skill.

The matter of what resources are required for media production is significant because it speaks directly to the questions of how the media are organized, who owns the media, and whether they are owned for profit, for public service, for advocacy, for prestige, or for some combination of these. Questions about resources have a direct bearing on the kinds of books, music recordings, video games, films, and magazines that are produced and made available to us.

We may not normally think of time as a resource, but, of course, it takes an investment of time to produce media content. This is particularly significant in the case of content that is produced on a speculative basis, such as the time invested in writing a book with no assurance of publication, or content produced by amateurs in their spare time, such as videos or music posted to YouTube. But it applies as well to the production of waged or salaried workers.

The category of labour includes all of the human resources required. This can range from a single individual writing and uploading a daily blog to the hundreds involved in the production of a big-budget feature film. The number of people and their skill levels will have a noticeable impact on the quality and cost of the production. The media bring together people specialized in particular creative processes and those skilled in the business side of the operation. The larger the media company, the greater the divide between these groups tends to be.

Technology refers partly to the equipment and, increasingly, to the specific software applications media organizations require. Clearly, some mass media (e.g., film, television, sound recording, computer games) require more investment in hardware and software than others. But, as we noted in Chapter 6, technology can also refer to the step-by-step processes by which production and dissemination are organized, and how, or whether, labour is divided among the various production tasks. Typically, large media organizations divide the production process into a series of specialized tasks—like an assembly line—while smaller organizations commonly require workers to perform several separate tasks. Digitization has made multi-tasking easier, allowing large media companies to cut staff and either outsource production tasks or combine them in-house as a cost-saving measure.

Capital refers not simply to money, but to money that is invested in media enterprises with the expectation of a return on investment. Most commonly, the return is financial, but there are other kinds of returns. In the case of commercial media, investors are seeking a financial return at least comparable to what they would receive for investing in any other enterprise. But they may also be interested in the prestige that accrues from being involved in media. Power and influence are other forms of return for commercial investors. Governments that own, or invest in, mass media have a primary interest in returns such as cultural development, regional industrial development, nation-building, job creation, or the expansion of the variety of cultural products and the range of voices within their jurisdictions. Non-profit societies, cooperatives, and interest groups may participate in media to fill what they perceive to be gaps in media content or for the sole purpose of advocacy.

The media use material resources, too: paper to print books, magazines, and newspapers; plastics to produce video games and cellphones; metals to produce TV sets, cameras, computers, game consoles, and sound systems; chemicals to produce ink and to fuel delivery vehicles.

Much of the excitement about digital media, in fact, is that they are much less resource intensive than their old-media cousins. This translates into significant cost savings for old-media producers, but it also lowers what economists call the **barriers to entry** for new participants in media production. Establishing a website, for instance, requires relatively few technological and capital resources, although it can require human resources comparable in number and skill level to old media if the site is to maintain quality standards and thereby compete with all the other similar websites to generate an audience.

There are two aspects to economic markets. The first is the good or service offered, and the second is the physical boundaries within which this offer takes place. Media economist Robert G. Picard explains: "A market consists of sellers that provide the same good or service, or closely substitutable goods or services, to the same group of consumers" (Picard, 1989: 17). The Canadian market has a number of distinguishing features that must always be taken into account in considering media economics in Canada, as Box 9.1 explains. There have been significant changes to both aspects of media markets in recent years. In some cases, there are more providers of media content to Canadians in areas such as international news, television programming, and music. In other cases, media choices are severely restricted. With respect to content, sources of local news, for example, are dwindling and in some instances are non-existent (see Hodson and Malik, 2018). As for media platform services, Canadians have limited options when it comes to choosing a wireless phone service or a cable or satellite company. At the same time, the global reach of digital communication networks means market boundaries have shifted, especially for content, opening up some media markets to the world.

Media markets are distinguished from other kinds of markets in that they serve two markets at the same time: the audience market and the advertising market (see Picard, 1989: 17). Audiences pay for access to media content with money, with their time, as well as with the personal information they provide about their consumption habits (e.g., through cookies that track internet-browsing activity). Advertisers pay media producers for access to audiences whose demographic characteristics fit with the customers they seek to attract.

Two points should be made here. First, consumers have never paid the full cost of producing and distributing media content. Aside from advertising, the two main financial supporters of media content have been governments (through subsidies, tax concessions, provision of infrastructure, etc.) and wealthy patrons (through donations, direct funding, the establishment of charitable foundations, etc.) (CMCRP, 2017: 58). Second, advertising revenues as a portion of the overall media economy are in decline, and subscriber fees are assuming a much more significant portion of media revenues. Based on 2016 figures, total subscriber fees were almost five times greater than advertising revenue in the media economy, especially given the costs Canadians pay for internet access, wireless phone service, and cable and satellite television. But even in the media content realm, consumers are being asked to make up for dwindling advertising revenues through **paywalls** and subscriptions to specialty services (see Mirtle, 2018). Subscriptions, for example, accounted for more than half of all TV revenue in 2016 (CMCRP, 2017: 7–8).

Satisfying Needs and Wants

Each society makes decisions about how to structure its economy to satisfy its needs and wants. Western democracies have predominantly free-market or capitalist economies, in which individuals are at liberty to engage in private enterprise, producing and consuming according to their own interests. But no economy is completely free; governments at all levels participate in the economy, in some instances providing the infrastructure that allows private enterprise to thrive—for example, building roads, delivering water and electricity, funding public education, providing subsidies, establishing favourable tax rates—and at other times tempering market forces when they feel it is in the public interest. Typically, governments mitigate market forces both through restrictions and via incentives.

For most of the twentieth century, the Canadian state took an interventionist stance toward the cultural industries, as we noted in Chapter 7. But, since the early 1980s, governments have become much more willing to let markets dictate the rules of the game. The application of free-market economics is becoming more common worldwide, and even ostensibly communist countries like China are keen to become part of international organizations devoted to freer trade. The crumbling of international trade barriers and advancements in technology have increased the global flow of communication

9.1 The Canadian Market

The very particular characteristics of the Canadian media market inform all of the economic decisions made by media companies, governments, and labour organizations. Although Canada constitutes an attractive market based on its affluence and technological sophistication, we have a relatively small population—35 million—dispersed across a huge land mass, with most of us clustered within 100 kilometres of a border shared with the world's most productive and lucrative media market: the United States. If most Canadians share a common language with Americans, we also have a significant French-language population concentrated in Quebec, which constitutes a media market of its own. Canada has a diverse population, based on race, ethnicity, and religion, as well as on the regions in which people live. These characteristics of the Canadian market speak to our limited market power.

As users and consumers of media, we want access to the best the world has to offer, and in that sense we belong to a world market for popular culture. We want our artists, musicians, writers, and performers to be able to participate in that world market. And a great number—among them Rachel McAdams, Justin Bieber, Seth Rogen, Adam Gopnik, Margaret Atwood, Drake, Alice Munro, Douglas Coupland, Atom Egoyan, David Cronenberg, Samantha Bee, Jean-Marc Vallée, Jim Carrey, Sarah Polley, Ryan Gosling, Kiefer Sutherland, Kim Cattrall, and Robert Lepage—have succeeded internationally.

But we also need a distinct and viable market for Canadian media products and services, those that may not have much reach beyond Canada's borders, yet remain invaluable. As all peoples do, we want books and films and songs that speak to, teach us about, and keep a lasting record of our unique experiences. We want news and information that keep us abreast of what is happening here—locally, regionally, nationally—and that reflect our own views and interests. We want to be able to see ourselves—literally, figuratively—in poems and plays and in the visual arts.

When we look at how the media in Canada are structured, we need to consider these particularities of the Canadian market.

services across borders, resulting in the availability of many more cultural choices from abroad than we've ever had before. And the globalization process, which we discuss in Chapter 11, calls into question conventional notions of community and place; people's sense of how they belong to the national community has changed. All in all, it is becoming more and more difficult for states to govern cultural production on behalf of their constituents, often prompting concerns of national sovereignty over information networks (see Powers and Jablonski, 2015).

These changes pertain to matters of how the mass media are structured, and for what purpose. Some media organizations are privately owned—by individuals and companies—and respond to the profit motive, negotiating a compromise between the most profitable products and consumer demand. Others are publicly owned—by governments, non-profit societies, and cooperatives—and respond to what they perceive to be collective needs and wants, mostly in areas where private enterprise cannot satisfactorily meet those collective needs and wants. Media products and services, that is, have value, both to individuals and to societies, serving us at different times in different ways. Sometimes, they serve us as citizens, and their value derives from the extent to which services are accessible and content informs and enlightens. Other times, they serve us as consumers, and their value derives from their ability to generate markets and revenues. Still other times, media industries serve our career aspirations, serving us as places to earn a living or to satisfy our need for expression. In Canada, historically, we have attempted to strike a balance among these values, although there is an increasing tendency to perceive the most popular media products and services as the best, and to devalue those that serve minority or fringe audiences. As Box 9.2 explains, success in the marketplace is not a foolproof gauge of value.

A fundamental problem is the tendency, especially among economists, to apply the free-market perspective to sectors of the economy in which it may not be entirely appropriate. While the merits of **economism**—the perception of cultural production as commercial enterprise—can certainly be debated, further consideration takes us back to our earlier discussion of returns on economic investment. Not all returns are financial. Not all returns are immediate. And further, not all costs are financial. This point strikes at the heart of how we perceive cultural production and what role we assign the mass media in society.

Economists talk about **market externalities**, which are the costs and benefits of economic activity that are not accounted for by—i.e., that are external to—the immediate economic transaction between buyer and seller. For example, critics of graphically violent films and video games claim that such films and games exact social costs—in law enforcement, in health care, in social welfare—that are not part of the production cost or sale price of these items. Instead, those costs are assumed by society at large. On the flip side, externalities can be positive: the benefits of public libraries and a good public education system—literacy, numeracy, critical-thinking skills, specialized knowledge, and so on—spread beyond library patrons and students to society at large.

Market economies have a number of other limitations. In its comprehensive survey of state involvement in cultural activity in Canada, the Applebaum–Hébert Committee (Canada, 1982: 64–71) noted that governments often intervene in the cultural sphere in cases of **market failure**, when the market does not or cannot serve adequately the cultural needs of society. Markets, for example, typically do not recognize the longevity of cultural products, which may be produced by one generation and maintain their value through subsequent generations. Think of the number of artists—Van Gogh, Rembrandt, or our own Emily Carr—who are today recognized for their genius, but who were not adequately compensated for their creations in their own lifetimes. Markets may also fail to accommodate infant industries: new, domestic industries that cannot compete right away with well-established and large-scale transnational industries. Canadian feature film and dramatic television are good examples of industries that have struggled to find markets in the context of Hollywood's long-standing dominance of this country's commercial theatre and television screens. Cultural production also confounds market economics because it entails a large element of risk and requires a substantial investment of a society's resources, and because the public has a "limitless variability of tastes." The most common instance of market failure in the cultural sphere, however, involves the market failing "to register the full benefits conferred" by cultural activity (Canada, 1982: 64–71). It is hard to imagine how many forms of communicative expression would exist if they were solely dependent upon market dynamics (e.g., poetry, alternative forms of live theatre, avant-garde literature or fine art, scholarly research, etc.).

Free-market or laissez-faire economics reduces all goods and services to the status of commodities, objects that attain their value strictly through marketplace exchange: their **exchange value**. While we often believe a market economy to be responsive to consumer demand for choice, the cultural theorist Raymond Williams (1989: 88) reminds us that the organization of communication within a capitalist economy imposes "commercial constraints" so that "you can say that at times freedom in our kind of society amounts to the freedom to say anything you wish, provided you can say it profitably." Commodities, by definition, are "validated" strictly through sale. If we perceive books as, first and foremost, commodities, then their value is measured in retail sales.

Economism also casts individuals as consumers playing a narrow role in the economy rather than as citizens with a larger role to play in

9.2

The Myth of Meritocracy

Myths are stories we tell ourselves to help us understand the way the world works. The myth of meritocracy is a story about the egalitarian nature of the media marketplace, whereby consumers discriminate among cultural products solely on the basis of universally accepted conceptions of worth. It asserts, in essence, that those books or records or movies that deserve to be made will be made, and find an appreciative audience in the marketplace. While we might all like to believe that the media marketplace works without bias, the myth of meritocracy discounts completely the political economy of cultural production.

Merit, of course, is not completely irrelevant; audiences don't simply watch happily everything that's put in front of them, and we can all point to fine works that we've read, watched, or listened to that have proved to be immensely popular. But the notion of merit is greatly overstated. For one thing, consumer demand is a product of industry supply. When we choose a television program or a movie to watch, our choice is restricted to what's available. When we browse the magazine racks, our choices are limited to what's being displayed. Most often, we have no say in what is offered to us.

Second, the myth of meritocracy denies the market power behind certain cultural producers. The major Hollywood film companies, for example, are tied into international distribution networks and theatre chains, ensuring themselves screen time in movie theatres around the world and narrowing the field of competition considerably by erecting significant barriers to entry. Their market power also allows them to hire the greatest star actors and directors to create, produce, and publicize the film.

Finally, the myth of meritocracy ignores the question of whose tastes determine the qualitative norm against which all other productions are measured, and how those tastes are determined. Commercial radio, for instance, sets constraints pertaining to the length of songs, the language used in lyrics, and the subject matter, which clearly favour easy listening over more challenging or provocative selections. We tend to buy the music we hear on the radio. Similarly, commercial television favours 30- or 60-minute dramatic programs with recognizable personalities and formats as well as accessible, non-threatening storylines. Programming that doesn't fit these broadcast parameters usually isn't aired, and certainly not during prime time. The sites offering us digital content typically promote the "most popular" or the "most shared," whether they are YouTube videos, book selections on Amazon, or stories on Yahoo News.

The World Wide Web has vastly increased the size of the marketplace and created at least some room for alternatives (see Anderson, 2006). This innovation addresses, in part, our first point about audience choice, but it does nothing to address either the question of market power or of qualitative norms.

The media market most certainly has a commercial bias—the greater the size of the audience a book, movie, or song is likely to appeal to, the better the chance it will be produced and benefit from its producer's market power. But commercialism is only one particular kind of worth, rendering cultural production as commodity production and appealing to the tastes of the majority. Other values (e.g., cultural worth, educational worth, minority taste, intellectual challenge) are largely excluded from this equation.

There can be other kinds of biases, too, when, for instance, decision-makers determine that audiences aren't interested in works about women, or about people of colour, or stories that address explicitly people in exotic places like . . . Canada. Canadian popular music and literature fought such biases half a century ago; today, we don't think twice now when a Canadian musician/performer wins a Grammy or a Canadian writer wins the Man Booker or Nobel Prize. But Canadian dramatic television and, especially, Canadian feature films still face hurdles in screen markets, at home and abroad, in large part because they tend to be distinctly Canadian and they don't always subscribe to Hollywood's production formulas.

democratic society. Television programs, theatrical performances, and museum exhibits are not simply goods or services that we buy and sell but opportunities for the kind of communication that is fundamental to the understanding of culture. They are expressions of a way of life and of a system of beliefs and moral values. They are expressions of ideas and perceptions that help people to imagine themselves within the culture and to articulate their personal contributions to its priorities. Their worth, that is, derives from their **use value**.

There is no denying the tensions between the public good and private commercial interest. Canada's *Broadcasting Act* recognizes these tensions by assigning social responsibilities to all radio and television licence holders, including minimum Canadian-content regulations and special additional responsibilities for the public sector. Section 19 of the *Income Tax Act* provides recognition in the form of effectively restricting majority ownership of Canadian newspapers, magazines, and broadcasting stations (i.e., any medium that accepts advertising) to Canadians. The public goals of communication are also recognized in the support policies of the Department of Canadian Heritage for cultural industries, even if these programs are under review by a federal government committed to balancing its books and under pressure from the United States, particularly through World Trade Organization challenges. These programs are also under pressure because new international streaming services like Netflix are not subject to the same requirements—Canadian-content regulations, collection of sales taxes, etc.—as domestic media companies (see Pilieci, 2018).

Historically, cultural production is associated with *both* Enlightenment values and the emergence of a capitalist economy. The Enlightenment was distinguished by an intellectual approach based on a scientific and rational perspective of the world, a fundamental shift in worldview that championed science over religion, justice over the abuse of power, and a social contract that specified individual rights and freedoms over the absolutist rule of kings and clerics. **Capitalism**, which traces its roots to the late fifteenth century, is an economic system based on exchange relations, the **private ownership** of the **means of production** (see Box 9.3), and the clear separation of capital (owners of the means of production engaged in the pursuit of profit) and labour (workers who satisfy their material needs—food, shelter, clothing—by exchanging their labour for a wage).

Pictorial Press Ltd /Alamy Stock Photo.

Media content has both exchange value and use value. If the exchange value of a feature film like *Black Panther* includes the cost distributors pay for distribution rights, the cost exhibitors pay to screen it, and the cost we pay for a ticket at the movie theatre, how might we understand its use value?

Organizing Structures

No media industry in Canada is governed exclusively by free-market economics. Governments, both provincial and federal, are implicated in one form or another in the structure of every media industry: as proprietors (CBC, NFB, Canada Post), custodians (museums, galleries, theatres), patrons (commissions, grants, sponsorships), catalysts (tax incentives, subsidies), or regulators (CRTC). The result is that our media are organized as a complex mixture of public and private enterprise.

Newspaper publishing comes closest to an exclusively private enterprise, but given the industry's struggles in the shift to digital—225 Canadian newspapers closed between 2008 and 2018 due to corporate mergers and lost advertising revenues (LNRP, 2018)—governments are being pressured to intervene. Even here, though, section 19 of the *Income Tax Act* ensures that Canadian newspapers remain Canadian-owned; the newspaper industry is protected by the state from foreign takeover and foreign competition. Newspapers are considered by the state to be relatively untouchable because they are so closely associated with the historical struggle for freedom of the press (and, subsequently, other mediated forms of expression). In 2017, the Quebec government introduced a $36.4-million program to support the transition of newspapers to digital (Papineau, 2017). The Canadian government in its 2018 budget promised $50 million over five years for local news organizations in underserved areas, in addition to the possibility of granting charitable status to newspapers to allow them to receive tax-deductible donations for certain kinds of reporting projects (Leblanc, 2018). Magazine publishing in Canada is distinguished from the newspaper business by its considerable dependence on both government subsidies (e.g., direct grants) and protectionist legislation (the *Income Tax Act*) for its survival in a marketplace dominated by US publications (see Dubinsky, 1996).

The state presence is much more apparent in the broadcasting sector. Radio, for example, has private, commercial stations operating alongside publicly owned broadcasters (i.e., CBC and the French-language Radio-Canada) and community stations. CBC and Radio-Canada compete with the commercial broadcasters for audiences, and to some extent for advertising. Public radio in Canada had been completely commercial-free since 1974, leaving the public broadcaster wholly dependent on federal government funding for its operations. But given its financial pressures, CBC received permission from the CRTC in 2013 to run four minutes of national advertising per hour on its secondary services: CBC Radio 2 (now CBC Listen) in English and Espace Musique (now ICI Musique) in French (Infantry, 2013). CBC'S principal radio services remain ad-free. Its website is largely ad-free, with the exception of commercial messages preceding video clips. Community radio stations are run by non-profit societies with a democratic management structure, and raise money from a combination of advertising, government subsidies, and fundraising activities. As we discussed in Chapter 8, all radio stations are regulated by the CRTC; they are required to meet the specific conditions of their broadcast licence as well as Canadian-content quotas. The domestic sound recording industry, though owned by private interests, has been the principal beneficiary of Canadian-content regulations on radio.

Television, too, is a mix of private, public, and community broadcasting stations. A significant difference is that the stations of CBC and Radio-Canada, including the CBC News Network and Ici RDI, compete with the commercial broadcasters for both audiences and advertising. This competition for advertising has long been a sore point with the private broadcasters, who feel that CBC encroaches on their business, especially when the public broadcaster goes after programming particularly attractive to audiences and advertisers (e.g., professional sports, game shows, blockbuster films) but seemingly unrelated to its public service mandate. However, CBC contends that, due to cuts in government funding, it needs this revenue to make ends meet while producing quality Canadian programming. Besides, as Leonard Brockington, the first chair of CBC, argued in the 1930s, CBC is the only broadcaster that delivers 100 per cent of the revenues it earns from advertising back to taxpayers in the form of Canadian programming. The profits of private broadcasters go to shareholders, not to the public.

Both private and public television in Canada are regulated (e.g., licensing, Canadian-content quotas, advertising limits), and both private and public broadcasters benefit from federal and provincial subsidies for the creation of Canadian film and television programming. Television will bear particularly close scrutiny in the years ahead as various forms of broadcasting (e.g., speciality

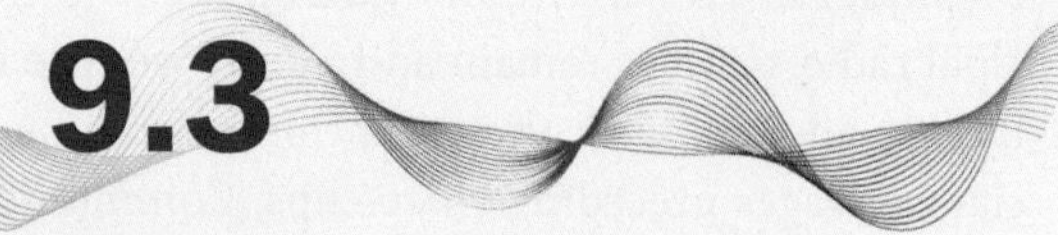

9.3 The Means of Production

When economists refer to the means of production, they are talking about the mechanism or process by which we satisfy our material needs for food, clothing, and shelter, and thus ensure our survival and the survival of our dependents. The means of production are, bluntly, the means of life.

In older, agrarian societies, peasants had direct access to the means of production; by working the land they could literally live off the land, eating what they grew and gathered, slaughtering livestock for food, leather, fur, and other necessities, felling trees for fuel, and collecting stones to use with wood to construct shelters. By controlling the means of production, they had direct access to, and control of, the means of their own survival. Most of us today would regard this means of survival as meagre and not particularly appealing. But the point we want to make is that peasants' relation to the means of production was fundamentally different from our own living today. Capitalism is a very specific economic and political system. A capitalist economy is an exchange economy mediated always by market relations.

Capitalism separates workers from the means of production. Instead of having direct access to the means by which to produce our life needs, we exchange our labour for wages and, in turn, exchange those wages for food, clothing, and shelter. As the historian Ellen Meiksins Wood (2002: 7) explains, "Material life and social reproduction in capitalism are universally mediated by the market, so that all individuals must in one way or another enter into market relations in order to gain access to the means of life." When we apply for a job, for instance, we are entering the job market, offering our labour in exchange for wages. In turn, we take those wages and enter the housing market, the food market, and the clothing market, exchanging our wages for our life needs. This is the sense in which we mean the market mediates between individuals and the necessities of life.

If our access to the means of production is governed by market relations, so is our access to the products of our own and of others' labour. Even when our work is devoted to the production of food, clothing, or home-building supplies, we don't own those products but must purchase them as we would any other commodity.

Why is this important?

Some people today argue that digital communication technologies return ownership of the means of production to ordinary people. The inference is that those who wish to engage in media production themselves no longer need to work for the corporate media conglomerates but can set up shop themselves. The further inference is that corporations no longer wield the economic power they once did, that **corporate concentration** in the media industries is no longer the concern it once was.

But this is where an important distinction must be made between the means of production and workplace tools. A carpenter who owns her own set of tools, no matter how extensive, does not own the means of production. She must engage in the capitalist economy by exchanging her specialized labour for a wage. Only when she establishes her own business—which requires all of the infrastructure necessary to secure and fulfill contracts, and ultimately to make a living—can she be said to own the means of production, to own the means of satisfying her material needs. Even then, all of the carpenter's business relations are conducted through the market, where she must compete with all of the other woodworking businesses for customers.

Similarly, someone with a website or a blog does not own the means of production—he owns only the tools with which to produce his website or blog. Those tools do not constitute the means of production in and of themselves, nor do they necessarily constitute the means with which to satisfy the blogger's material needs of survival.

Yes, personal computing grants individuals unprecedented access to the mediascape, as the millions of personal blogs, social media accounts, and small websites attest. But a distinction must be made between communicating as a hobby, a pastime, or some other kind of personal project and communicating to make a living.

channels, pay-per-view, streaming services) bring new players into the picture and fragment audiences, altering substantially the media landscape (see CMCRP, 2017: 32–39). The film industry in Canada is a special case because it has both public and private production houses, but the distribution and exhibition sectors of the industry are organized along principles of private enterprise. Governments in Canada have been involved in film production—as patrons, catalysts, and regulators—since early in the twentieth century. Hollywood began to dominate the burgeoning commercial film industry in the 1920s. The federal government established the National Film Board of Canada in 1939 as a means of asserting a greater Canadian presence on cinema screens. The NFB, though, has largely been confined to producing the kinds of films that tend not to be shown in commercial theatres—documentary, experimental, animation, and sponsored films—leaving the production of dramatic feature-length films to the (mostly American) private sector. Even the private producers of feature films in Canada rely heavily on government subsidies and tax breaks for production, distribution, and marketing, and public television has been one of Canadian cinema's most dependable exhibition venues.

James Brittain-VIEW / Alamy Stock Photo.

La Maison symphonique, a concert hall at Place des Arts in Montreal, was built in 2011 based on a public-private partnership, meaning it was funded by both government sources and the private sector.

For most of the twentieth century, telephone service was defined by Ottawa as a "natural monopoly," and Canada had both private (e.g., BC Telephone, Bell Canada) and provincial state monopolies (e.g., Sasktel, Manitoba Telecom Services) operating side by side. The CRTC, however, opened up long-distance telephony to competition and in 1994 opened all telephone services to competition. Similarly, the Crown corporation Canada Post monopolized mail service until the 1980s, when private companies created a market for specialized courier services.

Even art galleries, theatres, concert halls, and museums, insofar as they can be seen as mass media, are characterized by a mix of public and private ownership, with content generated by both public- and private-sector sources. The international web of computer networks we call the internet has no single owner, but it, too, counts on both public- and private-sector initiatives for its operation and its content. Cyberspace is a medium of exchange for all kinds of communication and defies any simple structural category.

Dual goals—creating and maintaining national and regional cultures while at the same time stimulating economic growth—remain in perpetual tension in the communication sphere, and the various ownership structures of the media in Canada speak to the ongoing struggle to keep both objectives in view. Where the Canadian people fit into this picture is an important question. Canadians are, at the same time, citizens, audience members, workers, consumers, and taxpayers with diverse interests, and their support for both private enterprise and public service contributes to the tension around ownership structures.

Public Ownership

The central difference between public and private forms of ownership relates to the question of return on investment. If private enterprises are interested primarily in a financial return, public enterprises seek other kinds of return: cultural development, industrial development, job creation, national identity formation, and so on. **Public ownership** is devoted to providing communication as some kind of public service based upon public goals: to enable citizenship, to foster a sense of community on regional and national scales, and to promote regional and national cultures. (It's worth noting here that the term *public ownership* has a dual meaning, as we explain in Box 9.4.) Private ownership is devoted to providing communication for profit. Regardless of the mix of private and public enterprise described above, this distinction is fundamental and needs always to be kept in view if we are to make the link between the ownership structure of a medium and the purpose of the communication it provides.

The idea of public service is to employ the mass media for social goals. This can mean the provision of universal and equitable service to all Canadians, as in the telecommunication, postal, radio, and television industries. It can mean foregrounding the educational component of communication, which informs all cultural policy to some extent. Or it can mean ensuring a Canadian voice in film, radio, TV, publishing, and popular music, where there has been, and remains, a clear risk of being drowned out by American voices. Communication as public service is inherently inclusive, addressing audiences as *citizens* rather than as *consumers*, and asserting citizens' rights to communicate and to be informed.

The public service ideal, of course, is not without shortcomings when it comes to putting principles into practice. In Canada, public service has often meant national service; in other words, communication in the service of nationalism, to the possible detriment of regional expressions of distinction or dissent. It has also meant the concentration of media services in Central Canada, creating a hierarchical distinction between the "national" preoccupations of Ontario and Quebec and the "regional" concerns of the other provinces and territories.

The central ethic of the public corporation, though, is connected to the democratic ideal. More specifically, it is to provide a public service to both the users of the service and to the population as a whole. Public enterprise, that is, employs a cost structure in which the users of the public service

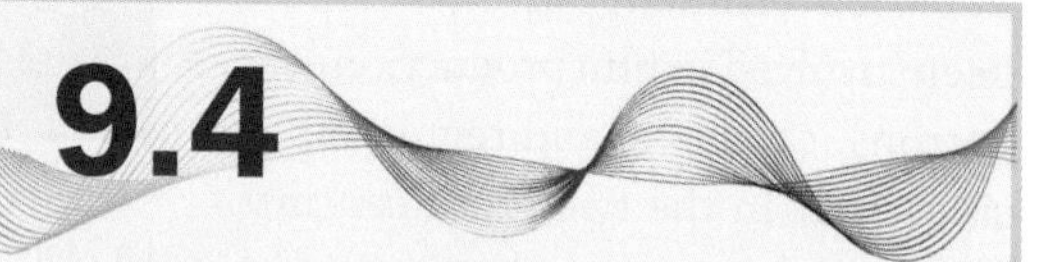

Public Ownership

Public ownership is a slippery term used in two contradictory ways by economists: sometimes to mean ownership by the state on behalf of its citizens—*the public*—and at other times to mean ownership by a group of self-interested shareholders. These are very different kinds of ownership.

The first sense of public ownership refers to Crown corporations like Canada Post or the Canadian Broadcasting Corporation, which are owned by the state on behalf of the Canadian people.

The second sense of public ownership refers to corporations whose shares are publicly traded through the stock exchange. They are "public" in the sense that shares in these companies can be bought and sold by anyone with the means to do so. Rogers Communications is an example of a publicly traded company; anyone can buy an ownership share.

Economists use the term *public* to mean "publicly traded" because there are also *private* companies owned privately—typically by a family or a small group of owners—whose shares are not for sale through stock exchanges. Brunswick News, for example, is a private media company owned by J.K. Irving of New Brunswick.

In this book, we use *public ownership* to mean state-owned, and *private ownership* to mean either shareholder-owned or privately held.

do not pay the full cost of that service; the costs are shared by all taxpayers. For example, visitors to the National Gallery in Ottawa pay an admission fee, but those fees do not recover the full costs of operating the gallery or of purchasing and maintaining the art collection contained therein. The remaining costs are covered by the federal government via tax revenues—money collected from every Canadian, most of whom have never visited and are unlikely ever to visit the National Gallery. The rationale for such a cost structure is the need to promote national culture and the conviction that a strict user-pay system would not meet this objective. The government-owned mail system, Canada Post, has a slightly different cost structure, but the same principle applies: we all share in the costs of maintaining a basic and essential communication service. In the case of Canada Post, rather than determine the cost of posting a letter on the basis of the costs of delivery (e.g., it costs less to send a letter across town than across the country), Canada Post charges us the same rate for the same stamp whether our letter is mailed three blocks away or across three time zones within Canada. The rationale for this cost structure is the need to provide equitable mail service to all Canadians, whether they live in concentrated urban centres or remote northern communities.

Public enterprise has a long and distinguished tradition in every Western country. Canada has made extensive use of public enterprise throughout its history, with the most common form being the Crown corporation. But, again, it is not without its drawbacks. As noted by Marc Raboy in his classic 1990 study of Canadian broadcast policy, *Missed Opportunities: The Story of Canada's Broadcasting Policy*, *national* communication services can become *nationalist* services, catering to the goals of the nation rather than to the divergent and possibly contrary goals of the various regions of the country. CBC, for example, struggles constantly to accommodate the great diversity of perspectives that constitute our national culture. Similarly, the production headquarters of these services tend to be centralized—in Toronto for English Canada, in Montreal for French Canada—distancing them from the communities they are mandated to serve. In a country as large and diverse as Canada, this can have repercussions for access to these institutions—as audiences, as cultural producers—as well as for the interests and concerns they serve. That said, privately owned media operating on a national stage face similar challenges (e.g., the Toronto-based *national* newspapers *The Globe and Mail* and the *National Post*, and the private TV networks CTV, Global, and TVA).

Public ownership also removes the element of choice from our decisions about media consumption and can cause resentment among those who have to pay for services through their tax dollars but don't use the services. We all pay for CBC radio and television broadcasts, NFB documentaries, and performances at the National Arts Centre, but not all of us are faithful consumers, and some of us may very well object to their programming choices.

Public ownership grants a tremendous amount of responsibility and power to governments in deciding when, where, and how to

CMHR-Aaron Cohen.

We all pay for CBC radio and television broadcasts, National Film Board documentaries, and displays at the Canadian Museum for Human Rights in Winnipeg, such as this exhibit on the life of Nelson Mandela. What are some of the advantages and disadvantages of public ownership?

intervene in the communication economy. As governments change, so can the state's cultural priorities. More importantly, public ownership creates an opportunity for political interference. Even though public media companies are managed at arm's length from the government of the day, they nonetheless depend upon governments for their mandates and their operating budgets. CBC, for example, has seen its annual appropriation from Parliament—its largest revenue source—shrink over the past 20 years, from about $1.5 billion in the early 1990s to $1.21 billion in 2017–2018, while at the same time being made responsible for more services (CBC, 2018).

Though direct political interference is rare—and can also be brought to bear on privately owned media companies—a number of high-profile incidents serve as a reminder that the state retains this power to pressure public institutions. In 1990, the National Gallery drew heavy criticism for its $1.8-million purchase of a modernist painting by the New York artist Barnett Newman called *Voice of Fire*. Among the critics was Progressive Conservative MP Felix Holtmann, the chair of the House Communications and Culture Committee (Geddes, 2010). In 1992, CBC Television attracted the ire of Canadian war veterans and Senator Jack Marshall, the chair of the Senate Subcommittee on Veterans Affairs, for its three-part World War II series *The Valour and the Horror*, produced by the Montreal documentary filmmakers Terence and Brian McKenna (Nash, 1994: 526–33). Parts two and three of the series were particularly critical of Canadians' participation in the blanket bombing of German cities and in the Normandy invasion. During Senate subcommittee hearings, CBC was condemned for airing the series, and the CBC ombudsman produced a report concluding that the series was "flawed and fails to measure up to CBC's demanding policies and standards" (531). In 2008, Stephen Harper's Conservative government adopted Bill C-10, an amendment to the *Income Tax Act*, allowing the federal government to deny tax credits to film and television projects considered offensive for reasons of violence, hatred, or sexuality. The bill was reportedly prompted by the release in 2007 of a Canadian film comedy entitled *Young People Fucking*.

Private Ownership

Private-sector ownership assumes two basic forms. The ownership of a company can be closely held, either by an individual or by a very small group (often family members). Or ownership can be widely held by a large group of shareholders, who buy and sell their interest in the company through the stock market. In the latter case, a company will form a board of directors answerable to its shareholders.

The overriding ethic of the private or commercial media outlet, in all instances, is survival and growth in a marketplace driven by profit. If publicly owned media have an obligation to serve all Canadians, private media serve only those who constitute their target market: those audiences most attractive to advertisers.

Because the bottom line in the private sector is profit, private media companies have considerable latitude in changing course to maximize their economic returns. In radio broadcasting, this can mean a repositioning in the market, either through the introduction of new program segments or through a complete change in format, from, say, all-news to golden-oldies music. A book publisher might decide to stop signing contracts for poetry or avant-garde fiction and focus on how-to books or celebrity biographies. More radically, a communication company can move into other industries altogether, whether those markets are in the sphere of communications or not. Consider the example of Thomson Corporation. Now known as Thomson Reuters, the company started as a small newspaper publisher in Timmins, Ontario, in the 1930s, and it became one of Canada's two largest newspaper owners by the 1980s, boasting significant newspaper holdings in the United States and the United Kingdom by the 1990s. The company that was primarily a newspaper publisher for half a century had completely abandoned the newspaper industry by 2003 for what its directors perceived as greener pastures in other industries: financial, legal, scientific, and health-care publishing, as well as medical and travel publishing. Thomson returned to journalism only when it merged with Reuters, one of the world's largest news services, in 2008 (Thomson Reuters, 2009). The Thomson family returned to the newspaper business in 2010 when its Woodbridge subsidiary reacquired an 85 per cent stake in *The Globe and Mail* (Ladurantaye, 2010)—and it assumed full ownership of the *Globe* in August 2015.

Within the private sector there exists a considerable variety of ownership structures. The single enterprise is, as its name suggests, a form in which owners confine themselves to one business with no connections to other companies. It is a single, independent firm that usually operates on a small scale. Some examples persist, particularly among magazines, community newspapers, and small-town radio stations, but single enterprises are fewer and fewer as chains both large and small gobble them up or force them out of business.

Chain ownership, a common form of media organization in Canada, is the linking, or horizontal integration, of a number of companies in the same business—typically newspapers, radio stations, or television stations—occupying different markets. Chains are usually geographically dispersed, but sometimes members of the chain will occupy the same location and aim for distinct audiences. Vancouver's two daily newspapers, the *Vancouver Sun* and *The Province*, for example, are both part of the larger Postmedia chain, but they seek different readers and advertisers within the Lower Mainland of British Columbia. Member companies in a chain may have agreements to buy and sell services from each other. Postmedia newspapers, for instance, share editorial content (stories and pictures) among member papers. In addition, chains often consolidate administrative resources, so that accounting and marketing services or departments responsible for technological innovation will be able to serve all members in the chain. Television networks are also chains; CTV, for example, has affiliate stations in eight provinces, co-ordinating programming through its Toronto headquarters (CTV, 2018). Such sharing of resources offers chain operations tremendous cost advantages over single enterprises. Typically, chain ownership provides the advantages of reducing competition and creating economies of scale.

Vertical integration is the concentration of firms within a specific business that extends a company's control over the entire process of production and distribution. A vertically integrated company, for instance, will have subsidiary companies involved in every aspect of an industry. The most common example of vertical integration is the Hollywood studio system, in which the major Hollywood companies not only own production studios and distribution companies, but they also have subsidiaries involved in exhibition networks to ensure their films reach audiences and generate revenues. For example, the Hollywood studio Warner Bros., in association with Heyday Films, produced the film *Harry Potter and the Deadly Hallows: Part Two*. Warner Bros. Distribution distributed the film, and it was promoted and marketed by several Warner Bros. affiliates: HBO, CNN, and *Time* magazine. The Warner Bros. International Cinemas chain screened the film worldwide, and HBO broadcast its television premiere (ABL Media, 2012). The advantages inherent in vertical integration are substantial. A **vertically integrated company** assures itself of resource supplies and sales markets, and it minimizes other uncertainties, such as competition, related to the circuit of production.

Conglomerate ownership is characterized by large companies with a number of subsidiary firms in both related and unrelated businesses. Besides the advantages of scale, shareholder risk is reduced because the conglomerate is not dependent for its profits on any one industry. **Convergence** is the name given to the economic strategy media conglomerates employ in an attempt to create synergies among their media properties. One of Canada's most converged conglomerates is Quebecor Inc. Through its various subsidiaries, Quebecor owns two leading daily newspapers and more than 50 magazines. Quebecor is also in the business of television (TVA), telecommunications and cable distribution (Vidéotron), new media (Canoe), publishing (TVA Publishing), film production (MELS), and retailing (Vidéotron Le Superclub). The company is also behind the bid for the return of a National Hockey League franchise to Quebec City. See Table 9.1 for more about converged conglomerates.

TABLE 9.1
Converged Conglomerates in Canada

Quebecor Inc.

Platform Media

- **Vidéotron:** wireline and mobile telephony; internet service provision; residential and business cable services
- **Fibrenoire:** data hosting services
- **4Degrees:** data hosting services
- **Distribution Select:** music and video distribution
- **Messageries ADP:** book distribution
- **SETTE:** digital program distribution

Content Media

- **Newspaper publishing:** Le Journal de Montréal, Le Journal de Québec, 24 heures, QMI news agency
- **Magazine publishing:** 50 magazines, including 7 Jours, TV Hebdo, Elle Canada, Elle Québec
- **Book publishing:** Sogides Group (18 publishing houses), CEC Publishing (textbooks)
- **Television:** TVA (the largest French-language television network), plus 7 specialty services, including TVA Sports, LCN, and MAtv community channel
- **Internet:** Canoe.ca web portal
- **Cinema:** MELS studio space, post-production services, special effects; SETTE post-production services; Goji support services for online video content producers
- **Music:** Musicor recording label
- **Advertising:** Bus and bus shelter advertising

Other

- **Entertainment:** Centre Vidéotron arena; Gestev show organization, marketing; Quebec Remparts and Armada de Blainville-Boisbriand junior hockey teams
- **Retail:** Vidéotron Le Superclub sales of Vidéotron telecommunications services, movie, TV, video-game rentals

Shaw Communications Inc.

Platform Media

- **Shaw Cablesystems:** residential cable TV service
- **Shaw Direct:** direct-to-home satellite service
- **Shaw Broadcast Services:** distribution of 570 TV and radio signals to broadcast redistributors
- **Shaw Business:** fibre-optic backbone network providing data, video, voice, and internet services to businesses
- **Shaw Home Phone:** wireless phone service
- **Freedom Mobile:** wireless phone service
- **Shaw Internet:** internet service provision

Rogers Communications Inc.

Platform Media

- **Rogers Cable:** residential TV service
- **Rogers Wireless:** wireless phone service
- **Fido:** wireless phone service
- **chatr Mobile:** wireless phone service
- **Rogers Telecom:** residential and business wireline services
- **Rogers Ignite:** internet service provision
- **Fido Internet:** internet service provision
- **Rogers Smart Home Monitoring:** security service

Content Media

- **Magazines:** Maclean's, Chatelaine, Today's Parent, Hello! Canada
- **Television:** Sportsnet, City TV, OMNI, TSC, FX, FXX, Outdoor Life Network
- **Radio:** 55 AM and FM stations
- **Video:** Dome Productions

Other

- **Entertainment:** Toronto Blue Jays baseball club; Rogers Centre stadium

BCE Inc.

Platform Media

- **Bell Satellite TV:** satellite tv service
- **Bell Fibe TV:** internet protocol TV service
- **Bell Home Phone:** domestic wireline phone service
- **Bell MTS:** domestic wireline phone service (Manitoba)
- **Bell Mobility:** wireless phone service
- **Virgin Mobile Canada:** wireless phone service
- **Bell Fibe Internet:** internet service provision
- **Bell Aliant:** internet service provision (Atlantic Canada)

Content Media

- **Television:** CTV network; 30 specialty channels including TSN and RDS; 4 pay television channels; Crave TV
- **Radio:** 109 licensed radio stations; 215 music channels
- **Internet:** Crave TV; GO video streaming; 200 websites
- **Advertising:** Astral
- **Video:** Iconic Entertainment Studios; Pinewood Toronto Studios; Dome Productions

Chain ownership, vertical integration, and convergence are all forms of corporate concentration, whereby the ownership of media properties is concentrated in relatively few hands. Corporate concentration grants a media company considerable market power, allowing it, for instance, to dominate resource, labour, advertising and audience markets, to limit competition from smaller players, and restrict both the kinds of content in circulation, as well as the range of viewpoints expressed through that content. Corporate concentration has been a particular concern in Canada's news industry (see Edge, 2016; Couture, 2013).

Media companies are no longer confined to their previous industry *silos* because they now have a digital presence as well. For much of media history, it made sense to talk about various analog media forms—books, newspapers, radio, television, cinema—as distinct technologies belonging to separate industries. With computerization and the translation of all types of information into the common digital language of 0s and 1s, these media silos have broken down. The combination of digitization and computer networking has resulted in the integration of all media, enabling the immediate and global exchange of every kind of content (Gasher, 2013).

Implications of Private Media Ownership

For those who believe that communication in all its forms involves much more than satisfying markets, the appropriation by private enterprise of a greater and greater share of the mediasphere is of great concern. While economists argue that the free-market organization of cultural production is the most efficient means of giving consumers what they want, political economists maintain that the commercial organization of cultural production limits choice and discriminates between those members of the public who have disposable income to spend on advertised products and media services and those who don't. This is particularly the case when corporate concentration limits the number of, and distinctions between, producers and distributors (see Mosco, 2009: 158–75).

In the realm of the mass media, private enterprise is seen as having two particular social benefits. First, it stimulates the provision of affordable goods and services for which consumers have expressed a need or desire through their purchasing decisions. Second, because advertising subsidizes the media, consumers are able to receive content either free or at minimal cost. These benefits, of course, are not as straightforward as they may seem. First of all, anticipating what consumers will buy is an inexact science, notwithstanding polls and focus groups. Consumers can make choices only among products and services already offered—supply to a large extent governs demand—and media managers have been frustrated time and again in trying to determine which new services will attract consumers. Media economists have demonstrated, for example, that most major Hollywood movies lose money, and the studios depend on their blockbuster hits to make up for their far more numerous flops (see Gomery, 2004). The same applies to television series; each new fall season introduces more losers than winners, shows that are cancelled after only a few weeks. Advertising, social media alerts, and other forms of publicity, of course, play a role in generating excitement and consumer demand around new films, TV shows, music recordings, and book releases, but consumer tastes remain very hard to anticipate.

Second, it is not entirely accurate to say consumers receive some media programming free of charge. Instead, consumers pay for it indirectly. As media have digitized, for example, we have to pay to access media services such as internet, wireless telephony, and cable and satellite connection. Further, even if we do not hand over any money to a radio station to listen to its programming, or to a commuter newspaper to read its articles, we pay for that content nonetheless every time we buy an advertised product. Advertising costs, in other words, are built into the sale price of potato chips and breakfast cereal, so that a share of the money we spend on groceries, snacks, clothing, beer, gasoline, and cosmetics pays for media programming.

Media economists also argue that we pay with our time—we literally *pay attention*—whenever we consume media services, and that time and attention is what advertisers seek. The key point to understanding how commercial media work within the economic system is that to generate profits, managers of commercial media seek to attract audiences to their programming to sell those audiences to advertisers. Communications theorist Dallas Smythe (1994: 270–1) famously pointed out that what advertisers buy is not simply air time or newspaper space, but "the services of audiences with predictable specifications who will pay attention in predictable numbers and at particular times to particular means of communications." Through increasingly sophisticated audience-measurement techniques, media managers collect data on their audiences—not only the size of the audience is determined, but also demographic factors such as income, education, age, and sex—and sell advertisers access to the kinds of audiences that will be interested in buying their product or service. Mass media content, therefore, is merely "an inducement (gift, bribe, or free lunch) to recruit potential members of the audience and to maintain their loyal attention." Dallas Smythe writes that "the free lunch consists of materials which whet the audience members' appetite and thus (1) attract and keep them attending to the programme, newspaper or magazine, and (2) cultivate a mood conducive to favourable reaction to the explicit and implicit advertisers' messages" (1994: 270–1).

Private ownership of the communication media raises four particular concerns. The first is that private enterprise casts cultural production as commercial enterprise, whereby the goal of communication becomes the generation of profit. This form of organization imposes commercial constraints on communication. Communication as a commercial enterprise creates pressures to maximize entertainment value and to minimize difficulty and complexity, and to provide communication in an advertising- or consumption-friendly environment. In the digital mediascape, competing content is only a click away. Programming that is difficult, challenging, or slow-paced may have trouble holding the attention of audiences, and it could be hard for media organizations to support.

A second concern is that the increasing convergence of media properties reinforces the profit motive and moves owners further and further from their core areas of business. That is, conglomerates are in business to make money rather than to make movies or newspapers or books or video games. By privileging the profit motive above all else, the creation of conglomerates weakens the owners' commitment to core areas of business; media properties may become a lesser priority within the conglomerate than, for example, its real estate holdings. Managers can revise the conglomerate's mandate, or abandon media initiatives altogether for more lucrative industries.

Related to this is a third concern. The broader a conglomerate's reach becomes, the more businesses it is involved in, the greater the chance for a conflict of interest between its media business and its other holdings. Critical themes (e.g., environmentalism, labour practices, poverty) in newspaper and magazine stories, TV and film documentaries, or radio programs could threaten the earnings or community standing of the conglomerate's other holdings. In such cases, the conglomerate's media properties may feel pressure to avoid certain subject areas, depriving the public of a full airing of important social issues or confining their discussion within safe parameters. The issue of climate change, for example, raises serious questions about capitalism as an economic system (see Klein, 2014).

Finally, the trend toward corporate concentration has reduced substantially our sources of information at precisely the point in history when our dependence on communications media for our knowledge of the world has increased. The plethora of TV and radio channels, websites, books, magazines, newspapers, music recordings, and videos available to us is largely illusory; it disguises the fact that many of these media are the products of a mere handful of large corporations, and that others (e.g., websites) are primarily distribution channels for other media, rather than generators of original content. If we are to take seriously our role as citizens in democratic society, we should be encouraging the greatest variety of information sources possible, as well as an increase in distinct media channels for us to express ourselves. Taken together, these trends of private ownership have reduced our sources of information and narrowed the range of what can be said and how it can be expressed.

New Labour Issues

The transformations we have been discussing have had a huge impact on media workers. As Box 9.5 explains, media work is increasingly precarious and flexible (see also Salamon, 2015, 2016; Curtin and Sanson, 2016). An estimated 10,000 Canadian media jobs were lost between 2008 and 2013 through a combination of layoffs and buyouts (Wong, 2013), and the losses have continued at major employers such as Rogers Media, Bell Media, Torstar, and Postmedia (see Jackson, 2018; Doherty, 2017; Watson, 2017). An increasing amount of the work that used to be produced by full-time, salaried workers is contracted out to temporary workers or freelancers at rates that are much lower than those paid to full-time employees and that do not include benefits. Freelance journalists, for example, are paid rates that have not changed in 30 years, even though their work may be used on a number of platforms and even archived for future sales (Coxon, 2018; Cohen, 2012). Some of this media work, too, has been handed to unpaid interns (see McKnight and Nursall, 2014); Canada's journalism, communications, and film schools are full of students eager to break into the industry through internships and other volunteer arrangements, altering dramatically the supply–demand relationship in labour markets.

For those media workers who remain, their jobs are characterized by increasing flexibility. This can mean a number of things: hiring and releasing workers as production demands shift, rendering jobs more temporary; adjusting employees' hours as immediate production demands rise and fall (see Dyer-Witheford and de Peuter, 2006, 2009; Frankel, 2017); dividing labour processes into separate tasks carried out in distinct locales, often internationally (see Christopherson, 2006); combining previously distinct tasks, typically using digital technologies and software applications; and requiring workers to repurpose their work for several media platforms.

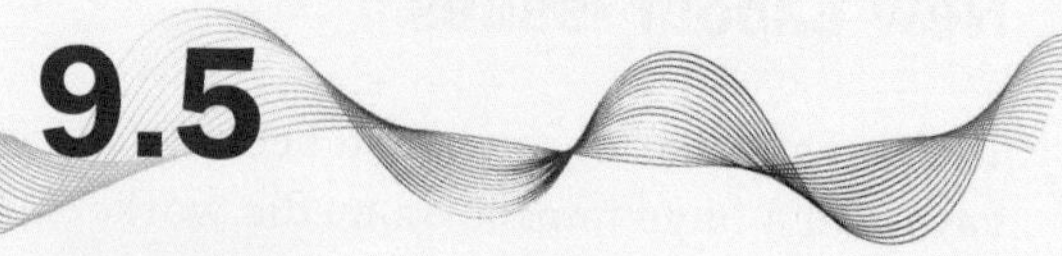

9.5 Precarious Labour

By Errol Salamon

Precarity is a term that describes a transformation of employment conditions throughout the twenty-first century and workers' responses to these transformations. There are three key characteristics of precarious labour across media industries (Salamon, 2018). First, the number of jobs has decreased. For instance, the total number of journalists, broadcast technicians, announcers, and other broadcasters dropped between 2001 and 2016, according to Statistics Canada (Salamon, 2019). Second, there has been an increase in employment that is neither permanent nor full-time, which refers to freelance, contract, temporary, or self-employment, and internships (Salamon, 2015, 2018). For instance, Statistics Canada data reveal that the proportion of self-employed journalists, broadcast technicians, film and video camera operators, and audio and video recording technicians jumped between 2001 and 2016 (Salamon, 2019). Third, precarious media workers tend to earn low pay compared to full-time and permanent employees. For example, a Professional Writers Association of Canada survey reveals that the average annual income of freelance writers dropped from $25,000 in 1979 to $24,035 in 2005. According to a 2015 Writers' Union of Canada survey, women writers have been disproportionately affected, earning 55 per cent of the income of their male counterparts. By comparison, the mean annual income for all occupations increased from $29,267 in 2000 to $37,231 in 2015, according to Statistics Canada figures.

Yet precarious media workers have organized labour unions to advocate for higher pay, along with long-term and full-time employment opportunities (Salamon, 2018, 2019). The Canadian Media Guild Freelance Branch, established in 1998 and affiliated with CWA Canada, represented 600 freelance workers at CBC and 183 independent freelance workers as of July 2017. Likewise, the Canadian Freelance Union, formed in 2009 and affiliated with Unifor, had about 250 independent members as of April 2016. These unions welcome freelance workers across media industries, including writers, journalists, photographers, videographers, technicians, graphic designers, and web producers.

Errol Salamon is a post-doctoral associate in Media, Popular Culture, Diversity, and Inclusivity in the Hubbard School of Journalism and Mass Communication at the University of Minnesota.

Related to the point made about internships and other volunteer work above, the generation of content by users is becoming a form of unpaid apprenticeship for some aspiring media workers (see Shepherd, 2013). Facebook, for instance, has become one of the largest media companies in the world without producing any original content; its content consists solely of posts by its unpaid users. Musicians, videographers, and writers post material to social media sites hoping to gain a following and perhaps follow the path of discovery laid by Justin Bieber and Alessia Cara (see Adib, 2009). In a case study of four such Montreal apprentices, Tamara Shepherd defines the labour behind such user-generated content as "a non-remunerated training ground" driven by "the promise of notoriety that begets autonomous future employment" (2013: 41). Most user-generated content is posted to, and becomes the property of, commercial digital platforms, creating value for corporations out of this free labour. And unlike apprenticeships for electricians, plumbers, or carpenters, such media apprenticeships are completely unorganized and beyond the scope of cultural-policy mechanisms (Shepherd, 2013: 42).

If the field of user-generated content is rife with the potential for exploitation, the provision of this free content, some of it of excellent quality, also drives down the value of the work performed by those trying to make a respectable living in the cultural industries. While labour organizations have suffered membership losses with layoffs, buyouts, and contract work (e.g., Quebecor hired back just 62 of the 253 unionized *Journal de Montréal* workers the company locked out because of a contract dispute between 2009 and 2011), the deterioration of working conditions in the cultural industries may enhance the raison d'être of trade unions in the long run. Overextended workers in the video-game industry are looking to organize (Dyer-Witheford and de Peuter, 2009, 2006: 612), and the unions themselves are combatting the power of converged media corporations by also converging (Mosco and McKercher, 2006). The two principal labour unions for media workers are the Canadian Media Guild—representing 6,000 workers in such organizations as CBC/R-C, Canadian Press, the Aboriginal Peoples Television Network, as well as freelancers—and Unifor, Canada's largest private-sector union with over 300,000 members in every sector of the Canadian economy, including more than 36,000 media workers.

Media Democratization

The barriers to media ownership and participation have decreased considerably with digitization and the greater accessibility of a range of communication technologies, from personal computers to digital cameras and sound recorders (see Gillmor, 2004; Shirky, 2008). **Media democratization** implies greater involvement by citizens in the production and distribution of all kinds of media content. We have already made reference to user-generated content, but democratization would include structured initiatives such as the establishment of organizations dedicated to expanding public participation and broadening media perspectives, especially in the areas of news and current affairs.

The idea of democratizing the media has a history dating back at least to the 1960s and '70s, when cooperative radio stations, film and video collectives, and alternative or "underground" newspapers were established. In the 1960s, for example, the NFB launched its Challenge for Change program, putting film cameras in the hands of citizens to tell their own stories. And in the 1970s, Canada's Native Communication Program helped establish a number of indigenous newspapers (Skinner, 2012: 37). Recently, however, the relative accessibility of the internet, the inadequacies of both public and private forms of ownership described above, and the hyper-commercialism that has accompanied globalization have combined to reinvigorate movements for media reform and the establishment of **alternative media** organizations.

Proposals for reforming the existing media include the following: imposing limits on ownership concentration, and especially cross-media ownership; amending the *Competition Act* to account for diversity in the expression of news and ideas; legislating a code of professional practice or a code of ethics for media organizations; restructuring provincial press councils and/or establishing a national media commission; and enacting right-of-reply legislation, which would permit editorial redress for persons misrepresented in the media (Skinner, 2004: 16–17). David Skinner argues that "these reforms would help ensure some diversity in corporate news voices, provide journalists some independence from their corporate employers and provide some checks on the relationship between the media and the public" (18). Reform initiatives, however, leave standing the fundamental structures of public and private media institutions.

Alternative media initiatives, on the other hand, pursue communication and cultural production to broaden public debate, to construct community, to advocate for social justice, and to challenge concentrated media power; see Kozolanka et al. (2012), who note that "these media occupy contested and shifting terrain, and that the news and ideas they contain are not marginal in any larger social sense, but indicate sustained efforts for more democratic media and society as one and the same" (2). Among the media organizations serving these goals are campus and community radio stations, community television channels, magazines such as *Spacing*, *Briarpatch*, *Canadian Dimension*, *This Magazine*, and *The Tyee* (online only), as well as online news providers like *The National Observer* and

The Dominion (Skinner, 2012: 37–43). The challenge for alternative media organizations and their corporate cousins is to achieve economic sustainability. As David Skinner notes, "For the most part, these media have developed out of a concern for the expression of a particular set of ideas and values, and consideration of a business model has generally taken a back seat to this goal" (26). Alternative media organizations tend to be small and enjoy few economies of scale, and those who work for them often do so for little or no pay. The size and demographic profile of their audiences is often unknown, making it hard to generate advertising and subscription sales, and their ideological content can limit their appeal to advertisers (26).

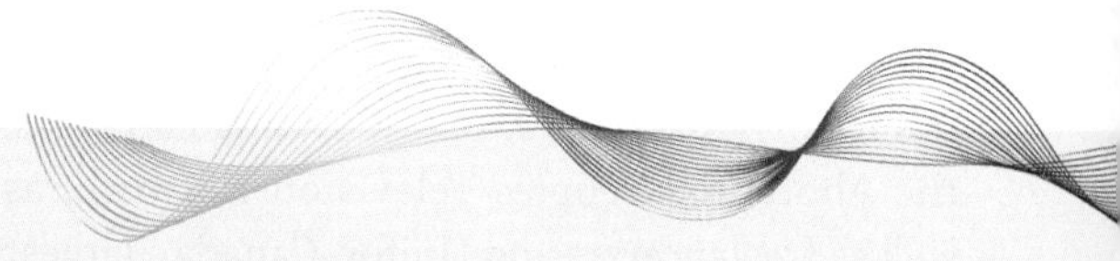

SUMMARY

There is no natural or inevitable way to organize the mass media. They are social institutions structured in various ways according to their technological characteristics, the resources they draw upon, and the socio-political context in which they operate. But if all media organizations have something in common, it is that they participate in the economy by generating revenues for media owners, providing communication services to their audiences, advertising goods and services, and providing employment.

The mass media in Canada are owned both privately and publicly, but all operate in a mixed economy. No media industry in Canada is governed exclusively by free-market economics. Even newspaper publishing, which comes closest to an exclusively private enterprise, is subject to federal government regulations regarding ownership intended to protect newspapers from foreign takeover and competition. Nor is any media organization in Canada immune to the demands of the marketplace; even the publicly owned CBC must pay attention to ratings and advertising revenues.

The critical difference between public and private forms of media ownership pertains to their bottom lines. Public ownership is devoted to providing communication as a public service, to employ the mass media for social or national goals. Private ownership is devoted to providing communication for the profit of media owners. These distinctions are fundamental because they speak to the role communication is assigned in Canadian society. The economistic view perceives communication, first and foremost, as commercial enterprise, subjecting all forms of cultural production to commercial criteria of supply and demand. The culturalistic view regards cultural products as much more than commodities to be exchanged in the marketplace—they are expressions of a culture as a way of life and as a system of beliefs and values, and expressions of ideas and images that help a culture to imagine itself and to articulate its priorities. As private enterprise has encroached on more and more areas of mediated communication in Canadian society, concerns have been raised over the commercialization of cultural production, conglomerate ownership of media organizations, conflicts of interest between media companies and other businesses owned by the same parent, and corporate concentration.

Media as workplaces have also changed dramatically with the combination of reductions in full staff at major media companies; the increased use of casual, contract workers, and interns; and the proliferation of user-generated content online.

Moves to democratize the media have assumed two forms: *media reform*, which seeks to find ways to diversify and render existing media organizations more accountable, and *alternative media*, or the establishing of new independent media outlets dedicated to serving defined communities.

KEY TERMS

alternative media, p. 243
barriers to entry, p. 225
capital, p. 224
capitalism, p. 230
chain ownership, p. 237
conglomerate ownership, p. 237
convergence, p. 237
corporate concentration, p. 232
economism, p. 228
exchange value, p. 228
labour, p. 223
market, p. 223
market externalities, p. 228
market failure, p. 228
means of production, p. 230
media democratization, p. 243
paywall, p. 226
private ownership, p. 230
public ownership, p. 234
resources, p. 224
use value, p. 230
vertical integration, p. 237
vertically integrated company, p. 237

RELATED WEBSITES

Canadian Media Concentration Research Project: www.cmcrp.org
The website of a research project led by Dwayne Winseck of Carleton University, the CMCRP tracks and analyzes the state of corporate concentration in the media sector of the Canadian economy. The site is an excellent source of current data and government policy initiatives.

Quebecor: www.quebecor.com
This site provides a detailed look at one of Canada's largest media companies, which has been a champion of media convergence.

FURTHER READINGS

Stuart Cunningham, Terry Flew, and Adam Swift. *Media Economics*. 2015. London: Palgrave. This is an accessible textbook explaining how economics works in the specific instances of the media industries, and assessing the contending approaches to understanding media economics today.

Heilbroner, Robert L. 1980. *The Worldly Philosophers: The Lives, Times, and Ideas of the Great Economic Thinkers*. New York: Simon & Schuster. This very readable reference guide covers history's leading economic theorists.

Kozolanka, Kirsten, Patricia Mazeppa, and David Skinner, editors. 2012. *Alternative Media in Canada*. Vancouver: UBC Press. This collection of essays provides a thorough assessment of the move to create a media sector that forms a true alternative to the dominant corporate media.

Mosco, Vincent. 2009. *The Political Economy of Communication: Rethinking and Renewal*, 2nd ed. Los Angeles: Sage. Mosco's theoretical work applies contemporary political-economic thought to communication and cultural industries.

STUDY QUESTIONS

1. What important changes have taken place in the media economy in recent years?
2. What resources do media organizations draw upon?
3. What is the rationale for state intervention in the cultural economy?
4. What are *market externalities* and how are they pertinent to the discussion of media economics? Cite an example of a positive externality and a negative externality.
5. What are the principal distinctions between public and private forms of ownership?
6. Name three forms that private ownership of the media can assume.
7. What is media convergence, and what does it imply for media content?
8. What does it mean to say media "sell audiences to advertisers"?
9. In what ways is the current labour market "precarious" for media workers?
10. What is media democratization and what forms can it take?

10

Journalists as Content Producers

The arts of rhetoric can serve either democracy or self-interested factions. Journalism is one of those arts. —*Stephen J.A. Ward*

National Geographic Image Collection / Alamy Stock Photo

Opening Questions

- What does it mean to say that news stories, like other kinds of media content, are produced or constructed? Why is this important?
- How is *networked journalism* different from the pipeline model of news production?
- What does it mean to say that journalism is a practice of representation?
- How do news stories produce meaning?
- What are the ideals that govern journalism as a practice of knowledge production?
- What economic challenges does journalism face as it becomes increasingly digital and networked?

Introduction

Content producers are central to all media organizations. Radio hosts, magazine photographers, web designers, television producers, film editors, and songwriters all have vastly different job descriptions and work environments, but they all produce media content. The stories and images we see and hear, whether based on fact or fiction, are never presented "naturally," but are instead highly constructed by people with particular sets of technical and aesthetic skills, organized within a specific production environment, and guided by ideals, ideologies, conventions, regulations, and institutional demands. These stories and images, in other words, are products of **mediation**. Mediation involves a series of choices about what content to create—how, for what purpose, and for whom, regardless of whether those choices are made consciously or unconsciously. User-generated content entails the same kinds of choices, even if those choices are less structured, and even if users are less aware of, or attentive to, the various contextual parameters within which they are operating.

In this chapter, we posit journalism as a particular practice of content production, and an especially interesting one given the ways it is evolving, in sometimes positive, sometimes negative directions. On the positive side, new openings have been created for people to participate in the production and circulation of news and commentary, along with fresh opportunities for people to take up discussion of news stories and events. The emergence of sites like the *National Observer*, *The Tyee*, *The Conversation*, *iPolitics*, and *The Discourse*, among many others, has diversified Canadian news coverage and analysis, providing alternatives to mainstream news providers.

Of course, these new openings in the mediascape have also allowed for the increased circulation of extremist commentary, misinformation, and the outright fabrication of news stories; if US President Donald Trump uses the charge of "fake news" to undermine legitimate news coverage, social media networks have been used to spread invented or distorted stories and images for political purposes. In what some have called a "post-truth" era, when suspicion is cast on many of our knowledge-producing institutions (e.g., government agencies, educational institutions, the justice system), journalism as a fact-finding and truth-seeking enterprise has also suffered (see McIntyre, 2018). Some of this, certainly, can be blamed on the news industry's own failings: instances of bias and partisanship, closures of longstanding news providers, cutbacks to newsroom staff and consequent reductions in coverage, the collapse of the so-called "wall" between the advertising and editorial functions of news organizations, etc. The widespread concern over these developments testifies to the fact that journalism remains an indispensable democratic communication system.

News reporting is a particular kind of media content, and journalists operate within a specific context, guided by ideals, storytelling conventions, and audience expectations that distinguish this practice from other kinds of content production. And the majority of original news reporting—however we access it—is still produced by journalists who work for legacy news organizations, those who attend the meetings, conduct the interviews, do the original research, and craft the original story (see Charles, 2014: 48–50; Dahlgren, 2013: 160).

Journalism is an especially suitable communication form for this chapter because we might not normally think of it as being manufactured or produced; some reporters still claim they simply mirror reality—that they simply record actuality. After all, journalism's self-appointed mission is to provide us with transparent accounts of newsworthy people, institutions, events, and trends, along with informed analysis. In its simplest definition, journalism provides the public with factual information and informed commentary about current events by addressing the most basic questions of who, what, when, where, why, and how. But as we will see, it is in all cases a manufactured product.

Journalism is also suitable for study because, like other types of media content, it is no longer the exclusive domain of professionals, but the product of an interactive and multi-source network.

News as Content Production

Like all forms of content, news is produced and, much like other media products, is presented in story form. News items are typically referred to as *stories*, in that they consist of characters, conflicts between characters, temporal and geographical settings, and narratives that take us from a beginning to an end. News stories, while based on actual events and real people, never simply mirror reality. A mirror, after all, shows us only what is placed before it, nothing more and nothing less, and in the proportions presented to it; the person holding the mirror may have control over where to point it, but the depiction the mirror offers is always a simple, direct, and unorganized reflection. The mirror metaphor and the associated notion of reflection do not adequately describe the role of journalists as content producers.

Nor is news simply gathered. Such a conception of journalism underestimates the degree of selection that goes into producing a news report and the extent to which events must meet the producer's understanding of "newsworthiness." Even those individuals who simply redistribute news through social media or submit photos or video clips to news organizations operate from some sense of what they think is important and worthy of people's attention.

Journalists make choices about what to cover based on what they perceive to have "news value," what fits within their organization's particular areas of coverage (politics, business, sports, crime, the arts) and what they believe will interest their audience. Deciding what is news is a subjective operation, involving journalists in a complex, consultative, and sometimes hotly contested process of selection. While news judgment is most often exercised intuitively by journalists under time pressure in the field, based on their experience and expertise (see Schultz, 2007), media scholars have identified a number of criteria that render some events news and others not news. Melvin Mencher (2006: 58–65), for example, identifies seven determinants of newsworthiness: *timeliness* (events that are immediate or recent); *impact* (events that affect many people); *prominence* (events involving well-known people, places, or institutions); *proximity* (events that are geographically, culturally, or "emotionally" close to the audience); *conflict* (events pitting two sides against each other); *peculiarity* (events that deviate from the everyday); and *currency* (long-simmering events that suddenly emerge as objects of attention).

Clearly, these **news values** require journalists to exercise subjective judgment about what is new, what is important, and what the target audience should know about. News is not an account of mundane activities, but a digest of extraordinary, unusual, significant, or unexpected events. To cite a simple example, normal rush-hour

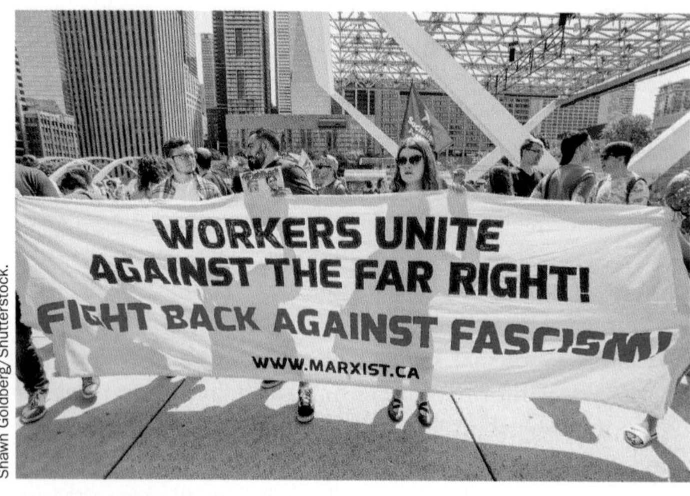

Shawn Goldberg/Shutterstock.

All news stories are told from someone's perspective.

10.1 Networked Journalism

What do we mean by "journalism" in a period when the production and distribution of news, commentary, and analysis are conducted not only by those who self-identify as journalists but also by ordinary citizens, hobbyists, bloggers with particular interests, community groups, and advocates of every stripe? Journalism is both a practice (reporting and commenting on current affairs) and an institution (the production and distribution system within which reporting occurs). If for most of the twentieth century, journalism was the bailiwick of professional reporters and editors working for legacy news organizations, this changed with the interactivity and accessibility of digital media. C.W. Anderson et al. put it this way: "We are living through a shock of inclusion, where the former audience is becoming increasingly intertwined with all aspects of news: as sources who can go public on their own, as groups that can both create and comb through data in ways the professionals can't, as disseminators, syndicators, and users of the news" (2012: 80). If Peter Dahlgren insists that mainstream reporting remains the predominant source of news and user-generated journalism largely operates "symbiotically," the result is that "facts and opinions, debates, gossip, nonsense, misinformation, the insightful, the deceptive, the poetic, are all mixed together, scrambling the traditional boundaries between journalism and non-journalism" (2013: 160).

Breaking down this dichotomy between what Dahlgren calls "mainstream journalism" and "participatory journalism," current scholarship perceives journalism today as *networked* rather than as a simple "pipeline" between news media and audiences (see Anderson, 2013; Anderson et al., 2012; Sheller, 2014; Archetti, 2014; Benkler, 2011; Clark and Van Slyke, 2011). Journalism, in other words, is the product of the perpetual and dialogic interactions among information sources of all kinds, news providers of all kinds, and news consumers who can tap into a vast array of information sources. As Figure 10.1 illustrates, professional journalists draw on story leads and information from their traditional sources (experts, actors in their field, news releases, news conferences) as well as from other information providers (websites, social media sites, blogs, and audience feedback). Bloggers contribute to this network by drawing on mainstream news reporting, other blogs, websites, social media sites, their followers' comments, and their own expertise. News consumers, similarly, develop an understanding of a news event from whatever combination of information sources they frequent; increasingly, this means gleaning information and analysis from a variety of traditional and non-traditional media—what Mimi Sheller calls "source promiscuity" (2014: 8). News consumers, too, can make their own contributions to this journalism network.

Journalism scholar C.W. Anderson maintains that "we need to think about networks of journalistic expertise, with both human agents and non-human objects networked together in complex strands of material practice and knowledge production" (2013: 1021). He writes, "By looking at 'newswork as network,' we can better factor in the cultural residue of a particular profession that constrains both its mental worldview and its available repertoire of action" (1021).

While *networked journalism* is a useful concept, it risks conflating the significant disparities between simpler forms of information production (e.g., content based on personal observation, recycled material, off-the-cuff analysis) and much more sophisticated and labour-intensive material (e.g., investigative reporting, expert data analysis, conflict reporting). The concept can, in other words, overlook or trivialize the skill set, experience, work effort, resources, commitment, even moral and physical courage, required to produce professional-grade journalism. In a study of citizen journalism practices in local UK newspapers, Lily Canter distinguishes between "low-level" and "high-level" categories of reporting. Low-level reporting is deemed to be the field of non-professionals, comprising such things as community events, charity events, "bottom-tier" council meetings, and self-interest news. High-level reporting, seen as best done by professionals, includes court cases, investigative reporting, major events, and breaking news (2013: 1100). Similarly, Anderson et al. see journalists as being displaced rather than replaced in the news ecosystem, moving higher up the editorial food chain where the emphasis is on their skills of **verification** and interpretation (2012: 22).

(continued)

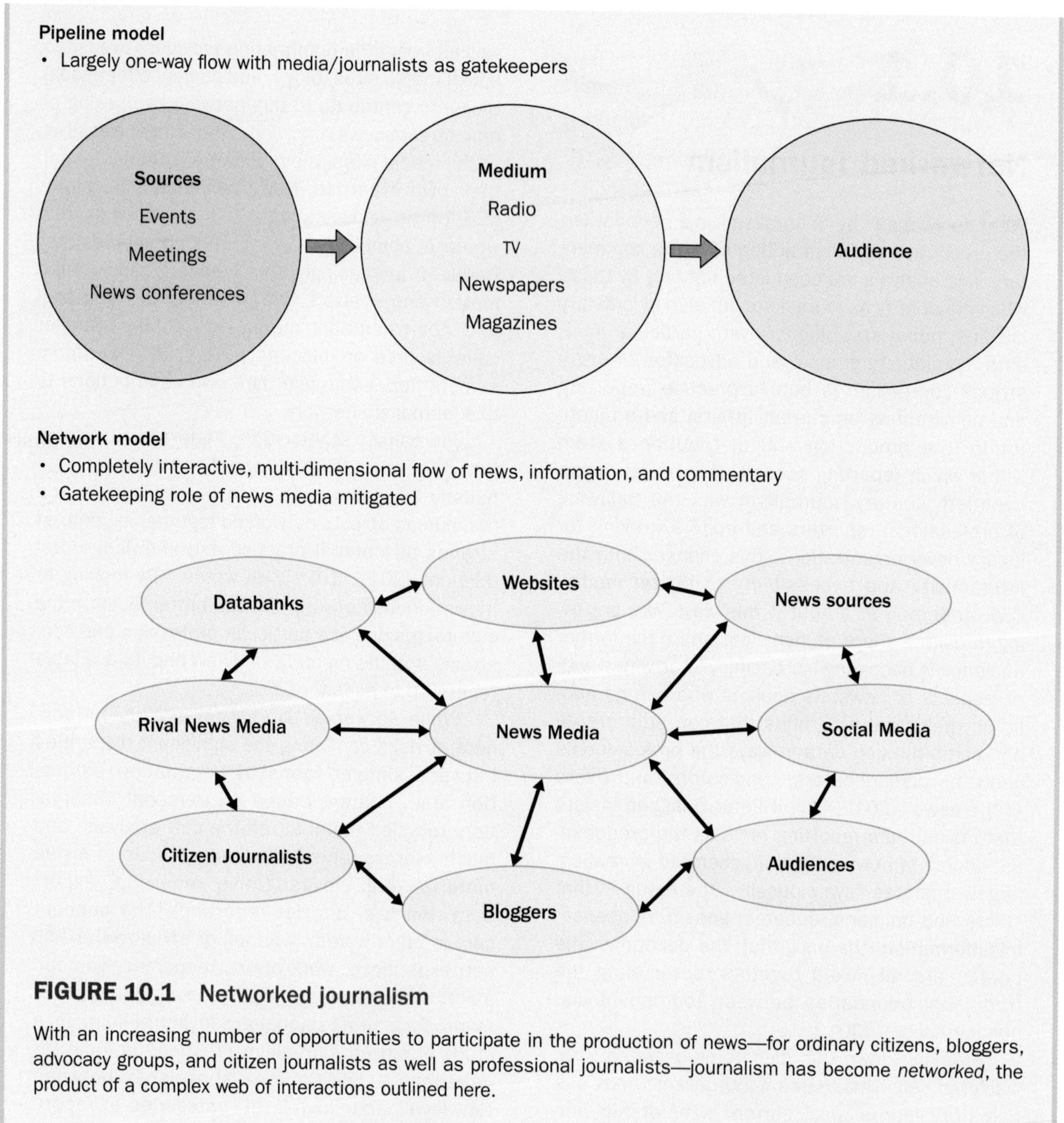

FIGURE 10.1 Networked journalism

With an increasing number of opportunities to participate in the production of news—for ordinary citizens, bloggers, advocacy groups, and citizen journalists as well as professional journalists—journalism has become *networked*, the product of a complex web of interactions outlined here.

traffic volume on a local urban freeway is not news, while a seven-car pileup that kills three people and closes several lanes of the freeway for a number of hours is definitely news. This process of selection has compelled some theorists to perceive journalists—especially editors and news directors—as gatekeepers, people who sift through a huge number of events and decide which will be covered and which stories will be circulated. But **gatekeeping** is only a partial explanation of the news production process, applicable only to some stages of selection.

If gatekeeping accounts for the question of *what* the news organization will cover, it leaves aside the equally important issue of *how* an event will be covered. It ignores, for example, the extent to which wire-service stories are revised by editors and the different *play*—length and prominence—they receive from one news organization to the next. Every news medium assigns relative importance to news stories by how it plays them—whether prominently or buried under mounds of other content. The same event may receive completely different treatment from one news provider to the next.

The gatekeeping metaphor also ignores the creative nature of news production. Every news organization establishes a brand: a particular identity through the style of journalism it practises (e.g., serious and thorough, entertaining and concise). Developing and maintaining that identity is achieved by establishing a certain kind of editorial presence through the assignment of resources and the shaping of content. Tabloid newspapers like the *Toronto Sun* and *Le Journal de Montréal*, for example, pay a considerable amount of attention to crime stories, covering the police beat and the courthouse quite heavily. Their news stories are relatively short and written in a lively and provocative style, and their pages are filled with bold headlines and lots of photographs. Tabloids are typically populist newspapers, devoted to what they perceive to be the interests of the everyday person. More sober broadsheets like *The Globe and Mail* and *Le Devoir*, on the other hand, pay much more attention to political, foreign-affairs, and cultural reporting. They tend to feature much longer and in-depth stories. These newspapers cater to what they perceive to be a more discriminating audience and aspire to be read by society's opinion leaders; they define news differently. This idea of branding is especially applicable in today's crowded mediascape, in what has been termed an "attention economy." Examining how any news organization's editorial style is created opens up the selection process to many more factors than the notion of gatekeeping can accommodate.

A useful exercise for the student of media is to examine the content of a favoured news provider and consider the ways in which it puts together a particular package of news. What topics does it cover? Is it specialized in one or a few topics (e.g., politics, business) or does it offer a broad range of subject matter? Then, how does it cover those topics? What kind of language does it use? What aspects of the story does it highlight? Whose voices and images are included? What references does it make to other events, people, or institutions? To what extent does it feature its own original reporting and commentary? How much material has been sourced elsewhere? The answers to these questions provide clues about what kind of audience the news provider aims to build, as well as its particular biases, understood here as the topics it highlights and the perspective it adopts.

A more precise way to think of journalists as content producers is through the metaphor of the frame. Through words, images, sounds, and story themes, journalists "frame" reality. If we think of the blank page or the blank screen as an empty frame, it is journalists who decide how to fill that frame, by inserting into the frame particular stories, visuals, and graphics and by deciding what to leave out. They also decide how to depict those events and what prominence to assign the story, what aspects or angle of the story to emphasize, whose voices are heard, what meanings they encourage audiences to take away from the story. It is useful to remind ourselves that every element of the news story, the news page, the news broadcast, the news site, has been inserted—at the expense of other content.

The metaphor of the frame implies, first of all, that there are limits to what a news organization can properly present as news. These limits are defined by such practical considerations as the size of the "news hole" (the space or time available), the costs involved in producing the coverage, and the availability of reporting staff or other sources of information. Even the producers of online news sites, with much more capacity for content, make decisions about what to include and exclude, and which content to feature prominently on their home page. These limits are also governed by the more subjective criteria of an event's news value and how well it suits the news organization's particular approach to coverage, as we touched on above. News coverage is also shaped by a given news organization's particular political stance or bias, whether or not this position is ever explicitly stated. Think about how news organizations may react differently, even if the distinctions are subtle, in their coverage of labour–management disputes, same-sex marriage legislation, cuts in social spending, or environmental issues.

No news organization can cover every event from every possible angle. As we have suggested, the practice of **framing** occurs within a production environment shaped by a number of factors: the ideals that distinguish journalism from other kinds of content production; the use of language—textual, aural, and visual—and the shaping of news reports into stories that give news events meaning; the specific sociopolitical culture in which news stories are produced; the laws and regulations that govern journalism; the economics of news production; and the technological infrastructure available to journalists.

Ideals of Journalism

If news is constructed, it is also subject to particular ideals that distinguish journalism from other forms of storytelling—and that distinguish journalism as it is practised in Western democracies like Canada from the way it might be practised elsewhere. We can be justifiably skeptical about how well journalists and their news organizations live up to these ideals. Ideals, after all, are lofty principles, even standards for perfection, but they nonetheless provide the yardsticks by which critics, practitioners, and audiences alike evaluate performance. These ideals form a kind

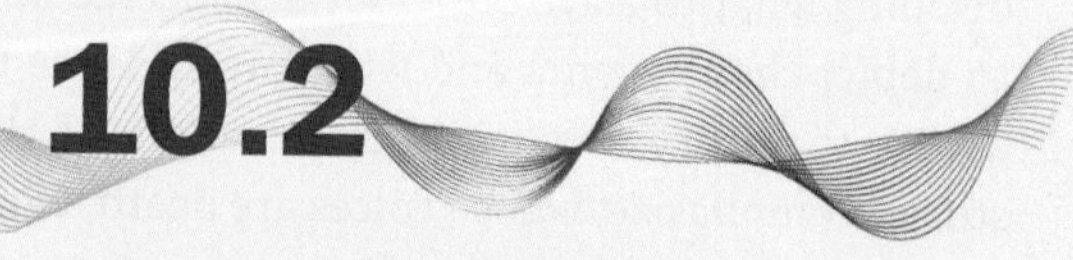

Pushing and Pulling

Until recently, it has been left to news providers to determine what to offer news consumers, through an imprecise calculation of what editors and producers think audiences want to know and need to know and what kinds of content will attract audiences that advertisers will want to reach. Legacy media like newspapers, magazines, and radio and television broadcasters are examples of **push technologies**, media that push content toward audience members, calculating that their supply will satisfy audience demand (see Sheller, 2014).

The interactive capacities of digital technologies have shifted the supply–demand dynamic, and can be understood as **pull technologies**. News consumers no longer need to rely on push technologies; they can *pull, or search out and retrieve,* whatever kinds of news content they prefer, whenever and wherever they want. If you want to know who is leading the Tour de France or whether the ceasefire in Syria is holding, you don't need to wait for the next newscast or breaking-news bulletin.

This erodes somewhat the power of commercial news organizations by breaking their monopoly hold on news production, opening them up to competition not only from other commercial news providers worldwide, but also from an assortment of news aggregators, alternative news sites, digital independents, bloggers, even the principal actors in the news themselves (government departments, think tanks, university researchers, non-governmental organizations, advocacy groups, and so on) who can address audiences directly. It has changed dramatically how we consume news; no longer are we confined to the packages that news organizations provide for us because we can pull individual stories from numerous news and information providers.

This change strikes at the heart of the question, *What is journalism for?* Relatedly, it speaks to concerns about journalism's standing as a democratic communication system. What are the implications for notions of citizenship and community if we get only the news we want—whether by push or by pull? Can we have a healthy democracy or any sense of local community without a shared body of knowledge about current affairs?

of gold standard for what "good journalism" is, and help to distinguish journalism from other communication practices.

It was the best of times. It was the worst of times.

(Depending upon which paper you read.)

Same day.
Same story.
Two points of view.
Which one represents you?

THE TORONTO STAR

Torstar Syndication Services.

As demonstrated by this *Toronto Star* advertisement, individual media organizations, as well as individual journalists, can tell vastly different stories about the very same event.

Journalism as we know it in Canada has a fundamental guiding ideal: the quest for truth. This quest is idealistic because the truth is not always accessible to us as fallible human beings, and certainly not readily accessible within the constraints placed on most journalists. Even the most conscientious, hard-working, and ethical journalists face constraints: time, access—to people, to documents, to events—and their own limits of expertise and analytical skill. The seemingly simple task of reporting on what happened—during a meeting, during a battle, during a public demonstration—is also always inflected with people's perception, interpretation, and pre-conceived ideas. Increasingly, we recognize that there is usually more than one truth at play; we might agree on a basic set of facts, but how those facts are made meaningful can produce many truths. Nonetheless, journalism derives its authority from providing the public with credible accounts of current affairs. Credibility is the currency that the news media trade in, and no news organization wants to be perceived as lacking in credibility.

A serious threat to journalistic credibility has emerged in the form of fake news, whereby individuals, organizations, or states disseminate fabricated or significantly altered texts and images to deceive and manipulate audiences (see Box 10.3).

The performance of journalism's truth-seeking function is related to a second ideal: serving democracy. Truth-seeking is the foundation for **freedom of the press**, a fundamental freedom for all democracies that can be traced back to the Enlightenment (see Box 10.4) and that is explicitly noted in Canada's *Charter of Rights and Freedoms* (section 2[b]). Journalism is tasked with the production and circulation of information and ideas for the benefit of all, extending the basic democratic right of freedom of expression granted to all individuals into the realm of the mass media. In their appraisal of the state of contemporary journalism, Kovach and Rosenstiel insist that "[t]he primary purpose of journalism is to provide citizens with the information they need to be free and self-governing" (2001: 17).

Fake News

The proper functioning of democratic society depends on a number of institutions providing its citizens with information that is factual, accurate, verifiable, trustworthy, and credible: government (through agencies such as Statistics Canada), the legal system (courts, police), the education system (through both research and teaching), the medical establishment (from doctors to researchers), and journalism. Factual information forms the basis of every kind of decision-making process.

If fake news has a long history—think of the trashy tabloid newspapers and celebrity magazines displayed at supermarket checkouts—it has become a much more serious problem given the ease with which social media networks can be deployed to fabricate or distort news reports and images.

The erosion of public trust is a serious threat, as media theorist Roger Silverstone argues: "For the media to be viable they have to be trusted by their addressees" (2007: 124). Once that trust is lost, Silverstone maintains, it is almost impossible to restore.

Bill Kovach and Tom Rosenstiel have described journalism as a "discipline of verification" as opposed to a "discipline of assertion." They write, "In the end, the discipline of verification is what separates journalism from entertainment, propaganda, fiction, or art" (2001: 71).

Methods of verification have taken on renewed importance given the increasingly open access to media networks, and social media in particular. The Knight Foundation (Hindman and Barash, 2018) conducted a study of "the fake news ecosystem" in the aftermath of the 2016 US presidential election, which was subjected to numerous and sophisticated disinformation campaigns. Analyzing 10 million tweets from 700,000 Twitter accounts linked to more than 600 "fake and conspiracy news outlets" in a 30-day period in spring 2017, the Knight Foundation concluded that "disinformation continues to be a substantial problem postelection." It tracked 4 million tweets linked to fake news and conspiracy producers, estimating that 70 per cent of the sites were automated (3–4).

The subsequent Donald Trump presidency in the United States has been noteworthy in prompting news organizations like the *Washington Post* (see Rizzo, 2018) and the *New York Times* (see Qiu, 2018) to publish regularly the results of fact-checking White House statements. And, of course, news consumers have greater capacity to do their own fact-checking (see Silverman, 2007).

A number of scholars have critiqued this normative definition of journalism as a democratic practice. Journalism historian Michael Schudson argues, "There is no doubting . . . the importance of the press to a democracy. But the press by itself is not democracy and does not create democracy" (2003: 198). The political scientist Anne-Marie Gingras concurs, citing a serious misunderstanding in the relationship between the media and democracy, based on what she terms three "confusions." First, while freedom of expression is an essential condition for the functioning of democracy, it does not guarantee political representation of the broad spectrum of society, nor does it establish the mechanisms necessary for a true dialogue between civil society and the state. Second, freedom of expression does not speak to the quality—specifically, the veracity—of media messages. Third, communication does not guarantee harmony or consensus (Gingras, 2006: 3–4). The media, Gingras argues, are caught in a conflict between their commercial interests and their political responsibilities; producing quality information does not ensure commercial success, nor does commercial success necessarily result in quality information (8).

The struggle for freedom of the press is ongoing, and journalists are at the forefront of efforts to extend public **access to information** in both formal and informal ways, as we discuss in Box 10.5.

Journalists are often highly dependent on official sources and their own contacts for information, and the news media's role as **fourth estate** grants journalists the moral authority to gain access to the people and institutions that

John Milton's *Areopagitica*

One of the earliest and most forceful arguments for freedom of the press came in a speech to the English parliament in 1644. In John Milton's speech, titled *Areopagitica*,* he objected to England's Licensing Order, by which publishing was restricted to government-licensed printers, and written works had to be pre-approved before printing (read the full speech here: www.gutenberg.org/files/608/608-h/608-h.htm). Milton's appeal was unsuccessful—the Licensing Order remained in place until 1692—but his speech remains a classic Enlightenment text, and his reasoning informs free-speech arguments to the present day.

If *Areopagitica* reflects Enlightenment thinking, it also appealed to the Christian sensibilities of Milton's audience. For example, Milton argued that God gave humankind free will, the capacity to choose between good and evil. "He that can apprehend and consider vice with all her baits and seeming pleasures, and yet abstain, and yet distinguish, and yet prefer that which is truly better, he is the true warfaring Christian." He questioned the practicalities of assigning fallible beings the responsibility for licensing and argued that knowledge and truth emerge precisely through the process of reading and discussion. "Where there is much desire to learn, there of necessity will be much arguing, much writing, many opinions; for opinion in good men is but knowledge in the making."

*The full title is *Areopagitica: A Speech for the Liberty of Unlicensed Printing to the Parliament of England*.

populate their reportage: politicians, bureaucrats, police officers, community leaders, celebrities, Parliament, the court system, the stock exchange, and so on.

The news media today fulfill the role of the fourth estate by reporting on legislative debates and other government business, and by pressuring governments to increase access to information. Of all the coverage the news media provide, political reportage is considered to be the most closely related to journalism's role in democratic society. If the original notion of the fourth estate was to be a watchdog over our governors, it has been expanded to include watching over all institutions of power, including the corporate sector. But, as with the other core journalistic values we have discussed, the fourth estate ideal is subject to critique. While the news media can serve as watchdogs on power, they can serve equally as lapdogs when they report uncritically on governments and corporations.

This fourth estate notion is connected to journalistic *independence*. Ideally, journalists are independent agents in service to the public, concerned only with the public good and beyond the influence of powerful private interests. This is, of course, another ideal that is difficult to live up to. For one thing, journalists are subjective beings with their own values and beliefs. And even the most conscientious journalist is not immune to the influences that can be brought to bear by the political or commercial agenda of the reporter's own news organization; by the public relations industry that serves governments, corporations, and other organizations; and by the motivations of the actors in the story who supply information and commentary, often for their own purposes. Moreover, mainstream news organizations are not at all independent from either corporate Canada or political Canada, but have instead become closely intertwined with these institutions of power. A principal raison d'être of the alternative news providers that have emerged in recent years is precisely to reassert journalistic independence from political and economic power.

Perhaps the most contentious ideal of journalism is *objectivity*. It has become commonplace to assert that there is no such thing as objectivity. This is, however, too simplistic, given that we have some expectation of objectivity not only from journalism but from other institutions as well: the legal system, the research community, the medical system. Too often, objectivity is thought of as an absolute; in other words, a claim is treated

10.5 Freedom of the Press

Constitutional guarantees and universal declarations are important, but they define freedom of the press in largely abstract terms. The real, concrete meaning of freedom of the press is derived from its daily exercise by those journalists who push at the boundaries of what can be screened, aired, and published.

Journalists exercise freedom of the press when they report what is truly new and important to the public interest; when they broaden the range of debate; when they expand the horizons of what can be reported, imagined, revealed, and criticized. Journalists also exercise freedom of the press when they hold their own news organizations to the standards and ideals of their journalistic calling, especially when a news organization may have to pay a political or economic price for its reportage.

Freedom of the press would be meaningless as a human right if journalists never exposed scandal; if they never revealed information that government officials preferred not to divulge; if they never quoted critics of powerful people and powerful institutions; if they never drew attention to hypocrisy, greed, or arrogance—if, in other words, they never gave anyone cause to restrict press freedoms.

The right to freedom of the press is exerted not only in exceptional, headline-grabbing cases—for example, the Somalia Affair (see Amad, 2018), the Federal Sponsorship Scandal (CBC News, 2006), the spying activities of the Communications Security Establishment of Canada, or the National Security Agency in the United States (see Greenwald, 2014)—but also on a daily basis, in countless small ways. Journalists are giving meaning to freedom of the press every time they reveal more than their sources are willing to share with the public, every time they undermine the propaganda disseminated by corporate and political communication officers, every time they introduce factual evidence to accompany the opinions of decision-makers.

as either 100 per cent objective, or not objective at all. But if freedom were defined this way—as absolute freedom—we would say that there is no such thing as freedom either. Both terms are best understood as relative; by objectivity, that is, we are really talking about *relative objectivity*.

Objectivity remains one of journalism's core values, at least within mainstream journalism. Journalists are supposed to report objectively, which means separating clearly the reporting of verifiable facts from the assertion of values and opinions. In a conventional news report, facts are typically declared in the reporter's voice and values are attributed to others, whether as direct quotations or as paraphrased statements. The convention in newspapers is to distinguish physically news reports from commentaries—columns, editorials, letters to the editor, op-ed submissions—by placing them on clearly identified pages or in separate sections. News providers operating on other platforms usually apply similarly transparent measures to distinguish for their audiences facts and values.

Separating facts from values or opinions is much easier said than done, of course. For one thing, as noted above, journalism involves selection, which immediately brings into play a number of subjective judgments: *What is news? Why is it newsworthy? What angle to the story should be pursued? Who should be interviewed? What does this news event mean to the public?* Second, the language choices used to describe news events unavoidably attribute meaning to those events. And finally, news, by definition, is what is perceived by journalists to be important or significant to the public interest; that is the first meaning given to any story, and it is further amplified by the amount and the type of coverage the story is granted.

Rather than reject objectivity altogether, there are more nuanced ways to think about it. We summarize two approaches: the *critical realism* of communication scholars Robert A. Hackett and Yuezhi Zhao and the *pragmatic objectivity* of the ethicist and former journalist Stephen J.A. Ward.

Hackett and Zhao reject the *positivist* model of objectivity, which perceives truth as the relatively simple product of direct observation and accurate recording. The positivist model asserts that all that stands between reality and journalistic accounts of that reality is good reporting practice, an assertion that fails to account adequately for the mediating presence of the journalist, the language she employs, and the socialization she has undergone (1998: 109–66). Hackett and Zhao, however, also reject the postmodern position, which dismisses objectivity as unattainable because the real world cannot be perceived directly without the mediation of conventional concepts, theories, ideologies, and values, without the mediation of language (in all forms), and, often, without the mediation of people describing the world on our behalf.

Instead, their critical realist approach acknowledges the limitations of both positivism and postmodernism but nonetheless insists that the real world is accessible, knowable, and describable. Coming to know the truth about the world, they maintain, is a never-ending process, with knowledge constantly produced and revised, subject to the mediation of our categories, concepts, values, and conventions, and emerging only as a result of "the interactive or dialectical to and fro between subject and object, concepts and reality" (129). In other words, if knowledge about the real world cannot be taken at face value through direct observation, and if knowledge production is always subject to various layers of mediation, knowledge and truth can nonetheless emerge through careful and reflexive investigation. "The world is knowable—but not at first sight" (130).

Ward, too, rejects what he calls "traditional objectivity" because it operates from dualisms of fact/value and truth/interpretation, which "distort our understanding of how we know, interpret and value" (Ward, 2004: 261). His redefinition of objectivity as *pragmatic objectivity* is a reflective and practical approach with an emphasis on process.

Ward insists, first of all, that the pursuit of truth is always a work in progress, producing "tentative results" subject to revision. He notes, secondly, that all forms of inquiry—whether in journalism or in other truth-seeking endeavours—are based on interpretation. The inquirer is never passive, but "an active, purpose-driven agent in a social setting" (264–5). Finally, these acts of interpretation are "holistic" in the sense that they are based on larger systems of knowledge or conceptual schemes. When, for example, the sun appears red at sunset, we understand that it hasn't changed colour during the day, but that its light is being refracted through Earth's atmosphere (272). Acts of interpretation are also "ubiquitous" in that we are constantly interpreting "because we have no direct, cognitive contact with reality." Ward concludes: "We judge an interpretation to be objective if it has good support, according to the best available standards of a conceptual system" (280).

Some journalists prefer to substitute the values of balance and fairness as a means of dodging the objectivity question, but these substitutes are highly flawed. Balance typically means presenting both sides of the story. This makes a number of presumptions that cannot be sustained. For one thing, there are many more than two sides to a story, and limiting the presentation to two often means choosing the most polarized positions, leaving aside more moderate views, and rendering the two polarized positions irreconcilable (see Lynch and McGoldrick, 2005). For another, the concept of balance can imply that the two views presented in a story are equally valid. News coverage of climate change, for example, often creates the impression that there is a serious debate about human causes of climate change by giving voice to both scientists and those who dispute their claims, granting comparable weight to both sides' positions. By refusing to discriminate among opinions, journalists do not bring us closer to the truth.

Similarly, fairness is a poor substitute for objectivity. Fairness is most often exercised in journalism by providing those with an opinion a fair hearing. Such opinions, however, may not be

Patrick T. Fallon/Bloomberg via Getty Images.

Journalists serve as a fourth estate when they report on government affairs and question politicians on behalf of citizens.

fair to the truth, as in the climate change example above. Both balance and fairness render journalists mere stenographers, absolving them of their responsibility for verification or discrimination between viewpoints.

Journalism as a Textual Practice

News stories are told through the medium of language, employing a range of symbolic systems: written or spoken words, images, sounds, symbols, gestures. News stories are texts; rather than faithful reproductions of the world, they are highly constructed representations or depictions of the world through language. Cultural theorist Stuart Hall (2013: 2) defines **representation** as "the production of meaning through language." In other words, journalists *represent* the objects of their reportage. To represent is to make present, or depict, or symbolize, through language(s): in this case, through news photos, audio clips, television reports, newspaper articles, multimedia packages, and so on. In so doing, journalists unavoidably give those objects meaning.

At the simplest level, deciding to cover an event as news in the first place defines it as important, significant, relevant, or interesting. A second level of meaning pertains to precisely how the story is covered. How should the story be framed? Why is it newsworthy? Is it good news or bad news, positive or negative, a natural disaster or a human-made tragedy? Is it a business story, a consumer affairs story, or a labour story? Is it worth prominent and extensive treatment or is it simply a news brief? Finally, what words are chosen to label the event? What images are selected to depict the event and its principal actors? Whose voices are heard? As Dahlgren notes, "Language use is . . . always already implicated in social horizons, pre-understandings, and power relations; ideologically charged discourses can shape the meanings of reported events, intentionally or not" (2013: 166–7).

If language is the medium through which meaning is produced, how does the process work?

The Swiss linguist Ferdinand de Saussure demonstrated that language works to produce meaning in the relationship between a **signifier**—an utterance of language (e.g., a word, an image, a symbol, a gesture, a sound)—and a **signified**—the image in our heads that is created when we see or hear a specific language utterance. While we normally do this unthinkingly, this is precisely the process we engage in when we acquire language skills as an infant, and what we might do if we later decide to acquire a second or third language. To cite a simple example, when we hear or see the word *tree* (the signifier), we picture in our minds a woody, leafy plant (the signified), even if we may not know which specific tree is being referred to. The signifiers *arbre*, *Baum*, or *coeden*, on the other hand, mean nothing to us unless we understand French, German, or Welsh.

If this seems obvious, the process quickly becomes more complicated—even contentious—when we read or hear everyday words like *family* or *marriage*. What exactly do these words mean? For some of us, *family* denotes a nuclear family; for others, an extended family. We might exclude from that association other kinds of family: same-sex parents with an adopted child, unmarried parents with children, and so on. When journalists use the word *family*, then, what exactly do they mean? Similarly, what do we think of when we see the word *marriage*? What kinds of couplings does this include and exclude? Can two people of the same sex be married? Can two people who have been living together for years without having any kind of official wedding ceremony or marriage licence be considered married? The very definition of marriage is frequently the subject of news stories. In Quebec news reports, the term *Québécois* can have an inclusive meaning (all residents of Quebec) or an exclusive meaning (French-Canadian residents of Quebec). The distinction is significant, particularly during discussions about Quebec sovereignty and nationhood. Even simple signifiers like *we* and *us* can have particular meanings when news reports pertain to, for example, immigration or multiculturalism. Journalists' use of these terms can promote particular understandings depending on the larger context of the news story in question, thus privileging certain definitions.

Journalists typically begin with the signified—the event, person, or institution they seek to describe—and need to assign signifiers to the object of their coverage. They choose language to label and describe what they are covering, and those labels have meaning. Think about the ways in which journalists describe demonstrators at a protest, for example. Are they portrayed as engaged citizens exercising their democratic rights, or as rabble-rousers and troublemakers? Which demonstrators are chosen to illustrate the event in news videos: the peaceful, conservatively dressed marchers, or violent protestors breaking plate-glass windows and confronting police? The same demonstrators, and the same demonstration, can be made to mean, through news stories and images, a range of things.

While some journalists may make these choices deliberately, these meanings more often are produced unconsciously by journalists who are simply following news conventions (e.g., the violent demonstrator makes a more compelling photo than the peaceful marcher) or by subscribing to what they perceive to be their audience's common-sense viewpoint (e.g., a labour–management dispute as a disruptive inconvenience to the public). Regardless of whether we can establish intent, subjectivity and conventional notions of news reporting once again come into play.

The point here is that journalists are implicated in this process of *meaning production* in three specific ways:

- Journalists decide what is news.
- Journalists attach relative importance to news events.
- Journalists interpret those events through their language choices.

This production of meaning is significant because, as communication scholar Tony Bennett (1996: 296) observes, "The power which the media derive from their reality-defining capability is attributable to the service they perform in making us the indirect witnesses to events of which we have no first-hand knowledge or experience."

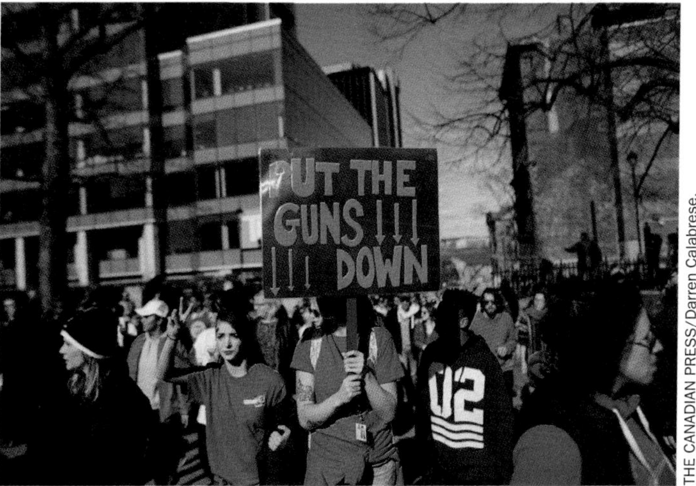

THE CANADIAN PRESS/Darren Calabrese.

A news photograph of a demonstration captures only a fragment of the entire event at a precise moment in time, but it nonetheless becomes the picture of that event for the news consumer. Think about the type of demonstrator shown in this news photograph, how the people are depicted, and how this image shapes our understanding of the larger event.

Journalism as a Sociocultural Institution

Journalism is a sociocultural institution in the sense that it both informs and is informed by the society and culture in which it is practised. As a social institution journalism is integrated politically because, in a democratic society such as Canada, it assumes the role of serving democracy through its fact-finding mission. Journalism is integrated economically because it is an industry in and of itself, and the news media are a key advertising vehicle.

Journalism is cultural because journalists produce texts that describe the communities in which we live, privilege certain community values and behaviours, define issues of central importance, and situate our community within the larger world. News reportage identifies society's central institutions of power and its most influential players.

Through the media we are presented with a picture of our community, its members, and their central preoccupations. The media also offer value judgments about right and wrong, legitimate and illegitimate, whether concerning how we behave, what we wear, how we drive, what we eat and drink, or what beliefs we hold. Similarly, news coverage draws boundaries around *here* and *there*, and determines what is considered important and relevant to a particular community of people (see Gasher, 2015). In this way, journalism makes distinctions between community insiders and community outsiders, establishing a sense of *us* and *them*. As communication scholar John Hartley (1992: 207) has argued, the news "includes stories on a daily basis which enable everyone to recognize a larger unity or community than their own immediate contacts, and to identify with the news outlet as 'our' storyteller." The boundaries between those defined as us and them are not coterminous with any formal political boundaries but can be drawn from any number of bases: for example, gender, race, class, religion, birthplace, or ethnicity. The role of ethnic or ethnocultural media is important in this regard (see Box 10.6).

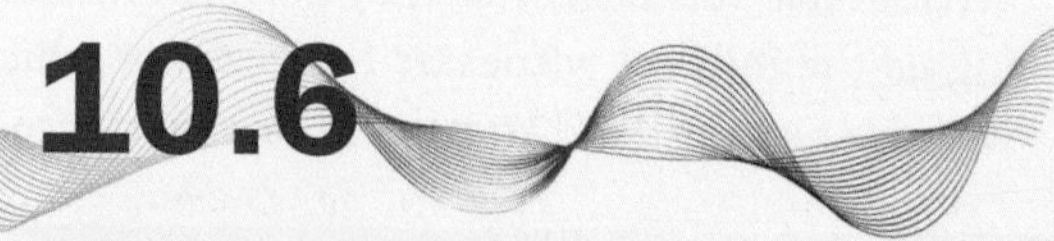

Ethnocultural Media

By April Lindgren

Ethnocultural or ethnic media are news media produced by and for immigrant groups and linguistic, cultural, and racialized (visible) minorities. At their best, when they adhere to journalistic standards and generate news that is timely, accurate, transparently reported, and independently produced, they perform important functions in their communities. They provide a counter-narrative to stereotypes in mainstream news media, tell stories that create a sense of community and fuel civic engagement, contribute to the preservation of cultures and languages, help newcomers understand their adopted society, and keep immigrants informed about what is happening in their country of origin.

There is no comprehensive listing of ethnic media in Canada (Yu, 2016). A directory run by the Canadian Ethnic Media Association, however, lists just over 1,300 ethnic news operations, including 537 radio stations, 437 publications, 232 television stations, and 106 online operations. These news sources are increasingly sought out by politicians and governments who want to get their messages out to Canada's diverse population in languages other than English or French.

The 2016 Statistics Canada census reported that 41 of the country's 338 federal ridings have populations where visible minorities—in most cases immigrants—actually form the majority. In more than 90 other electoral districts, visible minorities make up 20 to 50 per cent of the population (Griffith, 2017). Political parties now regularly have ethnic media strategies in place and, particularly during election campaigns, their leaders make a point of doing interviews with journalists from key ethnic news outlets (Lindgren, 2014; Yu, 2016). At the local level, municipal governments have also turned to ethnic media in a bid to keep their diverse citizenry more informed (Lindgren, 2015).

April Lindgren is a professor and the Velma Rogers Research Chair in the School of Journalism at Ryerson University.

Providing a picture of our community is a complex task for journalists. There is always a gap between community life as we experience it and the constructed reality the news media provide us—that is, between the material world and the news world. Nonetheless, in mass societies such as Canada, where most of us live in large and diverse metropolitan areas, journalism remains a key component of what the political theorist Jürgen Habermas (1996: 55) termed the **public sphere**:

> By "public sphere" we mean first of all a domain of our social life in which such a thing as public opinion can be formed. Access to the public sphere is open in principle to all citizens. A portion of the public sphere is constituted in every conversation in which private persons come together to form a public. . . . Citizens act as a public when they deal with matters of general interest without being subject to coercion; thus with the guarantee that they may assemble and unite freely, and express and publicize their opinions freely. When the public is large, this kind of communication requires certain means of dissemination and influence; today, newspapers and periodicals, radio and television are the media of the public sphere.

Habermas traces the emergence of an idealized public sphere to the eighteenth century, a period in the development of democracy when private persons gathered as peers in salons, cafés, and pubs to consider and discuss the issues of the day and come to some determination about them—that is, to form public opinion. This public sphere provided a forum for private citizens without formal political power to come together and influence political authority through rational argument. The newspapers of the day became "the vehicles and guides of public opinion" (58). Habermas regrets that the public sphere in contemporary society no longer operates on the basis of rational argument among private citizens coming together as equals, but has become instead "a field for competition among interests in the cruder form of forcible confrontation" (59). If the media provide some space for citizens to speak—increasingly so in the digital era—the focus of news coverage is almost exclusively on what are termed *opinion leaders*: politicians, business people, administrators, pollsters, public relations spokespeople, researchers, intellectuals, and other assorted experts and officials. These people are not speaking for themselves or impartially, but often on behalf of society's most powerful vested interests. This, again, explains the potential significance of alternative journalism forms, such as blogs and citizen journalism sites, that seek to restore citizens' voices and perspectives to the mediascape.

The news media's role in the public sphere is significant, given the extent to which we depend on the media for knowledge about our world. When, as citizens, we consider current events like the civil wars in Syria or Yemen, immigration, gun violence, or climate change, we typically rely on the news media for our knowledge of these issues, and it is through the media that responses to these issues are proposed to us by opinion leaders.

The media serve, too, as **socializing institutions** for all kinds of public attitudes about race, ethnicity, immigration, gender roles, the aged, youth culture, and so on, not only in news reports, of course, but also in advertisements, films, music videos, and television programs. It is through media representations that we are offered pictures of our society, and it is where we "meet" the fellow community members and community leaders with whom we have no actual personal contact.

Roger Silverstone sees the media as constituting an environment, and emphasizes "the significance of the media for our orientation in the world. . . . The media are both context and contextualized. They both construct a world, and are constructed by that world" (Silverstone, 2007: 6). What he calls the "mediapolis" is a significant moral space where we confront, and make judgments about, others: "There is in all of these frameworks a narrative of us and them, of origins and futures, of boundaries and the articulation of difference, without which our culture, indeed any culture, could not survive" (62).

For these reasons, journalists can be seen as social actors heavily implicated in the process of representation. Unfortunately, precise data on the makeup of Canada's corps of journalists are difficult to come by, and the task of gathering this information has become ever more complicated as the mainstream media reduce the size of their newsrooms, and as a vast array of alternative news organizations emerge. Nonetheless, there remains widespread concern that journalism continues to be an exclusive occupation and that the newsrooms responsible for producing the bulk of our original reporting fall far short of reflecting the gendered, racial, or ethnic makeup of the Canadian population (see Paradkar, 2016; Hemmadi, 2017; Ramanujam, 2016; Dhillon, 2018; Zoledziowski, 2019). With respect to women in journalism specifically, we have more information. A 2017 survey determined that 42 per cent of national newspaper columnists were women and that women represented 37 per cent of columnists in regional papers. The 2015 Global Media Monitoring Project, which studied 23 Canadian news organizations, found that 43 per cent of reporters were women (El Azrak, 2018).

In the state-regulated broadcasting sphere, inclusivity is a prominent theme of the *Broadcasting Act* (1991). Section 3(d)(iii) of the Act declares that the Canadian broadcasting system should

> through its programming and the employment opportunities arising out of its operations, serve the needs and interests, and reflect the circumstances and aspirations, of Canadian men, women and children, including equal rights, the linguistic duality and multicultural and multiracial nature of Canadian society and the special place of aboriginal peoples within that society. (Canada, 1991)

Inclusivity is an important issue in a period of globalization and in a country as diverse as Canada. Clearly, who reports the news has implications for what gets covered, how, and to whom news reports are addressed (see Nielsen, 2009; Nielsen et al., 2016).

As we noted earlier, there is considerable room for interpretation in news coverage. Therefore, the life experiences of journalists —their assumptions, their biases, their prejudices, their values—affect their reportage. In a report to the Canadian Race Relations Foundation, researchers Frances Henry and Carol Tator (2000: 169) concluded that journalists' "own sense of social location, experiences, values and world views, as well as the interests and positionality of publishers and newspaper owners, act as an invisible filter to screen out alternative viewpoints and perspectives." A relatively young reporting staff, for example, may be less aware of, and less sensitive to, issues that pertain to an aging Canadian population, such as the future of the Canada Pension Plan or the costs of prescription drugs. A predominantly male newsroom may be less receptive to issues of particular relevance to women, such as child care, reproductive rights, and sexism, and may be prone to patriarchal views of certain issues that especially involve women, such as sexual assault, spousal abuse, and pay equity (see Goodyear-Grant, 2013; Kimmel and Holler, 2011; Gidengil and Everitt, 2011; Poindexter et al., 2008).

This is what journalism educator John Miller (1998: 137) means when he argues that a lack of diversity among journalists results in "blind spots" in news coverage.

The point is not to turn the news media into organs of advocacy for the disenfranchised. Instead, Kovach and Rosenstiel (2001: 108) explain, "The ultimate goal of newsroom diversity is to create an intellectually mixed environment where everyone holds firm to the idea of journalistic independence. Together their various experiences blend to create a reporting richer than what they would create alone. And in the end that leads to a richer, fuller view of the world for the public."

Legal Parameters Governing Journalism

Freedom of the press is one of the most fundamental rights of a democratic society, and journalism in Canada is practised in a free-press environment. Section 2 of the 1982 *Canadian Charter of Rights and Freedoms* protects both freedom of expression and freedom of the press under the heading "Fundamental Freedoms":

2. Everyone has the following fundamental freedoms:
   (a) freedom of conscience and religion;
   (b) freedom of thought, belief, opinion and expression, including freedom of the press and other media of communication;
   (c) freedom of peaceful assembly; and
   (d) freedom of association.

The Canadian constitution is careful to extend the historical right of freedom of the press to all other media. As the journalism educator and former journalist Dean Jobb points out, "Books, plays, television documentaries, websites, videos, DVDS, Internet chat groups, online magazines, social-networking sites, new forms of media technology yet to be invented—whatever the medium, Canadians are free to publish and disseminate images and ideas" (Jobb, 2011: 59), subject only to the "reasonable limits" of "a free and democratic society," as section 1 of the *Charter* notes.

This does not mean, however, that journalists are free to report whatever they want. Press freedom in Canada is constrained by laws that ensure that journalists' freedoms do not compromise the security of the state or the freedoms of other Canadian citizens.

If freedom of the press is a core right of all modern democratic states, it is not interpreted the same way by all democracies, compelling journalists to work within both national and international legal and policy frameworks. At the international level, Article 19 of the International Covenant on Civil and Political Rights (United Nations, 1966) provides the ethical foundation. It states,

1. Everyone shall have the right to hold opinions without interference.
2. Everyone shall have the right to freedom of expression; this right shall include freedom to seek, receive and impart information and ideas of all kinds, regardless of frontiers, either orally, in writing or in print, in the form of art, or through any other media of his/her choice.
3. The exercise of the rights provided for in paragraph 2 of this article carries with it special duties and responsibilities. It may therefore be subject to certain restrictions, but these shall only be such as are provided by law and are necessary:
   (a) For respect of the rights or reputation of others;
   (b) For the protection of national security or of public order (ordre public), or of public health or morals.

Article 12 of the Universal Declaration on Human Rights (United Nations, 1948) also addresses infringement of privacy and attacks on honour and reputation: "Everyone has the right to the protection of the law against such interference or attacks." These two rights, free speech and the right to privacy, always exist in tension with each other. Journalists may have rights, but they also have legal obligations and ethical responsibilities.

In addition to the codes of ethics and regulatory bodies that guide Canadian journalists in providing fair and accurate reporting (see McCarten, 2013; Ward, 2014), particular Canadian laws aid or constrain the news production process. These statutes are designed to protect the public interest and cover areas like access to information, defamation, privacy, and contempt of court.

Access-to-information laws, for example, have recently been enacted in North America as a way of extending the right to freedom of information. Canada's federal government and all the provincial and territorial governments have access-to-information legislation, which outlines what kinds of government information are subject to scrutiny and how journalists and ordinary citizens can obtain access (see Jobb, 2011: 191–5).

While freedom-of-expression laws define the positive foundation of journalism, restraint laws define the negative constraints within which journalists must operate. For example, **defamation** (more commonly known as *libel*) is the publication or broadcast of a statement that is both false and damaging to a person's or organization's reputation (Jobb, 2011: 91). This includes the posting of material online. Jobb writes, "Defamation . . . is a form of tort law that gives everyone the right to protect their good name from being sullied by the unjustified allegations or criticisms of others" (90). Truth and fair comment are defences against an accusation of defamation (109–15).

Among the greatest legal restraints faced by Canadian journalists concerns coverage of criminal and civil court cases. The large and complex category of **contempt of court** ensures the integrity of the court system and brings into play the constitutional right of the accused to a fair trial. Among the most common restrictions imposed on journalists are publication bans, which prohibit the identification of victims of sex-related crimes or of witnesses to those crimes who are under the age of 18 (Jobb, 2011: 281) and which shield the identity of youth offenders and any victims or witnesses under the age of 18 (299–301). The Canadian government clarified the legal question of journalists' protection of confidential sources by passing the *Journalistic Sources Protection Act* in 2018. The law broadened the definitions of "journalist" and "journalistic source," putting the onus on the party seeking to reveal the identity of sources to demonstrate that the sources' information cannot be secured by any other means, and that the public interest in the administration of justice outweighs the public interest in protecting the sources' identity (see Sumar, 2018; Safayeni and Gonsalves, 2018). In Canada, then, freedom of the press is defined in the context of existing laws and judicial interpretations of constitutional guarantees informed by legal precedents.

Economics of News Production

As we discussed in Chapter 9, the economics of media production have changed dramatically in the era of convergence. We are in a period when news organizations are searching for new economic models because the old ones—based on some combination of paid subscription, paid advertising, and/or government funding—appear to be collapsing beneath them. It is far too premature to declare the death of the news industry, or even the newspaper industry, but significant changes clearly are in store (see Edge, 2014).

While it is tempting to blame digital media for the economic challenges legacy news organizations face, a growing number of scholars insist that the problems of the news industry began in the 1970s—two decades before the advent of the World Wide Web—as news organizations became part of concentrated corporations (see Compton, 2010; McChesney and Nichols, 2009; Cooper, 2011; and Edge, 2014). Mark Cooper states bluntly, "Quality journalism was undermined by the commercial corporate business model that sought to squeeze high rates of profit out of highly concentrated markets by pressuring variable costs—reporters—to produce more with less. As the quality of the product declined, so too did the value of the business" (2011: 320). Between 1970 and 2000, Cooper found, news organizations' net advertising revenues grew, but these monies were not reinvested in journalism (329–30). James Compton argues that the corporatization of the news industry in Canada since the 1970s not only has resulted in intensified competition for mobile capital investment and increasing sensitivity to stockholders, but it also imposes flexibility on news workers (2010: 592). This translates into pressures to further commercialize by shaping content to target the most attractive audience markets, compelling journalists to supply content to several media platforms, while at the same time reducing costs, whether that means paying down accumulated debt or reducing payroll, including the number of reporters and editors in newsrooms.

Exacerbating this decades-old trend, the networked environment in which journalism functions today creates more competition for audiences and revenues, whether those revenues come from advertising or subscription. On the one hand, it is a multimedia form of competition for audiences in which news providers, regardless of platform, compete with one another. On the other hand, this multimedia competition largely erases the physical boundaries of conventional news markets; while there remains a strong appetite for local or regional news coverage, local media now compete with brand-name national and international players in the general news category, as well as with specialty media in areas such as business and sports, as content is gradually "unbundled" from the omnibus news packages of the legacy media (see Anderson et al., 2012: 8).

The competition for advertising is similarly double-edged. News organizations in the same market continue to compete for advertising, but what is new is that an increasing amount of advertising is moving to digital platforms. This has had a negative impact on the news industry because digital advertising revenues do not come close to replacing advertising revenues on legacy platforms, and a significant portion of digital advertising goes to sites that do not produce original reporting. In 2016, for example, three-quarters of the $5.5 billion spent on digital advertising by Canadian companies went to Google and Facebook. Daily newspaper advertising fell to $1.3 billion from $2.7 billion just a decade earlier (Jackson, 2018b).

The economic uncertainty of today's news industry has a profound impact on both the working conditions and the resources available to journalists, whether they work for commercial news organizations or online start-ups; whether they are permanent employees, contract workers, or freelancers; or whether they are entering the job market straight out of school. Journalism is first and foremost a product of human labour. A story idea, the research behind it, the interviews that inform it, and the final presentation of the news item itself all require skilled labour. As Anderson et al. describe it,

> Getting key bits of descriptive information out of eyewitnesses, aggressively challenging the verbal responses of a seasoned government bureaucrat, knowing exactly where to find a key document, or navigating the routines and idiosyncrasies of complex modern organizations is a non-trivial intellectual endeavor, and a public good to boot (2012: 23).

When Canadian newsrooms downsize, there is a qualitative impact on the journalism those newsrooms produce. The reporters who remain are squeezed to produce more content and to provide updates to online and mobile platforms and promotional feeds to social media networks. Such pressures result in fewer opportunities for enterprise reporting; more single-source reports; more stories based primarily on news releases, news conferences, and official announcements; stories that are inadequately researched or fact-checked; and more stories produced by journalists who have little experience or knowledge of the topics they cover. As news organizations downsize their newsrooms, more journalists work on short-term contracts or try to survive on freelance rates that have not increased since the 1980s (see Coxon, 2018; Cohen, 2012).

Among these pressures, journalists are being asked to play a more active role in building audiences to sell to advertisers. The notion of journalistic independence used to mean, in part, maintaining a clear separation between the editorial and the business sides of news organizations, particularly at newspapers. This so-called wall was never completely impenetrable; the travel and automotive sections of newspapers have more to do with selling ads than with journalism, and newspapers have often featured **advertorials**, or promotional material thinly disguised as a news story (usually with a different typeface and identified by the advertorial label). But the wall between the advertising and editorial departments is crumbling further.

Even the most reputable newspapers now allow advertisements on their front pages, and editors are often asked to team up with salespeople in planning distinct content sections around special events: major sporting events, cultural festivals, trade shows, and so on. The latest steps in this direction are called **brand journalism** and **native advertising**, in which journalists are being recruited to produce content that becomes a deliberate hybrid between journalism and promotion (see Box 10.7).

The Future of Journalism

No one can tell us exactly what journalism as a practice or as an institution will look like 10 years from now. Will legacy news organizations evolve and survive? If so, which ones? Will newspapers continue to print and deliver hard copies, or will more of them close up their printing plants and go completely digital? Will digital start-ups assume a more significant share of the original reporting that is the foundation of journalism? Which of those start-ups will establish a viable business model and be able to pay journalists fairly for their work? Will we see increasing topic specialization and the continued treatment of audiences as markets?

All of these unanswered questions mean it is an exciting time to be studying media because we can watch these developments as they take place, possibly even participate in them. But we have to temper our wishful thinking—for a digital revolution, a new golden age of journalism, or at least a corporate media comeuppance—with careful analysis of what is going on. Journalism is restructuring, creating new conditions for the production of news. What will those new conditions be?

10.7

The Marriage between Journalism and Marketing

Two recent trends are bringing journalism and marketing together. Brand journalism consists of stories produced by journalists and paid for by companies or associations seeking to draw attention to their sphere of activity, if not directly to specific products or services. Typically, they are published in a magazine or posted to a website owned by the brand sponsor. Examples include articles about automobile travel and maintenance in *CAA Magazine*, articles about food and drink in the appropriately named *Food and Drink*, a glossy produced by the Liquor Control Board of Ontario, and blog posts and DIY videos posted on the Home Depot website (Basen, 2012; Ostrikoff, 2013). Journalist Ira Basen writes, "Brand journalism is storytelling meant to draw readers to a company's field of expertise, without laying on the hard sell. . . . The stories may be fairly and accurately reported by respected journalists . . . but the fundamental aim remains marketing" (2012: F1).

Native advertising is a form of sponsored content published in newspapers and magazines, similar to what used to be called advertorials. They are articles constructed as news stories with the difference that they carry a label identifying them as sponsored content and are typically set in a different typeface than the neighbouring news stories. Native advertising generates revenue for the news organization and allows advertisers to better integrate their messages by avoiding the "ad ghetto" (Basen, 2012). "The essence of native advertising is that content that originates from a brand should be given the same prominence on the page or the screen as editorial content." A number of newspapers and magazines respected for their journalism have entered the native advertising market: *The New York Times*, *The Washington Post*, *The Economist*, and *The Globe and Mail*. The *Globe* launched its native advertising initiative in April 2014; the content is produced by freelancers under the direction of the advertising department, and the resultant articles carry "sponsored content" labels and are set against a yellow background to distinguish them from news stories (Baluja, 2014).

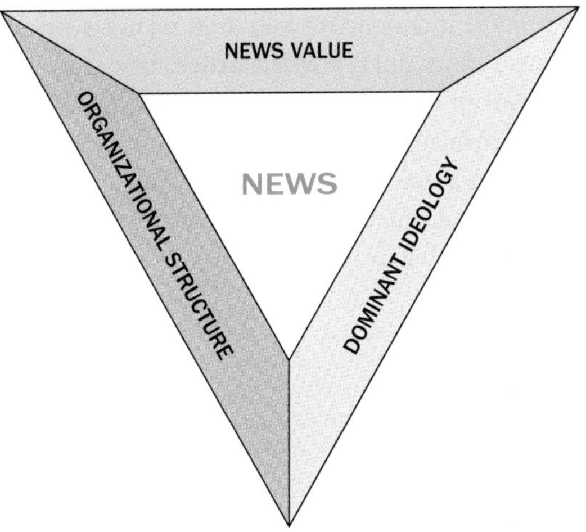

FIGURE 10.2 Defining the news

News can be seen as a product of the complex tension among the factors that inform news value; the economic, time, and space constraints of organizational structure; and the beliefs that make up the dominant ideology in society.

Alternatives to mainstream journalism have existed since at least the 1960s: campus radio stations and newspapers, non-profit community radio, community-access television, documentary film cooperatives, "underground" or alternative weekly newspapers (see Skinner, 2010: 225–31). These media tell different stories and adopt distinct storytelling styles. But there has been a veritable explosion of news providers and distributors since the mid-1990s. They initially capitalized on the accessibility and distributive powers of the internet, and more recently have taken advantage of increasingly ubiquitous hand-held communication devices, resulting in what Natalie Fenton (2010) calls "the expansion of the locus of news production." This new media ecology includes social-networking sites as both research resources (e.g., Twitter, Facebook, WikiLeaks) and circulation sites (e.g., Twitter, Facebook, YouTube). Although the bulk of the hard work, and most of the best journalism, still is produced by mainstream news organizations, it seems clear that the future of journalism will be digital and will include many more "born-digital" news providers.

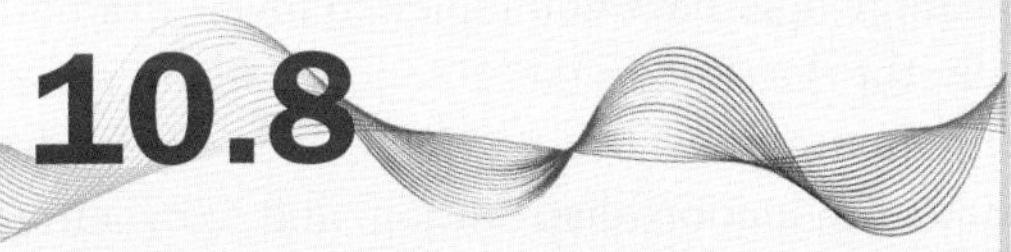

Journalism without Journalists?

The newsrooms of Canadian news organizations have been hard hit by economic uncertainty in the media industries. The Canadian Media Guild, a trade union representing 6,000 media workers, has estimated that 10,000 Canadian media jobs were lost between 2008 and 2013 through a combination of layoffs and buyouts (Wong, 2013). And the job reductions continue. Bell Media laid off 50 people in November 2017, and Rogers Media cut 75 jobs in June 2018, representing one-third of its digital content and publishing staff (Doherty, 2017; Jackson, 2018a). Along with the closure of six local newspapers in Alberta and Ontario, publishing company Postmedia announced in June 2018 that it was cutting staff costs by a further 10 per cent, the second round of buyouts and layoffs since 2016, when it sought to cut its cross-company salary outlay by 20 per cent (Canadian Press, 2018). A total of 290 newspaper jobs were lost in 2017— 244 at Postmedia and 46 at Torstar—when the two companies swapped 41 newspapers and closed most of them (Watson, 2017).

Some of these losses have been offset by the emergence of digital start-ups like the *National Observer* and *The Athletic*, but given the labour-intensive nature of news reporting, the trend is cause for concern, especially in those rural areas of Canada that have become news deserts (see Hodson and Malik, 2018; Lindgren, 2018).

The traditional news media were among the first to jump on the internet bandwagon in the mid-1990s, and they continue to evolve their online presence and attract significant audiences, even if they have been slow to invest resources in their digital operations (see Box 10.9). But the ease of use and affordability of digital technology, the accessibility of the internet, and the increasing media production skills of more and more people have combined to lower dramatically the barriers to entry to journalism, spawning thousands of new participants in the fields of news production, distribution, and commentary. Some, like *The Tyee* (thetyee.ca), *Rabble* (rabble.ca), *The Dominion* (www.dominionpaper.ca), and *The Real News Network* (therealnews.com), seek to provide independent and original news reporting and commentary. Many other sites aggregate news from other providers (e.g., nationalnewswatch.com, o.canada.com, salutbonjour.ca) or house the personal blogs of professional and amateur commentators on every topic under the sun (e.g., www.blogscanada.ca).

10.9

Podcasting

By Andrea Hunter

The term podcasting is largely attributed to journalist Ben Hammersley, who used it in a 2004 article for *The Guardian* when he was trying to find a word to describe online radio that could be downloaded (Hammersely, 2004). The word stuck, and today podcasting is a broad term used to describe any type of audio program that is available in digital form and can be downloaded onto a personal listening device.

It is no exaggeration to say that podcasting has taken off in recent years. While at the turn of the millennium many were worried that interest in radio was on the decline, podcasting has reinvigorated interest in audio programs. A recent market survey found that more than 10 million adult Canadians (about 36 per cent of the population) have listened to a podcast in the past year. Most people who listen to podcasts are in the youngest age demographic, between the ages of 18 and 34. The most popular type of podcast is comedy, but also high on the list are podcasts about society and culture, as well as news and politics (Audience Insights and Ulster media, 2018).

The fact that podcasts are mobile—you can listen to them anytime, anywhere—has a great deal to do with their popularity, but the podcast format has also given more people the chance to experiment with audio and has democratized the medium somewhat. There are many different types of podcasts, including those made by amateurs at home and those created by professional journalists and performers. Where once only professionals, such as journalists and those in charge of recording studios, had access to the necessary technology, now anyone with simple recording devices and software can produce professional-quality podcasts at home, which they can then upload and distribute via the internet.

Established radio programs that have been running for decades in Canada, such as *The Current* and *As It Happens* on CBC Radio, now package their programs for digital download and call them podcasts. These podcasts contain much of the same content as their regular radio programming. But podcasting has also sparked people's imaginations and creativity, and there are now many news and current affairs podcasts that deal with material that does not make it into a regular broadcast. For instance, Shauna Hunt, currently a Toronto-based City TV journalist, has created a podcast called *The Legal Potcast*. As the play on words suggests, this podcast deals with the legalization of marijuana in Canada. While the legalization of marijuana has been covered regularly in the news, the podcast gives room to cover stories in a more in-depth way and is described as "a look into the backrooms of Canada's newest industry" (Collie, 2018).

Podcasting also allows journalists to experiment with new ways of storytelling. Perhaps the most famous example is the widely popular podcast *Serial*, created by National Public Radio in the United States, which looks into a murder case in Baltimore in 1999. The case is reinvestigated over a series of twelve episodes, drawing the listener in with what has been described as "show-your-work journalism" (Levin, 2014). The listener is taken through the whole process of investigative journalism, including hearing the producers trying and failing to get interviews with key players in the story and weighing the validity of the evidence that is being collected. This is material that normally stays behind the scenes in journalism, but *Serial* lays it all out on the table, bringing the listener along on the journey.

Andrea Hunter is an associate professor in the Department of Journalism at Concordia University in Montreal.

Clearly, some trends appear to have staying power. Anderson et al. (2012) outline what they call the new "post-industrial journalism" as consisting of the **unbundling** or specialization of content (what they call "expert journalism"); increased forging of partnerships with other information providers (e.g., WikiLeaks, foundations, university research centres); increased use of publicly available data; increased reliance on crowds and computer programs for data collection and analysis; and greater collaboration in general between journalists and members of the public, experts in all fields, and technology. From the perspective of news consumers, it would seem clear that mobility is part of this future; we will access news when and where we want it. If newspapers and magazines were the original mobile media (Sheller, 2014), digital hand-helds have become ubiquitous. A report on digital media usage by media analysis company

10.10

Will Canadians Pay for Online News?

The widespread and free provision of online news and commentary has been a serious challenge for commercial news organizations, which typically pay for the costs of their original news production through a combination of subscription fees and advertising. These legacy media are responsible for the most significant and popular online news sites, but their attempts to charge subscription fees and erect paywalls for their electronic editions have had mixed results, and they do not attract the advertising revenues their printed editions used to command. Some newspapers, like *The Globe and Mail*, *The Times* of London, *The Wall Street Journal*, *The New York Times*, and Montreal's *Le Devoir*, continue to charge visitors to their sites for access to at least some portions of their news packages. Others, like *The Guardian*, allow free access but ask their readers for a donation. Canadian broadcasters like CBC, CTV, and Global provide free access to their news sites, and, of course, a considerable amount of news produced by mainstream news organizations circulates via social media channels.

If news consumers have until now been reluctant to pay for news, these attitudes may be changing, particularly as more and more of the quality and specialty news organizations retreat behind paywalls and comparable information cannot be found free of charge. After all, Canadians quickly got used to paying for drinking water when they were sold on the idea that bottled water was superior in purity and taste to freely available tap water.

A 2014 survey of news consumption habits in 10 countries found increasing numbers of people willing to pay for online subscriptions to news sites: 47 per cent of respondents in France, 63 per cent in the United Kingdom, 68 per cent in the United States, and 75 per cent in Denmark (Newman and Levy, 2014).

The *New York Times* reported a $24-million US profit in 2018, in large part because of an increase of 109,000 digital-only subscribers, which offset the newspaper's decline in print advertising. Of the paper's 3.8 million subscribers, 2.9 million subscribe to its digital edition (Peiser, 2018). *The Guardian*'s digital revenues surpassed print revenues for the first time in 2018, with 155 million monthly visitors to its website. If the Guardian Media Group—which also owns *The Observer* in the UK—lost £19 million in 2018, it was nonetheless encouraged by a significant increase in its financial supporters, from 500,000 in 2017 to 575,000 in 2018 (Waterson, 2018).

In Canada, news providers continue to seek paying customers, whether through subscriptions or donations (see Welch, 2018). A significant problem for the Canadian news industry has been the widespread and free sharing of news stories on social media networks without copyright recognition (see Orms, 2018). If the federal government has been reluctant to enforce copyright protection, its fall 2018 fiscal update promised a five-year, $595-million package of benefits to the news industry, which would include a tax credit allowing news subscribers to deduct a share of their subscription payments, a tax credit for the labour costs of news providers, and charitable status to non-profit news organizations (see Leblanc, 2018).

Comscore reported that, internationally, more than 80 per cent of the users of mobile devices searched for news and information, and the figure rose to 95 per cent for Canadian mobile and desktop users (Comscore, 2018: 31; see also Papineau, 2018).

As intriguing as these new possibilities are, a central issue remains the question of resources. How sustainable is the sphere of digital start-ups, alternative media, and citizen journalism initiatives? Are people willing to pay for access to news services? As we emphasized above, journalism is produced by people with a skill set for obtaining newsworthy information, making sense of it, and relating it to audiences in a concise and compelling manner. Such journalists tend to work best when they have the support of a reputable and well-resourced news organization, which allows them appropriate amounts of time and funding for their work, editorial assistance, and legal support (if required), not to mention a regular paycheque.

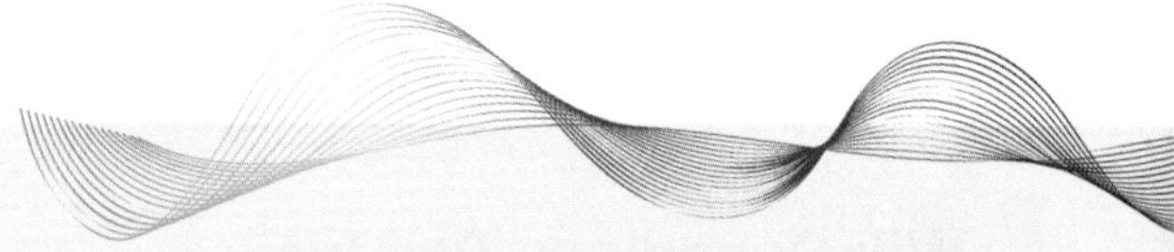

SUMMARY

It is easy to forget how much productive activity can go into media content, and this is particularly the case with journalism, which seeks to present news events as unobtrusively as possible. News is constructed or produced within a specific context, and it is informed by professional ideals, the nature of its textual forms, the sociocultural particularities of the diverse communities that journalism serves, the restrictions of Canada's legal system, the economic imperatives of news production, and the emergence of a networked and more competitive mediascape.

As a form of storytelling, journalism frames the material world, selecting particular events, people, and aspects of a story as newsworthy, while excluding many others. News texts unavoidably attribute meaning to events, which is a significant matter when we depend on the media for so much of our knowledge of an increasingly interconnected world.

Journalism shares some of the characteristics of other forms of storytelling, but it is distinguished by its guiding ideals of truth-seeking, independence, and objectivity; the ethical and legal rights and obligations of the practice in a free-press environment; and the institutional context of news production.

Similarly, most original news production is conducted by media organizations that need to sell audiences to advertisers. The economics of news production is changing dramatically, and all news providers—commercial news organizations as well as digital start-ups—are searching for new and viable business models. This has become the principal concern facing journalism in Canada today.

The most exciting development in journalism, of course, is the emergence of new news providers, and new multi-platform initiatives by legacy news organizations. This ongoing experiment is creating new openings in the mediascape and new answers to the questions of what journalism is for and what role it is to play in contemporary society. To what extent will journalism be just another form of commodity production, and to what extent can it live up to the ideal of being a central component of a democratic communication system?

KEY TERMS

access to information, p. 254
advertorials, p. 265
brand journalism, p. 266
contempt of court, p. 264
defamation, p. 264
fourth estate, p. 254
framing, p. 252
freedom of the press, p. 253
gatekeeping, p. 250
mediation, p. 247

native advertising, p. 266
news values, p. 248
public sphere, p. 261
pull technologies, p. 252
push technologies, p. 252
representation, p. 258
signified, p. 258
signifier, p. 258
socializing institutions, p. 261
unbundling, p. 269
verification, p. 249

RELATED WEBSITES

Canadian Association of Journalists: www.caj.ca
The CAJ is a national organization of journalists, which both advocates on behalf of Canadian journalists and promotes excellence in journalism. The site contains news pertaining to journalism as well as a calendar of upcoming talks and meetings across the country.

Canadian Journalism Foundation: www.cjf-fjc.ca
The mission of this non-profit foundation is to promote and reward excellence in journalism. It contains news of interest to journalists as well as a calendar of events and programs it sponsors across Canada.

Canadian Journalism Project: j-source.ca (English); projetj.ca (French)
A joint initiative by journalism educators across Canada, this comprehensive site brings together a wealth of news, commentary, and reference information about journalism and journalism education in Canada. The CJP has English- and French-language sites.

***In the Field*: www.caj.ca/In_the_Field**
An online series in which journalists discuss the methods and challenges they confront in producing important news stories.

Fédération professionnelle des journalistes du Québec: www.fpjq.org
This association of Quebec journalists publishes a very good French-language magazine, *trente*, and holds a conference each fall addressing the practice of journalism and the theoretical issues facing the news industry.

Local News Research Project: localnewsresearchproject.ca
A collaboration between Ryerson University's School of Journalism and the University of British Columbia's SpICE Lab, this research project employs crowd-sourced data to track developments in local newspapers, broadcast outlets, and online news sites.

FURTHER READINGS

Anderson, C.W., Emily Bell, and Clay Shirky. 2012 (November). *Post-Industrial Journalism: Adapting to the Present*. New York: Tow Center for Digital Journalism. This study provides a good look at the ongoing transformation of journalism, and while it delves into prognostication, the research is based on current trends.

Jobb, Dean. 2018. *Media Law for Canadian Journalists*, 3rd ed. Toronto: Emond Montgomery Publications. This is a current and comprehensive guide to the legal environment in which Canadian journalists operate.

McChesney, Robert W., and Victor Pickard, editors. 2011. *Will the Last Reporter Please Turn Out the Lights: The Collapse of Journalism and What Can Be Done to Fix It*. New York and London: The New Press. This collection of essays by scholars, journalists, and activists addresses the current crisis in journalism and proposes ways to both salvage and improve the institution.

Silverstone, Roger. 2007. *Media and Morality: On the Rise of the Mediapolis*. Cambridge: Polity Press. This thought-provoking study posits the media as a contemporary social space in which we come to moral judgments about sameness and difference.

Stuart, Allan, editor. 2010. *The Routledge Companion to News and Journalism*. London and New York: Routledge. This comprehensive treatment of journalism covers a broad range of topics in both classic texts and new studies.

STUDY QUESTIONS

1. In what ways are news stories highly constructed?
2. Why does it matter that news stories are constructed?
3. What is the problem with the mirror metaphor as it is applied to journalism? What is a more appropriate metaphor?
4. What challenges do journalists confront in trying to produce truthful, fact-based news stories?
5. What is the critical realist approach to objectivity? What is pragmatic objectivity?
6. How does the language of a news story produce meaning?
7. In what ways does journalism act as a socializing institution?
8. Why does it matter who journalists are, in terms of their age, sex, race, ethnicity, education level, and so on?
9. Freedom of the press in Canada is not an absolute right. What are some of the legal limits on this constitutional guarantee?
10. We have described journalism in this chapter as "networked." What does this mean and what is the danger in perceiving journalism in this way?
11. What are the challenges facing both legacy media and newly established news organizations today?

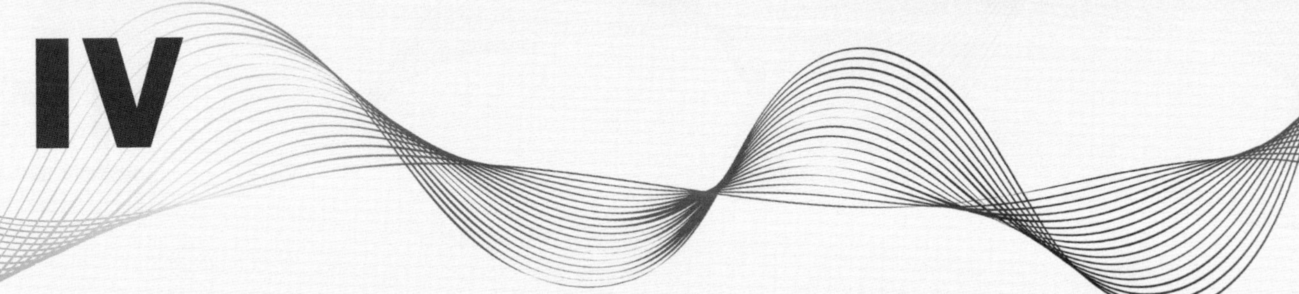

IV

An Evolving Communication World

Lee Yiu Tung/Shutterstock

11

Globalization

The local is increasingly lived under the shadow of the global.
—*Stephen Coleman and Karen Ross*

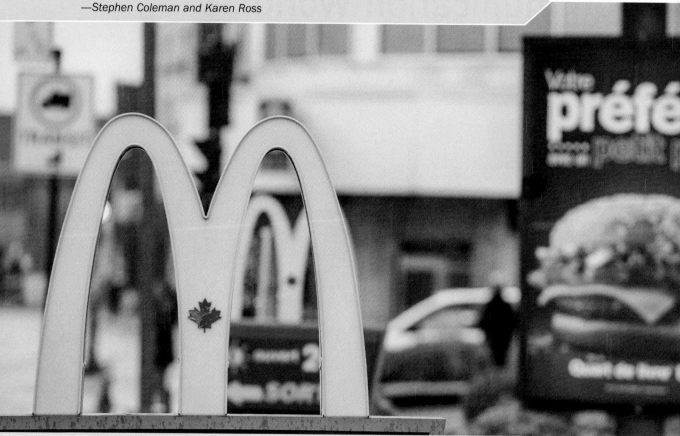

Jerome Cid / Alamy Stock Photo

Opening Questions

- What do we mean by globalization?
- How does globalization affect the ways we communicate?
- In what ways can the media be perceived as agents of globalization?
- What challenges does globalization present for the international flows of communication goods and services?
- What is the digital divide, and how is it relevant in the Canadian context?
- How does globalization affect our sense of community, our sense of place?

Introduction

As has been evident throughout the book, the communication practices of Canadians, government policy formation, and the activities of our cultural industries are in no way confined by municipal, provincial, or national borders. In an era of globalization, national communication systems can be seen as subsystems within an increasingly integrated global communication system, influenced and shaped by extra-national social, political, and economic currents, as well as by the everyday practices of media users, whether they are downloading music or video, accessing social networking sites, or reading news from abroad. In fact, the development of new information technologies has been very much part of the global reorganization of the capitalist economy since the mid-1970s. In this chapter, we examine globalization in broad terms and consider what globalization means for how each of us lives and communicates.

The activities and institutions we have described under the heading of "mediated communication in Canada" are not, and never have been, exclusively Canadian. In television, radio, and magazines, and on the web, foreign, particularly American, media abound in Canada. Similarly, Canadians' communicative practices have always been tied into international circulation. Federal and provincial cultural policy always has been informed both by universal covenants (e.g., freedom of expression, the sharing of the radio broadcast spectrum) and by the policies of neighbouring jurisdictions. Canadian media institutions were established and have continued to evolve in the context of other national media (particularly those of the United States). What distinguishes the current epoch is that the reach and speed of the media have increased so dramatically that borders, which in the past partially shielded one nation's communication system from those of other nations, have become increasingly porous. Distance is less an impediment to communication, and the distinctions between "here" and "there" are increasingly fuzzy. Globalization has altered our **media geography**, shifting dramatically the parameters of the world in which we live and in which we engage in communicative activities.

Many are tempted to look at technological innovation as the principal determinant of this global integration. But, as we have discussed, if technology has played an undeniably significant role in enabling global communications, so, too, have communication law and cultural policy, trade liberalization, and changing social and cultural conditions. We explain at length what globalization means, describe the ways in which the mass media serve as agents of globalization, and document briefly the general patterns of global information and communication flows. We follow with a discussion of how theorists have come to understand the importance and impact of globalization, and then we focus on policy debates surrounding the New World Information and Communication Order in the 1980s and the World Summit on the Information Society in the 2000s. Finally, we consider how our globalized communicative activities have affected our sense of place.

Defining Terms

While the term *globalization* is often used to refer to the world's increased economic interdependence—formalized by the **World Trade Organization (WTO)**, the **Canada–US–Mexico Agreement (CUSMA)**, and the ASEAN Free Trade Area—we define globalization as the set of processes by which social, cultural, political, and economic relations extend farther than ever before, with greater frequency, immediacy, and facility. More specifically, globalization refers to the increased **mobility** of people, capital, commodities, information, and images associated with the post-industrial stage of capitalism; with the development of increasingly rapid and far-ranging communication and transportation technologies; and with people's improved—though far from universal or equitable—access to these technologies. Simply put, globalization means we are more closely integrated with the rest of the world than ever before, even if these connections have significant gaps and are not shared equally by all Canadians, let alone by all citizens of the world. The central questions explored here are how globalization changes the world in which we live and how this process influences the way Canadians communicate.

In economic terms, globalization means that many of us work for companies with operations in a number of countries around the world and that we consume products and services in a global marketplace. When we shop, we buy clothes made in China, wine made in Chile, and furniture made in Sweden. When we go out to eat, we choose among Chinese, Japanese, Thai, French, Italian, Lebanese, and Indian foods. The specific job we do may be part of a production process organized as a transnational assembly line, coordinated from a distant head office, and the product or service we offer likely is destined for export markets. Nike shoes, for example, are produced through a global supply chain, comprising 150 factories in 14 countries, among them Vietnam, China, and Indonesia (Soni, 2014). Those countries, their business leaders, and especially their workers compete with other governments, investors, and workers from all over the world to attract or maintain local economic activity. Globalization also means that Canadian media producers and distributors participate in an increasingly global marketplace.

In the political arena, globalization means that governments are increasingly implicated in events that occur well beyond their own borders, whether through international governing bodies like the United Nations or on their own initiative. Whether the misfortune is famine, disease, war, or natural disaster, political leaders feel increasingly compelled to aid countries many of us cannot easily locate on a map. Canada, for example, had by 2018 accepted an estimated 40,000 refugees fleeing the civil war in Syria (Issawi, 2018). Globalization has added further layers of supranational governance, which means that Canadian communications and cultural policy must respect a growing list of international covenants.

In the social sphere, globalization means that friendships and family ties extend around the world and that our neighbours come from half a dozen different countries, speak different languages, wear different clothes, and worship within different religions. This means that, on a personal level, we are increasingly implicated in world affairs, in large part through our leisure and consumption activities, including media consumption. During the men's 2018 World Cup in Russia, for instance, the English, Croatian, and French teams were followed as closely in Toronto, Montreal, and Vancouver as they were in London, Zagreb, and Paris.

In the cultural sphere, globalization means that some Hollywood movies are as popular in Tokyo and Madrid as they are in Los Angeles. It also means that we come into contact with more and more cultures through social media links, vacation travel, and foreign-language acquisition. The internet connects us to a global newsstand, and to online radio stations and podcasts from places we've never been. What we consider to be Canadian art and cultural performance are increasingly infused by an array of international influences. Indeed, many of Canada's leading writers and performers have their roots in the Philippines, the Caribbean, Egypt, India, and Sri Lanka. Similarly, people around the world consume Canadian cultural exports, from films and television programs to popular music; Alice Munro won the Nobel Prize for Literature in 2013 for an oeuvre of short stories set primarily in small-town southwestern Ontario.

In the environmental sphere, we are increasingly aware that how we use natural resources—air, water, land, minerals, plants, fish—in one corner of the world has significant implications for the rest of the planet. Debates over international climate-change agreements and oil pipeline expansion symbolize both the difficulty and importance of collective struggles to come to terms with how we are degrading the global

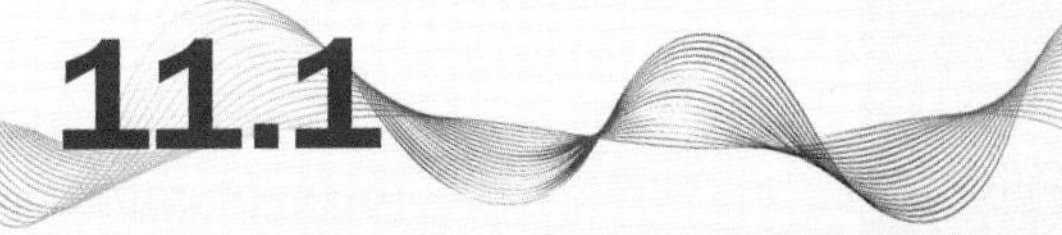

Canada's Changing Profile

It should be clear by now that serving Canada, with its vast geography and its scattered population, is one of the greatest challenges facing media organizations, whether their content is music, news, or dramatic entertainment. But that task is even more formidable in an era of globalization when the Canadian population is more diverse than at any time in its history, meaning media audiences may affiliate with any number of communities. The 2016 census conducted by Statistics Canada reported a Canadian population of just over 35 million people who claimed more than 250 ethnic origins (Statistics Canada, 2016, 2017). Diversity, of course, consists of much more than ethnicity; difference can be based on skin colour, maternal language, religious belief, and sexual orientation, as well as on age, sex, education, and income levels.

Immigrants to Canada accounted for almost 22 per cent of the population in 2016. The largest share of recent immigrants—arriving between 2011 and 2016—came from Asia (62%), primarily from the Philippines, India, and China (Statistics Canada, 2016, 2017).

More than one in five Canadians (22%) self-identify as belonging to a visible minority group, and 6.2 per cent of Canadians are indigenous (2016).

English remains the mother tongue of more than half of Canadians (55%), 20 per cent report French as their first language, and another 21 per cent have a first language other than English or French (2016).

Canada's changing demographic profile is of great significance for media organizations, especially when media managers try to imagine, and ultimately serve, their target audiences. How do they account for such differences of background, language, religion, culture, belief, and life experience? This is a matter of great concern because, as Henry et al. (2000: 296) note, the media "are major transmitters of society's cultural standards, myths, values, roles, and images." Because racial-minority communities tend to be marginalized in mainstream society at large, "many white people rely almost entirely on media for their information about minorities and the issues that concern their communities" (296). This applies to all media forms because they all participate in the practice of representing, or offering us a depiction of, Canadian society, through advertising, music, art, video games, films, news reports, blogs, and television dramas and sitcoms.

One response to Canada's increasing diversity has been the establishment of media dedicated to serving these distinct communities. The National Ethnic Press and Media Council of Canada (NEPMCC), for example, reports that 400 ethnic and community newspapers and magazines serve 12 million Canadians in a variety of languages besides French and English (NEPMCC, 2018). Canada has a national television network serving the indigenous population—the Aboriginal Peoples Television Network—and newspapers devoted to the gay and lesbian population (e.g., *Xtra,* Pink Triangle Press).

A second response—albeit much slower—has been the conscious attempt by mainstream media organizations to diversify their staffs, to normalize the depiction of Canadian society as multicultural, multi-racial, multi-faith, and so on.

Diversity, however it is defined, is a particularly important issue for Canadians, because the communication media have been assigned such a central role in creating a sense of national community, a theme that permeates federal cultural policy. The media are a principal source of images of our country, our fellow Canadians, our place in the larger world, and they play, therefore, a central role in our understanding of who we are as a society. As a socializing institution, either the media can continue to exclude people of colour and exacerbate racism and xenophobia or they can become more inclusive, reflecting Canada's changing demographic profile and facilitating this ongoing social transformation.

environment. Diseases, too, travel globally and quickly. A 2018 measles outbreak in Europe, for example, prompted health officials to encourage Canadians to ensure their vaccinations were up to date (Crowcroft, 2018).

The term *globalization* can be misleading, however, if it implies that all significant social relations now occur on a global scale. Clearly, this is not so. For one thing, we do not all share in the mobility that globalization affords. Second,

REUTERS/Andy Clark.

What we consider to be Canadian art and cultural performance are increasingly infused by an array of international influences. Similarly, people around the world consume Canadian cultural exports; Alice Munro won the Nobel Prize for Literature in 2013 for an oeuvre of short stories set primarily in small-town southwestern Ontario.

different aspects of our lives operate at local, regional, provincial, and national scales. Globalization more properly refers to an intensified relationship between social activity on local and global scales (Massey and Jess, 1995: 226). Once predominantly local, face-to-face, and immediate, social interactions now commonly stretch beyond the borders of our local community so that "less and less of these relations are contained within the place itself" (Massey, 1992: 6–7). While we still talk to our neighbours when we meet them on the street, we also communicate regularly with friends, relatives, and associates—by text messaging, social media, Skype—at the other end of the country and on the other side of the world. Globalization has altered dramatically the nature of human mobility as our travels, whether for business, school, or pleasure, carry us farther and farther afield, expanding the bounds within which most of us live.

Many of the features of globalization are not new. In fact, some theorists argue that the process of globalization is as old as humankind itself (see Lule, 2012: 22–3). International migration, for instance, is not new, nor is the mobility of investment capital or the global circulation of cultural products. What is new about globalization is its intensity: the expanded reach, facility, and immediacy of contemporary social interactions. The migration of people, whether regional, intranational, or international—whether voluntary or forced—has become a more common experience, and many of those who migrate return frequently to their countries of origin. There is a greater circulation today of people seeking to improve their lives, whether they are refugees fleeing intolerable conditions, youths seeking educational and employment opportunities away from home, or executives conducting business in markets around the globe.

Investment capital, too, has become increasingly mobile as companies seek business opportunities wherever they can be found and flee from regions deemed uncompetitive or hostile to free enterprise. Regions of the world are seen primarily as markets—sales markets, resource markets, labour markets—and corporate executives demonstrate less and less loyalty to their traditional places of business. American automakers, for instance, do not need to confine their operations to the Detroit area if cars and trucks can be made more cheaply with comparable quality standards in Canada or Mexico. Similarly, if Hollywood producers seek to reduce costs, they can film in places like Canada or Australia that may offer advantages in terms of currency exchange rates, labour costs, subsidies, and regulatory conditions. Recent Hollywood films shot at least partly in Canada include *The Shape of Water*, *Star Trek Beyond*, *Deadpool 2*, and *Skyscraper*.

Nowhere has capital been more successful at penetrating world markets than in the cultural sphere. The geographer Warwick Murray (2006: 232) cites six factors explaining this: the emergence of new global technological infrastructures, a rise in the velocity of cross-border

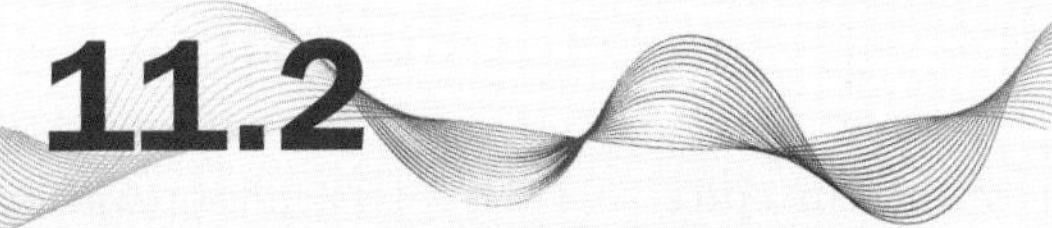

Indigenous Media Activity

The World Indigenous Television Broadcasters Network was established in 2008 "to retain and grow indigenous languages and cultures" by providing an international forum, support, and program exchange network for indigenous cultural producers who often work in minority languages and serve minority populations in their home jurisdictions. Canada's Aboriginal Peoples Television Network (APTN) was a founding member, joining broadcasters from Australia, Hawaii, Ireland, New Zealand, Norway, Scotland, South Africa, and Taiwan.

If the APTN may be considered Canada's most visible outlet for indigenous current-affairs and dramatic television programming, there are numerous other channels for indigenous media interventions, both within mainstream cultural institutions (e.g., CBC, the National Film Board) and beyond. Such interventions provide indigenous peoples an important voice as well as access for non-indigenous Canadians to perspectives that differ, and often run counter to, dominant media narratives (see Brady & Kelly, 2017).

Examples available through mainstream media institutions include CBC Radio programs *Unreserved* and *Reclaimed*, and the NFB films of Alanis Obomsawin (e.g., *Incident at Restigouche, Kanehsatake: 270 Years of Resistance, Trick or Treaty?*).

High-profile indigenous journalists include Tanya Talaga of the *Toronto Star*, author of *Seven Fallen Feathers* and the CBC Massey lecturer for 2018; Duncan McCue, host of CBC Radio's *Cross Country Checkup*; and freelancer Ossie Michelin (osmich.ca). Indigenous musical voices include Tanya Tagaq, A Tribe Called Red, Leela Gilday, Burnt Project 1, and Digging Roots. Among Canada's best-known writers are Richard Wagamese (*Indian Horse, Keeper'n Me*), Tomson Highway (*The Rez Sisters, Dry Lips Oughta Move to Kapuskasing, Kiss of the Fur Queen*), and Thomas King (*Medicine River, Green Grass, Running Water, The Truth about Stories*).

In their book about indigenous media tactics, Miranda J. Brady and John M.H. Kelly (2017) note as well the significance of the media-reported public statements during the hearings of Canada's Truth and Reconciliation Commission (Chapter 1), the multimedia platform IsumaTV (Chapter 2), the disruptive paintings of artist Kent Monkman (89–98), and Toronto's annual imagineNATIVE Film + Media Arts Festival (Chapter 4). Countering the photographic, literary, film, and television images widely circulated from the late nineteenth century to the present day, Brady and Kelly write:

> The cases we investigate illustrate the diversity of Indigenous media tactics as interventions into sites of power and a careful negotiation between mixed and pan-Indigenous audiences. They also illustrate the broader concerns important to contemporary Indigenous communities and the ways in which these concerns are placed firmly at the forefront of public consciousness (5).

cultural exchanges, the rise of Western culture as the central driver of global cultural interaction, the rise of transnational corporations in the culture industries, the rise of business culture as the main driver of cultural exchange, and a shift in the geography of cultural exchanges. David Morley and Kevin Robins (1995: 1–11) refer to a "new media order" in which the overriding logic of media corporations is to get their product to the largest possible number of consumers.

Media images also serve as a reminder of how far our social interactions stretch, the extent to which those relations are mediated, and the implications of such mediation. As Morley and Robins argue:

> The screen is a powerful metaphor for our times: it symbolizes how we exist in the world, our contradictory condition of engagement and disengagement. Increasingly, we confront moral issues through the screen, and the screen confronts us with increasing numbers of moral dilemmas. At the same time, however, it screens us from those dilemmas. It is through the screen that we disavow or deny our human implication in moral realities (141).

Consider, for example, the stark images of war and displaced people that television and internet news channels screen for us daily and what this means for our experience of the people, places, and events depicted.

The screen metaphor also applies to globalization itself, the processes of which filter out large segments of the population. This is a point easily ignored by those of us with easy, cheap, 24/7 access to communication technologies. We assume that everyone enjoys these advantages, but globalization's impact is in fact decidedly uneven, dividing people along class lines, in particular. While relatively wealthy, educated urban dwellers have considerable access to the fruits of globalization, those with less mobility and more immediate priorities—food, clean water, shelter, personal safety—are largely excluded, wherever they are in the world. Think of how often we have walked past a homeless person begging in the street while we are using our smartphone.

Not all of us are in a position to reap the benefits of global interconnectivity because we don't all enjoy the same degree of mobility, even in a country like Canada. In fact, many Canadians have been hit hard by the new-found fluidity of investment capital—when, for example, sawmills are closed in British Columbia and automotive manufacturers leave Quebec and Ontario because their owners can simply move in search of more hospitable investment climates. In such instances, those who control global capital are the only true "global citizens." As Zygmunt Bauman (1998: 2) states, "Globalization divides as much as it unites; it divides as it unites—the causes of division being identical with those which promote the uniformity of the globe."

Mass Media as Agents of Globalization

Sophisticated and accessible transportation and communication technologies are enablers of globalization. As we saw in our discussion of Harold Innis's ideas in Chapter 6, transportation and communication networks have the ability to "bind space," to bring people and places closer together. They enable people to maintain close contact in spite of their physical separation. Airline connections between major cities allow business leaders and politicians to fly to a meeting in another city and to return home in time for dinner. Frequent email or text messaging connects friends and colleagues in remote locations, minimizing the implications of their actual separation.

Since the end of World War II, globalization has prompted a new layer of international governance to coordinate the increasing number of integrated spheres of activity. Initially this meant the creation of the United Nations in 1945, which addresses military, economic, health, education, and cultural affairs between states. Today, the list of international governing agencies includes the North Atlantic Treaty Organization, the World Trade Organization, the Association of Southeast Asian Nations (ASEAN), the African Union, the Group of Seven, the Latin American Integration Association (LAIA), the European Union, and many others.

The flip side of this international cooperation is international interference in cases where states' interests conflict, and there has been a recent backlash by some states against these integrating forces (see Box 11.3). Globalization means that national governments no longer enjoy uncontested **sovereignty** within their own borders. This has significant policy implications when issues such as Canadian-content regulations, subsidization of cultural production, enforcement of online hate-speech laws, or enforcement of copyright laws are raised. Countries can choose to ignore international law—something of which China has been accused with respect to international copyright agreements—or they can exert their political and economic might to derail legislation. The United States uses this latter tactic with any country's attempt to protect its domestic film industry against Hollywood's dominance of commercial theatre screens.

11.3

Second Thoughts about Globalization

The governments of some countries are having second thoughts about the increased interdependency that globalization portends. The United Kingdom, for example, held a referendum in 2016 on its future membership in the European Union, and a small majority (52%) voted in favour of withdrawal (known as Brexit). The administration of US president Donald Trump has adopted an America First foreign policy, prioritizing the country's own political and economic interests and stepping back from internationalist ventures.

Perhaps most concerning is the reluctance of governments to work together to combat climate change. The US has announced it is withdrawing from the 2016 Paris agreement on climate change, and the governments of Australia and Brazil, in particular, have been criticized for their refusal to see climate change as a global crisis (see *The Guardian*, 2018). In Canada, the federal government has proposed a nationwide carbon pricing policy (while supporting the expansion of the Trans Mountain oil pipeline), but the governments of Ontario and Saskatchewan have vowed to contest the plan on constitutional grounds (see Giovannetti, 2018).

The mass media play four specific roles in the globalization process. First, they are the media of encounter, putting us in touch with one another, whether via mail, telephone, email, text messaging, social media, or so on. Second, they are the media of governance, enabling the centralized administration of vast spaces and dispersed places, whether by governments, businesses, or non-profit service organizations. Third, they situate us within the world, offering us a regular picture of where we are, who we are, and how we relate to other people and places in the world. Fourth, they constitute a globalized business in and of themselves, conducting trade in information and entertainment products. Taken together, these roles alter fundamentally the geographical parameters within which we live our lives.

While face-to-face interaction remains integral to interpersonal relations in even the most globalized of environments—on the street, in the park, at work, at school—**proximity** no longer constricts our social interactions. Communication technologies like the cellular telephone and personal computer bind social spaces and enable people to maintain contact across distance, rendering the communication industry "a primary channel of social interaction" (Jackson et al., 2011: 56). There are perhaps no better examples of this than social networking sites like Facebook, Snapchat, and Instagram. Often, of course, these media complement face-to-face interactions.

At the same time, as communication theorist Harold Innis points out, communication media enable the centralized governance of a political community on the scale of the modern nation-state and the centralized administration of a transnational corporation that spans the globe. Both national forms of governance and global forms of capitalism require efficient means of communication to establish a coherent agenda, to disseminate instructions and information, to monitor the activities of remote departments, and to receive reports from local managers or governors in the field. If a country as large and diverse as Canada is difficult to govern, its governance would be virtually impossible without modern communication and transportation technologies.

The scale on which governments and organizations function today can also, paradoxically, isolate nearby regions and peoples, if they are not deemed integral to the networks of governance or of commerce, or if they don't have a population base large enough to constitute either an important political constituency or a viable market (see Castells, 1999, 2001). On a global scale, Murray

(2006: 225) notes that Tahiti is one of the most physically remote islands on earth but remains culturally connected to the industrial West, whereas the Solomon Islands and Papua New Guinea are much closer to Western nations but much more culturally isolated. Even in Canada, isolation can occur when transportation companies cut service to some cities and towns because those routes are deemed not economically viable. When, for example, Greyhound Lines cancelled all of its Western Canadian bus routes in the fall of 2018, it increased the isolation of people along the route who depend on that connection; Greyhound's route between Winnipeg and Calgary, for instance, featured 46 stops in small communities (Lambert & Graveland, 2018).

The media also provide us with a sense of place and identity. They represent to us who we are, where we live, how we are connected to one another, and how we differ from other peoples and places. These depictions contain value judgments, sometimes expressed explicitly, but more often inferred. Media scholar Roger Silverstone describes media work as "boundary work"; this is "their primary cultural role: the endless, endless, endless playing with difference and sameness" (Silverstone, 2007: 19). For example, advertisements often seek to portray "typical" Canadians engaged in "normal" Canadian activities, offering us a definition of what typical and normal *Canadian-ness* is and suggesting what we look and act like. This is a key theme in, for example, Tim Hortons' corporate branding. Consider, too, the portrayal of the family in Canadian Tire commercials, the representation of Canadian males in Molson beer ads, or the gender roles assigned to men and women in commercials for any number of household cleaning products.

Finally, the media have become a central constituent of globalization in what is called the *information age* or the **network society**. This means, first, that the cultural industries are conducting a greater proportion of global trade by serving as the conduits for the exchange of information and entertainment commodities, including trade in hardware, such as computers, television sets, and sound systems, and in cultural products, such as books, magazines, DVDs, and music and video downloads. Instead of trading regionally or nationally, these goods and services are increasingly traded on an international or global scale; the world is their market. Second, information and ideas are becoming increasingly important to an economy that now depends on innovation in all industrial sectors. Ideas that can lead to new product development, greater productivity, and the expansion of markets have become essential to maintaining growth in a capitalist economy.

The economic role that the mass media play has considerable implications for how we define communication as *commodity* or as *cultural form* (see Chapters 2 and 9), for who gets to speak (on both the individual and the collective levels), and for what kinds of messages become privileged.

By making information an exploitable resource, the democratic ideal of free speech and freely circulating information has been

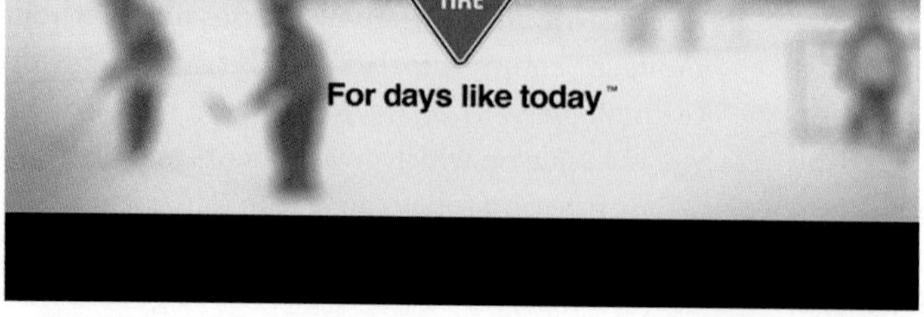

Advertisements often seek to portray "typical" Canadians engaged in "normal" Canadian activities, offering us a definition of what typical and normal Canadian-ness is and suggesting what we look and act like. What does this Canadian Tire ad convey about "typical" Canadians?

transformed—at least in many sectors—into the freedom of media proprietors to exploit world markets with that speech and with that information.

This problem is offset somewhat by the emergence of individuals and public-service organizations seeking to employ the same communication technologies for quite different purposes—perhaps to combat economic globalization or militarism, to support environmental or human-rights measures, or simply to create their own cultural products. The question, Dave Sholle (2002: 3) points out, is whether new media technologies "will be an agent of freedom or an instrument of control."

These technologies enable the emergence of alternative media organizations; they are alternative in the sense that they present a non-commercial media model that emphasizes "the promotion of public dialogue, the exchange of ideas, and the promotion of social action" (Skinner, 2010: 222). Such media include newspapers (the *Georgia Straight* in Vancouver, *The Coast* in Halifax, *Le Mouton Noir* in Rimouski), magazines (*This Magazine*, *Canadian Dimension*, *Briarpatch*), radio (Radio Centre-Ville in Montreal, Vancouver Co-operative Radio), podcasting (Indian and Cowboy, Canadaland), and, of course, online news services (Rabble.ca, TheTyee.ca).

Global Information Trade

Like other aspects of globalization, the cultural sphere is witnessing the expansion and intensification of a trend that already has a substantial history. This history reveals that international cultural exchanges have always been uneven, with a few sources of communication serving many destinations. This asymmetry intensified dramatically in the second half of the twentieth century as trade flows became increasingly concentrated; 20 countries accounted for 75 per cent of international trade in merchandise and fifteen countries accounted for 65 per cent of the international trade in services (Murray, 2006: 107–9). Murray argues that such economic flows form a "global triad," comprising the European Union, the United States, and East and Southeast Asia (110–1). He adds, however, that when we look closer at the global economy, "we see that most investment and trade actually takes place between specialized industrial spaces" (110–2).

Terhi Rantanen (1997) points out that a handful of European news agencies—Havas, Reuters, Wolff—began to dominate global news coverage in the mid-nineteenth century, and the development of the telegraph and submarine telegraph cables during those years meant that, for the first time, information could reliably travel faster than people.

Herman and McChesney (1997: 13–4) describe the film industry as "the first media industry to serve a truly global market." By 1914, barely 20 years after the advent of the motion picture, the United States had captured 85 per cent of the world film audience, and by 1925, US films accounted for 90 per cent of film revenues in the United Kingdom, Canada, Australia, New Zealand, and Argentina, and over 70 per cent of revenues in France, Brazil, and the Scandinavian countries. Hollywood's hegemony in the film world continues to the present day.

Such developments have been criticized as instances of **media imperialism**—the exploitation of global media markets to build political, economic, and ideological empires of influence and control. If what used to be called media imperialism is now usually described more palatably as *media globalization*, concerns nevertheless remain that the mediasphere has come to be dominated by the world's largest media companies, the majority of them based in Western Europe and North America. The resources of these large, global media companies (e.g., Alphabet, 21st Century Fox, Bertelsmann, Facebook, Baidu, CBS News Corporation, Viacom, Disney, Comcast) give them tremendous advantages over smaller, independent producers in terms of their ability to hire skilled professionals (including stars), the aesthetic quality of their productions, the power of their corporate brands, their access to distribution networks, and their ability to advertise and promote their products worldwide (see McChesney, 2003). Their use of digital platforms has only enhanced their ability to penetrate global markets. Global spending on media and entertainment was US$1.6 trillion in 2015 (the latest date for which figures are available), with broadband services and in-home video entertainment accounting for almost half of that amount. Three regions—Asia Pacific, North America, and Western Europe—accounted for 86 per cent of that spending (McKinsey and Company, 2016: 8-9).

The point is that the interdependence inherent in globalization is rarely symmetrical. The decidedly uneven flow of information and entertainment products creates a situation in which a few countries, and relatively few companies, produce and profit from the vast majority of media content, leaving most of the world, to a great extent, voiceless. As shown in Table 11.1, Hollywood films dominate box offices around the world; theatre screens throughout the world have become a global market for the same Hollywood films we see in North America. Table 11.2, on the other hand, shows that the international popular music scene is somewhat more diverse, even if the bulk of music flows from transnational media companies based in the West, and particularly the United States and United Kingdom (see Murray, 2006: 252–8).

Public broadcasting systems, which operate on a public-service model, are under siege in Canada and around the world. In spite of increasing demands on CBC/Radio-Canada, the public broadcaster has had its parliamentary appropriation reduced repeatedly since the early 1990s,

TABLE 11.1
Top Grossing Films, Selected Countries, May 2018

Germany	*Avengers: Infinity War*	USA
	Deadpool 2	USA
	Solo: A Star Wars Story	USA
France	*Avengers: Infinity War*	USA
	Solo: A Star Wars Story	USA
	Deadpool 2	USA
Italy	*Avengers: Infinity War*	USA
	Solo: A Star Wars Story	USA
	Deadpool	USA
Finland	*Avengers: Infinity War*	USA
	Solo: A Star Wars Story	USA
	Truth or Dare	USA
Australia	*Avengers: Infinity War*	USA
	Deadpool 2	USA
	Solo: A Star Wars Story	USA
Venezuela	*12 Strong*	USA
	Avengers: Infinity War	USA
	7 Days in Entebbe	USA/UK
China	*Avengers: Infinity War*	USA
	How Long Will I Love You	China
	Us and Them	China

Sources: Box Office Mojo (www.boxofficemojo.com), Internet Movie Database (www.imdb.com). Table compiled by Scott Baird.

TABLE 11.2
Top Five Music Singles, Selected Countries, May 2018

Austria	"Maserati"/RAF Camora	Switzerland
	"No Tears Left To Cry"/Ariana Grande	USA
	"Friends"/Marshmello & Anne-Marie	USA/UK
	"Paradise"/George Ezra	UK
	"Wake Me Up!"/Avicii	Sweden
United Kingdom	"One Kiss"/Calvin Harris & Dua Lipa	UK
	"No Tears Left To Cry"/Ariana Grande	USA
	"Nice for What"/Drake	Canada
	"Freaky Friday"/Lil Dicky & Chris Brown	USA
	"2002"/Anne-Marie	USA
Denmark	"Holder Fast"/Hennedub, Gilli & Lukas Graham	Denmark
	"One Kiss"/Calvin Harris & Dua Lipa	UK
	"Sydpa"/Bro	Denmark
	"Better Now"/Post Malone	USA
	"Friends"/Marshmello & Anne-Marie	USA/UK
Spain	"Lo Malo"/Aitana Ocana & Ana Guerra	Spain
	"Te Bote"/Nio Garcia, Casper, Darell, Nicky Jam, Bad Bunny & Ozuna	Puerto Rico
	"X"/ Nicky Jam & J Balvin	US/Colombia
	"Dura"/Daddy Yankee	Puerto Rico
	"Me Niego"/Reik, Ozuna & Wisin	Mexico/Puerto Rico
New Zealand	"Nice For What"/Drake	Canada
	"Psycho"/Post Malone & Ty Dolla $ign	USA
	"Freaky Friday"/Lil Dicky & Chris Brown	USA
	"No Tears Left To Cry"/Ariana Grande	USA
	"Love Lies"/Khalid & Normani	USA

Source: Top40-Charts (www.top40-charts.com). Table compiled by Scott Baird.

prompting a series of job cuts. The Liberal government of Justin Trudeau sought to reverse this trend in its 2016 budget, pledging an additional $150 million annually through 2021 (Bradshaw, 2016). Even the venerable BBC, which has come to symbolize the best of public broadcasting, has adopted commercial strategies in some aspects of its operation (e.g., BBC World News Television, BBC Studios) (BBC Studios, 2018).

What has emerged is a tiered global media market, dominated by US-based companies, which can capitalize on the competitive advantage of having "by far the largest and most lucrative indigenous market to use as a testing ground and to yield economies of scale" (Herman and McChesney, 1997: 52). In recent decades, for example, Canada became an important site of Hollywood film and television production, as US film companies took advantage of the lower Canadian dollar and comparable technical expertise of crews north of the border (see Elmer and Gasher, 2005; Gasher, 2002; Pendakur, 1998). The Hollywood animation industry has similarly taken advantage of the cheap yet stable labour markets of India, South Korea, Australia, Taiwan, and the Philippines for the time-consuming and labour-intensive execution of animation projects originally conceived in Los Angeles (Breen, 2005; Lent, 1998).

The large, transnational media companies are particularly interested in the world's most affluent audiences because these audiences have the money to spend on advertised products and services. This means, for example, that the poorest half of India's 1.3 billion people is irrelevant to the global media market, and all of sub-Saharan Africa has been written off. The global media are most interested in markets in North America, Latin America, Europe, and Asia.

That said, the global media market does see some two-way traffic. The Globo and Televisa television networks in Brazil, for example, have succeeded in capturing a respectable share of Brazil's domestic market, and their telenovela productions are major exports (Hopewell, 2014).

Canada, too, has begun to tap export markets in both the film and television industries, and it has quickly become a significant international video games producer (see ESAC, 2017). A renaissance in Canadian feature-film production since the mid-1980s means that directors like David Cronenberg (*Crash*, *ExistenZ*, *A History of Violence*, *Maps to the Stars*), Atom Egoyan (*Ararat*, *The Sweet Hereafter*, *Where the Truth Lies*, *Chloe*, *The Captive*, *Remember*), Deepa Mehta (*Fire*, *Earth*, *Water*, *Midnight's Children*, *Anatomy of Violence*), Denis Villeneuve (*Polytechnique*, *Prisoners*, *Enemy*, *Sicario*, *Arrival*, *Bladerunner 2049*), Jean-Marc Vallée (*C.R.A.Z.Y.*, *Café de Flore*, *Dallas Buyers Club*, *Demolition*), and Xavier Dolan (*J'ai tué ma mère*, *Mommy*, *Juste la fin du monde*, *The Death and Life of John F. Donovan*), among many others, have made names for themselves in international film markets. And Canada is increasingly drawing attention as an exporter of television programming. If in the past it has been a leading exporter in the episodic, children's, and animation categories, it has more recently had international successes in the drama category, with such productions as *Pure*, *Bad Blood*, *Mary Kills People*, *19-2*, *Orphan Black*, and *Cardinal*, the last of which has been sold to more than 100 markets worldwide (Wong, 2017, 2018; CMPA, 2018)..

All of this commercial activity, of course, both opens up and limits the circulation of communication goods. What digital technology on the one hand enables is access to a greater variety of both commercial and independently produced cultural products and services. Chris Anderson (2006), the editor-in-chief of *Wired* magazine, talks about the *long-tail* phenomenon, which allows companies to increase their inventory of books, films, and music as digitization reduces the costs of storage; iTunes, for example, can afford to offer older, more obscure, or less popular music because the costs of storing digital recordings for the handful of customers who might want to download them is minimal. Digital technology also allows budding musicians to distribute their music directly to listeners, via their own websites, through social media, or their own YouTube channels.

The TV crime drama *Cardinal*, which is broadcast in French and English, has been sold to more than 100 international television markets.

That said, it is still all about markets; to sustain the production of a diverse array of cultural materials, content producers need to be compensated. The corporate structuring of the media privileges the production and distribution of the most commercially viable products and services. It also grants media companies the power to inhibit, even prohibit, the production and circulation of products or services with limited appeal, or products that are critical or threatening in some way; Apple, for example, carries only those applications it approves in its App Store and restricts music downloaded from iTunes to Apple devices or software (see Murphy, 2017) .

Theories of Globalization

There is a growing body of theoretical work on globalization, some celebratory, some critical. In a survey of the major thinkers, Andrew Jones (2010: 11–15) identifies three areas of consensus on globalization and three points of dispute. Theorists agree, first of all, that globalization is part of a long history of societal integration (dating at least as far back as the Roman Empire), that the contemporary period of globalization (since the 1950s) is qualitatively different from previous periods, and that globalization has a complex impact on nation-states. There is disagreement among theorists, however, on whether globalization constitutes a coherent system or whether it consists of several independent processes, whether it is ultimately positive or negative, and what the key drivers behind it are.

The predominant account of globalization to date has been **world systems theory**, as articulated by Immanuel Wallerstein (1974, 2007). Wallerstein's theory posits globalization as an economic phenomenon and, as the name of his theory suggests, he sees it as systemic. He argues that even though humans have engaged in trade for thousands of years (see Bernstein, 2008), a European, capitalist "world economy" emerged in the late fifteenth and early sixteenth centuries. This extra-national economy involved long-distance trade that forged links between Europe and parts of Africa, Asia, and what came to be known as the West Indies and North and South America (Wallerstein, 1974: 15–20). World systems theory focuses on the relationship between nation-states—the world system—rather than on nation-states themselves, and demarcates three zones in the integrated world economy: the core states, characterized by industrialization and the rise of a merchant class; the periphery, comprising state economies based on resource extraction; and a semi-periphery, made up of in-between states whose economies share some characteristics of both the core and periphery (100–27). "Since this is a constantly changing phenomenon, not always for the better, the boundaries of a world-economy are ever fluid" (349). Wallerstein proposes that capitalism requires a world system (2007: 24) because its participants seek constantly to expand markets and to exploit the most favourable labour markets, regulatory regimes and infrastructure, access to resources, and access to investment capital and government support.

The world system's asymmetry, particularly with regard to trade in cultural materials, drew the attention of communication scholars in the post–World War II period and led to the development of two closely related theories: *media imperialism* and *cultural dependency*. Oliver Boyd-Barrett (1977: 117–8) used the term *media imperialism* to characterize the unidirectional nature of international media flows from a small number of source countries. Media imperialism research grew out of a larger struggle for decolonization in the aftermath of World War II (Mosco, 2009: 55).

Cultural dependency is a less deterministic means of characterizing cultural trade. Whereas *imperialism* implies "the act of territorial annexation for the purpose of formal political control," Boyd-Barrett (1996: 174–84) maintains that cultural dependency suggests "de facto control" and refers to "a complex of processes" to which the mass media contribute "to an as yet unspecified extent."

While both approaches contributed a great deal to documenting communication flows within the world economy and drew attention to an obvious problem, neither theory offered a sufficiently complex explanation of the power dynamics behind international cultural trade, nor did they provide satisfactory descriptions of the impact of such asymmetrical exchanges. The media imperialism thesis tends to be too crudely applied, assuming too neat a relationship between the all-powerful source countries and their helpless colonies.

While slightly more nuanced, the cultural dependency thesis shared a number of the shortcomings of the media imperialism thesis. Like media imperialism, Vincent Mosco (2009: 101–3) argues, the concept of cultural dependency created homogeneous portraits of both the source and the target countries. It concentrated almost exclusively on the role of external forces and overlooked "the contribution made by local forces and relations of production, including the Indigenous class structure." Cultural dependency also portrayed transnational capitalism as rendering the target states powerless. Like media imperialism, cultural dependency did not adequately account for how audiences in the target countries used or interpreted media messages that originate elsewhere. Current research seeks to account for the heterogeneity of national cultures, the specificity of particular industries and corporate practices, and how cultural products are actually used by audiences (see Lessig, 2008).

Nonetheless, the clear asymmetry of globalization remains an important issue for researchers who study cultural policy and the political economy of communication from a range of perspectives. And it is particularly pertinent to the Canadian case. Canada's relatively small, dispersed population, as well as its shared majority language and shared border with the United States, have made it an easy target for the US media powerhouse.

A New Media Ecology

Anthony Giddens studies globalization through the lens of sociology. He argues that globalization has transformed our sense of time and space, "disembedding" social relations from their local contexts and restructuring them across "indefinite spans of time-space" (Giddens, 1990: 21; see also Jones, 2010: 39). He writes, "In the modern era, the level of time–space distanciation is much higher than in any previous period, and the relations between local and distant social forms and events become correspondingly 'stretched'" (Giddens, 1990: 64). This "stretching process" is what we mean by globalization. Departing from Wallerstein's exclusive focus on economics, Giddens provides a four-dimensional model of globalization, with the world capitalist economy, the world military order, the nation-state system, and the international division of labour serving as its component parts. The media serve as the "global extension of the institutions of modernity" (70–1).

Manuel Castells places communication technologies at the centre of global economic—and by extension, social and political—interactions.

Castells describes a "network society" that, as its name suggests, is an interconnected world, which is less international than internodal, placing major global cities, rather than nations, at the centre of its analysis.

Castells argues that the internet has allowed people to forge a new kind of sociability—"networked individualism" (2001: 127–9)—and a new global geography—"a space of flows" (207–8). Communication technologies form the "unifying thread" that links globalizing processes, so that the "space of flows" creates "a distributed network with clusters around nodes and hubs" (Jones, 2010: 55–9). This interconnected world, then, has considerable implications for the inclusion and exclusion of people and places from the network of global **information flows**. Internet use, Castells notes, is highly concentrated within a network of "metropolitan nodes" (2001: 228), which become the new dominant hubs of economics, politics, and culture. For this reason, Castells places a new onus on democratic governments to ensure political representation, participatory democracy, consensus building, and effective public policy (278–9).

Saskia Sassen (1998:, p. xxv) sees in this network society "a new economic geography of centrality" in which certain global cities concentrate economic and political power and become "command centers in a global economy." If Sassen agrees with Castells that this new geography is produced by the internet's most prominent and active users (xxvii), she is nonetheless concerned with the conflict that necessarily ensues between "placeboundedness"—those peoples, activities, and institutions bound to a specific place, often in support of the network infrastructure—and "virtualization"—those peoples, activities, and institutions capable of exploiting Castells's virtual space of information flows (Sassen, 1998: 201–2).

The political economist Vincent Mosco describes the process of overcoming the constraints of space and time as **spatialization**, and he attributes to communication a principal role as an enabling mechanism. He cautions that the global commercial economy does not annihilate space but transforms it "by restructuring the spatial relationships among people, goods, and messages. In the process of restructuring, capitalism transforms itself" (2009: 157) by becoming increasingly mobile and, following Castells, by clustering together certain communicative activities in "agglomeration" zones (169). One of the oldest and clearest examples of such spatial agglomeration is Hollywood, which clusters together companies and workers devoted to film and television production, from the writers, actors, and directors to the specialists in editing, lighting, set design and construction, and costume design.

Clearly, what has emerged in the context of globalization is a new media ecology. James Carey has argued that the internet "should be understood as the first instance of a global communication system," displacing a national system that came into existence in the late nineteenth century with the development of, initially, telegraphy and railroad transportation, and later, national magazines, newspapers, radio, and television (Carey, 1998: 28). Carey underscores the point here that this new media ecology requires a cultural level to complement its global infrastructure; that is, an imagining and an articulation of community on a global scale, enabled, but not automatically produced, by communication or transportation technologies alone.

All this is not to say that national (or subnational) boundaries are obsolete. They may be more porous, but the governments within those boundaries remain primarily responsible for creating the economic, political, and cultural conditions for globalization's various activities. National governments establish the supporting infrastructure, laws, policies, incentives, and the health, education, and safety standards that businesses—including those in the cultural industries—require. Similarly, governments determine through policy measures what communication is for, and determine and protect the freedoms citizens enjoy in engaging in communication activities. Nation-states are also the representatives of their citizens' interests in international forums.

New World Information and Communication Order (NWICO)

Cees Hamelink (1994: 23–8) observes that two features of international communication emerged in the last half of the twentieth century: the expansion of the global communication system and tensions in the system across both east–west and north–south axes. East–west tensions (i.e., Cold War tensions between the totalitarian Eastern Bloc led by the Soviet Union and the Western democracies led by the United States) were most prominent in the 1950s and '60s. North–south tensions (i.e., tensions between the industrialized nations of the northern hemisphere and the post-colonial Global South) arose in the 1970s as the Global South took advantage of its new-found voice in the General Assembly of the United Nations, and they remain pertinent today. A number of United Nations initiatives led to a proposed New World Information and Communications Order (NWICO), which sought compromise between the US advocacy of the free flow of information and the Global South desire for a balanced flow.

The free-flow doctrine met its stiffest opposition from the Soviet Union, which insisted on the regulation of information flows and complained that the Americans' freedom-of-information position endorsed, in fact, the freedom of a few commercial communication monopolies. Nevertheless, the free-flow doctrine was largely endorsed by the United Nations, and Article 19 of the 1948 Universal Declaration on Human Rights states, "Everyone has the right to freedom of opinion and expression; this right includes freedom to hold opinions without interference and to seek, receive and impart information and ideas through any media regardless of frontiers" (Hamelink, 1994: 152–5).

The issue of communication flows was revisited at the behest of Global South countries in the 1970s when it became clear that the free-flow doctrine was a recipe for Western cultural hegemony, as the Soviets had anticipated.

The major global institutions addressing communication issues at the time—the United Nations, the UN Educational, Scientific and Cultural Organization (UNESCO), and the International Telecommunication Union—all included majorities of Global South countries and sympathetic totalitarian states.

The international debate at that time focused on three points, as it still does to some extent. First, historically, communication services together with evolved information technologies have allowed dominant states to exploit their political and economic power. Second, the economies of scale in information production and distribution threaten to reinforce this dominance. Third, a few transnational corporations had mobilized technology as a vehicle for the exploitation of markets rather than as a means of serving the cultural, social, and political needs of nations.

Pressure from the Global South compelled the United Nations to broaden the concept of free flow to include "the free and balanced flow of information." International debate over the design of a New World Information and Communication Order coalesced around the final report of the 16-member International Commission for the Study of Communication Problems (the MacBride Commission), established by UNESCO in December 1977 (UNESCO, 1980).

The MacBride Commission advocated "free, open and balanced communications" and concluded that "the utmost importance should be given to eliminating imbalances and disparities in communication and its structures, and particularly in information flows. Developing countries need to reduce their dependence and claim a new, more just and more equitable order in the field of communication" (UNESCO, 1980: 253–68). The MacBride Commission's conclusions were based on "the firm conviction that communication is a basic individual right, as well as a collective one required by all communities and nations. Freedom of information—and, more specifically, the right to seek, receive, and impart information—is a fundamental human right; indeed, a prerequisite for many others" (253).

The MacBride Commission pointed to an essential conflict between the commercialization and the democratization of communication and thus clearly favoured a movement for democratization. The report stated, "Every country should develop its communication patterns in accordance with its own conditions, needs and traditions, thus strengthening its integrity, independence and self-reliance" (254).

The MacBride Report also criticized the striking disparities between the technological capacities of different nations and described the right to communicate as fundamental to democracy: "Communication needs in a democratic society should be met by the extension of specific rights, such as the right to be informed, the right to inform, the right to privacy, the right to participate in public communication—all elements of a new concept, the right to communicate" (265).

From NWICO to WSIS

The MacBride Report proved to be a better manifesto on the democratization of communication than a blueprint for restructuring international communication exchanges. Even though UNESCO adopted its key principles—eliminating global media imbalances and having communication serve national development goals—the NWICO was poorly received in the West "because it gave governments, not markets, ultimate authority over the nature of a society's media" (Herman and McChesney, 1997: 24–6). Communication scholar Kaarle Nordenstreng argues that the NWICO was seen by its opponents as a curb on media freedom, "while in reality the concept was designed to widen and deepen the freedom of information by increasing its balance and diversity on a global scale" (Nordenstreng, 2012: 37).

Western countries in the 1980s, led by the United States under Ronald Reagan and the United Kingdom under Margaret Thatcher, chose the more aggressive path of pursuing liberalized global trade. In the face of concerns over the ways NWICO reforms would affect their media industries, the United States and the United Kingdom pulled out of UNESCO in 1985, severely undermining the organization's budget and making the recommended reforms impossible (34). Even Canada, which was one of the affluent industrialized nations identified by the MacBride Commission as being dominated by cultural imports, began to pursue the neoliberal agenda of free trade and budget cutbacks in the 1980s. Very little has changed since in Canadian government policy. Such issues as deficit reduction and freer trade continue to dominate the political agenda, and the ministers of industry, international trade, and finance enjoy as much influence over cultural policy as the minister with the culture portfolio (see Gasher, 1995).

International bodies like the World Trade Organization have become more important to the major cultural producers than the United Nations, and the rules of the game for international communications have been written in such treaties as CUSMA and the Treaty on European Union.

The New World Information and Communication Order, in other words, was almost immediately supplanted by what Herman and McChesney (1997: 35) call the "new global corporate ideology." Nonetheless, as Mosco (2009: 178) puts it, the struggle continues to be to "build a more democratic process grounded in genuinely global governance."

New concerns for the Global South arose in the 1990s with the emergence of digital information networks, the creation and expansion of cyberspace, issues pertaining to internet governance, and the financing of digital activities (Masmoudi, 2012: 25). The International Telecommunication Union (ITU) launched the World Summit on the Information Society (WSIS, 2010), which took the form of international conferences bringing together scholars, civil society groups, governments, and policy experts in Geneva in 2003 and Tunis in 2005. The Geneva conference laid out a 67-point declaration of principles and an action plan, and the Tunis conference addressed the financial implementation of the action plan, including the creation of the Digital Solidarity Fund.

Three decades after MacBride, the digital divide between the information-rich and the information-poor remains a central concern. According to 2017 ITU figures, less than half (48%) of the world's population is online, with significant disparity between connection rates in the world's developed countries (94.3%), those of the developing countries (67.3%), and what the ITU terms the world's least-developed countries (30.3%) (ITU, 2017). Internet access in Europe, for example, is 95.7 per cent, while in Africa it is 21.8 per cent. And there remains a global gender gap as well, with 50.9 per cent of men with internet access compared to 44.9 per cent of women. There is a comparable gulf in penetration rates for mobile broadband subscriptions: 98 per cent in the developed world, 49 per cent in the developing world, and 22 per cent in the least-developed countries. Further, the cost of access to information and communication technologies remains inversely proportional to the economic wealth of a territory. For example, entry-level data plans range from an average of $15.40 (in international dollars) in the developed countries to $41.10 in the least-developed countries. Even more than access to digital networks, though, communication scholar Jérémie Nicey argues that computer literacy needs to be seen as a basic human right (2012: 172). (See Box 11.4 for more about the digital divide.)

The international news agencies that were implicated in originating global information disparities continue to play a role in the digital divide. The world's three major wire services—Associated Press, Reuters, and Agence France-Presse—have used the internet to reinforce their dominance and have developed audio-visual services to supply international all-news television networks like CNN, BBC, and Al Jazeera (Laville and Palmer, 2012: 179–84). This dominance is enhanced by a general withdrawal from international news coverage by most daily newspapers and national television networks.

The Geneva declaration expressed the desire to create an information society "where everyone can create, access, utilize and share information and knowledge, enabling individuals, communities and peoples to achieve their full potential in promoting their sustainable development and improving their quality of life" (WSIS, 2010). Sadly, though, as Robert Savio (2012: 237) argues, what has emerged instead is a "New Information Market Order" characterized by corporate concentration and commercialization.

© IMNATURE/iStockphoto.

Appadurai argues that the world we live in today is characterized by a new role for the imagination of social life; globalization comprises distinct processes rather than a coherent system. How could Appadurai's five 'scapes appear in a crowded subway car?

Changing Notions of Place

A number of scholars have attributed to the communication media a significant role in how we imagine, define, understand, and experience place. The Canadian philosopher Charles Taylor (2005: 23) refers to this as the "social imaginary," which he defines as "the

The Digital Divide

The digital divide refers to the gap between the information-rich and the information-poor; it can be measured on both a global scale (between the regions and countries of the world) and a national scale (between individuals based on where they live, their access to digital networks, and demographic characteristics like household income, education level, age, and sex). The existence of this divide is a clear reminder that not everyone, even in our own communities, enjoys the same access to digital communication technologies. Given the importance of information and connectivity in modern society, the digital divide represents a measure of inequality that can have a serious impact on quality of life.

Jan A.G.M. van Dijk (2005: 15) captures the significance of the digital divide and at the same time explains why, as a negative feedback loop, it persists and worsens:

1. Categorical inequalities in society produce an unequal distribution of resources.
2. An unequal distribution of resources causes unequal access to digital technologies.
3. Unequal access to digital technologies also depends on the characteristics of these technologies.
4. Unequal access to digital technologies brings about unequal participation in society.
5. Unequal participation in society reinforces categorical inequalities and unequal distribution of resources.

At stake here is full participation in, or exclusion from, contemporary society. The digital divide also provides a measure of the economic health of nations and peoples.

Van Dijk (2012: 196) describes four types of access to computer networks: motivation; material or physical access; digital skills; and usage. *Motivation* affects an individual's decision "to purchase a computer and network connection, to learn the requisite skills, and to use the interesting applications" (197). Motivation can be influenced by a person's available time, by affordability, by need, and by a person's inclination to learn and use the internet (198). *Material or physical access* refers to the affordability and availability of computer hardware and network connections, whether in the home or in a public place. Van Dijk notes that the material access divide between haves and have-nots is decreasing in developed countries like Canada, but widening in developing countries (198–9). *Digital skills* are "the collection of skills needed to operate computers and the internet, to search and collect information in them, to communicate with them, and to use them for one's own purposes" (2012: 199). *Usage*, finally, refers to the need, opportunity, obligation, time, and effort that govern whether those with other kinds of access actually use computer networking (201–2).

Even if Canadians are among the best-connected people in the world, clear and persistent distinctions in internet usage remain, depending on income and educational levels, age, and community size. The most recent Canadian Internet Use Survey conducted by Statistics Canada in 2012 found that, overall, 83 per cent of Canadian households had internet access, up from 79 per cent in 2010. This ranged from a low of 77 per cent in New Brunswick to a high of 86 per cent in both Alberta and British Columbia. Among households with internet access, 97 per cent had a high-speed connection. Access figures ranged considerably based on income, however: 98 per cent of households with income of $94,000 or more had internet access, compared to 58 per cent of households with income of $30,000 or less. Similarly, only 28 per cent of Canadians 65 and over in the lowest income quartile used the internet, compared to 95 per cent aged 16 to 24 in the same income category (Statistics Canada, 2013).

Internet Penetration Rates (Selected Countries)

Country	Penetration (percentage of population)
Iceland	96.5
Norway	95.0
Canada	90.9
United States	84.2
Russia	76.1
Brazil	70.7
China	54.6
South Africa	53.7
Chad	5.0
Niger	4.3
Eritrea	1.4

Source: Internet World Stats, 2013.

ways people imagine their social existence, how they fit together with others, how things go on between them and their fellows, the expectations that are normally met, and the deeper normative notions and images that underlie these expectations." The widespread commercialization of cultural production, communication, and information exchange, and the extent to which we rely on these media for our communicative activities, raise a number of questions about the relationship between communication and culture. The perpetual flows of people, capital, goods, services, and images that characterize globalization carry significant implications for how we experience and imagine place, how we define community, and how we constitute identity.

The social anthropologist Arjun Appadurai (1996) argues that the world we live in today is characterized by a new role for the imagination of social life, and he perceives globalization as comprising distinct processes rather than a coherent system. The imagination, for Appadurai, is a "social practice," and he proposes five "'scapes" that create fundamental "disjunctures" between economics, culture, and politics (1996: 31–3). The *ethnoscape* is the "landscape of persons who constitute the shifting world in which we live." *Technoscapes* are formed by the global configuration of technology. *Finanscapes* are "the disposition of global capital." **Mediascapes** are "image-centered" and "narrative accounts of strips of reality." Finally, *ideascapes* are "concatenations of images" that reflect dominant ideologies and counter-ideologies (33–6). These five 'scapes form the "building blocks" of our "imagined worlds; that is, the multiple worlds that are constituted by the historically situated imaginations of persons and groups spread around the globe" (1996: 33; see also Appadurai, 1990; Jones, 2010: 209–26).

These contending 'scapes have profound implications for how we situate ourselves in the world, for how we relate to our own immediate community and other parts and peoples of the world. Doreen Massey (1991: 24) asks, "How, in the face of all this movement and intermixing, can we retain any sense of a local place and its particularity?" Globalization has intensified struggles over the meaning of place. This is particularly the case in countries like Canada, whose citizens tend to be more familiar with cultural imports than with the ideas and expressions of their own artists and intellectuals. This struggle also owes something to Canada's policy of multiculturalism, as Canada—urban Canada, especially—becomes a mixing ground for peoples of diverse backgrounds, beliefs, and traditions. Benedict Anderson defined the nation as "an imagined political community" and depicted eighteenth-century newspapers and novels as implicated in the projects of nation-building and nationalism. The nation, he wrote, "is imagined because the members of even the smallest nation will never know most of their fellow-members, meet them, or even hear of them, yet in the minds of each lives the image of their communion" (Anderson, 1983: 15).

In a similar vein, John Hartley maintains that publics are created by institutions and discourses, arguing that "the media are simultaneously creative and participatory. They create a picture of the public, but it goes live, as it were, only when people participate in its creation, not least by turning themselves into the audience" (Hartley, 1992: 4). Audiences, thereby, are "discursive productions" (Hartley, 1996: 67). But Hartley points out that media can exclude as well as include, creating divisions between those who belong and those who don't. Communities, that is, are largely defined by their distinction from other communities and by specific membership criteria. For example, the news, Hartley argues, is organized around strategies of inclusion and exclusion from our community, creating domains of *Wedom* and *Theydom*, dividing people into "us" and "them" (Hartley, 1992: 207).

As noted above, the various flows we associate with globalization are not new. What globalization has done, however, has been both to increase the traffic—human, material, electronic—across some borders and to reconfigure others (see Box 11.5). This heightened permeability of borders has been met, among some, by the desire for a more rooted, or more secure, sense of place. Places, and the experiences we associate with places, both as individuals and as members of a group, inform memory and our sense of belonging. This sense of belonging is critical to understanding the relationship between identity and a particular locale (Rose, 1995). We might, therefore, detect a very different sense of belonging between native residents of a place and migrants. Migrants such as refugees and exiles, who have not moved of their own free will, may feel little sense of belonging to their new place of residence.

Culture is another means by which identities of place are constructed and sustained. Stuart Hall argues that we tend to imagine cultures as "placed" in two ways. First, we associate place with a specific location where social relationships have developed over time. Second, place "establishes symbolic boundaries around a culture, marking off those who belong from those who do not" (Hall, 1995: 177–86).

At the same time, Hall explains, "There is a strong tendency to 'landscape' cultural identities, to give them an imagined place or 'home', whose characteristics echo or mirror the characteristics of the identity in question."

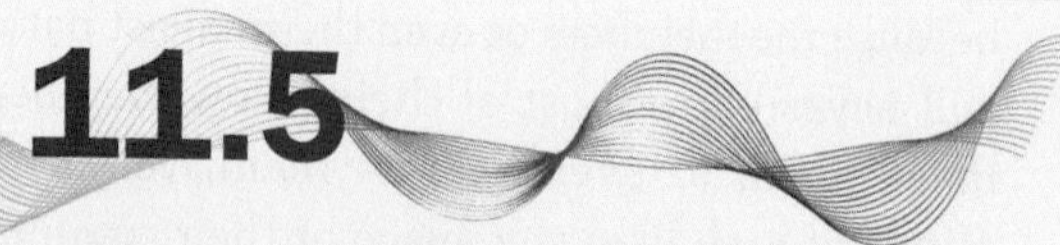

The Age of Migration

The movement of people, both across and within national borders, has been one of the most visible features of globalization in the first two decades of the twenty-first century. Stephen Castles, Hein de Haas, and Mark J. Miller have dubbed this period "the age of migration," situating the phenomenon within the larger context of globalization. "Migrations are not isolated phenomena: movements of commodities, capital and ideas almost always give rise to movements of people, and vice versa" (Castles et al., 2014: 7).

The United Nations put the number of international migrants worldwide in 2017 at 258 million; if this figure includes those who immigrate for work or family reasons, it also includes 25.9 million asylum seekers and refugees fleeing war (e.g., from Syria or South Sudan), political turmoil (e.g., the Democratic Republic of Congo) or some form of persecution (e.g., the flight of Rohingya from Myanmar into Bangladesh). The vast majority of asylum seekers and refugees (82.5%) are being hosted by developing countries (United Nations, 2017: 4-8).

The UN Refugee Agency reported 68.5 million displaced people worldwide (those forced to migrate, both within and across borders) by the end of 2017, setting a new high for the fifth straight year (UNHCR, 2018). More than half of them (53%) were children. Of the total, 40 million were internally displaced, 25.4 million were refugees (defined as people forced from their homeland), and 3.1 million were asylum seekers (defined as those claiming refugee status, but whose cases await evaluation). Two-thirds of the refugees came from five countries: Syria, Afghanistan, South Sudan, Myanmar, and Somalia.

Canada describes itself as a country of immigrants, meaning "most of its people originated from another country and moved to Canada in their generation or in previous generations" (Li, 2003: 9). Canada has a long history of immigration; only its 1.7 million indigenous peoples can truly claim not to be immigrants. Immigration, from Europe, was a central plank of Canada's National Policy in the late nineteenth century, in recognition of the need to populate the West's agricultural regions, build a national economy, and ward off feared annexation by the United States. And immigration has continued to be a central part of federal government policy to the present day (Li, 2003: 14–37). As we have noted, almost 22 per cent of Canadians are immigrants who report more than 250 ethnic origins or ancestries (Statistics Canada, 2016, 2017).

As with other aspects of globalization, migration can be welcomed by some—migrants' families, humanitarian relief agencies, businesses in need of workers—and opposed by others—those with concerns, legitimate or otherwise, over the social and cultural integration of migrants into the host society.

The widespread migration of peoples so prevalent in our time brings together people with very different roots, histories, traditions, and values. In some instances these differences are embraced. But at other times they can be perceived as threatening to our sense of community, of place, of culture, of identity. If much of our engagement with our community takes place through the media, and our understandings of Canadian histories, traditions, and values come not only from news reports but from music, film, television, and printed sources (e.g., books, magazines), then it is through media that we often first meet those who are different from ourselves, and where our understandings of those people originate.

If one impact of globalization has been to call into question the notion of "place" as the basis for identity or culture, postmodernism and improved networks of transportation and communication facilitate the imagination of communities based on gender, race, ethnicity, sexual orientation, social class, and so on. Proximity, in other words, is not a necessary element of identity formation. If culture and identity are not confined to a particular place, it follows that any one place is not confined to a single culture or identity—hence the Quebec conundrum of interculturalism and of its being a distinct society. This issue of identity formation has precipitated localized struggles over immigration and language as well as over urban development, architecture, and foreign investment.

The conventional container of identity and culture that has come under greatest challenge from the reimagining of community prompted by globalization has been the nation-state. Questions of citizenship and questions of identity have been increasingly dissociated (Morley and Robins, 1995: 19). We should not overreact to these changes, however. Canadians still have democratically elected national, provincial, and municipal governments, which, as we discussed in Chapters 7 and 8, continue to pass laws and pursue policies that form the basic framework within which media organizations operate in Canada. No media industry is untouched by them. Globalization alters the context in which mass communication takes place, but local conditions of cultural production remain both pertinent and central to the ways in which it is undertaken.

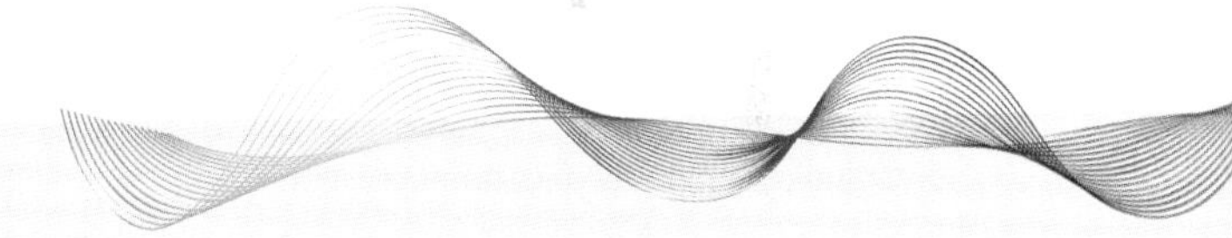

SUMMARY

We hear the term *globalization* used all the time, such that we can be unclear about its precise meaning and unaware of the implications this has on our lives, and particularly on how we communicate.

This chapter began with an extended definition of globalization and showed how it is not simply an economic phenomenon but an intensification of social relations across time and space that touches every aspect of our lives, from how we shop to what we see on our television and computer screens. We then outlined four roles the communication media play in the globalization process: as media of encounter; as media of governance; as media situating us within the world; and as globalized businesses in and of themselves. We subsequently reviewed the predominant theories to explain international communication flows and their implications, beginning with Immanuel Wallerstein's *world systems theory*, touching briefly on *media imperialism* and *cultural dependency*, and concluding with Manuel Castells's notion of the *network society* and Vincent Mosco's discussion of *spatialization*.

On this conceptual groundwork, we traced the history of international communication exchanges, concentrating particularly on the period from the 1940s to the present. We discussed the doctrine of *free flow* promoted by the United States, and then we explained the rise, and subsequent downfall, of the New World Information and Communication Order, whose proponents sought to alleviate communication imbalances between national communities in the 1970s and to promote the "right to communicate" as a fundamental human right. Instead, the period from the 1980s onward has been characterized by further trade liberalization and the reinforcement of the commercial view of communication as commodity exchange. We summarized briefly the 2003 and 2005 conferences of the World Summit on the Information Society as the latest coordinated efforts to democratize communication on a global scale.

We concluded the chapter with a discussion of the impact of globalization on how we think about *place*, *community*, and *identity*, given the importance of communication and cultural exchange to our sense of belonging, and we expanded on Castells's ideas about the new forms of sociability and the new global geography that characterize our time.

KEY TERMS

Canada–US–Mexico Agreement, p. 275
cultural dependency, p. 287
information flows, p. 288
media geography, p. 275
media imperialism, p. 283
mediascape, p. 293
mobility, p. 275
network society, p. 282
proximity, p. 281
sovereignty, p. 280
spatialization, p. 288
world systems theory, p. 286
World Trade Organization, p. 275

RELATED WEBSITES

European Union: europa.eu/index_en.htm
The official site of the European Union includes an institutional overview, regular news dispatches, and official reports.

International Telecommunication Union: www.itu.int/
The ITU is an international organization through which governments and private corporations coordinate telecommunications networks and services.

UNESCO: www.unesco.org/
The principal objective of the United Nations Educational, Scientific and Cultural Organization is to contribute to global peace and security by promoting international collaboration through education, science, culture, and communication.

World Summit on the Information Society (WSIS): www.itu.int/wsis/index.html
Taking the form of two international conferences, WSIS is a coordinated effort to democratize the institutions of mass communication and to eradicate communicative inequalities between peoples and nation-states.

World Trade Organization: www.wto.org
The WTO governs trade between nations and seeks to promote trade liberalization throughout the world.

FURTHER READINGS

Bauman, Zygmunt. 1998. *Globalization: The Human Consequences*. New York: Columbia University Press. This book looks at globalization from a critical and human perspective, considering its political, social, and economic implications on people's daily lives.

Castells, Manuel. 2001. *The Internet Galaxy: Reflections on the Internet, Business, and Society*. Oxford: Oxford UP. Written by one of the foremost contemporary theorists on international communication networks, this book examines the internet from a number of perspectives, including its history and how it affects the way people work, consume media, and interact socially.

Castles, Stephen, Hein de Haas, and Mark J. Miller. 2014. *The Age of Migration: International Population Movements in the Modern World*. New York and London: The Guilford Press. This book adopts a global perspective on migration, examining its consequences for both the source and destination countries for migrants.

Frau-Meigs, Divina, Jérémie Nicey, Michael Palmer, Julia Pohle, and Patricio Tupper, editors. 2012. *From NWICO to WSIS: 30 Years of Communication Geopolitics*. Bristol, UK: Intellect. The essays in this collection trace key communication policy issues from the time of the MacBride Commission to the present.

Held, David, and Anthony McGrew, editors. 2003. *The Global Transformations Reader: An Introduction to the Globalization Debate*. Cambridge: Polity Press. This is a comprehensive reader with concise chapters from leading scholars covering every aspect of globalization, from its economics to its political, social, and cultural implications.

Jones, Andrew. 2010. *Globalization: Key Thinkers*. Cambridge: Polity Press. As its title suggests, this book summarizes the arguments of globalization's principal theorists, contextualizes their ideas, and provides succinct analysis of each of their positions.

Morley, David, and Kevin Robins. 1995. *Spaces of Identity: Global Media, Electronic Landscapes and Cultural Boundaries*. London: Routledge. This is a provocative look at how the globalization of communication has undermined and altered conventional notions of national and cultural belonging. The ideas proposed in this book remain current.

Raboy, Marc, and Jeremy Shtern, editors. 2010. *Media Divides: Communication Rights and the Right to Communicate in Canada*. Vancouver/Toronto: UBC Press. This book contains a number of important essays that follow up on the work of the MacBride Commission and WSIS in the Canadian context.

Taylor, Charles. 2005. *Modern Social Imaginaries*. Durham, NC, and London: Duke University Press. An accessible philosophical study of the way we imagine our world and constitute identity in a period of significant political, economic, and social upheaval—a period of "multiple modernities."

UNESCO. 1980. *Many Voices, One World: Report by the International Commission for the Study of Communication Problems* (MacBride Commission). Paris: UNESCO. The controversial MacBride Report was critical of the free-flow doctrine promoted by the United States and proposed measures to ensure more equitable and balanced communication flows between nations.

Wallerstein, Immanuel. 2007. *World-Systems Analysis: An Introduction*. Durham, NC, and London: Duke University Press. This is an up-to-date introduction to world systems theory, which describes the emergence of an extra-national economy involving long-distance trade links between Europe and parts of Africa, Asia, and what came to be known as the West Indies and North and South America.

STUDY QUESTIONS

1. The term *globalization* is often used to mean economic globalization. Besides economics, what other globalizing forces affect the communication sphere?
2. In what ways do the mass media act as agents of globalization?
3. Is media globalization the same as media imperialism? Why or why not?
4. What is the argument in support of the free flow of communication? What is the basis for criticism of this position?
5. What was the MacBride Commission's position on international communication flows?
6. What is the World Summit on the Information Society?
7. What is world systems theory?
8. What does Manuel Castells mean by *a space of flows*?
9. How is globalization liberating? How is it confining?
10. In what ways can you say that you live globally in your day-to-day activities?

12

Media and Communication
Looking Back, Looking Forward

Where is the knowledge we have lost in information? —*T.S. Eliot*

Marshall Ikonography / Alamy Stock Photo

Opening Questions

- What does it mean to approach the study of media and communication from a critical perspective?
- What are some of the key theoretical perspectives in communication studies?
- What is the role of public policy in the media and communication industries?
- What are some of the problems of thinking of media and communication in simply economic terms?
- What are the key issues facing media in Canada today?

Introduction

Communication media pervade practically all facets of our lives. They encompass traditional media—film, books, magazines, television and radio broadcasting, newspapers, telecommunications—as well as an increasing range of digital information and communication technologies.

We began our study of media and communication by considering the shifting nature of communication technology, reflecting on how media and communication systems are central to the functioning and operation of society, and examining how they orient our understanding of the world and our actions within it. We considered the broad history of media and the ways they have been implicated in political, economic, and social development. We looked at a wide range of media theories, considered the different perspectives they provide on the broad processes of communication—particularly encoding and decoding—and weighed the different accents they put on the importance of structure and agency. We examined the dimensions and character of advertising and promotional culture and how, as forms of communicative practice, they are deeply tied to our economy and culture. We also reviewed the formal institutions of communication and the influence that professional values have on their operation, and we considered the role of larger social forces, such as politics and economics, in shaping the development and character of these organizations' activities.

As we have seen, the influence exerted by these media ranges across all dimensions of society: politics, economics, education, culture, the family, and individual lives. The media also have an enormous impact on our worldview and our frame of reference on events. But, as we have seen, media are incomplete and imperfect tools for understanding our world. To study the dynamics of media, as we have been doing in this book, is to attempt to understand the dynamics of representation and the ways in which it informs our understandings of the world and our place within it.

This final chapter summarizes the various ideas and perspectives on media and communication that we have considered, and points the way to future study and directions of growth and development of the field.

The Shifting Character of Media

Media are central to how we understand culture and society and share in them. In this context, we have approached the study of media and communications from a *critical perspective*. That is, we have been considering how media are implicated in our knowledge and understanding of the world.

Our discussion of oral, literate, and electronic forms of communication introduced how media of communication can influence social form and structure. Our discussion of oral communication, for instance, illustrated that media shape the production and transmission of knowledge. An examination of written or literate communication shows how media can shrink social distance and shift relations of political power. Digital electronic communication does all this and more. It can have both binding and fragmenting effects as barriers to constructing relationships across space collapse. While many digital divides continue to cause inequalities both at home and internationally, the electronic media overall contribute to shrinking social, political, economic, and geographic distances. Who will reap the majority of the benefits from these changes remains to be seen.

But as we have discussed, technology is not the sole defining feature of media systems. While specific types of media might have particular propensities, media systems are the product of a much larger set of political, economic, social, and cultural forces. Broadly speaking, in the context of Western societies, contemporary media reflect cultural forms and social practices engendered by the shift from feudal to industrial society, and the migrations and divisions of labour that characterized that shift. Moreover, in a large industrial nation such as Canada, the media are complexly woven into the social and cultural fabric. The unique characteristics of Canada, such as its large land mass, a small population spread primarily along the border with the United States, its regionalism, two official languages, and multiculturalism, have all laid their stamp on the structure and character of the Canadian media.

Rising from these circumstances, media both orient and animate social life. On the one hand, they reflect the larger set of social and cultural values that frame our lives. On the other hand, we come to know our society—its institutions, organizations, relationships—and the ideas, values, beliefs, and art forms that make up our culture largely through media and our engagement with them. Set in this context, some of the questions we have considered are the following: *Does it matter who owns the media? How does advertising influence what we see in the media? What roles do the media play in the economy? . . . in globalization? . . . in the construction of our tastes and desires and personal identity? Does it matter if Canadian media are dominated by foreign, mainly US, media products? Are television sitcoms, shows promoting celebrities, and other seemingly innocuous programs simply entertainment, or do they play other roles in our lives? In other words, whose or what interests do media serve, and what roles do they play in creating and maintaining social relationships, particularly relations of wealth and power?*

In considering these questions we have seen that communication technology, and the social forums it creates, are currently key sites of social change and struggle as a range of social interests fight for position in the shifting social landscape. Some might shy away from terms like *social struggle*. Neo-liberal critics might prefer "new, open, more competitive markets" or, as those of a more idealist bent might put it, a "new chance for democracy." But a social struggle it is.

Because they are embedded in a larger set of social and political circumstances, changes in our media systems signal much broader social change. In the current environment, we are not merely throwing out a bunch of old machines and bringing in some new, sleek, quieter, more effective ones. Rather, we are setting in motion the revision and reformation of the jobs associated with those machines. We are encouraging the reorganization and perhaps the re-establishment of associated organizations and institutions. We are opening up for reconsideration the foundations of **public policy** governing those activities and institutions. And we are recasting the dimensions of the economy, the location of labour, and the role of the consumer. In some ways, we are also recasting notions of citizenship.

Practices and institutions of mass communication are currently being undermined by the fragmentation of media markets and the rise of a sophisticated, publicly accessible transmission system—the internet. Internet television, radio, and podcasting, for example, can circumvent the state and commercial apparatus controlling mass broadcasting. Independent recording labels and bands who sell their music via the internet have been able to get around the control of the recording industry giants, such as Sony, EMI, Universal, and Warner. Consider as well open-source software, which is a concerted effort on the part of digital labourers to undermine the centralized production and market domination by a handful of companies such as Microsoft. News production, once generally the purview of large media corporations, is being taken up by bloggers, citizen journalists, and a host of small and financially tenuous news producers (see Box 12.1). Similarly, social media sites like Facebook, Twitter, Instagram, and YouTube offer an increasing range of new forms of social interaction. These are but a few examples in the growing range of interactive communications.

At the same time, the shifting structure and character of media industries is raising a host of new political, economic, and cultural issues. Over-the-top program distributors like Netflix and Amazon Prime TV are circumventing regulations, undermining the viability of Canadian screen industries, and raising new concerns about cultural sovereignty. Traditional jobs in journalism and the media are becoming

12.1

The Media Co-op

One of the most innovative online media organizations in Canada is The Media Co-op (www.mediacoop.ca), which was founded in 2006 and has three types of members—readers, contributors, and editors—all with their own respective interests and roles in the organization. In an effort to promote a more **horizontal relationship** between readers and the news organization, reader members are invited to participate in decision-making in terms of both developing story ideas and administrative issues. Journalist members are the main-story contributors, and the editors do the administrative work for the organization. While some of the published material is contributed by volunteers, the cooperative pays contributors wherever possible, in both cash and exchange. The organizational goal is to set up local media cooperatives across the country that produce news at both the local and national levels. At present, there are local cooperatives in Halifax, Toronto, and Vancouver, and more are said to be on the way. Each of these organizations has its own website for local news as well. Despite the ongoing struggle of raising money and developing resources, the cooperative has been operating for over 12 years.

increasingly precarious. There is a growing digital divide both domestically and internationally, and multiplying concerns over privacy as both industry and government strive to more closely track our activities.

The foundations of this change from mass distribution of centrally produced media products to mass communication by and through an expanding range of people and institutions can be understood by recalling the definitions introduced in Chapter 1:

- Mass communication is the centralized production and wide dissemination of information and entertainment.
- Mass communication is the decentralized production and wide accessibility of information and entertainment by means of public access to the internet.
- Mass communication is the interactive exchange of information (or messages or intelligence) among a number of recipients.

As we have seen, the latter two meanings of the term *mass communication* are relatively new. The processes they describe are not new: decentralized, widespread production of content describes early newspapers and small literary magazines; widespread person-to-person communication by means of the postal system is very old; and the telegraph and telephone have been with us since 1846 and 1876, respectively. What is new in the case of widespread production of cultural products is vastly increased ease of access and interaction. The greater variation of media text, sound, and image, together with the capacity for immediate transmission, storage, and manipulation, greatly extends the capabilities of traditional media. The social challenge new media present is how they might be put to work in the broader **public interest** rather than the interest of large private corporations—particularly foreign corporations with little to no concern for issues of Canadian sovereignty.

Communication and Democracy

Developments in communication media may interact with the fundamentals of democracy, particularly in terms of how ownership and control of media may enable or constrain the range of ideas and perspectives found in those media.

The history of this interaction can be traced back at least to the printing press in the mid-fifteenth century, which at first was controlled by the state or governing elite. But as the potential of communication technology for undermining and shifting the bases for political power became apparent, struggles over its control ensued. First, in the case of religion, in sixteenth-century Europe, Protestants such as Martin Luther sought to undermine the social control held by the Catholic Church. Later, governments sought to control the press and the flow of ideas that might stem from it. And in the twentieth century, the corporate control of media became a central question of concern. Should media organizations be free to use their potential power to advance their biases in favour of business, certain political parties, and specific policies (such as free commercial speech)? Or should they act in a more constrained fashion, as self-aware institutions with a privileged position in society and, consequently, a responsibility to act for the social good of all, for a larger public interest? These questions exemplify how communication interacts with notions of democracy.

We saw in Chapter 2 that the social responsibility thesis, particularly in Canada, has provided a backdrop against which media performance in this regard might be measured—at least until the late twentieth century—not only in the press but also in the founding of broadcasting and specifically through the creation of a national public broadcasting service. Even more than the press, broadcasting was seen as a potential harbinger of greater social coherence, public expression, and responsibility in the media, offering enlightenment to individuals and encouraging the pursuit of democratic ideals. Drawing on Canada's tradition of governmental or public enterprise, CBC gave the state the chance to finance a medium of communication on behalf of the people and the nation itself that would counterbalance the commercial media, which are often financed 80 per cent or more through commercial advertising.

At the international level, the efforts of **UNESCO**—beginning in the 1970s and carrying through to the 2000s—to extend the ideals of public communication through a new world order were founded on a similar idea of social responsibility. Dubbed "fair flows of information" rather than "free flows" (where the strongest in the market were free to dominate), the New World Information and Communications Order was championed by UNESCO in the 1980s as the possible impact and potential of new communication technology was becoming apparent. In large part, however, these efforts were squelched by the United States and the United Kingdom when they withdrew their support for UNESCO. The desire of these two countries to maintain their predominance as exporters of information, entertainment, and ideology to the world overrode any sense either had of social justice or of the value of celebrating diversity on a worldwide scale. Canadian policy was mostly set against this kind of imperialism, and with the help of favourable government policy, this country built up cultural industries capable of carrying Canadian creative content to domestic audiences in the face of the dominance of US media products in Canadian markets. More recently, given the ongoing advantages enjoyed by US and other foreign media producers, pressures have mounted to revisit current Canadian regulation that allows for more open markets. Critics have been raising questions as to the continued ability of Canadian perspectives to maintain their place in the Canadian mediascape.

In the digital age, because of the opportunities new media present for expanding public participation in formerly cloistered venues of decision-making, the question is perhaps how quickly and extensively large corporations will move to consolidate their predominance and, hence, their control of changing media and media markets. This is already happening in terms of concentration of ownership of traditional media; the vertical integration of content producers, such as television networks and newspapers, with the telecommunications companies that provide access to the internet; and corporate consolidation and control of web-based media organizations such as Google, Facebook, and Netflix. In the face of this ongoing consolidation, media policy becomes a particularly important vehicle for ensuring public participation and representation in both the development of new media and, perhaps more importantly, issues of governance in general. As illustrated in Box 12.2, "Advocating for Change," struggles to help ensure that the media are responsible to the greater public interest have a long history in Canada and continue today.

Content and Audiences

When we study communication, especially content, we are generally studying practices or processes of representation—that is, the act of putting ideas into words, paintings, sculpture, film, plays, television programs, websites, podcasts, or any other medium of communication. In this context, communication, or the making of meaning, is an active process that requires specific engagement at the levels of both encoding and decoding.

In the study of communication, the importance of a statement is not limited to whether it predicts events, can be refuted by others, or generates other interesting hypotheses—all standards used in science. The focus is on how an act of communication represents or reconstructs something, and what gives a particular representation its force or its ability to persuade. Whatever makes a particular novel, painting, or film more popular or revered than another—or perhaps even a novel more powerful than a film—cannot be satisfactorily discussed by reference to the relative truth of each communication. Such media and individual works are discussed by communication scholars in terms of their rhetorical force or in terms of the nature or style of their representation.

Communication researchers use a range of analytical theoretical perspectives to wrestle content into some meaningful framework so that they might better understand how it is generated and how it frames our understanding of the world. Each theoretical perspective provides a particular point of view on understanding content. And different perspectives can be deployed as the situation demands. From a critical theoretical perspective, however, our task is not to understand variables affecting communication in an effort to attain seemingly perfect communication, as a mathematical model might lead us to do in another field of study. Indeed, as we have seen, because everybody approaches the act of communication with different histories and assumptions, such an ideal is impossible. Our task is instead to understand the social processes involved in the creation and transmission of meaning.

In approaching this task, we can focus, for example, on the agency of the individual producers: on the life and intent of the author and the dynamics involved in the publication of a particular media text. Working from another direction, we can consider the ways in which larger social structures and processes impose limits and pressures on the media and media messages. Like structuralists and semioticians, we can consider how both the organizational dimensions of a story and the signifiers deployed refer back to a larger set of social circumstances and ideas, how the sign system is itself part of a larger set of social processes and circumstances, or, following the lead of the post-structuralists, we can delve into the particularities of the meaning system that has been created by audience members in the act of interpretation.

Similarly, political economy offers insight into how politics and economics give form to media content. From this perspective, we can examine the production of content in terms of the interests of the producers and those paying for production, as well as the impact on content of government regulation, professional codes and values, and, especially, the profit motive. This perspective provides an account of why certain kinds of content are produced and disseminated while other kinds are not.

At quite a different level again, organizational analysis provides insight into how the characteristics of specific organizations—such as whether an organization is mandate driven or profit

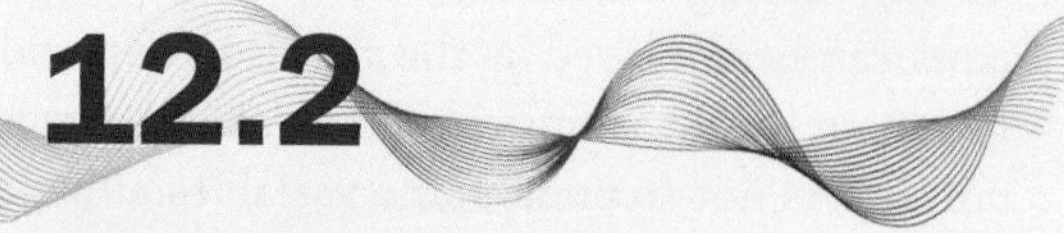

12.2

Advocating for Change

Efforts by citizens' groups to encourage the development of comprehensive media and telecommunications systems have a long history in Canada—sometimes to encourage the growth of public ownership and/or Canadian-owned industry; other times to mitigate the effects of market forces on the cost and character of services and products. Precedents go back at least to the early decades of the twentieth century and the fight by citizens of the Prairie provinces of Alberta, Saskatchewan, and Manitoba to establish public ownership of telephone systems (Babe, 1990: 102–11). As distinctions were drawn between content and carriage during that period, however, telecommunication and media regulation began to develop largely independently of each other (202–07). In that process—driven by values such as the need for an informed citizenship, access to a diversity of media, and cultural sovereignty—media regulation took on a higher public profile.

In this regard, federal government inquiries and commissions have often played an important role in animating public debate around media. In 1929, for instance, the government struck the first major inquiry into media: the Royal Commission on Radio Broadcasting (Aird Report). The struggle for public broadcasting developed out of this inquiry, with the Canadian Radio League using it as a springboard to develop a broad public campaign that led to the institution of the Canadian Radio Broadcasting Commission—the predecessor to today's Canadian Broadcasting Corporation—in 1932.

As media industries expanded through the middle part of the twentieth century, government sponsored inquiries continued to play an important role in highlighting and bringing forward issues concerning their growth and development. Pressures to increase profits encouraged escalating concentration of ownership, which took a toll on content. The overall number of reporters and editorial voices declined as newspapers and broadcast newsrooms shared stories and other material across the chain, and owners took increasing liberties in shaping stories and other editorial content.

Public outcries spawned several inquiries through the 1970s and '80s, including the 1970 Special Senate Committee Report on the Mass Media and the 1980 Royal Commission on Newspapers (Canada, 1971; Canada, 1981). These investigations provided forums for expressing public discontent on the state of these industries, and, rising from those concerns, pressure from activists helped shape the development of alternatives to corporate media, such as community television and radio (see Goldberg, 1990; Girard, 1992; Hackett and Carroll, 2006: 167–8). However, in terms of large corporate media, few of the recommendations of these inquiries were ever acted upon (Skinner et al., 2005: 56–64).

Following changes in regulations that had been designed to keep newspaper, broadcasting, and telecommunications companies separate, a series of cross-media ownership deals were struck in 2000 that radically altered the Canadian mediascape. This was the first round of corporate consolidation designed to reap the supposed economic benefits of technological convergence. However, layoffs and corporate tinkering with editorial policy followed, prompting public calls for a federal inquiry into the effects of these mergers. And, in the mid-2000s, more public inquiries were conducted to look into the impact of concentration of ownership on the media, particularly news and editorial content.

Today, organizations such as Friends of Canadian Broadcasting (www.friends.ca)and the Canadian Internet Policy and Public Interest Clinic (cippic.ca) continue to lobby governments and advocate on broadcasting and telecommunications issues on behalf of the public.

FRIENDS OF CANADIAN BROADCASTING

By permission of Friends of Canadian Broadcasting.

Founded in 1985, Friends of Canadian Broadcasting is a strong advocate for public broadcasting and Canadian journalism and storytelling.

oriented—impinge on media content. We can also gain an understanding of content through analyzing the characteristics of particular media forms, such as news stories, ads, soap operas, documentaries, and music videos: how ads are constructed to draw us in; how news presentation privileges the news anchor or one of the protagonists in a story; how investigative television can present a convincing veracity where there may be none at all; and how soap operas captivate audience members in their presentations of fictional characters. Each of these perspectives contributes to the richness of our understanding of both referents (signifieds) and the symbols (signifiers) used to represent them.

With the overall understanding these various perspectives make possible, we can then extend our understanding of the nature and roles of the media in society. We can understand, for example, how the media are separate from, yet intrinsic to, society. We can appreciate the role they play in incorporating content from subcultures, making it part of the culture as a whole, or how they can reject as legitimate perfectly normal styles of living that are a part of any culture. We can also gain a sense of how autonomous the media are in their capacity to create their own realities, what their inherent shortcomings are, and, by extension, why we might need mechanisms that help ensure they cannot entrap us in a world of their own construction.

But the encoding or construction of media messages is only one side of the equation. Decoding, or how they are received, is another. Thus, we have also considered how audience members engage with the media—what they take from the media and how.

The first principle in understanding content–audience interaction is recognizing that it is an active process. Even when distracted, audience members are meaning-generating entities. That is, they filter information and entertainment through their own histories and understandings of the world, through established opinions and knowledge, and through situational variables—fatigue, their assessment of the presentation, other pressing concerns of the day, their anticipation of certain events, their position in the workforce, and so on. Similarly, the media are active generators of meaning insofar as they create programs targeting certain audiences, with certain intensities, designed to engage audience members in a certain fashion.

Early studies of audiences perceived them as relatively passive, and the media as having direct effects on human behaviour and attitudes. While evidence for this latter notion is controversial at best, the argument that media serve some sort of agenda-setting function, or that they work to cultivate particular conceptions or attitudes, has gained some credibility among researchers. From this perspective, media don't so much tell people *what to think* as they do *what to think about*. Another perspective drawn from early effects research that we considered was uses and gratifications research, which analyzes the uses to which audience members put media content and the satisfaction and reward audience members feel they derive from media content.

Working from a different starting point, we also considered theories that focus on the ways that the media position audiences to reproduce dominant social ideas and values. Marxist perspectives on media, for instance, illustrate how they often serve to promote the ideas and values associated with capitalism, while the Frankfurt School's examination of the industrialization of the production of information and entertainment illustrates how economics structures cultural form in general.

In the face of these critiques, researchers of British cultural studies strove to better understand the complexity of the dynamics between media and audiences. Working with youth subcultures and social movements, their emphasis was on audience members as active agents and the numerous ways different groups of people engaged with media content. Working from yet another direction, feminist research illustrates how media and practices of communication contribute to social inequalities in terms of sex and gender.

Industry-based research approaches audiences from another direction, as commodities to be sold to advertisers. Such a perspective emphasizes quite different variables. At a first level, the number of people in the audience is of central importance. Then come their age, education, gender, income level, location, and so forth, followed by a consideration of how these elements are indicative of certain characteristics, such as specific attitudes; consumption patterns of particular products; and the time they spend listening, reading, or watching. Such information is valuable for the business of buying, selling, renting, and accessing audiences, and is also valuable in understanding general patterns in society.

The media and audiences tend to engage each other in diverse ways, and the resulting interaction creates many social issues. The various starting points and perspectives we use to gain insight into what audiences make of content reflect that diversity. In simple terms, media content, such as hate speech, may serve as an igniting spark for anti-social behaviour—a good reason for us to be concerned about content generation and how media might contribute to anti-social behaviour. But media content may also inspire lifelong ambition, grand humanitarian gestures, respect for individual freedom, social plurality, cultural values, and the building of community. This positive spark is even more important to understand.

As interactive public communication systems become more common in society, it is increasingly important to understand how media systems and content frame and animate social life.

The Social Dimensions of Media and Communication

Having acquired some understanding of the character and history of media, as well as some of the key perspectives on their content and interaction with audiences, we can turn to some of the larger social dimensions of media and communications: (1) advertising and promotional culture; (2) policy, or, more comprehensively speaking, law and policy; (3) ownership and control of communication institutions; (4) the role and actions of professionals; and (5) information and communication technology and globalization.

Advertising and Promotional Culture

As we have discussed, advertising is ubiquitous in our society and has taken over many public and private spaces and places. It is an integral component of modern culture and creates a vast system of symbols and ideas that reflect and shape our cultural values and understandings. By creating awareness and demand for products and services, it is a fundamental component of our economic systems and structures, and lies at the very foundation of the commercial mass media, financing the production and distribution of most information and entertainment.

Embedded in our culture, advertising is a system of meaning making with ideological and cultural dimensions that shape, inform, and reflect our views on social issues. It serves to hide or mask the conditions of production and instill commodities with new meanings that appear to be inherent in the commodities themselves, such as fashion, strength, athleticism, wealth, and love. In this context, branding is a key element of advertising and promotional culture. A brand is a promise, a set of values and expectations attached to a name/logo. Branding is about giving products and companies human characteristics and extends beyond products or companies to a wide range of institutions and organizations, including churches, universities, countries, political parties, and people. In the digital world, the business of advertising focuses on collecting and monetizing information about consumer behaviour (thus raising concerns about privacy).

But advertising has more profound impacts than simply communicating product information. It is an entire cultural system, a social discourse whose unifying theme is promoting consumption. Our voracious appetites for consumer goods have had a huge impact on the environment, and, in the face of global warming, the effects of advertising and promotional culture may be catastrophic.

Public Policy

Policy provides a set of rules and regulations governing the way information and media products are created and consumed. For instance, the *Broadcasting Act* describes the roles and responsibilities of the various elements of the broadcasting system, helping ensure that Canadian ideas and perspectives are represented in Canadian media content. Copyright legislation works to develop markets for media products and other forms of intellectual property. Privacy legislation works to protect the rights of individuals. Advertising regulations frame the kinds of claims advertisers can make and the kinds of products they may advertise. Libel laws structure the way journalists and news organizations operate. And income tax policies encourage advertisers to spend their ad dollars with Canadian media outlets and ensure Canadian ownership of newspapers.

Creating a Place for Canada

At a more basic level, policy also creates opportunities for Canadian media producers. As we have seen, the market is itself a form of regulation, and left to its own devices favours some interests over others. Because of the economies of scale involved, it is simply much cheaper for Canadian broadcasters to buy foreign programming than it is to produce their own. Thus, particularly in English Canada, without Canadian-content regulations there would be even more US programming on television than there is now.

Similarly, as we have seen, prior to the enactment of content regulations for radio in the 1970s, less than 5 per cent of the music played on domestic radio stations was Canadian. This was not because Canadians did not make good music, but because of the marketing and publicity spilling over from US markets into Canada, as well as other factors. It was simply more lucrative for Canadian radio owners to play American music. As well, there is not the same market in the States for Canadian cultural materials as there is in Canada for US products. Again, this is not because Canadian products are somehow of inferior quality but the result of simple economics. American producers generally supply more than enough product to meet demand in their home markets and—due to economies of scale—it is cheaper to use that product than to purchase Canadian content. These economics necessitate some form of regulation if Canadian media products are going to find space on the shelves in their home markets. The situation is somewhat different in Quebec, where a range of cultural factors allow homegrown products to compete successfully with foreign fare.

In short, public policy shapes the ground—particularly the economic ground—on which media products are created and, in turn, influences the character of those products and the ways they represent the world.

Ownership

A longstanding focus in Canadian media policy has been concerned with forms of **ownership**, and the interests of owners are seen to have significant effects on the content and character of media. In the face of cheap US media products, Canadian ownership and content regulations have been used to create an economics of Canadian production and to prevent Canadian media companies and markets from becoming simple extensions of their American cousins. In the broadcasting, cable, and telecommunications industries, legislation imposes limits on foreign ownership. In the newspaper industry, tax policy ensures that newspapers stay in Canadian hands.

At the same time, as we saw in Chapter 7, a number of public inquiries have voiced concern about how the economic forces underlying private ownership lead to escalating concentration of ownership and a narrowing range of voices and perspectives in the media. Consequently, issues of ownership in Canada have been framed by various government regulations that, on the one hand, have tried to keep the ownership of

Canadian media in Canadian hands and, on the other hand, have wrestled with the drawbacks and supposed benefits of allowing for large, privately owned media companies to get a foothold in the industry. As a result, no media industry in Canada is governed exclusively by **free-market economics**; the industries are framed by regulations that, in some cases, reflect a complex mixture of public and private enterprise.

The central difference between public and private forms of ownership pertains to the mandate or purposes that guide their operations. In contradistinction to privately owned media that foreground the profit motive, public and community media are mandated to serve broad social purposes. As laid out in the 1991 *Broadcasting Act*, section 3(1)(l), for instance, CBC is to "provide radio and television services incorporating a wide range of programming that informs, enlightens and entertains." Just as CBC did in the development of television, in the face of shifting technologies today, it has moved to develop a range of web-based services. Chief among these are an increasing number of television programs, shows, podcasts, documentaries, French programming, and more than 50 music streams that can be accessed from its *Gem* website (gem.cbc.ca).

Community media also are expected to fulfill social goals. For instance, while the mandate of community television stations is not enunciated in legislation, in its 2016 Community Television Policy the CRTC specifies that "community

12.3

National Campus and Community Radio Association / *Association Nationale des Radios Étudiantes et Communautaires* (NCRA/ANREC)

Broadcasting in over 60 languages, member stations of the NCRA/ANREC employ over 220 full-time (equivalent) staff and 7,000 volunteers, who work an estimated 25,000 hours per week. Community radio is about volunteerism, social engagement, independent music, learning by doing, community capacity building, citizen journalism, and more. The NCRA has more than 192,000 watts of broadcasting power.

Source: www.ncra.ca/about-cc-radio.

Used with permission of Zoe Ludski and Deepi Leihl.

On the left is NCRA volunteer Cousin Awd (Zoë Ludski), host of CJMP's *42 Fish* in Powell River, BC, meeting with Vancouver-based CITR volunteer news reporter Deepi Leihl at the National Community Radio Conference hosted by CFUV in Victoria.

programming should reflect the communities served and that community channels should reflect the official languages, ethnic and Aboriginal composition of the community" (CRTC, 2016). Similarly, but set at the organizational level, the Statement of Principles of the National Campus and Community Radio Association / Association Nationale des Radios Étudiantes et Communautaires (NCRA/ANREC), which represents 80 campus and community stations across the country, notes "that mainstream media fails to recognize or in many instances reinforces social and economic inequities that oppress women and minority groups of our society" and commits members to "providing alternative radio to an audience that is recognized as being diverse in ethnicity, culture, gender, sexual orientation, age, and physical and mental ability" (NCRA, 1987).

Still, private ownership is the dominant ownership form within the media system, and, in the face of ongoing pressure to tie the expansion of Canadian media to the profit motive, to what degree a larger set of public purposes might be maintained within the system is in question.

One of the central features of Canadian media policy has been to protect the revenues of Canadian media producers in order to ensure that they are profitable enough to invest in production. Yet, as we have seen, particularly in the broadcasting sector, it has always been a struggle to get the big private corporations to invest in quality Canadian programs, and changes in technology are working to narrow the range of private corporations at work within the Canadian mediascape.

With the digitization of information, communication systems that were once capable of carrying only one type of message can now carry a range of signals. Telephone, cable, and satellite systems all can be used to transmit television, telephone, and computer data. Webcasting is poised to supplant traditional television and radio broadcasting, and traditional newspaper and periodical delivery as well. And information-based products, like news and advertising, once destined for one medium, are now tailored for use across a range of media. Spurred by this technological convergence, companies in what were once separate industries, like newspapers and television or cable television and telecommunication, have broken into each others' markets and fuelled corporate convergence—in other words, concentration of ownership.

With companies trying to capture cost savings by forging new economies of scale and scope, recent trends toward concentration of ownership have raised particular concerns. Some of the important *synergies*—as the efficiencies gleaned from consolidation are sometimes called—sought by these corporations are reduced labour requirements, cross-promotion of media products, larger and more flexible advertising markets, the *repurposing* of content created for use in one medium for use in another, the integration of executive and administrative functions, and vastly increased barriers to entry for would-be competitors. Consequently, concentration is seen as narrowing the range of perspectives and distinct voices available in the media, while new editorial policies and sanctions evolving through these changes are raising fears for editorial independence.

But as we have seen, while the internet presents many new opportunities for producing and distributing media content, it is not the fountain of alternatives to traditional media that some pundits claim. High-quality media content is expensive to produce. Most of the news found on the internet comes from professional organizations, and most blogs and posts simply republish or comment on it.

Professionalism

Professionalism governs communication and cultural production in its own way. Cultural producers are not, strictly speaking, "professionals" in the same manner that lawyers and doctors are. Law and medicine require accredited formal training and permission to practise from recognized licensing bodies, and they are subject to their own specialized regulatory authorities. But cultural producers nonetheless derive a sense of professionalism from their specialized skills, their practice-specific codes of ethics, recognized sets of qualitative conventions, and, above all, the conviction that their work is an essential contribution to *culture* in the fullest sense of the term. Like other kinds of professionals, cultural producers owe some allegiance to their employers or clients, and they remain subject to laws particular to the communication field, such as those pertaining to libel, copyright, privacy, and access to information. But their professionalism means that cultural producers are especially responsible for upholding and advancing the recognized standards of their practice and earning the respect of their peers.

Cultural producers' sense of professionalism is tied very closely to the Enlightenment ideals of freedom of speech, freedom of expression, and freedom of the press, of questioning and challenging received wisdom and other forms of authority. They promote the notion that mass communication, in all its manifestations, is a key element of a democratic society. While we might attribute these ideals most readily to journalists, most cultural producers might make the claim that their communicative activities serve the cultural, political, social, and economic goals of society.

This sense of professionalism, though, is being eroded. Employers are increasingly treating cultural producers simply as workers like any others—replaceable parts in the assembly line of production, subject to layoffs and buyouts, relegated to contract work, compelled to emphasize quantitative efficiencies over qualitative merits. Newsrooms are shrinking across all platforms, television dramas share prime time with reality formats, radio hosts are replaced by computerized music programming, and freelance magazine writers work for the same rates they were being paid 30 years ago. The government policies that promote cultural production in Canada, as we described in Chapters 7 and 8, do little to protect cultural producers within their own industries.

Faced with fragmenting audiences and shrinking revenues, media corporations are laying off full-time employees and turning to contract workers or freelancers who are generally paid less and have little if any job security, and few benefits. For people trying to get their first job in media, unpaid internships have become a seemingly necessary rite of passage. But paid employment often remains elusive for many, and governments have recently begun to crack down on internships that they perceive to be illegal and exploitative (Global News, 2016). At the same time, labour unions such as the Canadian Media Guild (www.cmg.ca) have been focused on helping to improve conditions for this new army of part-time workers through a range of supports, including training and mentoring.

Weekend Images Inc/iStockphoto.

Many students do internships as a way to get experience in the field and on-the-job training. The Canadian Intern Association (www.internassociation.ca) advocates against the exploitation of interns and aims to improve the internship experience for both interns and employers.

Information and Communication Technology and Globalization

Technology does not exist in a vacuum or as a social force on its own. While different theoretical perspectives on technology afford both its developers and adopters differing levels of agency, as we have seen, technology is the product of a complex set of political, economic, and social forces that work to shape and configure its development. Policy also helps to set the context for technology. Whether in terms of government aid for research and development, licensing that allows organizations to offer particular technological services (e.g., cellphones, cable or satellite TV), tax incentives that encourage individuals or organizations to adopt particular technologies (or ownership mandates), policy can play a number of important roles in technological development. In communication, policy issues—such as who can use what technology for what purpose, who can control that technology, and how that control can be exploited—are critical.

Because technology encompasses machines, techniques, and social institutions, it has a substantial impact on the structure and functioning of society as a transformative agent, an agent of change that may bring both negative and positive consequences. And while we often think of information and communication technology (ICT) in terms of content, such as film, video, television, or music, one of the most dramatic changes it might be implicated in is a shift in the locus of control: the greater the ability to communicate, the further the control system can be from the phenomenon being controlled. As the history of communication illustrates, communication developments have often led to increased centralization of control. Whether in terms of the centralization of political control, as in the case of the railway and communication technology enabling early Canadian governments to exert east–west control over the northern territory of North America, or in the case of the centralization of economic control, as today's transnational corporations harness information technology to coordinate supply and demand in global markets (media markets and others), ICT is often a key vehicle for addressing issues of spatialization.

ICTS are not the first set of technologies that have been seen as reshaping society (see Box 12.4), but the social changes arising from the widespread implementation of ICTS are far-reaching, and they are central to the industrial restructuring taking place both at home and abroad.

The global economy is not a new development; there has been strong global trade for over 500 years. But since the mid-1970s economic recession and the lure of cheap labour have fuelled international trade agreements and the investment of manufacturing capital in places like Southeast Asia, China, northern Mexico, and the American Sunbelt. To combat this competition, companies remaining in traditional industrial centres restructured, reducing staff and adopting labour-saving technologies.

Through facilitating the movement of capital and goods, ICT has been important in facilitating this shift in labour processes, providing a vital link between the newly industrialized countries where these goods are now produced and

Scott Greene, *Channel Babel*, oil on canvas, 1998. Courtesy of the artist and Catherine Clark Gallery, San Francisco, California, USA.

Communication and accompanying media pervade our lives in modern society. The power of both the worldwide transmission of messages and the transformation that digital communication offers is the foundation for the remaking/reordering of society.

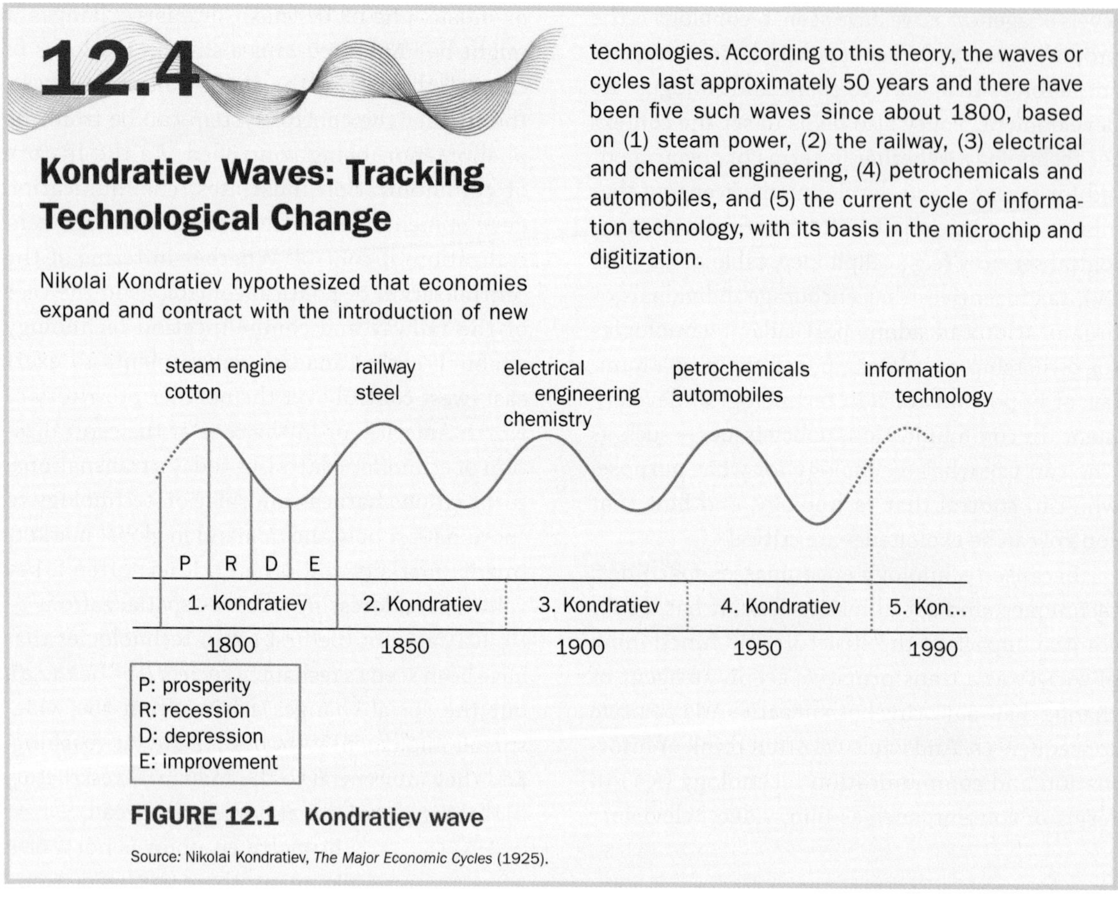

12.4 Kondratiev Waves: Tracking Technological Change

Nikolai Kondratiev hypothesized that economies expand and contract with the introduction of new technologies. According to this theory, the waves or cycles last approximately 50 years and there have been five such waves since about 1800, based on (1) steam power, (2) the railway, (3) electrical and chemical engineering, (4) petrochemicals and automobiles, and (5) the current cycle of information technology, with its basis in the microchip and digitization.

FIGURE 12.1 Kondratiev wave

Source: Nikolai Kondratiev, *The Major Economic Cycles* (1925).

the markets in old industrialized centres, such as North America and Western Europe, where they are consumed. ICT also has been central to the reorganization of industry in these old industrial centres, where it has been used to centralize control over operations, amalgamate responsibilities and functions, and more closely monitor and coordinate employees as companies have restructured to confront new global competitors.

As the information economy has taken form, ever-growing types of information commodities, both products and services, have been created. Changes in copyright legislation, for instance, provide legal sanctions against the unauthorized copying of computer software, video and sound recordings, television programs, and other forms of data, and these changes have been instrumental in developing and expanding multi-million dollar markets for these products. Similarly, sanctions against photocopying for other than personal use and royalties on public photocopiers and blank CDs have created new revenue streams for media companies and creators. Twenty-five years ago, professors often copied class readings and other course materials and handed them out to students for the cost of the copying. Today, such behaviour might be subject to heavy fines or even imprisonment. The television universe available via cable, satellite, and the internet also has expanded dramatically, as has the cost. Video games have become big business. Education, a necessarily information-based activity, has become increasingly commercialized and responsible to market forces. The internet has given rise to an expanding range of new web-based businesses and services, and access to the internet itself has become an increasingly costly service. With a whole new set of mobile telecommunications and internet-based services and products soon to hit the market, the information economy is proceeding apace.

Issues and Policy Trends

In the shifting field of communication various new issues are rising, and old concerns are taking new form.

Over-the-Top Video

As we illustrated in Chapter 8, online or *over-the-top* (OTT) video delivery services such as Netflix and Amazon Prime threaten to overwhelm the Canadian television system. Because the CRTC has previously ruled that that it would not regulate internet content, these services lie outside the regulatory system. Consequently, without the obligation to contribute to the production of Canadian programming, or even to ensure that Canadian programs are available on their systems, they sidestep the regulations that literally make Canadian television possible.

While some people argue that it is impossible to regulate the internet, and that we should finally surrender to the logic of the market, as we have seen in previous chapters, new technologies have long threatened to overwhelm the Canadian broadcasting system with foreign programming. And, with varying degrees of success, regulators have found ways to meet with those challenges.

In 1932, for instance, as a flood of US radio signals threatened to smother the nascent Canadian radio broadcasting system, the Canadian Radio Broadcasting Commission was put into place to help counter that threat. In 1952, with US television signals rolling across the border and attracting Canadian audiences, CBC and the government mounted a feverish campaign to build a Canadian television system. And in the mid-1960s, when cable TV was set to overwhelm the adolescent Canadian system with popular US channels, the 1968 *Broadcasting Act* made cable companies responsible to the broad social purposes of broadcasting, and a series of regulations like simultaneous substitution helped make the industry a responsible player within the system. In the 1980s, and again in the early 1990s, signals from US satellite broadcasters sent regulators scrambling to find ways to keep Canadians tuned in to the system. Scores of new pay-TV channels and a boost to the Canadian production industry was the response to that crisis.

In the face of all these technological threats to the domestic mediascape, regulators were able to forge a system that delivered Canadian perspectives to Canadian viewers. As its many critics point out, the current regulatory system is not perfect. And if history is to be our guide, any regulatory solutions to the current problems facing the system will inevitably be temporary and fleeting. To surrender to the latest technology, however, might well lead to the representation of Canadian ideas and values being overwhelmed by foreign programming on the growing range of screens watched by Canadian audiences. Solutions to these concerns, such as geo-blocking, do exist. Whether the CRTC and/or the federal government choose to exercise these options remains to be seen.

Foreign Ownership

Increasing foreign ownership of Canadian media is also a developing issue. Some argue that increasing foreign ownership in the telecommunications sector will boost investment in the industry and result in lower mobile telephone prices and better services. Others, however, point out a number of problems with this plan. First, given the growing cross-media ownership between telecommunications and broadcasting companies, allowing foreign ownership of telecommunications will inevitably lead to foreign ownership of broadcasting and a decline in investment in Canadian media production. Second, they argue that there is no incentive for foreign companies to invest in providing services in areas that present little return, such as in rural communities and the Far North—the areas most in need of investment to bridge digital divides. And third, there is concern that regulators are less able to exert control over foreign-owned companies than over their domestic counterparts. How this issue plays out could affect Canadian control over the long-term development of both the telecommunications and broadcasting fields.

Digital Divides

At another level, **digital divides** at the local, regional, national, and global levels threaten to split the information society into a world of *haves* and *have-nots*. Without computers and high-speed access to the internet, or the knowledge of how to use these technologies effectively, many people are excluded from the political, economic, and social benefits enabled by these technologies. As acquiring information increasingly hinges on the ability to pay for it, it is difficult for schools, universities, and public libraries to keep up with the rising cost. Consequently, the quality of education and general availability of information are being reduced and those people and organizations that cannot pay for it are in danger of being deprived of these crucial communication resources. Digital literacy is also an issue, as low-income people and people living in remote communicates can experience difficulty accessing training to acquire digital skills (CBC, October 19, 2018).

There are also many places on earth outside the wired world and, thereby, outside the reach of information technology. In Canada, rural areas with small populations such as in the Prairies and the North don't present the economies of scale to make it profitable for large corporations to invest in communication infrastructure and to supply services. Such areas, then, are sometimes left outside the digital world. Similarly, in many areas of the Global South, people simply cannot afford to buy into the communication transformation taking place.

Privacy

Privacy, too, is of rising concern. As social life is increasingly mediated by ICT, information about our activities is being monitored and collected by numerous organizations and government agencies. The unauthorized use of this information threatens our privacy in a number of ways. In the workplace, ICT can be used to monitor email and telephone conversations, or to count keystrokes and attempt to measure the volume of work undertaken by employees. (Charles Frederick Taylor, the originator of scientific management in the workplace in the early twentieth century, would be pleased!) Insurance companies purchase health and accident records in an attempt to assess the potential risk of applicants, sometimes denying coverage on this basis. Law-enforcement agencies are considering ways to use the information contained in databases to identify potential criminal suspects. And in both Canada and the United States, there is ongoing debate between law-enforcement agencies and public-interest groups over the right of government agencies to monitor electronic conversations and data flow.

These concerns are compounded by the fact that both personal information and important social, legal, and economic information is often stored and processed outside the country. Private corporations, governments, universities, libraries, and the legal and engineering professions all sometimes use data services and networks outside Canada to process and store personal tax, credit, and medical data, as well as educational materials and information on natural resources and other matters of national import. Because this trans-border data flow places the information outside of the reach of national laws and regulation, it raises a host of issues for both Canadian sovereignty and the economy, and it leaves Canadians vulnerable to a host of potential problems, including trade sanctions, bankruptcies, and theft.

Regulation

Keeping regulatory frameworks relevant in the face of rapid technological change is also an issue. As convergence accelerates, for instance, the CRTC is faced with trying to improve the overall coherence of the regulatory framework, and there are discussions around merging the Broadcasting and Telecommunications Acts. A concern here is what might happen to the cultural objectives of broadcasting should such a merger take place.

Shifting Economic Currents

The changing media environment is not only animating change in the realm of public policy, but, as some critics argue, it is also shifting the economics of media production.

The Long Tail

Popularized by Chris Anderson, editor-in-chief of *Wired* magazine, in a book of the same title, the **long-tail** phenomenon refers to what appears to be a change in the economics of media production brought on by the electronic storage and distribution of media productions.

The book begins with a bow in the direction of blockbuster hits, which, as Anderson points out, are the foundation of massive media and entertainment industries. Hits rule, he says, and, thus, the factors that are fundamental to making hits also rule: centralized production, celebrities, huge production budgets, massive marketing campaigns, restricted distribution systems, and formulas that attract members of the mass public, who are seeking entertainment. Everyone makes money when a hit comes along. The author J.K. Rowling earned a substantial amount of money when each new title in the *Harry Potter* series was published; sharing in the economic windfall were her agent, her publishers around the world, the designers, the editors, the warehouse staff, the booksellers, the filmmakers, the actors, the theatre owners, and the lawyers who draw up the movie rights, toy rights, and product rights. In fact, everyone benefits financially—right down to the babysitter who fills in because the usual sitter must go and see the latest movie adaptation.

So lucrative are hits that the entire industry is hooked on finding the next blockbuster. Potential sales channel and determine retail opportunities, whether space on a bookshelf, music store shelf, or magazine rack, screen time in a movie theatre, or a time slot or playlist on television or radio. To gain exposure, a product must fit an established category that sells. In books, such categories are mysteries, biography, romance, politics, self-help; on TV they are drama, reality TV, news, current events, game shows, and sports. Once comfortably slotted into a consumer category, the product must perform in comparison with established norms—it must sell at a certain pace from the opening days of its availability or else it vanishes unsold from the mainstream marketplace.

Cultural markets work in such a manner because the distribution and display system is both costly and highly competitive. Hits are the high flyers, but for the normal to slow sellers, it is a dog-eat-dog world; sales monitored week by week tell the tale of what products will survive and which will vanish. If a product isn't selling as quickly as retailers think it should be, away it goes and a new version takes its place.

The point Anderson makes in his book, however, is that distribution/display costs are much more forgiving in the online world. Once digital copies of a piece of music, a book, a film, or a game are uploaded into an online inventory, they can stay available indefinitely at a very low cost, perhaps selling only a few copies each year. Figure 12.2 has been adapted from an online essay of Anderson's which illustrates this point (available at www.wired.com/2004/10/tail). It depicts a typical *long-tail* distribution and describes the different sales and availability at Walmart (a "bricks-and-mortar" chain) and Rhapsody (one of the first music streaming services): Walmart carries 39,000 titles; Rhapsody well over 200,000. At the left-hand side of the graph are the hits and other bestsellers, with the vertical axis representing the number, or frequency, of sales. Moving to the right, we see the pattern of sales for those titles that are not bestsellers.

As the curve suggests, most surprisingly, a high percentage of the products available on the right side of the curve are accessed by consumers. In other words, a significant number of sales come from this extended inventory.

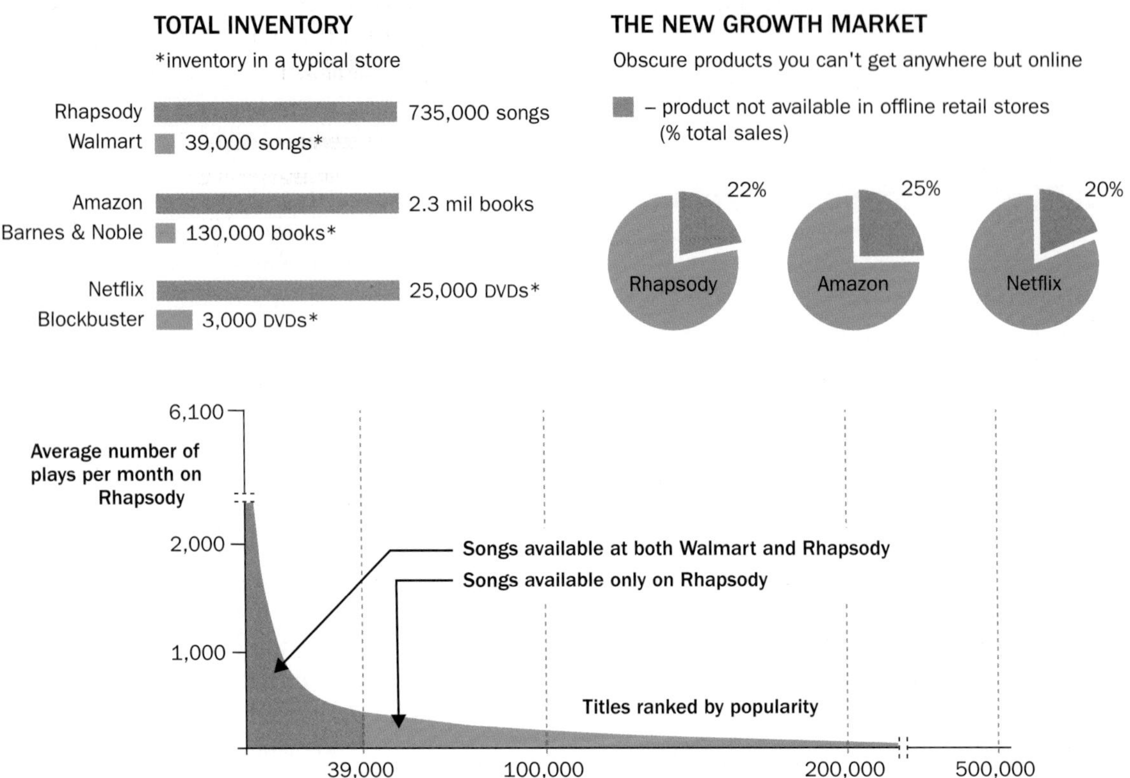

FIGURE 12.2 Anatomy of the long tail

Online services carry far more inventory than traditional retailers. Rhapsody, for example, offered 19 times as many songs as Walmart's stock of 39,000 tunes. The appetite for Rhapsody's more obscure tunes (charted in dark blue) made up the so-called long tail. Meanwhile, even as consumers flock to mainstream books, music, and films (bottom), there is a real demand for niche fare found only online.

The pie graphs in Figure 12.2 indicate that the sales of music not carried by Walmart and other major music stores are not trivial. They account for 20 to 25 per cent of the profit for an online retailer like Amazon. True, they may represent as much as 90 per cent of inventory, but when the cost of holding and managing the inventory is reduced to close to zero, as it can be with digital products and computerized control, there is a viable business.

Online services carry far more inventory than traditional retailers. In Anderson's example, for instance, Rhapsody offers 19 times as many songs as Walmart's stock of 39,000 tunes. The appetite for Rhapsody's more obscure tunes (charted in dark blue) makes up the so-called long tail. The selection enabled by this kind of inventory provides online retailers a distinct advantage over bricks-and-mortar ones. Moreover, having such an expanded inventory provides more sales opportunities, as consumers purchasing a copy of a currently popular song, film, or book can be automatically directed to similar products found in the long tail. As the automated message one receives after making an online purchase reads, "Customers interested in (insert popular song, book, film title you purchased here) were also interested in (insert long-tail title here)." More recent research appears to illustrate that the long tail is a key part of the marketing strategy for companies such as Spotify and Netflix (Flanagan, 2016; Arzavi, 2015).

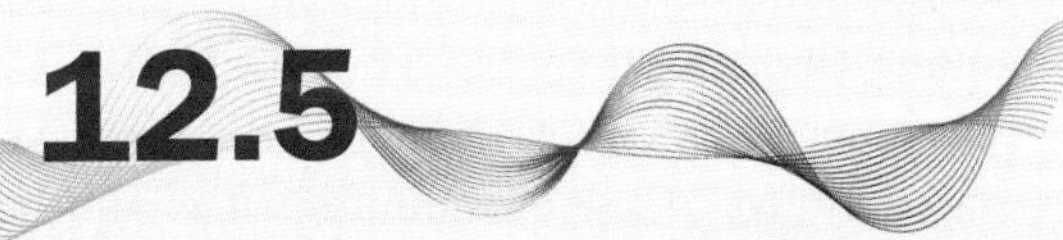

The Radical Fringes of the Long Tail

As we have seen, working with what Chris Anderson (2006) described as the "long tail phenomenon" (Figure 12.2), online retailers and video and music streaming companies like Amazon, Apple, and Walmart have created demand for a wide range of relatively obscure books, songs, and videos that otherwise may have gone unnoticed by potential audiences. But while recommending products that seemingly resemble those that people search for on online platforms seems to both increase consumer choice and feed the profits of large online companies, as Conor Friedersdorf points out in a March 2018 article in *The Atlantic*, algorithms that exploit the long tail can have a darker side.

Citing the work of internet scholar Zeynep Tufekci, Friedersdorf illustrates that watching relatively moderate political content on YouTube can quickly lead to radical fringes. As Friedersdorf states, Tufekci

> was watching Donald Trump rallies while conducting research, sitting through clip after clip, when eventually she noticed "autoplay" videos "that featured white supremacist rants, Holocaust denials and other disturbing content." Then she watched a bunch of Hillary Clinton and Bernie Sanders videos. Soon, "I was being directed to videos of a leftish conspiratorial cast," she wrote, "including arguments about the existence of secret government agencies and allegations that the United States government was behind the attacks of Sept. 11."

Consequently, Friedersdorf writes, "YouTube is unwittingly radicalizing some of its viewers through the videos that it automatically recommends that they watch next."

Whether or not people buy into the ideas and perspectives propounded by this radical content requires serous research. However, the fact that misguided algorithms may lead people wanting to learn more about the politics of the day into a dark web of dangerous and misleading misinformation should be a point of concern for the public and regulators alike. For more on this story, see Conor Friedersdof, "YouTube Extremism and the Long Tail" (March 12, 2018), www.theatlantic.com/politics/archive/2018/03/youtube-extremism-and-the-long-tail/555350/.

"Free" Market for Cultural Products?

Is the unfettered market the best way to produce and consume social resources? As a society, we don't seem to think so in terms of big issues like health care, education, and the environment. In fact, leaving such important social resources to a simple calculus of commercialism would necessarily lead to greater social inequity and environmental devastation as the market sorted between the services and activities that were the most profitable and those people that could afford to pay to access them. In other words, particularly in terms of education and health care, we would end up with fewer options and fewer people being able to access them—in short, greater ignorance and illness. In terms of the environment, such a rationale would allow natural resources to be put to the purposes commanding the highest price, with little regard to the interests of the people or other flora and fauna that depend on the natural world for their survival. Global warming and the wholesale devastation of forests, fish, and other wildlife species are clear evidence of where this path leads.

By the same token, in the context of ICT and the media it encompasses, should our perspectives, knowledge, and understandings of the world be subject to a purely economic rationale? Historically, as we discussed in Chapter 7, the Canadian public and policy-makers have answered with a resounding "No." For over a century, governments and others have recognized the need for regulation if Canadians are to enjoy fair and affordable access to communication services and media as well as cultural content that represents the breadth of Canadian perspectives. Common-carriage regulation in telecommunications, the founding of CBC, ownership regulations, Canadian-content regulations, production funds, and numerous other regulatory initiatives have been put into place to help ensure these purposes are met.

Yet over the last several decades, a pattern has emerged of cutting back on various forms of media regulation in favour of leaving business to market forces alone. Cuts to CBC's budget, a gradual loosening of ownership regulations, including those governing foreign ownership and concentration, a winnowing of support for community and indigenous broadcasting, and the CRTC's reluctance to regulate the internet all exemplify this trend.

Although the internet is often touted as the solution to the traditional problems plaguing our media systems, left to simple market economics, the internet holds little promise for increasing the range of media products and perspectives available to us. For film and television products, the internet does nothing to address the economic advantages conferred by economies of scale, and just as our television, movie, and computer screens are now dominated by US products, so, too, will they probably continue to be as the internet takes on a greater role in the distribution of such products. Although bloggers, citizen journalists, and a number of web-based news sites seem to have increased the range of news available to us, quality news production requires a high degree of knowledge and skill on the part of the people producing it, and because of this expense most internet news sites act as aggregators rather than producers of original news reports. Bloggers tend to offer little more than opinions gleaned from professionally produced news. At the same time, and perhaps most importantly, cross-media companies that count newspapers, broadcast, and web-based media among their holdings have business strategies that hinge upon repurposing media content generated for use in one medium for use in another. Consequently, whichever medium we turn to for news, the content is virtually the same.

The Cultural Commodity?

Compounding these problems is the fact that, as commodities, information and cultural products have quite different economic characteristics than other products such as soap, clothes, or cars. As Canadian lawyer Peter Grant and journalist Chris Wood point out in their book, *Blockbusters and Trade Wars: Popular Culture in a Globalized World* (2004), laws fundamental to economic thinking do not apply in the same way to information and cultural production. Rather, information and cultural products display a number of anomalies, or different economic characteristics, from other types of commodities:

- *Anomaly 1:* Cultural products such as TV programs, movies, and music are not consumed—in the sense that they are not destroyed in our use of them. Your listening to music does not deprive the next person from listening to the same music on the same CD. The market for cultural products behaves differently from normal commodities markets.
- *Anomaly 2:* The relationship between first-copy costs and run-on costs is dramatically different in cultural production than in the production of other commodities. In other words, the cost of making the "first copy" of a cultural product—such as a film, a television program, a concert, a novel, or a textbook—is enormous compared to the cost of subsequent copies. For instance, reportedly the budget for the film *The Hobbit: The Desolation of Smaug* was $225 million—that, then, is the cost of the "first copy." Making an electronic copy of the film, however, costs little more than the cost of download or a DVD (a few cents). Compare that dynamic to theatrical performances for which the players

must gather each night to put on the play; or manufacturing automobiles, where each "copy" requires a substantial outlay in parts and labour. For the cost of a cultural product to be the same as other kinds of commodities, the creation of each CD or DVD would require an artist to record anew. Similarly, for normal economic laws to hold, concert-goers would each suck out a little of the sound so that with a maximum audience there would be no sound left over. For books, the implications of consumption would be that as each page was read (perhaps not by the first, but let's say by the fiftieth reader) the print would disappear and by the end, the book would collapse into dust.

- *Anomaly 3:* Consumption patterns of cultural products and services are also different. Certain cultural products—blockbusters—command a major share of the market, while others don't come close to earning back their costs of creation. For instance, as few as one in ten feature films make big profits, three to five may break even, and the others lose money. Moreover, reduced pricing is rarely successful in persuading a person to watch an unpopular movie, read a bad book, or listen to a dull, tedious piece of music.
- *Anomaly 4:* Hidden consumer subsidies in the form of advertising or grants (by governments or those with a vested interest) can make cultural commodities available at a much lower price than their cost of production (e.g., magazines, newspapers) or, at times, even "free" to consumers (e.g., TV). Indeed, those with a vested interest can buy their way into cultural products—such as product placement in movies—so that the cultural consumer inadvertently consumes images that cause him or her to associate a product with a certain social dynamic (e.g., Apple laptops and powerful people).
- *Anomaly 5:* The appeal of any particularly cultural good is not readily predictable, a characteristic that is captured by Grant and Wood with the phrases "Nobody knows" (whether a cultural product will succeed in the marketplace) and "All hits are flukes." With normal commodities, most manage to capture some share of the market at some price.

These anomalies illustrate the fact that cultural products are quite different from standard industrial commodities. They call into question the appropriateness of applying standard economic theory to cultural products and underline the importance of regulations to help nurture and support the economic development of cultural industries at the local, regional, and national levels.

One other particularly important anomaly rests on the fact that information is not value-neutral. Economic analysis generally assumes that similar commodities are substitutable for one another. For instance, all things being equal, a stove from the United States is seen to be as good as one from Peru; or clothes made in China are as good as those made in Montreal. While there are a number of problems with this assumption, a key concern when applying this idea to media and information products is that the information such products contain is not value-neutral.

As we have seen, Canadians often seem to know more about US politics, history, and culture than about their own. In this regard, media and information products reflect particular ideas and attitudes, and those ideas provide specific ways of approaching and thinking about the world. Do imported educational materials, for example, incorporate Canadian values of diversity, tolerance, and common purpose, or are they underwritten by notions of competitive individualism that place the interests of the individual over the community at large? Do reports and studies authored elsewhere in the world and used by Canadian governments and industry to formulate policy and investment decisions take into account local and national environmental and community concerns, or are they simply based on abstract global economics?

As the lives of Canadians are spun in an ever-growing global web of dependencies, it is in our interest to consider carefully how media and information products are shaping our understanding of the world. The degree to which distinctive Canadian ideas and values are nurtured and carried into the future may, at least in part, hinge on the future of media regulation and its ability to keep those ideas circulating in our media.

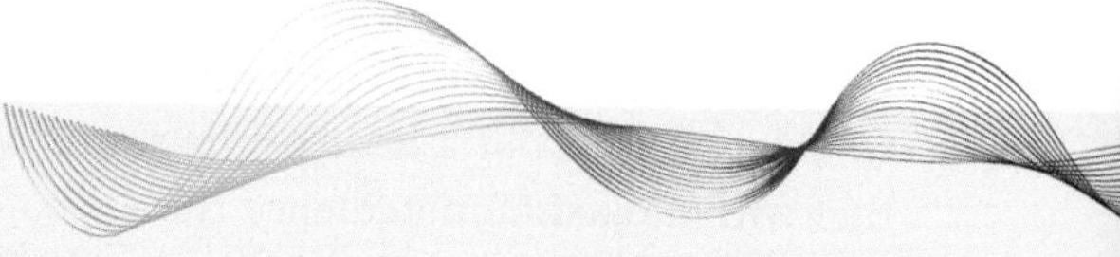

SUMMARY

In this book, we have examined the nature of communication in contemporary Canadian society. This final chapter has echoed the major themes, issues, and ideas treated in the preceding chapters. We have also gone beyond the analysis provided in the preceding chapters and discussed some of the directions in which the development of media and communication technology appear to be headed and the issues that these developments raise.

KEY TERMS

digital divides, p. 314
free-market economics, p. 308
horizontal relationship, p. 301
long tail, p. 315
ownership, p. 307
policy, p. 307
privacy, p. 314
public interest, p. 301
public policy, p. 300
UNESCO, p. 302

RELATED WEBSITES

Kondratiev Waves: www.kondratieffwavecycle.com/kondratieff-wave
A site devoted to discussion of the Kondratiev wave phenomenon.

The National Campus and Community Radio Association: www.ncra.ca
One of Canada's largest alternative media organizations.

Canadian Freelance Union: www.canadianfreelanceunion.ca/
An organization started by Unifor—Canada's largest private sector union—in an effort to provide some benefits and job protections to freelance journalists, photographers, illustrators, writers, and editors in Canada.

STUDY QUESTIONS

1. Is the world being transformed by the internet, or will the internet soon be largely captured by corporate interests such that its democratic potential will be lost?
2. Are the media alone a solid foundation for democracy?
3. While the media industries look at audiences in one manner, scholars tend to view them in another. Are these two approaches reconcilable?
4. Name and discuss three key issues facing media today.
5. Name three ways that media products differ from other kinds of commodities.

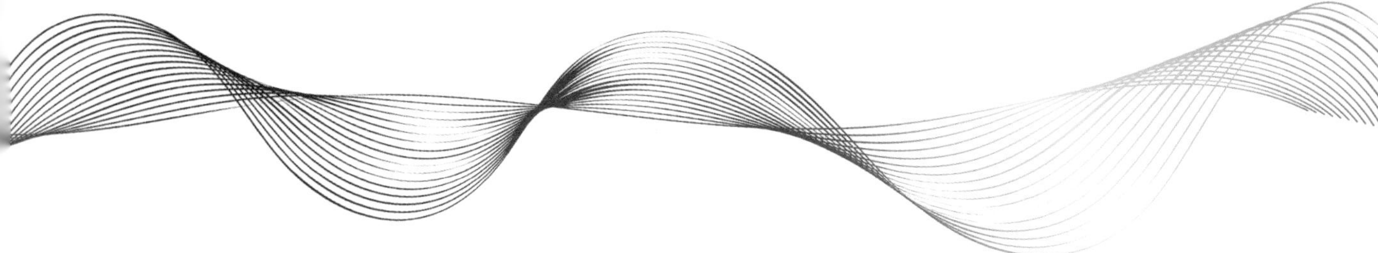

Glossary

access to information Related to the concept of freedom of information, it refers to the principle that information collected by governments belongs to the Crown, and citizens must appeal to governments for access to this information; this is the operating principle in Canada. In the United States, *freedom of information* is the more appropriate term because information collected by governments belongs to the people.

Adbusters A Canadian media activist group.

advertising Media content designed to promote broad awareness of a product, service, program, or organization. Typically, media space or time is purchased for advertising, and it thus serves as an important revenue source for media companies. However, advertising can also appear in unconventional, non-media spaces—such as bathroom walls and the floors of subway stations, or anywhere that it can attract attention.

Advertising Standards Canada An advertising lobbying group.

advertorials Promotional articles in magazines and newspapers thinly disguised as news stories, usually printed in a different typeface and identified by the advertorial label. As the name suggests, they are a cross between advertisements and editorial material.

agenda-setting function The process by which priorities are established, usually referring to elite actors or media owners and managers using their influence to shape society's priorities.

algorithms Computer formulas that enable media organizations to target consumers based on their profiles and habits.

alternative media Organizations that pursue communication and cultural production in ways alternative to, or distinct from, private, commercial, or state-owned media. Typically, alternative media seek to broaden public debate, construct community, advocate for social justice, and challenge concentrated media power.

ARPANET A project (circa 1969) that connected computer systems at five US universities, enabling information and message exchange between them; a precursor to the internet.

audience commodity The way in which audiences are packaged for sale to advertisers.

audience fragmentation The breakup of traditional television audiences because of the proliferation of TV channels in the last 25–30 years; the increasing draw of the internet has also further fragmented the audience.

backbone providers Organizations that develop communication infrastructure and make it available to users, typically as a business. Telephone and cable companies are examples of backbone providers.

barriers to entry An economic term that refers to the impediments one must overcome—e.g., raising investment capital, purchasing equipment or technology, finding a market niche, finding labour expertise—to enter into a new business enterprise.

Berne Convention The basis of international copyright law, which requires, among other things, that foreign authors be treated in the same way as domestic authors and that there be a minimum number of years of protection for a copyrighted work.

Birmingham School The media scholars at Birmingham University in the United Kingdom who developed the Marxist-derived critical school of thought that became cultural studies.

bourgeoisie A new land-owning class that emerged during the *Enlightenment* with the development of capitalism; this class generally controlled the means of production.

branded Referring to content sponsored and funded by an advertiser and created according to the advertiser's demands.

brand equity The value that is built up in a brand. Often, a branded product will sell more easily and for more money than the same product without a brand; but brand equity can also be lost when a brand begins to take on negative connotations.

branding A form of promotional culture that goes beyond advertising to include sponsorships and logo licensing.

brand journalism Content that is a deliberate hybrid between journalism and promotion.

British cultural studies An approach to social analysis that began in the 1950s and was led by scholars Richard Hoggart, Raymond Williams, and Stuart Hall; it extended a Marxist class analysis to include race, gender, and other elements of cultural history, and asserted the legitimacy of popular culture forms as objects of study.

Broadcasting Act (1991) Federal legislation governing all forms of broadcasting in Canada.

Canadian content A legal definition of material that either has been developed by Canadians or contains Canadian information; in broadcasting, filmmaking, and publishing, Canadian content is defined by reference to a specific set of production criteria, rather than content per se, designed to encourage the production of Canadian cultural materials by Canadians.

Canadian Radio League A lobby group founded in 1930 by Graham Spry and Alan Plaunt to lead a campaign to support the Aird Commission's central recommendation of a national public radio system for Canada.

Canadian Radio-television and Telecommunications Commission (CRTC) The federal agency that enforces the rules and regulations for broadcasters and telecommunications companies in Canada, as set out in the 1993 *Telecommunications Act*.

capital Funds invested, or available to be invested, for the express purpose of generating profits; not to be confused with money proper.

capitalism An economic system based on the private ownership of the means of production and the clear separation of capital (exemplified by the owners of the means of production engaged in the pursuit of profit) and labourers, who satisfy their material needs (e.g., food, shelter, clothing) by exchanging their work for a wage.

chain ownership A common form of media organization in Canada—the linking, or horizontal integration, of a number of companies in the same business (typically newspapers, radio stations, or television stations) occupying different markets.

commodities Goods sold in the marketplace valued primarily for the earnings they can generate through market exchange.

commodity fetishism A state in which a brand's value is not a reflection of its production but, instead, its enchanted meanings, which can be transferred to other products.

common carriage Telecommunications services provided to all members of the public at equitable rates; a common carrier is in the business of providing carriage services rather than content.

communication The act of transmitting and exchanging information and meaning through any form of language. While communication typically refers to exchanges through verbal, written, and electronic forms of transmission, clothing, gesture, architecture, and so on are also forms of communication.

conglomerate ownership A company that contains within it many companies carrying on a variety of businesses not necessarily related to one another. A media conglomerate does the majority of its business in the media; a general or non-media conglomerate has its foundation in non-media firms.

connotative meaning Implicit, suggesting, implying—a connotation is an implied meaning; in communication theory, words and messages are said to have connotative as well as *denotative* (or explicit) meanings.

conservative A political stance oriented to preserving current conditions and power structures rather than adapting to, embracing, or instigating changed, often more egalitarian, conditions.

constructivism A point of view arguing that technology is constructed by members of society and shaped by social forces, giving it both technical and social logic.

contempt of court A ruling by which a court of law determines that a person or an organization has disobeyed or contravened the authority of the court.

content analysis A quantitative research method that establishes units of analysis—specified ideas, phrases, sentences, column inches, placement, accompanying illustrations, categories of spokespersons quoted or cited—and counts them to try to analyze the meaning or perspective of a particular communication, such as a newspaper article or television news story.

convergence Generally, bringing together once separate communication technologies, such as telephone, broadcasting, computers, and sound and video recording, into one technological platform (e.g., the internet). The key to this *technological convergence* is the digitization of media content such that it can be translated into a common format. Similarly, concentration of ownership is sometimes referred to as *corporate convergence*, as media companies combine the resources and content of two or more different media properties to realize cost savings in content production and crosspromotional opportunities.

copyright The exclusive right to reproduce a work requiring intellectual labour; this right belongs to the author and constitutes (1) a property right, which may be assigned to others, and (2) a moral right, which may not be assigned but may be waived.

corporate concentration An economic term used to describe a particular industry ownership pattern whereby ownership of the participating companies is concentrated in only a few hands.

critical theory Generally, theoretical perspectives that focus on the ways in which wealth and power are unequally distributed in society.

cultivation analysis An examination of content for the way in which it may encourage or cultivate a positive attitude in the audience member toward a particular person or perspective.

cultural dependency A relationship in which one country comes to rely on the media products of stronger, exporting countries to satisfy the cultural and entertainment needs of its population.

cultural industries Groups of companies that employ large-scale, industrial methods to produce cultural products.

cultural sovereignty The capacity of a state or group to govern cultural activity (i.e., form policy, establish laws and conventions) independent of interference from other governments or groups.

culture Most commonly used to refer to a group of people's particular way of life (i.e., its anthropological definition), it can also refer to a process of human development (from the idea of cultivation) or to a group of people's finest artistic, literary, and intellectual works.

CUSMA (Canada–US–Mexico Agreement) A 2018 trilateral trade agreement that replaces the 1994 *North American Free Trade Agreement* (NAFTA).

cyborg An entity combining biological and technological elements. Used metaphorically, it refers to the symbiotic relationship between humans and technologies.

decoding Interpreting or meaning-making; for example, to interpret or make meaning from an advertisement, television program, or film, one must decode the signs and symbols used to construct those media texts.

defamation Injuring a person's good reputation by means of insults, or interference with the course of justice.

demographic (1) As an adjective, related to the statistical study of populations through the identification of characteristics of a given population (e.g., age, sex, education, income level); (2) as a noun, a specific group that may be identified through such analysis.

denotative meaning Explicit, literal meaning of a communication; in communication theory, words and messages are said to have both denotative and *connotative* meanings.

deregulation The process by which the state gradually withdraws from regulating particular spheres of activity and allows freer market activity. The term is, however, something of a misnomer because market forces are also a form of regulation, producing simply an alternative form of governance. For this reason, some commentators prefer the term *reregulation*.

deskilling The simplification of complex tasks into components that are readily mastered by workers, who often are working in conjunction with sophisticated machines.

digital A universal code that reduces sounds and images to a series of 0s and 1s; digitization allows the easy transfer of communications from one medium to another, enabling convergence.

digital divide The (increasing) difference in the development and use of information and communication technology between rich and poor countries, and between the haves and have-nots within a society.

digitization The process by which all forms of information—textual, visual, aural—are translated into a common computer language of 0s and 1s so that content produced originally for one digital platform can be used on all other platforms.

discourse analysis In popular usage, all forms of text and talk; in communication studies, text and talk about a particular topic or field of activity.

economies of scale Efficiencies in costs that can be achieved via repetition of some aspects of the production and distribution processes—for example, the reduction of the per-unit cost of printing 10,000 copies of a book once the presses have been set up, as opposed to printing just 1,000 copies.

economism The reduction of complex phenomena and institutions to their economic characteristics; such a view foregrounds and privileges economic values to the exclusion of political, cultural, or other social considerations.

effects The direct results of the media influencing human behaviour.

encoding Placing meaning in a particular code; for instance, language, digital signals, song.

Enlightenment An early-eighteenth-century change in Western European worldview distinguished by an intellectual approach based on a scientific and rational perspective on the world, a fundamental shift in worldview that championed science over religion, justice over the abuse of power, and a social contract that specified individual rights and freedoms over the absolutist rule of monarchs and popes.

epistemology A theory of knowledge—of what gets defined as knowledge and the sources and structures of that knowledge.

exchange value Worth placed on an object based on marketplace exchange.

fake news A term used in two senses: (1) to describe particular news items that are totally fabricated, usually to undermine a political foe or de-legitimate an idea; (2) to describe particular news outlets that a politician or political party sees as generally undermining the general image or message they would like to portray to the public.

fan fiction Works that use characters or settings from films, books, televisions shows, comics, or other media products that were originally the products of other creators.

feminist research A perspective critical of the character of modern societies for the male domination of women (patriarchy) that has led to profound human inequalities and injustices.

Fordism The concentration of production on a single site modelled after Henry Ford's automobile assembly lines whereby raw materials are turned into standardized finished products as part of a single, multi-faceted mass-production process.

fourth estate The media—referring to the role of the media in watching over the other powerful institutions in society.

frame/framing Both noun and verb, drawing attention to the boundaries a picture, story, or other means of communication places on that to which it refers; boundaries that tend to limit the range of interpretation by audiences or privilege particular readings.

Frankfurt School A school of thought led by the German intellectuals Max Horkheimer, Theodor Adorno, and Herbert Marcuse, who argued, among other things, that cultural life in modern times has been profoundly changed by the detrimental impact of capitalist methods of mass production.

freedom of the press (1) The constitutional right granted to the press and other media to exercise the right to free speech, usually in the name of the public good; (2) also understood as the right granted to press and other media owners to pursue market interests unhindered by the state; this freedom is not absolute, but subject to certain legal limits.

free-market economics A general approach to commerce, positing that a free market is the most efficient way of creating and allocating social resources.

frequency allocation The assignment by the International Telecommunication Union of frequency bands within the earth's electromagnetic spectrum for use by specific communication services, such as radio, television, and emergency communications.

functionalist A term referring to a theory based on the assumption that media function to serve some kind of audience need, and then researchers set out to discover what that need is.

gatekeeping The control of access to media publication or broadcast that determines which reported events will be covered, according to the identity or character of the media outlet.

globalization The processes by which social, political, and economic relations extend further than ever before, with greater frequency, immediacy, and facility.

horizontal relationship A unique arrangement between readers and a news organization, in which reader members are invited to participate in decision making in terms of both developing story ideas and administrative issues. Journalist members are the primary story contributors, and the editors do the administrative work for the organization. While some of the published material is contributed by volunteers, such a cooperative pays contributors whenever possible, in both cash and exchange.

icon A sign that looks like the object it describes. Maps and photographs are both icons.

ideology A coherent set of social values, beliefs, and meanings; in Marxist terms, it is a critical concept that refers particularly to dominant or ruling-class values, beliefs, and meanings—what came to be called the *dominant ideology*.

index A sign related to the object it represents. Smoke is an index of fire and a sneeze is an index of a cold, allergy, or irritant.

Industrial Revolution The application of growing scientific knowledge to production and industry that began to dominate in the late eighteenth century in Western Europe.

influencer As defined by Alison Hearn and Stephanie Schoenhoff, a person who generates a form of celebrity capital by "cultivating as much attention as possible and crafting an authentic personal brand via social networks, which can subsequently be used by companies and advertisers for consumer outreach."

information flows Patterns of circulation of information commodities or products (e.g., movies, magazines, television programs); a summary concept describing the imports and exports of goods, specifically information and entertainment products.

information and communication technology (ICT) Technologies used to store, access, and transmit information.

information society A society in which the production, distribution, and consumption of information take on growing and significant political, economic, and social importance.

instrumentalism A philosophical position whereby an adherent perceives technology as a value-neutral tool that can shorten the path to natural ends or, alternatively, social goals; technology here is simply a means to an end and can be used for whatever purpose we choose. Technology, from an *instrumentalist* perspective, is simply a tool for our use.

intellectual property The set of rights that accrue to an author by virtue of the work expended in the creation of a literary, dramatic, artistic, or musical work; the owned expressions of intellectual work derived from copyright law. Intellectual property carries two sets of rights—moral rights and property rights.

interactivity As a descriptor of media, the inclusion of user-created content as part of what is presented to the audience. While it may be claimed that such devices as letters to the editor are an interactive element of newspapers and magazines, they are placed in separate sections from the content produced by the publication itself. Interactivity is strongest when the boundary between the content producers and the audience is least. To use a theatrical analogy, in strongly interactive media the boundary between the stage and audience vanishes.

International Telecommunication Union A United Nations agency that coordinates standards and regulations for international information and communication technologies.

intertextuality The idea that the meaning we make of one text depends on the meanings we have drawn from other sets of signs we have encountered.

labour The human resources necessary to produce and distribute communications. This can include people working individually on their own creative products (e.g., novels, websites) and those working within an industrial production setting (e.g., large media companies). The category includes those directly involved in media production (e.g., writers, actors, photographers) and those in supporting roles (e.g., truck drivers, press operators).

legislation Acts, statutes, and laws passed either by Canada's federal Parliament or by provincial/territorial governments.

long tail A concept, introduced by Chris Anderson of *Wired* magazine, whereby the distribution/display costs are much more forgiving in the online world. Because of very low costs for display and distribution, and because item costs are low but access is easy, consumers choose widely rather than focusing their choices solely on hits.

market Generally, any arena in which sellers of goods and services are brought together with potential consumers of those goods and services. Today, buyers and sellers can be brought together virtually (e.g., through e-commerce) or physically (e.g., in a shopping mall). The term can also be used to refer to a specific market, meaning either a particular place (Calgary) or a specific group of consumers (luxury home buyers).

market externalities The costs and benefits of economic activity that are not accounted for by (i.e., are external to) the immediate economic transaction between buyer and seller.

market failure The inability of the free market to reflect the true value of (or provide) a good or service; for example, a work of art, which may be sold for a small sum during the life of the artist but for increasingly greater sums after the artist's death.

market segmentation The organization of consumers into smaller, tighter groups based on their demographic characteristics, lifestyles, and social values.

mass audience A convenient shorthand term for the great numbers of people who constitute the mass entertainment audience; rather than being conceived as homogeneous, vulnerable, and passive, the mass audience is better thought of as a great number of individuals of heterogeneous backgrounds who use the media for a great variety of purposes.

mass communication Historically, a term used to describe communication to a large undifferentiated group. More recently, the term has also been used to describe communication between a large number of individuals.

mass culture A culture or way of life that is largely constructed through mass media and industrial production. In this context, people are often seen as being relatively easily manipulated by the media and satisfied by cheap industrial goods.

mass media Newspapers, magazines, film, television, radio, advertising, book publishing, the internet, and popular music.

means of production The mechanism or process by which we satisfy our material needs for food, clothing, and shelter, and thus ensure our survival.

media convergence Either (1) the merging of previously distinct media technologies through digitization and computer networking or (2) a business strategy by which the media properties of a communication conglomerate work together.

media democratization A movement seeking to democratize media organizations through public or cooperative ownership, and by opening these organizations' decision-making processes to broad public participation.

media geography The physical space that any given media organization occupies and seeks to serve. For example, a national television network occupies and serves audiences and advertisers within a given country.

media imperialism The use of the media to build empires of influence and control.

media silos In a converged, multi-platform media environment, specific media platforms (e.g., radio, television, newspapers, magazines) that are not converged.

mediascapes "Image-centered" and "narrative accounts of strips of reality" (as defined by the social anthropologist Arjun Appadurai). Thus, the environment that media create and present to audiences.

mediation A process of making a series of choices about what content to create—how, for what purpose, and for whom—regardless of whether those choices are made consciously or unconsciously.

medium Any vehicle that conveys information; plural: *media*.

mobility A characteristic that refers to the relative portability or transportability of people, cultural products, investment capital, organizations, etc.

narrowcasting Used in contrast to *broadcasting* to describe media (largely radio and television) services targeting a small or niche audience with very specific characteristics.

native advertising A form of sponsored content published in newspapers and magazines (similar to ***advertorials***) consisting of articles constructed as news stories, the difference being that they carry a label identifying them as sponsored content and are typically set in a typeface different from the neighbouring articles.

net neutrality Internet service providers (ISPs) treating all content and applications equally, without degrading or prioritizing service based on their source, ownership, or destination.

network society Taken from the work of Manuel Castells, a description of contemporary society as bound together less by physical location than by globalized social, communication, and economic networks.

new media Technologies, practices, and institutions designed to encourage public participation in information creation, production, and exchange (i.e., communication) on a mass scale either by means of increased access to production facilities (decentralized production) or through ***interactivity***. They are usually, but not always, digital media.

news values The criteria journalists apply to determine whether a particular person or event is newsworthy, and the extent to which the person or event merits news coverage.

non-governmental organizations (NGOs) Non-profit citizens' organizations, independent of governments, designed to provide a social or political service on a regional, national, or international basis.

open-source software The production and development of software that allows users and others to see source code and thereby make adjustments to it to suit their needs.

ownership In the context of media influence, the location and identification of owners (of creation, production, copyright, distribution) of cultural property is of policy concern.

paywall A digital gateway that requires subscribers to enter a username and password in order to access the site of a digital medium that charges a subscription fee for access to its content.

peer-to-peer system A form of communication network in which there is no central point. The internet was developed as a peer-to-peer system, arranged like a web, in which points on the network are redundantly interconnected; the route by which any particular piece of information travels is guided by software rather than by the physical connections, and all points on the internet are designed to be equal as peers.

phishing A form of online fraud in which computer users are deceived into providing sensitive personal information. Typically, computer users are sent an email from someone posing as a legitimate service—e.g., a bank, the government, a telephone company—requesting username and password information. That information is then used for an illegal purpose, such as theft.

politics The social process whereby people make collective decisions. This definition includes formal processes of government, but it also includes a much wider range of activities that frame and animate formal government policies and activities, as well as informal discussions of social norms and values. From this perspective, politics is a key element in many aspects of social life. Whenever we are discussing or otherwise are engaged with issues of collective concern with other members of society, be it in a large or small group, or simply with just one other person, we are engaging in politics.

policy A set of rules and regulations governing the way information and media products are created and consumed.

polysemic The idea that a sign may have many meanings. Depending on the context, an image of an apple might be interpreted as knowledge, as a computer company, or simply as fruit.

position In the context of visual media, the point of view constructed for the viewer through filmic techniques—that is, how the viewer is "put in the picture."

primary definers Terms used to define the important elements of a news story; also used to designate those people who are first to assert a meaning to news events; primary definitions tend to be difficult to change.

privacy The right of people to protect certain aspects of their personal lives from the media. Such rights do not exist in Britain in any formal way, and they are weak in the United States.

private ownership Ownership by individuals or corporations, including of publicly traded companies, as opposed to ***public ownership***.

privatization The transfer of publicly owned enterprises into the hands of private individuals or corporations.

primary definers Interviewed politicians, experts, military figures, etc. who are routinely allowed to frame the issues, express their opinions, and offer interpretations of events and circumstances.

product placement The insertion of identifiable commercial products into the content of entertainment or information media for the purpose of promoting awareness of them.

promotional culture Articulating how the boundaries between advertising, marketing, promotion, the media, and public relations are blurring and destabilizing.

prosumers People who are both media producers and media consumers at the same time.

proximity The degree of closeness, which can be physical, cultural, or emotional closeness.

public interest The investment that a national group or other polity has in preserving or developing the best of its values and ideals.

public ownership Ownership by arm's-length government agencies (e.g., CBC) or by groups of individuals (e.g., cooperatives), which members of the public can join for a token membership fee. Public ownership contrasts with commercial or ***private ownership*** of commercial companies, some of which are publicly traded and therefore called, in business circles, *public companies*.

public policy The set of government-sanctioned rules, laws, and practices that govern social, political, and economic life.

public relations The practice of controlling, managing, and maintaining communication between a person, company, or organization and its publics.

public sphere A place or space where people can meet to discuss and debate issues and ideas of common concern.

pull technologies Media forms that allow people to seek out—or *pull* out—content from a seemingly infinite array of options found within a seemingly unlimited range of sources. The internet is an example of a pull technology, with an emphasis on user demand.

push technologies Media forms that present—or *push* toward—audience members a limited range of content options within a finite number of sources. Conventional television, for example, offers the viewer a number of programs from which to select at a given time from a relatively limited array of channels. The emphasis on push technologies is with the supply on offer.

reach The percentage of audience members who tune into a broadcast program at least once during a specified time period.

reception analysis A research method that investigates how and in what context audiences consume media products.

regionalism A political ideology that emphasizes a primary identification or affiliation with a particular region. In Canada, for example, some people may identify themselves as westerners or Quebecers first, and as Canadians second.

regulations Rules that address the details and practical applications of pieces of legislation. The authority to make regulations related to a particular government act is assigned within the act itself; regulations have the full force of law.

re-intermediation Refers to the reintroduction of intermediaries in digital communications, resulting from the emergence and growth of corporate aggregators. The filtering and sorting capacities of these services counter the initial trend of the internet, meant to allow users direct, or unmediated, access to online content.

Renaissance A cultural movement between the fourteenth and seventeenth centuries in Western Europe that highlighted a return to classical forms of learning and knowledge.

representation The production or construction of ideas or images in a communicative form; the depiction through language of an idea, event, person, or institution.

resources The elements necessary for media production—specifically, time, labour (workers), technology (hardware, software), capital (money to invest), and physical materials (paper, plastics, metals, and so on).

rhetoric A persuasive form of communication; a research method in which communications are studied as examples of persuasive speech.

right to communicate The expansion of the notions of *freedom of expression*, *freedom of speech*, and *freedom of the press* to include the right to be informed, the right to inform, the right to *privacy*, and the right to participate in public communication.

royal commissions High-level inquiries established by government to investigate problems of significant public concern and recommend solutions. Members are appointed by the governor-in-council and have the power to subpoena witnesses and request documents. They are more ambitious undertakings than task forces and have a higher profile, but they are limited to making recommendations to government, which may or may not heed them.

scientific management The study and implementation of methods to maximize the efficiency of workers' contributions to production processes. It is sometimes called *Taylorism*, after Frederick Winslow Taylor, who in the early twentieth century conducted time and motion studies to break down work-related tasks into their component parts and determine the most efficient means of organizing such tasks. Scientific management was ideally suited to industrialized, mass-production processes that combined workers and machinery in various forms of assembly line.

semiotics The study of signs and sign systems and the ways in which they create meaning.

share The percentage of the average audience that tunes into a program or channel over any specified time period.

sign (1) A physical form (a word, gesture, even an object like a rose) used in communication to refer to something else (an object, a feeling) and recognized as such; (2) the totality of associations, thoughts, understandings, or meanings brought about by the use of symbols in reference to an object, person, phenomenon, or idea.

signified The mental concept of what is referred to—for instance, an object as we think of it when we hear a word (e.g., the image of table when we hear the word *table*).

signifier The physical form of the *sign*—for instance, symbols such as words.

socializing institutions Those institutions in society, such as the education system, the media, and the family, through which social norms and values are communicated and either reinforced or contested.

socially contingent A point of view emphasizing that technology arises and takes a particular form reflecting the dynamics of the society in which it emerges.

social theory Generally, a representation of the social world—a set of ideas about how the world is organized and functions.

society A general term referring to a specific group of people and their interactions with one another and the institutions they have established over time.

socio-technical ensemble A term coined by Wiebe Bijker to describe a technical apparatus to reflect the fact that built into all commonly used technology are both social dynamics and technical feasibility (and history).

sovereignty The quality of independence, typically referring to the ability of nations to self-govern.

spatialization The process of overcoming the constraints of space and time, typically applied to organizations such as media companies.

streaming The process by which audiovisual communications—e.g., music, all types of radio and television programming, films—are delivered over digital platforms.

structuralism A method and theory that emphasizes how the formal elements of a linguistic or social system limit or determine the agency of the individuals that use that system.

substantivism A point of view that sees technology as operating according to its own inexorable logic, and that this logic is at the expense of human concerns and hence humanity.

subvertising An amalgam of *subverting* and advertising. *Subvertisements* imitate the look of advertisements but are parodies of the ads in order to make political messages; they can impact a company's brand equity.

symbol A sign that bears no direct resemblance to what it signifies, such as words. Communication is based on the exchange of systems of symbols that form various kinds of language.

task forces Bodies of inquiry, whose members are appointed by the governor-in-council, assigned to investigate a particular problem on behalf of government. They differ from royal commissions in that their objects of inquiry are typically less significant, they operate with smaller budgets, their reports are less extensive and typically reflect the government's point of view, and they do not have to be made public.

technological determinism The notion that technology is an autonomous and powerful driving force in structuring society or elements of society.

technological hubris A form of human conceit. A position whereby a person perceives technology as contributing inherently to progress—a naive position that ignores or downplays technology's limits or its potential downsides.

topsight The electronic recording and collection of online transactions for the purpose of creating a body of data that can provide a big picture of online activity and subsequently be mined for valuable information.

trade liberalization The process by which trade in goods and services between national and subnational jurisdictions is gradually freed from various forms of government regulation.

unbundling The breaking up of the content packages assembled by legacy media, such as radio, television, magazines, and newspapers. New media technologies allow users to access individual articles and programs from the websites or apps of legacy media organizations themselves or through social media.

UNESCO The United Nations Education, Scientific and Cultural Organization, a specialized agency of the United Nations.

Universal Declaration of Human Rights Global declaration of basic rights adopted by United Nations General Assembly in 1948, Article 19 of which is specific to freedom of opinion and expression.

uses and gratification research (U&G) A theory of media focusing on how audience members use the media (e.g., for information, for entertainment, for conversation) and what satisfaction they derive from media.

use value Worth derived from utility.

verification The process whereby a claim or a statement is authenticated as truthful or factual.

vertical integration A group of companies linked by common ownership that exist in a supply–demand relation to one another, such as a sound recording company and a radio network.

viewing time The number of hours spent viewing, expressed over the course of a day, week, or longer period of time.

Web 2.0 The extension of web applications though the addition of new communication and interaction options that replace static informational sites with social media applications that allow people to discuss, collaborate, or otherwise interact.

wireless spectrum Electromagnetic and radiation frequency bands used by wireless communication services.

world systems theory A theory articulated by Immanuel Wallerstein that focuses on the relationship between nation-states in a global economic system. The theory categorized nations as core, peripheral, or semi-peripheral states, depending on the role they play in the international economic system.

World Trade Organization (WTO) An intergovernmental body that governs trade and is committed to reducing trade barriers between member nations.

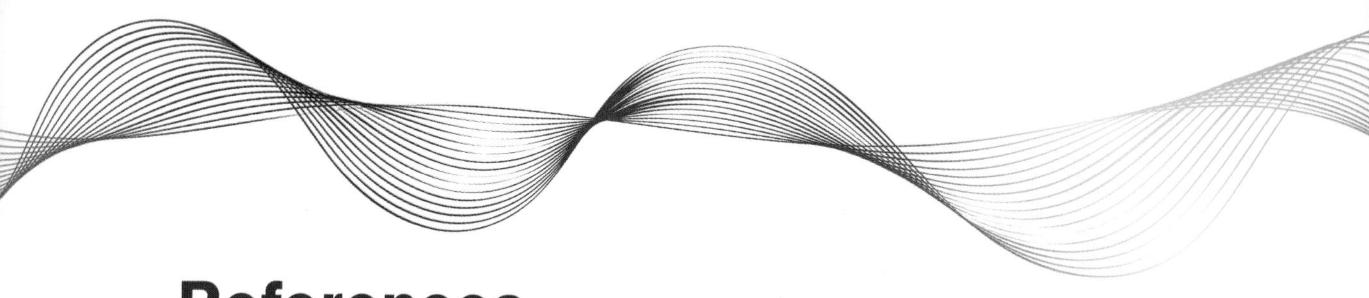

References

Chapter 1

Anderson, Benedict. 1983. *Imagined Communities: Reflections on the Origin and Spread of Nationalism*. London: Verso.

Benkler, Yochai. 2006. *The Wealth of Networks*. New Haven, CT: Yale UP.

Canada. 2017. *Creative Canada Policy Framework*. Ottawa: Department of Canadian Heritage. Accessed at www.canada.ca/en/canadian-heritage/campaigns/creative-canada/framework.html.

Carey, James W. 1989. "Technology and ideology: The case of the telegraph." In *Communication and Culture: Essays on Media and Society*. Boston: Unwin Hyman, 201–30.

CBC. 2017 (19 September). "Canada's privacy commissioner 'very concerned' about U.S. border phone searches." Accessed at www.cbc.ca/news/politics/us-border-cellphone-password-search-1.4296331.

Chadwick, Andrew. 2013. *The Hybrid Media System: Politics and Power*. New York: Oxford UP.

Chung, Emily. 2013 (21 October). "Muzzling of federal scientists widespread, survey suggests." Accessed 21 November 2013 at www.cbc.ca/news/technology/muzzling-of-federal-scientists-widespread-survey-suggests-1.2128859.

CIRA. 2018. *Canada's Internet Factbook 2018*. Accessed at cira.ca/factbook/canada%E2%80%99s-internet-factbook-2018.

Coulter, Natalie. 2014. "From the top drawer to the bottom line: The commodification of children's cultures." In *Mediascapes: New Patterns in Canadian Communication*, 4th ed., edited by Leslie Regan Shade. Don Mills, ON: Nelson Education, 409–26.

CRTC. 2017. *Communications Monitoring Report 2017*. Accessed at publications.gc.ca/site/eng/371392/publication.html.

Eastwood, Joel. 2014 (18 March). "Recording industry earns more from fan videos than from official music videos." *Toronto Star*. Accessed 24 April 2014 at www.thestar.com/entertainment/music/2014/03/18/recording_industry_earns_more_from_fan_videos_than_from_official_music_videos.html.

Fuchs, Christian. 2012. "Google Capitalism." In *tripleC* 10(1): 42–48. Accessed at www.triple-c.at/index.php/tripleC/article/view/304.

Guynes, Sean, and Dan Hassler-Forest, editors. 2017. *Star Wars and the History of Transmedia Storytelling*. Amsterdam: Amsterdam UP.

Habermas, Jürgen. 1989. *The Structural Transformation of the Public Sphere: An Inquiry into a Category of Bourgeois Society*. Cambridge: Polity Press.

Jenkins, Henry. 2006. *Convergence Culture: Where Old and New Media Collide*. New York: New York UP.

Jhally, Sut. 1997. *Advertising and the End of the World* (video). Northampton, MA: Media Education Foundation.

Katz, Elihu, and Paul Lazarsfeld. 1955. *Personal Influence: The Part Played by People in the Flow of Mass Communications*. New York: Free Press.

Kluft, David. 2016 (18 October). "10 Copyright Cases Every Fan Fiction Writer Should Know About." In *Copyright and Trade Law*. Accessed at www.trademarkandcopyrightlawblog.com/2016/10/10-copyright-cases-every-fan-fiction-writer-should-know-about/.

Leiss, William, Stephen Kline, Sut Jhally, and Jaqueline Botterill. 2005. *Social Communication in Advertising*, 3rd ed. New York: Routledge.

Lessig, Lawrence. 2008. *Remix: Making Art and Commerce Thrive in the Hybrid Economy*. New York: Penguin.

Lievrouw, Leah. 2011. *Alternative Media and Activist New Media*. Malden, MA: Polity Press.

Lorimer, Rowland. 2002. "Mass communication: Some redefinitional notes." *Canadian Journal of Communication* 27(1): 63–72.

McCarthy, Shawn. 2015 (17 February). "Anti-petroleum movement a growing security threat to Canada, RCMP say." *The Globe and Mail*. Accessed 5 March 2015 at www.theglobeandmail.com/news/politics/anti-petroleum-movement-a-growing-security-threat-to-canada-rcmp-say/article23019252.

Murray, Ben. 2015 (22 March). "Remixing Culture and Why The Art Of The Mash-Up Matters." In *Tech Crunch*. Accessed at techcrunch.com/2015/03/22/from-artistic-to-technological-mash-up/.

Nguyen, Tina. 2018 (26 July). "For the Trump White House, Even the Weather Has Become Fake News." *Vanity Fair*. Accessed at www.vanityfair.com/news/2018/07/white-house-weather-fake-news.

O'Sullivan, T., J. Hartley, D. Saunders, and J. Fiske. 1983. *Key Concepts in Communication*. Toronto: Methuen.

Peters, John Durham. 1999. *Speaking into the Air: A History of the Idea of Communication*. Chicago: University of Chicago Press.

Shannon, Claude E., and Warren Weaver. 1949. *The Mathematical Theory of Communication*. Urbana: University of Illinois Press.

Silverstone, Roger. 1999. *Why Study the Media?* Thousand Oaks, CA: Sage.

Stanford, Jim. 2008. *Economics for Everyone: A Short Guide to the Economics of Capitalism*. Black Point, NS: Fernwood.

Thompson, John B. 1995. *The Media and Modernity*. Stanford, CA: Stanford UP.

Toffler, Alvin. 1980. *The Third Wave*. New York: Bantam.

Toronto Star. 2018 (6 May). "Doug Ford evades real scrutiny by hiring his own reporter." Accessed at www.thestar.com/opinion/editorials/2018/05/06/doug-ford-evades-real-scrutiny-by-hiring-his-own-reporter.html.

Watters, Haydn. 2015 (18 June). "C-51, controversial anti-terrorism bill, is now law. So, what changes?" Accessed 30 July 2015 at www.cbc.ca/news/politics/c-51-controversial-anti-terrorism-bill-is-now-law-so-what-changes-1.3108608.

Weir, Ernest Austin. 1965. *The Struggle for National Broadcasting in Canada*. Toronto: McClelland & Stewart.

Wood, Ellen Meiksins. 2002. *The Origin of Capitalism: A Longer View*. London: Verso.

World Atlas. 2017. "Countries Where People Spend the Most Time Online." Accessed at www.worldatlas.com/articles/top-countries-which-spend-the-greatest-amount-of-time-online.html.

Chapter 2

Armstrong, Robert. 2016. *Broadcasting Policy in Canada*, 2nd ed. Toronto: University of Toronto Press.

Babe, Robert E. 1990. *Telecommunications in Canada*. Toronto: University of Toronto Press.

Bennett, R.B. 1932. "Speech in support of Bill 94, respecting radio broadcasting." Document 16 in *Documents of Canadian Broadcasting*, edited by Roger Bird (1988). Ottawa: Carleton UP, 111–14.

Canada. 1981. *Report of the Royal Commission on Newspapers* (Kent Commission). Ottawa: Minister of Supply and Services.

Canada. 1987. Department of Communications. *Vital Links: Canadian Cultural Industries*. Ottawa: Minister of Supply and Services.

Canada. 2017. *Creative Canada Policy Framework*. Ottawa: Department of Canadian Heritage. Accessed at www.canada.ca/en/canadian-heritage/campaigns/creative-canada/framework.html.

Charland, Maurice. 1986. "Technological nationalism." *Canadian Journal of Political and Social Theory* 10(1), 196–220.

Commission on Freedom of the Press. 1947. *A Free and Responsible Press*. Chicago: University of Chicago Press.

Darnton, Robert. 1982. *The Literary Underground of the Old Regime*. Cambridge, MA: Harvard UP.

Daschuk, James. 2013 (19 July). "When Canada used hunger to clear the West," *The Globe and Mail*. Accessed 15 July 2014 at www.theglobeandmail.com/globe-debate/when-canada-used-hunger-to-clear-the-west/article13316877.

Grant, Peter S., and Chris Wood. 2004. *Blockbusters and Trade Wars: Popular Culture in a Globalized World*. Vancouver: Douglas & McIntyre.

Hackett, Robert A., and Yuezhi Zhao. 1998. *Sustaining Democracy? Journalism and the Politics of Objectivity*. Toronto: Garamond Press.

Klass, Benjamin, Dwayne Winseck, Marc Nanni, and Fenwick McKelvey. 2016 (June). "There ain't no such thing as a free lunch: Historical and international perspectives on why common carriage should be a cornerstone of communications policy in the Internet age." Submitted before the Canadian Radio-television and Telecommunications Commission Telecom Notice of Consultation CRTC 2016-192, Examination of differential pricing practices related to Internet data plans. Accessed at www.cmcrp.org/wp.../CMCRP_Intervention_to_TNC_CRTC_2016-192_Jun2016.pdf.

Moll, Marita, and Leslie Regan Shade, editors. 2008. *For Sale to the Highest Bidder: Telecom Policy in Canada*. Canadian Centre for Policy Alternatives. Accessed 5 August 2014 at www.policyalternatives.ca/sites/default/files/uploads/publications/National_Office_Pubs/2008/For_Sale_To_The_Highest_Bidder_contents_intro.pdf.

Moll, Marita, and Leslie Regan Shade, editors. 2011. *The Internet Tree: The State of Telecom Policy in Canada 3.0*. Canadian Centre for Policy Alternatives. Accessed 5 August 2014 at www.policyalternatives.ca/sites/default/files/uploads/publications/National%20Office/2011/06/Internet_Tree_0.pdf.

Mosco, Vincent. 2009. *The Political Economy of Communication*, 2nd ed. London: Sage.

Peers, Frank. 1969. *The Politics of Canadian Broadcasting, 1920–1951*. Toronto: University of Toronto Press.

Peers, Frank. 1979. *The Public Eye*. Toronto: University of Toronto Press.

Raboy, Marc. 1990. *Missed Opportunities: The Story of Canada's Broadcasting Policy*. Montreal and Kingston: McGill-Queen's UP.

Roth, Lorna. 2005. *Something New in the Air: The Story of First Peoples Television Broadcasting in Canada*. Montreal and Kingston: McGill-Queen's UP.

Rutherford, Paul. 1990. *When Television Was Young: Primetime Canada*. Toronto: University of Toronto Press.

Schudson, Michael. 1978. *Discovering the News: A Social History of American Newspapers*. New York: Basic Books.

Sontag, Susan. 1999. "On photography." In *Communication in History: Technology, Culture and Society*, edited by David Crowley and Paul Heyer. Don Mills, ON: Longman, 174–7.

Sotiron, Minko. 1997. *From Politics to Profit: The Commercialization of Daily Newspapers, 1890–1920*. Montreal and Kingston: McGill-Queen's UP.

Thompson, John B. 1990. *Ideology and Modern Culture: Critical Social Theory in the Era of Mass Communication*. Stanford, CA: Stanford UP.

Vipond, Mary. 2011. *The Mass Media in Canada: Who Decides What We Read, Watch, & Hear?* 4th ed. Toronto: James Lorimer.

Weir, Ernest Austin. 1965. *The Struggle for National Broadcasting in Canada*. Toronto: McClelland & Stewart.

Williams, Raymond. 1974. *Television: Technology and Cultural Form*. Glasgow: Fontana Collins.

Williams, Raymond. 1976. *Keywords: A Vocabulary of Culture and Society*. London: Fontana.

Chapter 3

Babe, Robert E. 1990. *Telecommunications in Canada*. Toronto: University of Toronto Press.

Bach, Natasha. 2017 (9 October). "Dove Removes 'Racist' Ad That Seemed to Suggest Black Women Were Dirty." *Fortune*. Accessed at fortune.com/2017/10/09/racist-dove-facebook-ad-taken-down/.

Bahadur, Nina 2017 (6 December). "Dove 'Real Beauty' Campaign Turns 10: How a Brand Tried to Change the Conversation about Female Beauty. *Huffington Post*. Accessed at www.huffingtonpost.ca/entry/dove-real-beauty-campaign-turns-10_n_4575940.

Baltruschat, Doris. 2009. "Reality TV Formats: The Case of *Canadian Idol*." *Canadian Journal of Communication* 34(1). Accessed 6 August 2014 at www.cjc-online.ca/index.php/journal/article/view/2032.

Barthes, Roland. 1968. *Elements of Semiology*, translated by A. Lavers and C. Smith. New York: Hill and Wang.

Barthes, Roland. 1972. *Mythologies*. London: Jonathan Cape.

Barthes, Roland. 1977a. *Image-Music-Text*, translated by Stephen Heath. New York: Hill and Wang.

Barthes, Roland. 1977b. "The death of the author." In Barthes, 1977a: 142–9.

Bennett, Tony, and Janet Woollacott. 1987. *Bond and Beyond: The Political Career of a Popular Hero*. New York: Methuen.

Bredin, M., editor. 2013. *Media Policy in Canada: Sources for Critical Analysis*. Dubuque, IA: Kendall-Hunt.

Budinsky, Jennifer, and Susan Bryant. 2013 (June). "'It's not easy being green': The greenwashing of environmental discourses in advertising." *Canadian Journal of Communication* 38(2), 207–26.

Clements, Mikaella. 2018 (8 August). "From Star Trek to Fifty Shades: How fanfiction went mainstream." In *The Guardian*. Accessed at www.theguardian.com/books/2018/aug/08/fanfiction-fifty-shades-star-trek-harry-potter.

Curran, James. 1990. "The new revisionism in mass communication research: A reappraisal." *European Journal of Communication* 5(2–3), 135–64.

Doherty, Mike. 2018 (18 May). "Music videos can be too powerful to ignore—and artists know it." In *Maclean's*. Accessed at www.macleans.ca/culture/music-videos-powerful-artists-know/.

Druick, Zoë, and Aspa Kotsopoulos. 2008. *Programming Reality: Perspectives on English-Canadian Television*. Waterloo, ON: Wilfrid Laurier UP.

Eco, Umberto. 1982. "Narrative structure in Fleming." In *Popular Culture Past and Present*, edited by B. Waites et al. Milton Keynes, UK: Open UP.

Eco, Umberto. 1986. "The multiplication of the media." In *Travels in Hyperreality*. New York: Harcourt Brace Jovanovich, 148–69.

Fairclough, Norman. 2010. *Critical Discourse Analysis: The Critical Study of Language*. New York: Routledge.

Felt, Mylynn. 2017. "News Portrayals of Cyberbullying as the Product of Unstable Teen Technological Culture." *Canadian Journal of Communication* 42(5), 893–912.

Fornas, J., U. Lindberg, and O. Sernhede. 1988. *Under Rocken*. Stockholm: Symposium.

Foucault, Michel. 1980. *The History of Sexuality*, translated by Robert Hurley. New York: Vintage Books.

Foucault, Michel. 1988. *Madness and Civilization: A History of Insanity in the Age of Reason*, translated by Richard Howard. New York: Vintage Books.

Foucault, Michel. 1995 [1979]. *Discipline and Punish: The Birth of the Prison*, translated by Alan Sheridan. New York: Vintage Books.

Fuchs, Christian. 2012. "Google Capitalism." *tripleC* 10(1), 42–8. Accessed at www.triple-c.at/index.php/tripleC/article/view/304.

Gasher, Mike. 2007. "The view from here: A news-flow study of the on-line editions of Canada's national newspapers." *Journalism Studies* 8(2), 299–319.

Geraghty, Christine. 1991. *Women and Soap Opera: A Study of Prime-Time Soaps*. Cambridge: Polity Press.

Giddens, Anthony. 1984. *The Constitution of Society: An Outline of a Theory of Structuration*. Berkeley: University of California Press.

Goffman, Erving. 1959. *The Presentation of Self in Everyday Life*. Harmondsworth, UK: Penguin.

Gunster, Shane. 2011. "Covering Copenhagen: Climate politics in B.C. media." *Canadian Journal of Communication* 36(3). Accessed 6 August 2014 at www.cjc-online.ca/index.php/journal/article/view/2367.

Hackett, Robert A., and Richard Gruneau. 2000. *The Missing News: Filters and Blindspots in Canada's Press*. Ottawa and Aurora, ON: Canadian Centre for Policy Alternatives and Garamond Press.

Hall, Stuart. 1993. "Encoding, decoding." In *The Cultural Studies Reader*, edited by Simon During. London: Routledge, 507–17.

Herman, Edward S., and Noam Chomsky. 2002. *Manufacturing Consent: The Political Economy of the Mass Media*. New York: Pantheon Books.

Heyer, Paul. 2003. "America under attack 1: *The War of the Worlds*, Orson Welles, and 'media sense.'" *Canadian Journal of Communication* 28(2): 149–65. Available online at www.cjc-online.ca/index.php/journal/article/view/1356/1421.

Hirji, Faiza. 2014. "The colour of difference: Race diversity and journalism in Canada." In *Mediascapes: New Patterns in Canadian Communication*, 4th ed., edited by Leslie Regan Shade. Don Mills, ON: Nelson, 390–408.

Jhally, Sut. 1997. *Advertising and the End of the World* (video). Northampton, MA: Media Education Foundation.

Jensen, Klaus Bruhn. 1990. "The politics of polysemy: Television news, everyday consciousness and political action." *Media, Culture and Society* 12(1), 57–77.

Jiwani, Yasmin. 2010. "Rac(e)ing the nation: Media and minorities." In Shade, 2010: 271–86.

Kluft, David. 2016 (18 October). 10 Copyright Cases Every Fan Fiction Writer Should Know About. In *Copyright and Trade Law*. Accessed at www.trademarkandcopyrightlawblog.com/2016/10/10-copyright-cases-every-fan-fiction-writer-should-know-about/.

Krippendorf, Klaus. 2004. *Content Analysis: An Introduction to Its Methodology*. Thousand Oaks, CA: Sage.

Kristeva, Julia. 1969. "Le mot, le dialogue et le roman." In *Sèmiòtikè: Recherches pour une sémanalyse*. Paris: Editions du Seuil.

LaGuardia, Robert. 1977. *From Ma Perkins to Mary Hartman: The Illustrated History of Soap Opera*. New York: Ballantine Books.

Lévi-Strauss, Claude. 1969. *The Raw and the Cooked*, translated by John and Doreen Weightman. London: Jonathan Cape.

McCurdy, Patrick. 2018. "From the Natural to the Manmade Environment: The Shifting Advertising Practices of Canada's Oil Sands Industry." *Canadian Journal of Communication* 43(1), 33–52.

Meyrowitz, Joshua. 1994. "Medium theory." In *Communication Theory Today*, edited by David Crowley and David Mitchell. Stanford, CA: Stanford UP, 50–7.

Mirrlees, Tanner. 2013. *Global Entertainment Media: Between Cultural Imperialism and Cultural Globalization*. New York: Routledge.

Moll, Marita, and Leslie Regan Shade, editors. 2008. *For Sale to the Highest Bidder: Telecom Policy in Canada*. Canadian Centre for Policy Alternatives. Accessed 5 August 2014 at www.policyalternatives.ca/sites/default/files/uploads/publications/National_Office_Pubs/2008/For_Sale_To_The_Highest_Bidder_contents_intro.pdf.

Moll, Marita, and Leslie Regan Shade, editors. 2011. *The Internet Tree: The State of Telecom Policy in Canada 3.0*. Canadian Centre for Policy Alternatives. Accessed 5 August 2014 at www.policyalternatives.ca/sites/default/files/uploads/publications/National%20Office/2011/06/Internet_Tree_0.pdf.

Mosco, Vincent. 2009. *The Political Economy of Communication*, 2nd ed. London: Sage.

Murray, Stuart. 2012. "Nous sommes avenir / à venir: The voice of the we yet to come." *Canadian Journal of Communication* 37: 495–97.

Murray, Susan, and Laurie Ouellette. 2004. *Reality TV: Remaking Television Culture*. New York: New York UP.

Pendakur, Manjunath. 1990. *Canadian Dreams and American Control: The Political Economy of the Canadian Film Industry*. Toronto: Garamond Press.

Pedwell, Terry. 2017 (16 July 16). "Not enough diversity on Canadian television, report says." *Toronto Star*. Accessed at www.thestar.com/news/canada/2017/07/16/not-enough-diversity-on-canadian-television-report-says.html.

Propp, Vladimir. 1970. *Morphology of the Folktale*. Austin: University of Texas Press.

Quail, Christine. 2015. "Producing Reality: Television Formats and Reality TV in the Canadian Context." *Canadian Journal of Communication* 40, 185–201. Accessed at www.cjc-online.ca/index.php/journal/article/view/2828/2555.

Radway, Janice. 1984. *Reading the Romance: Women, Patriarchy, and Popular Literature*. Chapel Hill, NC: University of North Carolina Press.

Richter, Solina, Kathy Kovacs Burns, Yuping Mao, et al. 2011. "Homelessness coverage in major Canadian newspapers, 1987–2007." *Canadian Journal of Communication* 36(4). Accessed 6 August 2014 at www.cjc-online.ca/index.php/journal/article/view/2417.

Saussure, Ferdinand de. 1974. *Course in General Linguistics*. London: Fontana.

Shade, Leslie Regan, editor. 2010. *Mediascapes: New Patterns in Canadian Communication*, 3rd ed. Toronto: Nelson Education.

Silverman, Kaja. 1983. *The Subject of Semiotics*. New York: Oxford UP.

Smythe, Dallas. 1981. "Communications: Blindspot of economics." In *Culture, Communication and Dependency: The Tradition of H.A. Innis*, edited by William H. Melody, Liora R. Salter, and Paul Heyer. Norwood, NJ: Ablex.

Smythe, Dallas. 1994. *Counterclockwise: Perspectives on Communication*, edited by Thomas Guback. Boulder, CO: Westview Press.

van Dijk, Teun A. 1985. *Handbook of Discourse Analysis*. 4 vols. London: Academic Press.

van Dijk, Teun A. 1997. *Discourse as Structure and Process*. Thousand Oaks, CA: Sage.

van Dijk, Teun A. 2014. *Discourse and knowledge : A socio-cognitive approach*. Cambridge: Cambridge UP.

Williams, Carol T. 1992. *It's Time for My Story: Soap Opera Sources, Structure, and Response*. London: Praeger.

Williamson, Judith. 1978. *Decoding Advertisements: Ideology and Meaning in Advertising*. London: Boyars.

Winseck, Dwayne. 1998. *Reconvergence*. Cresskill, NJ: Hampton Press.

Winseck, Dwayne. 2017. *Media and Internet Concentration in Canada, 1984–2016*. Accessed at www.cmcrp.org/media-and-internet-concentration-in-canada-results/.

Winseck, Dwayne, and Dal Yong Jin. 2012. *The Political Economies of Media: The Transformation of the Global Media Industries*. New York: Bloomsbury Academic.

Chapter 4

Adorno, Theodor, and Max Horkheimer. 1977 [1944]. "The Culture Industry: Enlightenment as Mass Deception." In *Mass Communication and Society*, edited by J. Curran, M. Gurevitch, and J. Woollacott. London: Edward Arnold, 349–83.

Al-Mahadin, Salam. 2017. "Gendered soundscapes on Jordanian radio stations." *Feminist Media Studies* 17(1), 108–11.

Anderssen, Erin. 2014 (2 October). "Big data is watching you. Has online spying gone too far?" *The Globe and Mail*. Accessed at www.theglobeandmail.com/life/relationships/big-data-is-watching-you-has-online-spying-gone-too-far/article20894498/?page=all.

Arnott, Peter D. 1989. *Public and Performance in Greek Theatre*, London: Routledge.

Barker, Chris. 2012. *Cultural Studies: Theory and Practice*. Thousand Oaks, CA: Sage.

Beauvoir, Simone de. 1957 [1949]. *The Second Sex*, translated and edited by H.M. Parshley. New York: Knopf.

Blumler, Jay, and Elihu Katz, editors. 1974. *The Uses of Mass Communications: Current Perspectives on Gratifications Research*. Beverly Hills, CA: Sage.

Bryce, J. 1987. "Family time and TV use." In *Natural Audiences*, edited by T. Lindlof. Norwood, NJ: Ablex, 121–38.

Cavalcante, Andre, Andrea Press, Katherine Sender. 2017. "Feminist reception studies in a post-audience age: Returning to audiences and everyday life." *Feminist Media Studies* 17(1), 1–13.

CMCRP. 2019. *The Growth of the Network Media Economy in Canada, 1984–2017* (updated). Accessed at www.cmcrp.org/wp-content/uploads/2019/01/The-Growth-of-the-Network-Media-Economy-1984-2017-01142019.pdf.

Cohen, Nicole. 2008. "The valorization of surveillance: Towards a political economy of Facebook." *Democratic Communiqué* 22(1), 5–32.

Coté, Mark, and Jennifer Pybus 2011. "Learning to Immaterial Labour 2.0: Facebook and Social Networks." In *Cognitive Capitalism, Education and Digital Labor*, edited by Michael A. Peters and Ergin Bulut. New York: Peter Lang. Available on Moodle.

Croteau, David, and William Hoynes. 2003. *Media/Society*, 3rd ed. Thousand Oaks, CA: Pine Forge.

CRTC. 2017. *Communications Monitoring Report 2017*. Accessed at crtc.gc.ca/eng/publications/reports/policymonitoring/2017/cmr4.htm#s42v.

Curtis, Liz. 1984. *Ireland, the Propaganda War: The Media and the "Battle for Hearts and Minds."* London: Pluto Press.

Eagleton, Terry. 2007. *Ideology: An Introduction*. London: Verso.

Erlichman, Jon. 2018 (6 July). "One in 100: Canada's 'embarrassing' lack of female CEOs among top TSX companies." BNN Bloomberg. Accessed at www.bnnbloomberg.ca/female-ceos-noticeably-absent-from-canada-s-c-suite-1.1103584.

Facebook. 2018. *Lookalike Audiences*. Accessed at www.facebook.com/business/help/465262276878947.

Friedan, Betty. 1963. *The Feminine Mystique*. New York: Norton.

Fuchs, Christian. 2013. "Theorising and analyzing digital labour: From global value chains to modes of production." *The Political Economy of Communication* 2(1), 3–27. Accessed at www.polecom.org/index.php/polecom/article/view/19.

Gajjala, Radhika, and Yeon Ju Oh, editors. 2012. *Cyber-Feminism 2.0*. New York: Peter Lang.

García-Galera, M. Carmen, and Angharad Valdivia. 2014. "Media Prosumers. Participatory Culture of Audiences and Media Responsibility." *Comunicar* 43(22), 10–13.

Garnage, Shashini Ruwanthi. 2018. "Soap operas, women, and the nation: Sri Lankan women's interpretations of home-grown mega teledramas." *Feminist Media Studies* 18(5), 873–7.

Gerbner, George. 1969. "Towards 'cultural indicators': The analysis of mass-mediated public message systems." *AV Communication Review* 17(2), 137–48.

Gerbner, George. 1977. *Trends in Network Drama and Viewer Conceptions of Social Reality, 1967–1976*. Philadelphia: Annenburg School of Communications, University of Pennsylvania.

Glasgow Media Group. 1976. *Bad News*. Boston: Routledge & Kegan Paul.

Gray, Ann. 1999. "Audience and reception research in retrospect: The trouble with audiences." In *Rethinking the Media Audience: The New Agenda*, edited by P. Alasuutari. Thousand Oaks, CA: Sage, 22–37.

Grossberg, Lawrence, Ellen Wartella, D. Charles Whitney, and J. Macgregor Wise. 2006. *MediaMaking: Mass Media in Popular Culture*, 2nd ed. Thousand Oaks, CA: Sage.

Gunster, Shane. 2004. *Capitalizing on Culture*. Toronto: University of Toronto Press.

Hale, James Loke. 2019. "More Than 500 Hours of Content Are Now Being Uploaded to YouTube Every Minute." *Tubefilter*. Accessed 7 May 2019 at www.tubefilter.com/2019/05/07/number-hours-video-uploaded-to-youtube-per-minute/.

Hall, Stuart. 1980. "Encoding/decoding." In *Culture, Media, Language*, edited by Stuart Hall et al. London: Hutchinson; Birmingham, UK: Centre for Cultural Studies, 128–38.

Hall, Stuart et al. 1978. *Policing the Crisis: Mugging, the State and Law and Order*. London: Macmillan.

Hartley, John. 1987. "Invisible fictions." *Textual Practice* 1(2), 121–38.

Hebdige, Dick. 1979. *Subculture: The Meaning of Style*. London: Methuen.

Hermes, Joke. 2006. "Feminism and the politics of method." In *Questions of Method in Cultural Studies*, edited by Mimi White and James Schwoch. Oxford: Blackwell, 154–74.

Hoggart, Richard. 1992 [1957]. *The Uses of Literacy*. New Brunswick, NJ: Transaction.

Ingham, Tim. 2016. "YouTube earnt $9bn in revenue last year, towering over Spotify. In *Music Business Worldwide*. Accessed at www.musicbusinessworldwide.com/who-we-are/.

Israel, Solomon. 2017 (8 March). "StatsCan on gender pay gap: Women earn 87¢ to men's $1." Accessed at www.cbc.ca/news/business/statistics-canada-gender-pay-gap-1.4014954.

Jay, Martin. 1974. *The Dialectical Imagination*. London: Routledge.

Jenkins, Henry. 1992. *Textual Poachers: Television Fans and Participatory Culture*. New York: Routledge.

Jhally, Sut, director. 2010. *Killing Us Softly 4* (video). Northampton, MA: Media Education Foundation.

Kimmel, Michael S., and Jacqueline Holler, editors. 2011. *The Gendered Society*. Don Mills, ON: Oxford UP.

Kleinman, Alexis. 2012 (19 December). "12 items Walmart considers more dangerous than assault weapons." *Huffington Post*. Accessed 3 October 2014 at www.huffingtonpost.com/2012/12/18/walmart-banned-products_n_2324382.html.

Larrain, Jorge. 1979. *The Concept of Ideology*. London: Hutchinson.

Larrain, Jorge. 1983. *Marxism and Ideology*. London: Macmillan.

Lee, Richard E. 2003. *The Life and Times of Cultural Studies*. Durham, NC: Duke UP.

McGuigan, Jim. 1992. *Cultural Populism*. London: Routledge.

McGuigan, Lee, and Vincent Manzerolle, editors. 2014. *The Audience Commodity in the Digital Age*. New York: Peter Lang.

McInturff, Kate. 2014 (1 May). "Where are all the women on Canada's 100 top CEOs list?" Canadian Centre for Policy Alternatives. Accessed 3 October 2014 at www.huffingtonpost.ca/kate-mcinturff/canada-100-top-ceos_b_454681.

McQuail, Denis. 2010. *McQuail's Mass Communication Theory*, 6th ed. Thousand Oaks, CA: Sage.

Mathieu. David. 2015. "The Continued Relevance of Reception Analysis in the Age of Social Media." *Trípodos* 36, 13–34.

Matsakis, Louise. 2018. "YouTube's Latest Shake-Up Is Bigger Than Just Ads." In *Wired*. Accessed at www.wired.com/story/youtube-monetization-creators-ads/.

Modleski, Tania. 1984. *Loving with a Vengeance: Mass-Produced Fantasies for Women*. London: Methuen.

Morley, David. 1980. *The "Nationwide" Audience: Structure and Decoding*. British Film Institute Television Monographs, 11. London: BFI.

Morley, David. 1986. *Family Television: Cultural Power and Domestic Leisure*. London: Comedia.

Mulvey, Laura. 1975. "Visual pleasure and narrative cinema." *Screen* 16(3), 6–18.

Napoli, Philip. 2011. *Audience Evolution*. New York: Columbia UP.

Potter, James W. 2014. "A Critical Analysis of Cultivation Theory." *Journal of Communication* 64(6), 1015–36.

Press, Andrea L. 2000. "Recent developments in feminist communication theory." In *Mass Media and Society*, edited by James Curran and Michael Gurevitch. New York: Oxford UP, 2–43.

Radway, Janice. 1984. *Reading the Romance: Women, Patriarchy, and Popular Literature*. Chapel Hill: University of North Carolina Press.

Reuters. 2013 (8 April). "77 percent of people use their computers while watching TV: Survey." *Huffington Post*. Accessed 1 October 2014 at www.huffingtonpost.com/2013/04/09/tv-multitasking_n_3040012.html.

Sarikakis, Katherine, and Leslie Regan Shade. 2008. *Feminist Interventions in International Communications*. Lanham, MD: Rowman & Littlefield.

Savage, Philip. 2014. "Audiences are key." In *Mediascapes: New Patterns in Canadian Communication*, 4th ed., edited by Leslie Regan Shade. Don Mills, ON: Nelson Education, 127–49.

Sawchuk, Kim. 2014. "Beyond the f-word: A constellation of feminist concepts for media researchers." In *Mediascapes: New Patterns in Canadian Communication*, 4th ed., edited by Leslie Regan Shade. Don Mills, ON: Nelso n Education, 59–80.

Schlesinger, Philip. 1983. *Televising "Terrorism": Political Violence in Popular Culture*. London: Comedia.

Schulman, Norma. 1993. "Conditions of their own making: An intellectual history of the Centre for Contemporary Cultural Studies at the University of Birmingham." *Canadian Journal of Communication* 18(1), 51–74.

Seiter, Ellen, Hans Borchers, Gabrielle Kreutzner, and Eva-Maria Warth, editors. 1989. *Remote Control: Television, Audiences, and Cultural Power*. London: Routledge.

Signorielli, Nancy, and Michael Morgan, editors. 1990. *Cultivation Analysis*. Beverly Hills, CA: Sage.

Silverstone, Roger. 1981. *The Message of Television: Myth and Narrative in Contemporary Culture*. London: Heinemann Educational Books.

Smythe, Dallas. 1977. "Communications: Blindspot of Western Marxism." *Canadian Journal of Political and Social Theory* 1, 1–27.

Smythe, Dallas. 1994. *Counterclockwise: Perspectives on Communication*, edited by Thomas Guback. Boulder, CO: Westview Press.

Storey, John. 1993. *Cultural Theory and Popular Culture*. London: Harvester Wheatsheaf.

Sullivan, John L. 2013. *Media Audiences: Effects, Users, Institutions, and Power*. Thousand Oaks, CA: Sage.

Thomas, Sherry. 2016. "A virtual life: How social media changes our perceptions." In *Insight*. Accessed at www.thechicagoschool.edu/insight/a-virtual-life/.

Thompson, Edward P. 1980 [1963]. *The Making of the English Working Class*. Harmondsworth, UK: Penguin.

Turner, Graeme. 1990. *British Cultural Studies: An Introduction*. London: Routledge.

Waylen, Georgina, Karen Celis, Johanna Kantola, and S. Laurel Weldon, editors. 2016. *The Oxford Handbook of Gender and Politics*. Oxford UP.

Williams, Raymond. 1958. *Culture and Society: 1780–1950*. New York: Columbia UP.

Williamson, Judith. 1978. *Decoding Advertisements: Ideology and Meaning in Advertising*. London: Boyars.

Willis, Paul. 1977. *Learning to Labor*. New York: Columbia UP.

Winseck, Dwayne. 2018. *The Growth of the Network Media Economy in Canada, 1984–2017*. Ottawa: Canadian Media Concentration Research Project.

Wober, J. Mallory, and Barrie Gunter. 1986. "Television audience research at Britain's Independent Broadcasting Authority, 1974–1984." *Journal of Broadcasting and Electronic Media* 30(1), 15–31.

Women's Studies Group. 1978. *Women Take Issue: Aspects of Women's Subordination*. Birmingham, UK: Centre for Cultural Studies.

Chapter 5

Abidin, Crystal. 2016. "'Aren't These Just Young, Rich Women Doing Vain Things Online?': Influencer Selfies as Subversive Frivolity." *Social Media and Society*: 1–17. doi.org/10.1177/2056305116641342.

Aronczyk, M. 2018. "Consume This! Advertising and Consumer Data." ASA (American Sociological Association) Section on *Consumers and Consumption*. Accessed at asaconsumers.wordpress.com/2018/07/30/consume-this-advertising-and-consumer-data/.

Asquith, K., and A. Hearn. 2012. "Promotional Prime Time: 'Advertainment', Internal Network Promotion, and the Future of Canadian Television." *Canadian Journal of Communication*, 37(2), 241–57.

Belisle, D. 2011. *Retail nation: Department stores and the making of modern Canada*. UBC Press.

Brady, M.J., and M. Aronczyk. 2015. "Branding history at the Canadian Museum of Civilization." *Canadian Journal of Communication* 40, 165–84.

Cohen, Nicole. 2008. "The valorization of surveillance: Towards a political economy of Facebook." *Democratic Communiqué*, 22(1), 5–32.

Comrack, P., and J. Cograve. 2018. "'Always fresh, always there'. Tim Hortons and the consumer citizen." In *Advertising, Consumer Culture and Canadian Society*, edited by Kyle Asquith. Don Mills, ON: Oxford UP.

Cook, D. 2004. *The Commodification of Childhood: The Children's Clothing Industry and theRise of the Child Consumer*. Raleigh, NC: Duke UP.

Cook, D. 2011. "Commercial epistemologies of childhood: 'Fun' and the leveraging of children's subjectivities and desires." In *Inside Marketing: Practices, Ideologies, and Devices*, edited by D. Zwick and J. Cayla. Oxford: Oxford UP, 257–68.

Elmer, G. 2003. "A diagram of panoptic surveillance." *New Media & Society* 5(2), 231–47.

Ewen, S. 1976. *Captains of consciousness: Advertising and the social roots of consumer consciousness*. New York: McGraw-Hill.

Gleeson, S. 2018 (8 September). "Study: Nike online sales surge 31 percent days after Colin Kaepernick ad released." *USA Today*. Accessed at www.usatoday.com/story/sports/2018/09/08/study-nike-online-sales-up-after-colin-kaepernick-ad/1240378002/.

Hearn, A., and S. Schoenhoff. 2016. "From celebrity to influencer: Tracing the diffusion of celebrity value across the data stream." In *A companion to celebrity*, edited by P. David Marshall and S. Redmond. New York: Wiley, 194–212.

Horkheimer, Max, and Theodor Adorno. 2006 [1944]. "The Culture Industry: Enlightenment as Mass Deception." In *Media and Cultural Studies: KeyWorks*, edited by M.G. Durham and D.M. Kellner. Malden, MA: Blackwell, 41–72.

Jhally, Sut. 1987. *The Codes of Advertising: Fetishism and the Political Economy of Meaning in the Consumer Society*. New York: Routledge.

Jhally, Sut. 1997. *Advertising and the End of the World* (video). Northampton, MA: Media Education Foundation.

Jhally, Sut. 2006. *The spectacle of accumulation: Essays in culture, media, & politics*. New York: Peter Lang.

Johnson, R. 2018. "A Professional Ideal." In *Canadian Contributions to the Study of Advertising. Advertising, Consumer Culture and Canadian Society,* edited by Kyle Asquith. Don Mills, ON: Oxford UP.

Klein, Naomi. 2000. *No Logo: Taking Aim at the Brand Bullies*. Toronto: Knopf Canada.

Langlois, G. 2014. *Meaning in the age of social media*. New York: Palgrave Macmillan.

Lapowsky, I. 2017 (26 October). "What Did Cambridge Analytica Really Do for Trump's Campaign?" *Wired*. Accessed at www.wired.com/story/what-did-cambridge-analytica-really-do-for-trumps-campaign/.

Leiss, W., S. Kline, S. Jhally, and J. Botterill. 1990. *Social communication in advertising*. London.

McGuigan, L. 2019. "Canadian Contributions to the Study of Advertising." *Advertising, Consumer Culture and Canadian Society*, edited by Kyle Asquith. Don Mills, ON: Oxford UP.

McGuigan, L., and V. Manzerolle, editors. 2014. *The Audience Commodity in a Digital Age: Revisiting a Critical Theory of Commercial Media*. New York: Peter Lang.

Marchand, R. 1985. *Advertising the American dream: Making way for modernity, 1920–1940*. Berkeley: University of California Press.

Meehan, E.R. 2005. *Why TV is not our fault: Television programming, viewers, and who's really in control*. Lanham, MD: Rowman & Littlefield.

Noble, S.U. 2018. *Algorithms of Oppression: How search engines reinforce racism*. New York: New York UP.

Novy-Williams, Eben. 2018 (4 Novemeber). "Kaepernick Campaign Created $43 million in Buzz for Nike." *Bloomberg*. Accesseed at www.bloomberg.com/news/articles/2018-09-04/kaepernick-campaign-created-43-million-in-buzz-for-nike-so-far.

Qiu, J.L. 2017. *Goodbye iSlave: A manifesto for digital abolition*. Urbana: University of Illinois Press.

Slater, P. 1970. *The Pursuit of Loneliness*. Boston: Beacon.

Smythe, D.W. 1977. "Communications: Blindspot of Western Marxism." *CTheory* 1(3), 1–27.

Terranova, T. 2012. "Free labor." In *Digital Labor*, edited by Trebor Scholz. New York: Routledge, 41–65.

Wernick, A. 1991. *Promotional culture: Advertising, ideology and symbolic expression*. Newbury Park, CA: Sage.

Williams, Raymond. 1980. "Advertising: The magic system." In *Problems in Materialism and Culture*. London: Verso, 170–95.

Zwick, D., and J. Denegri Knott. 2009. "Manufacturing customers: The database as new means of production." *Journal of Consumer Culture* 9(2), 221–47.

Chapter 6

Anderson, Chris. 2006. *The Long Tail: Why the Future of Business Is Selling Less of More*. New York: Hyperion.

Bermejo, Fernando. 2011. "The evolution of audience labor: Appropriating online activities." In Park et al., 67–82.

Bijker, Wiebe. 1993. "Do not despair: There is life after constructivism." *Science, Technology & Human Values* 18, 113–38.

Blok, Anders, and Torben Elgaard Jensen. 2011. *Bruno Latour: Hybrid Thoughts in a Hybrid World*. New York: Routledge.

Braverman, Harry. 1974. *Labor and Monopoly Capital: The Degradation of Work in the Twentieth Century*. New York: Monthly Review Press.

Bruns, Axel. 2008. *Blogs, Wikipedia, Second Life, and Beyond: From Production to Produsage*. New York: Peter Lang.

Croteau, David, and William Hoynes. 2014. *Media/Society: Industries, Images, and Audiences*, 5th ed. Los Angeles: Sage.

Crow, Barbara, Michael Longford, and Kim Sawchuk, editors. 2010. *The Wireless Spectrum: The Politics, Practices and Poetics of Mobile Media*. Toronto: University of Toronto Press.

CSEC (Communications Security Establishment Canada). 2014. "What we do and why we do it." Accessed 23 July 2019 at www.cse-cst.gc.ca/en/inside-interieur/what-nos.

Dahlberg, Lincoln, and Eugenia Siapera, editors. 2007. *Radical Democracy and the Internet: Integrating Theory and Practice*. New York: Palgrave Macmillan.

de Kerckhove, Derrick. 1995. *The Skin of Culture: Investigating the New Electronic Reality*. Toronto: Somerville House.

Dredge, Stuart. 2011 (14 September). "Apple bans satirical iPhone game Phone Story from its App Store." *The Guardian*. Accessed 9 November 2018 at www.theguardian.com.

Ellul, Jacques. 1964. *The Technological Society*. New York: Knopf.

Elmer, Greg. 2004. *Profiling Machines: Mapping the Personal Information Economy*. Cambridge, MA: MIT Press.

Feenberg, Andrew. 1999. *Questioning Technology*. New York: Routledge.

Fekete, Jason. 2013 (10 October). "Spy agency meets industry regularly; CSEC says its foreign intelligence activities follow Canadian law." *Edmonton Journal*, A15.

Flew, Terry, and Richard Smith. 2014. *New Media: An Introduction*, 2nd Canadian ed. Don Mills, ON: Oxford UP.

Foucault, Michel. 1995 [1979]. *Discipline and Punish: The Birth of the Prison*, translated by Alan Sheridan. New York: Vintage Books.

Franklin, Ursula. 1996. *The Real World of Technology*. Concord, ON: House of Anansi Press.

Fuchs, Christian. 2009. "Information and communication technologies and society: A contribution to the critique of the political economy of the internet." *European Journal of Communication* 24(1), 69–87.

Gasher, Mike. 2013. "Media convergence." *The Canadian Encyclopedia*. Accessed at www.thecanadianencyclopedia.ca/en/article/media-convergence.

Goggin, Gerard. 2011. "Telephone media: An old story." In Park et al., 231–49.

Goody, J.R. 1977. *The Domestication of the Savage Mind*. Cambridge: Cambridge UP.

Greenwald, Glenn. 2014. *No Place to Hide: Edward Snowden, the NSA, and the U.S. Surveillance State*. Toronto: McClelland & Stewart.

Greenwood, John. 2014 (6 June). "Rogers had nearly 200K data requests." *National Post*, FP1.

Grofman, Bernard, Alexander H. Trechsel, and Mark Franklin, editors. 2014. *The Internet and Democracy in Global Perspective: Voters, Candidates, Parties and Social Movements*. Cham, Switzerland: Springer.

Haraway, Donna. 1991. "A cyborg manifesto: Science, technology, and socialist-feminism in the late twentieth century." In *Simians, Cyborgs and Women: The Reinvention of Nature*. New York: Routledge, 149–81.

Harris, Kathleen. 2017 (13 March). "Federal officials say no personal information leaked in 'credible' software security threat." *CBC News*. Accessed 2 November 2018 at www.cbc.ca.

Hindman, Matthew. 2018. *The Internet Trap: How the Digital Economy Builds Monopolies and Undermines Democracy*. Princeton, NJ: Princeton UP.

Hirst, Martin, John Harrison, and Patricia Mazepa. 2014. *Communication and New Media: From Broadcast to Narrowcast*. Canadian ed. Don Mills, ON: Oxford UP.

Holmes, Nancy. 2008 (September). *Canada's Federal Privacy Laws*. Ottawa: Library of Parliament. Accessed 18 June 2014 at www.parl.gc.ca/Content/LOP/researchpublications/prb0744-e.pdf.

Innis, Harold. 1950. *Empire and Communications*. Toronto: Oxford UP.

Innis, Harold. 1951. *The Bias of Communication*. Toronto: University of Toronto Press.

ITU (International Telecommunication Union). 2017 (July). *ICT Facts and Figures 2017*. Accessed 25 September 2018 at www.itu.int.

Jenkins, Henry. 2006. *Convergence Culture: Where Old and New Media Collide*. New York: New York UP.

Kobie, Nicole. 2019 (21 January). "The complicated truth about China's social credit system." *Wired*. Accessed 27 March 2019 at www.wired.co.uk.

Leblanc, Daniel, and Tu Thanh Ha. 2014 (16 April). "RCMP charge teen in relation to Heartbleed bug attack on CRA." *The Globe and Mail*. Accessed 23 June 2014 at www.theglobeandmail.com/news/national/rcmp-charge-teen-in-relation-to-alleged-heartbleed-bug-theft/article18041007/.

Lessig, Lawrence. 2008. *Remix: Making Art and Commerce Thrive in the Hybrid Economy*. New York: Penguin.

Lyons, Daniel. 2010 (5 April). "Think really different." *Newsweek*, 47–51.

MacCharles, Tonda. 2014 (13 June). "Police need warrant to get internet customers' identities, Supreme Court rules." *Toronto Star*. Accessed 24 June 2014 at www.thestar.com/news/canada/2014/06/13/police_need_warrant_to_get_internet_customers_identities_supreme_court_rules.html.

McChesney, Robert W. 2013. *Digital Disconnect: How Capitalism Is Turning the Internet against Democracy*. New York: The New Press.

McDiarmid, Jessica. 2013 (28 November). "Canada let US spy at G20, report says: Documents released by Snowden show Ottawa allowed surveillance in 2010." *Toronto Star*, A3.

McDonald, Joe. 2019 (22 February). "China bars millions from travel for 'social credit' offenses." *AP News*. Accessed 27 March 2019 at www.apnews.com.

McKercher, Catherine. 2002. *Newsworkers Unite: Labor, Convergence, and North American Newspapers*. Lanham, MD: Rowman & Littlefield.

McLuhan, Marshall. 1962. *The Gutenberg Galaxy: The Making of Typographic Man*. Toronto: University of Toronto Press.

Mosco, Vincent. 2014. *To the Cloud: Big Data in a Turbulent World*. Boulder, CO: Paradigm Publishers.

Mosco, Vincent. 2017. *Becoming Digital: Toward a Post-Internet World*. Bingley, UK: Emerald Publishing.

Nieborg, David B., and Anne Helmond. 2018. "The political economy of Facebook's platformization in the mobile ecosystem." *Media, Culture and Society* 41(2), 196–218.

Park, David W., Nicholas W. Jankowski, and Steve Jones, editors. 2011. *The Long History of New Media*. New York: Peter Lang.

Powers, Shawn M., and Michael Jablonski. 2015. *The Real Cyber War: The Political Economy of Internet Freedom*. Urbana: University of Illinois Press.

Schulte, Stephanie Ricker. 2011. "Cutting the cord and 'crying socialist wolf': Unwiring the public and producing the third place." In Park et al., 37–54.

Shirky, Clay. 2008. *Here Comes Everybody: The Power of Organizing without Organizations*. New York: Penguin Press.

Shirky, Clay. 2010. *Cognitive Surplus: Creativity and Generosity in a Connected Age*. New York: Penguin Press.

Slack, Jennifer Daryl, and J. Macgregor Wise. 2007. *Culture and Technology: A Primer*. New York: Peter Lang.

Srnicek, Nick. 2017. *Platform Capitalism*. Cambridge: Polity Press.

Statistics Canada. 2013. "Households with home internet access." Accessed 6 May 2014 at www.statcan.gc.ca/daily-quotidien/131116/t131126d001-eng.htm.

Taras, David. 2015. *Digital Mosaic: Media, Power, and Identity in Canada*. Toronto: University of Toronto Press.

Tarkka, Minna. 2011. "Labours of location: Acting in the pervasive media space." In *The Wireless Spectrum: The Politics, Practices, and Poetics of Mobile Media*, edited by Barbara Crow et al. Toronto: University of Toronto Press, 131–45.

Taylor, Frederick Winslow. 1997 [1911]. *The Principles of Scientific Management*. Mineola, NY: Dover Publications.

Trottier, Daniel. 2012. "Interpersonal Surveillance on Social Media." *Canadian Journal of Communicaton* 37, 319–22.

van Dijk, Jan A.G.M. 2012. *The Network Society*, 3rd ed. London: Sage.

Williams, Raymond. 1974. *Television: Technology and Cultural Form*. Glasgow: Fontana Collins.

Chapter 7

Abramson, Bram Dov, and Marc Raboy. 1999. "Policy globalization and the 'information society': A view from Canada." *Telecommunications Policy* 23, 775–91.

Baeker, Greg. 2002. "Sharpening the lens: Recent research on cultural policy, cultural diversity, and social cohesion." *Canadian Journal of Communication* 27, 179–96.

Bird, Roger, editor. 1988. *Documents of Canadian Broadcasting*. Ottawa: Carleton UP.

Canada. 1929a (19 January). Order-in-Council 2108. *Canada Gazette*, 2306.

Canada. 1929b. *Report of the Royal Commission on Radio Broadcasting* (Aird Commission). Ottawa: F.A. Acland.

Canada. 1951. *Report of the Royal Commission on National Development in the Arts, Letters and Sciences, 1949–1951* (Massey–Lévesque Commission). Ottawa: Edmond Cloutier.

Canada. 1957. *Report of the Royal Commission on Broadcasting* (Fowler Commission). Ottawa: Edmond Cloutier.

Canada. 1982. *Report of the Federal Cultural Policy Review Committee (*Applebaum–Hébert Committee*)*. Ottawa: Minister of Supply and Services Canada.

Canada. 1987 (April). Department of Communication. *Vital Links: Canadian Cultural Industries*. Ottawa: Minister of Supply and Services Canada.

Canada. 2014a. Department of Canadian Heritage. *Book Distribution and Bill 51 in Quebec*. Accessed 30 October 2014 at www.pch.gc.ca/eng/1372789992292/1372790043461#h2.

Canada. 2014b. Department of Canadian Heritage. *Canada Book Fund*. Accessed 28 October 2014 at www.pch.gc.ca/eng/1268182505843.

Canada. 2014c. Department of Canadian Heritage. Canada *Periodical Fund*. Accessed 30 October 2014 at www.pch.gc.ca/eng/1268240166828.

Canada. 2014d. Department of Canadian Heritage. *Canadian Arts Presentation Fund*. Accessed 31 October 2014 at www.pch.gc.ca/eng/1267553110077.

Canada. 2014e. *Digital Canada 150*. Accessed 14 October 2014 at www.ic.gc.ca/eic/site/028.nsf/eng/00576.html#item3.

Canada. 2017. *Creative Canada Policy Framework*. Ottawa: Department of Canadian Heritage. Accessed at www.canada.ca/en/canadian-heritage/campaigns/creative-canada/framework.html.

Forsey, Eugene A. 2006. "Order-in-council." *The Canadian Encyclopedia*. Accessed 25 November 2014 at www.thecanadianencyclopedia.ca.

Fowler, Robert. 2014 (4 October). "We've got to get nasty, or get the hell out." *The Globe and Mail*. Kindle edition.

Hamelink, Cees J. 1994. *The Politics of World Communication*. London: Sage.

Kelly, Brendan. 2018 (20 July). "Cultural milieu hopeful Rodriguez will back them; Entertainment industry banking on new heritage minister's support of 'Netflix tax.'" *Montreal Gazette*, A2.

Law Central Alberta. n.d. "Statutes and Regulations (Federal)." Accessed 12 November 2015 at www.lawcentralalberta.ca/en/know/laws-canada/statutes-regulations-federal.

McChesney, Robert W. 1997. *Corporate Media and the Threat to Democracy*. New York: Seven Stories Press.

Raboy, Marc. 1990. *Missed Opportunities: The Story of Canada's Broadcasting Policy*. Montreal and Kingston: McGill-Queen's UP.

Raboy, Marc, and Jeremy Shtern, editors. 2010. *Media Divides: Communication Rights and the Right to Communicate in Canada*. Vancouver: UBC Press.

Shea, Albert A. 1952. *Culture in Canada: A Study of the Findings of the Royal Commission on National Development in the Arts, Letters and Sciences (1949–1951)*. Toronto: Core.

Spry, Graham. 1931 (April). "Canada's broadcasting issue." In *Canadian Forum*.

Statistics Canada. 2016. "Census Profile, 2016 Census." Accessed 17 September 2018 at www12.statcan.gc.ca/census-recensement/2016/dp-pd/prof/details/page.cfm?Lang=E&Geo1=PR&Code1=01&Geo2=&Code2=&Data=Count&SearchText=Canada&SearchType=Begins&SearchPR=01&B1=All&TABID=1.

Vaidhyanathan, Siva. 2001. *Copyrights and Copywrongs: The Rise of Intellectual Property and How It Threatens Creativity*. New York: New York UP.

Vipond, Mary. 1992. *Listening In: The First Decade of Canadian Broadcasting, 1922–1932*. Montreal and Kingston: McGill-Queen's UP.

Chapter 8

Advertising Standards Canada. 2015. *The Broadcast Code for Advertising to Children*. Accessed 12 July 2019 at www.adstadards.com.

APTN (Aboriginal Peoples Television Network). 2018. "About." www.aptn.ca.

Armstrong, Robert. 2016. *Broadcasting Policy in Canada*, 2nd ed. Toronto: University of Toronto Press.

ASC (Advertising Standards Council). 2018. "About us." www.adstandards.com.

Association of Canadian Publishers. nd. About. Accessed 10 December 2018 at publishers.ca.

Babe, Robert E. 1979. *Canadian Broadcasting Structure, Performance and Regulation*. Ottawa: Economic Council of Canada.

Bernard, Elaine. 1982.*The Long Distance Feeling*. Vancouver: New Star Books.

Boggs, Jeff. 2012. "Book publishing: Dying one Chapter(s) at a time?" In *Cultural Industries.ca: Making Sense of Canadian Media in the Digital Age*, edited by Ira Wagman and Peter Urquhart. Toronto: James Lorimer, 94–109.

BookNet Canada. 2018. *The Canadian Book Market 2017*. Accessed 10 December 2018 at www.booknetcanada.ca.

Canada. 1991. *Broadcasting Act*. https://laws.justice.gc.ca/eng/acts/B-9.01/]

Canada. 1996. *Convergence Policy Statement*. Accessed at www.ic.gc.ca/eic/site/smt-gst.nsf/eng/sf05265.html.

Canada. 2017 (21 July). Department of Canadian Heritage. *Revised Foreign Investment Policy in Book Publishing and Distribution*. Accessed 21 December 2018 at www.canada.ca/en/canadian-heritage/services/cultural-sector-investment-review/foreign-investment.html.

Canada. 2018a. Department of Canadian Heritage. *Canada Book Fund*. Accessed December 17, 2018 at www.canada.ca/en/canadian-heritage.html.

Canada. 2018b. Department of Canadian Heritage. *Canada Periodical Fund*. Accessed 17 December 2018 at www.canada.ca/en/canadian-heritage.html.

Canada. 2018c. (5 June). Department of Canadian Heritage. "Government of Canada launches review of Telecommunications and Broadcasting Acts." Accessed at www.canada.ca/en/canadian-heritage/news/2018/06/government-of-canada-launches-review-of-telecommunications-and-broadcasting-acts.html.

Canada Council. 2018. "Funding." Accessed 21 December 2018 at canadacouncil.ca.

Canada Post. 2014. *Annual Report, 2013*. Accessed 26 October 2014 at www.canadapost.ca.

Canada Post. 2018. *Annual Report, 2017*. Accessed 20 December 2018 at www.canadapost.ca.

CBC. 2014 (23 September). "Netflix refuses CRTC demand to hand over subscriber data." Accessed at www.cbc.ca/news/business/netflix-refuses-crtc-demand-to-hand-over-subscriber-data-1.2774921.

CBC Radio. 2018 (19 October). "The digital divide leaves more Canadians offline than you think." Accessed at www.cbc.ca/radio/spark/410-1.4868830/the-digital-divide-leaves-more-canadians-offline-than-you-think-1.4868857.

CBSC (Canadian Broadcast Standards Council). 2018. "About us." www.cbsc.ca.

CIRA. 2018. *Internet Factbook*. Accessed at cira.ca/factbook/canada%E2%80%99s-internet-factbook-2018.

CMCRP. 2018. *The Growth of the Network Media Economy in Canada, 1984–2017*. (Updated January 2019). Accessed July 2019 at www.cmcrp.org/wp-content/uploads/2019/01/The-Growth-of-the-Network-Media-Economy-1984-2017-01142019.pdf.

CMF (Canadian Media Fund). n/d. "Funding streams." Accessed 20 November 2014 at www.cmf-fmc.ca/funding-programs/overview.

CMPA (Canadian Media Producers Association). 2017. *Profile 2017: Economic Report on the Screen-Based Media Production Industry in Canada*. Accessed 3 December 2018 at cmpa.ca.

Cohen, Nicole. 2012 (12 September). "How much do freelance journalists make?" *J-Source*. J-Source.ca.

Coxon, Lisa. 2018 (11 October). "What it's like to earn a living freelance writing in Canada." *J-Source*. Accessed 19 October 2018 at j-source.ca.

CRTC (Canadian Radio-television and Telecommunications Commission). 1999. "Broadcasting Public Notice CRTC 1999–84." Accessed at crtc.gc.ca/eng/archive/1999/pb99-84.htm.

CRTC. 2009 (21 October). "Telecom Regulatory Policy CRTC 2009-657: Review of the Internet traffic management practices of Internet service providers." Accessed at crtc.gc.ca/eng/archive/2009/2009-657.htm.

CRTC. 2010. *Navigating Convergence: Charting Canadian Communications Change and Regulatory Implications*. Ottawa. Accessed 13 October 2011 at www.crtc.gc.ca/eng/publications/reports/rp1002.htm.

CRTC. 2013 (September). *CRTC Communications Monitoring Report*. Accessed 15 August 2013 at www.crtc.gc.ca.

CRTC. 2015 (12 March). "Let's Talk TV: CRTC announces measures to support the creation of content made by Canadians for Canadian and global audiences." News Release. Accessed 12 November 2015 at news.gc.ca/web/article-en.do?nid=947269.

CRTC. 2017a. *Communications Monitoring Report*. Accessed at crtc.gc.ca/eng/publications/reports/policymonitoring/2017/index.htm.

CRTC. 2017b. "Telecom Regulatory Policy CRTC 2017-104: Framework for assessing the differential pricing practices of Internet service providers." Accessed at crtc.gc.ca/eng/archive/2017/2017-104.htm.

CRTC. 2018. *Communications Monitoring Report*. Accessed at CRTC.gc.ca/eng/publications/reports/policymonitoring/2018/cmr.htm.

CRTC. n.d. *Your Consumer Rights for Mobile Phones (The Wireless Code of Conduct)*. Accessed at crtc.gc.ca/eng/phone/mobile/code.htm.

Dewar, Elaine. 2017 (9 June). "How Canada sold out its publishing industry." *The Walrus*. Accessed 9 June 2017 at thewalrus.ca.

Ebner, D. 2009 (3 August). "Toronto Scores Points in the Video Game Sector." *The Globe and Mail*. Accessed 10 January 2019 at www.theglobeandmail.com/technology/toronto-scores-points-in-video-game-sector/article4281020/.

Elliott, Patricia. 2017. "National Dreams and Neoliberal Nightmares: The Dismantling of Canadian Heritage's Periodical Assistance Programs, 1989–2015." *Canadian Journal of Communication* 42, 805–27.

Elmer, Greg, and Mike Gasher, editors. 2005. *Contracting Out Hollywood: Runaway Productions and Foreign Location Shooting*. Lanham, MD: Rowman & Littlefield.

Filion, Michel. 1996. "Radio." In *The Cultural Industries in Canada: Problems, Policies and Prospects, edited by* Michael Dorland. Toronto: James Lorimer, 118–41.

Gasher, Mike. 2002. *Hollywood North: The Feature Film Industry in British Columbia*. Vancouver: UBC Press.

Gendreau, Bianca. 2000. "Moving the mail." In *Special Delivery: Canada's Postal Heritage*, edited by Francine Brousseau. Fredericton, NB, and Hull, QC: Goose Lane Editions and Canadian Museum of Civilization, 125–39.

Gooderham, Mary. 2009 (9 October). "Career Satisfaction – and a Life." *The Globe and Mail*. Accessed 10 January 2019 at www.theglobeandmail.com/report-on-business/small-business/career-satisfaction---and-a-life/article1207070/.

Gouglas, S., et al. 2010. *Computer Games and Canada's Digital Economy: The Role of Universities in Promoting Innovation*. Report to the Social Sciences and Humanities Research Council, Knowledge Synthesis Grants on Canada's Digital Economy.

Hamelink, Cees J. 1994. *The Politics of World Communication*. London: Sage.

Harris, Sophia. 2018 (8 May). "Canadians pay some of the highest wireless prices in the world — but report says they're worth it." *CBC News*. Accessed at www.cbc.ca/news/business/wireless-prices-cell-phone-plan-canada-1.4652550.

IBISWorld. 2017. *Magazine and Periodical Publishing – Canada Market Research Report*. Accessed 18 December 2018 at www.ibisworld.ca.

IBISWorld. 2018 (April). *Book Publishing – Canada Market Research Report*. Accessed 18 December 2018 at www.ibisworld.ca.

Jackson, Emily. 2017 (7 December). "CBC, media producers, actors call for internet and Netflix tax – again." *Financial Post*. Accessed at business.financialpost.com/telecom/cbc-media-producers-actors-call-for-internet-and-netflix-tax-again.

Kamenetz, A. 2013 (11 July). "Why Video Games Succeed Where the Movie and Music Industries Fail." *Fast Company*. Accessed 10 January 2019 at www.fastcompany.com/3021008/why-video-games-succeed-where-the-movie-and-music-industries-fail.

Lessig, Lawrence. 2008. *Remix: Making Art and Commerce Thrive in the Hybrid Economy*. New York: Penguin.

Lorimer, Rowland. 2012. *Ultra Libris: Policy, Technology, and the Creative Economy of Book Publishing in Canada*. Toronto: ECW Press.

McKenna, Barrie. 2014 (7 October). "Mail delivered directly to your door—only $20 a month." *The Globe and Mail*, B1, B11.

McSween, Pierre-Yves. 2017 (le 31 mai). "Vivre de sa plume au Québec, une réalité pratiquement impossible." *La Presse*. Accessed 17 November 2018 at plus.lapresse.ca.

Magder, Ted. 1985. "A featureless film policy: Culture and the Canadian state." *Studies in Political Economy* 16, 81–109.

Masthead. 2014 (7 April). "Ontario Labour Ministry cracks down on unpaid internships." Accessed 28 October 2014 at www.mastheadonline.com.

Morris, Peter. 1978. *Embattled Shadows: A History of Canadian Cinema, 1895–1939*. Montreal and Kingston: McGill-Queen's UP.

Music Canada. 2012 (12 April). *Economic Impact Analysis of the Sound Recording Industry in Canada*. Accessed 31 October 2014 at www.musiccanada.com.

Music Canada. 2013. *Music Canada Statistics 2013*. Accessed 31 October 2014 at www.musiccanada.com.

Music Canada. 2017. *The Value Gap: Its origins, impacts and a made in Canada approach*. Accessed at musiccanada.com/resources/research/the-value-gap-report/.

Nawotka, Ed. 2018 (14 September). "Canadian publishing in 2018." *Publishers Weekly*. Accessed 10 December 2018 at www.publishersweekly.com.

Nordicity. 2015. "Canada's Video Game Industry in 2015." Accessed at theesa.ca/.

Nordicity. 2017. "Canada's Video Game Industry in 2017." Accessed at theesa.ca/.

Nordicity. 2018 (July). "The Canadian English-language Book Publishing Industry Profile." Accessed 10 December 2018 at publishers.ca.

Ontario Arts Council. 2018. "Grants." Accessed 21 December 2018 at www.arts.on.ca.

Ontario Media Development Corporation. 2018. "Funding Programs." Accessed 21 December 2018 at www.ontariocreates.ca.

Paddon, David. 2018 (17 December). "Bell, Rogers, Telus will offer range of lower-priced data-only wireless plans: CRTC." *Financial Post*. Accessed at business.financialpost.com/telecom/crtc-wireless-carriers-agree-to-offer-range-of-lower-priced-data-only-plans.

Patch, Nick. 2018 (6 January). "How Amazon is pushing publishers' buttons." *The Globe and Mail*, R3.

Québec. 2018. Ministre de la Culture et des Communications. "Loi sur le développement des entreprises québécoises dans le domaine du livre." Accessed 21 December 2018 at www.mcc.gouv.qc.ca.

Raboy, Marc. 1995. "The role of public consultation in shaping the Canadian broadcasting system." *Canadian Journal of Political Science* 28(3), 455–77.

Roth, Lorna. 2005. *Something New in the Air: The Story of First Peoples Television Broadcasting in Canada*. Montreal and Kingston: McGill-Queen's UP.

SODEC (Société de développement des entreprises culturelles). 2018. Livre et Édition. Accessed 21 December 2018 at sodec.gouv.qc.ca/.

Statista. 2018. *Magazines in Canada: Statistics and Facts*. Accessed 18 December 2018 at www.statista.com.

Statistics Canada. 2018 (23 March). "Book publishing industry. 2016." *The Daily*. Accessed 10 December 2018 at www150.statcan.gc.ca.

Sumanac-Johnson, Deana. 2018 (17 November). "Well-established but not well-off: Canada's authors struggle to make ends meet, study says." *CBC News*. Accessed 17 November 2018 at www.cbc.ca/news.

SuperData. 2018. *2017 Year in Review: Digital Games and Interactive Media*. Accessed at www.superdataresearch.com/.

Wijman, T. 2018 (30 April). "Mobile Revenues Account for More Than 50% of the Global Games Market as It Reaches $137.9 Billion in 2018." *Newzoo*. Accessed 10 January 2019. newzoo.com/insights/articles/global-games-market-reaches-137-9-billion-in-2018-mobile-games-take-half/.

Willis, John. 2000. "The colonial era: Bringing the post to North America." In *Special Delivery: Canada's Postal Heritage*, edited by Francine Brousseau. Fredericton, NB, and Hull, QC: Goose Lane Editions and Canadian Museum of Civilization, 35–46.

Wingfield, N. 2014 (15 October). "Feminist Critics of Video Games Facing Threats in 'GamerGate' Campaign." *New York Times*. Accessed 10 January 2019 at www.nytimes.com/2014/10/16/technology/gamergate-women-video-game-threats-anita-sarkeesian.html.

Winseck, Dwayne. 2010. "Financialization and the 'crisis of the media': The rise and fall of (some) media conglomerates in Canada." *Canadian Journal of Communication* 35, 365–93.

Yerema, R., and K. Leung. 2018 (8 November). "Ubisoft Canadian Studios." *Mediacorp Canada*. Accessed 10 January 2019 at content.eluta.ca/top-employer-ubisoft-entertainment.

Chapter 9

ABL Media. 2012. *Vertical Integration in Warner Bros*. Accessed 18 October 2018 at ablmedia.blogspot.com.

Adib, Desiree. 2009 (14 November). "Pop Star Justin Bieber is on the Brink of Superstardom." *ABC News*. Accessed 23 October 2018 at abcnews.go.com.

Anderson, Benedict. 1983. *Imagined Communities: Reflections on the Origin and Spread of Nationalism*. London: Verso.

Anderson, Chris. 2006. *The Long Tail: Why the Future of Business Is Selling Less of More*. New York: Hyperion.

Canada. 1982. *Report of the Federal Cultural Policy Review Committee* (Applebaum–Hébert Committee). Ottawa: Minister of Supply and Services Canada.

CBC (Canadian Broadcasting Corporation). 2018. *Annual Report 2017-2018*. Accessed October 18, 2018 at www.cbc.radio-canada.ca.

Christopherson, Susan. 2006 (September). "Behind the scenes: How transnational firms are constructing a new international division of labor in media work." *Geoforum* 37(5), 739–51.

CMCRP (Canadian Media Concentration Research Project). 2017. *The Growth of the Network Media Economy in Canada, 1984–2016*. Report. Ottawa: Canadian Media Concentration Research Project.

Couture, Toby D. 2013. "Without Favour: The Concentration of Ownership in New Brunswick's Print Media Industry." *Canadian Journal of Communication*, 38, 57–81.

Cohen, Nicole. 2012 (12 September). "How much do freelance journalists make?" *J-Source*. J-Source.ca.

Coxon, Lisa. 2018 (11 October). "What it's like to earn a living freelance writing in Canada." *J-Source*. Accessed 19 October 2018 at j-source.ca.

CTV. 2018. *Corporate Information*. Accessed 18 October 2018 at www.ctv.ca.

Curtin, Michael, and Kevin Sanson, editors. 2016. *Precarious Creativity: Global Media, Local Labor*. Oakland: University of California Press.

Doherty, Brennan. 2017 (21 November). "Bell Media lays off 50 people." *Toronto Star*, B3.

Dubinsky, Lon. 1996. "Periodical publishing." In *The Cultural Industries in Canada: Problems, Policies and Prospects*, edited by Michael Dorland. Toronto: James Lorimer.

Dyer-Witheford, Nick, and Greig S. de Peuter. 2006. "'EA spouse' and the crisis of video game labour: Enjoyment, exclusion, exploitation and exodus." *Canadian Journal of Communication*, 31, 599–617.

Dyer-Witheford, Nick, and Greig de Peuter. 2009. *Games of Empire: Global Capitalism and Video Games*. Minneapolis: University of Minnesota Press.

Edge, Marc. 2016. *The News We Deserve: The Transformation of Canada's Media Landscape*. Vancouver: New Star Books.

Frankel, Todd C. 2017 (11 November). "Sounding off: In $24-billion video-game industry, voice actors struggle to make a living in a demanding craft." *Vancouver Sun*, E2.

Gasher, Mike. 2013. "Media convergence." *The Canadian Encyclopedia*. Accessed at www.thecanadianencyclopedia.ca/en/article/media-convergence.

Geddes, John. 2010 (21 January). "Voice of fire: Are we over this yet?" *Maclean's*. Accessed 3 August 2010 at www2.macleans.ca/2010/01/21/are-we-over-this-yet.

Gillmor, Don. 2004. *We the Media: Grassroots Journalism by the People, for the People*. Sebastopol, CA: O'Reilly.

Gomery, Douglas. 2004. "The economics of Hollywood: Money and media." In *Media Economics: Theory and Practice*, 3rd ed., edited by Alison Aleander et al. Mahwah, NJ, and London: Lawrence Erlbaum Associates.

Hodson, Jaigris, and Asmaa Malik. 2018 (11 July). "The future of local news is one bound with our own." *J-Source*. Accessed 23 October 2018 at j-source.ca.

Infantry, Ashante. 2013 (1 October). "CBC wades gently into on-air commercials." *Toronto Star*. Accessed 15 September 2014 at www.thestar.com/business/tech_news/2013/10/01/cbc_wades_gently_into_onair_commercials.html.

Jackson, Emily. 2018 (14 June). "Rogers Media axes 75 jobs, slashing one-third of its digital content and publishing team." *National Post*. Accessed 23 October 2018 at nationalpost.com.

Klein, Naomi. 2014. *This Changes Everything: Capitalism vs. the Climate*. Toronto: Knopf Canada.

Kozolanka, Kirsten, Patricia Mazeppa, and David Skinner. 2012. "Considering alternative media in Canada: Structure, participation, activism." In *Alternative Media in Canada*, edited by Kirsten Kozolanka, Patricia Mazeppa, and David Skinner. Vancouver: UBC Press, 1–22.

Ladurantaye, Steve. 2010 (11 September). "Bell ushers in new era with CTV deal." *The Globe and Mail*, 1, 18.

Leblanc, Daniel. 2018 (27 February). "Federal budget 2018: Ottawa opens door to charitable status for news organizations." *The Globe and Mail*. Accessed 27 February 2018 at theglobeandmail.com.

LNRP (Local News Research Project). 2018 (1 October). *Local News Map Data, October 1, 2018*. Toronto: Local News Research Project.

McKnight, Zoe, and Kim Nursall. 2014 (28 March). "Province cracks whip on unpaid internships." *Toronto Star*, A16.

Mirtle, James. 2018 (31 January). "Why The Athletic has a paywall." *The Athletic*. Accessed 11 August 2018 at theathletic.com.

Mosco, Vincent. 2009. *The Political Economy of Communication*, 2nd ed. London: Sage.

Mosco, Vincent, and Catherine McKercher. 2006. "Convergence bites back: Labour struggles in the Canadian communications industry." *Canadian Journal of Communication* 31, 733–51.

Nash, Knowlton. 1994. *The Microphone Wars: A History of Triumph and Betrayal at the CBC*. Toronto: McClelland & Stewart.

Nelson, Jacqueline, and Nicolas Van Praet. 2018 (8 May). "La Presse goes non-profit as Desmarais family lets go." *The Globe and Mail*. Accessed 23 October 2018 at theglobeandmail.com.

Papineau, Philippe. 2017 (5 décembre). "Québec aidera la presse écrite à coup de projets." *Le Devoir*. Accessed 5 December 2017 at ledevoir.com.

Picard, Robert G. 1989. *Media Economics: Concepts and Issues*. Newbury Park, CA: Sage.

Pilieci, Vito. 2018 (3 February). "A tale of Netflix, sales taxes and non-existent loopholes: Federal government has set awkward precedent with digital streaming service." *Ottawa Citizen*, A3.

Powers, Shawn M., and Michael Jablonski. 2015. *The Real Cyber War: The Political Economy of Internet Freedom*. Urbana: University of Illinois Press.

Raboy, Marc. 1990. *Missed Opportunities: The Story of Canada's Broadcasting Policy*. Montreal and Kingston: McGill-Queen's UP.

Salamon, Errol. 2015. "(De)valuing Intern Labour: Journalism Internship Pay Rates and Collective Representation in Canada." *tripleC: Communication, Capitalism & Critique* 13(2), 438–58. doi.org/10.31269/triplec.v13i2.573.

Salamon, Errol. 2016. "E-lancer Resistance: Precarious freelance journalists use digital communications to refuse rights-grabbing contracts." *Digital Journalism* 4(8), 980–1000.

Salamon, Errol. 2018. "Precarious E-Lancers: Freelance Journalists' Rights, Contracts, Labor Organizing, and Digital Resistance." In *The Routledge Handbook of Developments in Digital Journalism Studies*, edited by Scott A. Eldridge II and Bob Franklin. New York: Routledge, 186–97.

Salamon, Errol. 2019. *Digital Media Labor@Work: Reforming Press Freedom Through Networked Freedom of Association*. Book manuscript in preparation.

Shepherd, Tamara. 2013. "Young Canadians' apprenticeship labour in user-generated content." *Canadian Journal of Communication* 38, 35–55.

Shirky, Clay. 2008. *Here Comes Everybody: The Power of Organizing without Organizations*. New York: Penguin Press.

Skinner, David. 2004. "Reform or alternatives? Limits and pressures on changing the Canadian mediascape." *Democratic Communiqué* 19(Spring), 13–36.

Skinner, David. 2012. "Sustaining independent and alternative media." In *Alternative Media in Canada*, edited by Kirsten Kozolanka, Patricia Mazeppa, and David Skinner. Vancouver: UBC Press, 25–45.

Smythe, Dallas. 1994. *Counterclockwise: Perspectives on Communication*, edited by Thomas Guback. Boulder, CO: Westview Press.

Thomson Reuters. 2009. "About us." Accessed 15 December 2009 at www.thomsonreuters.com.

Watson, H.G. 2017 (27 November). "Torstar and Postmedia swapped 41 newspapers and are closing most of them." *J-Source*. Accessed 23 October 2018 at j-source.ca.

Williams, Raymond. 1989. *Resources of Hope: Culture, Democracy, Socialism*, edited by Robin Gable. London: Verso.

Wong, Jan. 2013 (19 November). "Canadian Media Guild data shows 10,000 job losses in past five years." *J-Source*. Accessed 18 August 2014 at j-source.ca.

Wood, Ellen Meiksins. 2002. *The Origin of Capitalism: A Longer View*. London: Verso.

Chapter 10

Allan, Stuart, editor. 2010. *The Routledge Companion to News and Journalism*. London and New York: Routledge.

Amad, Ali. 2018 (14 March). "Remembering the 'Somalia Affair,' Canada's Forgotten Abu Ghraib Moment." *Vice*. Accessed 22 November 2018 at vice.com.

Anderson, C.W. 2013. "What aggregators do: Towards a networked concept of journalistic expertise in the digital age." *Journalism* 14(8), 1008–23.

Anderson, C.W, Emily Bell, and Clay Shirky. 2012 (November). *Post-Industrial Journalism: Adapting to the Present*. New York: Tow Center for Digital Journalism.

Archetti, Cristina. 2014. "Journalism and the city: Redefining the spaces of foreign correspondence." *Journalism Studies*. Accessed 5 August 2014 at dx.doi.org/10.1080/1461670X.2014.894354.

Audience Insights & Ulster Media. 2018. *The Canadian Podcast Listener*. Accessed at canadianpodcastlistener.ca/the-report.

Baluja, Tamara. 2014 (16 April). "*Globe* launches pilot native advertising project." j-source.ca.

Basen, Ira. 2012 (4 August). "Is that an ad or a news story—and does it matter which?" *The Globe and Mail*, F1.

Benkler, Yochai. 2011. "Giving the networked public sphere time to develop." In *Will the Last Reporter Please Turn Out the Lights: The Collapse of Journalism and What Can Be Done to Fix It*, edited by Robert W. McChesney and Victor Pickard. New York and London: The New Press, 225–37.

Bennett, Tony. 1996. "Media, 'reality,' signification." In *Culture, Society and the Media*, edited by Michael Gurevitch et al. London and New York: Routledge, 287–308.

Canada. 1991. *Broadcasting Act*. https://laws.justice.gc.ca/eng/acts/B-9.01/]

Canadian Press. 2018 (26 June). "Postmedia to close more local newspapers, cut staff cost by 10 per cent." *J-Source*. Accessed 10 September 2018 at j-source.ca.

Canter, Lily. 2013. "The source, the resource and the collaborator: The role of citizen journalism in local UK newspapers." *Journalism* 14(8), 1091–109.

CBC News. 2006 (26 October). "Federal Sponsorship Scandal." *CBC News: In Depth*. Accessed 22 November 2018 at cbc.ca.

Charles, Alec. 2014. "The abuse of power: Savile, Leveson, and the internet." In *The End of Journalism 2.0: Industry, Technology and Politics*, edited by Alex Charles. Oxford: Peter Lang, 1–52.

Clark, Jessica, and Tracy Van Slyke. 2011. "How journalists must operate in a new networked media environment." In *Will the Last Reporter Please Turn Out the Lights: The Collapse of Journalism and What Can Be*

Done to Fix It, edited by Robert W. McChesney and Victor Pickard. New York and London: The New Press, 238–48.

Cohen, Nicole. 2012 (12 September). "How much do freelance journalists make?" *J-Source*. J-Source.ca.

Collie, Meghan. 2018. "The legal potcast: A look into the backrooms of Canada's newest industry." *CityNews*. Accessed at toronto.citynews.ca/2018/10/18/the-legal-potcast-a-look-into-the-back-rooms-of-canadas-newest-industry/.

Compton, James R. 2010. "Newspapers, labor and the flux of economic uncertainty." In *The Routledge Companion to News and Journalism*, edited by Stuart Allan. London and New York: Routledge.

Comscore. 2018. *Global Digital Future in Focus: 2018 International Edition*. Accessed 8 March 2018 at comscore.com.

Cooper, Mark. 2011. "The future of journalism: Addressing pervasive market failure with public policy." In *Will the Last Reporter Please Turn Out the Lights: The Collapse of Journalism and What Can Be Done to Fix It*, edited by Robert W. McChesney and Victor Pickard. New York and London: The New Press, 320–39.

Coxon, Lisa. 2018 (11 October). "What it's like to earn a living freelance writing in Canada." *J-Source*. Accessed 19 October 2018 at j-source.ca.

Dahlgren, Peter. 2013. "Online journalism and civic cosmopolitanism: Professional vs. participatory ideals." *Journalism Studies* 14(2), 156–71.

Dhillon, Sunny. 2018 (29 October). "Journalism While Brown and When to Walk Away." *Medium*. Accessed 19 November 2018 at medium.com.

Doherty, Brennan. 2017 (21 November). "Bell Media lays off 50 people." *Toronto Star*, B3.

Edge, Marc. 2014. *Greatly Exaggerated: The Myth of the Death of Newspapers*. Vancouver: New Star Books.

El Azrak, Lama. 2018 (15 March). "Women Journalists and the Glass Ceiling." *J-Source*. Accessed 19 November 2018 at j-source.ca.

Fenton, Natalie. 2010. "News in the digital age." In Allan, 2010, 557–67.

Gasher, Mike. 2015. "Geographies of the news." In *Mediated Geographies/Geographies of Media*, edited by Susan Mains, Julie Cupples, and Chris Lukinbeal. New York: Springer, 127–40.

Gidengil, Elisabeth, and Joanna Everitt. 2011. "Unconventional politicians: Gender and media coverage of Canadian leaders' debates, 1993, 1997, 2000." In *The Gendered Society Reader*, edited by Michael S. Kimmel, Amy Aronson, and Amy Kaler. Don Mills, ON: Oxford UP, 304–17.

Gingras, Anne-Marie. 2006. *Médias et Démocratie: Le Grand Malentendu*, deuxième édition. Québec: Presses de l'Université du Québec.

Goodyear-Grant, Elizabeth. 2013. *Gendered News: Media Coverage and Electoral Politics in Canada*. Vancouver: UBC Press.

Greenwald, Glenn. 2014. *No Place to Hide: Edward Snowden, the NSA, and the U.S. Surveillance State*. Toronto: McClelland & Stewart.

Griffith, Andrew. 2017 (15 December). "The growing diversity within federal ridings." *Policy Options Magazine*. Accessed at policyoptions.irpp.org/magazines/december-2017/the-growing-diversity-within-federal-ridings/.

Habermas, Jürgen. 1996. "The public sphere." In *Media Studies: A Reader*, edited by Paul Marris and Sue Thornham. Edinburgh: Edinburgh UP, 55–9.

Hackett, Robert A., and Yuezhi Zhao. 1998. *Sustaining Democracy? Journalism and the Politics of Objectivity*. Toronto: Garamond Press.

Hall, Stuart. 2013. "The work of representation." In *Representation*, 2nd ed., edited by Stuart Hall, Jessica Evans, and Sean Nixon. Milton Keynes, UK: The Open University, 1–47.

Hammersley, Ben. 2004. "Audible revolution." *The Guardian*. www.theguardian.com/media/2004/feb/12/broadcasting.digitalmedia.

Hartley, John. 1992. *The Politics of Pictures: The Creation of the Public in the Age of Popular Media*. London and New York: Routledge.

Hemmadi, Murad. 2017 (12 May). "On diversity, Canadian media is throwing stones in a glass house." *Maclean's*. Accessed 19 November 2018 at macleans.ca.

Henry, Frances, and Carol Tator. 2000. *Racist Discourse in Canada's English Print Media*. Toronto: Canadian Race Relations Foundation.

Hindman, Victor, and Vlad Barash. 2018. *"Fake News" and Influence Campaigns on Twitter*. Miami, FL: John S. and James L. Knight Foundation. Accessed 12 March 2019 at knightfoundation.org.

Hodson, Jaigris, and Asmaa Malik. 2018 (11 July). "The future of local news is one bound with our own." *J-Source*. Accessed 23 October 2018 at j-source.ca.

Jackson, Emily. 2018a (14 June). "Rogers Media axes 75 jobs, slashing one-third of its digital content and publishing team." *National Post*. Accessed 23 October 2018 at nationalpost.com.

Jackson, Emily. 2018b (23 August). "Senate panel urges Liberals to rethink tax rules for digital ads." *Edmonton Journal*, B10.

Jobb, Dean. 2011. *Media Law for Canadian Journalists*, 2nd ed. Toronto: Emond Montgomery Publications.

Kimmel, Michael S., and Jacqueline Holler, editors. 2011. *The Gendered Society*. Don Mills, ON: Oxford UP.

Kovach, Bill, and Tom Rosenstiel. 2001. *The Elements of Journalism: What Newspeople Should Know and the Public Should Expect*. New York: Crown.

Leblanc, Daniel. 2018 (27 February). "Federal budget 2018: Ottawa opens door to charitable status for news organizations." *The Globe and Mail*. Accessed 27 February 2018 at theglobeandmail.com.

Levin, Josh. 2014. "*Serial* wasn't a satisfying story: It was a master class in investigative journalism." *Slate*. Accessed at: slate.com/culture/2014/12/serial-as-investigative-journalism-the-hit-podcast-was-a-master-class-in-reporting.html.

Lindgren, April. 2014. "Toronto-area ethnic newspapers and Canada's 2011 federal election: An investigation of content, focus and partisanship." *Canadian Journal of Political Science* 47(4), 667–96.

Lindgren, April. 2015. "Municipal communication strategies and ethnic media: A settlement service in disguise." *Global Media Journal: Canadian Edition* 8(2), 49–71.

Lindgren, April. 2018 (26 March). "How Ottawa should spend its $50-million to support local news." *The Conversation*. Accessed 27 March 2018 at theconversation.com.

Lynch, Jake, and Annabel McGoldrick. 2005. *Peace Journalism*. Stroud, UK: Hawthorn Press.

McCarten, James, editor. 2013. *The Canadian Press Stylebook: A Guide for Writers and Editors*, 17th ed. Toronto: The Canadian Press.

McChesney, Robert W., and John Nichols. 2009. *The Death and Life of American Journalism*. New York: Nation Books.

McIntyre, Lee. 2018. *Post-Truth*. Cambridge, MA: MIT Press.

Mencher, Melvin. 2006. *News Reporting and Writing*, 10th ed. New York: McGraw-Hill.

Miller, John. 1998. *Yesterday's News: Why Canada's Daily Newspapers Are Failing Us*. Halifax: Fernwood.

Newman, Nic, and David A.L. Levy, editors. 2014. *Reuters Institute Digital News Report, 2014*. Oxford: Reuters Institute for the Study of Journalism.

Nielsen, Greg. 2009. "Framing dialogue on immigration in *The New York Times*." *Aether: Journal of Media Geography* 4, 22–42. Accessed at 130.166.124.2/~aether/volume_04.html.

Nielsen, Greg, Amanda Weightman, James Gibbons, and Mike Gasher. 2016. "Dialogic Journalism: Bringing marginalized communities into the implied audience." In *The Praxis of Social Inequality in Media: A Global Perspective*, edited by Jan Servaes and Toks Oyedemi. Lanham, MD: Lexington Books, 21–38.

Orms, Mary. 2018 (13 October). "News media group urges Canada to act: No appetite to confront world's tech giants, industry advocate says." *Toronto Star*, A12.

Ostrikoff, Lisa. 2013 (31 January). "Farewell 'push' marketing, hello brand journalism." *The Globe and Mail*. Accessed 26 August 2014 at www.theglobeandmail.com.

Papineau, Philippe. 2018 (26 juillet). "90% des 18-34 ans s'informent surtout sur les plateformes numériques." *Le Devoir*. Accessed 10 September 2018 at ledevoir.com.

Paradkar, Shree. 2016 (4 November). "Lack of racial diversity in media is a form of oppression." *Toronto Star*. Accessed 19 November 2018 at thestar.com.

Peiser, Jaclyn. 2018 (8 August). "New York Times Co. reports $24-million profit, thanks to digital subscribers." *New York Times*. Accessed 10 September 2018 at nytimes.com.

Poindexter, Paula, Sharon Meraz, and Amy Schmitz Weiss, editors. 2008. *Women, Men, and News: Divided and Disconnected in the News Media Landscape*. New York and London: Routledge.

Qiu, Linda. 2018 (19 November). "Trump's misleading claim that he warned about Osama bin Laden." *New York Times*. Accessed 22 November 2018 at nytimes.com.

Ramanujam, Priya. 2016 (7 December). "What should diversity in Canadian media look like?" *This Magazine*. Accessed 19 November 2018 at this.org.

Rizzo, Salvador. 2018 (19 November). "President Trump's crowd-size estimates: Increasingly unbelievable." *Washington Post*. Accessed 22 November 2018 at washingtonpost.com.

Safayeni, Justin, and Andrea Gonsalves. 2018 (26 October). "The Journalistic Sources Protection Act: A Primer." *Centre for Free Expression*. Accessed 19 November 2018 at cfe.ryerson.ca.

Schudson, Michael. 2003. *The Sociology of News*. New York: W.W. Norton & Co.

Schultz, Ida. 2007. "The journalistic gut feeling: Journalistic doxa, news habitus and orthodox news values." *Journalism Practice* 1(2), 190–207.

Sheller, Mimi. 2014. "News now: Interface, ambience, flow, and the disruptive spatio-temporalities of mobile news media." *Journalism Studies*. Accessed 5 August 2014 at dx.doi.org/10.1080.1461670X.2014.890324.

Shade, Leslie Regan, editor. 2010. *Mediascapes: New patterns in Canadian communication*, 3rd ed. Toronto: Nelson Education.

Silverman, Craig. 2007. *Regret the Error: How Media Mistakes Pollute the Press and Imperil Free Speech*. New York: Sterling.

Silverstone, Roger. 2007. *Media and Morality: On the Rise of the Mediapolis*. Cambridge: Polity Press.

Skinner, David. 2010. "Minding the growing gaps: Alternative media in Canada." In Shade, 2010: 221–36.

Sumar, Al-Amyn. 2018 (10 October). "Source protection key to freedom of press." *London Free Press*, A7.

United Nations. 1948. *Universal Declaration of Human Rights*. Accessed at www.unhchr.ch/udhr/lang/eng.htm.

Ward, Stephen J.A. 2004. *The Invention of Journalism Ethics: The Path to Objectivity and Beyond*. Montreal and Kingston: McGill-Queen's UP.

Ward, Stephen J.A. 2014. "Ethics resources." *Media Morals*. Accessed 26 August 2014 at mediamorals.org/ethics-resources/.

Waterson, Jim. 2018 (24 July). "Guardian Media Group digital revenues outstrip print for first time." *The Guardian*. Accessed 10 September 2018 at theguardian.com.

Watson, H.G. 2017 (27 November). "Torstar and Postmedia swapped 41 newspapers and are closing most of them." *J-Source*. Accessed 23 October 2018 at j-source.ca.

Welch, Cam. 2018 (17 August). "Will people pay for hyper-local news?" *J-Source*. Accessed 15 November 2018 at j-source.ca.

Wong, Jan. 2013 (19 November). "Canadian Media Guild data shows 10,000 job losses in past five years." Accessed 18 August 2014 at j-source.ca.

Yu, Sherry S. 2016. "Instrumentalization of ethnic media." *Canadian Journal of Communication* 41(2), 343–51.

Zoledziowski, Anya. 2019 (12 March). "Working as the Newsroom's 'Diversity Hire'." *The Tyee*. Accessed 15 March 2019 at thetyee.ca.

Chapter 11

Anderson, Benedict. 1983. *Imagined Communities: Reflections on the Origin and Spread of Nationalism*. London: Verso.

Anderson, Chris. 2006. *The Long Tail: Why the Future of Business Is Selling Less of More*. New York: Hyperion.

Appadurai, Arjun. 1990. "Disjuncture and difference in the global cultural economy." *Theory, Culture and Society* 7, 295–310.

Appadurai, Arjun. 1996. *Modernity at Large: Cultural Dimensions of Globalization*. Minneapolis: University of Minnesota Press.

Bauman, Zygmunt. 1998. *Globalization: The Human Consequences*. New York: Columbia UP.

BBC Studios. 2018. "About Us." BBC Studios. Accessed 20 September 2018 at www.bbcstudios.com.

Bernstein, William J. 2008. *A Splendid Exchange: How Trade Shaped the World*. New York: Grove Press.

Boyd-Barrett, Oliver. 1977. "Media imperialism: Towards an international framework for the analysis of media systems." In *Mass Communication and Society*, edited by James Curran, Michael Gurevitch, and Janet Woollacott. London: Edward Arnold.

Boyd-Barrett, Oliver. 1996. "Cultural dependency and the mass media." In *Culture, Society and the Media*, edited by Michael Gurevitch et al. London and New York: Routledge.

Bradshaw, James. 2016 (22 March). "Federal budget pledges $675-million in CBC funding." *The Globe and Mail*. Accessed 20 September 2018 at www.theglobeandmail.com.

Brady, Miranda J., and John M.H. Kelly. 2017. *We Interrupt This Program: Indigenous Media Tactics in Canadian Culture*. Vancouver and Toronto: UBC Press.

Breen, Marcus. 2005. "Off-shore pot o' gold: The political economy of the Australian film industry." In *Contracting Out Hollywood: Runaway Productions and Foreign Location Shooting*, edited by Greg Elmer and Mike Gasher. Lanham, MD: Rowman & Littlefield, 69–91.

Carey, James. W. 1998. "The internet and the end of the national communication system: Uncertain predictions of an uncertain future." *Journalism and Mass Communication Quarterly* 75(1), 28–34.

Castells, Manuel. 1999. *End of Millennium*. Oxford: Blackwell.

Castells, Manuel. 2001. *The Internet Galaxy: Reflections on the Internet, Business, and Society*. Oxford: Oxford UP.

Castles, Stephen, Hein de Haas, and Mark J. Miller. 2014. *The Age of Migration: International Population Movements in the Modern World*. New York and London: The Guilford Press.

CMPA (Canadian Media Producers Association). 2018. *Profile 2017: Economic Report on the Screen-Based Media Production Industry in Canada*. Accessed 25 September 2018 at cmpa.ca.

Crowcroft, Natasha. 2018 (17 September). "Canada shouldn't let its guard down on measles." *Toronto Star*. Accessed 20 September 2018 at thestar.com.

Elmer, Greg, and Mike Gasher, editors. 2005. *Contracting Out Hollywood: Runaway Productions and Foreign Location Shooting*. Lanham, MD: Rowman & Littlefield.

ESAC (Entertainment Software Association of Canada). 2017. *Essential Facts About the Canadian Video Game Industry*. Accessed 25 September 2018 at theesa.ca.

Frau-Meigs, D., et al., editors. 2012. From NWICO to WSIS: 30 Years of Communication Geopolitics. Bristol, UK / Chicago, USA: Intellect.

Gasher, Mike. 1995. "Culture lag: The liberal record." *Point of View* 26(Winter), 22–4.

Gasher, Mike. 2002. *Hollywood North: The Feature Film Industry in British Columbia*. Vancouver: UBC Press.

Giddens, Anthony. 1990. *The Consequences of Modernity*. Cambridge: Polity Press.

Giddens, Anthony. 1999. *Runaway World: How Globalization is Reshaping Our Lives*. London: Profile Books.

Giovannetti, Justin. 2018 (5 October). "Doug Ford joins Jason Kenney at rally to rail against carbon tax: 'The biggest lie in Alberta history.'" *The Globe and Mail*. Accessed 9 October 2018 at www.theglobeandmail.com.

Hall, Stuart. 1995. "New cultures for old." In Massey and Jess, 175–214.

Hamelink, Cees J. 1994. *The Politics of World Communication*. London: Sage.

Hartley, John. 1992. *The Politics of Pictures: The Creation of the Public in the Age of Popular Media*. London and New York: Routledge.

Hartley, John. 1996. *Popular Reality: Journalism, Modernity, Popular Culture*. London: Arnold.

Henry, Frances, Carol Tator, Winston Mattis, and Tim Rees. 2000. *The Colour of Democracy: Racism in Canadian Society*. Toronto: Harcourt Brace.

Herman, Edward S., and Robert W. McChesney. 1997. *The Global Media: The New Missionaries of Global Capitalism*. Washington: Cassell.

Hopewell, John. 2014 (27 January). "Brazilian TV giant innovates in services, sales, shows." *Variety*. Accessed 25 April 2014 at variety.com/2014/tv/global/globo-unveils-newsource-movies-new-tv-fiction-1201072733/.

Internet World Stats. 2013 (30 June). "Usage and Population Statistics." Accessed 9 October 2018 at www.internetworldstats.com.

Issawi, Hamdi. 2018 (19 August). "Language still a major barrier for settling Syrian refugees in Edmonton: report." *Toronto Star*. Accessed 20 September 2018 at thestar.com.

ITU (International Telecommunication Union). 2017 (July). *ICT Facts and Figures 2017*. Accessed 25 September 2018 at www.itu.int.

Jackson, John, Greg Nielsen, and Yon Hsu. 2011. *Mediated Society: A Critical Sociology of Media*. Don Mills, ON: Oxford UP.

Jones, Andrew. 2010. *Globalization: Key Thinkers*. Cambridge: Polity Press.

Lambert, Steve, and Bill Graveland. 2018 (10 July). "'Feel cut off:' Loss of Greyhound bus service leaves few options in rural areas." *National Post*. Accessed 20 September 2018 at nationalpost.com.

Laville, Camille, and Michael Palmer. 2012. "The international news agencies (and their TV/multimedia sites): The defence of their traditional lead in international news production." In Frau-Meigs et al., 175–85.

Lent, John A. 1998. "The animation industry and its offshore factories." In *Global Productions: Labor in the Making of the "Information Society,"* edited by Gerald Sussman and John A. Lent. Cresskill, NJ: Hampton Press.

Lessig, Lawrence. 2008. *Remix: Making Art and Commerce Thrive in the Hybrid Economy*. New York: Penguin.

Li, Peter S. 2003. *Destination Canada: Immigration Debates and Issues*. Don Mills, ON: Oxford UP.

Lule, Jack. 2012. *Globalization and Media: Global Village of Babel*. Lanham, MD: Rowman and Littlefield.

McChesney, Robert W. 2003. "The new global media." In *The Global Transformations Reader: An Introduction to the Globalization Debate*, edited by David Held and Anthony McGrew. Cambridge: Polity Press, 260–8.

McKinsey and Company. 2016. *Global Media Report 2016*. Accessed 24 September 2018 at www.mckinsey.com.

Masmoudi, Mustapha. 2012. "Correlations between NWICO and information society: Reflections of a NWICO actor." In Frau-Meigs et al., 17–28.

Massey, Doreen. 1991. "A global sense of place." *Marxism Today* (June), 24–9.

Massey, Doreen. 1992. "A place called home?" *New Formations* 17, 3–15.

Massey, Doreen, and Pat Jess, editors. 1995. *A Place in the World? Cultures and Globalization*. New York: Oxford UP.

Morley, David, and Kevin Robins. 1995. *Spaces of Identity: Global Media, Electronic Landscapes and Cultural Boundaries*. London: Routledge.

Mosco, Vincent. 2009. *The Political Economy of Communication*, 2nd ed. London: Sage.

Murphy, Mike. 2017 (3 August). "Apple's 'walled garden' approach to content has paid off massively." *Quartz*. Accessed 9 October 2018 at qz.com.

Murray, Warwick. 2006. *The Geographies of Globalization*. London: Routledge.

NEPMCC (National Ethnic Press and Media Council of Canada). 2018. *A Report to all Canadians*. Accessed September 25, 2018 at www.nepmcc.ca.

Nicey, Jérémie. 2012. "The notion of access to information and knowledge: Challenges and divides, sectors and limits." In Frau-Meigs et al., 163–74.

Nordenstreng, Kaarle. 2012. "The history of NWICO and its lessons." In Frau-Meigs et al., 29–40.

Pendakur, Manjunath. 1998. "Hollywood North: Film and TV production in Canada." In *Global Productions: Labor in the Making of the "Information Society,"* edited by Gerald Sussman and John A. Lent. Cresskill, NJ: Hampton Press.

Rantanen, Terhi. 1997. "The globalization of electronic news in the 19th century." *Media, Culture and Society* 19(4), 605–20.

Rose, Gillian. 1995. "Place and identity: A sense of place." In Massey and Jess, 1995.

Sassen, Saskia. 1998. *Globalization and Its Discontents*. New York: New Press.

Savio, Robert. 2012. "From New International Information Order to New Information Market Order." In Frau-Meigs et al., 233–37.

Shade, Leslie Regan, editor. 2010. *Mediascapes: New Patterns in Canadian Communication*, 3rd ed. Toronto: Nelson Education.

Sholle, David. 2002. "Disorganizing the 'new technology.'" In *Critical Perspectives on the Internet*, edited by Greg Elmer. Lanham, MD: Rowman & Littlefield, 3–26.

Silverstone, Roger. 2007. *Media and Morality: On the Rise of the Mediapolis*. Cambridge: Polity Press.

Skinner, David. 2010. "Minding the growing gaps: Alternative media in Canada." In Shade, 2010: 221–36.

Soni, Phalguni. 2014 (2 December). "An Overview of NIKE's Supply Chain and Marketing Strategies." *Market Realist*. Accessed 20 September 2018 at marketrealist.com.

Statistics Canada. 2013. "Households with home internet access." Accessed 6 May 2014 at www.statcan.gc.ca/daily-quotidien/131116/t131126d001-eng.htm.

Statistics Canada. 2016. "Census Profile, 2016 Census." Accessed 25 September 2018 at www12.statcan.gc.ca.

Statistics Canada. 2017 (25 October). "Ethnic and cultural origins of Canadians: Portrait of a rich heritage." Accessed 25 September 2018 at www12.statcan.gc.ca.

Taylor, Charles. 2005. *Modern Social Imaginaries*. Durham, NC: Duke UP.

The Guardian. 2018 (8 October). "The Guardian view on climate change: a global emergency" (editorial). Accessed 8 October 2018 at www.theguardian.com.

UNESCO. 1980. *Many Voices, One World: Report by the International Commission for the Study of Communication Problems* (MacBride Commission). Paris: Unipub.

UNHCR (UN High Commissioner for Refugees). 2018. *Global Trends: Forced Displacement in 2017*. Accessed 23 July 2019 at www.unhcr.org.

United Nations, Department of Economic and Social Affairs. 2017. *International Migration Report 2017*. Accessed 27 September 2018 at www.un.org.

van Dijk, Jan A.G.M. 2005. *The Deepening Divide: Inequality in the Information Society*. Thousand Oaks, CA: Sage.

van Dijk, Jan A.G.M. 2012. *The Network Society*, 3rd ed. London: Sage.

Wallerstein, Immanuel. 1974. *The Modern World-System: Capitalist Agriculture and the Origins of the European World-Economy in the Sixteenth Century*. New York: Academic Press.

Wallerstein, Immanuel. 2007. *World-Systems Analysis: An Introduction*. Durham, NC: Duke UP.

Wong, Tony. 2017 (23 December). "Who said Canadian television is dead? While a dark time for the industry, 2017 has been the best year for homespun dramas." *Toronto Star*, E1.

Wong, Tony. 2018 (8 September). "Why Canadian authors are hot in Hollywood." *Toronto Star*. Accessed 25 September 2018 at www.thestar.com.

WSIS (World Summit on the Information Society). 2010. Accessed 23 June 2010 at www.itu.int/wsis/index.html.

Chapter 12

Anderson, Chris. 2006. *The Long Tail: Why the Future of Business Is Selling Less of More*. New York: Hyperion.

Arzavi, Hananeh. 2015. "Netflix Case Study: The Long Tail." Accessed at netflixcasestudy.blogspot.com/p/the-long-tail.html.

Babe, Robert E. 1990. *Telecommunications in Canada*. Toronto: University of Toronto Press.

Canada. 1970. *The Uncertain Mirror: Report of the Special Senate Committee on the Mass Media* (Davey Committee), vol. 1. Ottawa: Information Canada.

Canada. 1981. *Report of the Royal Commission on Newspapers* (Kent Commission), vol. 1. Ottawa: Minister of Supply and Services.

CBC. 2018 (19 October). "The digital divide leaves more Canadians offline than you think." CBC Radio. Accessed at www.cbc.ca/radio/spark/410-1.4868830/the-digital-divide-leaves-more-canadians-offline-than-you-think-1.4868857.

CRTC. 2016. "Broadcasting Regulatory Policy CRTC 2016-224: Policy framework for local and community television." Accessed at crtc.gc.ca/eng/archive/2016/2016-224.htm.

Flanagan, Andrew. 2016. "Where's the Long Tail? Spotify Touts Its Artist Discovery." *Billboard*. Accessed at www.billboard.com/articles/business/7385830/wheres-the-long-tail-spotify-artist-discovery.

Friedersdorf, Conor. 2018 (12 March). "YouTube Extremism and the Long Tail." Accessed at www.theatlantic.com/politics/archive/2018/03/youtube-extremism-and-the-long-tail/555350/.

Girard, Bruce, editor. 1992. *A Passion for Radio: Radio Waves and Community*. Montreal: Black Rose Books.

Global News. 2016. "Ontario government blitz cracks down on unpaid internships." Accessed at globalnews.ca/news/2670439/ontario-government-blitz-cracks-down-on-unpaid-internships/.

Goldberg, Kim. 1990. *The Barefoot Channel: Community Television as a Tool for Social Change*. Vancouver: New Star Books.

Grant, Peter S., and Chris Wood. 2004. *Blockbusters and Trade Wars: Popular Culture in a Globalized World*. Vancouver: Douglas & McIntyre.

Hackett, Robert A., and William F. Carroll. 2006. *Remaking Media: The Struggle to Democratize Public Communication*. New York: Routledge.

NCRA (National Campus and Community Radio Association). 1987. "The NCRA statement of principles." Accessed 29 July 2004 at www.ncra.ca/business/NCRAStatement.html.

Skinner, David, James Compton, and Mike Gasher, editors. 2005. *Converging Media, Diverging Politics: A Political Economy of News Media in the United States and Canada*. Lanham, MD: Lexington Books.

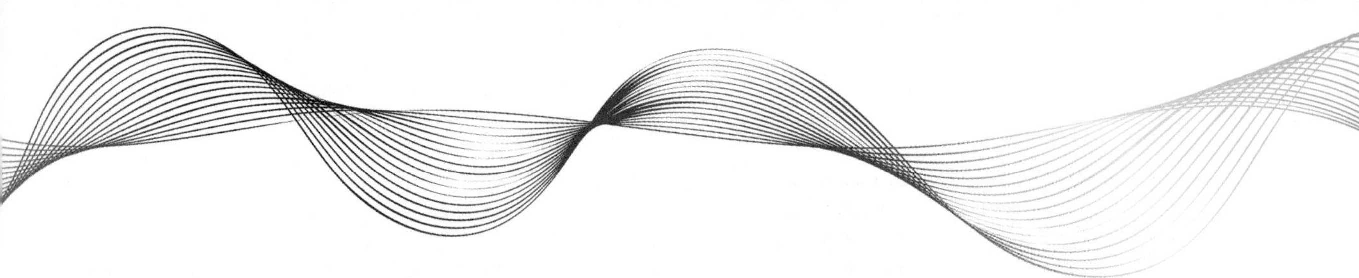

Index